Corporate Governance in Modern Financial Capitalism

Corporate Governance in Modern Financial Capitalism

Old Mutual's Hostile Takeover of Skandia

Markus Kallifatides

Associate Professor, Stockholm School of Economics, Sweden

Sophie Nachemson-Ekwall

MSc, Stockholm School of Economics, Sweden

Sven-Erik Sjöstrand

Matts Carlgren Professor of Management, Stockholm School of Economics, Sweden

Edward Elgar

Cheltenham, UK • Northampton, MA, USA

Published by
Edward Elgar Publishing Limited
The Lypiatts
15 Lansdown Road
Cheltenham
Glos GL50 2JA
UK

Edward Elgar Publishing, Inc.
William Pratt House
9 Dewey Court
Northampton
Massachusetts 01060
USA

A catalogue record for this book
is available from the British Library

Library of Congress Control Number: 2009940654

ISBN 978 1 84844 684 7

Printed and bound by MPG Books Group, UK

Contents

List of figures x
About the authors xi
Preface xii
Introduction xiii

PART I ON CORPORATE CONTROL AND GOVERNANCE PROCESSES IN FINANCIAL CAPITALISM

1 A theoretical platform 3
1.1 The purpose of this work 3
1.2 Setting the scene: early twenty-first century financial capitalism 4
1.3 An extensive empirical case study 7
1.4 Actors and institutions 10
1.5 Two perspectives on the corporation 14
1.6 Towards a revised theory of corporate governance 17
1.7 Shareholder rationales differ 21
1.8 Institutional differences create arbitrage opportunities 24
1.9 A few concluding remarks 31

PART II A CASE OVERVIEW

2 The Old Mutual–Skandia case: actors and context 39
2.1 A changing context 39
2.2 A turbulent period 40
2.3 Skandia in the early twenty-first century 41
2.4 Old Mutual up to the millennium 42
2.5 The main ingredients in our narration 44
2.6 Book overview 47

PART III A TARGET COMPANY: SKANDIA BEFORE APRIL 2004

3 A success – and a crash 55
3.1 Skandia 2003 – a troubled company 55

3.2 Shareholding restrictions 55
3.3 Skandia's successful unit-linked business 57
3.4 The embedded-value method 60
3.5 A crash 62
3.6 A tarnished brand 64

4 Skandia Life UK 68
4.1 A strained relationship 68
4.2 The acquisition of Bankhall 71
4.3 A power struggle 72

5 A takeover target 74
5.1 Changes in shareholding and board composition 74
5.2 A nomination committee 76
5.3 Passive shareholders 78
5.4 Turning the page with a new chair 80
5.5 Trying to form a future 81
5.6 A cancelled merger plan 82
5.7 A bonus scandal 84
5.8 Further shareholder changes 85
5.9 Skandia – a post-crisis company 86

PART IV THE ACTORS IN THE SKANDIA TAKEOVER: SKANDIA 2004

6 A new CEO, board and shareholder composition 91
6.1 A new CEO: Hans-Erik Andersson 91
6.2 A new set of shareholders 93
6.3 The new board of directors 96

7 Rebuilding Skandia 107
7.1 A platform 107
7.2 The AGM on 15 April 2004 108
7.3 A change of leadership 109
7.4 Governance ambiguities 113

8 Working for a stand-alone case or heading for a structural deal? 116
8.1 Internal problems 116
8.2 Presenting the 'Glue plan' 119
8.3 Project Pegasus 122
8.4 Skandia goes for stand-alone 125
8.5 Reporting the second quarter 2004 127
8.6 Shareholder activity 129
8.7 Skandia's CEO still in the driving seat 131

9 New kinds of shareholders enter the scene 136
9.1 Christer Gardell looks for allies 136
9.2 Skandia becomes a target 138
9.3 Chair Bernt Magnusson: Skandia open to sale 140
9.4 Activist Gardell acts 143

10 Old Mutual 147
10.1 The history of Old Mutual 147
10.2 Old Mutual expands abroad 149
10.3 An emerging interest for Skandia 150

PART V OLD MUTUAL GOES FOR SKANDIA (DECEMBER 2004 TO AUGUST 2005)

11 Growing unease on the Skandia board 159
11.1 The Skandia board meeting on 22 December 2004 159
11.2 Christmas activities 160
11.3 Skandia's Turbo plan 162
11.4 Board dispute about the Morgan Stanley agreement 163
11.5 A first visit from Old Mutual 166
11.6 Growing tension on the Skandia board 168
11.7 Icelandic support for Cevian 171
11.8 Settlement with former chair Lars Ramqvist 172
11.9 Old Mutual prepares a bid 176

12 An indicative bid leaks out 179
12.1 New attempts to control the businesses in the UK 179
12.2 Old Mutual enters the arena 180
12.3 Structuring a cross-border bid 182
12.4 Old Mutual's proposal leaks out 185
12.5 Sceptical media 188
12.6 A board agreement on the Turbo plan 191

13 Summer of due diligence 195
13.1 Different opinions regarding Old Mutual's indicative bid 195
13.2 The suitors 198
13.3 A difficult board meeting 202
13.4 A letter from Fidelity 205
13.5 Lengthy due diligence 207
13.6 Attempting to sell parts of Skandia 208

14 Old Mutual's friendly bid 213
14.1 Trouble with financing the bid 213

14.2 The Morgan Stanley agreement 214
14.3 An eroding Skandia contest 215
14.4 A formal bid from Old Mutual 216
14.5 Meeting with Skandia's larger institutional shareholders 221

PART VI OLD MUTUAL ACQUIRES SKANDIA (SUMMER 2005 TO SPRING 2006)

15 A divided board 227
15.1 The Fourth National Pension Fund states its position 227
15.2 Different opinions on Old Mutual's qualities 230
15.3 Two camps emerge on the Skandia board 232
15.4 A second shareholder meeting 235
15.5 A week of media speculation 237
15.6 Soft irrevocables from shareholders 242
15.7 The public bid 243

16 A controversial bid 247
16.1 Old Mutual's bid for Skandia 247
16.2 Early reactions to the bid 249
16.3 Initiating a board document 252
16.4 Emerging shareholder activity 252
16.5 Old Mutual top management meets the Skandia board 254
16.6 A cascade of arguments 256

17 Trying to keep Skandia independent 260
17.1 Activities in and around the Swedish AP funds 260
17.2 A critique of Morgan Stanley 263
17.3 The conflict with the Brits continues 264
17.4 Publishing the Turbo plan 265
17.5 A delicate political issue 266

18 A hostile bid 269
18.1 Public relations problems 269
18.2 Short selling Skandia shares 270
18.3 Planning for a blocking minority 271
18.4 Board vote and press conference 272
18.5 Swedish institutions acting in concert 275
18.6 Lowering the acceptance hurdle? 276
18.7 The question of national interest 277

19 Hedge funds intervene 281
19.1 Paulson & Co. takes a strong position in Skandia 281
19.2 Skandia's chair Bernt Magnusson resigns 282

19.3 Active hedge funds 283
19.4 Swedish institutional investors sell out 284
19.5 Playing by a new set of rules 286
19.6 The defence document 289
19.7 Bid reactions in South Africa 291

20 Facing a new reality 295
20.1 In search of a 'white knight' 295
20.2 Skandia Liv 296
20.3 Swedish minority rights 298
20.4 A letter from Skandia chair Lennart Jeansson 299
20.5 Skandia road show 300
20.6 A new nomination committee 302
20.7 Emerging markets' rally 303
20.8 Raising the bid? 306

21 Old Mutual acquires Skandia 310
21.1 Waiving the 90 per cent threshold 310
21.2 A winning strategy 312
21.3 The minority organizes its opposition 315
21.4 Old Mutual's final plan 316
21.5 Old Mutual in control 318
21.6 Further selling of Skandia shares 320
21.7 Epilogue 322

PART VII CONCLUSIONS

22 Some conclusions on corporate control and governance processes in financial capitalism 329
22.1 Chapter overview 329
22.2 General observations 331
22.3 Differing views of the purpose of a limited company 335
22.4 The financial rationale dominates the scene 345
22.5 The functioning of the Skandia board and related agencies 361
22.6 Institutional competition 374
22.7 Where do we go from here? 382

Appendix A methodological note 389
References 395
Name index 413
Subject index 417

Figures

1.1	Two corporate governance flows	18
1.2	Four ideal-type rationalities of corporate control	20
2.1	The competitive landscape	43
2.2	The focal arena	44
2.3	Major events in the process leading to Old Mutual's (OM's) acquisition of Skandia	48
2.4	The two 'opposing camps' in the Skandia context	49
2.5	Skandia share price, 1996–2006	50
5.1	Shareholding in Skandia, 1994	75
6.1	Major owners of Skandia shares in July 2003 and March 2004	95
21.1	Skandia's largest owners as of 1 December 2005	313
22.1	A changed relationship between the two corporate governance flows	360

About the authors

Markus Kallifatides (b. 1972) is an associate professor at the Stockholm School of Economics. His research interests span the social and cultural construction of managerial leadership, the role of the corporation in global relations, and corporate governance. He has contributed to *Invisible Management* (Thomson, 2001) and *Corporate Citizenship in Africa* (Greenleaf, 2006) and has recently been published in *Critical Discourse Studies* and *Corporate Social Responsibility and Environmental Management*.

Sophie Nachemson-Ekwall (b. 1964) is an award-winning business journalist who has worked for a variety of leading news publications in Sweden for the past 20 years. She is the co-author of two books: *Lethal Management: The History of the ABB Crash* (Ekerlids Förlag, 2004), and *Rain of Gold: The Tale of Skandia* (Månpocket, 2005). She has been enrolled as a doctoral candidate at the Stockholm School of Economics since 2006, where she is pursuing research in corporate governance with a particular interest in the evolving European regulatory framework of contests of corporate control and takeovers.

Sven-Erik Sjöstrand (b. 1945) has been Professor of Business Administration at the Stockholm School of Economics (SSE) since 1978, and is the current holder of the Matts Carlgren chair in Management. He has also been the Head of SSE's Centre for Management Studies since 1977, where he leads a staff of about 20 researchers. His own ongoing research addresses corporate government, corporate control and general management issues. Sjöstrand has been a board member on both listed companies and large state-controlled organizations, and has also been a senior adviser to controlling shareholders, boards of directors and CEOs of large Nordic corporations. Sjöstrand's list of publications in English includes: *Organizational Myths* (Harper & Row, 1979); *Institutional Change: Theory and Empirical Findings* (M.E. Sharpe, 1993); *On Economic Institutions – Theory and Applications* (Edward Elgar, 1995); *The Two Faces of Management: The Janus Factor* (Thomson, 1997); *Invisible Management* (Thomson, 2001); and *Aesthetic Leadership* (Palgrave, 2007). Sjöstrand has also published books in Chinese, Finnish, German and Swedish (approximately 25 titles).

Preface

This book is the result of extensive fieldwork that could not have been completed without the most generous support from a great number of individuals, all of whom have devoted substantial time sharing their insights and knowledge with us. Many have also spent even more hours checking and double-checking the accuracy of the voluminous and complex empirical materials that form the heart of the book. For all these dedicated, unreserved and thorough contributions, we express our deepest gratitude.

This publication is the outcome of an ongoing research programme called 'Corporate Governance in Financial Capitalism', which is led by Sven-Erik Sjöstrand at the Stockholm School of Economics' Centre for Management Studies. *Handelsbankens forskningsstiftelser* generously provided funding for this programme. Additional support for this particular project was given by *Fjärde AP-fonden*, *Alecta*, Foundation for Economics and Law, and the Stockholm School of Economics.

We also owe a great many thanks to Professor Lars Östman for reading the manuscript and providing advice, particularly regarding the empirical material, and to Professor Erik Nerep for checking the parts of this text that address the Swedish Companies Act and related legislation and regulations (Chs 1 and 2). We would also like to thank Ingrid Kollberg for her assistance in the production of the manuscript, and Karyn McGettigan for her extensive professional language editing and advice.

The responsibility for all the contents of this book, of course, remains with the authors.

Markus Kallifatides
Sophie Nachemson-Ekwall
Sven-Erik Sjöstrand

Stockholm, June 2009

Introduction

On 2 September 2005, the London-listed and South-Africa-dominated financial and insurance house, Old Mutual, presented a public bid for Skandia, the Stockholm-listed and Swedish-dominated insurance company. After a process that proved to be long, drawn out, complicated, heavily debated, dubious and, in the end, 'hostile',[1] Old Mutual finally declared control over Skandia on 14 February 2006. As a consequence, Skandia's chief executive officer (CEO) resigned, a new board was formed, and Skandia was ultimately delisted from the Stockholm Stock Exchange (SSE).

This book focuses on corporate governance processes: the systems by which companies are directed and controlled. The arena is early twenty-first century financial capitalism and the market for corporate control, characterized by a 'bricolage' of institutions that provide both many and contradictory norms. Numerous actors are involved, coming from several different countries and representing many organizations. We focus upon actual as well as potential shareholders, directors and top managers in the two focal corporations: Old Mutual and Skandia. Other important categories of actors in this market for corporate control include advisers, financial analysts, business journalists and politicians. We have chosen the Skandia board as the nexus for our description of this hostile takeover process.

The basic subject matter of this book is how various kinds of actors are positioned in financial capitalism and how they act on their knowledge about the institutional context, as well as on their understanding of their own positions and the expected rationales of others. Thus our overall ambition has been to describe, problematize and explain some of the institutions and rationales linked to human action in the context of financial capitalism, particularly those with implications for corporate control and corporate governance in a global environment.

NOTE

1. A hostile bid is defined as one that lacks support from the board of the target company.

PART I

On corporate control and governance processes in financial capitalism

1. A theoretical platform

1.1 THE PURPOSE OF THIS WORK

This book has both a theoretical and an empirical purpose. The theoretical purpose is to try to improve socioeconomic theories addressing corporate control and corporate governance, and the empirical ambition is to provide an extensive case study of a hostile cross-border takeover process that helps in understanding corporate control struggle practices in early financial capitalism. Both of these purposes come as responses to the substantial changes in the global economic system that have occurred in recent decades. Taken together, these changes primarily represent a strengthening of predominantly US and UK (Anglo-Saxon) ideals and practices regarding financial markets and corporate governance throughout the rest of the world. Gaining momentum in the 1980s, this diffusion of what we designate as 'financial capitalism' has created both uncertainty and controversy in, as well as across, nations and corporations. We focus on the way large listed and globally active corporations in the early twenty-first century are controlled and governed. The marketing of (US) financial capitalism represents both a challenge and a threat to Europe – particularly those countries outside the UK. This is a challenge because it forces (continental) Europeans to weight the pros and cons of their own differing systems, and a threat due to the often-overwhelming power of US economics on the world stage.

In this chapter we describe our theoretical platform. The chapter is divided into eight sections, first setting the scene and presenting our chosen empirical case study: Old Mutual's hostile takeover of Skandia (Section 1.3). Section 1.4 elaborates on the three basic 'forces' that we claim are involved in the struggle for corporate control: actors, institutions and culture. Following that, we centre on the concept of the corporation and deal with perspectives on the (limited) company (Section 1.5), focusing particularly on the difference between shareholder and stakeholder views. In Section 1.6 we introduce a theory of corporate governance that identifies and visualizes the basis for the different forces that make up the control and direction of the publicly traded company. Based on this theoretical platform, we also describe the activities of various kinds of investors that have been particularly active in corporate control struggles in the era of financial capitalism.

In Section 1.7 we look at shareholder-value bases, time horizons, investment strategies, risk attitudes and kinds of governance behaviour. The following section starts with a brief outline of some of the more important global differences concerning corporate governance systems. We continue on this line and deepen the discussion by focusing on the ingredients that characterize the corporate governance systems involved in this empirical case study: those that fall under the categories of the Anglo-Saxon and the Swedish. In Section 1.8 we look at how the similarities and the differences in such systems could be utilized in cross-border corporate governance efforts. Section 1.9 concludes the chapter with a short description of the increasingly complex practice of corporate governance.

1.2 SETTING THE SCENE: EARLY TWENTY-FIRST CENTURY FINANCIAL CAPITALISM

Financial markets are essentially made up of traded contracts that directly or indirectly refer to underlying assets. A characteristic of these markets is that they are immaterial in character; it has long been argued that their abstract quality feeds much of the 'casino character' of many of the contract markets.[1] Sophisticated actors in more or less coordinated forms speculate upon both various future developments and upon the (re)actions of less sophisticated actors. The well-documented herd mentality of particularly the latter category further contributes to considerable volatility in both prices and volumes on these markets. Those fluctuations sometimes develop into 'bubbles' when the value of the traded contracts loses meaningful connection to the underlying assets (be it in markets for tulips, real estate or stock derivates).[2] For this reason, financial markets have been subject to various regulatory efforts within and across states. One aim has thus been to attempt to prevent this financial market instability from spilling over into the real economy of goods and services. This has proven to be very difficult in practice, as the deep global financial crisis that erupted in 2008 has once again made apparent.[3]

'Financial capitalism'[4] is used in this case to refer to the conditions resulting from financialization, which is conceptualized as 'the increasing role of financial motives, financial markets, financial actors, and financial institutions in the operations of the domestic and international economies'.[5] This evolving state of affairs, which became a force in the world economy from the 1980s and onwards,[6] has also been characterized by huge credit expansion, volatile interest rates, exploding volumes of trade in derivates and other financial instruments, increasing employment and exceptional incomes in the financial sector, extreme asset price fluctuations and amplitudes due to speculation, wide dissemination of elusive risks and moral hazards (separating the decision-makers and receivers of the rewards of risk-taking from those who pay the costs).[7] In sum, financial perspectives have taken the lead and also determine the conditions for the 'real' economy.

With this financialization, a new set of shareholders has entered the scene and has begun to influence the ways in which many business organizations are governed. In general, institutional investors such as pension funds, retail funds and different kinds of hedge funds have captured a dominant shareholding in many corporations in the USA and the UK; they have also taken substantial positions in several other Western countries including Sweden. These investors are subject to the rationale of the financial market, competing for capital on the global scene (i.e. from private savings). They usually receive compensation in ways (performance-based bonuses) that make them target shares in companies that are expected to adopt a strategy that, in the short run, drives its share price upwards. At the company level, this financial primacy has spurred equity-related compensation schemes for management, share redemptions, increased dividends, new forms of debt (making increased leverage possible), a core-competence rhetoric, downsizing, a drift away from prudential (i.e. conservative) accounting principles, a reporting aligned to analysts' expectations, and a pivotal role of (mostly US) investment banks as advisers to corporate managers and other governing bodies.[8]

This financialization has also been characterized by the strong growth of investment banks and other (particularly US-based) financial institutions,[9] which function as intermediaries between investors and corporations. These investment banks act as creditors, underwriters, advisers, investors, and even regulators, all at the same time. Above all, they act as mediators between the wide range of investment funds and the corporations on the global stock market, thus canalizing and influencing the flows of capital between listed companies, industrial sectors and countries.

An arena in which the functioning of the financial markets and the various corporate governance methods is particularly visible is the one where corporate control is ultimately decided. The concept of control then refers to an actor (in this case: shareholder) being in command of a unit, while the concept of governance is used to refer to how such actor control is executed. We focus on contracts linked to this market for corporate control: to those that involve shares and related financial instruments. Therefore, since shares regularly come with voting rights (i.e. opportunities for corporate control and governance efforts), there is an explicit and crucial link between those instruments and the corporations from whom they are issued. In spite of this, however, many of the actors on that market treat company stocks as objects of pure trade; to them, such market transactions are considered simply as shifts in portfolios.[10]

Classical financial theory regards the development of an efficient market for corporate control as beneficial for society at large: for example, one that facilitates mergers and acquisitions. The market for corporate control is, therefore, often viewed as an arena in which managerial teams compete for the right to manage corporate resources,[11] and also have the legal means to do so. On this market, 'better-performing' managers (assumed to be indicative of better-performing companies) can replace 'poorer-performing' managers (assumed to be indicative of poorer-performing companies). Thus the idea is that an efficient market for corporate control reduces agency costs, since the shareholders obtain an instrument (current share prices) through which they can better monitor the actions of the managers.[12] The opportunity for any capitalist to pursue a hostile takeover can be seen, in this context, as a condition that encourages management to do its best to avoid being replaced. We put particular emphasis on the governance and control aspects of such takeover processes.[13] To most classical financial theorists, there are also two other ways to reduce agency costs: aligning management with the shareholders through executive compensation; and board composition.

However, the theoretical ideas behind the classical financial model of the market for corporate control may be challenged. The global market for corporate control was very active during the period 2003–07; this is often described as the sixth takeover wave.[14] However, this activity was not primarily the outcome of increased market efficiency. Instead, many deals within Europe were the result of phenomena such as cross-border differences regarding laws, regulations and customs addressing market views, institutional arrangements and corporate governance models. Another important driving force was the extensive presence of (new kinds of) institutional investors that, in a period with low interest rates and a competitive race to boost the rate of return on capital, spurred both an increase of leverage and higher risk-taking at the corporate level. This focus on short-term profits rather than on long-term value creation worked as a breeding ground for special kinds of institutional investors (e.g. hedge funds and activist funds) who were able to stimulate the occurrence of various kinds of 'events', such as mergers and acquisitions (M&A), and make profits from taking short positions in those struggles for control.

One can claim that financial capitalism has moved control and governance processes to the forefront and placed managerial activities in the background. This more financially based struggle for corporate control has created governance bodies and methods that have often been considered new to continental European and Nordic stakeholders and shareholders. In this novel and rather unfamiliar context, actors draw different conclusions regarding what governance means are available, appropriate, legitimate and effective.

The extensive changes of governance ideals and practices have arguably blurred the corporate positions as stakeholder, shareholder, director and CEO. These role ambiguities have increased the frequency in clashes between various systems for corporate control and governance, and it is those agents that most successfully master this mixture of old and new ways of corporate governance that will dominate the formation of (business) capital for the coming decades. All actors are not equally well prepared for such struggles for corporate control on the contemporary market. There may be significant differences in their knowledge about the changing institutional settings and about the emerging new actor rationales.

We believe that all these changes, basically linked to the transformation of industrial capitalism to financial capitalism, create a need for a reconsideration of the existing theories addressing corporate control and governance processes. Therefore our main purpose in this book is to try to improve the existing theories in these areas. We present the theoretical platform for our efforts in Section 1.4. Before this, however, we would like to add and emphasize that our theoretical ambition is built upon, and intertwined with, an extensive case study of a cross-border hostile acquisition process that involves one Swedish company (AB Skandia) and one UK corporation with a South African heritage (Old Mutual plc). We also believe that our empirical investigation will in itself contribute to a better understanding of national, as well as cross-national, struggles for corporate control and how governance processes develop under conditions of financial capitalism. This extensive empirical platform, as presented in Parts III–VI, then constitutes the basis for the theoretical conclusions that are presented in the final chapter of the book.

1.3 AN EXTENSIVE EMPIRICAL CASE STUDY

There are very few (if any) extensive in-depth studies of cross-national hostile takeover processes carried out in the context of contemporary financial capitalism.[15] However, there are several biographical and journalistic descriptions of such activities.[16]

Our extensive case description is based upon unique access to the actors involved and the statements they made, as well as to some of their private notes and materials. We have also used other kinds of written sources, such as texts published in newspapers and journals, and have even had access to documents that were otherwise labelled as classified. Therefore we have had the opportunity to base our study upon an extraordinary amount of rich and detailed empirical material. This has helped us in our ambition to open the 'black box' in a most delicate field – that of the functioning of the increasingly global market for corporate control.[17]

We have been able to incorporate various kinds of investors, board directors, senior managers, investment bankers, legal advisers, management consultants, politicians and other centrally placed actors.[18] In doing so, we have tried to meet the strong demand for scientifically based empirical investigations of what corporate control and governance processes actually look like in the context of global financial capitalism. The intention behind that effort is to enable a much more grounded discussion about how various kinds of actors interpret this economic system and act upon this understanding when they influence activities in and around corporations. This should provide a better foundation for evaluating various theoretical and normative conceptions presented in the vast amount of academic literature that deals with the phenomenon of corporate takeovers.[19]

Old Mutual's hostile acquisition of Skandia in 2006 was chosen as our 'unit' of investigation because it represented precisely the kind of process that we wanted to study: a cross-border takeover attempt involving the globalized market for corporate control and its many actors and institutions. That recent European power struggle almost perfectly matched these criteria, and involved many of the kinds of actors that are usually active in corporate governance processes. Thus it was not solely the shareholders, directors and managements of the two companies that were expected to be vital in the takeover attempt; many other actors were also considered important contributors both to the process and to the final outcome (hedge funds, activist funds, event-driven funds, arbitrage funds, investments banks, management consultancy firms, analysts, business journalists, auditors, legal advisers and politicians). However, it should be noted that this case also 'chose itself' to a certain extent, because several key actors approached us and asked if we were interested in making a study of Old Mutual's acquisition of Skandia.[20]

The Old Mutual–Skandia case was also chosen because it could easily be contrasted with the classical acquisitions in the era of industrial capitalism, where the market for corporate control was local and there were both fewer and less-differentiated investors. There are some empirical in-depth scientific studies of those earlier acquisitions that provided knowledge about the institutions and actor rationales of the time; unfortunately, they were not many. In a Swedish context, one such extensive study from the 1980s addressed a struggle for control in the pulp and paper industry, where two globally integrated pulp, paper and packaging companies (Stora and MoDo), which were linked to different Swedish bank spheres, competed for the international Swedish-listed packaging company Iggesund.[21] Among large listed global Swedish companies, this takeover effort was the first hostile one of its kind. However, as were most of the acquisitions at the time, it essentially involved local (i.e. Swedish) actors. Another example from the era of late industrial capitalism occurred in the early 1990s when the attempt was made to merge the French vehicle company Renault and Swedish counterpart Volvo.[22] This was a European cross-border effort and could, therefore, be seen as part of the capital market's transformation period from 'industrial' to 'financial' capitalism. Despite this, it still mostly involved local actors (French and Swedish ones).

Both the Iggesund contest and the merger attempt between Renault and Volvo differ substantially from the Old Mutual–Skandia case. These differences illustrate some of the significant changes that have occurred during the past two decades. The former two attempts were local matters with regard to the shareholders, institutional investors and banks involved, and they were linked to the classic ideals and functioning of industrial capitalism (i.e. a strong presence of stakeholder perspectives). The Old Mutual–Skandia case of 2004–06 should instead be examined through the lens of financial capitalism, increasingly sophisticated financial markets, a strong focus on shareholder value, and the influx of globally active institutional investors and investment banks to formerly rather closed national markets for corporate control. Thus the Old Mutual–Skandia case makes visible and concrete the transposition of ideals and practices regarding corporate governance that has occurred when the market for corporate control has changed its basic way of functioning. As mentioned earlier, the purpose of this book is not solely theoretical: our ambition is also to provide an in-depth description of a cross-border struggle for corporate control in early financial capitalism.

Our choice of Skandia (and not Old Mutual) as the nexus of the case has further explanations than the ones just presented. Skandia was not just any large Swedish public company in the late twentieth century – it had also been one of the 'crown jewels' of Swedish business life. This position was based on the fact that its mutually run pension arm Skandia Liv and its previous activity in the property-and-casualty market (P&C market) had made it both a large shareholder in many other large Swedish corporations listed on the Stockholm Stock Exchange (SSE), and a financial corporation of particular importance for a Sweden trying to maintain its position as a financial centre of northern Europe (in the Nordic and Baltic countries).[23] Moreover, its recent history of successful internationalization of a fast-growing financial services industry had won it international fame, which also made it an appropriate candidate for the focal position in the case.

1.4 ACTORS AND INSTITUTIONS[24]

In the theoretical framework presented here, corporate control struggles and corporate governance processes are generally regarded as being influenced by three 'forces': actors, institutions and culture. Almost any social phenomenon can be approached with these concepts, and almost any investigation would require adding particular occurrences or events in order to attain a 'full picture' of the phenomenon in question. Culture is perhaps the most elusive of the three aforementioned concepts, for which academic literature has provided many meanings. For us, culture signifies the overall world-view and ethos prevalent in a society that instantiates itself in certain common attitudes, postures, emotional patterns and practices.[25] An institution is then part of that general (societal) culture that represents a specific system of embedded and enforced social norms of some duration that shape and are shaped by human action.

A society is constituted by, and constitutes, numerous institutions that may be complementary, competing, de-coupled, as well as unrelated. They are continuously constructed, reproduced, exceeded, changed and destroyed by human activity. At the same time, however, institutions influence – enable and constrain – individual actions. In doing this, they have the power to mould the dispositions of human beings; they even have the capacity to change people's ideals, attitudes and aspirations. Institutions emerge, develop and change over time, which makes them historical forces that materialize in physical artefacts (e.g. buildings) as well as in explicit discourses (e.g. economic theory) and invisible dispositions (e.g. tacit knowledge). In this way, history provides the material, mental and habitual resources for the thinking, talking and acting of individuals. Institutions can, therefore, function as a kind of macro-actor in society. They work as arbitrators between individuals and influence the relative power of each actor; in this way, institutions become tools for mobilizing human efforts.

Previous struggles have established the current system of norms (i.e. institutions). Some of these are encoded in laws; others are encoded in customs or professional traditions. Each institutionalized norm and its associated practice is also supported by some kind of sanction (physical, economic or social). As already mentioned, there is a multitude of institutions that, as grounds for their actions, could be enacted by individuals.

These institutions together form what could be called a 'bricolage'.[26] This concept is introduced here to underscore the fact that institutionalized norms applicable to a certain situation may not only be numerous; they may often be conflicting or even contradictory to one another.

When turning to human action, we see individuals as driven by combinations of ideas, values and interests (i.e. gain). These three items are, in some respects, interrelated. This does not, however, imply that individuals always know what ideas, values and interests to promote. Such things may change over time and also emerge in (reflecting upon) actions. We assume, however, that individuals often – but not always – have intentions linked to their actions. Like everybody else, however, we are prevented from knowing directly the intentions of others. What we do have is the possibility of interpreting verbal communication and body language as if such 'perceivable' human expressions are linked to purpose.[27] Such interpretations are always part of the formation of a story; hence they are part of a certain narrative tradition.[28]

When putting ideas, values and interests into practice, individuals must deal with uncertainties of various kinds, since the present is never perfectly known and the future always unknown (although more or less qualified guessing can often be done). These (remaining or genuine) uncertainties refer both to other people and to the gradually emerging contexts (culture, institutions and occurrences/events). Uncertainties that are essentially associated with individual action can be dealt with in two ways: intrapersonal and interpersonal. Intrapersonal ways include handling uncertainty through the use of cognition, emotions, intuition and aesthetic judgement, while interpersonal ways include gaining confidence in unknown others, establishing reliance upon partly known related others, and building trust in well-known close others.[29]

Our model of the human actor stems from the classical one that has long dominated the economic sciences, usually labelled economic man or *Homo oeconomicus*. In this book, however, this notion of the human being is qualified in several ways. The classical construct was built upon the notion that an individual is perfectly informed, has unlimited calculative capability and is, therefore, able to maximize her or his utility. There are many problems associated with this theoretical construct, particularly for those who carry out empirical studies. There is an overwhelming amount of both experimental studies and fieldwork that shows how human beings act in much more diversified and complex ways than is implied and prescribed by the construct *Homo oeconomicus*.[30] However, the relevance, prominence and applicability of this rationale, which is based upon human capacity for calculation, are often taken for granted. To many people, calculation represents a generally valid way of approaching the various decisions that must be made, representing 'the undisputed path'. There is perhaps a largely illusory sense of confidence associated with its use.[31]

In practical contexts, however, it is very difficult to apply a purely calculative rationale with confidence, except in very simple cognitive or transparent situations. There are several reasons for this shortcoming. One is contingent on the bounded rationality associated with human beings, which means that people usually have to tackle complexities with the help of 'non-rational' simplifications such as, for example, various heuristics. Another reason is that many decisions involve dimensions that are hard or even impossible to measure in a meaningful way. It is then not possible to use calculations (i.e. mathematical methods), statistics and other quantitative approaches. In such situations, individual judgements must be added and they are, to a large extent, based on non-cognitive intrapersonal methods. However, judgement is also an important ingredient in most interpersonal uncertainty-handling processes.[32]

Thus a problem with using *Homo oeconomicus* as a scientific model is its strictly cognitive character. As mentioned earlier, this ideal type[33] of a construct disregards the fact that individuals also have emotions, intuitions and aesthetic preferences, and that they also make use of those qualities when coping with uncertainty. This means that human actors can, over time, develop strong emotional ties not only to certain ideas, values or interests, but also to particular individuals; such 'dispositions' in certain situations will guide their decisions and actions. This also means that intuition (individual experiences that are difficult to explain to others in an unambiguous way, e.g. through calculations), are used in intrapersonal attempts to reduce uncertainty. The same reasoning also applies to aesthetics, which means that something that looks or sounds good (cf. rhetoric) is often put into practice. If one combines these four intrapersonal bases for human acting (cognitions, emotions, intuition and aesthetics), a revised construct of the human being emerges: that of *Homo complexicus* or the multi-rational[34] individual.

We add to the construct *Homo complexicus* the idea of the individual as a social and interactive being. This then enables the interpersonal path for dealing with uncertainties. This means that, in all their actions, individuals take into account the activities of others: those already experienced through past interactions, current ones, and those expected to occur. The word 'action' should, therefore, be read and understood as representing a mutuality or an 'interaction'. Past actions often represent a long period of time, while the present is no more than a 'split second', which makes the traces of earlier actions important. This 'history of actions' then influences how people's cognitive maps and emotional memories develop, although the past is concurrently redefined in their ongoing actions. The future is then built both upon the past and the present since human beings, at least to a certain extent, are planners who consider the consequences to which the present might lead.

Since individuals in societies are dependent upon numerous others, and as these others are usually either unknown regarding their personalities or are perceived as distant in other respects, individuals can only (at best) know these others in terms of their positions and functions. Thus, in spite of all these dependencies, most individuals are essentially anonymous to each other, neither interested nor capable of identifying the specific actors involved in particular exchanges. A specific human method has emerged over time to cope with this particular kind of uncertain situation: the classic calculative rationale.

Dependent individuals, however, are not always anonymous to each other. Many such relationships – perhaps even most of them – take place between individuals who have at least some knowledge about the others involved. In order to handle uncertainties both in current contexts and regarding the future, people usually also put faith in the judgements made by known or even selected others. Actors then develop reliance on people whose ideals and values they share, but where the rest of their personalities may be essentially unknown. In this way, a value-based rationale builds relationships and ties between individuals that significantly influence their actions. Such shared values contribute to common understandings among people, and may even bridge many substantial gaps and distances – human, geographical and temporal. A judgement based on this rationale could even be so important in a certain situation that it supersedes a position built on a classic calculative one.[35]

A closer or stronger human relationship has the potential to build what we denote here as trust: a stronger form of interpersonal belief than both the calculative-based confidence and the value-based reliance, since it develops in particularly close and lasting relations between individuals. Trust emerges among the best-known others, such as friends, life partners, cohabitants, family members and other very close people. Trust grows from such relations that then, in turn, relate to matching personalities as well as shared or complementary values, experiences, interests and the like. These trusted others often constitute one or several specific groupings of individuals. One common such bloc denotes a clan, as it refers to individuals tied together by various kinds of kinship. Another bloc denotes a circle, as it is built upon friendship ties. In both of these groupings – clan and circle – affinity and solidarity develop that sometimes lead to well-organized alliances or units (e.g. a family business, an aristocracy or a mafia). Both clans and circles make it possible for actors to handle crucial uncertainties by putting faith in certain others and trusting their judgements. As they know these individuals particularly well – their heritage, experiences, personalities, networks and so on – they can evaluate the underlying bases for their suggestions and advice. They can also be almost sure that these close individuals do their very best and do not try to deceive or betray them. Private, delicate and crucial information can, therefore, be shared and exchanged in such groupings of trusting individuals.[36]

To summarize this section, this book will address the actors, institutions and culture that shape struggles for corporate control and governance processes. We shall interpret actors as complex and multi-rational human beings who deal with uncertainty in several ways, by both intrapersonal and interpersonal paths. Particular attention will then be given to circles as platforms for individual actions, as well as to more temporary organized efforts such as coalitions.

1.5 TWO PERSPECTIVES ON THE CORPORATION

The limited company is a fairly recent human invention, dating back to the nineteenth century. This is a prime example of the productivity of institutions, in this case law. As mentioned earlier, institutions (e.g. legislation) not only constrain human agency; they also enable action.[37] Institutions such as laws are then part of the general production of beliefs, social processes, and goods and services in a society. One particularly prominent feature of the limited company is that it attributes limited liability to the involved human beings for the activities carried out in its name.

The limited company was constructed with the explicit intention to move risks from the individual to an artificial (juridical) person. This lowered the threshold for people to participate in risky investments, since they could do so on a controlled and modest basis. This opportunity attracted a larger number of individuals to participate in different ventures with some of their savings (capital). Individuals did not have to risk their total economic (and social) standing, since only the amount of capital they had put into the corporation could be lost. This shift from human actors to 'super-human' legal actors (limited companies) raised the general risk level in society, and made it possible for its citizens to obtain more wealth.[38] Because this construct of the 'limited corporation' is upheld as a legal possibility by the state, and because its basic purpose is to contribute to general progress in a society, there is a legitimate reason for many categories of actors to participate in the monitoring processes of such organizations. This position is also supported by the fact that many company activities have substantial external consequences on the natural, social and economic environment.[39, 40]

A crucial question then arises whether the basic idea behind the limited corporation is to increase wealth for those that control the company's stock (the shareholders) or if it exists for the benefit of all actors involved. Those who advocate the former more restricted view claim that the limited corporation exists for the benefit of its shareholders: its purpose is to maximize 'shareholder value'.[41] Those who advocate the latter broader view of the corporation (a stakeholder-value perspective) claim instead that limited corporations exist for the benefit of society (i.e. people) in general.[42,43] However, 'shareholder value' is not an unambiguous concept; on the contrary, there are several possible interpretations of what such a perspective represents.[44] Many of its advocates claim that favouring the shareholders' wealth will at the same time benefit the people at large in a society, something that, however, has been difficult to prove (or disprove). However, one could note that most societies have introduced both legislation and regulations that restrict the power and discretion of shareholders, and that could be taken as an indication of certain problems associated with a more 'radical' interpretation of the shareholder-value view.

Actors advocating a shareholder-value view do not always refer to the same interpretation of the concept. A particularly important differentiation of the notion of shareholder value refers to the time horizon applied. Some of the promoters of shareholder value tend to focus on the *current* shareholders in a company, basically acting in a short-run perspective. In such cases, there is rather seldom an evaluation of the various qualities (values, ambitions, experiences and competencies) associated with the shareholders and the shareholding (i.e. no 'discrimination' takes place). However, other advocates of the shareholder-value view instead put the emphasis on the value created for *all* shareholders, current as well as future, and in their actions apply a long-term perspective.[45] Their ambition tends to be a successful (re)production of 'sustainable business structures', providing wealth to all shareholders over time. Some of those who advocate a long-term perspective also often talk about 'reputational costs', which are hard to measure and are, therefore, difficult to include in a short-term rationale. However, regardless of the kind of shareholder-value view promoted – short-term or long-term – the limited company is looked upon as a nexus of incomplete contracts, with the shareholders as the ultimate decision-maker and as the receiver of the residual (profit).[46,47] Those who advocate the shareholder-value view also stress that profit is the best way to measure the company's performance and, thus, management accountability; they claim that the stakeholder perspective blurs actor responsibility.

Those who make use of a stakeholder-value perspective tend to focus on what benefits the corporation as a whole and as a unit; a position they share with many of those who apply a long-term shareholder-value view. In its most 'radical' form, the stakeholder-value view provides no primacy for the shareholders when it comes to governance and control. However, in most cases, stakeholder views tend to add dimensions to long-term shareholder positions by bringing up – and strengthening – specific values that are not immediately associated with – or necessarily advocated by – actors promoting shareholder-value views. Relatively speaking, those who uphold either long-term shareholder views or stakeholder-value views tend to put considerable weight on the corporation's operations, while those taking short-term shareholder views basically treat the corporation as a 'financial unit'.[48] Thus, to several advocates of a shareholder-value view, corporations serve mostly as arenas for investors (foremost for those using a short time horizon); while to many other advocates of a shareholder-value view, corporations function as attractors of capital (investors) to its businesses (especially for those using a long time horizon).

Applying a long-term shareholder rationale or a stakeholder-value-based view means giving more say to customers, suppliers, employees, creditors, the state and civil society at large. The use of these kinds of rationale provide more time for recurrent dealings with all of these actor categories, which build persistent business structures that, in the long run, might create greater value for all shareholders. Conversely, the application of a short-term shareholder-value-based rationale means putting a greater emphasis on the needs of the current actors on the financial markets, including the more speculative ones. To the world outside the corporation, stressing almost any kind of shareholder-value view implies massive increases in information regarding the shares of listed companies, the demand for corporate reporting, the number of professional analysts, and the use of the terminology associated with a shareholder-value view (by managers, directors, shareholders, journalists, politicians, union representatives, academics, ordinary citizens and so on). The use of this rationale within the corporation usually means that decisions and actions become directed towards phenomena that are measurable. Consequently, it also often inspires mergers and acquisitions, share redemptions, higher dividends and attempts to govern by way of monetary incentives.

For at least a century, variants of the long-term shareholder-value view and stakeholder perspectives have dominated most parts of Europe. From the 1980s, however, when financial capitalism made its worldwide breakthrough, this situation has been challenged. In just one or two decades, short-term shareholder-value views have grown in influence, adding to a general strengthening of shareholder perspectives in and around the globalized capital markets colonizing economic life.[49,50,51] In the Old Mutual–Skandia takeover process, both short-term and long-term shareholder-value views, as well as stakeholder perspectives, have their advocates among actors both inside and outside the two merging corporations. Some of them regard it as the fiduciary duty of a board to try to maximize shareholder value for the current shareholders ('short-termism'); some stress a board's duty to secure long-term shareholder value instead. Others see the duty of the board to govern more in the interest of (some of the) stakeholders. These varying perspectives on the limited company bring about differences when it comes to balancing between, on the one hand, financial issues and values, and, on the other, operational matters and business rationales. There may also be differences of opinion regarding how the impact of a company on society as a whole should be handled.

1.6 TOWARDS A REVISED THEORY OF CORPORATE GOVERNANCE

We have described above the basic idea behind the (limited) corporation. Investigating the main forces involved in global struggles for corporate control and interconnected governance processes requires a more elaborate view of the corporation that integrates legal, financial and operational aspects.[52] Many of the more recent capital-market-flavoured studies of corporate control and governance have almost exclusively made use of a financial perspective, ultimately based on the notion of an underlying 'effective' (or even perfect) capital market. They also often concentrate on the functioning of the capital market, and show less interest in its consequences for corporations. This assumed presence of an 'effective' capital market has provided the basis for capital-based corporate governance processes founded on a financial rationale.

For clarity (visualization), this capital-market-based flow will, henceforth, also be described as the 'vertical' governing process (see Figure 1.1). This is a manifestation of a classical and rather uncomplicated view of the principal–agent relationship (cf. mainstream agency theory), where the shareholders (principals) simply define the goals, and the executives (agents) attempt to realize them. Thus it generally puts the shareholders of corporations – not the board or the senior management – in the driving seat.

In this financial perspective, a corporation is regarded as a bundle of assets that it is possible to capitalize either one by one, or in its entirety. The assumption is, furthermore, that shareholders act to maximize the return on the assets (i.e. the capital invested). It is also assumed that the shareholders are able to uphold a superior position – that they are the best

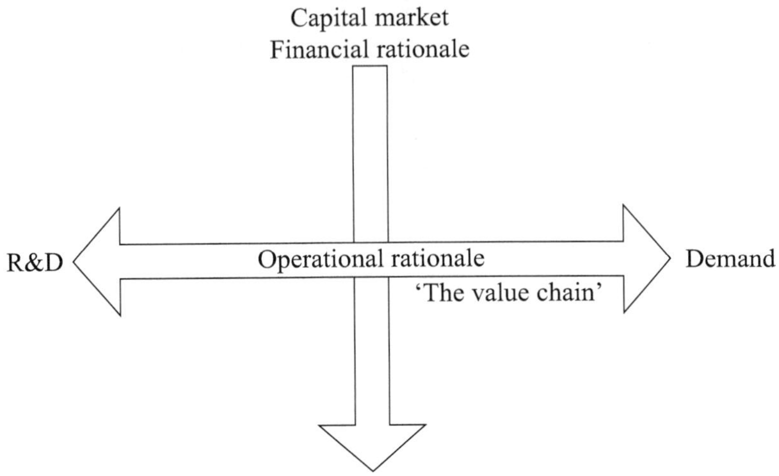

Figure 1.1 *Two corporate governance flows*

informed about the possible future paths for a corporation. Unfortunately, however, academic studies of such capital-based governance processes seldom embrace the core ingredients of the businesses (taking into consideration the actual operations involved). Thus actors deal exclusively with corporate enhancement through the reallocation of capital on the market for corporate control in theories that focus upon capital-based governance processes.

Most management studies of corporate control and governance have focused instead on the actual businesses of corporations, that is, the operational rationale has taken precedence. This governance process utilizes an operational perspective that corresponds to what business administration literature has often called the 'value-chain view', putting the board of directors and the CEOs of corporations in the driving seat. For clarity, this operational flow is also described as the 'horizontal' governance process (see Figure 1.1). Unlike the capital-based vertical governance process that basically goes in one direction (top to bottom), the horizontal process flows both ways (shown as left–right and right–left). One basic driving force is R&D (left to right); the other is market (e.g. customer) demand (right to left). The operational process represents business enhancement through the employment – 'locking in' – of resources for a certain period of time. Thus capital in its general form, financial capital or money, is transformed to a specific use/application as real or fixed capital. Thus actors in the horizontal processes deal mostly with corporate enhancement through the development and recombination of the resources engaged.

Both of these constructs – the capital market determined vertical principal–agent process and the operations-focused horizontal value-chain process – are here amalgamated to form a more complex construct. Thus the financial rationale and the operational rationale are treated as two simultaneous and equally important ingredients in the total corporate governance process. We also add to this complexity by making room for several kinds of actors in both governance flows, all contributing in some way to the outcome of the total integrated process. In the vertical flow, various (kinds of) shareholders participate in the governance activities, as do directors and management, investments bankers, financial analysts, business journalists,[53] credit-rating suppliers, credit providers, regulators and so on. In the horizontal flow, we find not only management and employees in general, but also various kinds of consultants, union representatives, customers, resource suppliers, head-hunters, local politicians and so on. Many of the interactions between actors in these two governance flows occur directly (face to face), but a growing amount of the interaction is mediated (i.e. takes place through the mass media or other intermediaries).[54]

The necessary translation of horizontal processes into assets (and vice versa) is an intricate matter. By implicitly or explicitly allocating assets to processes (or processes to assets), internal corporate accounting does precisely that, but never in a self-evident manner. In any complex organization, it is most difficult to determine which processes are productive and which are not. Financial analysts make the same kind of judgement, although it is usually based on much more limited information.

An important difference between the two flows is that the financial one gains a great deal from transparency, and that quality is usually also demanded by the actors involved in the governance process. The operational process generally benefits from the secrecy that may go with technological and market development. Competitive strengths are usually built on some confidentiality regarding operational core competencies and activities. This difference regarding the two governance flows can sometimes create tension inside and outside corporations.

The corporate governors involved in governing the 'super-human' legal actor of the corporation are constantly dealing with questions concerning operational risk and financial risk (see the arrows in Figure 1.1). We map the possibilities as ideal-type cases (see Figure 1.2). Each of the four generic possibilities that we identify coincides with forms of capitalist practice that are easily read into historical practice.[55] We refer to these four possible combinations as ideal-type corporate control rationalities. 'Entrepreneurial capitalism' is then referred to as the combination of high operational risk-taking and high financial risk-taking. Such practices can often be seen in a particular corporation's initial phases, often with

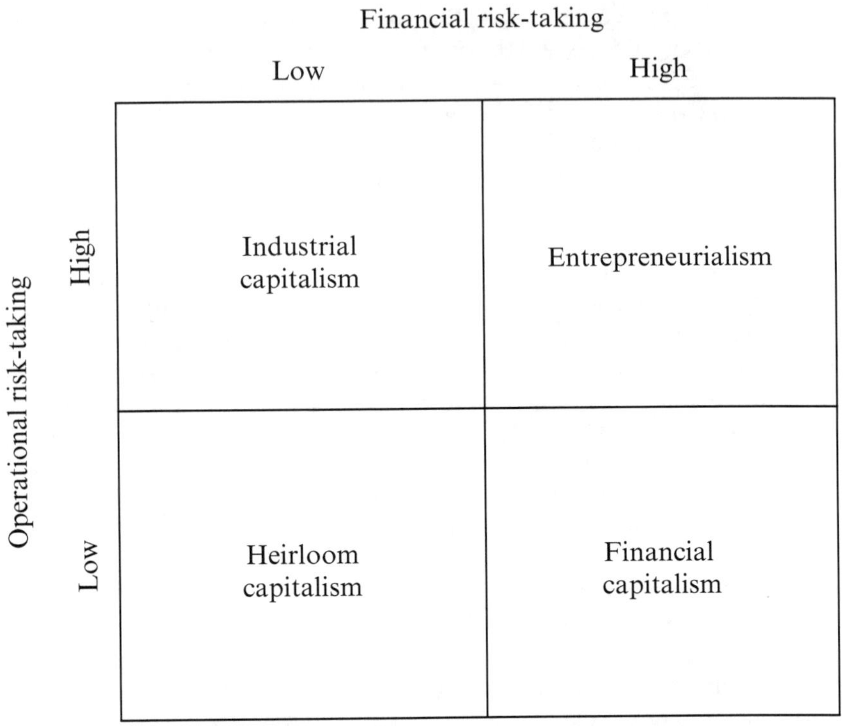

Figure 1.2 Four ideal-type rationalities of corporate control

a founder/owner at its formal head. Initially self-financed, the person(s) with a business idea takes on substantial debt to finance the firm's rapid growth, and also takes all-or-nothing risks in operations.[56]

If the corporation survives the entrepreneurial beginnings, it can evolve in three directions. In many cases, inheritors of the equity of such a corporation develop much more conservative 'heirloom capitalism' in which both financial and operational risks are kept low.[57] In many cases, however, the corporation has slipped from the hands of its initial founders into those of more dispersed shareholders. One path from such a situation has been the practice of 'industrial capitalism' in which there is a cautious approach to financial risk and substantial operational risk-taking.[58] The alternative path is that of 'financial capitalism', with acceptance of financial rather than operational risk.

All these forms of capitalist practice are discernible in all advanced capitalist nations in recent and more distant history. The relative 'weights' or significance of these forms vary and have, indeed, varied over time and between nations. A growing number of authors in recent years have argued that many nations have seen a rather unidirectional shift in prevailing corporate governance regimes – in the direction of financial capitalism.

1.7 SHAREHOLDER RATIONALES DIFFER

Shareholders are treated in a rather simplified way in many approaches to corporate control and corporate governance. They are assumed to attempt solely to maximize the value of their shares. But many shareholders also often want something else, and such ambitions are usually also legitimate.[59] A conclusion is that shareholders are allowed to exercise influence over a corporation on the basis of their personal values in a way that sometimes actually moderates (although not eliminates) the (maximum) profit ambitions, which makes room for the whole repertoire of human rationales. Such a possibility is particularly interesting if a limited company is listed and has several (kinds of) shareholders – both direct (private) and indirect ones (institutional). One could add that there is so much uncertainty involved regarding what actions that, in the long run, actually lead to corporate profit maximizing that the room for human discretion in any case is substantial.

Thus personal values and preferences matter when it comes to direct private shareholding, although they usually play at least some role regardless of the position from which the power of a shareholding is executed. One must keep in mind, then, that direct private shareholding varies a great deal in scale: from a situation where a single individual has a controlling block of shares in a corporation to one where the individual holds only an infinitely small part of a company's stock. In the latter case, the ultimate shareholder's values could be many, differing and disorganized, thus making them rather difficult to promote. In many countries, however, there are associations that try to canalize or mobilize the interests of the small private shareholders.[60] For many of these intermediaries (institutions) there is only a formal link between the principals (ultimate investors) and the agents (middlemen) that handle the shareholding and the governance opportunities in the corporations.[61]

The status and impact of shareholder values can become very problematic, particularly in situations where indirect shareholding is significant. This is because the shareholding in such situations is decided and executed by other actors – middlemen – than by the (ultimate) stockowners. Thus two different sources of values are linked to the market for corporate control: those of the (representatives of the) investing intermediaries and those of the (collective of the) ultimate investors.

The establishment of units (e.g. funds) for indirect shareholding rests upon the expectations that such an arrangement brings several advantages to investors: economies of scale, early and exclusive information, and benefits from specialization (i.e. expertise). Such shareholding – where people buy shares in funds or other intermediaries that are entrusted to place at least some of their capital in corporate stock – has grown substantially in recent decades, not least in Sweden.[62] A repertoire of such funds and institutions, located between the ultimate private investors and the listed corporations, has emerged in the decades around the millennium. This explosion of different kinds of intermediaries could be seen as a market response to the assumed (as well as expressed) variations in investor values, preferences and rationales. However, these new units could also be seen as organizations for producing or encouraging such differences – and to boost and/or to segment the savings or investment market.[63]

A particular feature of larger institutional investors is that they, as intermediaries, take on the characteristics of 'universal shareholders' in a wide range of corporations. This inevitably forces their theoretically rational interests away from those investors with shareholdings in a single or a limited number of corporations, regardless of time horizons and risk attitudes.[64]

The largest category of 'modern' institutional investors is pension funds, with asset pools that are supposed to generate stable growth over a long period of time; these are considered modern compared to investment companies, insurance companies, trusts and so on. These may be national (run by the state) or private (e.g. linked to corporations or other kinds of associations), and they are often among the biggest institutional investors in many countries, controlling considerable amounts of capital.

Another kind of institutional investor that has become a particular important actor category in the era of financial capitalism is the mutual fund, which essentially represents a collection of stocks and/or bonds and other securities, and seeks relative returns. This category includes retail funds that are sold to individual investors through dealers on a competitive market. A mutual fund has a fiduciary obligation to act in the sole interest of investors, who can reclaim their money at short notice. Quarterly, monthly and even daily performance is tracked for these mutual fund investors, and the pressure from competition ensures that they continously try to get the best return on the capital invested (cf., 'index tracking'). Thus this type of institutional investor has an inbuilt focus on short-term earnings. Moreover, if they participate in corporate governance processes, they will have an interest in pushing the board of directors to pursue, for example, share-redemption programmes and mergers and acquisitions, as well as to support incentive programmes that are supposed to align the top executives with the interest of the current short-term shareholders.[65]

A third category of modern institutional investors is usually denoted hedge funds. They deal with getting the most out of fluctuations and amplitudes on markets for assets of various kinds. Hedge funds are typically open only to a limited range of professional or wealthy investors, which provides them with an exemption in many jurisdictions (e.g. US Securities and Exchange Commission) from regulations governing short selling, derivative contracts, leverage, fee structures and the liquidity of interests in the fund.[66] As a category, hedge funds have exploded in the relatively short era of financial capitalism. Nobody really knows the total size of these institutions, since they are often set up in tax havens or countries that do not furnish such information to the general public. The impact of these funds, however, far exceeds the amount of capital deposited by the owners (sometimes by a factor of 100).[67] Some of these funds have become significant actors on the stock market and have participated in corporate control struggles – either in their role as early catalysts or as late-trading arbitrageurs.

A fourth kind of actor in financial capitalism is the activist fund, which often locks in capital for a 3–5-year period. This typical US financial capitalism invention is particularly well positioned to force a board of a supposed underperforming listed company to take measures to increase its shareholder value. Following the millennium, this particular investment style spread to Europe, where Sweden emerged as one of the more popular target markets for such investors. An activist usually agitates – even publicly – for substantial corporate changes. The idea is that if the activists can obtain support from other investors (such as hedge funds or retail funds), then they can influence the decisions of the boards and even gain control over some board seats, and have a chance to change the path of the company, make its business more profitable, and perhaps boost its share price and earn a profit. The power of the activist fund, thus, depends a great deal on the combination of the shareholding composition and governance features of a targeted company. The chance of success is, therefore, highest in a corporation with an open shareholder structure in a country that has an 'open' shareholder-value-oriented governance model (e.g. by giving even moderately strong shareholders the opportunity to influence the composition of boards).

The increased presence of new actors such as mutual funds, hedge funds and activists does not mean that other kinds of institutional investors have disappeared, but their role has been reduced, especially at a global level. There are several 'classic' kinds of (mostly domestic) investors that were influential actors in twentieth-century industrial capitalism that are still important in the corporate struggles of the early years of the new millennium. The foundation is one such basis for investors that play an important role in the context of the new financial capitalism. Foundations have varying allocation and governance policies, ranging from securing control for some shareholder sphere to using the dividends for some stipulated purpose (research, education, charity and so on). Another important kind of classic investor is the investment company, which usually takes a high specific risk by investing in few companies, and actively participates in the governance of these units. The insurance company is yet another type of substantial investor that is still active in the twenty-first century; it is characterized by the dual task involved in its business (i.e. it is both a large investor and a provider of financial services). Finally, there is also the (nation) state (including sovereign wealth funds), which is often a direct shareholder in corporations, expressing varying investment and governance policies and practices.

This discussion indicates that listed corporations in general constitute arenas where many differing, conflicting, and even incompatible shareholder values and rationales often compete. This tendency is strengthened in the era of financial capitalism, where diluted and differentiated shareholdings have become more common. Diluted, in this case, refers to the growing absence of a single dominant (private) shareholder in large listed corporations (most of the shares are controlled instead by either institutional investors or unorganized small investors) and differentiated denotes the fact that shareholder rationales have become more varied on the global scene. The content and form of pressure from the principals (ultimate shareholders) on their agents (middlemen) varies a great deal for all these forms of shareholding (i.e. funds). What is usually lower for long-term investors, such as pension funds, is often stronger for the more sophisticated short-term investors, such as specialized hedge or activist funds, which are all ready to take a stake in a target company.

1.8 INSTITUTIONAL DIFFERENCES CREATE ARBITRAGE OPPORTUNITIES

There is no shortage of academic literature on the many different institutions that are linked to corporate governance.[68] Corporate governance regimes are both varied and complex. Here, we shall limit ourselves to a brief comparison of some aspects of alternative governance regimes, giving rise to a rich landscape in which there are many 'varieties' of capitalism.[69]

Institutions of corporate governance develop as part of the politics of any given nation.[70] Governments, political parties, employer associations, labour unions, social movements, 'big business', lobbyists, 'think-tanks', professional associations and academic disciplines appear as the types of actors most heavily involved in the negotiated order, that is the corporate governance regime in any particular nation. In line with the theoretical framework previously outlined, these actors must be understood in relation to economic structures and (usually national) culture in order to complete the picture.[71] Any particular corporate governance regime forms a more or less coherent whole. Hence changes in any particular institution, actor or cultural aspect may appear as something of an 'irritant' to other institutions and actors, as well as to the general culture.[72] Overall, corporate governance regimes can be expected to be rather resistant to such irritants, as changes will constitute challenges to established and usually rather powerful groups of actors, and the institutions and cultural basis they rely on.[73]

The most important mode of corporate governance around the world is the one that falls under the common rubric of the Anglo-Saxon model. This form, most associated with the 'liberal market economy' of the USA and the UK, is characterized by the importance it accords to the liquidity of financial markets. Furthermore, neither corporate nor labour law puts too many limits on the discretionary powers of managers in this model. The dominating idea has been that liquid markets supply rewards to good managers and credible threats of takeovers to bad ones.[74] The main way for shareholders to exercise control over managers is by entry or exit (i.e. buying or selling their shares). Hence shareholders have been particularly interested in liquid markets, so that they are practically able to 'vote with their feet' at a reasonable cost (not having to accept a much lower price when selling).

In Germany, to provide a contrasting example to the Anglo-Saxon model, both corporate and labour law subject management to strong constraints, forcing it to negotiate with stakeholders in the process of governing the corporation. These negotiations take the form of both formal and informal coordinations and were built up around the banks that (through loan giving) emerged as influential corporate shareholders after the twentieth-century world wars (and sometimes they also involve actors representing the federal economy). The German model serves as an example of a rather different governance regime and of a 'coordinated market economy'. The banks' basic governance idea has been to promote low risk-taking rather than a high return on the capital submitted to corporations by the shareholders. The German governance model became a divided one that made a distinction between an executive board (*Vorstand*) and a supervisory board (*Aufsichtsrat*). The latter includes an equal number of shareholders and employee representatives, with the shareholders choosing the chair.

With the growth of financial capitalism, it has been assumed that there has been a rapid global convergence of governance regimes towards the Anglo-Saxon model. However, a closer look at the empirical basis for that thesis provides no safe conclusion on this point. Convergence seems to have been the rule for a decade or so, especially when it pertains to the regulation of financial markets. Corporate law and labour law (two other important pillars in any corporate governance regime) show stability or even sometimes increased divergence when comparing the US, Nordic, German and emerging EU models.[75]

In conjunction with 'Americanization' of financial markets, the opening up of capital markets for flows across national borders has challenged the varying national institutional arrangements manifested throughout the world. The markets for corporate control have transformed from being local (e.g. Swedish or English) or regional (e.g. Nordic or British) to being international, with no effective separation of the national borders involved. In this globalized arena, corporations established in different countries face new and unexpected restrictions, as well as possibilities. The fact that regulations of corporate control and governance processes vary across nations has created a 'new kind' of competition – one that directly concerns the quality, content and enforcement of the relevant institutions. The special takeover regulations, which represent interesting cross-sections of governance regulation, are noteworthy for their contradictory and complex pattern of evolution.[76] In that clash of regulations (legislation, custom, codes and so on), some systems have turned out to be stronger than others. In the late twentieth century the Anglo-Saxon ideals and practices took command by circulating their shareholder-value ideal around the world.

Old Mutual's acquisition of Skandia, which provides the empirical material used in this book, illustrates a clash between the dominant Anglo-Saxon tradition and a continental European one (in this case a Swedish/Nordic model). To understand this process and its final outcome, one has to know something about the basics of the different regulatory systems involved, and about the ways of thinking associated with both of these governance traditions.

As the Swedish market for corporate control and governance principles has been significantly influenced by the Anglo-Saxon ones during the last decades, it is important to know something also about the more recent changes in that country in order to understand the takeover process studied here. Thus there is both what could be described as the 'new' Swedish model and the 'older' one; both are briefly described here. One or the other (or sometimes both) is present in the minds of the Swedish actors, and this consequently affects their decisions and activities.

The older Swedish model is associated with classical Nordic and continental European industrial capitalism, and was built upon a basically regional Swedish or Nordic market for corporate control and governance processes. This was characterized by a long corporatist tradition that secured cooperation, mutual understanding and acting in concert between the (then) dominant political power (the Social Democratic Party) and the economic power centres (certain families and bank spheres). In this context, the rhetoric of national interests was central.[77]

In the twentieth century, there was a particular focus on the needs of the many large Swedish international corporations, which was visible, for example, when national regulations and taxation issues were discussed. There was also an emphasis on ownership stability to ensure that the founders or entrepreneurs could continue to control the growing companies through various types of shares (with different voting power), and the allowance of corporate cross-holdings of stock. Stability was also manifested in the presence of bank spheres of interest, and deals across these borders were rather rare (as were CEO and director recruitments).

Generally, the Swedish Companies Act gave great power to shareholders over executives, although certain other regulations restricted that freedom (e.g. labour market law, taxation laws, environmental protection regulations and so on). Many of these laws and regulations stimulated the retaining of earnings in the company, thereby stimulating investments in people and other non-financial resources, while backing the operational dimension of a corporation.

In the late twentieth century, strong pressures were put on Swedish actors to abolish several of the country's distinguishing features that had been inspired by the (then) global rush for deregulation of capital markets and the spreading of financial capitalism. The Swedish exchange and currency regulation was removed in the 1980s, and, within a few years, foreign investors increased their shareholding in Swedish listed companies. Institutional shareholders such as pension funds and mutual funds – both Swedish and foreign – then became strong voices demanding more openness to better match the control and governance ideals and traditions linked to financial capitalism, and to be able to challenge controlling blockholders. The previous rather closed Swedish market for corporate control opened up, cross-company shareholding was significantly reduced, some corporations changed[78] or even abolished voting restrictions, and new listed firms often issued only one set of shares with equal voting rights. However, most old listed companies retained the differentiated voting rights, which made that construction an important condition in the modelling of an early twenty-first-century Swedish governance code.

The Swedish (Nordic) governance system was based upon a clear-cut distribution of functions – duties as well as responsibilities – between three different agencies: the shareholders' meeting (i.e. Annual General Meeting – AGM), the board of directors and the CEO. In Swedish company law, the shareholders at the AGM suggest and appoint the directors on the board according to one-year mandates (a few other board members are appointed by the local unions). The board appoints the CEO, the person solely in charge of the operations of the company. He or she might be a member of the board; however, this is not always the case. Directors are non-executives and are, thus, independent of the corporation; this rule is also valid for the chair. Thus Swedish directors are 'dependent' on (and chosen by) the large shareholder(s). The Swedish Companies Act, however, states that all directors must act so that all shareholders are treated alike (the bigger ones cannot be favoured) – they are obliged to act in the best interest of the entire corporation. The capacity of the AGM to exact influence is strong. The AGM exerts a more direct influence upon the running of the company, since it is free to decide on any unannounced matter (but its decisions obviously remain constrained by law and the corporate constitution; moreover, consensus is usually required).[79] Especially with regard to the board of directors there are certain differences compared to the Anglo-Saxon model.

In the British Anglo-Saxon model, a group of independent directors on the board suggest new board members. The board is composed of both executives (often the CEO and the CFO) and non-executives (in this tradition, the latter category is referred to as 'independent').[80] However, there are notable differences between UK Anglo-Saxon governance and the US model, where the latter has traditionally put more power into the hands of the CEO (who, historically, has also acted as chair). Since a US board of directors suggests the names for which to vote, and many directors are voted in for a few years at a time, the immediate influence of shareholders is restricted. In Sweden, the large shareholders are expected to be on the board and even to control the chair.

A new 'independent' corporate governance body between the AGM and the board was formally introduced in Sweden in the early twenty-first century, namely the 'nomination committee' where members represented the shareholders,[81,82] and requirements were raised for putting independent directors on the boards (independent from the dominating shareholders). This meant that the Swedish nomination committee's standing differed from its Anglo-Saxon counterpart, where it is a body made up of independent directors from the board. To ensure that shareholders, especially foreign, understand the duties of the nomination committee and the responsibility of Swedish directors, the Swedish Code of Corporate Governance (established in 2005; revised 2008) states that 'good governance' means ensuring that companies are run as efficiently as possible on behalf of the shareholders. The confidence of existing and potential shareholders that such is the case is crucial to their interest in investing in companies, thus securing corporate Sweden's supply of risk capital.

The Swedish and the US cases might be seen as mirror images of each other. In Sweden, dominating shareholders potentially marginalize the board function, sometimes against the wishes of management, and sometimes to the (unintended) detriment of the corporation. In the USA, dominating CEOs potentially marginalize the board function, sometimes to the (unintended) detriment of dispersed shareholders and the corporation. In both cases, and on both sides of the Atlantic, there have been ambitions to resurrect corporate boards as a viable agency for 'proper' corporate governance.[83] In the UK version of Anglo-Saxon governance, the work to strengthen the standing and independence of the directors has been carried out since Sir John Cadbury's first Code of Corporate Governance was adopted at the London Stock Exchange (LSE) in 1992.[84]

The USA and the UK must also be treated separately regarding takeovers – especially hostile ones. In the UK, a takeover bid should be presented directly to the shareholders, with limited possibility for the board to stop it; the same applies when a takeover bid is hostile (see the British takeover rules[85]). In the USA, the board of directors has plenty of possibilities to prevent shareholders from accepting a non-recommended bid.[86] It should be noted that the European takeover directive adopted in 2004 was developed with reference to the UK counterpart, although it was less strict and less detailed. German regulations, for instance, strongly influenced by employee representatives on the board, allow the use of 'poison pills' to protect the company from hostile takeovers.[87]

Swedish and UK takeover regulations are pretty inviting to unfriendly takeovers, although there are important differences between Swedish and Anglo-Saxon governance that become particularly visible in certain situations. Takeovers have for long been an important feature on the Swedish stock market. Since the 1990s its market for corporate control has been second only to that of UK.[88] One explanation is the large presence of voting differences. This may simplify the bidders' negotiations with target shareholders (as some of them often control shares with strong voting power), while at the same time it reduces the attractiveness for the remaining minority shareholders to remain owners.[89] A taxation system that discourages direct shareholding by Swedish households may also be a reason.[90] An even more complicated bricolage of features and activities seems to emerge in the Old Mutual–Skandia study, which focuses on both a hostile bid and a Swedish context, in which certain adjustments to some of the UK Anglo-Saxon governance principles in the late twentieth and early twenty-first century play an important role.

Agents work through the various toolkits that their environment provides: laws and regulations, formulas for calculation, established arenas and networks, socially enforced custom and traditions, and the media. The Swedish toolkit of immediate relevance for actors involved in corporate control processes has, in recent years, been transformed. The Old Mutual–Skandia takeover process, therefore, includes several novelties (i.e. new to the Swedish market) such as nomination committees, due diligence procedures and 'soft irrevocables'. This struggle for control also involves several forms of national 'soft regulations'. In Sweden, there is the Swedish Securities Council (Aktiemarknadsnämnden), the Swedish Industry and Commerce Stock Exchange Committee (Näringslivets börskommittée), and the Takeover Rules (Offentliga erbjudanden om aktieförvärv). There are also national 'hard regulations', most of which have long been established in the country's legal systems: for instance The Companies Act (Aktiebolagslagen), the Insurance Companies Act (Försäkringsrörelselagen), and a number of laws or regulations that address insider trading in stocks and derivatives. These laws and regulations together form the basic – and, at the same time, partly changing – toolkit for agency on the Swedish market for corporate control. Since the corporate scandals of the late 1990s, this toolkit has been subject to recurrent renegotiations with a manifest government interest in the processes.[91]

As initially mentioned in this section, institutional differences between countries present opportunities for actor discretion (i.e. strategic interpretations and manoeuvring). The decades before and after the millennium have provided particularly favourable conditions for such activities, since the institutional arrangements around the world that relate to corporate control and governance matters have changed dramatically (the emergence of financial capitalism). Skilful agency will, therefore, be partly theorized as an aptitude for making use of other (countries') agents' historical legacy, and as acting to obtain benefits from it. We introduce two concepts to capture these activities: rule arbitrage and moral arbitrage.

Arbitrage is a concept used to denote forms of trade where actors attempt to obtain the rewards of differences in the pricing of equivalent assets (e.g. shares) on different markets (e.g. stock markets around the globe). In an analogous yet more complex way, there may be earnings from following rules in one place (e.g. country or stock exchange) when acting in another – we call this rule arbitrage. Yet another form of arbitrage can be said to exist when some actors in a marketplace do precisely what others would not do – we call this moral arbitrage.

1.9 A FEW CONCLUDING REMARKS

Corporate governance regimes differ between nations and regions. They are here seen as temporary, but quite stable, negotiated orders formed by multi-rational actors, historically constructed and contested institutions, imperfectly integrated culture, and events that always carry unintended and unforeseen effects.

One rather unilateral trend, sparked by the lifting of local currencies (e.g. in the EU) and capital controls, has been under way for three decades. A specific corporate governance regime – US financial capitalism – has spread across the globe. It has then been injected and/or drawn into the ongoing dynamic power struggle that forms corporate governance regimes throughout the world. This poses both opportunities for and threats to many incumbent actors, and to the institutions and culture that form the medium through which they act. This also spurs the formation of new kinds of actors (such as new forms of shareholders in corporations) and, hence, affects the overall appearance of the playing field. Together, new and old kinds of shareholders participate in what might be seen as an increasingly complex practice of corporate governance. With these conceptions and theoretical ideas, and with the ambition to both substantiate and elaborate upon them, we now turn to a particular case of corporate governance and a struggle for corporate control.

NOTES

1. Sjödin (2006) provides an elaborate philosophical grounding and updated application of this fundamental conception of financial markets.
2. Cf. Brenner (2002).
3. In fact, as Brenner (2002) and others have warned, following the bursting of the ICT bubble and the notorious events of 11 September 2001, the US Federal Reserve has officially acted to promote such spillover effects from the financial markets into the real economy (through what is known as 'the wealth effect'). Unsurprisingly, such spillover effects work both in times of booming financial markets and when they turn downwards. Cf. Palley (2008), Pérez Caldentey and Vernengo (2008), and D'Arista (2008) for updated analyses.
4. This view is contrasted with the 'previous period', which is often referred to as 'industrial capitalism'.
5. Cf. Epstein (2005b), p. 3.
6. The deregulation of domestic economies and opening up of the financial markets that began in the USA and the UK in the early 1980s are seen as the starting point of a low-growth expansionary cycle in the global economy, marked by widening domestic and global inequalities that came to an abrupt end with the bursting of the housing market bubble in the USA in 2007–08.
7. Cf. Krugman (2009), who particularly stresses that borrowed money tends to breed moral hazard.

8. Aglietta and Rebérioux (2005). See Bebchuk and Fried (2004) for a devastating argument on managerial compensation.
9. Five US investment banks dominated the global market for corporate deal-making up to 2008: Morgan Stanley, Goldman Sachs, Merrill Lynch, JP Morgan Chase and Lehman Brothers. German Deutsche Bank was among the few non-US-based among the top actors, alongside Swiss UBS.
10. Cf. e.g., Hawley and Williams (2000).
11. Cf. Jensen and Ruback (1983).
12. For a thorough description of agency cost, see Berle and Means (1932), who coined the famous formula of the 'separation of ownership and control'. In companies that have hundreds of thousands of shareholders, small shareholders are no longer able to assert their right of ownership and control.
13. In the 1990s, this was also an important aspect of the works by the European Commission in its goal to strengthen Europe's corporations *vis-à-vis* US and Asian competition through the formation of European champions. To achieve this, the Commission and its member states pressed for the creation of a level playing field targeting the deregulation of previous captive markets (e.g. power generation, telecommunications and banking) and opening up the market for cross-border mergers. Part of this work was to create a market for hostile takeovers.
14. Previous takeover waves broadly refer to the first (1893–1904), second (1919–29), third (1969–73), fourth (1984–89), and fifth (1993–2000).
15. There were, however, some studies carried out in the era of industrial capitalism (e.g. Sjöstrand, 1997).
16. Journalists are trained and habituated to catch an opportunity when it occurs, so they are often able to start to collect empirical material at very short notice, and then report on what has happened. Many of these business journalists have access to statements from the key actors, and sometimes they also acquire classified material.
17. One will search in vain in widely used textbooks for materials based upon observation or deep interviewing with actors involved in practice (cf. Brealey and Myers, 1991).
18. The dominance of journalistic reporting rather than academic investigation is particularly evident in a US context. Cf. the work by Kim and Nofsinger (2007), or consult the huge work by Monks and Minow (2004).
19. We hope that our study is of relevance to, and makes use of insights from, several fields of enquiry. Among them we find the fields of 'political economy' (cf. Lazonick and O'Sullivan, 2000, Aglietta and Rebérioux, 2005 and Epstein, 2005a), 'historical institutionalism' and 'organizational institutionalism' (cf. Fligstein, 2001 and Campbell, 2004), 'social studies of finance' (cf. Knorr Cetina and Preda, 2004, MacKenzie, 2006 and Froud et al., 2006), and 'corporate governance' (cf. McCahery et al., 2002, Roe, 2003 and Clarke, 2004, all of which, irrespective of their differences, contain significant challenges to textbook economics.
20. Carried out as a part of our ongoing research programme at the Economic Research Institute at the Stockholm School of Economics, addressing the consequences of the transformation from industrial to financial capitalism for corporate control and governance processes.
21. Cf. Ericson (1990) and Sjöstrand (1997).
22. Cf. e.g., Sundquist (1994).
23. In 'long-only' fund quarters in Sweden, Skandia was the *exemplum* of the need for better and active corporate governance on the part of stand-in owners like themselves (cf. Bengtsson, 2005).
24. This section is based on Sjöstrand (1995).
25. Our approach to culture follows that of Jackall (1988). On an even more foundational level, see Geertz (1973), who puts significant emphasis on the incompleteness of social integration via what we refer to as institutions, although his overall theory is one of integration rather than of social disorder. Jackall, in his magisterial analysis of US managerial culture, tells a tale of such culturally integrated, while endemically contested, institutions.

26. Campbell (2004) chooses this term in his exposé of institutional social theory. Another concept that is often used by anthropologically inspired theoreticians is 'hybridization'. In his 1985 exposé of social theory, Sjöstrand used the concept of 'empirical forms of emanation' to express the notion that practice never realizes clear-cut ideology, but rather a bricolage (Sjöstrand, 1985). The idea is traceable to nineteenth-century German philosopher G.W.H. Hegel in his *Phenomenology of Spirit* (*Mind*), and to Hegel's personal experience of institutional bricolage (Pinkard, 2000).
27. Already meticulously elaborated upon by, for instance, Schütz (1932/1967).
28. Cf. e.g., Ricœur (1983/1984).
29. Cf. Sjöstrand (1997).
30. Cf. Sjöstrand (1997). The following paragraphs also build upon this volume.
31. The tradition represented by Callon and Muniesa (2005) places particular emphasis upon faith in calculative tools of various kinds in the construction of economic interaction.
32. Cf. Gonzales Guve (2003).
33. 'Ideal type' (cf. the German *Gedankenbild*) has nothing to do with the usual definition of ideal as meaning 'to be preferred above all else'.

    > Instead, ideal types refer to established constructions with a distinct and commonly accepted scientific meaning. Ideal types are formed by accentuating certain selected characteristics that are ascribed to an empirical phenomenon (some scholars even suggest that ideal types represent constructions of theoretical extremes; cf. McNeil, 1981). Hence an ideal type expresses conceptual purity and is, thus, similar to an elaborate construct with no obvious empirical counterpart. In other words, ideal types do not simply reflect empirical phenomena, nor do they correspond to anything wholly separated from empirical knowledge. Ideal types are usually based upon scientific exploration, explicitly or implicitly involving empirical elements. Therefore they are based on ingredients drawn from the best existing scholarly knowledge. The value of a construct of this kind is not only determined by testing single ideal types against single empirical organizations; rather, its prime value is often revealed when the whole theoretical *repertoire* (the system of theoretical ideal types) is confronted with empirical material for analysis. In brief, the relationship between ideal types and empirical phenomena is, thus, an analytical one – ideal types represent tools of an 'as if' kind for use in theorizing (cf. Collin, 1990, p. 73). Human organizing, it is assumed, occurs *as if* it were governed by rationales associated with a mixture of ideal types. The ingredients that compose the 'as ifs' for each ideal type then play a crucial role in theory construction (Sjöstrand, 1997, p. 200).

34. The notion of the 'multi-rational' human being was introduced in Sjöstrand (1997).
35. Cf. Sjöstrand (1997).
36. Cf. Sjöstrand (1997).
37. Cf. Burchell et al. (1991); and Foucault (1975/1977). The former book is an introduction to the thought of French historian of ideas Michel Foucault, one of the prime explorers of the productivity of law, an idea he picked up primarily from German philosopher Friedrich Nietzsche and Karl Marx.
38. Cf. Tricker (2000); and Micklethwait and Wooldridge (2003/05).
39. According to many expressions of stakeholder-value ideology, it is as though there were no tension between shareholder and stakeholder interests, and as though human beings naturally work towards higher ideals or represent 'the higher good', i.e. as though a particular stakeholder were the representative of all.
40. Regarding this discussion about shareholder and stakeholder perspectives on the company, cf. e.g., Maher and Andersson (2002).
41. The shareholder-value view begins and ends by arguing as if there were no externalities to the firm's operations, as if all shareholders had equal opportunity to make reasoned judgements about the actions of 'their' corporation, as if financial markets

were 'efficient', and as if the legal system surrounding the corporation were working as planned. For a clear expression of the opinion that corporations should be directed to one objective only, see Jensen (2001), pp. 6–21.

42. See, e.g. Sternberg (2004); This author is particularly annoyed that stakeholder-theory talk continues to pretend to speak about corporate welfare when it is actually about promoting other interests than the protection of property rights and free enterprise – which she considers to be the solid rocks of civilization.
43. Samuelsson (2005).
44. Cf. e.g., Samuelsson (2005).
45. A shareholding changes 'continuously' in a limited company (in principle, there is a new shareholder distribution every minute, day, week, month, quarter, year etc.
46. But there are several alternative highly developed conceptualizations, both theoretical and normative: cf. Turnbull (1997b), Fraser (1998) or Aglietta and Rebérioux (2005).
47. This is due to the fact that shareholders in the construct chosen obtain their payments last – they carry the highest economic risk. Therefore, it is assumed that the shareholder's motivation to work for the effectiveness of the company is the strongest among all stakeholders. Cf. e.g., Sjöstrand (1985).
48. Cf. Östman (2009).
49. An important statement regarding this transformation, which addresses the strong connection between academic knowledge creation, education of managers and directors, and corporate practices, can be found in Fligstein (2001). Evidence of these transformations is given through the voices of experienced managers/directors in Swedish corporations in Brodin et al. (2000). The great impact of these transformations on CEO practice is demonstrated in Tengblad (2004). An investigation of the various expressions in this particular discourse to Swedish-dominated corporations can be found in Borglund (2006). An updated overview of the development of shareholder value as ideology and one empirical investigation of its implications for managerial and organizational practice in a Swedish context is presented in Blom (2007). A similar reasoning – one that puts it all in an even wider ideological context and, in doing so, by an explicitly 'neo-Marxist' theoretical framework related to the neo-Weberian (institutionalist) framework of Fligstein (2001) – is found in Ezzamel et al. (2008). Lazonick and O'Sullivan (2000) was perhaps the landmark prediction of the 2008 collapse in the US economy, as they launched a critique of shareholder value as a macroeconomically unsustainable principle for corporate governance.
50. Financial markets are seen as efficient, which makes short-term and long-term shareholder value the same thing. From the view of economic research, this perception of capital markets is peculiar given the production of cycles of speculation bubbles and crashes that continue on the world's financial markets (cf. Brenner, 2002).
51. A broad overview of corporate scandal mechanisms in the USA is presented in Mitchell (2001). An analysis of the insider legislation on the Swedish (and US) stock market is provided in Sjödin (2006). Both works describe the failures of legislation to achieve at least some of its stated objectives.
52. Cf. also Östman (2009).
53. Most of the time, it will be quite clear that the media and selected journalists are used by other agents to make their case, whereas in other instances certain journalists actively contribute to the process by producing analyses themselves or orchestrating news and events.
54. For a provocative statement on the profundity of the mediatization of modern life, see Baudrillard (1994).
55. Cf. Glete (1994).
56. A point made by Weber (1911–19/1978).
57. Emling (2000) recently showed the doubly risk-averse attitude prevailing in family-controlled corporations in Sweden. The term 'Heirloom capitalism' was inspired by the work of Karlsson Stider (2000).
58. E.g. Chandler (1977).

59. The Swedish Companies Act, e.g., does not demand that a limited corporation try to maximize its profit as its main purpose; to strive for (any level of) profit is sufficient (cf. e.g., Johansson and Nial, 2007).
60. Bengtsson (2005) details the problem with poor 'rational' incentives to engage in activism; this is an example of Olson's (1965) classic theory. Bengtsson also subjects this theory to (institutionalist) critique upon the basis of his empirical study of actual shareholder activism. In Sweden, for instance, the Swedish Shareholders' Association organizes and represents small private shareholders. The Association can vote by proxy at AGMs, and has historically been an important force in the development of both minority shareholder rights and governance.
61. Principals seldom hold agents responsible for their activities and results due to this weak connection and lack of interaction. However, institutional actors have such an agency function, with a fiduciary responsibility to generate 'optimum returns' to their principals. This 'return', however, is not always easy to determine, since the principals could be both numerous and constitute a rather heterogeneous 'crowd' that is not always interested in, or able to communicate, which allocations of capital and governance efforts they would like to see. Thus it is often difficult to identify a common denominator among the principals; therefore, middlemen often construct the allocation rules and earnings targets themselves.
62. Cf. Blyth (2002). Swedish citizens, as long as they are employed, cannot avoid being major indirect shareholders through collective pension schemes. Various governments since the 1980s have supported retail fund savings by creating tax incentives and by information campaigns. Individual holding of shares has also become vastly more common. Lindqvist (2001) examines the deep transformations of everyday life related to the practice of shareholding. The relative reduction of direct shareholding has varied between countries, regarding both speed and level. Institutional investors controlled 59 per cent of the London Stock Exchange in the early 1990s. At the same time 35 per cent of the capital came from institutional investors in the USA (48 per cent from private individuals) (cf. Charkham and Simpson, 1999). By 2005 institutional investors controlled 61 per cent of the capital. Despite the massive increase in household shareholding in Sweden, households halved their proportion of the total shareholding on the Stockholm Stock Exchange (SSE) from 30 per cent in 1983 to 13.5 per cent in 2007, while retail funds grew their part of total shareholdings from 5 per cent to 11 per cent (Statistics Sweden, 2008). The presence of Swedish insurance companies, investment companies and non-private institutions, such as foundations, fell back during the same period, thus creating space for an influx of foreign institutional investors. Foreign shareholding on the SSE grew from 8 per cent in 1990 to close to 40 per cent in 2000. Since then the figures have varied between 37 and 40 per cent.
63. A collected capital could have a specific ambition or allocation policy that is often expressed in quite a straightforward way. This could make it possible for investors who entrust capital to a fund or other kind of investing institution to express their values and preferences regarding value, risk, time horizon, industry and so forth.
64. Hawley and Williams (2000) provide ample arguments on this point.
65. For a description see, for example, Windolf (2008).
66. A hedge fund will typically commit itself to a particular investment strategy, certain types of investments and leverage levels via statements in its offering documentation, thereby giving investors some indication of the nature of the fund. A hedge fund manager typically receives both a management fee and a performance fee directly from the client. The presence of the latter is one of the characteristics of a hedge fund.
67. Dodd (2005) and Parenteau (2005) carefully analysed these developments, as did Brenner (2002) and Sassen (2001), in a more summarized way. Cf. also Krugman (2009, pp. 119–21).
68. E.g. Sjöstrand (1993), Aoki (2001), Hall and Soskice (2001), Fligstein (2001), Mantzavinos (2001), McCahery et al. (2002) and Campbell (2004).
69. Hall and Soskice (2001) was a contribution that received much attention. Overviews

of various systems of corporate governance around the world can be found in Mallin (2006a, 2006b).

70. Roe (2003) has a particularly strong argument on the centrality of national politics, although he may be seen to take consequences of governance regimes too much at face value, confounding shareholder influence on paper with shareholder influence in practice, for instance.
71. Gao (1998) brings it all together in an account of transformation of economic institutions in Japan.
72. Following Teubner (2001) specifically discussing the 'legal irritant' of 'good faith' as a legal principle injected from continental European legal systems to the UK one as part of European efforts at 'harmonization'.
73. Hall and Soskice (2001) was an attempt to highlight the importance of firms and, in particular cases, associations of firms in the 'negotiation' leading to the 'negotiated order' of national corporate governance regimes, and more broadly to the entire socio-economic fabric of nations.
74. Manne (1965/2000) introduced the concept of a 'market for corporate control'.
75. Cf. Roe (2003).
76. McCahery et al. (2002), and Aglietta and Rebérioux (2005).
77. Lindqvist (1996). His work focuses upon the older corporatist legitimating narrative used by corporate managers and shareholders (summarized as 'jobs in Sweden'). He also raised the question of whether Europe would come to replace the single nation as the new focal object in a new legitimating narrative.
78. For example, they changed the voting difference between A-shares and B-shares from 1:1000 to 1:10.
79. Carlsson (2007) presents an overview of Swedish corporate governance and its history.
80. Independent also means that an actor has not been on the board for longer than eight years. Directors should be submitted for re-election by shareholders at least every third year.
81. Given the special features of the Swedish model of corporate governance, the nomination committee (appointed by the AGM) had turned into a powerful force for shareholder activism, legitimizing actions in the corporate boardroom that, for example, were not allowed in the USA.
82. Through this, smaller shareholders are assured that a controlling shareholder – usually in control of between 10 and 30 per cent of the voting power, but sometimes above 50 per cent – will involve smaller minority shareholders in the composition of the board before the AGM. In companies with wholly dispersed shareholder bases, in which no shareholder has above 10 per cent of the voting power, the nomination committee is made up of the largest investors – usually institutional investors controlling a few per cent each.
83. E.g. Kim and Nofsinger (2007, ch. 4), Brodin et al. (1995), and Sjöstrand and Petrelius (2003).
84. *Cadbury Report*, December 1992: the basic document for the British Governance Code of Corporate Governance and included in the Combined Code. It has set the standard for governance in other parts of Europe, including Sweden.
85. Available at www.thetakeoverpanel.org.uk.
86. This especially manifests itself through the state of Delaware, which puts the board of directors in the target company in the forefront during a hostile takeover.
87. For a discussion on the development of European minority protection rights, see, e.g., La Porta et al. (2000); and Aglietta and Rebérioux, (2005).
88. Cf. Söderström (2003).
89. Cf. Burkart and Lee (2008). See also Bebchuk (1988).
90. Cf. Henrekson and Jacobsson (2002).
91. Cf. Lindberg (2005).

PART II

A case overview

2. The Old Mutual–Skandia case: actors and context

2.1 A CHANGING CONTEXT

AB[1] Skandia (Försäkringsaktiebolaget Skandia) had been listed on the Stockholm Stock Exchange (SSE) since 1863, and had been the most important supplier of insurance and life assurance for families and firms in Sweden for more than 150 years. Basically, its revenues had been founded upon the insurance premiums received from its policyholders; that is, its business had been built upon taking care of other people's money. This capital had been managed by the company staff on behalf of either its policyholders or its shareholders, depending upon the form of association in use (i.e. mutual life insurance – Skandia Life – or incorporated insurance company – Skandia).

During those years, it was very difficult for a single investor (or constellation of investors) to get control over the company. Voting rules did not permit any single shareholder to vote for more than 30 shares at the AGMs. This transferred a substantial amount of the power from shareholders to top management, particularly the CEO. In spite of that, a position at the board was seen as most attractive since Skandia's size and position in Sweden's business world provided a unique insight into many of the crucial flows of capital on the SSE. This information advantage was predominantly a consequence of particular allocation rules in the law, which regulated Swedish insurance companies (Försäkringsrörelselag) and allowed Skandia to invest only a maximum of 5 per cent of its insurance capital in any particular stock; this 'forced' the company to disperse its shareholdings, thus making it a substantial shareholder in quite a few of the larger companies on the SSE.

Skandia's standing as an 'impregnable' company changed during the years 1994–2000, when the voting restriction for its shareholders was removed in three distinct steps. In 1994, after the Swedish real-estate crisis, Skandia needed a substantial capital injection (close to 3 billion SEK), and several shareholders then conditioned their contribution to the new issue on a change of the voting rules. However, the entire matter resulted in a compromise, where a single shareholder was allowed to vote for up to 5 per cent of the stock. Two years later, that figure was increased to 10 per cent; and in 2000, the restriction was removed entirely. That development made Skandia vulnerable to corporate control struggles – particularly after the collapse of its share price from the year 2001 onwards, and also, at least in theory, from the mid-1990s (since coalitions among major shareholders became practically possible).

The changes in voting rules accompanied important contextual changes from the late 1980s, which also had an impact on the long-term shareholding in Skandia. As mentioned earlier, the company was most attractive to investors in Sweden, and from the late 1980s it had also become a target for those interested in participating in the consolidation of the Nordic 'bankassurance' sector. Similar to many other countries, Sweden had deregulated its capital market and become an integrated part of the emerging globalized financial system. Therefore Skandia opened up not only to Swedish investors who were looking to control the company. In the early 1990s, it had become open to all investors worldwide, regardless of their intentions. In other words, as a consequence of radical internal (abandoned voting restrictions) as well as contextual changes (emerging financial capitalism), the national 'heirloom' Skandia had in the early twenty-first century become both an actor and a potential takeover target on the emerging global market for corporate control.

2.2 A TURBULENT PERIOD

The early era of financial capitalism was to influence Skandia in two ways. In the late 1990s Skandia was positioned in the midst of the international speculation bubble that occurred on the global stock market.[2] In March 2000, company shares rose to valuation levels exceeding 12 times the (book value of) equity. At that time, Skandia was worth 250 billion SEK. In the aftermath of the stock market crash of 2001–02, with Skandia valued at only 11 billion SEK, it was easy to see that its model for success was built upon selling unit-linked assurance products on a rapidly rising stock market. Skandia's increase in its number of policyholders and its growing revenues were closely coupled with the exceptionally positive development of the stock market (and particularly for IT/technology shares).

In their valuations of Skandia (and many other companies) at the time, leading actors seemed to have taken buoyant markets almost as a long-term fact rather than as an expression of a strong trend that sooner or later would be broken.[3] Their valuations of Skandia were even more inflated as they were based upon what turned out to be a problematic path for the (stock market) valuation of its business: 'the embedded-value method'. On top of this, Skandia management added to the crisis by implementing an executive compensation scheme that rewarded (particularly) themselves. The scheme was based on the expected future results of current business (using the embedded-value method), rather than just on what was realized through actual cash flow. The actions and events concerning Skandia are described and explained in this book according to these basic facts about financial market instability and governance failures. Skandia is treated both as an actor and as an arena for those processes.

Some of the actors on the financial markets are those who contribute most to the inflation and deflation of asset prices, particularly those in repeated contact with one another, who jointly target different shares or who select companies with the purpose of forming new (although often temporary) corporate constellations, or quite simply to make a profit on trading securities. These actors include senior managers, financial analysts and various kinds of fund managers (event, hedge, activist and so on).[4] Rumours about emerging movements of share prices are disseminated among these categories of actors. Such information builds actor expectations and underpins the valuations of company shares. In this research, the Skandia share constitutes a focal point, as does the Old Mutual share. To a substantial extent, our narrative is woven around how these two share prices developed – particularly then how they were treated and traded during 2004 and 2005.

2.3 SKANDIA IN THE EARLY TWENTY-FIRST CENTURY

The collapse in the value of Skandia shares between summer 2000 and autumn 2003 was linked to a growing understanding among market actors that Skandia's prime business (unit-linked assurance products) was non-viable in the context of the less favourable 'bear markets' that followed the boom. Management capabilities and trustworthiness were also questioned at the time, primarily due to public scandals that revealed exceptionally favourable compensation schemes for some of the leading managers. This, along with Skandia's set of (dispersed) shareholders where no actor (or constellation of actors) showed any serious interest in taking the lead, created a difficult situation for the company.

Therefore the general impression of Skandia during the first years of the new millennium was one of a 'scandalous' company led by a combination of greedy top management and rather passive directors. The fact that such a view prevailed among both the public at large and the company's external stakeholders was well known within the walls of Skandia; its staff therefore regarded the situation of the organization (and their own situation) as most difficult. However, together with a new top management and board (2004), they worked hard to regain confidence among the stakeholders – particularly from customers, shareholders, business colleagues and suppliers. Moreover, Skandia was not weak overall; its client base was definitely a strength, as most of it was locked up in long-term contracts, and outside of Sweden, many of Skandia's operations – most importantly its UK business – remained quite unaffected by these scandals. There were also, at the very least, some actors on the market for corporate control who believed that the company still had potential and was undervalued on the stock exchange.

A new board and CEO took office in early 2004. At that time, the landscape of 'bankassurance' in a European perspective looked as in Figure 2.1. The largest actors on the Nordic market measured by market value were (from largest to smallest): Nordea, Danske Bank, Handelsbanken, Swedbank, SEB, DnB Nor, Sampo, Skandia and Storebrand. In the UK, Skandia was ranked in a second grouping next to the leading one – in tenth place. In a broad European or global 'bank-assurance' perspective Skandia was not among the top companies in terms of market value. Some of the largest actors in the business that were visible in this Old Mutual–Skandia case were Allianz, AXA, Aviva, Friends Provident and Prudential.

2.4 OLD MUTUAL UP TO THE MILLENNIUM

Old Mutual has a prominent role in this case: in early 2006 it finally acquired Skandia after a very long and trying process. At the time it was a slightly larger player than Skandia in the international financial and insurance markets, having been located in South Africa, it was a well-reputed company that was associated with the end of apartheid and the reopening of South Africa to the rest of the world. Old Mutual had embarked upon its journey from a national mutual insurance company to an international financial corporation – both later and differently than Skandia did. Old Mutual was the result of a demutualization process that was completed in 1999, as well as a subsequent listing on the London Stock Exchange (LSE) that raised new capital for its planned international expansion.

The early twenty-first century saw Old Mutual engaged in a long series of acquisitions outside its home country. The expansion mainly took place in the USA and in the UK. The timing of the formation of Old Mutual brought favourable conditions for expansion. During its first years as a listed company on the LSE, there were sharp rises in the stock market valuations of most companies. Despite the overall decline when the 'new

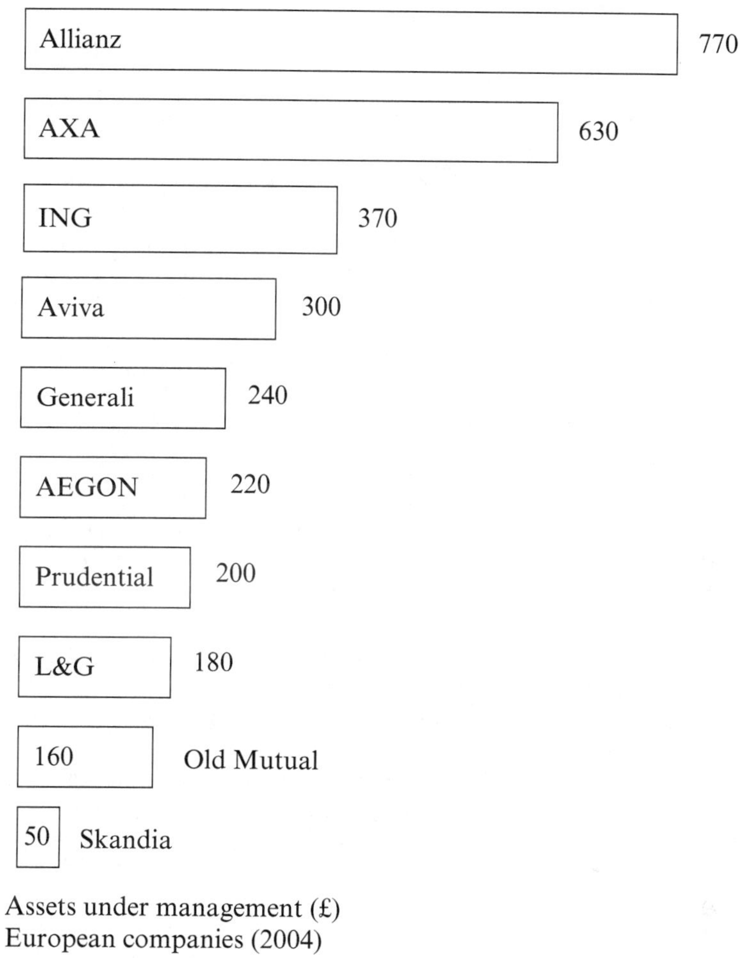

Figure 2.1 The competitive landscape

economy' failed on its promises, the Old Mutual share did not collapse. The company was never part of the speculative expectations surrounding many companies in the new millennium; it remained heavily involved in traditional insurance, property-and-casualty (P&C), and banking businesses rather than entering into the new more dazzling unit-linked kind of assurance. In 2003, its shares were still trading above the introductory level of 1999. By 2004, however, Old Mutual's growth prospective had come to a halt. Shareholders were dispirited, which pushed the share price down. The management team attempted to refocus the group towards growth in order to support the market valuation of the company, and in that strategy Skandia's unit-linked portfolio became the perfect target.

In 2005, Old Mutual exhibited a much less dispersed shareholder base compared to that of Skandia. A number of South African institutional investors held substantial stakes in the company, and this included the state. There was also a relatively strong element of cross-holdings between the mother company and its subsidiaries. Furthermore, primarily because of the Anglo-Saxon board of directors that generally acted more independently of its shareholders than the boards in Sweden, Old Mutual had a governance structure that differed from that of Skandia.

2.5 THE MAIN INGREDIENTS IN OUR NARRATION

Our extensive empirical investigation of the process that ended with Old Mutual's acquisition of Skandia focuses upon the period from early 2004 to early 2006, although our story also includes most of the important events, institutions and actors that had prior influence on what was to occur. We direct our study towards the major actors in the process, as was further elaborated upon in Chapter 1; that is, we focus on the activities conducted by the members of the Skandia board[5] and its CEO, and those actions for which they represented the primary target (see Figure 2.2). These processes are seen as interactive in character (see Chapter 1); therefore it can be assumed that interpretations of what others involved may think and do, as well as educated guesses about upcoming events, have

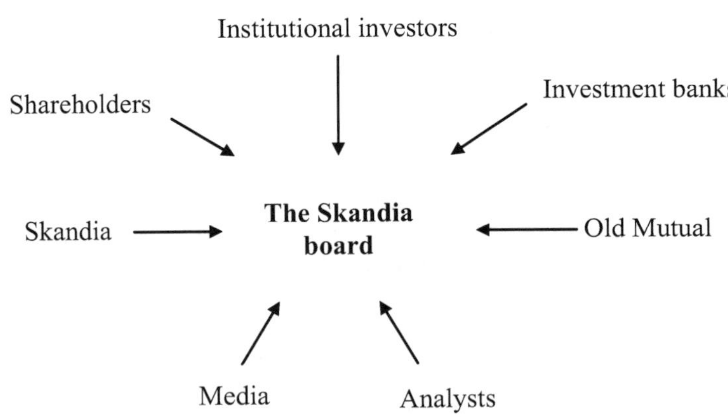

Figure 2.2 The focal arena

influenced the actors' decisions and performances. Thus our narration attempts to capture many of the complicated patterns of interaction.

In Chapter 1 we assumed that most human activities – in this case struggles for corporate control – are carried out in situations and contexts imbued both with calculable risk and genuine uncertainty. This, along with human shortcomings and limitations, makes drawn-out processes difficult to govern for any single actor. Strategic processes, such as those involving acquisitions, are seen as decisively marked by a lack of control. In these kinds of processes skilful agency springs both from an actor's location in relevant networks that provide a favourable basis for making qualified predictions about the future (including the future actions of others), and from an actor's aptitude for interpreting and thinking-in-action.[6]

Apart from the board and top management at Skandia, Old Mutual's leading actors – particularly its CEO – will receive particular attention in this case description. The various advisers to both Skandia and Old Mutual also play significant roles. Other important actors in this narration are the shareholders of the two companies – particularly the relatively larger ones that decided to express their opinions.

Old Mutual's acquisition of Skandia was most actively supported by the following actors/institutions: the (partly executive) board of Old Mutual; most shareholders in both companies; Fidelity International, shareholder in both companies; Deutsche Bank; advisory firms Merrill Lynch, Lenner & Partner, Linklaters, Kreab and Brunswick; three board members in Skandia (including both its chair and deputy chair); activist fund Cevian (represented on the Skandia board); SEB Funds; a number of globally active hedge funds; and, up to a certain point, the Second (Swedish) National Pension Fund (AP2). Conversely, those who most actively opposed the proposed deal were eight board members in Skandia, the CEO and other senior managers of the firm, and a range of Swedish institutional investors who had shareholdings in Skandia; these included the Fourth (Swedish) National Pension Fund (AP4) and, after some time, also the AP2. The opposition also included the Swedish Shareholders' Association, several politicians, some business leaders and parts of the business media.

As described in Chapter 1, our study attempts to capture what forces (actors, institutions, culture and events) were important in influencing the development of the process that culminated in Old Mutual acquiring Skandia. In doing so we have endeavoured to identify what positions the actors took and upheld over time, what kind of incentives they were exposed to, and what plans they actually put into practice. We have also tried to find out in which peer groups or professional networks these actors were active, since such memberships often establish an arena that favours the development and reproduction of particular dispositions and actions. Such controlled contexts usually tend to gather individuals with specific ideals and values, shared thought-and-action rationales, certain kinds of personalities, similar life paths, converging professional experiences and so on. We treat these emerging actor dispositions as embedded in a historically established tradition, making some sets of rules dominant, and rendering certain ethics and other kinds of (normative) beliefs more legitimate than others. Many of these institutionalized rules and norms were challenged in the Skandia contest, since agents with different cultural backgrounds and professional practices interacted. In particular, there was a clash between the Scandinavian/Nordic and the UK Anglo-Saxon legislations and traditions regarding corporate acquisitions and governance principles.

Thus individual action in takeover processes is seen as significantly influenced by certain 'toolkits' provided by forces in the environment: through institutions such as laws, customs, or other kinds of normative regulations (see Chapter 1). However, since the 1980s, this situation has become more complicated as both the content of the toolkit and the actor categories[7] and rationales have changed both in Sweden and elsewhere due to the globalization ('Americanization'[8]) of the financial markets. In the late twentieth century the Swedish regulations and customs were neither in tune with what many experts saw as appropriate, nor with what many citizens in Sweden considered 'fair and just'. In conformity with many other advanced capitalist states, these changes in the Swedish national regulations were carried out with a distinct government interest in the process.[9] All these 'hard and soft' regulations (along with several others of less importance) provided the agency guidelines on the Swedish market for company acquisitions from 2004 to 2006 when Old Mutual attempted to buy (and finally succeeded in acquiring) Skandia. However, in spite of all these standardizing institutions, one must keep in mind that there has also been plenty of room for various unconventional rule interpretations and creative strategic manoeuvring. Thus unorthodox formulas for calculations, unconventional platforms for power struggles, informal arenas for decision-making, and (new and old) ways of using the media and so on, have also significantly affected the Old Mutual–Skandia takeover process.

In Chapter 1 we indicated that it is not possible to get direct or certain knowledge of actors' intentions. All that a researcher can do is attempt to interpret the activities, verbal communications and documents produced, as if such expressions, statements and texts are indicative of actor purposes.[10] In this particular narration addressing the Skandia contest, actor intentions have been rather difficult to discover, as the fight for control has involved emotionally loaded activities and prestigious power struggles that do not always match 'classic Sunday-school ideals'. Some actors have, therefore, taken an interest in not talking too much about certain parts of the process (see the Appendix on methodology).

Our way to solve at least some of this dilemma of hidden agendas and activities, as well as *ex post* rationalizations, is to describe the individual actors (with their positions and names), present their decisions and actions (specified by date and arenas), and elaborate upon the contexts for the actors and their agency (describing the operating institutions and norms). All of this should give the reader an opportunity to acquire a coherent picture of what happened and, at the same time, the possibility to judge whether or not the presented narration seems to substantiate the conclusions drawn in the final chapter of the book.

As a consequence of this ambition to encourage and enable reader interpretation, the story describing how Old Mutual acquired Skandia will contain a great deal of quite detailed information. In order to simplify the Skandia contest story, this chapter ends with a chronological overview of the most important events, arenas and decisions, highlighting the major events in the process, in the view of those actors involved and the authors of this book. Figure 2.3 presents this summary in the form of a chronological illustration.

Something also worth mentioning in this outline is that, as the story unfolds, ownership in Skandia changed substantially. Although the foreign shareholding in Skandia was large throughout the early years of the twenty-first century, it should be noted, that before 2003, the largest known single shareholders were Nordic and Swedish institutions. In 2004 and – particularly – 2005, however, activist and event-driven funds run by private investors or large financial corporations took more significant shareholder positions. As the battle for control over Skandia continued, most of the actors – regardless of type – ended up belonging to one of two distinct camps: one in favour of Old Mutual's offer to buy the shares in Skandia; the other against it by advocating a Skandia 'stand-alone' case. When the Old Mutual bid was put on the market in September 2005, the two camps looked as illustrated in Figure 2.4.

2.6 BOOK OVERVIEW

The presentation of the Skandia contest is divided into four chronological parts (III–VI), each containing several chapters. Chapter 3 describes Skandia's previous success story, focusing on the years 1997–2000 and Skandia's extraordinary growth and skyrocketing share price (see Figure 2.5).

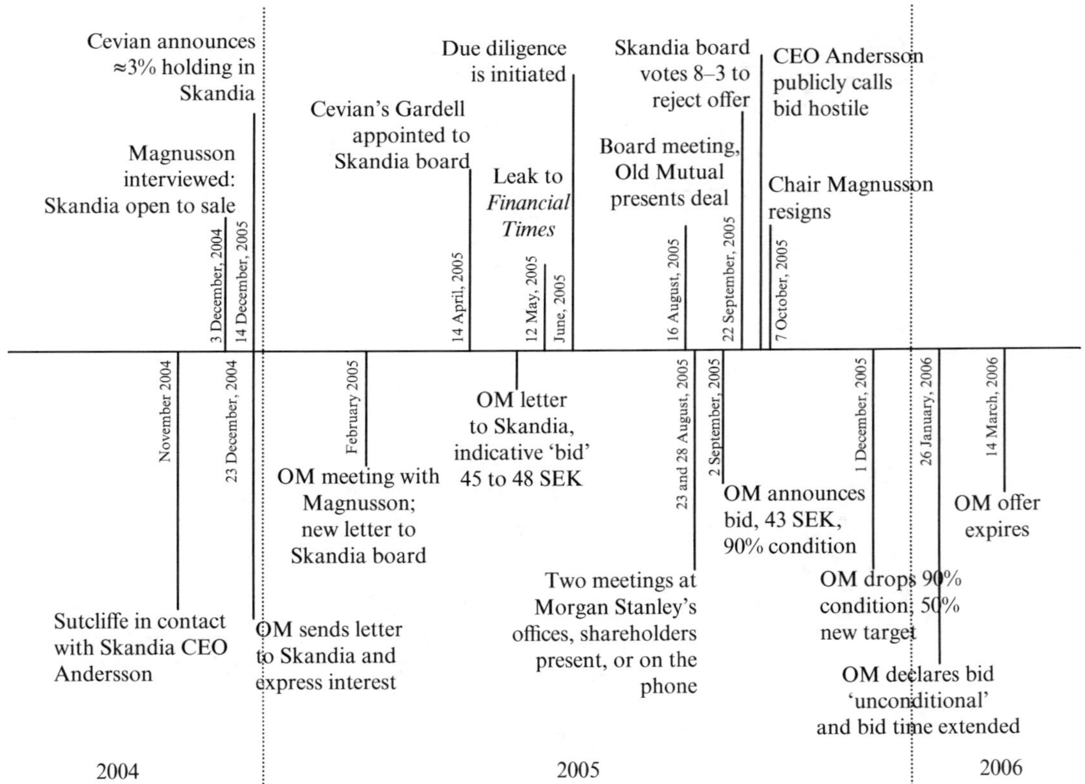

Figure 2.3 Major events in the process leading to Old Mutual's (OM's) acquisition of Skandia

Actors in favour of Old Mutual's acquisition of Skandia

Fidelity International,
Trelawney Williams
major stockholder in Skandia

Old Mutual's
CEO Jim Sutcliffe
offering to acquire Skandia

Merrill Lynch, advisers/brokers
to/for Old Mutual

AP2, Lars Idermark, major
stockholder in Skandia, member of
the nomination committee 2004–05

Bernt Magnusson, from April 2004
chair of the board, of Skandia;
resigned in October 2005

Björn Björnsson
deputy chair of the board, Skandia

Deutsche Bank
advisers to Old Mutual

Lenner & Partner
Lars Lenner
adviser to Old Mutual

Activist fund Cevian (major stockholder
in Skandia), and its head Christer Gardell,
member of the nomination committee 2004–05;
Skandia director from April 2005

SEB fund's Björn Lind, major
stockholder in Skandia; chair of
the nomination committee 2004–05

Birgitta Johansson-Hedberg,
board member, Skandia

Kajsa Lindståhl,
board member, Skandia

Lennart Jeansson,
chair of Skandia from October 2005,
board member 2004–06

Anders Ullberg,
board member, Skandia

Karl-Olov Hammarkvist,
board member, Skandia

Hans-Erik Andersson,
CEO, Skandia

AP2, Petter Odnhoff/Carl Rosén,
major stockholder in Skandia,
member of its nomination committee

AP4 Thomas Halvorsen,
major stockholder in
Skandia

Several distinguished Swedish
businessmen and a few leading
politicians

Actors in favour of Skandia's stand-alone path

Figure 2.4 The two 'opposing camps' in the Skandia context

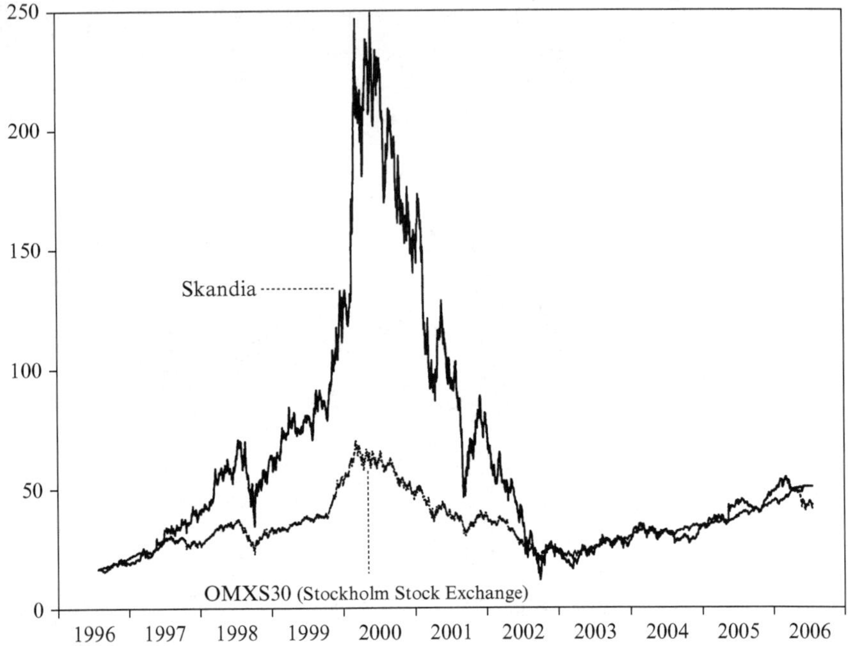

Figure 2.5 Skandia share price, 1996–2006

Later in the same chapter we discuss Skandia's stock market crash and scandals from the first years after the millennium – events and actions that suddenly turned Skandia into an insurance company with serious problems. In order to get a good understanding of the 'new' Skandia that had emerged in 2004, Chapter 4 describes Skandia Life UK, a subsidiary that both represents a large part of Skandia and plays an important role in the case. Chapter 5 shows how Skandia became a takeover target for other companies; and describes Skandia's new board and management that were established in April 2004.[11]

Part IV covers the period from January to December 2004, the year when a new Skandia board of directors and a new CEO formed the strategy for the company. Chapter 6 presents these leading actors. In Chapter 7 Skandia's internal problems are described, and also its attempt to rebuild both its brand and businesses. The basic strategic issue discussed in Chapter 8 is whether the new Skandia board and CEO should go for the 'stand-alone' alternative or aim for a structural deal from the very start. Several differing shareholder, board and management ambitions are introduced in this discussion. Chapter 9 describes the emerging new shareholder situation at Skandia, making the company a target for various hedge and activist funds. Around the same time (late December 2004) Old Mutual enters the scene, so Chapter 10 represents a brief description of that company, its plans for and growing interest in Skandia.

Part V covers the period from late December 2004 to August 2005. Chapter 11 indicates that there was a growing tension inside the Skandia board at the start of the year, related to different priorities and a growing lack of trust among directors. Chapter 12 describes the sudden leak of an indicative bid proposal from Old Mutual on Skandia, forcing the Skandia board to make several challenging decisions. Chapter 13 focuses on the issue of opening up Skandia for a limited due diligence, and a rather complex 'auction' process that followed the decision to do so. In Chapter 14 the outcome of these processes in the form of a friendly bid proposal from Old Mutual is described, along with the initial informal discussions among important shareholders of that proposal.

Part VI covers the period from August 2005 to the first months of 2006 in which Old Mutual acquired Skandia. Chapter 15 describes the formation of two distinct camps within the Skandia board, one in favour and one against the idea of a takeover, in turn leading up to it being presented with a more detailed bid proposal. The ensuing flood of public reporting and heated debate, particularly in Sweden, is described in Chapter 16. Chapter 17 revolves around the formation of a camp that in the public domain argued against the takeover. In Chapter 18, we describe the Skandia board's decision not to recommend the bid, and Old Mutual's subsequent presentation of the hostile bid. In addition, we draw on the activities of the major Swedish institutional investors who held Skandia holdings. Chapter 19 covers the intervention of hedge funds, the continuous selling of Skandia shares on the part of Swedish institutional investors, and the continuing publicity battle. In Chapter 20, the final attempts at securing another outcome than a takeover by Old Mutual are described. Chapter 21 covers the final moves by which Old Mutual gained control over Skandia and provides an epilogue to the main story in which the more recent fate of the enlarged Old Mutual is depicted.

In Part VII, finally, we present an interpretation of the events studied and relate that interpretation to the theoretical concerns initially raised in Chapter 1.

NOTES

1. In the text legal qualifications such as 'AB', 'Ltd', and 'Gmbh' are omitted for all the companies referred to.

2. This 'bubble' is described from an insider perspective by Kurtz (2000). Skandia's position in this bubble is portrayed in Nachemson-Ekwall and Carlsson (2004). See also Elmbrant (2005).
3. Nachemson-Ekwall and Carlsson (2004).
4. A connection with Michels', classical notion of the 'iron law of oligarchy' and modern financial markets can be found in Blomberg (2004). Financial analysts are found in different kinds of organizations: investment banks, retail banks, fund management companies, the press etc.
5. Based on the board composition established in April 2004.
6. See Sjöstrand (1997). Sjöstrand named his approach 'interactional institutionalism'.
7. See, for example, the growing importance of international hedge funds, activist funds, index trackers, insider traders and so on.
8. The initiated changes were predominantly inspired by Anglo-American values, legislation and traditions, and attuned to the interests of particular firms and industries based in the USA and the UK.
9. Lindberg (2005), pp. 27–48.
10. See, for example, Schütz (1932/1967).
11. Chapters 3–5 are to a large extent based on parts of Nachemson-Ekwall and Carlsson (2004).

PART III

A target company: Skandia before April 2004

3. A success – and a crash

3.1 SKANDIA 2003 – A TROUBLED COMPANY

At the time when Skandia became a target for takeover proposals in 2004, the company was still shaken by its series of recent scandals. The company had been heavily criticized by the Swedish public for handing out 4 billion SEK in bonuses to 100 senior staff during the years 1997–2002. The depth of the bonus scandal had been revealed on 2 December 2003 after seven months of gruesome internal investigations. The greater part of these bonuses was calculated on the basis of expected future profits. These profits had, therefore, not materialized when the bonuses were paid out, and it was uncertain whether there would be any expected profits at all and, if there were, if they would reach the shareholders' pockets.

The shareholders' upheaval concerning these bonuses was just the tip of the iceberg. Within a period of a few years around the turn of the millennium, Skandia – the oldest listed company on the Stockholm Stock Exchange (SSE) – had been transformed from a success story of international expansion in the life insurance industry to one of collapse and near bankruptcy. In 2002, Skandia lost billions of SEK through the sale of its former 'golden egg': its US subsidiary, American Skandia. The following year, the CEO of Skandia and several members of his top management team had to leave the company along with some of its board members, including chair Lars Ramqvist. However, before this deplorable situation emerged and reached its height in the early twenty-first century, Skandia and its stakeholders had experienced a long and, for the most part, impressive business journey.

3.2 SHAREHOLDING RESTRICTIONS

Skandia was formed back in 1855 as the first incorporated insurance company in Sweden. It grew through large mergers and acquisitions, especially during the 1960s,[1] to become the most powerful private insurance company in the country. Several well-known business families of Swedish society – such as Gyllenhammar, Palme, Roos and Söderberg – all made their imprint on Skandia. The control of the company even passed through generations, as fathers and sons subsequently upheld positions as directors or CEOs.

For decades different groups of investors had split the control of Skandia among them. Skandia never submitted to the Swedish tradition of a dual voting structure with A-shares and B-shares, the latter often with one-tenth of the voting power of the former. Instead, influence over Skandia was restricted by a rule that only allowed a single shareholder to vote for a maximum of 30 shares at AGMs. Whereas a dual share structure can secure power in the hands of a single or few shareholders with quite limited capital invested, the voting structure of Skandia transferred power from its shareholders to its top management.

During the 1970s and 1980s the Skandia group, including both the property-and-casualty company (Skandia P&C) and the traditional life assurance business (i.e. the mutual life arm Skandia Liv[2]), was the most influential institutional investor on the SSE. Skandia itself measured by market capitalization was just a mid-sized insurance company; however, its collected stock market portfolio reflecting the investments from 1.2 million policyholders in Skandia Liv and its P&C arm accounted for 3–4 per cent of the market value of the SSE. This was before foreign direct investment was allowed in the Swedish market,[3] and before the international fund industry and modern institutional investors had grown to become an important force in the global stock market arena, Sweden included. The influence from the Skandia group was especially challenged by the two strong power groupings that otherwise dominated Swedish business: the Wallenberg sphere through the Wallenberg foundations, the investment company Investor, and the commercial retail bank SEB; and the Handelsbanken sphere, with the investment company Industrivärden and the commercial retail bank Handelsbanken as its core organizations.

For many decades, a seat on the Skandia board had been an attractive position in Swedish business society. Although it did not furnish somebody with direct power because of the voting restriction mentioned above, it did give a unique insight into the activities at the SSE. The Wallenberg family was among those that always made sure they had seats on the board, owning their shares in Skandia through Investor. It was not until the year 2000 that the restrictive voting structure was fully abandoned, and a race for shareholder control over Skandia could start. By that time, Skandia had changed from a general insurance champion to a successful international niche player, as an intermediary on the market for savings and asset management.

3.3 SKANDIA'S SUCCESSFUL UNIT-LINKED BUSINESS

In the late twentieth century Skandia became renowned for its unit-linked life insurance business. This dated back to the middle of the 1970s, a decade of distress for traditional insurance companies in Sweden. For a Skandia that had already reached its limit in size in P&C on the home market, the way forward had been to seek opportunities to expand internationally. Consequently, Skandia grew in international reinsurance but it was obvious to many that it was a risky business including, for example, asbestos litigation, natural disasters and the dangers linked to breast implants.

Skandia CEO[4] at the time, Björn Wolrath, spearheaded quite a number of new ventures launched as the 1980s began. Similar to many others in the industry at that time, Wolrath was attracted by private life saving products. It was a market that was just beginning to take off throughout the Western world where a wealthy, but ageing, middle class was beginning to worry about the capacity and security of the public welfare system. A new product, the unit-linked life insurance then saw the light of day. This was originally an idea from South Africa that had been further developed in the Netherlands. A unit-linked policy is an insurance contract in which the savings benefit is linked directly to the value of units in a mutual fund or in a company's own internal fund, where the policyholders are running the investment risk.[5]

For an insurance company, the unit-linked business was attractive – it could be very capital efficient. The solvency requirement laid down for traditional insurance business in Europe at the time forced life insurers to hold (at least) 4 per cent of reserves compared to 1 per cent of a unit-linked policy.[6] Life insurers with a large portfolio of pure unit-linked business were, thus, required to hold less solvency capital. Throughout the 1990s, the unit-linked policies were to become increasingly popular as an alternative to traditional with-profit policies (in the UK), and to policies with a minimum guaranteed return (in continental Europe, which included the Nordic countries).

The idea of Skandia and its CEO Wolrath to start a company in life and pension savings came from a group of executives working at the UK insurance company, Abbey Life. Based on their experiences, Skandia Life UK was formed and started business on 4 July 1979. Over the years, this new offering in the pension market would become known both for its open architecture, where the policyholder could choose from a broad range of funds in which to invest, and for its modern flexible IT platform, which could swiftly be adopted according to customer needs. Customers then referred to the decisions made by independent financial advisers (IFAs) that sold the products to policyholders. The Skandia Life UK business especially attracted wealthy individuals as customers.

It took some years for Skandia's investment in its UK unit-linked business to take off; however, when the business model was finally in place, it became a huge success. During the 1990s, Skandia's unit-linked business grew rapidly in the UK, the USA and Sweden. The company also started similar businesses in 20 other national markets, including Australia and several countries in Latin America. Plans were also made to establish branches in Japan and China.

In the mid-1990s, many market actors and competitors around the world saw Skandia as an innovative financial service company. It proudly presented itself as positioned in the middle of the value chain in the savings market, capable to custom-fit, that is, to 'wrap', the offerings of more than 2000 fund-managing organizations worldwide to individual clients in its local markets. Skandia's unit-linked offering revolutionized the market for pension products, and soon became global standard practice.

Skandia's successful expansion sprang from a decentralized growth model; it was in tune with the classic Skandia ideals and followed the traditions already established in the company as early as the late 1960s by its former CEO Pehr G. Gyllenhammar.[7] Under the leadership of Jan Carendi, renowned head of Skandia's unit-linked business in the 1990s, Skandia speeded up the expansion of the united-linked franchise. This was done in an organization that showed federative-like qualities. This meant that the subsidiaries abroad were being run with loose control from the HQ in Stockholm. These local country managers had, from the start, very much run their 'own' businesses. Two subsidiaries particularly flourished: Skandia Life UK (with its HQ in the coastal town of Southampton) and American Skandia (located in Shelton, Connecticut, close to New York City). By the millennium, American Skandia held the number one position in the one-billion-dollar US market for variable annuities, the US equivalent to unit-linked assurance products. In the UK, Skandia had 13 per cent of the market for independent financial advisers, IFAs. In Sweden, Skandia's market share for new unit-linked products had grown to approximately 30 per cent. Between 1995 and 2000, Skandia group sales of unit-linked insurance and related fund-saving products grew from 30 billion SEK to close to 200 billion SEK. Added together these numbers were astonishing.

In the 1990s, Jan Carendi made a name for himself in the USA by leading the US variable annuity business. The growth even rendered American Skandia credit as a Harvard Business School case study illustrating a successful international expansion of a service company. There

Carendi was characterized as a modern charismatic leader empowering his employees with confidence.[8] In Sweden, Skandia CEO Wolrath retired in 1997 and was replaced by Lars-Eric Petersson, who came with experience from working with the reconstruction of a large part of the Swedish savings bank sector (which later became Swedbank) in the midst of the Swedish bank crisis in the early 1990s. Petersson spent his first years in charge cleaning out all the risky and sometimes loss-making business that Skandia had carried with it from the years of seemingly uncontrolled international expansion in both P&C insurance and international reinsurance.

The successful growth of the unit-linked business soon dwarfed what was left of the rest of Skandia and, as both businesses needed financial support, Petersson and his new team decided to focus Skandia's resources on the unit-linked business. The reinsurance business was sold in 1997 and, at that time, the P&C business was also put on the list to be considered for a future structural deal.[9] In line with the Anglo-American ideals that were spreading to continental Europe and the Nordic countries during the 1990s, with their messages about 'shareholder value' and stock-market-based governance methods, Skandia's board of directors awarded its top management stock options – a programme later to be known as 'Sharetracker'

In 1999, Skandia's P&C business partly merged with the Norwegian insurance company Uni Storebrand,[10] providing Skandia with around 6–7 billion SEK to use for its new core business expansion. The only substantial business to be left out of this selling process was the mutual life arm, Skandia Liv. In 2000 the main business of the Skandia group was split between new unit-linked policies (80 per cent) and mutual funds (20 per cent).[11]

Statistics seemed to support the positive sentiments from both investors in Skandia stock and from Skandia's management. In the USA, American Skandia was booming and statistics from Europe were just as exciting as those coming from the Swedish home market. Between 1996 and 2000, the unit-linked market in Europe grew by an annual rate of 24 per cent. Conversely, traditional participating business increased by an annual rate of only 5 per cent during the same period. In money terms, unit-linked premiums grew from €40 billion (1995) to €240 billion (2000). This corresponded to an increase of unit-linked premiums from 16 per cent to 45 per cent of total life insurance premiums. As one of the eight largest players in Europe, Skandia seemed correctly positioned to profit from this situation. The top management of Skandia also believed this. In March 2000 many investors also expected a bright future for Skandia.

In March 2000, when the world's stock markets reached their height before the bursting of the IT and telecom bubble, Skandia was valued at

250 billion SEK – 12 times the book value of the reported shareholder equity. The market value of Skandia had doubled each year since 1997 and the reputation of its CEO Lars-Eric Petersson grew, bringing with it an enhanced position in Swedish business life. Many financial analysts and investors in Skandia stock seemed to believe that the success would continue, and at the same rapid pace. The price/earnings multiple on the future embedded-value profits was around 50; this was on par with any hyped IT or technology stock at the time. To live up to these stock market expectations, Skandia had to continue growing by 20 to 30 per cent per year over the coming ten years.

3.4 THE EMBEDDED-VALUE METHOD

Swedish investors were late to join in on the Skandia share ride. Between 1994 and 1997, the proportion of shares controlled by foreign investors more than doubled to approximately 70 per cent. Well-renowned US institutional investors such as Fidelity, Scudder and Putnam invested. From time to time, the New-York-based hedge fund Viking, with roots in Norway, also appeared as an investor. From 2000, Swedish institutional investors started buying Skandia shares; however, foreign shareholders still held more than 60 per cent. This meant that Skandia maintained its position as the share listed on the SSE that (among large corporations) had the highest amount of foreign investors. On average, a listed company had around 30 per cent of stock in foreign hands. Skandia was also a heavily traded share, second only to the telecommunications giant Ericsson.

There were reasons for this delayed interest in Skandia among Swedish investors. They were slow to recognize the effect upon Skandia's results that had emerged from the use of a UK accounting method developed to 'better' reflect value created in life insurance: the 'embedded-value' method. With traditional Swedish statutory accounting, Skandia's new business area of unit-linked reported financial results strained by its rapid expansion of new businesses. A life insurer usually pays most of the acquisition commission to the sales agent up front, and then pays the rest over the following years. The main source of revenue to the life insurer then stems from annual fees earned from underlying assets. The asset-rich Skandia could handle this initial outflow of capital through selling off its other businesses, including P&C. However, it was difficult for Skandia's management to fully communicate the merits of the new business using statutory accounting; for that, the embedded-value accounting method was needed. Skandia's CFO Ulf Spång, in charge of finance since 1997, endorsed the use of these 'new' embedded-value calculations.

The embedded-value method transforms accounting according to the prudential principle of 'costs when they are suspected, and revenues when they are realized'. First of all, a company creates a balance-sheet item (deferred acquisition cost) instead of this being charged as a one-off cost in the year. The next step is to include the present value of calculated future surpluses from the annual fees paid by policyholders according to the contracts in force, instead of the fees actually paid in the year. The reported operating results of the group then include the change in these surplus values for the period.

In Skandia's case, the embedded-value numbers were huge. According to Swedish statutory accounting practice, during the years 1996–2000, Skandia's profit before tax totalled slightly more than 1 billion SEK. The cash flow from the business during the same five-year period was minus 2 billion SEK. With embedded-value accounting the reported profit had increased fourfold to 8 billion SEK, and Skandia's consolidated capital reached 37 billion SEK. At the height of 2000, when Skandia's market value hit 250 billion SEK, almost 85 per cent of this reflected expectations on future sales profits. During this heyday for financial analysts who were observing Skandia, betting on future surplus income from policy contracts became the number-one selling story.

There was nothing inherently wrong with the embedded-value accounting method. It was the norm in the UK, where it had worked well for years. When it was applied to Skandia, with a fast-growing US business, however, it seriously distorted the picture in two ways. First of all, the US policy buyers were different from the UK ones. The latter invested in traditional mixed funds with both shares and bonds, whereas US customers rushed into risky IT or general technology funds. In the late 1990s, the bubble years of 'the new economy', the value of these funds rose quickly, with the present value of future cash flows from policy charges exploding the stock market valuation of American Skandia. At the height of 2000, American Skandia, which was still being run with a negative cash flow, was perceived to be worth more than 100 billion SEK ($11 billion). When the stock market crashed, the value of the annual income stream from assets under management disintegrated at the same speed. The same happened with the stock market evaluation of American Skandia.

Second, the Skandia management that worked with the unit-linked business had a long-term incentive (L-tip) bonus programme during the years 1997–99 and part of 2000 (Wealthbuilder) that was attached to the growth in embedded value. Originally a UK construction, this bonus programme worked differently when it was applied to the results of the US business. As mentioned earlier, when policyholders in the UK invested in funds that contained a mixture of traditional stocks and bonds, business grew slowly and with a positive cash flow. In the USA, the situation was somewhat different: there, the management that was running the company was rewarded for future expected sales while the accompanying negative cash flows were left to the Skandia HQ in Sweden to handle. Due to this construction, the US management team had a strong personal incentive to promote investments in fast-growing IT/technology funds. When Skandia crashed, it became apparent to many actors that this kind of incentive programme was a mistake. In an ordinary share option programme, it is the shareholders who transfer part of the market value of a company to its management. In Skandia's case, the money to finance the bonus programme, which was based on embedded-value calculations, came from its own cash flow (and that was negative). In 2001, when it was time for Skandia to honour the bonus payments, many investors began focusing on this cash flow problem, and paid less attention to embedded value.

3.5 A CRASH

During the year 2000 several incidents indicated that times were changing for Skandia. After the New Year, when the stock market was still rallying, there was shareholder upheaval as a new favourable stock option programme was to be granted to top management, replacing the previous Sharetracker programme (the Wealthbuilder programme was at that time unknown to the shareholders). A group of Swedish institutional investors fought hard to stop this new programme, but their success was limited. In Skandia's annual report for 1999 published in the spring of 2000, it was revealed that two bonus and option programmes given to a group of top Skandia executives for the years 1997–99 totalled 1.1 billion SEK, or 12 per cent of the Skandia group's results before tax during the period. CEO Petersson, who had received 75 million SEK in bonus and stock options, had by then already officially accepted a reduction to 12 million SEK.[12]

Around the year 2000 the relationship between the CEO Petersson and his deputy Carendi had also become more and more strained, culminating in a power struggle that, on 31 May 2000, forced Carendi to leave his positions both as head of the unit-linked business and as CEO of American Skandia.[13] A mere two days later (on 2 June 2000), the Skandia share reached its all-time high at 252.5 SEK.

During the autumn of 2000, the downturn of the global financial market came knocking on Skandia's door. The sales of the unit-linked products in Europe and of variable annuities in the USA had severely decreased in the initial years of the millennium. Skandia was confronted with a 35 per cent inflation-adjusted decline in premiums earned between 2000 and 2001. Suddenly, American Skandia's continuous quest for cash to finance its expansion became both apparent and problematic. A business model built upon payouts to agents first, and income later, did not work when the value of the policyholders' funds had fallen.

It took some time for top management in Skandia to adapt to the altered market outlook. In 2001, CEO Petersson and CFO Spång were still focusing on the expected turnaround on the stock markets. For example, the top 100 managers of Skandia had met in late August 2001, in the Scottish town of St Andrews, to set out the course for the future. The Skandia share was then trading at approximately 70 SEK, having lost 70 per cent of its all-time-high value. Even then top management had talked about 'b-hags' (that is, 'big hairy audacious goals'), pointing to the possibility of growing the asset under management from 100 billion SEK in 2000 to 600 billion SEK by the end of 2005. If the goal was to be achieved, the expectation was that Skandia stock would increase by tenfold from its present level of 70 SEK to 700 SEK. The UK management had been more than sceptical regarding these numbers, as they believed them to be unrealistic HQ goals. The US management, which was in urgent need of cash, had been shaken when it realized that the Swedish management did not see the seriousness of its quest for support.

On 11 September 2001, one week later, two airplanes crashed into the World Trade Center in New York. That disaster put additional strain on an already depressed global financial market. By then, the continuous negative cash flow of American Skandia worried the credit-rating institute Moody's. However, it did not seem to be enough to worry the top management in Stockholm, where the Skandia board and CFO Spång sold off Skandia assets to free capital in order to invest in new unit-link businesses, particularly in the UK acquisition of the IFA network Bankhall (see Section 4.2).

The last blow to American Skandia came late in the summer of 2002. New US legislation – unknown to most Skandia shareholders, the Swedish management team, and the Skandia board – forced American Skandia to put up reserves for eventual losses on policies if a holder died before the payout of insurance money began. The mechanism in question was the 'guaranteed minimum death benefit' (GMDB). The problem was not going to be the actual payout of cash. People were not going to die before their time was up simply because the fund value of their policy had dropped. The problem was that Skandia did not have that amount of money to reserve on a passive account. However, this effect could have been minimized as American Skandia had reinsurance contracts in place in the late 1990s by the reinsurer Cigna. However, for various reasons, these reinsurance contracts were closed down – something that looked reasonable in 1999, but would later prove to be a mistake.[14]

In the autumn of 2002, Skandia was in desperate need of cash. There was no way Skandia could come up with the 10 billion SEK that the state of Connecticut demanded to be allocated to special GMDB reserves. On 8 October 2002, the Skandia share was trading at its lowest point: 10.8 SEK. At the end of that year, however, it had bounced back to 23 SEK. That price could be compared to Skandia's disclosure in the accounts of 2002 of a consolidated capital of 26 billion SEK (i.e. 26 SEK per share). At that time, its equity capital was approximately 15 billion SEK.

In December 2002 American Skandia was taken over by the US insurance company Prudential. Skandia then had to take a loss of 8 billion SEK before taxes on a subsidiary that one year earlier had been valued at no less than 100 billion SEK by investors on the stock market. The composition of the Skandia group was changed accordingly: Stockholm top management controlled a huge UK subsidiary that made up 70 per cent of Skandia's business.

3.6 A TARNISHED BRAND

The Skandia management in Stockholm, especially its CFO Ulf Spång, was renowned for its creativity in freeing cash to finance the expansion of the unit-linked business. During the mid-1990s up to the beginning of the new millennium, Skandia's stock holdings, various assets and side businesses were sold; in 1999, its P&C business merged with Finnish Pohjola and Norwegian insurance company Storebrand to create the pan-Nordic company, If P&C Insurance. However, a series of politically flavoured transactions between Skandia management and actors in the Finnish insurance sector lead Pohjola to leave the joint venture before closure. Instead, Finnish Sampo emerged in 2001 as a new third partner.[15]

There was also growing public concern about the wheeling and dealing that was going on between the mutual life arm Skandia Liv (the assets of which were owned by its policyholders) and the listed mother company Skandia (which was owned entirely by its shareholders). As long as the Skandia share kept rising, few took a serious interest in the matter. However, shortly after New Year 2002, things changed as Skandia announced that Norwegian Den Norske Bank[16] had bought the right to manage the assets of the 1.2 million Swedish life savers associated with Skandia Liv. Skandia received 3.2 billion SEK from selling the managing contract that had been packaged in its subsidiary, Skandia Asset Management. The company needed this money to support its troubled

US subsidiary, American Skandia; it also facilitated the Skandia Life UK expansion, including its acquisition of independent financial adviser Bankhall. This affair was carried out ahead of an expected deregulation of the UK financial advisory market. The Skandia share rose when the deal with Den Norske Bank was presented; however, many of the Skandia Liv's policyholders objected. They regarded the money from Den Norske Bank as theirs by right – that is, the policyholders' property, since it was their savings that were managed by Skandia Asset Management rather than anything emerging from the business of the mother company, Skandia.[17]

In 2002 and 2003, Skandia's trouble turned into a seemingly never-ending target for the Swedish press. Skandia had difficulties dealing with this serial story, although the effects of this negative exposure were reduced somewhat by the fact that Skandia was no longer a truly Swedish company; it had become international in terms of shareholders, and its unit-linked business grew first and foremost outside Sweden. However, there were also international problems for Skandia, although the collapse of American Skandia, the GMDB legislation and the intricacies of embedded-value accounting did not really make it to the headlines. Those difficulties were too technical and complicated for many journalists, most shareholders, and the general public to grasp.

In Sweden, the (known and rumoured) rewards granted to top managers were strongly criticized on the grounds of both their generosity and how they had been decided. At the same time, daily newspapers, radio, television and the Internet were full of opinions regarding Skandia actors. For example, it surfaced that rental apartments owned by the mutual arm Skandia Liv had been distributed to Skandia managers' children and other relatives. To add insult to injury, it became known that the refurbishing of apartments in very attractive locations in downtown Stockholm had been paid for directly by Skandia, the (listed) parent company of Skandia Liv – a fact that had been hidden from the public in the Skandia accounts. In Stockholm, a city where rents are regulated and apartments are in chronic shortage, this was far from appropriate.

From all of this it should be obvious that Skandia's chief information officer (CIO) Odd Eiken probably had one of the most stressful jobs in Sweden during 2003 and 2004; however, it was not only Skandia's lost confidence in the eyes of Skandia stakeholders and many others that engaged him. Another reason was that Skandia's chair Lars Ramqvist was forced to resign at the AGM on 15 April 2003;[18] then, a few hours after the AGM, the new board at its first meeting dismissed CEO Lars-Eric Petersson. But that was not enough; after the summer holiday CFO Spång followed suit, along with another manager from the top, Ola Ramstedt (head of human resources). Moreover, in the following years, Skandia was involved in several legal disputes with previous management in both Sweden and the USA, and with members of the Skandia board. There were also disputes with its mutual life insurance arm, Skandia Liv, and with Prudential, the buyer of American Skandia.

One major challenge remained within Skandia itself: at the time of his resignation Skandia's chair Ramqvist announced publicly that, following the sale of American Skandia, Skandia was almost debt free. This, however, was not the main issue for a Skandia going forward. The most crucial problem was that the cash flow was still negative. Moreover, there seemed to be no way to stop the outflow of capital. Skandia's federative kind of structure was built for growth, as were the internal accounting systems and follow-ups adopted for a continuous handout of cash from the head office in Stockholm to the subsidiaries abroad. Thus Skandia's control systems were not designed for a standstill – let alone a decline or crisis. Therefore, in the spring of 2003, it was obvious to management, board and shareholders that Skandia's structure and business model both had to be rebuilt. The 'independent' subsidiaries had to be more integrated into Skandia, and every unit-linked product had to be redesigned in order to generate a positive cash flow more quickly. The new HQ management team that took over after Petersson et al. regarded this as a feasible task, although they were well aware that this implied that Skandia would grow much move slowly and with a much less illustrious outlook for the share price. Above all, it meant gaining control over Skandia Life UK.

NOTES

1. For a historical account, see Englund (1982).
2. The Skandia group was made up of three parts: P&C, traditional life and international reinsurance.
3. The Stockholm Stock Exchange opened up for foreign investors to buy shares freely in 1993.
4. CEO from 1981 to 1997.
5. A strict definition from www.financialglossary.com describes unit-linked as 'a life assurance policy in which a portion of the premium is used to purchase life cover (the sum assured), with the balance invested in an authorised unit trust/trusts. The return on the policy is thus linked to the performance of the units in the unit trust. Unit-linked policies include single premium bonds or investment bonds, unit-linked endowment assurance and unit-linked whole life assurance. For the policyholders unit-linked is attractive since the product offers a spectrum of different investment alternatives. The savings fund could be composed of bonds or most likely stocks, and the investment is then linked to insurance with various conditions, including tax treatments'.
6. For descriptions of the legal regulation of insurance companies in Sweden and Europe we rely on Swedish Ministry of Finance (2006).
7. Gyllenhammar later became internationally renowned as CEO and chair of the Swedish vehicle company Volvo (between 1970 and 1993). In 2000 he took over as chair of the

UK insurance company Aviva, the result of the merger between Norwich Union and CGU to create Europe's fourth-largest life insurance company.

8. Bartlett and Mahmood (1996).
9. Source: Skandia's *Annual Report* 2000. The reinsurance business was sold to Hannover Re by Hans-Erik Andersson during his first period at Skandia. He later became CEO (between 2004 and 2006).
10. The Storebrand Group was a leading player in the Nordic markets for pensions, life and health insurance, banking and asset management. In 1991 it merged with the Norwegian competitor Uni Forsikring to create Uni Storebrand. The name Uni was later dropped from the company name.
11. These figures do not include the life arm Skandia Liv.
12. As would later be apparent in the internal Rydbeck-Tidström report that was made public in December 2003, the actual bonus and stock option programme to the top managers during the years totalled 4 billion SEK of which the CEO was allotted 175 million SEK. The SEK 175 million had been allocated to a pension trust; only 12 million SEK appeared in the annual accounts of 1999 (in a footnote).
13. Carendi was to focus on new markets, especially those emerging in Asia; however, as little as a year later (2001) he left Skandia. During the years 2003–06, he was head of the US life savings arm of German insurance company Allianz.
14. At the beginning of the 1990s, the State of Connecticut (American Skandia's domicile) changed accounting requirements for savings products. The regulatory authority demanded that an insurance company build up reserves to cover losses equivalent to the value after a 30 per cent fall in capital paid on policies – known as the GMDB. To cover this, Skandia bought reinsurance contracts from Cigna which, at that time, was a broader traditional US insurance company; however, the company stopped selling such contracts in 1999. This was in line with its evolution towards a focus on health insurance. The rules governing accounting practice in the USA for GMDB also hit other companies besides American Skandia, and the need for reserves has been subject to huge debate.
15. Pohjola was an old P&C insurance company based in Finland, part of a banking and insurance group that, since 2006, has also operated under the name Pohjola, which includes the former OKO Bank. In 1999, Swedish Nordbanken merged with its largest shareholder Meritabanken to create a cross-border Nordic banking champion. As a result, the shares in Pohjola were sold to Skandia, which seemed logical given the plans to merge the P&C businesses of the two groups. But Skandia resold the Pohjola shares to the latter's main domestic competitor, Sampo-Leoni, creating much upheaval in the Finnish business community. In May 2001 Sampo merged its P&C arm with the If Group and became the new leading partner.
16. Den Norske Bank was and remains the leading Norwegian banking group with businesses throughout Scandinavia. In 2003 the company name was altered to DnB.
17. On 2 October 2008 the arbitration panel, in a historic decision, finally found in favour of the mutually controlled Skandia Liv. The policyholders should be compensated by 600 million SEK plus interest, totalling 1.3 billion SEK.
18. Chair Lars Ramqvist announced his resignation in early February 2003.

4. Skandia Life UK

4.1 A STRAINED RELATIONSHIP

In the early twenty-first century British managers in Skandia Life UK were not – and had never been – particularly impressed with the activities carried out at the Swedish parent company. Above all, they frowned at what they saw as a growing focus on the US operations in American Skandia that, in their eyes, had a weak business model. Back in the 1980s and 1990s, the UK management had spent energy on keeping the Swedish management, that is, their owner, at some distance. This attitude was not taken out of the blue. The UK life insurance market differed from that of the rest of Europe. It was seen as more sophisticated, mature and competitive; thus the Skandia Life UK actors ran their own business. This was also Skandia's largest subsidiary. In 2003 Skandia Life UK (with its HQ in Southampton) and Royal Skandia[1] (with an office on the Isle of Man) employed a total of 2200 persons. The US business had at its height 1400 employees. During the same period Skandia Sweden had 1700 employees split between the mutual Skandia Liv, its unit-linked business, and Skandiabanken (its Internet bank).

Few people in Skandia Life UK talked about the Swedish parent company and its HQ. There were employees in UK who did not even know that the company had a Swedish mother company until the bonus scandal reached the UK press in 2003. Among those who did know about the Swedish business, some thought the roles were actually reversed, and that it was Skandia Life UK that controlled a Swedish subsidiary.

There was resentment on the UK management's side at having to work with its Swedish superiors at Skandia HQ almost from the start, that is, back in 1978. At that time a group of well-educated men in their early thirties left Abbey Life[2] to start a unit-linked business. The group included Mike Sullman, Frank Capon, Paul Bradshaw and Stewart Cohen. When seeking someone to finance the start-up they turned to Skandia; it invested £25 million, gaining control over 76 per cent of the equity. The remaining shares were split between the employees – at the time of inception, a total of 32 people, including five at the top of the organization. Alan Wilson, who later took over as CEO of Skandia Life UK, was the first person employed. He was also included in the original share allocation scheme at approximately half the value of the one provided to the founding actors. Those who joined six months later – such as Jim Roberts – were not included in this first partnership. Throughout the entire period that Skandia had control over Skandia Life UK, the profit-sharing between the Skandia Life UK management and Skandia remained an important, difficult and, for the most part, an unsolved issue.

Skandia Life UK management soon had problems with the top management of Skandia. They did not feel that the Swedes understood the business they tried to obtain. The UK management wanted to be left alone to run what they regarded as 'their own business'. The Swedes who held board seats in Skandia Life UK and those who were sent to work for the UK company were often ignored or viewed as 'spies', and were sometimes even treated less well. As the success of Skandia Life UK continued, the Skandia management team decided that they could live with the tension and leave the UK management very much on its own. In spite of that, Bradshaw (Skandia Life UK's first CEO) remained disappointed with the Swedish parent company. This was for several reasons, the first related to Skandia Life UK's debacle in the USA. In the mid-1980s, Skandia's CEO Björn Wolrath and his management team in Stockholm decided to expand the unit-linked franchise to other countries. Skandia Life UK was put in charge of that venture; however, the outcome of its effort was poor. The UK unit-linked model simply did not appeal to the Americans. Stockholm demanded results, and when they were lacking, Wolrath put a Swede – Jan Carendi – in charge (1986). He was picked to run what was to become a global unit-linked business. Even worse for Bradshaw and the UK management was that Carendi was asked to build up the US franchise in direct competition with his colleagues from the UK. This assignment produced another conflict between Bradshaw and the Skandia HQ in Sweden.

A further reason for the continuous tension between the UK management team and the Swedish HQ was the ownership situation in Skandia Life UK. As early as 1981, new solvency rules from the European Community stipulated that Skandia Life UK had to raise more capital. This meant that the partnership between Skandia Life UK management and Skandia was re-examined. In the initial 1978 deal between Skandia and Skandia Life UK, Skandia had promised the UK team that, in the future, they would be able to cash in on their stockholdings through a partial initial public offering (IPO) at the LSE. Such a Skandia buyout of the Brits was aimed to end the partnership between Skandia Life UK management and Skandia. However, in the late 1980s, Skandia changed its mind and decided to keep Skandia Life UK as a wholly owned subsidiary.

Bradshaw was unhappy with this change. He expected it to be very difficult for Skandia and Skandia Life UK to agree upon a price for the shareholding that the Skandia Life UK management had in the UK subsidiary – a shareholding that, over the initial years, had grown from 25 per cent to 33 per cent. When the negotiations began, the UK management valued the company at £600 million (using the embedded-value method). When a deal was finally struck in 1988, the Swedish management had succeeded in reducing the valuation to £100 million. This was four times more than Skandia had invested ten years earlier.

The UK management team, however, remained unhappy as they felt that the Swedish shareholder had exploited their team spirit, and that they had had no chance to finance a counter-bid for what they considered to be 'their firm'. In order to get everyone to accept the buyout, Skandia CEO Wolrath believed it necessary to give the UK management a new favourable bonus programme. This was to last for two years. By 1991, when the terms of the new incentive programme were reviewed, Bradshaw had had just about enough of Skandia and of Carendi, so he left.

In 1991, lawyer Alan Wilson took over as the new CEO of Skandia Life UK. Wilson had been at the company from the very beginning – it was he who had bought the off-the-shelf company Mackston that became Skandia Life UK. However, Wilson had received only £1.5 million from the old bonus programme (half as much as the other top managers). In his eyes the time had come for him and his new UK management team to benefit as well. Therefore he fought urgently for new lucrative incentive programmes for the UK management team. Wilson came up with the incentive programme that was to be based upon a complicated string of embedded-value calculations, with an extra bonus for the Skandia Life UK board members (including its chair Carendi). During the really good years of the 1990s, the leading actors received bonuses amounting to two, three or even four times their ordinary salaries. This was generous, since a standard incentive programme in the UK insurance industry seldom exceeded the equivalent of one year's salary. Carendi, however, endorsed the programme, claiming that it motivated people to become dedicated and work harder for success. The UK system that calculated the incentive programmes, the so-called 'L-tips' (long-term incentive programmes) soon became standard for most unit-linked companies in the group (including American Skandia); it also became a central part of the so-called 'Wealthbuilder' programme, the global Skandia incentive programme that eventually consumed a great part of Skandia's cash flow in 1998–2000. All of this was revealed to the public in the internal investigation that was carried out in December 2003 (see Section 5.7).

4.2 THE ACQUISITION OF BANKHALL

By the mid-1990s, Skandia Life UK was the exemplary model in unit-linked business. The UK management was very proud of 'their' company, and they all benefited from the lucrative incentive programmes. The Skandia HQ seemed no longer to interfere much with the UK management. Chair Carendi, for example, showed up only at the UK board meetings. This kind of autonomy fitted Skandia Life UK's CEO Alan Wilson like a glove. At that time (in 1997), Lars-Eric Petersson took over as Skandia's CEO, following Björn Wolrath. He continued to let Wilson act very much on his own. In the view of the local UK management, new Skandia CEO Petersson was a friendly and competent individual; however, he never fully believed in the rationale behind the unit-linked business. The UK managers looked upon Petersson as someone who knew how to restructure a business, but not as someone who knew how to develop a business and move it forward.

In late 1990s, many people inside and outside Skandia focused on the success of American Skandia. There were talks about a partial listing on the New York Stock Exchange (NYSE). Carendi did everything he could to prove that the US team was more successful than the UK team. Many actors believed him; the stock market obviously liked American Skandia. On 25 February 1998, investors flocked around Carendi at a capital markets day in London. Few called on Skandia Life UK's CEO. For UK management, Carendi's success was nothing but a nuisance.

In late 2001, when Skandia was losing its appeal and American Skandia was headed for a crisis, Skandia Life UK bought the IFA network Bankhall. CEO Wilson had pushed for the acquisition, and Skandia's CFO Ulf Spång had raised the necessary capital (mainly through the selling of Skandia Liv's asset management business to Norwegian Den Norske Bank). Skandia paid £210 million for Bankhall, accounting for 50 per cent of Skandia Life UK's embedded value. At that time, it seemed logical that Skandia Life UK would expand its coverage of the value chain.

The acquisition of Bankhall, however, soon proved to be a mistake, made at the extreme of the IT bubble, although there was nothing wrong with the industrial rationale underpinning the deal. Distribution of UK insurance products was changing, and the IFAs were gaining more power. Bankhall was the largest agent and provider of support services to IFAs in the UK, and the latter were obliged to be connected to an agent. Bankhall had an IT platform designed to service the IFAs that were authorized by the UK Financial Services Authority (FSA). The price, however, was (too) high and buying an IFA agent was risky; well-educated people who were less inclined to take instructions from others populated Bankhall.

Another problem was that the initial Skandia Life UK plan to sell off parts of Bankhall to other insurance companies never materialized. Moreover, Skandia Life UK never added any extra managerial resources to govern Bankhall. All of this contributed to the growing distrust between Skandia's Swedish management team and Bankhall's original founders, Paul Hogart and Simon Taylor, who had made a good financial deal selling to Skandia. Slowly, Bankhall fell apart.[3]

4.3 A POWER STRUGGLE

After the rush sale of American Skandia in December 2002, Wilson's UK organization, including Royal Skandia, accounted for two-thirds of the group's assets. Thus the power balance shifted in favour of Skandia Life UK. The UK management team began, once again, to dream of the day when Skandia would decide to sell them off. However, the trouble was that, by late 2002, the UK business no longer performed very well. Despite its size, the UK business accounted for only half of the total volume of new sales of unit-linked and mutual funds. Looking at the profits, the UK numbers lagged even more. Fierce competition on the UK market had put pressure on the results, which thus landed far below the average for the Skandia group.

After the millennium the UK management became a part of a power struggle at the Swedish HQ. The tension between the two Swedish top executives (CEO Lars-Eric Petersson and Deputy CEO Jan Carendi) had left the subsidiaries – including Skandia Life UK – more or less out of control. Petersson called upon Wilson to help out, hence his role and influence in Skandia grew. Following Carendi's departure in 2002, Wilson took on responsibility for the Asia Pacific region, including countries such as China and Australia. Wilson accepted this extensive responsibility; however, he did not recruit new managers to discharge him of his old undertakings in Skandia Life UK and Royal Skandia. Wilson spent a great deal of time travelling around the world, so the UK management in Southampton started to look thin at the same time as the Bankhall acquisition began to turn into a serious problem.

The basic conflict between the management of Skandia and Skandia Life UK concerned group integration, something that CFO Spång had already started to work at around the millennium. One of the important issues was about how to integrate the control of fund links using one common global fund platform as the device (this was known as Global Funds). That simplification would save a substantial amount of money. This line of thinking was not controversial *per se*; however, Skandia Life

UK did not want to participate in the project. It was necessary to achieve scale economies; Skandia Life UK accounted for half of Skandia's assets outside the USA. The UK opposition to almost any sort of coordination was to become a continuous problem for the management in Stockholm.[4]

When Global Funds was originally launched in the UK, management had cooperated fully in its creation. At that time, Alan Wilson chaired the company, and both members of UK management and representatives from the Swedish HQ were on its board. However, when Skandia selected a US model for Global Funds, the plans went too far in the eyes of the UK staff. Wilson resented this path, as he believed that it would never work in a UK context. In some ways, Wilson was probably right. The UK business, which was run with an open architecture, was different from the one carried out in continental Europe, which had more of a closed or guided one; that is, the insurance companies there selected the funds that were presented to the final customers. This gave the insurance companies power to direct the prices to the fund managers. In the UK, the policyholders were accustomed to choose funds freely by themselves. If the customers liked a particular fund, then there was no way that Skandia Life UK could remove it from its platform without losing the relationship. There were also tax issues and certain regulations that complicated setting up Global Funds in the UK.

Wilson believed that the Skandia Group would fall apart after American Skandia was sold in December 2002; for Skandia Life UK, the Skandia HQ in Stockholm had turned into a burden that slowed decision-making, damaged reputation and exaggerated control. In addition, Skandia Life UK could not make decisions on new incentive programmes.

NOTES

1. A leading provider of offshore savings products for customers all over the world and with office on the UK tax haven, the Isle of Man.
2. Abbey Life was a traditional closed-book life insurance company.
3. The greater part of the original £200 million investment was later reserved as write-offs in the Skandia accounts of 2004 and 2005.
4. Global Funds was to take over the responsibility of joint pre-selection and procurement of international fund offerings from actors such as Fidelity, Mangroup and Capital Group.

5. A takeover target

5.1 CHANGES IN SHAREHOLDING AND BOARD COMPOSITION

Skandia had been a target for structural deals since 8 October 1990, when Skandinaviska Enskilda Banken[1] (later SEB), along with the Wallenberg group as the dominating shareholder, acquired 28.2 per cent of the shares in Skandia; the aim was a full-fledged merger between the bank and the insurance company (both its life arm and P&C business). The plan was prepared before the change of European Community regulations, which opened up for a new financial sector, allowing banks and insurance companies to merge. In the late 1980s, such financial cross-sector mergers were very high-profile. The seller of the Skandia shares was the investment company Investor, which was controlled by the Wallenberg foundation and the family-owned publishing house Bonniers, of which Bengt Braun was the CEO. This planned deal was instantly met with opposition. Skandia's CEO, Björn Wolrath, did not like the way the proposed merger was presented by SEB, as the bank was aiming for a takeover and not a merger of two equal parties. This was a problem since SEB needed support from the Skandia board and management to overcome the voting rules that blocked control of the company.[2] Furthermore, SEB lacked financial resources to afford an outright hostile bid on the company, something that would demand a premium (and the bank was not interested in a passive investment in Skandia).

In 1991, SEB teamed up with three Nordic insurance companies: Norwegian Uni Storebrand, Danish Hafnia and Finnish Pohjola. This group of four companies controlled 60 per cent of the shares in Skandia and, in 1992, was prepared to vote for a change in the company by-laws at the upcoming AGM. The group, however, could not agree on how to structure a break-up of Skandia and divide the parts. At that time, a real-estate crisis spread throughout the Nordic region, hitting all financial institutions and, after summer 1992, the crisis effectively blocked all further plans for establishing a joint effort. Thus Wolrath had protected Skandia from two hostile deals. A year later, in June 1993, the investment banks Goldman Sachs[3] and Carnegie[4] placed the shareholdings from Hafnia[5]

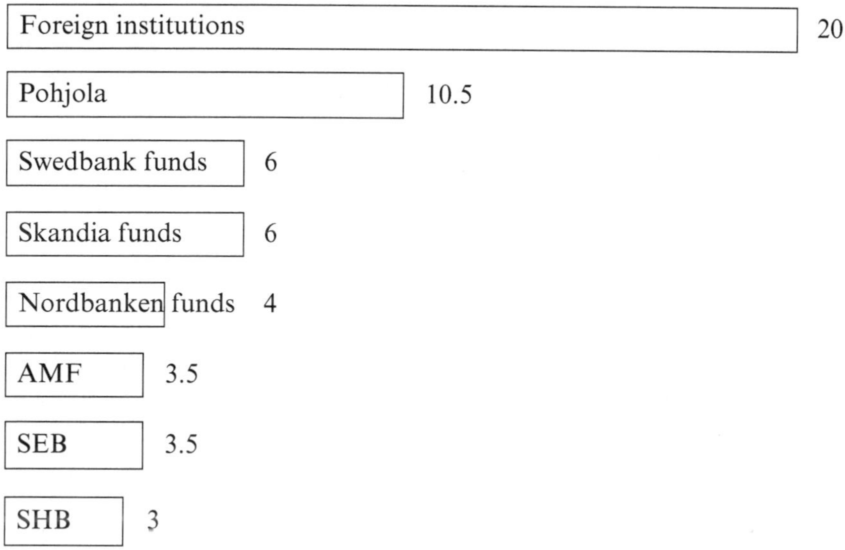

Figure 5.1 Shareholding in Skandia, 1994 (per cent)

and Uni Storebrand into the hands of 100 Swedish and international financial institutions. Thus Skandia did not get a dominant shareholder (coalition) at that time either. The major shareholders in Skandia at this time are shown in Figure 5.1.

By 1994, Skandia needed a capital injection, as did most other financial institutions in the Nordic region that had survived the real-estate crisis in Sweden. At the AGM in April, shareholders voted for a capital injection of 2.8 billion SEK. To gain shareholder support, Skandia had to abandon part of the voting restriction. The financial duo Sven Hagströmer and Mats Qviberg were the leading actors in this discussion among Swedish investors; it all resulted in a compromise where by an individual shareholder was allowed to vote for a maximum of only 5 per cent of the share capital in Skandia. In 1996, this voting restriction was raised to 10 per cent; in 2000, it was abandoned altogether (see Section 2.1).

Throughout the second half of the 1990s, competitors, banks, investors and insurance companies eyed Skandia continuously. Around the millennium it was no longer Skandia's assets and P&C business that were in focus, but rather its position as a successful niche player with a strong standing in the savings market directed to the fast-growing sector of unit-linked assurance products. For that reason Skandia could fit well in almost any financial house. Consequently, SEB calculated a new deal, and so did both the large Swedish savings bank Sparbanken Sverige[6] and the

Wallenberg-dominated investment company Investor. But all these new efforts fell through because of the tremendous success of the unit-linked arm of Skandia that spurred steady increases in the Skandia share price. The company became too expensive for those interested in acquiring it.

5.2 A NOMINATION COMMITTEE

When institutional investors increased their ownership in public corporations in the 1980s, the landscape for corporate control and governance changed; this had consequences for Skandia as well. A new kind of institutional investor emerged in the 1990s who wanted to have more say. That development had taken place earlier in the Anglo-Saxon countries; however, after the liberalization of the international financial markets, it also spread to continental Europe and the Nordic countries. In Sweden, institutional investors no longer complied with the traditional idea of main shareholders dominating the boardrooms; although they were all minor shareholders who each controlled (only) up to a few per cent of the stock, they wanted to influence the board composition, or at least have a say before new board members were presented at the AGM. Therefore, as a new and more significant governing force they also began to promote their own candidates.

The Swedish Shareholders' Association (Aktiespararna) was among the first to advocate the introduction of nomination committees in companies that were listed on the SSE. These bodies then had to be consulted before the main shareholders decided upon board members (at the AGM). Lars-Erik Forsgårdh, CEO of the Swedish Shareholders' Association,[7] described the current procedure as totally unacceptable, with shareholders arriving at the AGM without previous information of the names of the board of directors for whom they were expected to vote. Instead the names, Forsgårdh argued, should be presented well in advance so that all shareholders had time to evaluate the suggested candidates.

Back in 1993, the Swedish Shareholders' Association had already demanded the introduction of a Swedish code of conduct for corporate governance. This had been inspired by the 1992 British Cadbury Report. However, it was not until the Skandia scandals had been revealed that Sweden obtained a code of conduct of its own for all listed companies. In some important respects, it differed from its UK prototype. For example, since Swedish executives were seldom board members, the Swedish nomination committees never had to address the problem of balancing executive directors (insiders/managers) and independent directors (outsiders). In Sweden, a few large shareholders and their representatives (i.e. the outsiders) often dominated the board. Therefore the problem was rather about how to maintain a balance between different groups or kinds of influential shareholders and, at the same time, make room for actors who were independent of such dominant constellations.

With its voting restrictions and dispersed shareholder base, Skandia became a model case for the introduction of the Swedish Shareholders' Association's ambition to introduce nomination committees in listed Swedish companies. Through the years, Skandia CEO Wolrath and his successor Petersson had both been supportive of this idea. In the spring of 1994, Skandia became the first publicly listed company to open up for the establishment of such a shareholder committee with the explicit task of suggesting new board members. In a first tentative effort, its nomination committee was composed of representatives of both its largest shareholders and of representatives of a stakeholder perspective. Throughout the 1990s, the mutual pension fund company AMF Pension[8] (AMF) was the largest Swedish institutional investor in Skandia. Therefore its head of investments, Tor Marthin, was chosen to represent those investors in the nomination committee. He took on the role of coordinator, and collected different suggestions from the shareholders.

In 2000, when it was time to replace Skandia chair Sven Söderberg, who was about to turn 70, the nomination committee became involved (along with major shareholders).[9] This process had already begun back in 1998, when former Ericsson CEO and chair Lars Ramqvist became an elected board member of Skandia. When he took over as chair in 2000, he was a highly respected actor in Swedish business life. Ramqvist also held positions as chair of the global vehicle corporation, Volvo, and the Swedish Confederation of Industries (Industriförbundet). The following members made up the Skandia board at the time: Oonagh McDonald, financial consultant and former member of the UK parliament; Willem T. Mesdag, former Goldman Sachs investment banker, who came from the USA and had long experience as a deal-maker for Skandia; Günter Rexrodt, former German minister of finance; Eero Heliövaara, CEO of Skandia's partner, Pohjola, which had control of 10 per cent of Skandia shares; and Melker Schörling, who was a prominent Swedish businessman with his own listed investment company, and who was also a major shareholder in the service company, Securitas. Heliövaara's presence on the board reflected both an earlier partnership and continuity, while the others represented various capacities with which to deal with upcoming opportunities.

Following the bonus upheaval in the winter of 2000, many investors regarded Skandia's board – that had looked so good on paper – to be a rather weak agency that was very much in the hands of its top management. The latter also included the UK and US teams that constantly fought, both for autonomy from their Swedish superiors and for compensation in the form of lucrative bonus and stock option programmes. Consequently, the board did not do much to curb the financial risks that were connected with the star-performing subsidiary, American Skandia. Some Swedish institutional investors with particular insight complained about this to the chair of the Skandia nomination committee, Tor Marthin; however, nothing ever happened. Moreover, at that time, Ericsson ran into trouble, and Swedish institutional investors, who were also large shareholders in Ericsson, were reluctant to jeopardize Chair Ramqvist's standing.[10] Moreover, Skandia's dominant foreign institutional investors did not meddle. During the first years following the millennium, they remained a passive group of traders who hardly ever voiced any opinions regarding the composition of the boards of Swedish listed companies.

5.3 PASSIVE SHAREHOLDERS

Skandia had two quite large shareholders around the millennium: Finnish Pohjola and Swedish Industrivärden. At the time both were passive. This had a substantial effect on Skandia's capability (and method) to deal with the financial downturn following the millennium. Skandia, among others, ran into serious trouble. Finnish insurance company Pohjola, along with its major shareholders (the mutually run life insurance companies Suomi and Ilmarinen), were the largest shareholders in Skandia, controlling 10 per cent of the stock. That holding sprang from a cross investment by Pohjola and Skandia back in 1988 during the Wolrath era, when Skandia was still very much a traditional insurance company. By 2000, this cross-ownership became an ingredient in a fight over the control of the Finnish insurance industry; this resulted in Skandia's sale of its Pohjola shares to the latter's fiercest competitor, Sampo. When the dust had settled, Pohjola announced that its shareholding in Skandia was a pure financial investment. In the summer of 2000, this holding was worth 25 billion SEK, and it was publicly stated that the shares were to be sold as soon as the stock market climate made it possible. When Pohjola and its partners finally sold out in 2003, it was worth one-tenth of that. All along, Pohjola remained a passive shareholder in Skandia.

Another major private investor in Skandia at that time was Industrivärden – an investment company associated with the large Swedish retail bank Handelsbanken. Industrivärden had started buying shares in 1995 and, by 2000, the holding had grown to 3.9 per cent; its CEO, Clas Reuterskiöld, had ambitious plans for what then seemed to be a successful investment. In August 1999, Industrivärden had freed billions of SEK through the sale of a large stake in the listed Swedish commercial gas company, AGA to its German rival, Linde. Reuterskiöld was quoted in the media saying that Skandia had now turned into a 'core holding' for Industrivärden.[11] There were rumours that Industrivärden tried to buy Pohjola's shares in Skandia, but that the deal had fallen through when the Skandia share rose rapidly. By the year 2000, Industrivärden's holding in Skandia was 4.8 per cent; it was a holding that Industrivärden had paid 5 billion SEK to acquire, and was now valued above 12 billion SEK.

Industrivärden was never a dominant shareholder in Skandia; however, it had certainly been influential during the late 1990s. Thus, in 1998, Industrivärden had suggested Lars Ramqvist as the new chair of the Skandia board to nomination committee chair, Tor Marthin. During his time as CEO and chair of Ericsson, most actors saw Ramqvist as an Industrivärden/Handelsbanken ally. At that time, Industrivärden sought its own seat at the Skandia board but was stopped by the voting restrictions and had difficulty in gaining support from institutional shareholders. At the 2001 Skandia AGM, Industrivärden could, for the first time, suggest its own board member candidate (CEO Reuterskiöld). But Industrivärden did not take the lead in 2001 when Skandia was headed for trouble and Reuterskiöld was the sole active shareholder on the board, although, in 2002, Industrivärden, along with Pohjola, stopped an attempt from some of the institutional investors to remove Ramqvist as chair of Skandia.

Industrivärden was also active in the discussions about Skandia's distressed financial situation. In the autumn of 2001, American Skandia had difficulty meeting the solvency levels stipulated by the financial authority of the State of Connecticut in the USA. The rating institutes then informed the financial market that Skandia was in urgent need of a capital injection from its shareholders. With the assistance from the investment bank Goldman Sachs, CFO Ulf Spång calculated the capital needed to be approximately 1 billion USD. This request for new capital was met with resistance from Industrivärden's CEO and Skandia board member Reuterskiöld. At the time, Skandia was trading at around 70 SEK, and Industrivärden had already lost money on its Skandia investment; Reuterskiöld did not want Industrivärden to risk losing even more. Therefore Skandia had to make it on its own, selling subsidiaries, launching cost-saving programmes, and initiating creative financial deals with its Skandia Liv arm (such as the sale of the asset management contract to Den Norske Bank).

In the spring of 2002, the management of American Skandia (assisted by the investment bank Goldman Sachs) again asked for a capital injection in Skandia to secure its US business expansion. Skandia was then trading between 30 and 40 SEK per share. Reuterskiöld's message was the same as before: a clear 'no'. At that particular time, 'sphere' considerations also contributed to Reuterskiöld's refusal to support Skandia with fresh capital. Industrivärden's excess capital was targeted for its core holding (strong position) in Ericsson, which was another corporation that was squeezed by a financial crisis. In the autumn of 2002, it was Ericsson – not Skandia – that received a capital injection. Parts of the Swedish business community criticized Industrivärden for its lack of support for Skandia. Soon after, Reuterskiöld turned 60, and resigned as CEO of Industrivärden. Anders Nyrén replaced him, and he was even more negative about Skandia's outlook than his predecessor. Nyrén did not like the embedded-value method, and he expressed pessimism about Skandia's business model as one that was caught in the middle of a value chain. Industrivärden's new CEO argued to his own board for a Skandia exit, adding that it was also a company over which Industrivärden lacked control and was very much in the hands of top management.

5.4 TURNING THE PAGE WITH A NEW CHAIR

With the Swedish Shareholders' Association demanding in early 2003 an internal investigation of the bonus programmes given to management, the Swedish public, shareholders and journalists all expected the Skandia AGM in April to be a tough one. Its CEO Lars-Erik Forsgårdh had secured support from several other institutional investors, such as Alecta and Nordea Funds.[12] Former CEO Petersson made a surprise announcement at the AGM that he would offer his services as CEO for a salary amounting to 1 SEK. But he received no support for that offering.

Three new board members were elected at the AGM. Bengt Braun was appointed as chair, thus replacing Ramqvist. Braun, who was CEO of the family-owned publishing house Bonniers,[13] had served as director on the Skandia board throughout the 1990s (he was also deputy chair for a few years). He had been involved in the design of the first bonus programme Sharetracker that was launched in 1997 – which he made known to the members of the nomination committee when he was approached. In the beginning of 2003, however, the full breadth of the problems revolving around the bonus programmes was yet to be revealed. The committee, therefore, recommended Braun, who, in turn, suggested that Leif Victorin (a retired former head of Skandia's Nordic business) should join him as board member. Victorin soon took over as acting CEO. The committee also suggested independent financial and strategy consultant Björn Björnsson as new board member. He was regarded as a strong-willed and competent actor, and was particularly renowned for his troubleshooting capacity. Along with Reuterskiöld from Industrivärden, the trio Braun, Björnsson and Victorin formed an inner circle of board members with hands-on involvement in establishing a new strategy for Skandia. The search for a new permanent CEO was postponed until Skandia's future was ascertained.

5.5 TRYING TO FORM A FUTURE

In the spring of 2003, Bengt Braun had two solutions to Skandia's problem: he and the new CEO, Victorin, brought in the investment bank ABN Amro[14] (owner of the Swedish investment bank that was previously named Alfred Berg) to arrange a 'beauty contest', where various investment banks were invited to present their cases for what they thought Skandia should do. Braun's other major move was to call in a management consultant firm McKinsey, which had worked closely with units in the Bonnier group and whose former head of its Nordic business, Christian Caspar, was a member of its board of directors.

The McKinsey team, with the senior consultant Andrew Dowman in charge, worked in parallel with the management's day to day work to get Skandia's business back on track. The focus was to get the Nordic business back in shape and settle the problematic relationship between Skandia and its mutual funds arm, Skandia Liv. McKinsey was expected to come up with both a strategic plan and a business plan. Board member Björnsson was assigned to work closely with McKinsey on the matter of Skandia Liv and its future relationship with Skandia, including a possible demutualization. Management would work through matters such as a new investment policy and rebates for policyholders. Under the supervision of new CFO Jan-Erik Back and Head of Europe Michael Wolf, management returned within a few months with cost-cutting plans amounting to well over 1 billion SEK. The strategy included plans to sell off both the Japanese unit-linked business and Skandia Bank Switzerland, a costly heritage from earlier days. (An additional 0.5 billion SEK would later be added to this savings programme.)

In April/May 2003, Alan Wilson, CEO of Skandia's UK subsidiary Skandia Life UK, visited the new Skandia chair Braun, and the new CEO Victorin in Stockholm. Wilson presented a pile of overhead slides, the first of which displayed the words 'Don't panic'. This expression referred to the fact that Skandia Life UK was not doing well. However, Wilson claimed to have things under control, and he also assured the others that better times were to come. As Wilson saw it, the problem was a lack of substance to keep together the Skandia group of independent subsidiaries. Therefore he ended his slideshow by making a plea for an autonomous Skandia Life UK. His belief was that it ought to be separated from Skandia either through a partial listing or by way of a full management buyout. He left Braun and Victorin with the rhetorical question: 'What is Skandia's reason for keeping us in the group?' A few weeks later, Skandia's management held a meeting on 23 May at Heathrow Airport. Once again, they tried to get the UK more integrated into the Skandia group; this time, it was through its plan to merge the UK product format Multifund with all-Skandia Global Fund. Wilson remained negative about this idea. He stated that it could not be done – the UK could not be included.

Following the summer of 2003, the Skandia management had come far enough with the savings programmes and redesign of the unit-linked products for it to be confident that it could survive on its own. If the plans were fully implemented, then Skandia would also experience a positive cash flow. At the same time, Wilson and his UK management team had finally agreed to participate in the savings programme and cut costs.

5.6 A CANCELLED MERGER PLAN

CEO Lars-Eric Petersson had merged Skandia's P&C insurance arm with Storebrand and Pohjola back in 1999 (see Section 3.6). In the autumn of 2001, the Finnish partly state-owned financial house Sampo[15] replaced Pohjola as the Finnish co-investor in If P&C. At this time, Björn Wahlroos was Sampo's CEO. He quickly involved himself in the future strategy of If P&C, as both Skandia and Storebrand were more interested in developing savings products. If P&C was unprofitable and the three-part merger was still not in place, something had to be done. Sampo's COO, Kari Stadigh, took on the role of chair and became deeply involved in transforming If P&C into a profitable business.

Wahlroos had even bigger plans for Sampo, the If P&C business and the Nordic insurance sector. In the autumn of 2002, Sampo started to buy straight into Skandia. Skandia was then trading in the low 20s. Buying Skandia shares was regarded as a risky path to take, since this was before its subsidiary American Skandia was sold off. In Wahlroos's eyes, however, Skandia's portfolio of unit-linked contracts and assets under management was deeply undervalued. By early January 2003, Sampo had bought 5 per cent of the shares and, therefore, also had to announce its holding. At the April 2003 AGM, Sampo's shareholding was parked at 7.4 per cent. On average, Sampo paid 19 SEK per share. Shortly after the announcement of this stockholding and before the Skandia AGM in April 2003, the largest shareholders – AMF, Industrivärden and Pohjola – had invited Sampo to participate in the works of the nomination committee. However, Sampo turned down this invitation. AMF CEO Tor Marthin continued to act as chair of the nomination committee despite the fact that AMF had sold its Skandia shares dating back to 2000. By 2003, AMF had no Skandia shares left.[16]

In the spring of 2003, when the future of Skandia was to be ascertained, Wahlroos was not ready for a board membership. But he was convinced that something had to happen in the Nordic insurance market. His plan was to build a strong Nordic financial corporation, and to establish a situation where Skandia had to be split. In such a case, the jointly owned company If P&C had to be sold, as well as Skandia's UK subsidiary Skandia Life UK and the Skandia subsidiaries in far-reaching countries outside Europe (for example, Colombia and Japan). Wahlroos therefore visited institutional investors in Stockholm during the spring of 2003, where he presented his Nordic vision. He also contacted Skandia's CEO at the time, Lars-Eric Petersson, and had a meeting with Skandia's prospective chair Bengt Braun; he was to present ideas about a possible merger of equals. Braun politely told him to wait until after the upcoming Skandia AGM in April.

Following the summer of 2003, chair Braun and CEO Victorin spent some time talking to Sampo's CEO Wahlroos about keeping Skandia together. They claimed that integrating If P&C Insurance back into Skandia as a wholly owned company would mean access to a strong cash flow, and that could be enough to solve Skandia's financial problem. The Sampo team finally agreed to the suggestion.

The Sampo–Skandia plan of a merger of equals that was discussed in the autumn of 2003, however, never amounted to anything.[17] The independent consultant and Skandia board member Björnsson was hesitant the entire time, as he did not believe in Sampo's talk of a merger of 'equals'. Björnsson argued that the deal could end with a full takeover of Skandia by Sampo. Furthermore and more importantly, he believed that the pricing was wrong. In the autumn of 2003, Skandia shares traded at around 25 SEK. Björnsson regarded the company as a classic turnaround case with a share that could possibly rise quickly. According to Björnsson's calculations, the Sampo share was more than fully valued.

In the proposed merger, Skandia shareholders would get 45 per cent of the new company and Sampo shareholders would acquire 55 per cent. Björnsson's conclusion to this allocation of control between the two companies was that it was better for Skandia to continue as a stand-alone company. He had initially been rather alone in his negative view towards a merger with Sampo; however, he gradually gained support from the other board members. As the months passed, the initial enthusiasm from Skandia top management also began to fade away. Skandia Life UK management had been openly against being part of such a merger the whole time and was preparing for a management buyout. Following meetings with Wahlroos and deputy CEO Kari Stadigh, the Stockholm management returned disappointed. The impression was that the Sampo team acted more as short-term financial investors than long-term shareholders.

In October, Sampo changed tactics and talked about moving the Skandia HQ from Stockholm to Helsinki, suggesting that it should have the majority of the board seats, and asked for a mandate to change the composition of Skandia's top management. By that time, Björnsson had had enough of Sampo and acted accordingly. Chair Braun allowed him to ask the investment bank Morgan Stanley to deliver a second opinion on the proposed deal. Wahlroos's move in this situation was to make direct contact with the largest institutional shareholders, Alecta, Industrivärden and Robur.[18] Wahlroos argued that Sampo was the right partner to get Skandia in order, just as it had done with the partly owned If P&C business. Braun realized that it was time to give up on the idea of a merger with Sampo. After all, the investment bank ABN Amro's list of Skandia's potential partners included several alternatives to Sampo (such as Handelsbanken, Swedbank and Nordea).

Morgan Stanley was represented at the last Skandia board meeting in October 2003, before the deal between Sampo and Skandia was called off. The investment bankers from ABN Amro were present as well, and were still prepared with facts that supported a possible merger. In a last effort to get a deal, Braun suggested that Sampo, instead, should bid for the whole company. Wahlroos, however, did not want to pay an expected 20 per cent premium over the market price to get control of Skandia. The talks were finally called off at the beginning of November 2003.[19] Then, on 14 November, Braun presented a new CEO for Skandia: Hans-Erik Andersson.

5.7 A BONUS SCANDAL

On 1 December 2003, SVT (Swedish Television) broadcasted the outcome of the Skandia investigation live for the entire nation to see. Two of the main players in the TV presentation were distinguished lawyer Otto Rydbeck and experienced accountant Göran Tidström.[20] Many households in the country heard Otto Rydbeck address the issue of the two bonus programmes, stating that 'a small group of leading persons at Skandia who have already left the company have acted unethically and have also possibly committed crime'.[21] The fact that Skandia CEO Petersson had received 200 million SEK from a stock option programme called Sharetracker – a figure substantially different from the 12 million one that was published in the Skandia 2001 accounts – was just one of the delicate issues that was revealed. The rest of the money had been 'transformed to pensions' and had, therefore, been hidden from disclosure to both shareholders and a broader audience.

Bengt Braun, who had been a board member when the Sharetracker programme had been introduced, resigned as chair the very same day (on 1 December). He had been deputy Chair in 1997 when Chair Sven Söderberg – under pressure – had removed the cap for payouts in the Sharetracker programme. At that late stage, the board had accepted the removal of the cap as a *fait accompli*. On 1 December 2003, the entire Skandia board put up their seats for a re-election to be held at an extra shareholders' meeting set for the last week of January 2004. In the meantime, Björn Björnsson became acting chair.

5.8 FURTHER SHAREHOLDER CHANGES

As the scandals were revealed in the autumn of 2003, the Swedish Shareholders' Association was quite straightforward in its criticism of Industrivärden and some of the other large shareholders regarding their responsibility for the governance of Skandia. Chief lawyer Lars Milberg said: 'What has happened in Skandia is the result of flawed governance (. . .). The large shareholders should have acted earlier. It was really tough to get an investigation going. We had to push hard. The major owners were not convinced of the desirability of an investigation.'[22]

Being a large shareholder in Skandia at this period thus meant having to answer to an unhappy Swedish public. That seemed not to be in the interest of Skandia's main shareholders at the time, so they sold. The trio of Finnish insurance companies – Pohjola, Suomi and Ilmarinen[23] – all sold their holdings, amounting to almost 10 per cent. On 19 December 2003, only two weeks after the rather dramatic televised presentation of the Skandia investigation, its second-largest shareholder Industrivärden announced that it had sold all of its Skandia shares. This Industrivärden sellout had already started following Skandia's Q2 report on 29 October, although sales had been slower during the discussions between Skandia and Sampo. The shares were sold at 27 SEK each, with a net loss of 1.5 billion SEK. Thus, in a matter of a few months, 15 per cent of Skandia's more prominent shareholder base obtained a new domicile.

5.9 SKANDIA – A POST-CRISIS COMPANY

Skandia had held a central position in Swedish society for a very long time. It was a company that boasted a long successful history and to which 1.2 million Swedes entrusted their pension plans. Hence it was a major player on the SSE, transcending the two dominant business spheres in Sweden, in spite of the fact that various socially high-ranking members of these as well as other Swedish business circles had been involved in the company. Traditionally, Skandia had been an example of a governance regime that was based predominantly upon powerful and public CEOs; this was still the case around the millennium. As a result of the combination of the institutional bricolage and the dispersed shareholder base, Skandia was a company that was primarily under managerial – not shareholder or board – control. Skandia lacked a dominating principal.

The turmoil related to the bonus scandals was traumatic not only because of the negative media attention it attracted, but also because it signalled such a complete failure of the governance system that was supposedly in place. The top management had proved that it was not worthy of the great trust that was attached to it. This failure in governance also raised concerns that something similar could occur in other listed companies. Skandia became a symbol for something that was troublesome for many leading business managers in Sweden. The Wealthbuilder and Sharetracker programmes that had been the cause of so much trouble were seen as results of the importation of US governance theory and financial capitalism.

The challenge for the new set of directors and managers was to try to accomplish a more stable control of the company with the shareholders and board in charge. This task proved rather difficult, and the ongoing negative media attention made it even tougher to achieve. Furthermore, intending actors (including various advisers) targeted Skandia looking for a bargain, and (institutional) shareholders walked into and away from their positions. By 2003, it was also obvious to most actors inside the company (and to many outsiders as well) that the tense relationship between Skandia's UK operations and Swedish HQ had contributed to the process, which ultimately resulted in the bonus scandal. This problem also had to be solved in order to allow Skandia to realize its full potential.

NOTES

1. Skandinaviska Enskilda Banken, now branded SEB, was the result of a 1972 merger of Stockholms Enskilda Bank (the Wallenberg dynasty bank since 1855) and Skandinaviska Banken.

2. At that time, institutional investors and small shareholders were still expected to vote with the board's recommendation, in turn highly influenced by the stance taken by management.
3. Goldman Sachs has been a leading investment bank on a world scale throughout the twentieth century. After the financial market collapse in 2008, the organization reverted to a status as 'bank holding company' (along with long-standing rival Morgan Stanley). That, in some respects, brought 'the era of investment banking' on Wall Street to a close.
4. Carnegie was an investment bank owned by the partly state-controlled bank Nordbanken (today Nordea). In 1994, it was sold to UK merchant bank Singer & Friedlander and, up to 2001, was run as a partnership with management when Carnegie was listed on the SSE.
5. Hafnia, originally established in 1872, was a Danish insurance company in severe distress. In 1993, it declared bankruptcy, and the business was taken over by Danish life insurer Codan. In 2004, Codan was bought by Swedish SEB and merged with its mutual life arm Trygg Liv.
6. Swedbank, previously called FöreningsSparbanken, is one of the four major retail banks in Sweden. The group is basically the result of the 1997 merger between Sparbanken Sverige and Föreningsbanken. These were, in somewhat simplified terms, the banks (or credit unions) of the small-time savers and small businesses, particularly in rural areas and small towns. Both organizations had their roots in the early nineteenth century.
7. The Swedish Shareholders' Association had historically played an important role in governance issues in Sweden, partly as a result of a historically large household participation in the stock market, and partly related to its resonance with corporatist traditions in Sweden lending legitimacy to democratically organized associations. This represented individuals holding small numbers of shares in companies with the capacity for proxy voting at AGMs.
8. AMF Pensionsförsäkring (previously AMF Pension) is a mutual life insurance company that managed pension funds for one-third of Sweden's population. The Swedish Trade Union Confederation (LO) and the Confederation of Swedish Enterprise (Svenskt Näringsliv) owns the company in equal shares. In 1997 AMF controlled 5 per cent of the shares in Skandia. Pohjola had 10.5 per cent but was a passive shareholder supporting Skandia management (a cross-holding situation existed).
9. Skandia's CEO Lars-Eric Petersson was also involved in the procedure (similar to many CEOs in other listed companies with an open shareholder structure). At the time, Petersson was director of the board of telecommunications giant Ericsson, where Skandia had a shareholding and informally represented the interests of the Swedish institutional investors.
10. At that time he chaired both Ericsson and Skandia. The majority of the Swedish institutional investors were more heavily exposed to Ericsson than Skandia. That included Skandia's largest Swedish shareholder at the time, Industrivärden.
11. *Finanstidningen*, 17 Augusti 1999, 'Industrivärden lägger vantarna på Skandia', Robert Eriksson.
12. Alecta is a mutual pension fund company managing individual pension plans according to collective bargaining agreements and on behalf of predominantly white-collar employees in private enterprises. Its history dates back to 1917 as the Sveriges Privatanställdas Pensionskassa. Nordea Funds is the fund management arm of the retail bank Nordea that, in 2009, was the largest banking group in Northern Europe. It was formed in 2000, along with major businesses throughout Scandinavia and the Baltic region. The largest shareholder of Nordea is the Swedish state (with one-fifth of the shares). The group is the result of a large number or cross-border mergers.
13. Bonniers is the dominant media group in Sweden. The Bonnier-family-controlled group includes businesses in publishing, television and web-based media throughout Northern Europe.

14. A globally active Dutch banking group acquired in 2007 by the later destitute Royal Bank of Scotland.
15. Sampo, with CEO Björn Wahlroos, was formed in 2000 and 2001 as a banking and insurance company with businesses in the Nordic countries, the Baltic States and Russia. In 2007, it divested its banking arm and began to buy into Nordea instead.
16. In the aftermath of the Skandia scandals, Tor Marthin admitted that it had been a mistake to remain on the nomination committee.
17. It was only later that these discussions became publicly known.
18. The name of the retail fund arm within Swedbank.
19. Nothing was leaked to the press.
20. The public service TV company in Sweden has a very strong position in terms of credibility and number of viewers.
21. Petersson was found *not* guilty in a trial in 2008.
22. *Dagens Industri*, 24 October 2005, 'Industrivärdens fiasko', Henrik Westman.
23. A major Finnish mutual pension and insurance company formed in 1961.

PART IV

The actors in the Skandia takeover: Skandia 2004

6. A new CEO, board and shareholder composition

6.1 A NEW CEO: HANS-ERIK ANDERSSON

Hans-Erik Andersson was introduced as the new CEO of Skandia on 14 November 2003. Incumbent chair Bengt Braun and CEO Leif Victorin had put forward his name. A headhunter had approached Andersson in early June; however, due to the Sampo talks, the process had dragged on. Andersson had pursued two years of studies in statistics, law, economics and business at Stockholm University. In the early 1990s, he had worked with Skandia's international reinsurance, following which he obtained a position with the UK reinsurance company Mercantile & General,[1] where he remained for five years, restructuring the business until it was sold to Swiss Re[2] in 1996. A year later, Skandia's new CEO Lars-Eric Petersson asked Andersson to return and take care of its P&C business. In 1999, that business was merged with Storebrand P&C, thus creating If P&C.[3] Chair Braun thought that Andersson's time at Mercantile & General had provided him with valuable experience that he could bring to Skandia, since dealing with the UK management at Skandia Life UK would be an important part of the job. In 2003, Andersson worked for the US insurance broker Marsh & McLennan, where he had run its Nordic operations for a few years from an office not far from Skandia's HQ on Sveavägen in Stockholm. Andersson was not particularly well known in the Swedish business community at the time.

The new CEO Hans-Erik Andersson made his first public comment regarding Skandia in a press release issued on 14 November 2003:

> Today Skandia is entering an interesting and exciting period that offers great potential for development . . . Skandia operates on a growing market and has both the competence and the products to be successful. I am confident that we can offer our customers the best solutions and build a profitable business for our shareholders.

Andersson, however, had a troublesome start even before formally entering his new position. A story broke in the Swedish media a mere ten days after his appointment, concerning approximately 15 million SEK that

Andersson had received from Skandia when leaving the company a few years earlier. Before this, Andersson had publicly (correctly) stated that he had received about 6 million SEK from the Sharetracker programme. He had received the 15 million SEK when his term at Skandia was terminated in advance (in 1999).[4] Given the public upheaval at the time over any sort of payment to Skandia directors, any story that involved Skandia left the media with a taint of dishonesty.

Since Bengt Braun had resigned as board chair and the other directors had put up their seats for re-election, Andersson was forced to face this difficult situation very much on his own. At the time, several shareholders voiced their doubts regarding the soon-to-be CEO. For example, Lars-Erik Forsgårdh, CEO of the Swedish Shareholders' Association, publicly demanded that Andersson be replaced. The board, however, decided not to act. A few weeks before Christmas, and less than two months ahead of the extraordinary general meeting (EGM) that was arranged to elect a new chair and board, the then-current board decided that it was not the right time to search for a new CEO; its decision to let Andersson stay was made when Björn Björnsson took over as board chair. He had a meeting with Andersson and came to the conclusion that Andersson should stay on as CEO – at least until the new Skandia board had been installed and had formed its opinion. With a severely diminished share price and hot on the heels of the Rydbeck Report, the media intensely covered not only the new CEO but also the activities of many other (former as well as current) Skandia managers. In the winter of 2004, Skandia was a kind of Swedish 'Enron case',[5] so many of them suffered severe pressure.[6]

During December 2003 and January 2004, the newly appointed CEO spent a great deal of time and effort introducing himself to the members of the Skandia organization with the ambition of re-establishing good relationships between employees and top management. Andersson did gain the support of Skandia's top management – particularly from its CFO Jan-Erik Back – and from its Head of Europe, Michael Wolf. Back and Wolf represented a new generation of Skandia managers. The old Skandia management had enrolled both of them but they entered the organization too late to be part of, or associated with, the lucrative bonus programmes. Moreover, neither of them had grown up in the federative-like decentralized management structure of Skandia. Both had backgrounds as bankers: Back came from Handelsbanken and Wolf from SEB. The former started at Skandia as head accountant in 1998, while the latter began as head of Skandia Deutschland in 1999. Neither of them subscribed to the one-sided emphasis put on the embedded value as a method for top management to promote sales activities. Back and Wolf had spent the last few years trying to rebuild Skandia as a stand-alone company after the devastating near-collapse. They were among the few from the old management team that would work closely with new CEO Andersson.

Andersson's analysis of the Skandia case expressed optimism. In his view, the company had great potential, not having profited enough from its strong position on the Swedish savings market, and still growing rapidly abroad. Andersson had heard former CEO Lars-Eric Petersson say that he was waiting for the stock market to bounce back, but Andersson did not see that as a viable strategy. He claimed that Skandia needed a business model that allowed the company to finance its growth of the unit-linked franchise in a more balanced way. Consequently, Andersson focused on basic issues such as payback, profitability and return on invested capital. He liked Wolf's remaking of the product-offering constructs, which made the business react differently in a stock market downturn and resulted in quicker payback times. These measures, however, transformed Skandia into a less spectacular savings company, although keeping it as a company with growth potential.

Skandia did not wait for its new CEO to take charge. In December 2003, the board decided to sell Skandia's unit-linked business in Japan, since the Japanese regulators had increased the required level for reserve capital in the industry, among other things. The transaction was valued at 1.4 billion SEK – almost 1.5 times the book value of the business. In February 2004, the selling continued with Sampo buying Skandia's stake in If P&C; the deal valued the whole of that company at 24 billion SEK, and Skandia owned 19 per cent of it. Then, Skandia and its mutual arm Skandia Liv (that had been co-investors in If P&C throughout the years) together made a net profit of 2.2 billion SEK, of which 1.5 billion went to Skandia (to its shareholders) and the rest to Skandia Liv (indirectly to its policyholders).[7] After the sale, Skandia had become a pure life insurance company. Chair Björnsson stood behind the sale of If P&C, arguing that it would benefit Skandia's share price. Investment bank Morgan Stanley had been involved as an adviser, as well as CEO Andersson, who, for example, pursued talks with Storebrand's CEO Idar Kreutzer.

6.2 A NEW SET OF SHAREHOLDERS

Skandia's shareholder base changed dramatically during 2003 and 2004. This transformation had implications for the nomination committee that was to suggest new board members before AGMs. During 2003 and 2004, new 'large' shareholders (in this case defined as shareholders with at least some per cent of the stocks) would literally walk in and out of the nomination committee.

On 24 November 2003, the nomination committee that was to suggest board members for the 2004 AGM was composed of the following members: Björn Wahlroos, CEO of Sampo (chair); Carl-Olof By, CFO of Industrivärden; Bo Eklöf, of Robur Funds;[8] Ramsay Brufer, responsible for corporate governance issues in Alecta; Per Löfqvist, chair of Skandia's shareholder association;[9] and Lars Öberg,[10] appointed by the Stockholm Chamber of Commerce to represent the policyholders of Skandia Liv. Together, they represented around 20 per cent of the shares in Skandia. They received little guidance from the resigning board members in a press release dated 1 December 2004: 'After consulting with Skandia's major Swedish institutional shareholders, the board has decided to summon an extra general meeting. This will give Skandia's owners an opportunity to appoint the board members and the auditors they feel are best suited . . .'.

At the EGM on 28 January 2004, the nomination committee suggested four new board members: Karl-Olof Hammarkvist, adjunct professor at Stockholm School of Economics and a former Skandia manager; Birgitta Johansson-Hedberg, former director and CEO of FöreningsSparbanken (later renamed Swedbank); Lennart Jeansson, former deputy CEO at Volvo; and Christopher Taxell, former Finnish minister of justice and board member of Sampo. Two others were to remain on the board until the AGM in April 2004: Eero Heliövaara, CEO of Skandia former partner Pohjola; and Maria Lilja, Skandia Liv policyholder representative appointed by the Stockholm Chamber of Commerce. Björnsson was also to remain in his position as chair, but he made it clear to the nomination committee that he did not want to continue beyond the April AGM.

The new board immediately focused on Hans-Erik Andersson's future. Johansson-Hedberg raised this issue on 28 January 2004 at the first board meeting; Andersson was asked to leave the room while his prospects as CEO were discussed. The fact that it took a rather long time for the board to come to a conclusion made Andersson and his Skandia colleagues, who joined him outside the boardroom, think that he might get dismissed. The board, however, decided that Andersson should continue as CEO.

The composition of the Skandia nomination committee continued to change between the EGM in late January and the AGM in April 2004. Industrivärden had left the committee on 27 January, the day before the EGM. In February, Björn Lind of SEB Funds, who was in control of 3.4 per cent of the Skandia shares, was co-opted to the committee. In early March, Sampo followed Industrivärden, and sold its holding in Skandia, making a net profit of 1 billion SEK. At the same time, Wahlroos left as chair of the nomination committee. Goldman Sachs sold Sampo's block of

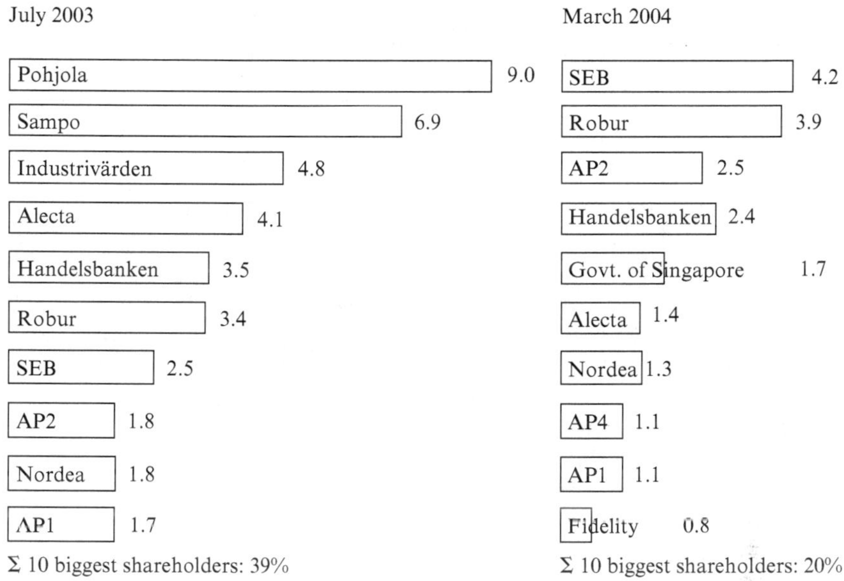

Figure 6.1 Major owners of Skandia shares in July 2003 and March 2004 (per cent)

shares straight into the market to a broad set of international institutional investors. Björnsson, however, was in touch with some Swedish institutional investors ahead of Sampo's actions, suggesting that they should buy the shares, but they refused. Skandia was then left with an uncoordinated and disorganized body of shareholders.

In a 4 March press release from Skandia's board, it was suggested that Bo Eklöf would be the new chair of the nomination committee. Eklöf represented Robur funds with a 3.3 per cent shareholding in Skandia. At the same time, Lars Idermark, CEO of the Second National Pension Fund (AP2), was co-opted to the nomination committee. AP2 owned 2.5 per cent of the Skandia shares.

Skandia's changing shareholder base during the second half of 2003 led to some difficulties in gathering a nomination committee able to suggest new board members. In summer 2003, almost 40 per cent of the capital was in the hands of Skandia's ten largest shareholders. Industrial investors such as Sampo, Pohjola and Industrivärden controlled half of this amount. With Lars Otterbeck[11] as CEO, Alecta had been in control of more than 4 per cent. In March 2004, however, the ten largest shareholders controlled only about 20 per cent of Skandia's capital (see Figure 6.1). Then, four Swedish institutional investors – Robur, SEB, Alecta and AP2 – led the nomination committee that, along with the representative of Skandia's Shareholders' Association, voted for about 15 per cent of Skandia.

6.3 THE NEW BOARD OF DIRECTORS

The board that was formed at the 28 January 2004 EGM was left in a kind of vacuum.[12] It had been impossible for the shareholders to agree upon a new chair. Sampo's CEO Björn Wahlroos, who at the time still controlled a significant part of Skandia shares, turned down most of the names that the nomination committee had put forward. He wanted a chair that he could be sure would not stop his plans to buy the If P&C shares from Skandia and Skandia Liv. Wahlroos suggested Casimir Ehrnrooth, a well-respected industrialist in Finnish business society.[13] Major Swedish shareholders argued that Skandia was not ready for a foreign chair, who would most likely lack the ability to deal with the public turmoil. A group of Swedish institutional investors suggested Marcus Storch, chair of the Nobel Foundation and former CEO of the commercial gas company, AGA. Storch refused to take the helm without the Skandia shareholders guaranteeing that he would be supported for a certain period of time. Since they both were sellers, neither Industrivärden nor Sampo could guarantee that support, and the regulations governing the Swedish retail funds made it difficult for them to provide it, even if they planned to remain as shareholders.

In early 2004, AP2 had begun to build a position in Skandia. Lennart Jeansson, deputy CEO at Volvo, was then suggested as a chair candidate. At AP2, both its chair Gunnar Larsson and its CEO Idermark tried to persuade him to take on the new role. SEB Funds' head Björn Lind flew from Stockholm to Gothenburg, where both AP2 and Volvo were located, to persuade Jeansson to take the chair position. At the time, Jeansson still had quite a few tasks to complete with Volvo (he retired from his position at Volvo on 1 July 2005), so he turned down the role as chair, but accepted a seat on the board.

In March, Bernt Magnusson's name came up as a serious candidate for the position of Skandia chair (he had been on the shortlist of conceivable chairs from the beginning). By March, Magnusson was the strongest name on that list, and the suggestion was made public on 16 March. Three days later, two new names had been added to the list of proposed directors: Anders Ullberg from the large Swedish steel corporation, SSAB, and Kajsa Lindståhl, who had a background as asset manager.

Following the 15 April 2004 AGM, Skandia had a board that was solely populated by Swedes, making it the only company among the large

Swedish listed corporations to have an all-Swedish board. This was particularly strange for Skandia given that 70 per cent of its business was done in the UK, yet the nomination committee thought that they had chosen the six directors with great care. The institutional investors on the nomination committee had suggested people for the board with an explicit aim to restore confidence in Skandia; they communicated an open mandate to the new board to come up with a plan for its future. Skandia's April 2004 board was composed of individuals who had been chosen for their individual experiences and qualities. The majority of the members had never worked closely together before.

The new directors were all well known in Swedish business society, and one must keep in mind that Sweden is a small country, which means that board members often have connections to each other (similar educational backgrounds, shared working experiences, membership on the same boards or associations, holiday homes in the same areas etc.). In the eyes of many investors, however, they were all viewed as independent in the sense that none of them was seen to be aligned with either of the two major power groups in Swedish business (the Wallenberg family and the Handelsbanken sphere). Five new directors were elected: Karl-Olof Hammarkvist, Lennart Jeansson, Birgitta Johansson-Hedberg, Kajsa Lindståhl and Anders Ullberg; former director (and chair) Björn Björnsson became deputy chair.

Karl-Olof Hammarkvist was an adjunct professor of business administration at the Stockholm School of Economics when he was appointed a member of the Skandia board. He had held the position as head of asset management and life insurance at MeritaNordbanken (subsequently Nordea) when, back in 2000, he had been the Nordea representative when large shareholders had criticized the bonus programmes at Skandia. Hammarkvist also had four years' experience with Skandia International during the late 1980s, a company which, at that time, was Skandia's listed reinsurance arm that also included its unit-linked business. When Hans Dalborg, his old friend from the Stockholm School of Economics and head of Skandia International, left for Nordbanken in 1990, Hammarkvist followed suit. Since 2000, he has held a position as deputy chair of the Fourth National Pension Fund (AP4). Hammarkvist was generally described as a diplomatic person who usually strives for consensus solutions.

Lennart Jeansson had been involved in several corporate transformations, none the least at the vehicle-maker Volvo, where he had served for 39 years. He was heavily involved in closing the initial deal between Swedish Volvo and French Renault: a spectacular attempt to merge two big European vehicle companies that culminated in its dramatic collapse in 1993. Jeansson had also managed the delicate issue of reopening the deal after Volvo chair Pehr G. Gyllenhammar had been challenged by his own management team and resigned. Jeansson was credited for his diplomacy in managing this process without insulting any of his French counterparts. He was president of Volvo Car Corporation during 1990–93 and earned particular respect for his rational standpoint. Jeansson had a low public profile, but was widely respected in Swedish society for his focus on facts and figures.[14] He was chair of the Swedish holding company Stena[15] when he was asked to become involved with Skandia. In 2004, Jeansson was also elected deputy chair of the board of the Sixth Swedish National Pension Fund (AP6), investing only in unlisted companies and with a slightly different profile from the rest of the National Pension funds. He was also deputy chair of Chalmers University of Technology in Gothenburg, and a board member of the Confederation of Swedish Enterprise. He was a board member of two of the divisions of Volvo, and was chair of Volvo's pension fund and insurance company, Volvia.

Birgitta Johansson-Hedberg was a psychologist by profession and became a well-known actor in Swedish business as CEO of FöreningsSparbanken[16] in 2000. When she became CEO, she had already been on the board of directors for five years. Before that, Johansson-Hedberg had worked for 15 years at the publishing house Liber and stayed on as CEO long after the firm had been sold to the Dutch publishing house Wolters Kluwer. For quite some time, she was the only female CEO of a large listed company in Sweden. She had remained loyal to her farmer roots throughout her professional life, through the years holding different positions within the agricultural and forest sector, where economic society, and thus membership control, was the preferred way to organize business activity. During her time at Liber/Wolters Kluwer and later at FöreningsSparbanken, she was chair of Lindex,[17] deputy chair at the AP4, board director at Södra Skogsägarna,[18] director of Telia[19] and Spira,[20] and director of Oriflame.[21] She had previously been a board member of Trygg Liv, a mutual pension fund that was later taken over by the bank SEB. In November 2003, just weeks before she resigned from FöreningsSparbanken, she became chair of the board of University of Umeå.

The press speculated that Johansson-Hedberg would take over as chair of Skandia. Her name was discussed; however, institutional investors hesitated, referring to the uncertainty as to why she had left as CEO of FöreningsSparbanken. In the autumn of 2004, Johansson-Hedberg became CEO of Lantmännen.[22] While at Lantmännen, she kept her position as board member of Sweden's largest forest-owner, state-owned Sveaskog. Its chair, Bo Dockered, was an influential person in the Swedish agricultural–forestry sector with close political ties to the Centre Party (previously called the Farmers' Party). He also upheld the position as deputy chair of AP2 in Gothenburg (subsequently a large shareholder in Skandia).

Anders Ullberg was CEO of the Swedish steel company Svenska Stål AB (SSAB)[23] when he joined Skandia's board. He had a degree (MSc; civilekonom) from the Stockholm School of Economics with a specialization in business administration (finance and control). Ullberg left research and teaching in the 1970s for the position of controller at Götaverken.[24] He was offered the job of CFO at SSAB in 1984. Ullberg came to play an important role when SSAB was semi-privatized in 1989.[25] He participated in refocusing SSAB from a decent regional Nordic player with a broad range of standard products to a leading global producer of specialized high-strength steel sheet and steel plate. The successful turnaround was a result of both a strong global quest for raw materials, and a niche strategy and customer focus that had given the company a certain pricing power. That was a kind of management experience that, in the eyes of Skandia's nomination committee, suited the troubled company.[26] Ullberg already had several board directorships, such as deputy chair of TietoEnator,[27] and member of the board of Atlas Copco,[28] when his name was suggested to the Skandia board.[29]

Kajsa Lindståhl was seen in some circles as the 'grand old lady' of Swedish asset management firms. She was the daughter of Gösta Bohman, former minister of finance and a right-wing party leader during the 1970s and 1980s. Lindståhl studied at the Stockholm School of Economics in the 1960s. Following graduation, she worked for 15 years on financial matters for the Bonnier publishing group before being offered the position of CEO of Banco Funds in 1985. Banco was one of the first asset firms in Sweden that worked independently from the large Swedish commercial banks. It was also one of the first to offer ethical funds based upon the United Nations Declaration of Human Rights. Lindståhl remained at Banco until her retirement in 2003, the final years as chair. In 2004, she chaired Aktiefrämjandet,[30] Tumba Bruk[31] and Amnesty Business Group.[32] Similar to her Skandia board colleague Hammarkvist, Lindståhl was also a director at AP4.

Björn Björnsson had a degree from Stockholm University. He began a career in the 1970s as financial analyst at the Wallenberg-dominated bank, Skandinaviska Banken (later SEB). He came to Skandia in 1976, where he became responsible for the company's shares and bonds portfolio, a position he took over after Wolrath (who later became Skandia CEO). During the 1980s, Björnsson returned to the Wallenberg sphere, first taking over as CEO of one of the smaller investment companies, and later as CEO of the Wallenberg-controlled private banking firm, Lancelot.[33] Björnsson's first experience as troubleshooter came during the Swedish real-estate and banking crisis of the early 1990s, when he was appointed acting CEO of Reinhold City, one of the real-estate companies that crashed early in the crisis.[34] In 1997, Björnsson made a name for himself as a board member of the troubled Trustor, a public investment company that had been subject to fraud. During its restructuring process, he acted as one of three liquidators and managed to reclaim a great deal of money for the shareholders.[35] Around the time of the millennium, he was a board member of AssiDomän, the state-owned forest company restructured under the leadership of Bernt Magnusson. In 2002, he was elected to the board of Bure Equity,[36] an investment company that nearly crashed in the aftermath of the telecoms bubble. Thus, when Björnsson was elected Skandia board member in 2003, he was well known and respected for his reconstructing work in troubled companies. He was also a board member of the forest company Billerud,[37] the construction group JM[38] and the state-owned broadcasting network and infrastructure company Teracom.[39]

Björnsson was known as not always being a team player; instead, he was seen as a man of integrity who often possessed rather firm views. He was regarded by many as a person with a no-nonsense attitude. When he was re-elected as Skandia board member in 2004, he had already made a name for himself within the company: first, when he as (the sole) board member had opposed its planned merger with Sampo in the autumn of 2003; and later, when he took a strong stance against the management of Skandia's mutual life arm, Skandia Liv.[40]

Björnsson had also been involved in trying to keep Skandia afloat during the four turbulent months from December 2003 to the April 2004 AGM. Since the new Skandia board needed some continuity, and as it was supposed to benefit from having an experienced troubleshooter on board, Björnsson was re-elected and appointed deputy chair. One of his main tasks was to take care of all the legal mess from the past, and he was also supposed to support the new chair Magnusson in helping to get Skandia back on track. One could note that, at this stage, Björnsson was the only board member who owned any shares in Skandia.

The chair was left to be chosen – a *primus inter pares* – who also had a particular responsibility to make board members work together in order to create a strong Skandia. Bernt Magnusson was chosen for that exposed position.

Bernt Magnusson grew up in Falun, one of the old industrial communities in the middle of Sweden known for its forestry, mills, waterpower and steel industry. Upon graduating in Economics and Business at Uppsala University in 1965, he received a position as executive assistant at the large pulp and paper company, SCA.[41] There, he worked with the industrial restructurer Björn Wahlström, who was well known in Scandinavia. It was as a member of his team that Magnusson would be known to wider circles in Swedish business life. Magnusson left SCA for Alfa-Laval[42] and that, in turn, led to a position in the large forest and power company, Uddeholm.[43] In 1984, Uddeholm merged with the steel company Avesta,[44] controlled by the troubled Nordstjernan[45] and owned by an old Swedish industrial dynasty (the Johnson family). A year later, Magnusson became CEO of the company. Magnusson's achievements in that position made him publicly known as one of the leading restructurers of the Swedish industrial sector. While working for Nordstjernan and the Johnson group, which was made up of around 320 different companies scattered around various countries and working in different industries, Magnusson predominantly sold, closed down and merged companies.[46] When the restructuring was finally complete, the group had been reduced and concentrated to a large property and construction company, Nordic Construction Company (NCC).[47] The road forward for the reconfigured Johnson group later included the first successful hostile bid for a listed Swedish company: namely JCC's bid in 1988 for its large Swedish construction competitor, ABV.

Magnusson obtained a prominent position in the financial sector when, in 1990, he joined Wahlström on the board of Nordbanken (which later became a substantial part of Nordea[48]) after it had crashed during the financial crisis earlier that same year. He then became a member of the bank's credit committee. There, Magnusson met Karl-Olof Hammarkvist, among others, who would later be one of his colleagues on the Skandia board. Magnusson kept his board position at Nordea until he left for Skandia. In the early 1990s, Wahlström supported Magnusson as chair at the Nobel group,[49] which had previously been owned by investor Erik Penser, and taken over by Nordbanken. Nobel was heavily indebted but the various consumer businesses were, for the most part, healthy. Magnusson sold the diversified Nobel companies one at a time. Later, in 1993, he was offered a board position at Swedish Match,[50] a company in the middle of a restructuring phase. In 1995, he became its chair. During the Magnusson era, the group was downsized and refocused in order to create dominant positions in niche markets such as snuff, chewing tobacco and cigarillos.

In 1999, the Swedish government asked Magnusson to take over as chair of AssiDomän, a large forest and paper company with the Swedish state as dominant owner. The government wished to reduce its investment in the business sector, and Magnusson had been instructed by the government to carry out a restructuring of the company. He was then almost free to choose the other board members, and asked (and got acceptance from) Björn Björnsson, as well as several other experienced Swedish businessmen that he knew quite well.[51]

It was Alecta's corporate governance-general Ramsay Brufer who, in 2004, began to promote the name of Bernt Magnusson as the new chair of Skandia. SEB's Björn Lind supported the suggestion once it was on the table. Lind then used AssiDomän (see above) as an example of Magnusson's ability to build shareholder trust. Some of the other institutional investors joined in, reckoning that Magnusson's name was the best around. At that time, they were also in a hurry to get the new board of Skandia working.

The name Bernt Magnusson as chair of Skandia had come to several shareholders as a surprise, as, at that time, business investors on the stock market focused very much on growth, either organically or by business combinations. Several journalists wrote critical articles questioning his appointment.[52] To them, the choice of Magnusson was not self-evident, as his previous experiences had been predominantly with the restructuring of heavy industries, trade companies and conglomerates. However, Magnusson had also been on the board of the Nordic bank Nordea for many years, so he had previous experience of participating in the development of a transnational financial industry. All in all, most Swedish financial actors and business journalists concluded that Skandia needed a period of peace and quiet and, given the current messy situation, Magnusson's rather tough management style was likely to work well. He was simply the best available person for the difficult and challenging position as new Skandia chair.

But it was not easy to persuade Magnusson to accept the position of Skandia chair. In the first press interviews, he explained his final acceptance of the appointment:

> I have been thinking about Skandia for some weeks. I am always hesitant to take on new tasks. But in this case, I am attracted by the interesting opportunities. I think one can develop the business . . . Over time, the position as chair of Skandia has gained a character of national military service. [In one way or the other] Skandia involves a great part of the Swedish people, and it is important that banks and insurance companies – key institutes in Swedish society – function properly and are trusted by the public.[53]

Magnusson knew that he had not been the nominating committee's first choice and that the group of shareholders that actively promoted his name controlled only approximately 15 per cent of the votes. But as passive and unknown small shareholders ultimately owned the remaining 85 per cent, it was unlikely that they would express an opinion on this matter; instead, their shareholding was represented by various kinds of foreign and Swedish institutional investors working at a distance, mainly through entry and exit behaviour. In this crucial way, Magnusson's role as chair of

Skandia differed from most of his previous experiences. For example, in both AssiDomän and Nordstjernan a dominant shareholder had been in control, who was able to set an agenda for Magnusson to implement. But Magnusson did not feel uneasy about Skandia's dispersed shareholding, as his involvement in Swedish Match also represented such an open situation. Magnusson commented in an interview with *Dagens Industri*:[54]

> These days most of the Swedish listed companies have a large presence of institutional shareholders and also a large presence of foreign owners. Skandia lacks a dominating owner, but I do not view this as a problem. The company will be driven forward on its own merits no matter the circumstances.[55]

On 19 March, Magnusson demonstrated his confidence in Skandia by buying 50 000 shares (he already owned 34 500).

Skandia's new CEO Hans-Erik Andersson and its new chair Bernt Magnusson met for the first time over lunch at Skandia on 19 March 2004, almost a month ahead of the AGM. That same morning, Magnusson had announced the dismissal of Swedish Match CEO, Lennart Sundén.[56] As a result, Magnusson had to speak to journalists about that decision on his mobile phone during a substantial part of the lunch. Throughout the remainder of the meeting, Magnusson told Andersson his views on how one could develop various parts of Swedish industry. The two men did not, at this stage, enter into more detailed discussions about the future of Skandia.

NOTES

1. The reinsurance division of British Prudential. It is a different company from the US-based Prudential Financial (which bought American Skandia). In 1996 Swiss Reinsurance, Swiss Re, paid £1.75 billion for M&G.
2. Swiss Re is a Zurich-based reinsurance company founded in 1863. After several major international acquisitions it became the largest company in global reinsurance.
3. A deal that Andersson opposed for both structural and financial reasons. At the time of the Storebrand merger Skandia was already working on integrating its P&C business with the P&C business of Norwegian Vestas that had to be sold off to get acceptance from the Norwegian Competition Authority.
4. When If P&C was created.
5. Enron was the US energy company that 'used sophisticated and complicated methods to generate inflated reported earnings' (Kim and Nofsinger, 2007, p. 34), eventually causing not only its own downfall, but also that of its auditing firm, Arthur Andersen.
6. An example of this extraordinary situation was that both Skandia's former CFO and its former head of human resources had to spend a few nights in police custody.
7. The deal was good for Sampo too. In the original 2001 deal, the three partners (Finnish Sampo, Norwegian Storebrand and Swedish Skandia) had agreed that, if any of them wished to list its shares or buy any of the others' shares in If P&C, the remaining

partners had to choose between bidding for the whole lot or selling their part. Sampo decided to suggest just that; the response from both Skandia and Storebrand was a sale of their stakes in If P&C to Sampo.

8. From 1993 to 2000, Bo Eklöf had been CEO of the occupational pension specialist, SPP. The SPP shareholding in Skandia had rendered him eligible to chair the Skandia nomination committee, and he had supported Ramqvist as Skandia deputy chair in 1998 and chair the following year. Eklöf left SPP when its traditional life portfolio was sold to Handelsbanken and SPP changed its name to Alecta. In 2003, he upheld different directorships and helped Robur funds with its governance in connection with board nomination committees. In June 2004, he was appointed chair of Skandia Liv.
9. A remnant of the time when Skandia had restrictive voting rights.
10. A former CEO of the Swedish investment company Custos.
11. In 2000, Lars Otterbeck replaced Bo Eklöf as CEO of SPP/Alecta. He left Alecta in 2004 when Thomas Nicolin from AP3 was appointed its new CEO. In 2006, Otterbeck was appointed board member of Old Mutual, chair of its subsidiary Skandia and director of Skandia Liv.
12. Christopher Taxell, Eero Heliövaara and Maria Lilja resigned as board members before the April 2004 AGM.
13. Casimir Ehrnrooth was a former chair of the Finnish mobile phone giant Nokia Corporation. His career began in the forest industry and later he was deputy chair of UPM-Kymmene (a large pulp and paper company) and Merita Nordbanken (before this, a pan-Nordic bank merged with Norwegian Kreditkassen to become Nordea).
14. 'It is facts and figures that are decisive. We did have the right numbers and the right analysis, Lennart Jeansson says, claiming to be uninterested in power games' (Jeansson's comment on the tough rationalizations at Volvo in *Dagens Industri* in July 2006, when he retired). That was one of his rare interviews.
15. One of the largest private companies in Sweden, owned by the family Dan Sten Olsson, based in Gothenburg and with interests in property, shipping and the mechanical industry.
16. Föreningssparbanken (later Swedbank) was the result of the merger between the Swedish savings bank Sparbanken and the Swedish farmers' cooperative bank, Föreningsbanken.
17. A listed Swedish female clothing retail chain. In 2003, Amaranth (later Cevian), led by activist fund head Christer Gardell, emerged as one of the largest shareholders, prepared with new ideas about how to run the company. In December 2004, Gardell took over as chair of Lindex. He later joined Johansson-Hedberg on the Skandia board.
18. Södra Skogsägarna is an economic society encompassing 50 000 forest-owners with major businesses in pulp, wood products and bio-energy.
19. Telia was formed as a corporation in 1993 out of what was previously the government-run teleoperator Televerket. In 2000, the Swedish state divested 30 per cent of the shares in the company. In 2002, Telia merged with its Finnish 'sibling' Sonera.
20. Spira is a subsidiary of Lantmännen (see note 22).
21. Oriflame is a company that sells cosmetics, using a workforce of non-employed individuals selling outside the traditional retail trade system. Its turnover amounts to several billion SEK.
22. A major agricultural economic association (cooperative firm) and producer of goods and services related to that sector.
23. SSAB had grown out of the state-owned steel industry. Since 1992 the state had relinquished all control of the company.
24. A large Gothenburg-based shipyard that was caught in the Swedish shipyard crisis of the 1970s. In 1977 it was taken over by the Swedish state and emerged as part of the state-owned shipbuilding company Svenska Varv (Swedish Shipyards).
25. The tough restructuring of Swedish steel industry and SSAB in the 1980s was, however, led by Björn Wahlström. The latter was famous in Sweden for having fostered a group

of four young men to top positions in large listed business companies. Amongst them was Bernt Magnusson.

26. 'We had to choose a new way. If we had not we would not have survived the competition . . . But specialization is not enough. We had to work close to our customers too', was the comment from Ullberg (*Dagens Industri*, 22 April 2006, 'Stålmannens sista dag på jobbet', Jan Wäingelin).
27. A large Finnish–Swedish IT consultant. Ullberg later became chair just before Tieto Enator, with a fairly open shareholder base, resisted a hostile bid from a private equity group.
28. One of Sweden's largest industrial companies and a world-leading provider of industrial productivity solutions such as compressed air and gas equipment, construction and mining equipment, and industrial tools.
29. He would later gain other prestigious board memberships as well. Ullberg left SSAB in 2006. The following year, he took over as chair at TietoEnator and Boliden. As with Skandia, both TietoEnator and Boliden were companies that had an open shareholder structure.
30. A foundation controlled by the Swedish Shareholders' Association with the aim of promoting stock ownership.
31. The company that produced and printed the Swedish national currency (owned by the Swedish Central Bank until 2002).
32. Amnesty Business Group is a freestanding association within Amnesty International set up with the purpose of assisting in the promotion of business support for human rights.
33. Lancelot Asset Management, based in Stockholm, offers asset management and advisory services.
34. Reinhold City was part of a group of Reinhold estate companies that were heavily indebted when the Swedish property and estate market crashed during the early 1990s.
35. Trustor was a holding company that controlled a group of industrial parts companies. The Trustor scandal of 1997 has been described as one of the largest frauds of a Swedish public company in modern times. A total of SEK 600 million was stolen from the company. See Lindstedt (2000).
36. Bure Equity is a mid-sized Swedish listed investment company focusing on non-listed companies.
37. Billerud is a Swedish-based company specializing in packaging based on paper. Its turnover is approximately 6–7 billion SEK.
38. JM is one of the larger listed construction companies in Scandinavia with a turnover around €1 billion.
39. Teracom is a Swedish state-controlled media and communication systems company separated out from Televerket when it was incorporated as Telia.
40. Björnsson was board member of Skandia Liv, representing Skandia as shareholder. He worked on the delicate issue of establishing proper governance rules between Skandia and the company when the latter demanded more independence.
41. A global consumer goods and paper company that develops, produces and markets personal care products, tissue, packaging solutions and solid-wood products.
42. A Swedish technology company that manufactures a wide range of equipment, systems, and services for liquid/solid separation, heat transfer and treatment, and fluid handling.
43. Specializing in tool (high-carbon) steel. Since 1991 a part of the Austrian steel corporation Böhler-Uddeholm, in its turn a part of Voestalpine (Linz).
44. Magnusson chaired the Uddeholm–Avesta steel group. In 1992 it was taken over by British Steel and renamed Avesta Sheffield. Magnusson stayed as a director until the millennium. Since 2001 it has been part of Finnish steel group Outokumpu.
45. See Larsson and Saving (1990).
46. Nordstjernan streamlined its operations. Some 180 companies and legal entities were sold over the coming years.

47. NCC became the second-largest construction group in the Nordic region.
48. In 1997, Finnish Merita Bank merged with Nordbanken and formed MeritaNordbanken. In 2001, MeritaNordbanken subsequently merged with Danish Unibank and Norwegian Christiania Kreditkasse, forming Nordea.
49. The Nobel group included a part of the Swedish defence industry (Bofors), chemical industry (Kema Nobel) and consumer products (Barnängen). German Henkel, Deutch Akzo, British BAE and Swedish Saab were among buyers of different parts.
50. Swedish Match was a consumer conglomerate focused on matches, tobacco products and lighters that had been in the control of Ivar Krueger, the legendary industrial magnate of the 1920s and early 1930s. In 1996, its dominant shareholders Volvo and the Swedish state sold its stock, leaving Swedish Match with an open shareholder base.
51. At that time, investors in AssiDomän were SEB Funds, the pensions company Alecta, the investment company Custos with Gardell as its CEO, and his American co-investor the Wall Street activist Carl Icahn, among others. The stock market and many institutional investors applauded the concentration of AssiDomän's business on just a few core business areas. The AssiDomän stock doubled in less than two years when different parts of the company were sold. In the autumn of 2001, the Swedish state-owned forest company Sveaskog bought what remained of AssiDomän, and the company was subsequently delisted. But the activities also received criticism from some institutional investors and the Swedish Shareholders' Association, as well as from former managers, all questioning the rationale behind the sellout. See *Dagens Industri*, 22 November 2000, 'Staten skapar nytt Domänverk', Per Braconier, Jan Wäingelin; *Dagens Industri*, 13 October 2001, Commentary, Lars Otterbeck and Staffan Grefbäck (CEO and CIO at Alecta); and *Dagens Industri*, 1 June 2001, 'Hur kunde statens klippare lägga ASSI på slaktbänken?', P.-O. Hemmar and Peder Waern-Bugge (former AssiDomän managers).
52. Business journalists in three leading newspapers in Sweden questioned this choice of Magnusson. They wrote critical evaluations of the AssiDomän and Nordstjernan transformations, and questioned the strategy of Swedish Match (see *Dagens Nyheter*, 17 March 2004, 'Analys: Han är inte okontroversiell', Bengt Carlsson; *Dagens Industri*, 18 March 2005, 'Livbolaget ratar Skandias nye chef', Karolina Palutko Macéus; and *Svenska Dagbladet*, 18 March 2004, 'Perspektiv: Bernt Magnusson – Har Skandias städgumma rent samvete efter NCC?', Nils-Olof Ollevik.
53. *Dagens Industri*, 17 March 2004, 'Bernt Magnusson tvekade länge innan han bestämde sig', Fredrik Sjöshult.
54. The largest daily business newspaper in the Nordic region of Europe (controlled by the Bonnier family group).
55. Se note 52.
56. In his capacity as chair of Swedish Match.

7. Rebuilding Skandia

7.1 A PLATFORM

In 2003, the world economy was slowly beginning to experience the momentum from the growth of the two biggest economies in Asia – China and India – and also from the activity in former Eastern Europe. Western economies followed suit, as did Skandia. The Skandia accounts for 2003 showed that sales rose 16 per cent to 75 billion SEK (2002: stagnant). New sales of unit-linked assurance rose 6 per cent (2002: minus 18 per cent). Funds under Skandia management increased to almost 310 billion SEK (2002: 240 billion SEK). According to embedded-value accounting, the estimated profit margin for new sales of unit-linked assurance stood at 14.6 per cent. The change in Skandia's financial situation was even more dramatic. Skandia went from 18 billion SEK in net debt in December 2002 to a 4 billion net debt at the end of 2003. At the end of the first quarter of 2004, after the sale of the unit-linked business in Japan and If P&C, calculations (in accordance with a solvency test marketed by Standard & Poor's) showed an excess capital of 5–6 billion SEK, not taking into account the legal exposure in the USA, which was money that financial analysts concluded could be returned to shareholders through dividends or share buyback programmes. In the spring of 2004, some financial analysts sold the story of an overcapitalized Skandia to the investment community.

At the beginning of 2004, Skandia's new management team went on its first road show to present Skandia to UK and US investors. Chair Björn Björnsson joined CEO Hans-Erik Andersson in London to introduce their presentations at a Capital Market Day with the message that the morale and atmosphere at Skandia were much better than investors actually thought. The question whether or not Skandia was overcapitalized was raised, which Björnsson confirmed was a relevant question. The proceedings, however, went somewhat off their intended track, as the message of Sampo's sellout of Skandia shares was voiced half an hour into the presentation.

Andersson's trip across the Atlantic Ocean to meet investors was the first visit from a Skandia CEO to the USA in over three years. The investors he met there included representatives of hedge funds, long-only funds and pension funds. His message was that the work had begun to rebuild Skandia and to establish it as a solid company. This included tending to its expensive federative-like decentralized structure, as well as to its fragmented global presence. It also meant that the efficiency programme that implied reducing the costs by 1 billion SEK was to continue.[1] Among the major investors that received this message were the Government of Singapore,[2] Fidelity, Third Avenue,[3] and Viking Global.[4] All these actors closely monitored their investments in Skandia the following year, as did most of the investment banks.

With the Sampo merger plan now cancelled, the door was wide open for new suggestions. In the spring of 2004, several financial analysts in London pointed to HSBC Bank[5] and the South African insurance company, Old Mutual, as the most likely candidates eyeing Skandia's UK business (Skandia Life UK and its offshore arm, Royal Skandia).[6] For the Swedish business, FöreningsSparbanken[7] and Nordea were the favourite suggestions, particularly the latter; to many actors, Nordea and Skandia's Swedish division was the perfect match. Within a few years, through mergers with banks in Norway, Denmark and Finland, Nordea had grown into a Nordic financial champion. But its position in the Swedish retail segment was lagging behind those of the three other big Swedish commercial banks, especially in the life savings field. Thus it should have been easy for the shareholders and executives of the two companies to open up merger discussions. Moreover, there were personal links on which to build, as Skandia's chair Magnusson had previously been director of Nordea, and Skandia director Hammarkvist had been a member of Nordea's executive team. One could also add that Nordea's CEO Hans Dalborg had worked for Skandia back in the 1980s and was in charge of its international operations, including the young unit-linked business. However, in the spring of 2004 when CEO Andersson met with many of the investment bankers, he turned them all down. He politely listened to what they had to say; yet in the end his response was a firm 'no'. His message was that it was too early for structural changes. The board and management had first to get Skandia in order.

7.2 THE AGM ON 15 APRIL 2004

The 15 April 2004 AGM became quite turbulent. The Swedish Shareholders' Association had fought hard to gain the support of Swedish institutional investors on a vote against discharging the previous Skandia board and, in particular, the works of its chair, Lars Ramqvist. Approximately 600 Skandia shareholders met in the Globe arena (Stockholm's main event facility). This was their chance to question and criticize, if not the refurbished departments or dealings with Skandia Liv, then at least the bonus payments that were handed out to top management during 1999–2003. It was revealed that the total sum of the latter amounted to 3.6 billion SEK, a sum that exceeded the total profits in the Skandia group for all of those five years. The Swedish Shareholders' Association's CEO Lars-Erik Forsgårdh pushed hard for the matter to be discussed at the AGM. Also, in Skandia the management infighting ahead of the AGM had been infectious. Jan-Michael Bexhed, Skandia's chief of legal affairs, had felt obliged to write to American Skandia's new owner Prudential in order to get its permission to make the story of the previous bonus payments to the US management team public information.

The dialogue with Skandia Life UK was complicated as well. A clarification of everything related to the 'scandals' did not suit the UK management. They believed that making the bonuses public would be detrimental to the company. Chair Björnsson did not agree, and had already informed the Swedish Shareholders' Association about the sums involved. However, Alan Wilson, CEO of Skandia Life UK, had refused to comply, telling Björnsson that, in the UK, it was illegal to disclose individual bonuses. Wilson even sent the board of Skandia a legal opinion on the issues of UK confidentiality and data protection law. Despite this, Björnsson answered 'yes' at the AGM when Forsgårdh asked whether the management of Skandia Life UK had received slightly more than £80 million in bonuses for the years 1999–2003.[8] However, it was not until mid-May that Skandia announced the more definitive numbers for the bonus payments including the L-tips, the Wealthbuilder and the Sharetracker programmes. These amounted to more than 4 billion SEK.

At the AGM, Staffan Grefbäck, Alecta's head of asset management (representing 1 per cent of Skandia shares), joined forces with the Swedish Shareholders' Association to deny discharging the previous Skandia board. The rest of the large shareholders joined in, albeit many of them reluctantly; all were well aware of the public pressure to deny discharge. The discussions continued for hours, with many shareholders making their positions well known. At the AGM, it was finally decided that Björnsson, as newly elected deputy chair of the board, would continue the work to sort out any legal issues.

7.3 A CHANGE OF LEADERSHIP

At the 15 April 2004 AGM, Bernt Magnusson was elected chair of the Skandia board, Björn Björnsson was to be deputy chair, and Karl-Olof

Hammarkvist, Birgitta Johansson-Hedberg, Lennart Jeansson, Kajsa Lindståhl and Anders Ullberg were all voted in as directors. All but Björnsson were new to the board. The nomination committee representatives, Ramsay Brufer of Alecta, and Björn Lind of SEB Funds, presented all the new directors with the same assignment: to consolidate Skandia's position. To regain customer and employee confidence was the most urgent matter. Ahead of the AGM these shareholders' message was phrased as four imperatives: get this house in order; sort out the legal issues get a proper incentive programme in place; and 'clean up'. The nomination committee also encouraged Chair Magnusson to approach his duties[9] 'with open eyes'; this included scrutinizing the new CEO. Still, at the AGM in April, Andersson's position among many investors was somewhat uncertain. He was rather anonymous with regard to both the public and the Skandia shareholders. Brufer had told Andersson that he had a high hill to climb; however, the board, which was led by Magnusson, decided to keep him in office.

As early as at the AGM, it was apparent that it was time to start working. The group of institutional investors behind the nomination committee decided that Magnusson and Björnsson should be granted special responsibility as chair and deputy chair of the board; they were both to have particular assignments. Magnusson was supposed to have more of an active role than what was the norm in most listed companies in Sweden, while Björnsson was to work mostly with legal issues. Putting Björnsson in charge of the 'old' problems would also enable the new chair to concentrate on Skandia's future strategy and other related matters. At the AGM, Magnusson stressed that Björnsson's special assignment had to be carried out in close cooperation with all the other board members, as well as with the representatives for the shareholders (i.e. some of the institutional investors).

Moreover, Magnusson would act as chair of the compensation committee, and Björnsson as chair of the audit committee. The two men were granted an office space adjacent to each other at Skandia's corporate HQ. As Ramsay Brufer and Björn Lind expressed it, there they could work at close proximity to CEO Andersson and support him in his job. Andersson was not appointed director of the board; he was co-opted on to it.[10] At the AGM, the board also decided upon a rather lengthy package for board compensation, which added up to approximately 5 million SEK; 1 million more than the previous year.[11]

There were quite a few important legal issues awaiting Björn Björnsson:

- Issues surrounding past conditions and circumstances that were uncovered by the Rydbeck investigation and during other inquiries that Skandia had commissioned in 2003. This responsibility pertained, above all, to Skandia's litigation with former senior executives such as Petersson and Spång. It also dealt with the Skandia Liv apartments, which involved manager Ramstedt.
- The arbitration proceedings between Skandia and Skandia Liv, concerning profit distribution in connection with Skandia's 3-billion SEK sale of its asset management business to Den Norske Bank.
- Questions posed at the AGM on 15 April with respect to previous bonus payments and the lack of discharge for the board of directors during part of 2003. The question of a legal case against former chair Ramqvist (in particular) was to be cleared up.
- Problems left over from the 2002 sale of American Skandia to Prudential were to be addressed. In connection with investigations by the US Securities and Exchange Commission and the New York Attorney General's office, several mutual fund and variable annuity assurance companies in the USA had been accused of allowing some investors to frequent trading or 'market timing' in fund units.[12]

Bernt Magnusson made his first speech in his new capacity as chair of the board at the AGM.

> I hope all of you understand that, at this stage, I refrain from grandiose declarations and dead certain statements. Important assignments (such as this one) demand respect for experience, and a need for listening and learning from others. . . . Serving around three million customers and having about 130 000 shareholders, Skandia has a relationship to almost all Swedish households. During more than 150 years, this company has been the most important supplier of economic security for families and firms in Sweden. As the sole genuinely international Swedish actor in the financial sector, Skandia is an important company for this country and, at the same time, it contributes to putting Stockholm on the financial world map. . . .
>
> But the fact that Skandia's position and development is important for Sweden should not hide the fact that this company is currently an international one. Skandia operates in twenty markets around the world; its 'home' market is not even its biggest: more than 80 per cent of sales are actually produced outside Sweden; more than half of the owners have other citizenships than Swedish; and more than 75 per cent of the employees belong to non-Swedish daughter companies. Moreover, the greatest opportunities for expansion are probably to be found in markets outside Scandinavia. . . .
>
> The board of directors appointed today is well aware that the future of Skandia depends on its ability to grow and develop as an international company. Our chances to be successful in creating such an international business are dependent on Skandia having a strong home market, and on its ability to establish a competitive business structure. Then, one has to keep in mind

> that the demands on such a structure are rapidly changing for most industries and markets. Before, a national structure was sufficient to be successful – later a Nordic one then became a necessity. Today, however, we have to develop a business structure that can match that of European, as well as, global competitors. . . .
>
> Several times, some of us on the board have been exposed to situations where tough actions were required in order to create competitive power. . . .
>
> If one accepts a responsibility like this board membership, then one must be prepared to carry out even unpopular actions, if necessary. But tough action is no merit in itself – the important task is to keep this company in order and to build proper structures and persistent businesses; it is particularly the latter activity that makes the future. . . .
>
> It is proposed that the most important task for the new board is to re-establish confidence in Skandia as a company – and I agree. A company is basically like a chain of trust relationships – ranging from owners who give an assignment to a board who, in turn, appoints a CEO who, in turn, creates a management team that, in turn, supervises all employees who (re)produce trust in their customer relations.
>
> Today, Skandia has presented a satisfactory closing of the books with a positive development of both profit and volume. We also notice that the Skandia of today meets one of the crucial conditions for healthy long-term development: a financial stability that provides us [the board and top management] with a certain freedom of action. . . .
>
> [So there are] . . . three good messages: [Skandia has] a business that creates satisfactory results, a good financial position, and there are strong underlying growth forces that support our industry. [All together] these have created conditions that make a future success possible. . . . On the international markets we [now] have to fight some of the most powerful corporations in the world.

Similar to most newly elected chairs in listed companies, Magnusson kept all doors open, while at the same time he stressed the problems that were linked to the current business by talking about 'law and order'. A problem of the old Skandia was the lack of routines and HQ control. Magnusson's message was that Skandia soon had to gain full control over its group of companies, where the managers of some of the subsidiaries had been acting for a rather long time as if they belonged to a loosely tied 'federation'[13] of companies. In his world, 'the church stood in the middle of the town overlooking the neighbourhood'. Magnusson also wanted that arrangement to materialize in Skandia. He said that a main challenge ahead was to build a solid Skandia that was capable of moving forward. However, he added that no one could guarantee that Skandia – or parts of it – would not be sold. Someone (anyone) might come up with a (too) good offer, he stated.

A minor board clash also occurred soon after that board had been elected. After the AGM on 15 April, journalists had flocked around new board members Kajsa Lindståhl and Birgitta Johansson-Hedberg, trying to get answers on what they were going to do to restore confidence in Skandia. Both of the women spoke to the press, and that upset Magnusson. He was not worried that they would say anything inappropriate; it was simply that, as directors, they were not expected to make any public statements about the company. This was solely the chair's task.[14] Magnusson even summoned a board meeting by phone the morning after the AGM to inform the directors of the rules regarding information. He expressed his thoughts in a rather harsh way, and both Lindståhl and Johansson-Hedberg expressed their discomfort.

7.4 GOVERNANCE AMBIGUITIES

On 4 May, Skandia's board issued a press release specifying the particular mandates given to Chair Magnusson and Deputy Chair Björnsson. Björnsson was given a 'special responsibility for pursuing and following up on the issues surrounding past conditions and circumstances that were uncovered by the Rydbeck investigation and other inquiries that Skandia commissioned in 2003'. The press release also touched on the board's responsibility for Skandia's development. Magnusson was quoted as saying:

> The task assigned to the board by the AGM mainly concerns Skandia's current and future challenges. We must, therefore, find a division of duties that will allow a thorough and serious follow-up of old issues, while at the same time allowing the board and management to focus on future matters. Björnsson's appointment on the board to monitor the lingering issues is an expression of this; at the same time, this does not change the fact that it is the board as a whole that carries the full responsibility for handling matters of the future, as well as of the past.

In the same press release, Lind (who represented from SEB Funds; one of Skandia's largest shareholders), and who was also chair of the nomination committee, expressed support for the arrangement: 'We think that this is a good solution that will allow Skandia to continue monitoring and conclusively deal with the results of the investigative work in a serious manner, while allowing the board and management to concentrate on developing Skandia's business activities.'

Some of the directors, however, were a bit concerned. It was still unclear what the extended mandate that shareholders at the AGM had given the chair would imply for the practical work of the board. The responsibilities of Deputy Chair Björnsson had been clearly stated, but the chair's role seemed less distinct. It was not a question of the extra pay that aroused concern – nor that both of them were given rooms at the Skandia HQ.

The fact that the chair had a room at Skandia was nothing unusual, since similar arrangements had also been made for the two previous chairs at Skandia: Sven Söderberg and Lars Ramqvist. The question was more whether or not Bernt Magnusson's seemingly strong mandate as chair, responsible for strategy, would make him a 'working chair' (and if so, what did that really mean?). The expression 'working chair' had actually been used in Sweden for a long time, often in connection with CEOs who had moved into the position of chair in the same company.[15] But the construction had often been problematic, since it might complicate the allocation of responsibility both between the chair and the CEO, and between the chair and the other board members. However, due to some criticism[16] and some dysfunctional consequences, that particular Swedish practice had withered away.

At the 10 May 2004 board meeting, Director Kajsa Lindståhl asked how responsibilities and information would be shared among the board members. Bernt Magnusson assured her that all directors would get full and continuous information. His message at the board meeting was that, when it came to decision-making, he and Björnsson would have no further role on the board than the other directors, and that everyone would receive all the necessary information. This statement calmed those board members who had been worried.

From the very beginning, Magnusson also acted to make sure that all board members were included in all discussions during every meeting. For example, Magnusson always gave every one of the directors the opportunity to state her or his view on important matters by explicitly asking them. Some of the other directors noted that Magnusson did not always include himself when passing the question from director to director. When one board member rhetorically asked Magnusson what his own view was on a certain topic, he said that he usually preferred to wait and summarize instead of stating his opinion in advance.

Following the AGM, Skandia CEO Hans-Erik Andersson spent some time trying to clarify and establish his role and authority in the company. When he made his first public appearance following the AGM, he tried to act so that the ambiguity that had existed during the winter regarding his standing would disappear. He went out in public stating that he wanted a Skandia that was held together as one group, where Swedish and UK management worked closely together. He frankly concluded that Skandia's HQ was located in Stockholm and this included responsibility for its UK operations. His statement also indicated that there were severe internal problems in Skandia that had to be handled in the rebuilding process.[17]

NOTES

1. That rationalization included a cut in the 600 million SEK overhead costs of the Stockholm office.
2. One of the world's largest sovereign wealth funds and long-term investor on the SSE.
3. A New-York-based hedge fund geared to long-term value investments.
4. A New-York-based hedge fund geared to long-term value investments, which earned a great deal of money short-selling Skandia shares during the 2001 crash.
5. Hong Kong and Shanghai Banking Corporation Limited.
6. For many years, the Skandia subsidiary Royal Skandia was a profitable tax-haven business for Swedes and other Europeans wishing to reduce their taxable income.
7. In 2006, the name of the banking group was changed to Swedbank and was, thus, given the name that the wholly owned investment bank already had.
8. The comment from Björnsson generated additional upheaval among the management in the UK. One UK manager even claimed later that Björnsson had publicly revealed the figures to deliberately destabilize the group, making the Skandia group tear itself apart.
9. There was no written documentation about these expectations from the shareholder representatives.
10. In listed Swedish companies, the common practice was to have the CEO as a formal member of the board (in 2004 around 70 per cent of the 50 biggest listed companies had such a solution). The idea of 'only' co-opting the CEO was however debated intensively in Sweden. The Swedish Code of Corporate Governance settled in 2005 that both models were acceptable.
11. For the elected period 2004/05, the chair of Skandia's board was to receive 1 million SEK and the deputy chair 600 000 SEK. Ordinary directors were to receive 350 000 SEK. In addition to this, Magnusson and Björnsson were to receive compensation for expected extra work amounting to 1 million SEK to be split between them. An additional 700 000 SEK was to be shared among directors for compensation for work on different committees. Moreover, there was a sum of 450 000 SEK that, in 2003, had been earmarked for a deputy chair, although he/she was never elected. It was, therefore, suggested that this sum go to Björnsson instead, as compensation for his extra work as chair from December 2003 to April 2004.
12. Market timing is a strategy of making buy-or-sell decisions about financial assets (often stocks) by attempting to predict future market price movements based on information not yet disclosed (from a position of temporal advantage in trading).
13. Describing Skandia as a federation began back in 1988 when Jan Carendi was on the quest for maximum independence for country managers in order to expand and quickly grow the unit-linked business. The legal structure of Skandia, however, was never a federation.
14. A common practice in listed companies in Sweden, but not legally regulated.
15. The position as 'working chair' has never existed in the Swedish Companies Act (Aktiebolagslagen) and has never had any legal implications. It was never used in Skandia.
16. For example, in Brodin et al. (1995).
17. *Affärsvärlden*, 21 April 2005, 'Intervju: Hans-Erik Andersson – Skandias framtid', Sophie Nachemson-Ekwall.

8. Working for a stand-alone case or heading for a structural deal?

8.1 INTERNAL PROBLEMS

In late April 2004, Skandia had a market capitalization of 30 billion SEK (equivalent to 30 SEK per share). According to the embedded-value model, this valuation reflected a slight premium compared to the consolidated capital. Financial analysts, who decided to include the present value of future cash flow of projected new sales in the valuation, arrived instead at 40 billion SEK. The business weekly *Affärsvärlden*[1] claimed that 'no one' would want to pay that much for Skandia. The risk built into the Skandia business model, largely in the hands of independent financial advisers (IFAs), was deemed too high. However, the risk of a downturn was argued to be lower than previously. During the first quarter of 2004, Skandia's sales of unit-linked assurance and mutual funds increased to 25 billion SEK, which corresponded to a rise of almost 50 per cent in local currency compared to the previous year. By that time, Skandia's cash flow was more or less in balance. *Affärsvärlden* also wrote that CEO Andersson had to successfully manage a Skandia turnaround and, if he did not deliver the expected results, the board – led by Chair Magnusson – would probably sell (parts of) Skandia.

The growth in the world economy and the improvement of Skandia figures did not, however, hide the fact that the Skandia group was unbalanced; it was structured into three groups: the Nordic region; Skandia Life UK including the offshore subsidiary Royal Skandia; and continental Europe, along with countries in Latin America and Asia. The two latter units were growing steadily. For Sweden, however, which was the second-largest market representing 16 per cent of the sales, numbers for 2003 were lagging. Moreover, during the first quarter of 2004, total sales in Sweden were decreasing, although an optimist could note that the rate of the decline was lower. Bad publicity was blamed for this sales problem.

The downturn in sales gradually altered Skandia's traditionally strong position on the Swedish insurance market. During 2003, the market share for Skandia Link (the subsidiary that sold unit-linked and fund products) had fallen from 29 per cent to 24 per cent. Skandia's share of new sales in the market was as low as 10 per cent. Conversely, competitors such as SEB's pension arm SEB Trygg Liv were doing well. Part of Skandia's problem in Sweden was its relationship with insurance brokers. The business model where the broker was paid up front on selling a new insurance policy was changed to a model where the payback was instead made over a period of years. This was better for Skandia's long-term cash flow, but less lucrative both for Skandia's in-house brokers and its free agents.

The relationship between Skandia and its mutual subsidiary Skandia Liv remained strained. The conflict of interest between mutual life insurance companies (such as Skandia Liv) and a controlling entity (such as Skandia) then became a governmental issue in Sweden. A commission was set up to analyse the effects of a law-enforcing demutualization. To silence public criticism of what had been perceived as an unhealthy relationship between Skandia Liv and its listed mother company Skandia, the latter's new board and management team worked hard to establish independent status for Skandia Liv. Concurrently, the new board and new management team of the former sought independence from Skandia. The old partnership, built upon the listed Skandia almost dictating how costs should be allocated between the life company and the rest of the business, no longer suited Skandia Liv. The dialogue between Skandia and its mutual subsidiary Skandia Liv was also complicated by the fact that Björnsson (Skandia's deputy chair and representative on the Skandia Liv board) and the Skandia Liv management team were not comfortable with each other. Björnsson's relationship with Urban Bäckström,[2] the new CEO of Skandia Liv, was strained. Both men, however, maintained a professional dialogue.

Skandia also had problems in the UK. Skandia Life UK was selling well, although the profit levels coming out of the UK subsidiary were lagging behind the rest of the Skandia group. In Sweden, the profit margin fell slightly in 2003 from close to 17 per cent to 16 per cent. In the rest of the world, profit margins rose from 18 per cent to 23 per cent. The UK (including Skandia Life UK and Royal Skandia) developed differently. There, an already low profit margin fell even further from 11 per cent to 9 per cent. These differences in profit margins were made public in the 2004 Q1 report which, for the first time ever, treated Skandia Life UK as a separate entity. Its profit margin, including the offshore arm Royal Skandia, was 12 per cent.

At the time, the Financial Services Authority (FSA), which is the regulating authority of all UK providers of financial services in the country, was investigating Skandia Life UK. It seemed that UK life insurance customers were overcharged for their policies. Skandia Life UK had identified the problems and informed the FSA. One difficulty was that an actuarial formula had been written with incorrect specifications. The formula had been written at Deputy CEO Nick Poyntz-Wright's department when he worked there in the early 1990s as an actuary. This purely technical error seemed to pop up time and time again in customer accounts. During 2004–06, this mistake cost Skandia Life UK £20 million to correct. The second problem stemmed from a guaranteed pension fund. The weak market development post-2000 had led to a fall in fund prices. It soon became evident that the customers had been charged wrongly. The fund closed in 2003 when Skandia Life UK had to admit to the FSA that it had made mistakes in its handling of the fund. The FSA demanded that, in order to compensate customers correctly, Skandia Life UK backtracked all payouts. All values had to be recalculated on a day-to-day basis at a cost to Skandia Life UK of £30 million.

Concurrently, the Skandia Life UK subsidiary Bankhall was not doing well. In 2003, its profit reached 84 million SEK (2002: 85 million SEK). This figure was calculated before a goodwill amortization of 136 million SEK (2002: 137 million SEK) that actually turned the statutory accounts into a loss. The idea behind the Bankhall investment in 2001 had been to benefit from expected structural changes on the UK IFA market. However, the market change dragged on: the re-regulation of the market for financial advice on life products was postponed for 18 months until 2005. In 2004, sector actors were talking about an 'evolution' (rather than a 'revolution') of market behaviour.

In early April 2004, CEO Hans-Erik Andersson and CFO Jan-Erik Back attended a board meeting at Skandia Life UK's HQ in Southampton. Swedish management expressed its concerns and claimed that the UK business lacked a coherent structure. Skandia Life UK, Royal Skandia and Bankhall were treated as three completely separate entities with no transparent allocation of capital between them. Therefore Skandia (as the mother company) could not make a continuous follow-up of the financial statements of these UK units. Instead, the Skandia Life UK group and its financial status were predominantly under the control of its CEO Alan Wilson. Andersson and Back wanted to change this. During the Southampton board meeting, the two suggested that Skandia should revitalize the old UK holding company that formally controlled the UK companies.[3] The ambition was to take full control over Skandia's capital flow.

At the meeting, Wilson made his point clear. He did not want Andersson and Back to look into 'his' books. Wilson wanted to run Skandia Life UK. He wanted to solve the problems with the FSA himself, and he wanted to carry out the necessary cost reduction programme his own way. Wilson's conclusion was that Skandia did not need to control Skandia Life UK as its business was already regulated by the FSA; he did not want to discuss the future for Bankhall either. Andersson later contacted the FSA to sort out the regulatory matters on the UK market. The authority welcomed and supported Skandia's interest in its UK affiliate, much to Wilson's dismay. But simultaneously, Wilson needed support from Skandia HQ. He wanted Skandia to finance the expansion of Skandia Life's Bankhall franchise into mortgages. The management team of Bankhall, Paul Hogarth and Simon Taylor, had big plans for the future. Andersson said that he was prepared to discuss the matter providing that Wilson came back with calculations that showed the money spent on such a new investment would yield a return, positive cash flow and future dividend payouts. Wilson never returned with such calculations; neither did Hogarth or Taylor.

8.2 PRESENTING THE 'GLUE PLAN'

During the four-month period that Björn Björnsson had been the chair of Skandia (December 2003 to April 2004), he had worked hard to figure out a possible strategy for the corporation. In the autumn of 2003, Björnsson had turned down the Sampo deal for one main reason: Sampo's bid was too low. This time, Björnsson turned to McKinsey, a consultancy firm that had been previously used by former Skandia chair, Bengt Braun. McKinsey had been working on a plan for Skandia's Swedish operations. This included a plan for the mutually run life insurance company, Skandia Liv.[4] At the beginning of 2004, McKinsey and its director-in-charge, Andrew Dowman, were also engaged in examining the relationship between the two firms (Skandia and its mutual arm, Skandia Liv). This included analysing the possibility of a demutualization of the latter. Since Björnsson was the director of Skandia Liv and since Andersson did not sit on its board for governance reasons, it became Björnsson's responsibility to sort out the delicate relationship between the mutual life company and its shareholder Skandia. Part of the job was to be presented in June when the new Skandia Liv chair Bo Eklöf was put in place.[5] For the first time, the mutual life company would have both a chair and a CEO (Urban Bäckström) who were fully independent of its owner.

Björnsson, however, wanted to expand McKinsey's tasks. He asked the firm to review the strategy for the entire Skandia group. Björnsson was eager to find out where the 'glue' was between the Nordic region, Skandia's international subsidiaries and its UK business – something that Wilson, the head of Skandia UK, considered was missing. Björnsson also wanted to know where the potential synergies were to be found in a more integrated group, and what the situation would look like in a structure where Skandia acted as a pure holding company.

Dowman presented a strategic plan to the Skandia board a few weeks before the AGM in April 2004. The strategy was founded upon a benchmarking analysis. The basic idea was to remove the Swedish operations from the European division, and to form a separate division for all Swedish and Nordic operations (i.e. Skandia Liv, Skandia Link, Skandia Lifeline and Skandiabanken). This meant that the Nordic operations were to be fully integrated for the first time, and that customers would face a common Skandia. The final report was presented at one of the first meetings of the new board, on 10 May 2004. McKinsey's ideas behind the separation of the Skandia group into three different companies with three separate balance sheets had been easy to appreciate by both Skandia board and management. Such a solution would facilitate the monitoring of cash flow, profitability, capital allocation and business in general. The controversial issue was a new savings plan that the consultants suggested.

McKinsey presented savings that amounted to 1 billion SEK. The largest share was expected to come from the UK, where the figures pointed to possibly large savings on back-office services. The new board members had responded positively to these ideas, but management was critical. CEO Andersson was not impressed at all. To him, the suggested savings were more a question of academic paperwork, which neither included a strategy for how the suggested savings were to be carried out, nor how the joint activities were supposed to work. Thus, to him, the report lacked realism. Andersson argued instead for a continuation of the works that had already been carried out by Monitor,[6] the consulting firm that had already gone through Skandia's international strategy for 2002 and 2003. Among other things, Monitor's plan had focused on the delicate issue of possible savings through coordinating activities of the unit-linked business across the whole of Skandia; this included its UK business.

The UK management loudly opposed such joint cooperation plans; the team argued that its operations differed from those both in Europe and elsewhere. Moreover, in the eyes of the UK management, the cultural differences between Sweden and the UK were simply too large for such a solution. Andersson argued that the UK management team was strong in entrepreneurship, sales and marketing, but was lacking in administrative capabilities and control. Skandia Life UK had also outgrown its established administrative practices, which resulted in high costs and low margins. During the internal discussions, Andersson cited the start-ups on the Continent as examples of excellent administration.

Skandia quickly moved to take firmer control of the UK subsidiary. On 1 May 2004, a mere two weeks after the AGM, the 1980s UK holding company structure, set to control the capital flows between UK companies, was back in place. Skandia CEO Andersson was appointed chair of the board. There were also two independent UK directors on the board as well: Ashok Gupta, who came from the UK life insurance industry and David Cranston, who had a military background and an education in finance. The two men joined the board along with members from both the UK and Swedish management. Andersson's plan was to get the UK group to work as an integrated part of the whole Skandia team, albeit with its own balance sheet.

Those at Skandia Life's UK HQ quickly understood that its new board had given Andersson the mandate to try to get a firmer grip on the UK management. There was suddenly a Swedish rulebook in place, and the UK management complained to each other about having to ask for approval for almost everything. Functions such as accounting, actuary, HR, IT, investment, marketing and so on had to report directly to Andersson, thus forming a matrix structure. Moreover, as of 1 May, all capital movements between the companies in the UK had to be approved by the board of the UK holding company. All this made CEO Wilson and his management team rather dissatisfied with the new Stockholm regime. At the same time, Wilson was involved in a big and complex salary discussion with his Southampton staff. In the new structure, such decisions required approval by the board of the UK holding company – and this irritated Wilson. Some of the managers at the UK subsidiary believed that Andersson had the new board's mandate of 'taming the UK management', and to squeeze Wilson so hard that he would be forced to resign. (All of the other top managers who had become wealthy by the previous incentive programmes had left the company.)

The UK management team flew to Stockholm on 10 May 2004, destined for the Skandia board meeting where the McKinsey report was to be discussed. The six on the plane were Alan Wilson, Nick Poyntz-Wright, Jim Roberts, Roger Phillips, Simon Burgess, Jamie Macleod and Paul Hogarth. They intended to try to persuade the board to sell the UK company. In the boardroom, Wilson showed slides displaying Skandia Life UK's future outlook. Three strategic options were presented on one of the last slides: sell it, separate it, or capitalize on its current value (for instance, by an IPO). The board just thanked Wilson for his presentation without offering any particular opinion.

Some of the members of the UK delegation left with the feeling that Wilson's message regarding the merits of an urgent selloff had not been clear. The only point that Wilson had been able to get across was that Skandia Life UK was a fantastic company, so why would Skandia want to sell it? They also had the impression that most of the board members were uneasy throughout the presentation. For example, they had interpreted Director Björnsson's body language as one of several expressions of his (and the board's) unwillingness to compromise. Following the meeting, Wilson told his disappointed team that he thought it would be better to come back later; he said that he was sure he could generate a sale. On 17 May, seven days after the board meeting in Stockholm, Wilson (who was 54 years old at the time) went for a walk in Hyde Park, where he suffered a heart attack. Nick Poyntz-Wright, number two in rank in Southampton, took over his responsibilities.[7]

8.3 PROJECT PEGASUS

The Swedish institutional shareholders in Skandia were pleased with what Bernt Magnusson had told them after he had been chair for a few months. During summer 2004, in meetings with a group of shareholders, he had referred to the management team's strategy using the classic 'hockey stick' metaphor: indicating that everything will turn out fine in a few years' time. Some institutional investors had the impression that the new chair was not convinced by what he had seen thus far of management's own plans for Skandia. Their impression was that merely aiming to make Skandia profitable was not a viable long-term strategy for Magnusson.

After the 10 May board meeting at which McKinsey had made its presentation of the 'glue' of the Skandia group, Magnusson turned to the investment bank Morgan Stanley for assistance in making a strategic review of Skandia ('Project Pegasus'). The investment bank already had an adviser agreement with Skandia since the Sampo deal in the autumn of 2003. In the spring of 2004, Morgan Stanley had concluded the sale of If P&C to Sampo on behalf of Skandia. Magnusson now approached Per Hillström, head of the Nordic region, and Jakob Lindquist, who was based in London. The two were asked to analyse the status of Skandia Life UK and Skandia's position in the life insurance industry as a whole; they were then to present the results to the Skandia board. The analysis was to be prepared in conjunction with Per Jungkvist, who was in charge of Skandia's financial strategy.

The Morgan Stanley consultants focused on the scattered geographical presence of the Skandia group and its various sizes of local subsidiaries. Bearing that in mind, they argued that Jungkvist's spreadsheets were inappropriate, at least if their purpose was any sort of continuous follow-up of cash flow, capital requirements and return on capital employed. In their analysis, Skandia's federative-like heritage – with local management acting independently of each other and with a full focus on sales volumes – still prevailed on both small and large markets, including Skandia Life UK. For the Skandia group, it was not possible to make cash flow follow-ups per division on a quarterly basis, and there were no separate balance sheets for the different companies. This was untenable to Morgan Stanley's people, particularly as the Skandia group showed a negative cash flow.

Project Pegasus was presented to the board for the first time at its meeting in June 2004, where Morgan Stanley presented a structural analysis of Skandia including several possible alternatives for how it could go forward. In a set of papers, Morgan Stanley had benchmarked Skandia against other European insurance and savings companies; it became evident that no other company in the industry looked like Skandia, with its full focus on unit-linked business. For example, when compared to AXA,[8] a French group that paralleled Skandia in having a broad international strategy, it became clear that AXA was larger in the local markets, and also seemed to have an expansion plan in place. Some of the board members' interpretation of all the comparisons made was that the competitive landscape had changed and that Skandia's current strategy – being a competent niche player in the market of unit-linked products – might not work in a long-term perspective. Moreover, Skandia's market position seemed to be eroding both in the Nordic region and the rest of Europe. Skandia also lacked economies of scale in many of its local markets; its presence was strong only in the UK and Sweden. Morgan Stanley also presented a few different ideas regarding possible future paths for Skandia: one was to further concentrate Skandia's market presence (e.g. by selling off its businesses in countries such as Colombia and Italy); another available option was to sell Skandia Life UK (an attractive business opportunity for many competitors).

Magnusson gave a great deal of credibility to the Morgan Stanley presentation. The chair's question to the other directors was whether a successful international company could have a size and structure like that of Skandia. This, along with the low confidence in the Swedish market, made room for another solution: Skandia could also be split up and sold in parts. Magnusson suggested that, in such a case, Skandia Life UK could be the first to opt out. However, most of the other board members did not share the chair's conclusion from the Morgan Stanley presentation, and were not at all convinced that Skandia's current niche strategy was bound to fail – at least not in the foreseeable future.

CEO Andersson and his Swedish management team were not convinced that the chair's view was the best for Skandia either. Outside the boardroom Andersson spoke with Magnusson and tried to convince him that it was too early to split up the Skandia group. Andersson wished that such suggestions be postponed until the planned programme for the turnaround had been implemented, and had provided value to the Skandia shareholders. But Magnusson still wanted to keep all doors open, although he also agreed that a preferred solution for an autonomous Skandia should be sorted out – at least it was needed as a 'fall-back' alternative. He saw several solutions for a Skandia going forward. During this period, both Magnusson and Andersson expressed their views, albeit only in very limited circles.

Two days after the Morgan Stanley presentation in early June, Magnusson sent a letter to Andersson with copies to the other board members. He wrote that he had noticed Skandia's international business differed significantly from its domestic business. It was obvious to him that Skandia lacked an adequate business structure. Therefore he suggested that Andersson should work to reallocate the capital to the different Skandia divisions, so that the balance sheets could be separated for each unit. This work would concurrently prepare Skandia for a possible future split, also to be further discussed at the Skandia board meeting in August.

The next board meeting was scheduled for 20 June 2004. Magnusson wanted a board mandate with Morgan Stanley to sort out the possible options for Skandia's future, and the board decided to approve his proposal. During the rest of the summer, Morgan Stanley outlined Project Pegasus, particularly the role of Skandia Life UK. As the summer went on, Morgan Stanley structured its Pegasus case, focusing on five alternatives: stand-alone for an integrated Skandia group, a break-up of the Skandia group, a sale of the Skandia UK businesses (Skandia Life UK and Royal Skandia), a demerger and partial listing of the UK businesses, and status quo.

The preparatory works during the summer months were not to be carried out in a vacuum. Nordea publicly announced on 29 June 2004 its interest in the Skandia's Nordic business when its CEO Lars G. Nordström was interviewed in the Swedish leading daily newspaper, *Dagens Nyheter*:

> We do not have a strong position in the Swedish life savings market, but would like to have it. One way forward is through acquisitions. Regarding Skandia, I am not yet confident that its Swedish position is stable enough. One needs to be out of the risk zone for unexpected negative surprises – of which we have seen a few – before we can begin to calculate. But, long term savings – including life savings – is an area that more and more people become interested in.[9]

A few days later, Göran Lenkel, head of Skandia's Internet bank, quit his job citing personal reasons. There were speculations that Skandia planned to sell Skandiabanken. It was one of the few new Internet banks that had gained a significant position in the Swedish banking market. Moreover, market rumours indicated that both Icelandic bank Kaupthing[10] and Danish bank Danske Bank[11] also evaluated Skandiabanken. In an interview published on 9 July in *Dagens Industri*, Sweden's daily business newspaper, Magnusson commented upon the plans for a savings programme that was to be announced later:

> If we have higher costs than others, we will lose out. That is the market's verdict . . . In a global world, structural change is a part of day-to-day matters. There is a pressure to become cost-efficient and this demand is increasing all the time. It is the same for all industries. Therefore, Skandia must also be open for structural rationalization. But first, we must have full control of our operations . . . [and that cannot] be allowed to take a long time. I must also add that no plans exist today for Skandia to participate in the structural transformations of the savings industry.

8.4 SKANDIA GOES FOR STAND-ALONE

In the summer of 2004, Nick Poyntz-Wright, Skandia Life UK's new CEO, did his best to balance the wills of the Skandia board and the management of Skandia. Poyntz-Wright was an actuary by profession and had joined Skandia Life UK in 1985. Former CEO Wilson later promoted him to chief operating officer (COO). At the time, Poyntz-Wright joined the Stockholm management to try to solve the troubling Bankhall case. Meanwhile, discussions between Stockholm and Southampton continued to be tense. Poyntz-Wright also continued working hard to establish an attractive incentive programme.

Morgan Stanley's summer work was to be presented at the Skandia board meeting on 12 August. Among other things, it included both a feasibility study and preparations for a possible demerger of Skandia Life UK. Poyntz-Wright and his management team were pleased with this work, believing that the Stockholm management would finally support the UK's desire to be separated out; therefore they supported Project Pegasus. A sale of Skandia Life UK, including Royal Skandia, was expected to bring in 16–17 billion SEK – more than half the value of the whole of Skandia. At the same time, Poyntz-Wright made his own plans to prepare for a demerger and a possible initial public offering (IPO). The UK management worked through an old contact with a private investment bank in London. There were also plans for a financial package for a partial management buyout (MBO).

Late that summer, something began to go wrong with the UK management's plans to demerge Skandia Life UK. It had become evident to the team that it would not be possible to convince the management in Stockholm, nor the board of directors, of the necessity of an IPO. However, before the 12 August board meeting, Poyntz-Wright received support from the independent board members of Skandia Life UK.

Together, they wrote a letter of support to the Skandia board, outlining the UK management's wish for a demerger of Skandia Life UK. They also expressed concern that the UK management team would otherwise resign. However, the letter did not help, and neither did the material that Morgan Stanley had prepared.

The feasibility study that was presented to the board described how Skandia Life UK could be launched as an IPO, and that a partial listing of Skandia Life UK could be valuable for Skandia's shareholders. The Skandia board was neither enthusiastic for the UK management demerger plan nor for the conclusion regarding value accretion to Skandia's shareholders. However, some board members did not subscribe to the underlying implications of turning down these alternatives. Björn Björnsson expressed concern that the Swedish top management team would fail to gain control over the management in the UK. This was a serious problem since Skandia Life UK, when all capital was allocated to the different units in Skandia, seemed to be in worse financial shape than expected. With the possible exception of Magnusson and Björnsson, the board members did not see any immediate need to make structural changes primarily to address financial matters. There were reasons for keeping Skandia together; without the UK businesses, that amounted to up to 70 per cent of Skandia's turnover, only a rather small part of Skandia would be left.

Some of the directors also saw Skandia as a turnaround case. In that context, its portfolio of businesses was approached analytically with particular reference to market shares (relative to competitors) and market growth. The directors then applied the classical Boston matrix[12] on the material. In doing so, they put Skandia in a segment of a savings industry that was growing quickly and that offered plenty of opportunities for profit. However, Morgan Stanley had not provided a large amount of material tailored to evaluate this particular strategic path.

Director Anders Ullberg's view differed from the one favoured by the chair. At the 12 August board meeting, he referred to his SSAB experiences – a company that many analysts had regarded as a hopeless case in the global consolidation of the steel industry. However, SSAB had survived, arguably by refocusing and working methodically in its selected niches. Ullberg had got the impression that Magnusson had been a bit surprised that the SSAB niche strategy had worked so well in an industry where scale of operations was deemed so important. Ullberg still argued that a similar strategy ought to work in Skandia as well; he was convinced that niche players (generally) could survive – and even thrive – in global markets.

The conclusion from the board meeting was that Skandia should continue to focus on the stand-alone alternative. Morgan Stanley's folder with Project Pegasus was to be put on the shelf.[13] Skandia Life UK should be retained at least until the rest of the company was operating well. The board entrusted Andersson with the work of gaining full control over the UK management and of implementing a new management retention system. Björnsson, however, expressed concern over what to do with the UK subsidiary.

When the directors left the 12 August board meeting, most of them were confident that management concentrated on rebuilding Skandia, cutting internal costs and looking for synergies. One board member expressed this: 'Finally we will devote ourselves to the business. What Skandia needs is peace and quiet, and it is going to receive that from now on . . . We cannot keep on following two parallel tracks. Skandia as a stand-alone company is the way forward.'

The board meeting minutes stated that the Morgan Stanley study on the UK activities was terminated, and that the overview was finished. Later, when reading these approved minutes, some of the directors noted that there was a passage stating there would be a continuous follow-up of the strategy. According to some of the directors, that particular issue had not been discussed during the August board meeting. There was, however, nothing controversial with that statement – a board of directors is always obliged to scrutinize a chosen strategy. Chair Magnusson had drafted the passage in the minutes, the secretary of the board, Jan-Mikael Bexhed, had cleared this addition.

8.5 REPORTING THE SECOND QUARTER 2004

Skandia presented its Q2 report on 13 August 2004, showing that the results continued to improve, just as they had already done in the first quarter. New financial targets were presented with the ambition of increasing the value of the new business compared to the rest of the industry. As for the Q1 report that had been presented in May, many analysts' reports highlighted the diminishing market share in Sweden, and the high costs incurred in the UK operations. In the light of speculations of share redemption, the message from Skandia's CFO Jan-Erik Back was that Skandia was not to return any money to its shareholders. He argued that this course was necessary to save Skandia from the effects of new accountancy rules concerning solvency levels in financial companies.[14] Andersson added that the 'excess' capital would be absorbed by Skandia's planned growth. On 13 August, the Skandia share fell once again to 26 SEK, giving Skandia a market value of 26 billion SEK. The company was, again, trading at about the same level as it had a year earlier, whereas the SSE had gained more than 15 per cent in that 12-month period.

Some investors and analysts were disappointed with Andersson's cost-cutting plans. It was revealed in the report that a provision for restructuring costs of approximately SEK 350 million was to be taken at the end of the year, of which approximately SEK 300 million pertained to Skandia's Swedish operations. Critical voices claimed that this was a very low number, dismissing the fact that Skandia had just lowered costs by 1 billion SEK. So much more had to be done to change the investors' future outlook for Skandia's Swedish franchise. Critics further pointed out that sales of new policies had dropped by 35 per cent during the first six months of 2004. This meant that Skandia's sales of new policies in Sweden had halved since 2001. Consequently, during a telephone conference on 13 August with Skandia management, several analysts and investors expressed strong criticism regarding management's capability of dealing with the situation. Those listening in could hear the disappointed voice of Tom Purcell of Viking Global Funds, who, during the winter and spring of 2004, had established a position in Skandia amounting to approximately 2 per cent.

Ahead of Skandia's Q2 report most analysts had a 'buy' recommendation. Deutsche Bank (controlling more than 1 per cent of Skandia's stocks), among others, was looking forward to hearing what management would say about the group's capital position, and whether any clear financial targets would be defined. The target price was 33.40 SEK; this was 16 per cent more than the current trading price of 28.80 SEK.[15] After the Q2 presentation, the Deutsche Bank analysts changed their recommendation from 'buy' to 'hold'. Their analysis stated:

> Skandia disappointed us on a number of levels. Firstly, the level of excess capital in the group was acknowledged, but with no repatriation to shareholders. One financial target was given, but we think the market will be concerned that a 13 per cent new business growth will be hard to achieve, given ongoing margin pressures across Europe – and with the larger players likely to start encroaching on Skandia's patch. And Sweden is hardly likely to help, with reputational issues still doing damage, and with the cash-rich banks seemingly buying up shares. The underlying results were reasonable, though not spectacular. The stock had outperformed by 15 per cent so far this year and, while today's reaction is well overdone in our view, it is difficult to see a further significant post-bounce outperformance with the last of the positive catalysts gone.[16]

The disappointed Deutsche Bank analysts set the new target price at 29.70 SEK, 5 per cent above the current trading price of 28.20 SEK. There was argued to be a new risk in the valuation – this time the upside risk of a 'bid approach'.

A month later, in an analysis dated 10 September, investment bank Merrill Lynch summarized in a note to investors some of these modified sentiments surrounding Skandia; concurrently, its recommendation was lowered from buy to neutral: 'Many analysts appear to have lost confidence in the Skandia stock after the Q2 report in August. We share part of that worry, but more importantly, we focus on the lack of short term catalyst to move the share upwards in the short term.'[17] According to Merrill Lynch, there was a risk that the investor community continued valuing the Skandia stock with a discount. At the time, this was a consequence of the following factors: the weakness of its market position in Sweden; the questions concerning its embedded-value accounting; the slowing of its market growth; the pending court cases in Sweden and the USA; the general frustration among investors concerning the lack of transparency in the financial accounts; and the lack of experience from a rather junior management team. Merrill Lynch thus lowered the value of Skandia's life business, reducing the multiples applied on new business from 15 to 10. This reduced the valuation of the Skandia share from 33 to 29.30 SEK. Merrill Lynch further argued that the growth in the unit-linked business was set to continue, although the growth numbers would be dampened. It also stated that the problems in Sweden would, in the short term, hold down the share price. Those at Merrill Lynch also believed that Skandia's cost level would be further lowered, resulting in new restructuring costs – something that should dampen enthusiasm in the investor community. All in all, Merrill Lynch expressed a rather negative view of Skandia's near future. Other analysts followed Deutsche Bank and Merrill Lynch, and lowered their recommendations as well.

8.6 SHAREHOLDER ACTIVITY

In the autumn of 2004, CEO Andersson was busy focusing on establishing Skandia as a stand-alone company, and made plans for the implementation of a growth strategy, which was how he had interpreted the assignment from the 13 August board meeting. Therefore the CEO signalled to his organization (including the management at Skandia Life UK) that he was satisfied with the mandate to concentrate on (re)building the Skandia business. The unit for Europe and the rest of the world, under the leadership of Michael Wolf, was to show the way forward. The next steps were then to work out a common IT platform, a savings programme, and a stable and integrated Skandia structure.

During a Skandia management conference in September, Andersson presented his new plan for the company. Tim Mann, who was in charge of Skandia Life's IT function, was told how he was to now report to Gert Engman[18] in Stockholm, and human relations manager Jennifer Ruhle was asked to introduce a standard training programme for all employees. On the plane back from the conference, the UK management talked about how they believed they had been 'defeated'.

In the autumn of 2004, the Skandia share traded between 26 and 28 SEK. Proposals from different investment bankers continued to arrive, and many analysts and investment bankers had their arguments in place: Skandia was too big to be a niche player and too small to achieve world-class economies of scale. Ideas of possible deals seemed to come from all over the place. For example, the French life group AXA called Bernt Magnusson, and a meeting was set up between him, Andersson, AXA's CEO Henri de Castrics and CFO Denis Duverne. Another interested party was UK company Friends Provident.[19] Jakob Grinbaum, head of corporate development at Nordea, with the help of his team, updated a booklet on Skandia. This preparation was discussed (among other structural issues) at a Nordea board meeting in September. Moreover, Jan Olsson, investment banker at Deutsche Bank, came to see Andersson in Stockholm to check Skandia management's interest in a structural deal with another party. The investment bank ABG Sundal[20] wrote in an analysis that Skandia and South African Old Mutual, among other insurance companies, would be a good combination.

However, Andersson turned down all suggestions. Magnusson reacted differently and, as he had usually done, kept all options open. He was not convinced that the board's expressed preference to go for the stand-alone alternative was the best solution. Magnusson expressed doubts about the calculations presented by the Skandia management, and distrust of the UK top executives. At the end of September 2004, Magnusson had lunch at Nordea, the board he had left a few months earlier. During lunch, there was some discussion about the two companies' opportunities to do something together, but it was only small talk that covered a full-fledged merger to cooperation in selected fields. Nordea's representatives raised many issues: they pointed out many of the complications regarding possible legal issues, the relationship with Skandia's mutual arm Skandia Liv and the DnB asset management contract, and Nordea's genuine lack of interest in Skandia Life UK. This talk somehow made it to the headlines ('talks on a deal between Nordea and Skandia'). This coincided with a small rally in the Skandia share.[21]

Magnusson and Björnsson met with the large shareholders as well: SEB Fund's Björn Lind and Lars Idermark from AP2, who, together, controlled approximately 6 per cent of Skandia. Lind was outspoken about his disappointment with the development of the Skandia share. It was trading in the high 20s and was still treated as 'pariah' at the SSE. Idermark was not impressed by the performance of the new Skandia top management, and did not believe in Skandia as a stand-alone company. He argued that Skandia needed a partner from the industry.

On 25 October, the large US retail fund Fidelity[22] announced a holding of 5 per cent of Skandia. The position might have been even larger at the time, possibly as large as 8–9 per cent. That would make the group the largest shareholder. The difference was due to Fidelity's structure with Fidelity International, which was run from London, and Fidelity Group, which ran from its head office in Boston (Fidelity International owned the announced 5 per cent holding). Fidelity, however, did not seek to get involved in the Skandia nomination committee, a procedure that was unfamiliar to Fidelity at the time. Around November, five large Swedish institutional investors controlled 22 per cent of the shares. This was a substantial increase compared to April, when they owned 14 per cent (and was even more impressive if compared to November 2003, where they only controlled 6 per cent).

The Skandia nomination committee – which was entirely Swedish – had its first meeting in early November. Björn Lind, who was backed by SEB's retail funds and the life savings arm SEB–Trygg Liv, and was in control of 5.7 per cent of the shares in Skandia, was the largest single investor, thus becoming the committee chair. The other three members were Lars Idermark of AP2, K.G. Lindvall of Robur and Olof Neiglick from Nordea Funds. The four met at SEB to discuss the composition of the board before the April 2005 AGM; Magnusson was invited too. He represented Skandia and was there to describe the company, outline its future, and help the nomination committee understand what kind of board competence Skandia might need when going forward. This time, Magnusson's message was clearer than the one he had delivered at the AGM seven months earlier. During this meeting, he talked about a financial industry in fast transformation and the need for consolidation. He also pointed to Skandia's diminishing market shares – both globally and in the Nordic region – and said that Skandia probably needed a partner. At this stage, he sought support from the shareholders to let Morgan Stanley initiate a serious review of the current stand-alone strategy. Both Idermark and Lind gave him this reassurance (the rest of the members of the committee made no clear statements on that issue).

8.7 SKANDIA'S CEO STILL IN THE DRIVING SEAT

As expressed in the August meeting and in accordance with the board decision, Morgan Stanley did not work with any special assignments for Skandia during autumn 2004. However, the Morgan Stanley agreement was not terminated the way some board members had perceived; it had its retainer agreement with Skandia that was rolling until Christmas, so it still did some work for Skandia.[23] Morgan Stanley's investment bankers also met with some of the Skandia board members at that time. One board member claims that some of the Morgan Stanley advisers had expressed concern about Skandia: they felt at times a bit uncomfortable in meetings, and thought that the directors 'did not walk in step'.[24]

During that same autumn, Andersson and his management team planned for structural savings, a common IT platform, and for the integration of all of Skandia's business activities (i.e. between the Nordic region, Skandia Life UK, Skandia Europe and 'the rest of the world'). He also intended to resolve the troubled relationship between the management teams in Stockholm and Southampton. On 20 October, the UK management had a meeting with Morgan Stanley and part of the Swedish management at Skandia House in London. As one actor later ironically described it, 'It was a wonderful meeting.' Another person referred to the day as a classic 'come to Jesus' meeting, where everybody was to give their own version on the matters of conflict.

At the meeting, Andersson talked about working together as a group in accordance with the stand-alone plans developed by the management team, with support from its Monitor consultants. However, such a path for the future upset the UK management team, which claimed that the Skandia board and management had put aside Morgan Stanley's feasibility study of a possible demerger of Skandia Life UK for the wrong reasons. One of the managers at the subsidiary told Andersson that he seemed to employ incompetent people at the HQ in Sweden. Some of the new managers that he (indirectly) referred to were Jennifer Ruhle (head of human relations), Gert Engman (responsible for Sweden and IT) and Steve Hardwick (actuary). Those criticized also included Jan-Erik Back, who was described as a perfectly good accountant, but who was a long way short of being a finance director of a listed company. However, things went Andersson's way. The new UK holding structure – Skandia Life Assurance Holding UK – was finally in place: Andersson was chair, and Skandia board member Karl-Olof Hammarkvist would join him on this board.

During autumn 2004, Andersson and Hammarkvist had been in close contact with the FSA and Skandia Life UK concerning the overcharged policies. Andersson and Poyntz-Wright had agreed that Bankhall must be sold. Meanwhile, at the HQ in Stockholm, Andersson's team was developing plans for what should be done if Poyntz-Wright refused to cooperate. By the time of the Q3 report, they had concluded that, if necessary, the top managers at Skandia Life UK were to be replaced one by one. Andersson even had a person ready to take over from Poyntz-Wright. The potential successor had been presented to Skandia Life UK's independent board members; however, for some reason, they decided to turn down the candidate.

Skandia continued to report improved results in late 2004. When the Q3 numbers were published on 18 November, Skandia revealed that sales in the UK and Asia had risen by 47 per cent to 12 billion SEK compared to the same quarter in 2003. In Europe and Latin America, sales had risen by 11 per cent. When added together, Skandia's sales rose by 29 per cent. The cash flow was also positive. Moreover, Andersson claimed that he had taken hold of Skandia Life UK. During a press conference, Andersson denied any speculations of a continuous disagreement between Skandia's HQ in Sweden and the management in the UK: 'Contrary to media speculations, we cooperate quite well. The purpose with the holding company structure is to speed up the process to get a more integrated organization.'

Changing Skandia's position on the Swedish market, however, was a different matter. When the Q3 report was published, management concluded that Skandia – for the first time ever – had lost its leading position in the Swedish market for unit-linked assurance. Its market share had fallen below 20 per cent; a year earlier, it had still been around 28 per cent. SEB had moved in the opposite direction from a market share of 26 per cent to 34 per cent. Moreover, Skandia's sales of new policies had fallen by 36 per cent compared to the third quarter in 2003. Gert Engman, head of Skandia Nordic, concluded that Skandia was the 'ugly duckling', but assured that it would come back and flourish. Skandia Liv was losing just as much. At the same time, however, Skandia's asset management was doing well, so the life customers who were locked into Skandia Liv's mutual fund had no reason to complain. This was one of the oldest life companies in Sweden and had a consolidated financial capital ratio that superseded the rest of its competition in the industry. The effect of this was that, throughout the years, Skandia could afford to accept a higher exposure to the volatile stock market than younger competitors. In 2004, a year of bull markets, this paid off in higher returns.

In the autumn of 2004, however, all these messages sent from Skandia's HQ competed with information from extraneous sources addressing other company issues. The media reported on matters such as the settlement between former CFO Ulf Spång and Skandia, the uncertainty surrounding the potential costs for the US court case, the lawsuits dealing with the costly renovations of apartments to Skandia top executives, the pending case between Skandia Liv and Skandia concerning asset management, and the possibility that the former board of directors would be sued for the flawed bonus programmes.

On 18 November the stock market responded negatively to the Skandia Q3 report. During that day, the Skandia share fell slightly to 27.70 SEK. Its presentation of a cost reduction programme, saving approximately 300 million SEK in the Swedish organization and reducing personnel by 200 people, did not seem to impress the vast majority of investors. The investment banks were also quick to mail sale recommendations to Skandia investors. It was obvious that the analysts still put a high discount on the Skandia share in their models. In the Q3 report, the net asset value, which reflected equity along with the present value of business in force, according to the embedded-value methodology, landed at 33 billion SEK. This figure, at the time, did not include income from future sales, Skandiabanken and the value of the retail fund portfolio.

NOTES

1. *Affärsvärlden*, 21 April 2004, 'Skandias framtid – Vilken väg tar Skandia?', Sophie Nachemson-Ekwall.
2. Urban Bäckström, former head of the Swedish Central Bank, became CEO of Skandia Liv in October 2003. He resigned in May 2005 after having been offered a position as CEO of the Confederation of Swedish Enterprise.
3. Skandia Holding UK had been a passive paper construction since the early 1980s when the UK management of Skandia Life UK had managed to 'freeze out' the Swedish manager in charge of the UK subsidiary.
4. Skandia Liv was a wholly owned subsidiary of Skandia AB, and run as a mutual. The constellation meant that Skandia AB 'only' owned and submitted the share capital, but had no right to claim the return that belonged instead to the 1.2 million policyholders.
5. Eklöf, with a background in SPP/Alecta, replaced Lars-Eric Ericsson on 23 June 2004 as chair of Skandia Liv. Concurrently, Gert Engman, new head of Skandia Sweden, was put on the Skandia Liv board. Cecilia Daun Wennborg, former head of Skandia Sweden, and Skandia secretary Jan-Mikael Bexhed resigned alongside Ericsson. Björn Björnsson stayed on, as did the three independent directors: Elisabeth Annell, Lars Öberg and Gunnar Holmberg. Thus Skandia's representation on the new board had been reduced from six seats to two.
6. A privately owned global management consulting firm, founded in 1983 by a group of six entrepreneurs who had ties to Harvard Business School.
7. Wilson did return to work after six months, but he was never again to be involved in executive matters. After an additional 15 months, he retired from Skandia Life UK for good, after having spent 27 years with the company.
8. A leading French insurance and asset management company. AXA was the result of a 1982 merger between Mutuelles Unies and the Drouot Group. Over the years, AXA grew to become a major international player in the financial sector.
9. *Dagens Nyheter*, 29 June 2004, 'Skandiaaffär i huvudet på Nordeachefen', Bengt Carlsson.
10. During the first years after the millennium, Kaupthing was one of three fast-growing Icelandic banks. In 2002, it bought the two securities firms Aragon and JP Nordiska Bank; in 2004, it bought Danish FIH Erhvervsbank and in 2005, the UK bank Singer & Friedlander (later Kaupthing Singer & Friedlander). In the midst of the global financial crisis in October 2008, Kaupthing went bankrupt and was nationalized.
11. During the years after the millennium, Danish Danske Bank Group was a fast-growing

bank expanding across borders through mergers in Sweden (1997 with Östgötabanken), Ireland (2006 with Northern Bank and National Irish Bank) and Finland (2007 with Sampobank).

12. www.en.wikipedia.org/wiki/Boston_matrix.
13. Moreover, in the minds of several board directors Skandia's advisory agreement with Morgan Stanley was to be terminated once it ran out in late autumn.
14. International Accounting Standards (IAS).
15. Deutsche Bank, 10 August 2004, 'Skandia Forsakring. Q2 preview', Spencer Horgan and Mark Cathcart.
16. Deutsche Bank, 13 August 2004, 'Skandia Forsakring. Friday the 13th', Spencer Horgan and Mark Cathcart (quotations from p. 1).
17. Reported by Swedish newswire Direkt on 10 September 2004: 'Skandia: Merrill Lynch sänker rek till neutral'.
18. Andersson had planned to appoint Jan Wangärd head of the Nordic region; however, he passed away, so the position was left vacant for some time. In June 2004, however, Andersson enrolled Gert Engman, a former head of IT at FöreningsSparbanken, as new head of the Swedish operations.
19. A life assurance business mainly based in the UK.
20. A listed Norwegian investment bank focused on equity research and corporate finance; its analysts Espen Bruu Syversen and Sigmund Håland had followed Skandia for many years.
21. *Dagens Industri*, 27 September 2005, 'Budplaner okända för Skandia', Jan Wäingelin. TT, 28 September 2005, 'Börsen vände uppåt', Peter Challis.
22. Fidelity is the largest US manager of mutual funds and one of the largest providers of financial services in the world; it managed and serviced several trillions of US dollars of assets.
23. Morgan Stanley's view was that the investment bank was entitled to do a follow-up analysis for the Skandia board during the autumn, all according to the retainer agreement (although that material was never presented at a board meeting).
24. However, there have been several different versions regarding the board's relationship to Morgan Stanley and its more informal opinions.

9. New kinds of shareholders enter the scene

9.1 CHRISTER GARDELL LOOKS FOR ALLIES

Activist investor Christer Gardell's profile was low when he entered the financial scene in Sweden. He did not say much when interviewed by the media.[1] His reply to most questions was: 'My ambition is to earn money.' He would follow up by adding that it was the 'fiduciary duty of boards of directors and management to work for the best of the shareholders'. It took a few deals until the wider Swedish business community understood the meaning of that latter wording in the context of financial capitalism, with its global mixture of international hedge funds, investment bankers, shareholder activists and media actors.

Gardell and his twin brother Rickard were born in 1960 and grew up in working-class quarters at Finntorp, 10 km from Stockholm. The twin brothers took the same path, both graduating from the Stockholm School of Economics with top grades and each awarded scholarships to other renowned business schools. They turned to management consultancy: Rickard was at Bain[2] in London and later Australia, where he founded Australia's largest private equity firm, Pacific Equity Partners; Christer founded Cevian a few years later.

Christer Gardell was employed at McKinsey in 1984, where it did not take long for him to rise to a star position. In 1995, he became a senior partner at Nordic Capital, one of the first Swedish private equity firms, but he stayed less than a year having been offered the job of turning around Custos,[3] a conservative and rather inactive Swedish investment company. Behind Custos stood the financial duo Sven Hagströmer and Mats Qviberg, representing a more traditional breed of Swedish corporate raiders acting on their own through boardroom infighting. It took Gardell six years to sell off most of Custos's holdings in listed companies; this included splitting old industrial conglomerates and opening up for hostile bids. Custos provided its shareholders, among them the team Hagströmer and Qviberg, with a return of nearly 300 per cent during this period. This figure exceeded the index by nearly 200 percentage points. Custos distributed a total of more than 11 billion SEK to its shareholders, including redemption proposals.

In 2001, Gardell left Custos along with Chief Investment Officer, Lars Förberg to start Amaranth (later known as Cevian). The announced plan was to act as a catalyst for Nordic midcap-listed companies that were underperforming, reveal hidden values, and then sell off the stakes after three to four years. Cevian's initial years coincided with the bursting of the telecoms bubble that depressed the financial markets. Thus it was difficult for Gardell to raise any money. Gradually, however, Gardell and Förberg got the ear of two of the Swedish National Pension Funds, namely AP1 and AP2, although their largest investor was Capital Z: a US investment fund sponsored by Zurich Financial Services. Carl Icahn, a renowned American corporate raider who had turned to shareholder activism, became another investor. Gardell and Förberg managed to raise a total of 3.1 billion SEK (of which Icahn invested 10 per cent).

Although Gardell was tight-lipped at the start, he did speak publicly about his close relationship with Icahn. He told the press and other interested parties that he had met Icahn in 1999 through a mutual Swedish friend. Over the years, Gardell had presented quite a few investment cases to him. One of the early ones was the Swedish forest company AssiDomän (with its Chair Magnusson and Director Björnsson). In Cevian, Gardell and Förberg copied Icahn's investment style of transforming US raiding methods from the 1980s to European shareholder activism of the early twenty-first century.[4] They also adopted the Icahn device of acting politely and correctly all the way, but not becoming friends with anybody. By 2005, the Cevian fund had 12 employees, most of them with degrees from the Stockholm School of Economics, and a few billion SEK in investments. Cevian started slowly by making investments in the debt collector Intrum Justitia[5] and in Lindex, where Birgitta Johansson-Hedberg was chair. Cevian also added a stockholding in Finnish construction company Metso to their portfolio. To the surprise of several other investors, Gardell's activities were impressive – the Lindex share increased four times during Cevian's three-year holding.

It soon became obvious to many actors in Stockholm's financial district that Cevian performed in a new way on the capital market. This difference was not just due to the fact that Gardell was an outsider; newcomers had tried to raid Swedish companies before. Nor was he the first Swedish actor who tried to make profits through challenging boards in office. What was new was his method of joining forces with predominantly international hedge and activist funds. In this new global financial context, Sweden became an attractive battlefield for these active shareholders.[6]

Another ingredient in Gardell's unusual toolkit was his skilful 'media management', which helped create a buzz around targeted stocks. Drawing in 'hot money' to a focused stock helped to show that Cevian's involvement in a corporation added value (i.e. a rising stock price). Such a development increased the fund's chances both of installing its own management team and acquiring board positions. These ideas and techniques distinguished Cevian from other Nordic funds, which allowed it to tackle disproportionately large targets.

9.2 SKANDIA BECOMES A TARGET

Cevian's junior analyst Martin Oliw followed Skandia in great detail for at least six months during 2004. Cevian had already looked at Skandia back in 2002 when the shares were trading around 10 SEK; however, at that time, its subsidiary American Skandia was problematic, and Cevian also lacked financial resources to act on its own in such a large company.[7] By late 2003, Gardell contacted the investment company Industrivärden, which held close to 5 per cent of Skandia, and suggested that it join forces with Cevian. A deal would entail that Gardell actually did the work needed to turn the company around, and Industrivärden would split the profit between the two partners. CEO Anders Nyrén, however, rejected the proposal as being incompatible with Industrivärden's way of working. In the winter of 2004, Gardell and Cevian made another attempt to buy a block of Skandia shares, namely Sampo's holding of 7 per cent. Gardell visited Sampo's COO Kari Stadigh and CEO Björn Wahlroos at their offices in Helsinki. The Finnish duo, however, turned him down – just as Nyrén at Industrivärden had done. Instead, Sampo preferred to sell its Skandia stake straight into the market.

The majority of analysts had reacted negatively to Skandia's six-month report in mid-August 2004. Many observers had been let down by the message that there would not be a buyback or redemption programme of 5–10 billion SEK. For Cevian analyst Oliw, this disappointment on the market was a trigger to look even more closely at Skandia. Financial engineering, such as redemption programmes, was precisely the sort of work Cevian could pursue. Therefore the Cevian team met with Skandia leaders: CEO Andersson, Chair Magnusson and Investor Relations Officer Harry Vos. Oliw would continue to talk with Vos on several other occasions during that autumn.

Skandia's open shareholder structure and the fact that Gardell knew some of its larger shareholders well were important ingredients in his ambition to become a substantial shareholder in the company. For example, Lind at SEB Funds lived only a few blocks away from the Gardell family in a Stockholm suburb; the two had also worked together on investments before. Moreover, SEB Funds had been investing in the retail chain Lindex before Cevian entered the scene, and it supported Cevian's decision to buy shares. Gardell also knew Skandia's next largest Swedish investor quite well; AP2 had been one of the co-investors in the Cevian fund. CEO of AP2, Lars Idermark had developed an investment rationale that fitted well with Cevian's plans for the future. AP2's Skandia holding was part of its strategic portfolio of long-term holdings where AP2 exercised its corporate governance rights and acted as active shareholder through nomination committees. Moreover, Gardell also knew Skandia Chair Magnusson, as Custos had been one of the investors in AssiDomän, which Magnusson had chaired. They also talked about Skandia in the autumn of 2004.

By November 2004 the Cevian team, which consisted of Gardell, Förberg and Oliw, decided that Skandia was either a perfect turnaround case or a break-up candidate. The team's line of argument was that the fundamental business of the company was strong and promising, was substantially undervalued and, at the same time, was having great difficulty with its costs. The HQ 'burned' approximately 650 million SEK a year, and they estimated that the number could be cut by half a billion SEK. If Cevian bought Skandia shares for the price of 28 SEK, they would pay the equivalent of its embedded value and, at the same time, receive 'for free': the profits from future sales of unit-linked products; the returns from Skandia's mutual funds portfolio; Skandiabanken, the niche Internet bank with around 850 000 customers worth an estimated 3 billion SEK; a balance sheet with heavy tax losses on the Swedish side (Skandia Sweden had not paid any tax for five years, and would probably not do so for the following years either); and Skandia Liv, which, if demutualized and fully controlled by Skandia, could be valued at least a minimum of 10 billion SEK.

Structurally, the Cevian team expected a large amount of interest from competitors in the industry both for Skandia's UK business (Skandia Life UK and Royal Skandia) and for its Swedish operations. The team regarded the management culture as being poor in both Sweden and the UK. Given a 3–5-year horizon, Oliw calculated the sum of the parts as 53 SEK per share (a rise of 85 per cent). He also added the value of a demutualized Skandia Liv, resulting in an estimate price for the Skandia share in the range of 60–70 SEK. However, at that time no one at Cevian spoke of a bid for the listed Skandia. The numerous legal issues and pending court cases were tantamount to poison for an interested investor.

In the autumn of 2004, Gardell sent investment specialists from Cevian to New York with the intention of sparking some interest from Icahn in the Skandia case. He wanted the Wall Street veteran to contribute some extra money outside the Cevian fund in a joint bet on Skandia. Icahn supported the idea; thus Cevian started buying Skandia shares on 18

November, the day after the Q3 report was made public. Over the next four days, Carl Icahn Co. Investment[8] and Cevian each invested close to 500 million SEK in Skandia. They bought approximately 3 per cent of the company, paying an average 25–26 SEK per share.

9.3 CHAIR BERNT MAGNUSSON: SKANDIA OPEN TO SALE

Late on 1 December 2004 Hans-Erik Andersson, the new CEO of Skandia as of January that same year, saw a text at his desk that was to be published the following morning in Swedish daily *Dagens Nyheter*. It was a printout of an interview with Skandia's chair, Bernt Magnusson. This interview was the first one he had granted since he took charge. Skandia's press department had checked both the content and the quotes presented in the article. By leaving an advance copy for Andersson, Magnusson wanted to be certain that his CEO was given the opportunity to read the text before it was published.

Andersson expressed surprise by what he read. The views conveyed in the interview were not the ones he had expected, and they had not been discussed with him in advance. The headline read: 'Skandia's chair open to sale'. Magnusson was pictured in an accompanying photo with his arms open wide, giving readers the impression that he invited 'everybody' to come up with ideas about the future structure of Skandia, even including a sale, in whole or in part, of the company. The article ran as follows:[9]

> 'Skandia may be sold [as a whole]: it can buy companies, merge with others or sell off subsidiaries. There are no taboos,' says Skandia's chair of the board, Bernt Magnusson. But for the time being, he concentrates on re-establishing the Skandia group. 'Skandia is financially a relatively strong company, on the whole doing quite well', Magnusson states in his first interview since becoming chair in April 2004.
>
> Despite the great difficulties on the Swedish market that are mainly due to the company's bad [home market] reputation, the situation is quite different in other markets. This is particularly valid for the United Kingdom and its subsidiary Skandia Life UK that makes up half of all operations in Skandia. In the UK, analysts and journalists have raised the question whether it would be better if Skandia Life UK was sold and listed on its own. Management in Sweden has, thus far, rejected that path; however, Bernt Magnusson made it clear that all alternatives are considered. 'Nothing is static. One must always be open to what is going on in the outside world. If there is a partner indicating interest to co-operate, if there is an attractive company (for Skandia) to buy or if there is an opportunity to sell, then maybe one should act', he argues.
>
> However, . . . structural deals are not on top of Bernt Magnusson's agenda. There one will find three other items: '[We must have] complete control of the

firm. [This means] trimming and making efficient what we have, and clearing up the Swedish situation', he says. He also states that all the legal disputes and processes that are going on involving Skandia function like effective 'shark-powder' against any structural deal. There are very few actors that are interested in mergers or acquisitions as long as it is unclear who has done what in the scandals, and who, in the end, will be forced to pay. On top of that, the board wishes to see next year's annual report in order to feel confident of having control. After that, it is time to consider the future. 'And then, nothing is taboo,' Magnusson says.

It has been almost eight months since his appointment. He arrived at a company in turmoil where employees were angry with previous management, and where middle managers were 'hesitant to fire their guns' – they did not dare do their job. At the same time (almost) everybody – that is, shareholders, board members, managers, and so on – were talking about the scandals and their repercussions. 'Everyone was running after the ball', as Magnusson expresses it. Therefore, his first main task was to delegate. Deputy chair Björn Björnsson was asked to handle historical matters: something that included contacts with lawyers investigating the (legal problems linked to the) scandals. CEO Andersson was to concentrate on Skandia's running business.

Magnusson had taken on the task himself of making Skandia less of a 'federation' and to make the company more of a consolidated group. Still, the strong independence of the local companies had been an advantage. There had been room for entrepreneurs, particularly in the subsidiaries, that had dared to invest in novelty. That spirit he wished to maintain: 'It is a delicate balancing act. One has to tiptoe cautiously about it'. In order to handle this balancing act, Magnusson has a strong mandate from the owners, stronger than usual in a company with institutions as the dominating owners.

Magnusson reports to the [Skandia] owners through the nomination committee: 'It must be absolutely clear who is in charge and, therefore, there must be a close connection between owners, the board, and management. I cannot think of another company where institutions have taken command so forcefully.' They stuck their necks out: the strong mandate also enables Magnusson to say things that many other chairs would hesitate to express. For example, after the semi-annual report, many actors were disappointed that Skandia did not, as it was rumoured, pay an extra dividend to shareholders: 'I had lots of calls from various institutions about it. To the last one calling, I said something that may have sounded a bit brutal: If you are that dumb that you think the board as its first measure would borrow x billion SEK and hand it out to shareholders with the history that we have behind us, then I think you should sell the shares.'

Bernt Magnusson had made a reputation for being a 'clean-up guy'; one who is called in to rescue various businesses in distress. Now, he is inside such a company in crisis. '. . . Skandia is a service company that is not suffering from economic problems. However, it has a problem with its image in Sweden and, as a consequence, it has lost market shares. . . . I do not want to underestimate the problem', he says laughing. 'This is the first company where I have not begun by going to the bank to borrow more money. In many of those other cases, it has been about surviving the day'.

These statements were not that different from the ones Magnusson had already expressed in his introductory speech at the shareholders' AGM eight months earlier. Yet, for many investment bankers, institutional investors and competitors in the pension savings market who had insight into Skandia, the chair's message was both new and clear. With this interview, Magnusson opened up all kinds of alternatives for Skandia – including selling the entire company. Although the board and top management obviously concentrated on the re-establishment of the company, for many actors the key point in the interview was that Magnusson had posted a 'for sale' sign on the entrance to the Skandia HQ. Everyone was invited to act. Therefore, during the first week of December, the Magnusson interview was an important topic among investment bankers, senior managers at other financial companies, financial and legal consultants, and this extended much further than Stockholm. Skandia was perceived to be a takeover target. Using the jargon of the financial industry, Skandia was 'in play'.

The *Dagens Nyheter* interview incited reaction among many Skandia actors. CEO Andersson was concerned about the content of the interview and spoke to people around him, referring to it as the 'opening of a dam'. A few days later, he asked Magnusson why he had said what he had, and Magnusson answered that the open-to-sale message was not a big issue since all companies must always be open to structural ideas. Some of the board members were, however, also concerned; they, too, regarded the information from the chair as new and rather controversial. Referring to his AGM speech in April 2004 (see Section 7.2), Magnusson argued that there was nothing really new in his words, except for the way he stressed the board's obvious task of looking at both internal and external issues simultaneously. Therefore he did not see any contentious or unusual facts in the article. After all, he had been given a special mandate by the shareholders. In the eyes of many actors, however, Skandia had changed its position between his AGM speech in April and the statements he made in the December interview.

The day after the interview in *Dagens Nyheter*, Magnusson sent a letter on 3 December to Hans-Erik Andersson, as well as board members Karl-Olof Hammarkvist and Björn Björnsson. The message was that the board needed to discuss the future for Skandia Life UK. Hammarkvist and Andersson were both directors of the Skandia Life UK board, and Björnsson was deputy chair of the Skandia board, so Magnusson consulted them on the matter and asked for their opinion. The letter began with the following words: 'Some factors speaking in favour of a demerger, IPO or sale of Skandia UK as soon as possible.' He expressed scepticism that it was feasible to force Skandia Life UK to obey the Skandia HQ, and added that a bigger structural change could also help to get rid of some of the negative press writings in Sweden regarding Skandia. He also mentioned that establishing partnerships with other Nordic players would be simplified if the Skandia Life UK problem was solved. He concluded by asking when such a possible demerger, IPO or sales process could be initiated and be made known to the general public.[10]

Both Hammarkvist and Andersson expressed surprise about the letter, since this theme had not been discussed at the Skandia board meetings during the autumn. Five days later, chair Magnusson sent out a second letter, this time addressed to Andersson with copies emailed to all directors. He explained the necessity of taking a further look at the structural opportunities for Skandia. The heading of the letter read: 'Short topics ahead of the Skandia board meeting on 22 December 2004'. Magnusson wrote: 'Brother, I have now been here for six months . . . Skandia is too divided. Skandia looks wrong. Skandia Life UK must be discussed and possibly be introduced separately on the stock exchange . . . The insurance business is entering a phase of consolidation.' Magnusson referred to Skandia as an investment company in the financial industry and therefore one must consider how the board could work to maximize its shareholder value. The chair wrote: 'How should this be done? The answer is always the same regardless of industry and geography – that is to establish a structure that is more competitive and efficient than the ones of the competitors.' He ended his second letter with some concluding questions addressing the future for Skandia UK, to be discussed at the upcoming board meeting on 22 December.

9.4 ACTIVIST GARDELL ACTS

On 13 December a report[11] was published that pointed to Skandia as the most likely takeover target at the SSE within the coming two years. The very same day, rumours began to circulate throughout trading rooms in London and Stockholm that Cevian, still operating under the name Amaranth, had bought shares in Skandia. By the afternoon, the Swedish-based wire service Direkt sent out the flash: 'rumours speculate that Amaranth has bought Skandia (shares)'. By 1 p.m. Skandia, the fourth-most traded stock that day,[12] had risen by 2 per cent to 30.30 SEK. This was a level Skandia had not reached since early summer.

Gardell called Magnusson that same day (13 December) and informed him that he had bought 3 per cent in Skandia. One of the large investors in Skandia also received a phone call from someone speaking on behalf of Cevian; the message was the same. Another actor received a similar message through 'a trustworthy bird'. *Dagens Industri* published this information the following morning, quoting Gardell himself.[13] The next morning, Cevian officially declared that it had bought 3 per cent of the shares in Skandia in a stock market announcement to the SSE. That same day, Gardell publicly declared that he was aiming for a seat on the board. The fact that Cevian had gained support from the Wall Street activist Carl Icahn was also reported. Cevian, along with the hedge fund Icahn Partners, had invested a total of 900 million SEK in Skandia, paying 26–27 SEK per share. Gardell was quick to answer questions from investors, wire services and paper media regarding this. *Dagens Industri* quoted Gardell as saying: 'We are now among the largest owners of the company. Of course our goal is to take a seat on the board of directors.' He also expected support from other shareholders: 'In the case of Skandia, everybody has complained over the lack of active owners.' The international coverage was also substantial. The fact that Wall Street raider Icahn had teamed up with an internationally unknown Swede to buy shares in Skandia hit the front page of the *Financial Times*[14] and was also covered by the *Wall Street Journal*.[15]

Investment bankers close to Gardell had the impression that his intention was to work for a break-up of Skandia: something that often resulted in short-term positive stock market movements and lucrative work for the advisers to different parties.[16] Activities increased for potential bidders. The aim was to take a stance soon on a possible bid for Skandia, either in whole or in part. Gardell publicly supported the Skandia board and its management: 'The value of the company is much higher than the stock price. We like companies that have had problems and are shunned (by investors). But, all in all, Skandia is in a good position.'[17] Gardell gave no further details regarding his ambitions for Cevian or the future Skandia.

Several media commentators raised a red flag. For example, Torbjörn Isacsson wrote in *Dagens Industri*:

> As CEO of Custos, Christer Gardell tried to split up all the companies in the portfolio. In some cases, it worked out well; in others, it did not. Icahn has the same track record from Wall Street . . . Now the speculation is that Skandia must sell off its profitable British unit . . . It is not likely that Christer Gardell and Carl Icahn will carry with them any long-term ideas for Skandia, but they will most likely do what they can to make things happen.[18]

In *Dagens Nyheter*, Bengt Carlsson pointed out that it is unusual for an investor to send out a press release announcing a shareholding of 3 per cent when the regulations require such a thing be done only when a holding reaches 5 per cent. Carlsson concluded by stating that 3 per cent was quite a small shareholding and far from a 'guaranteed' board seat.[19]

Following the public announcement of his investment in Skandia, Gardell engaged in intensive communications. He talked to former

Skandia CEO Petersson and also talked to former Deputy CEO Carendi who, after leaving Skandia, began working for the German insurance company, Allianz. A few days following the announcement, Gardell also flew to London to present his perspectives on Skandia to investors. He asked them for their support, suggesting that they vote for him as new director at the upcoming Skandia AGM in April 2005, and that they bought Skandia shares and made the stock price rise. In private meetings, Gardell, who had presented the information along with Oliw, indicated a valuation of Skandia in the range 60–70 SEK (no papers were however distributed). Gardell and Oliw argued that Skandia was the perfect break-up case, with very little risk.

In London, Gardell also met fellow Swede and graduate from the Stockholm School of Economics, Lars Bane, one of 12 fund managers at Noonday, a large US-based hedge fund managing $4 billion. Noonday was part of the Farallon Group,[20] which Bane had joined as a partner in 2002. Before that, Bane had worked as head of special situations equity sales at Enskilda Securities[21] in London. Noonday had been a large investor in Custos when Gardell was CEO, and had later also been a co-investor with Cevian in Lindex. In their talks, Gardell tried to sell his Skandia case. He suggested to Bane that Noonday should join him. Bane turned down the offer as he found the Skandia case too risky.[22]

Gardell also met with representatives of the Fidelity funds in London. The analysts shared Gardell's views; however, they never officially gave him their support. Gardell then continued on to New York, where he met a representative from Third Avenue Fund.[23] He also met Paulo Pellegrini from Paulson & Co. and Tom Purcell, CEO of Viking Global. Gardell and Purcell compared notes, and Viking Global afterwards doubled its position in Skandia to 3–4 per cent, although it never openly supported Cevian.

NOTES

1. *Veckans Affärer*, 11 April 2005, 'Porträtt: Christer Gardell – en playboy', Christer Berglund.
2. Bain is a globally active Boston-based strategy consulting group.
3. An old Swedish investment company with roots in the early twentieth century when new laws prevented banks from direct ownership in companies. Custos was the Skandinaviska Banken arm (the latter became a part of the Swedish bank SEB).
4. The raiding activities of the 1980s had mainly concentrated on leveraged buyouts, a market that closed after new US regulations were adopted in the 1990s. Around 2000 the 'raiders' turned to raising money in investment funds instead, which provided a mandate to act as 'activist' shareholders in listed companies. Skandia was the first large Swedish company where this new investment rationale was put into practice.

5. A Swedish-based debt collector founded in the early 1920s. It was listed on the LSE in 1990 but ran into trouble and was delisted in the late 1990s. In 2001 it was floated on the SSE.
6. For example, the Swedish Code of Corporate Governance came to require 'nomination committees', which provided small shareholders with a unique opportunity to influence board composition.
7. That limited financial capacity lived on as late as autumn 2003.
8. Carl Icahn became world-famous in 1985 when he invested in, and raided, the troubled American airline, TWA. He made a comeback in 2004 raising an activist fund – Icahn Partner Fund – with the aim of investing in US-based companies (with support from other co-investors). The fund grew to $7 billion, of which Icahn himself allocated $3 billion. Besides this 'small' Skandia investment, Icahn challenged the US business elite through placements in companies such as Motorola and Time Warner.
9. Pia Gripenberg and Dan Lucas wrote the article, published by *Dagens Nyheter* on 2 December 2004.
10. A summary of the most important parts of the letter.
11. Svensk Image, private provider of market research for analysts, investors and listed companies, among others renowed for its yearly 'Shareholder Barometer' for the Swedish Shareholders' Association.
12. During the previous 12-month period, Skandia had been traded as the ninth to tenth most active stock, according to statistics from OMX Nordic exchange.
13. *Dagens Industri*, 14 December 2004, 'Bolagsslaktare in i Skandia', Rafaela Bjäringer.
14. *Financial Times*, 14 December 2004, 'Icahn-backed fund builds up Skandia stake', Nicholas George.
15. *Wall Street Journal* (European edition), 14 December 2004.
16. Board members and investment bankers who were in contact with Magnusson around Christmas time 2004 heard him say that he was pleased that Skandia had at last one shareholder with a large investment – Christer Gardell – who shared his view that the company needed structural changes.
17. Quoted from Swedish business wire services Direkt, 13 December 2004, 'Skandia: Gardells Cevian storägare, vill in i styrelsen'.
18. *Dagens Industri*, 14 December 2004, 'Trögstartad riskkapitalist har fått upp farten', Torbjörn Isacsson.
19. *Dagens Nyheter*, 15 December 2004, 'Skandia behöver inga soloåkare', Bengt Carlsson.
20. A US company founded 1986 working as an asset management firm with different strategies, including the UK-based low-risk-profile hedge fund, Noonday.
21. The investment bank arm of SEB that, for many years, had a dominant role as deal-maker in Sweden.
22. In late autumn 2005, Noonday bought into Skandia (that is to say, after the bid from Old Mutual was publicly announced).
23. Third Avenue Fund was formed in 1986, and has been highly successful in its predominantly long-term investments. The fund would later buy 0.8 per cent of the Skandia shares.

10. Old Mutual

10.1 THE HISTORY OF OLD MUTUAL

Old Mutual had a history of more than 150 years as a South-African-based mutual society before its public listing in 1999. Back in 1845, a Scotsman named John Fairbairn led a group of 166 members in the formation of South Africa's first mutual life assurance society. Old Mutual grew strongly right up to the end of the nineteenth century, and soon claimed to be one of South Africa's leaders in the life assurance market. When the country gained self-government from the UK and became a member of the Commonwealth Union in 1910, Old Mutual became one of South Africa's most dominant institutions, capturing as much as one-third of the country's life assurance market. In the face of the government's strict exchange controls, Old Mutual – akin to many other South African companies – focused its energy primarily on the domestic market. Similarly, the society's investment portfolio reflected the increasing ostracism of the apartheid state. Unable to invest in corporations outside South Africa, Old Mutual became a major shareholder in a number of South African financial institutions such as Nedbank, Swiss-based Richemont, Rembrandt, Standard Bank, Barloworld and Anglo American.

Old Mutual's position in South Africa had become strong. Throughout its history, it had actively recruited South Africa's non-European population into its membership, in part by actively promoting group memberships and group-based insurance, and other financial products. By the 1990s, Old Mutual held 25 per cent of the country's industrial assets through its life and asset management operations, and it held a majority position in Nedbank. Old Mutual also had a majority holding in Mutual & Federal, the country's second-largest general insurer. Despite its focus on South Africa, Old Mutual none the less had established operations in other places on the African continent, such as Zimbabwe, Namibia, Kenya and Malawi. Old Mutual had also expanded its product range into mutual funds and unit trusts. By the beginning of the 1990s, Old Mutual ranked at 38 among the world's top insurance groups.

Frustration was growing as Old Mutual found it difficult to expand its base in a country isolated by international sanctions due to the government's apartheid policies. However, apartheid ended in 1994 with the electoral victory of the African National Congress led by Nelson Mandela. In 1995, Old Mutual set up new businesses in Boston, Hong Kong and in Guernsey. In 1997, Old Mutual acquired Capel Cure Myers, a leading private-client stockbroker and investment manager in the UK. A year later, it acquired a second UK-based provider of portfolio management and stock broking services – Albert E. Sharp – for more than £40 million. It subsequently merged with Capel Cure Myers to form Capel Cure Sharp. In a matter of two years, Old Mutual had built a group in the UK with more than £10 billion in assets under management.

In the late 1990s, many financial institutions around the world abandoned their mutual structures; UK companies such as Norwich, Halifax, Alliance & Leicester and Woolwich did so. South African companies such as Sanlam and Old Mutual followed suit. This development represented a milestone for South African business. A board of directors who very much represented the business elite of the past made the decisions at Old Mutual. A close cooperation with two international investment banks – namely Merrill Lynch (with James Agnew as co-head of corporate broking) and Warburg Dillon Read – was established in order to assist these directors in their efforts there. Agnew joined Deutsche Bank in 2002, where he soon became managing director and head of corporate broking. He continued to work with Old Mutual as a customer in this new position. Later, Agnew was also one of three investment bankers who became a member of the British Panel on Takeovers and Mergers.[1]

When Old Mutual argued in favour of a demutualization of the company, it officially formulated ambitions to expand internationally and to reinvent itself as a major asset management group. The claim was that demutualization would give Old Mutual the capacity to raise the required capital to implement this new global strategy. Although Old Mutual was not the only company in South Africa heading for London, demutualization was a controversial move. The board and management had to promise not to reduce the amount of people employed at the company's South African working sites in order to gain support from its policyholders. In May 1999, the policyholders in the South African Mutual Life Assurance Society approved demutualization, which gave more than 3 million policyholders the opportunity to become shareholders in the new company, some receiving shares equal to as much as one year's salary. The initial share price became 120 pence, giving the company a market capitalization of £3.9 billion.[2] The demutualization turned Old Mutual's principals into a dispersed group of shareholders. However, the largest shareholders were to remain South African. According to its annual report, Old Mutual Life Assurance Company owned 8.1 per cent of the shares in 2001. The South

African shareholder base represented 65 per cent of the investors in Old Mutual, whereas UK-based institutional investors held the remaining 35 per cent of the shares.[3] Old Mutual moved its HQ to London in order to obtain a listing there and join the FTSE 100 index,[4] and to get an exposure to the international investment community. Its first issue in the London market then raised £559 million, creating a foundation for its intended international expansion.

10.2 OLD MUTUAL EXPANDS ABROAD

Jim Sutcliffe was appointed to the board of Old Mutual in January 2000, where he took specific responsibility for the group's life assurance businesses. Sutcliffe was born in Malawi. He was educated at the University of Cape Town, and later he became a Fellow of the Institute of Actuaries. Sutcliffe, with 20 years experience in international insurance business, had been deputy chair of Liberty International,[5] chief executive UK of Prudential and COO of Jackson National, Prudential's US subsidiary. Thus he had a strong track record in the international investment and insurance industry, with experience in the UK, the USA and South Africa.

At the height of the IT/technology boom on the financial market in March 2000, Old Mutual paid £529 million to acquire the Gerrard Group, a prominent private-client stockbroker in the UK.[6] Old Mutual became one of the leading private-client wealth managers in the UK overnight. In August of the same year, UK citizen Julian Roberts was recruited to the position of group finance director with the executive management team. Roberts had gained a BA degree from Stirling University, and had later become a Fellow of the Institute of Chartered Accountants in England and Wales. Roberts' professional experience also included positions such as group finance director of Sun Life & Provincial Holdings and director and CFO of Aon UK Holdings.[7]

In September 2000, Old Mutual bought United Asset Management Corporation for $2.2 billion. The diverse group of more than 40 affiliated asset management companies was reconfigured and renamed Old Mutual Asset Management US. Old Mutual's official strategy was threefold: to create a world-class international financial services group; to provide a high-quality asset management capability to build and protect client assets; and to establish regional customer-facing platforms, upon which Sutcliffe placed particular importance. A full financial services offering was maintained in South Africa, including a comprehensive range of banking and short-term insurance businesses. In the USA, Old Mutual would focus on specialist asset management with a life business in order to provide some diversity. In the rest of the developed world, where the welfare systems were thought to be falling apart amidst an ageing population, 'open architecture' was assumed to be the key to success.

In March 2001, Old Mutual paid $25 million to acquire Unified Life; later renamed American Life, the insurance company was based in the USA with licences to operate in 43 states. In September of the same year, Old Mutual's US expansion was topped by the $635 million acquisition of Fidelity & Guaranty Life. This US-based insurance company was later named Old Mutual Financial Life.

Old Mutual had a poor result for 2001. During that autumn, the South African rand had weakened against the UK pound.[8] Given that 70 per cent of Old Mutual's assets were still in South Africa and accounted for in rand, the balance sheet shrank from £5.6 billion to £3.5 billion; this wiped out an embedded value of over £2 billion. Meanwhile, the adjusted operating profit fell from £911 million to £856 million; if measured in sterling (including writedowns), the group headed for a loss. The poor economic climate continued throughout 2002, and Old Mutual was once again hit hard by exchange rate fluctuations.[9] In 2002, operating profits rose by 8 per cent in rand terms, but were down 15 per cent in sterling at £724 million. In February 2002, Old Mutual shares at 93 pence were trading at a discount to accounted embedded value, indicating 104 pence per share. By 2003, media reports in South Africa characterized the company's acquisition history as a 'tragic' journey. The tide had changed: investors tended to avoid traditional life companies, and Old Mutual was 'out of fashion'.[10] Old Mutual's big stake in South African banking did not impress the analysts either, nor did its exposure to the South African rand or the complex deals made in the USA (despite its success in selling niche policies there). However, Old Mutual was seen as successful in keeping costs down by transferring some office operations from the UK to its cheaper South African base. In November 2001, Sutcliffe had become group CEO of Old Mutual and executive director on its board. He, therefore, remained in office.

10.3 AN EMERGING INTEREST FOR SKANDIA

During 2001, Old Mutual had launched its Selestia platform for life savings products in the UK market. This platform was Sutcliffe's baby. It was something completely new to the South African Old Mutual. The years working in the UK had assured Sutcliffe that there was a trend to move from traditional life assurance to unit-linked investment through an open architecture fund platform. Back in 1997, Sutcliffe had met Paul Bradshaw, Skandia Life UK's former head of business. Bradshaw had come up with the innovative open architecture concept, and introduced it to the UK market. Selestia was built as a copy of the model – the most successful 'wrap'[11] business in the UK at the time. Thus Old Mutual UK, with the Selestia platform in place, was set up as Skandia Life UK's direct competitor.

The Selestia platform offered the independent financial advisers a system through which they could access more than 700 funds offered by 57 fund managing companies in order to construct and maintain investment portfolios, taking into account the investors' risk profiles when making the asset allocation and fund selection. Selestia was reputed to have a modern technology platform built and maintained in South Africa, where costs were low. Technically, this was a success, even winning awards for the best offer of unit-linked products in the UK savings industry. In 2004, sales grew to £423 million; by 2005, to £704 million; Selestia gained 10 per cent of new sales on fund supermarkets, and £1 billion of assets under its management.

Selestia's UK expansion, however, did not seem to impress the analysts. Old Mutual was still regarded as an emerging-market investment, and the share traded on the LSE at a heavy discount compared to its European competitors. In the FTSE 100 and Fortune Global 500,[12] it was ranked as the tenth-largest European insurer. Old Mutual's geographical mix had shifted. By 2003, only 60 per cent of the group's business on an embedded-value basis came from South Africa, while the USA contributed to over 30 per cent, and the UK added the remaining 10 per cent. Furthermore, Old Mutual had over £125 billion in assets under its management, of which 60 per cent came from the USA. Thus the UK business that accounted for close to 10 per cent of Old Mutual's business was too small to receive full focus from analysts. On top of all this, a significant UK presence would make sense for Sutcliffe, given the fact that Old Mutual had its head office costs in the UK, but precious little UK revenue to match it.

At a press conference on 24 February 2003, Sutcliffe stated that the group was exploring ways to strengthen its UK business. During spring its balance sheet had been boosted by £1 billion, partly through a rights issue. However, Old Mutual's plans for expansion in the UK were put off again and again,[13] and its US activities continued to bring trouble. In 2003, life sales were down 14 per cent to $389 million. Similar to many other companies (including Skandia), Old Mutual was concurrently stuck in discussions with US financial regulators regarding possible market-timing irregularities at its Pilgrim Baxter subsidiary.

Old Mutual sold Gerrard Management Services[14] to Barclays Bank in December 2003 for £210 million, after having already sold GNI[15] (the derivatives broker) for £100 million and its own corporate and institutional brokerage business for £12 million. This added up to an overall loss of £200 million compared to the original Gerrard Group deal three years earlier. The *Financial Times* concluded that the sale 'was a neat example of what Warren Buffett has described as the "gin rummy"-school of management in which businesses are acquired and discarded at every turn. The net effect, as with Old Mutual, is normally value-destroying.'[16]

The falling profits in 2003 meant further disappointment on the market. The majority-owned South African Nedbank reported heavy losses from its investment portfolio and problems with funding issues relating to the acquisition of BoE,[17] which had been acquired two years earlier. In February 2004, Old Mutual announced a £0.42 billion[18] rights issue to enable Nedbank to meet minimum regulatory capital requirements. During that season, Old Mutual strengthened its South African general insurance holdings when it bought out the minority shareholders of its publicly listed Mutual & Federal subsidiary. The political and economic problems in South Africa brought one 'good' thing: they reconfirmed Old Mutual's need to substantially increase its UK businesses. The sale of the various Gerrard operations had significantly added to Old Mutual's financial resources, providing approximately £1 billion to spend on acquisitions.

John Deane joined Old Mutual with responsibility for M&A in January 2004. With substantial experience of M&A from the insurance sector, Deane's task was to help Old Mutual buy a 'closed block' of UK business.[19] In early 2004, Old Mutual conducted a due diligence investigation on the Henderson Group's[20] UK life book; however, its offered price was too low. Old Mutual's group CFO Julian Roberts stated that the company wanted to be bigger in the UK when the Q1 report was presented in May 2004, and that it had a team of people looking at this issue.

Old Mutual's market confidence was restored in August 2004; it reported 6.8 pence per share in adjusted operating profit for the six-month period ending 30 June. This was up from 5.6 pence per share from the same period in 2003. Although the strong rand flattered the results, the figure exceeded most analysts' forecasts. By the end of June, Old Mutual's assets under management were £130 billion, up by 12 per cent from 2003. The group's return on equity improved from 16 to 19 per cent during the same period. Furthermore, the embedded value per share was 114 pence at the end of June, up 9 per cent since the year-end. Old Mutual derived 53 per cent of its life insurance sales from its US activities for the first three months in 2004, and profit was up 43 per cent for the US asset business. Its US Life profit was up 18 per cent and the US life insurance business had margins of 22 per cent, the highest the group had ever experienced.

The UK expansion was in focus during that autumn. Julian Roberts described to the investor community in a presentation of the report for the first half of 2004 how Old Mutual continuously focused on buying closed life funds in the UK. However, it was obvious to him that it was more difficult than simply being expected to buy something that fitted Old Mutual's ambitions, since Old Mutual was not the only suitor. Both Britannic[21] and Chesnara[22] had also stated that they participated in the consolidation of the UK life fund market. Therefore prices were rising quickly and Old Mutual said it was keen not to overpay. John Deane, head of M&A, began to search further, that is, to look for an open block of business. Skandia Life UK fitted into such a specification.

In early 2004, Old Mutual's CEO Sutcliffe and Skandia's CEO Andersson had met in Florence at a McKinsey conference for industry CEOs. Although they were not necessarily close friends, they had worked together at Mercantile & General; therefore they knew each other quite well. Sutcliffe had suggested that Old Mutual and Skandia do something together, adding that such cooperation could be built upon the fact that other managers had met in the past and had always been friendly to each other. The connection between the two companies dated back to 1996, when Carendi – Skandia's 'superstar' of the time – had visited South Africa. In Florence, Sutcliffe invited Andersson to visit him the next time he travelled to London. In October–November 2004, Andersson made a courtesy visit to Old Mutual in London, and gave him a description of the Skandia group. Sutcliffe told Andersson that it would be great to discuss doing a deal of some kind with Old Mutual, if he were ever interested. But Andersson rejected such a possibility, stating that Skandia needed to focus on standing on its own feet in the near future. A month later, however, Sutcliffe heard about the December article in Sweden's *Dagens Nyheter*, where Skandia's chair Magnusson stated that the company was open to all suggestions.

Jan Olsson, who was the head of the Nordic operations at Deutsche Bank, talked to Magnusson over the phone following the publication of the *Dagens Nyheter* article (see Section 9.3). Magnusson's message was that selling Skandia was a viable alternative. Magnusson welcomed Deutsche Bank to come up with suggestions of likely candidates for possible structural deals addressing Skandia, in whole or in part. The other investment bankers who approached the chair received a similar response. Olsson called his colleagues at the London office who, incidentally, were already looking into the case. James Agnew, who was responsible for corporate broking, and Tony Burgess, who was responsible for European M&A, had been told that Morgan Stanley was doing some work for Skandia. Therefore they continuously updated their acquisition appraisal book on the company. Deutsche Bank also intensified contacts with customers who might be interested in participating in a Skandia bid (in whole or in part). One of the interested parties contacted was Old Mutual.

This development spurred Old Mutual's CEO to contact Skandia's CEO a few days following the media interview. Sutcliffe was straightforward on the phone, and asserted that the media article contained a different message from the one he had received from Andersson a month before. Andersson had confirmed that the message was different. Sutcliffe then asked Andersson for advice regarding what he should do in this situation. Andersson suggested that Sutcliffe should write a letter to the Skandia chair, Bernt Magnusson.

The Deutsche Bank team recommended that Sutcliffe take a serious look at the whole of Skandia – not only at its UK Life business. During the autumn, when they had considered Skandia, they concluded that it would be difficult to split up its business. A bidder for the entire company would probably be in an advantageous position. Old Mutual and Deutsche Bank regarded Skandia as an attractive company because of the high market shares that Skandia Life UK had in the UK, and Skandia's strong position at home in Sweden. However, there were probably many other interested parties looking at the company as well. Sutcliffe built his interest on the general trend towards more of an open architecture business, both throughout Europe and in Latin America and Asia. Singapore, Australia and Chile then provided the template for privatized pension markets. A deal with Skandia would increase Old Mutual's geographic diversity and reduce the proportion of earnings and assets exposed to fluctuations in the South African currency. In such a context, Skandia seemed like a hand-in-glove fit for Old Mutual. For Sutcliffe, it was a path worth exploring.

By Christmas, Old Mutual's stock was trading at 135 pence on the LSE, which, at the time, reflected only the embedded value from the Old Mutual books. It contained no value for a new life business to be written by Old Mutual (either in South Africa, where it was the largest life company, or in the USA, where it wrote over £2 billion of new businesses in 2005). According to analysts at Fox-Pitt, Kelton,[23] a stand-alone fair value of the company should be in the 170 pence range. That would allow for implied new business multiples of 5.2 for the South African individual business, 7.3 for the South African group business, and 10.1 for the US life business. This was still a fairly conservative valuation compared to the European average of approximately 12 times new business, and trading at 1.35 times its embedded value.

NOTES

1. The British Panel on Takeovers and Mergers is a self-regulatory body established in 1968 with the stated objective to ensure fair treatment in takeover bids for all shareholders.
2. The average currency exchange rate in 1999 was £1 = R9.85; an exchange rate of £1 = R9.93 was recorded for 31 December. Source: *Old Mutual Annual Report*, 1999. From a Swedish perspective, this could be translated to SEK100 = £7.3 and SEK100 = R137. Source: Swedish Central Bank (Riksbanken). The exchange rates between the three countries fluctuated greatly over the next ten-year period. In May 2005, the rates were SEK100 = £7.4 and SEK100 = R114. In September 2008 they were SEK100 = £8.3 and SEK100 = R82.
3. Over the following years, the largest investors in Old Mutual were to remain South-African-based. In the spring of 2005, the Public Investment Corporation of the Republic of South Africa was the largest investor with a holding of 5.6 per cent, followed by three Old-Mutual-related investors: Old Mutual Life Assurance Company with 5.1 per cent, Old Mutual Asset Management with 3.8 per cent, and the Old Mutual partly owned Legal and General Group with 3.1 per cent.
4. The leading index at the LSE reflecting the activity of the 100 most traded stocks.
5. A UK investment company with a focus on real estate.
6. The Gerrard Group included a wealth management business, as well as an online broker firm that was merged with OM's Capel Cure Sharp private banking business to create the then largest UK-based private stockbrokerage firm.
7. Sun Life & Provincial Holdings is a holding company formed in 1995 controlling such corporations as the Canadian insurance company, Sun Life. Aon UK Holdings was part of the Chicago-based insurance and consulting company, Aon.
8. On 31 December the relationship was £1 = R17.42, on 31 December 2000 it was £1 = R11.31. The average currency relation during the 12-month period for 2001 was £1 = R12.39; for 2000, the average was £1 = R10.52 (*Old Mutual Annual Report*, 2001).
9. On 31 December 2002 the relationship was £1 = R13.8. The average currency relation during the 12-month period for 2002 was £1 = R15.78 (*Old Mutual Annual Report*, 2002).
10. For example, a commentary in South African web paper *Personal Finance* 15 March 2003, and in *Business Day*, 5 June 2002: 'Old Mutual still has a lot to prove overseas. Having overpaid for some acquisitions, group must show they are good businesses', Hilary Joffe, and in *Financial Mail*, 7 September 2001, 'Old Mutual, still a huge integration task', Andrew McNulty.
11. Common name for unit-linked assurance products offered through an open architecture platform.
12. One of the many global stock market indices used by portfolio managers to compare their performances.
13. The media reported on Old Mutual eyeing the Britannic Group, Abbey National Scottish Provident, as well as Jupiter Asset Management. See *Telegraph*, 8 June 2003.
14. Part of Gerrard Group.
15. Also originally part of Gerrard Group.
16. *Financial Times*, 28 October 2003, 'The gin rummy school of management: Old story for Old Mutual', Philip Coggan.
17. A South-African-based private bank with 90 billion rand of assets under management.
18. Converted from rand. On 31 December 2003, the relationships were £1 = \$1.78 and £1 = R11.9 (*Old Mutual Annual Report*, 2003).
19. An actuarial term for a limited and defined group of policies and assets where the cash flow from the assets is used exclusively to support the policies.
20. A large UK financial asset and service group listed on the LSE; it also had a life service business that was sold in 2005.
21. Since the autumn of 2005 a part of Phoenix life group owned by Pearl Group. Other

companies include, e.g. Sun Alliance, Swiss Life and Abbey National Life. In 2008 Phoenix became Pearl Group.

22. A UK life assurance company closed for new business (formely a subsidiary of Countrywide Assured Group before its demerger from the group in May 2004).
23. A UK-based brokerage house with a focus on banks and insurance companies; it started in 1971 and, throughout the year, earned a reputation for high-quality analytical work in the finance sector. In 2005, Swiss Re was the owner, later selling to a private equity group that subsequently merged with Cochran Caronia Waller in 2007.

PART V

Old Mutual goes for Skandia (December 2004 to August 2005)

11. Growing unease on the Skandia board

11.1 THE SKANDIA BOARD MEETING ON 22 DECEMBER 2004

The Skandia share had been trading at around 28–29 SEK until 13 December, when activist Christer Gardell announced his Cevian fund investment. Before Christmas the share price then increased about 10 per cent, reaching 31.5 SEK. The general view among the board members was that Skandia was still trading at a discount. The low share price was attributed to several ongoing litigations, certain tax issues and uncertainties related to the embedded-value calculations.

The Skandia board held its last meeting for the season on 22 December 2004. For the first time since the 12 August meeting, advisers from Morgan Stanley were present. They were invited by Chair Bernt Magnusson to give an update on Skandia's business opportunities and lay a foundation for discussions about the future for Skandia Life UK. Morgan Stanley representatives mentioned a possible value of 41 SEK billion for the whole Skandia group. This was a sort of 'indicative group appraisal value', where the different divisions were valued separately. The adviser further talked about something they called 'Skandia's credibility gap', which, based on applying multiples similar to those applied to industry peers, referred to the difference between the share price and company valuations. The advisers also described two ways to close the gap. The 'Glue document', a report that McKinsey consultants had produced back in May 2004, described the first. It indicated cost synergies in the range of 600–800 million SEK. However, according to Morgan Stanley's presentation, there were risks associated with following that recommendation, particularly as long as Skandia Life UK's management claimed that they saw negative synergies in a more integrated Skandia group. Skandia's top management had also expressed doubts when the 'Glue document' was presented, regarding it as a rather abstract plan without specifications of actions to be taken. In December 2004, it still lacked internal support. The management at Skandia Life UK was particularly negative, fearing a loss of local UK focus if the UK staff had to participate fully in an internal group cost-savings programme. Skandia CEO Hans-Erik Andersson agreed to most of Morgan Stanley's analysis, and suggested that the cost synergies between the UK business and the rest of Skandia were probably lower than what McKinsey had indicated.

The second way that Morgan Stanley suggested of closing the credibility gap presumed that the board first answer four questions, and then act according to the conclusions drawn from that analysis. The questions were: what is Skandia today?; what can – and should – Skandia be in the future?; how does Skandia Life UK fit into a Skandia of the future?; and if Skandia Life UK does not fit in, what will be the 'end game' for Skandia? Furthermore, the board decided that, before the next board meeting (set for 14 January 2005), Morgan Stanley should go through all the alternatives regarding Skandia Life UK. Andersson was asked to prepare a presentation of his management team's own ideas regarding the future for the entire Skandia group.

However, neither the so-called credibility gap nor the future for Skandia Life UK was the main issue at the board discussions on 22 December. The directors had other more urgent topics to deal with, such as the possibility of legal action against former Skandia board members and its top management. Lawyers Peter Danowsky and Otto Rydbeck,[1] who had both conducted inquiries into the affairs of previous directors and management of Skandia, presented their arguments. Danowsky argued in favour of suing former Chair Lars Ramqvist, who, in his eyes, failed in his duty to provide the board with distinct information about the amounts allocated to the various top management incentive programmes. Ramqvist had also failed to inform the board about how former CEO Lars-Eric Petersson's 200 million SEK bonus from the incentive programme Sharetracker was turned into a pension. Rydbeck, however, argued against the legal case because he expected that such litigation would be too costly for Skandia shareholders.

The board spent several hours discussing the pros and cons of initiating a legal process. In the end, they unanimously agreed to a deal that they hoped would clear up the entire issue: Ramqvist would have to agree on returning the pay he had received during his three years as chair, which amounted to a total of 2.2 million SEK. In early February, Ramqvist accepted the proposed settlement. However, this agreement also required shareholder approval at the forthcoming AGM, set for April 2005.

11.2 CHRISTMAS ACTIVITIES

Christer Gardell was co-opted on 22 December 2004 to Skandia's nomination committee, which was publicly announced the same day. The committee was to suggest board members for the AGM decision, which was scheduled for 15 April 2005. The committee also included: Björn Lind, chair of SEB Funds; Lars Idermark from AP2; Karl Gunnar ('K.G.') Lindvall from Robur; Per Löfqvist of the Skandia Shareholders' Association; and Olof Neiglick, representing Nordea Funds. Altogether, they represented 19.2 per cent of Skandia's capital and votes.

One important matter was not discussed at the board meeting on 22 December: Deputy Chair Björn Björnsson did not call attention to the ongoing discussion with Morgan Stanley about its role in Skandia. That same day, Björnsson received a formal letter from Morgan Stanley's investment bankers, Per Hillström and Jakob Lindquist.[2] The letter included an agreement of the terms on which Morgan Stanley accepted to prolong its existing advisery agreement with Skandia, which had been in effect for the past 18 months. The letter also included the suggestion that Morgan Stanley should perform a continuous review of Skandia's strategic options, provide financial advice, deliver other preparatory work, and have the opportunity to act as adviser if (and when) a corporate transaction was to be conducted. The letter was addressed to both Magnusson and Björnsson, although it was Björnsson who eventually signed the contract. The other directors were not informed at the meeting about this imminent renewal of the agreement with Morgan Stanley. This contributed later to the emerging tension between some of the members of the board.[3]

The day after the board meeting, Old Mutual's CEO Jim Sutcliffe sent a letter to the Skandia board expressing his interest in a merger (or some other kind of cooperation) with Skandia. Deutsche Bank had been working on it to establish its formulations with Old Mutual's director of corporate development John Deane.[4] Bernt Magnusson received the letter during the Christmas holidays. At this time,[5] however, neither this letter nor other incoming proposals were communicated to the other directors.[6]

Christer Gardell's intentions for Skandia were discussed in the 27 December edition of *Dagens Industri*.[7] According to a 'reliable source', Gardell's secret plan for Skandia was 'to reduce Skandia's HQ costs by half a billion SEK, and to make a separate listing of its UK insurance arm: Skandia Life UK'. The latter was valued at 20 billion SEK, approximately 60 per cent of Skandia's total market value. Gardell's goal was to get the Skandia stock to move upwards. Therefore he tried to gain support for his plan both from the other shareholders and, later, as a result of his expected position at the board, from the other Skandia directors. He declined to elaborate on his plan, but stated: 'the costs are high and there should be room for further savings'. He added that Skandia's CEO had taken several steps in the right direction.

One month after Gardell had announced Cevian's investment, Skandia shares were trading above 33 SEK. Around this time, Magnusson wrote a letter to all board members suggesting that they should invest some of their own money in Skandia.[8] Magnusson told Andersson that he, who had received 6 million SEK as salary, but bought only 10000 shares for approximately 250000 SEK, ought to invest more in the company. In early January, Andersson doubled his investment to 20000 shares, and the board members followed suit.[9]

11.3 SKANDIA'S TURBO PLAN

At the 14 January 2005 board meeting, Andersson and his management team presented preliminary figures for 2004.[10] It had been a tough year for the Skandia group. Bankhall, Skandia Life UK's troubled independent financial adviser, was a prime candidate for a goodwill writedown of 931 million SEK. Skandia's market share for its unit-linked business was 17.9 per cent in Sweden, down from 25.9 per cent the previous year. There was also still trouble with the guarantees to Prudential covering American Skandia's involvement in the market-timing issues, which was subject to scrutiny by various US authorities. When American Skandia was sold in December 2002, Skandia had left a guarantee of $1 billion, one-fifth of the market capitalization of the Skandia group. Analysts' reports generally calculated that the settlement with American Skandia could come to a substantial sum, even though it was deemed unlikely that it would absorb the entire guarantee.[11]

Nevertheless, at the January board meeting Skandia's CEO was optimistic, reporting that most things were changing for the better. Skandia's top management had worked hard for internal coordination and cost control. During Q4 2004, the profit margin on new sales of unit-linked products rose to 21.8 per cent; this was up from 18.3 per cent in Q3. Skandia Life UK was the fastest-growing unit-linked company on the market in the UK, with sales rising by 50 per cent. In Sweden, the result from the banking arm Skandiabanken more than doubled, to 400 million SEK. Andersson also presented his budget and plans for 2005. He saw Skandia heading for a balanced growth, although it would probably take another six to nine months until shareholders could see the improvement in reported profits. Moreover, several operations in continental Europe were also budgeted to turn losses into profits. Andersson argued that economies of scale could be achieved in these operations, and this could be possible before even taking a changed organizational structure into account. Andersson summarized Skandia's budget as being really good. In his view, Skandia's strategy was to remain an international niche player with three distinctive advantages on the long-term savings market: its unit-linked assurance business, its product distribution through IFAs; and its open architecture platform (with local packaging adapted to tax and other regulations). The board appreciated these achievements and plans.

Andersson also presented an updated business development plan based upon the McKinsey review that Morgan Stanley had previously addressed. The plan stated that there were substantial synergies between Skandia's businesses in the UK, the Nordic region and the rest of the world. Calculations further indicated that Skandia's HQ in Stockholm was too expensive. Excessive costs also existed in Skandia Life UK, and Andersson added that there was ongoing disagreement with its management. The board members were also introduced to many other items, such as plans for the future IT infrastructure, internal services operations, upcoming rationalizations, more efficient product development processes and the consolidation of fund management across the Skandia group. Andersson further reported that both Gert Engman (head of the Nordic region) and Michael Wolf (head of Europe and Latin America) supported the plans; both wanted a mandate to work through the various alternatives. However, Chair Magnusson and Deputy Chair Björnsson were more sceptical of the Skandia management's intentions. They wanted to see an alternative to the McKinsey papers that, in the presence of the resentment from the UK office, lacked the necessary specificity. The CEO promised to come back with a 'turbo-charged version' of the McKinsey business development plan.[12] Andersson would ask Monitor – the management consultancy firm that previously had undertaken work for Skandia – to spend part of the spring ironing out an action plan with Skandia's management team.

11.4 BOARD DISPUTE ABOUT THE MORGAN STANLEY AGREEMENT

Tensions began to grow at the board meeting on 14 January 2005. Magnusson told the board that shareholders were approaching him, complaining that the stock price was too low (Skandia was trading at around 30 SEK). Moreover, the Skandia Life UK management still wanted to separate its business from Skandia, so he had asked the Morgan Stanley team to analyse different alternatives for the large unit. The chair also suggested that the board should consider the possible need for a strategic partner in the Nordic region.

Magnusson further mentioned that Morgan Stanley had been asked to go through all the different options for Skandia, including a full selloff, stating that Skandia had received ten foreign suggestions that indicated an interest in cooperating or merging with Skandia, both in whole or in part. Through Per Hillström, Morgan Stanley was assigned the task to sort out the most interesting suitors. Board members Birgitta Johansson-Hedberg and Kajsa Lindståhl expressed surprise when the chair mentioned these activities; as they saw it, the board's decision five months earlier at the 12 August meeting had been quite different. All matters regarding the structure of the Skandia group – including talks of a sale – were to be put aside for the time being. Neither saw the point of entering into such discussions again. In their analysis, the UK business was a 'poison pill' without which a competitor would most likely buy Skandia's businesses – particularly those in Sweden. Consequently, Morgan Stanley's mandate to work with those issues had been terminated.

Magnusson was taken by surprise, claiming that he had not perceived the discussions during the August 2004 meeting in the same way. He said that he remembered the meeting as of a different kind: one that centred on the future of Skandia Life UK. The approved minutes from the meeting also supported his recollection of what had actually been decided. Magnusson also referred to a letter signed on 22 December that contained details of an 18-month extension of the advisery agreement with Morgan Stanley. One director noted: 'At that moment, it became so quiet [in the room] that one could hear a pin drop.'

Magnusson and Björnsson then told the board that they had prolonged the retainer agreement since Skandia had been receiving a number of proposals from various potential buyers, and needed support in the primary analyses of the ambitions and capacities of these prospects. Moreover, they argued that it was also necessary for Skandia to have a relationship with an investment bank like Morgan Stanley for several other reasons: to continuously review various matters (including strategic options); to provide financial advice; and to carry out other running tasks. According to Magnusson, the standards practised in such contracting included the formulations that gave Morgan Stanley the opportunity to act as adviser if and when a possible transaction was conducted.

Karl-Olov Hammarkvist, Lennart Jeansson and Anders Ullberg, who were the other board members appointed at the AGM, did not comment on the prolonged Morgan Stanley advisery agreement. Birgitta Johansson-Hedberg finally concluded the discussion by stating that if the deal with Morgan Stanley were signed and sealed, then there was nothing the board could do but accept it. Ullberg added that Morgan Stanley must be kept on a 'tight leash', and Magnusson promised that he would do precisely that. One of the union representatives on the board, Anna Andersson, expressed concern that Morgan Stanley's mandate could be self-fulfilling if a transaction came to the fore. Later in the meeting, Johansson-Hedberg said that she wanted a clarification that the stand-alone alternative remained as the main path forward, and added that Skandia should 'hold onto itself' and wait for the 'right one'. By the end of the meeting, all board members agreed on five crucial points that Magnusson summarized as follows: (i) Skandia as a stand-alone company remained the main option; (ii) Morgan Stanley should not actively seek suitors; rather they would act only after interested parties had called Skandia and submitted concrete proposals; (iii) the Skandia board was to be continuously informed about all serious propositions; (iv) Morgan Stanley had the task of evaluating the tendering offers that the board selected; and (v) Morgan Stanley was to be kept under a 'tight leash'.

When the Morgan Stanley advisery agreement was discussed during the 14 January 2005 board meeting, CEO Hans-Erik Andersson remained silent. He was not a formal member of the board and had, therefore, chosen to speak only when a topic concerned Skandia's operations or if someone specifically asked for his opinion. Neither Andersson nor Skandia's head of Strategy, Per Jungkvist (who usually also worked with Skandia's investment banks) had been consulted regarding the prolongation of the Skandia/Morgan Stanley agreement. However, outside the board meeting, Andersson expressed to several directors his discontent about this procedure.

In the first weeks of 2005, intense rumours of the activities at Skandia continued to circulate in Stockholm. For the investment banking community, it was difficult to figure out what the directors on the Skandia board really wanted. Many investment bankers were convinced that Morgan Stanley had a mandate to sell Skandia, and that it was actively inviting parties to look at the company; some of them had the impression that not all the board members supported such a path. A few investment bankers who were closely connected to the board even heard directors deny the fact that Skandia was up for sale. One was Lars Lenner, head of the private corporate finance boutique Lenner & Partners, who scouted around for companies to partner with Skandia. Lenner was the previous head of M&A at Alfred Berg.[13] He and his Alfred Berg colleague, Patrik Tillman,[14] had ample experience dealing with the financial companies in Stockholm city and, similar to several other dealmakers, Lenner & Partners spread the belief that there was no future for a Skandia on its own.

A few weeks following the board meeting on 14 January 2005, some Skandia board members who attended meetings in Stockholm heard that Lenner had spoken to friends about the ongoing activities concerning Skandia in the investment banking community. Lenner had apparently said that many investment bankers were actually working to arouse an interest in various parts of Skandia. According to Lenner, most actors on the market believed that several investment bankers had obtained the board's mandate to come up with suggestions for structural deals so that the Skandia board had something to discuss at its February meeting. However, Lenner expressed doubts that a bidder for the company as a whole would emerge.

During winter 2005, Kajsa Lindståhl expressed worry that the board was not functioning well. The Skandia director had phoned some of the other board members complaining that the board had become two-tier: with an 'A-team' in control and a 'B-team' that sometimes lacked crucial information. Her impression was that the chair and the deputy chair had a hidden agenda whose hidden implications she wanted the rest of the board members to consider. Lindståhl revealed her concerns to Lennart Jeansson. He, however, had the impression that Magnusson was sincere and trustworthy, yet he promised to look into the matter. Anders Ullberg reacted pretty much in the same way when Jeansson voiced her concerns. As Ullberg saw it, the decision of the board was that Skandia's management should work with Morgan Stanley; and the chair and deputy chair, together with the management team, had prolonged the advisory agreement. The fact that top management worked with an investment bank was also the normal procedure in all companies, according to Ullberg, although he did promise Lindståhl to talk to the CEO about this issue. A while later, Ullberg asked Andersson why he so often turned to Morgan Stanley. Andersson's reply was brief: it had not been his decision, and he was not in control of the process.

11.5 A FIRST VISIT FROM OLD MUTUAL

On 23 December 2004, the day after the board of Skandia held its last meeting of the year, Old Mutual's CEO had sent the letter to Skandia's chair. The letter was not discussed at the next board meeting in January; however, several companies were mentioned in the minutes as expressing interest in talking with Skandia, and Old Mutual was one of those on the list. Magnussson had invited Old Mutual's CEO to come to Skandia later in January.[15] Jim Sutcliffe and his team, including representatives of Deutsche Bank, met Magnusson, Björnsson and Andersson, who listened to what Sutcliffe had to say. His team described Old Mutual's rationale for reaching some kind of a deal with Skandia – the main reason being that Old Mutual was a South African insurance company that was seeking to strengthen its position outside its home market (at the time, it had its sights set particularly on the UK). Sutcliffe and his team felt that the Swedes had reacted with disappointment to their presentation and messages. Deutsche Bank's head of Nordic operations, Jan Olsson, had assisted Old Mutual in the preparations for its presentation. He later communicated the same conclusion – Skandia's executives were not impressed. The benefits for Skandia to engage in such a deal had not been sufficiently highlighted.

The Deutsche Bank team concluded that the Skandia actors were expecting more 'logical' business suitors than Old Mutual, since the company was virtually unknown to most Swedish business people. Olsson had actually been disappointed by Deutsche Bank's choice of partner. In his view, it would have been easier to work with the German insurance company Allianz, the Swedish bank Nordea or another more obvious potential bidder. The latter two companies were also probably the kinds of suitors that the board and management of Skandia had in mind. Olsson said to colleagues that representing Old Mutual in talks with Skandia was 'a long shot'. The chances of closing a deal were small except for the fact that, in January 2005, Old Mutual seemed to be the only actor interested in bidding on Skandia as a whole. By the end of January 2005, Deutsche Bank received the formal mandate to represent Old Mutual in a public offer for Skandia. With full backing from London, Olsson became the Scandinavian representative of this British/South African dark horse in the quest for Skandia.

In February 2005 Jan Olsson contacted Linklaters, a global law firm known for its experience in dealing with cross-border takeovers in Europe (Old Mutual had previously used them). Old Mutual's corporate development team revealed their plans to bid for Skandia to Duncan Barber, a Linklaters partner in London, and to Fredrik Lindqvist, head of Linklaters' team in Sweden.[16] Old Mutual planned to prepare its bid for later use, although at least before midsummer (late June). With the assistance from Linklaters they headed for a smooth deal with no surprises or delays.

Later that February, Sutcliffe sent a second letter to Magnusson as a follow-up to the Stockholm meeting. The letter had been worked through in detail by the Old Mutual and Deutsche Bank teams, as well as by co-financial adviser, Merrill Lynch, the corporate brokerage house and market maker of Old Mutual shares on the LSE. The letter stated Old Mutual's interest in buying the whole of Skandia at an indicative price of 40 SEK per share: a share-for-share offer with a sufficient portion in cash to cover Skandia's outstanding legal liabilities (to be held in escrow). A split of 85:15 between shares and cash was suggested. However, this was just a 'sighting shot', as the Deutsche Bank's representatives put it – an attempt to see some kind of reaction from the Skandia camp. However, there was no response at all from Skandia. Yet Magnusson did speak with Sutcliffe on the phone, and signalled his and the other directors' and executives' preoccupation with the upcoming arduous Skandia AGM. Some actors interpreted this behaviour as stalling for time, while others saw it as a reasonable explanation for the lack of response to Old Mutual.

All this contact between Sutcliffe and Skandia was conducted in a friendly manner. This was important to Sutcliffe since his mandate from the board was to carry through a non-hostile takeover. Old Mutual was preoccupied with other corporate events (especially the Black Economic Empowerment transaction that was to turn non-European South Africans into Old Mutual shareholders). Therefore he let Skandia know that he had no problem waiting a month or two for a response.

11.6 GROWING TENSION ON THE SKANDIA BOARD

At the beginning of 2005, Skandia's CEO began to complain to people around him about Morgan Stanley's activities. Andersson said that he believed that the contacts he had previously had with different investment banks were slipping out of (his) control. Up until the 14 January board meeting, he had been the one dealing with the investment banks that were courting Skandia: Goldman Sachs, JP Morgan, Deutsche Bank, HSBC, CSFB,[17] Merrill Lynch and so on. Up to that point, investment bankers who came to the Skandia HQ went to the sixth floor, turned left and walked down the corridor to Andersson's office. Andersson politely showed them the door. After the January board meeting, however, this procedure changed. Now the investment bankers came to the sixth floor, turned right instead of left, and walked to the other end of the corridor where Magnusson and Björnsson had their offices. Andersson's frustration grew, as did the gossip among several board members that the chair and CEO did not get along as well as expected. Morgan Stanley actors also expressed frustration. In their case, they complained to the chair about the limited cooperation from the Skandia management, which seemed not so keen to sell the company after all.

The Skandia board of directors met once again on 25 February 2005.[18] This time, the important topic was the work that the Morgan Stanley staff had done during the winter. Morgan Stanley was not present at the meeting, but the board material included the adviser's Skandia calculations. This information could be found in the document called 'Valuation Overview', dated 18 February 2005. Morgan Stanley had prepared a total of seven different calculations. First, Morgan Stanley had made calculations of Skandia's value: its so-called 'fair trading value' (FTV). As a going concern, FTV was estimated at 34–38 SEK per share. This calculation included only official information, as perceived by the stock market. Morgan Stanley had also made a calculation based on management's assumptions of Skandia's outlook. This reflected the management's new business plan, as it had been compiled by Per Jungkvist after the 14 January board meeting. The FTV would increase to 37–40 SEK if the business plan were to be included and recognized by the stock market (although with some discount for uncertainty). However, if the shareholders gave full credit to the management's Turbo plan (actually believing that it could soon be implemented), and, thus, used the same discount factor as Skandia, then the value would land at 44–47 SEK. Moreover, if Skandia management's business plan were calculated using discounted cash flow,[19] the value could be calculated at 53–57 SEK. This calculation included current share price, full value of current business plan, as well as the net present value of the future business plan.

Morgan Stanley presented a valuation of Skandia in a separate calculation, which included the value of a possible partnership or partnerships. The value of Skandia would probably increase if based upon a 'sum-of-the-parts' calculation. In a deal where Skandia were split up and sold in pieces to industrial buyers capable of extracting synergies, the value of Skandia would be higher than for a stand-alone path. Three additional calculations were presented: FTV plus synergies, creating a value of the Skandia share of between 43 and 47 SEK (based upon a market value of 34–38 SEK); market FTV (plus synergies and including a discounted valuation of the management's business plan) giving a value in the interval 46–49 SEK; and management FTV (which implied that the market fully believed in the outcome of the management's business plan) indicating a value in the range 53–56 SEK. Taken together, the seven alternatives gave a value range of Skandia between 34 SEK and 57 SEK, with an average of 45.5 SEK.

Calculated in two groups, with the first four in one group and the other three in a second group, the average value would add up to 45.5 SEK and 49.5 SEK respectively. The average (47 SEK) would, for many of the directors, remain as the key outcome from the board meeting.

The board material from 25 February also included a first report of Morgan Stanley's 'sorting out' of proposals. There were several interested parties, although the appetite to purchase the whole of Skandia was somewhat limited, with the exception of Old Mutual. Some board members reacted with unease to this information, taking for granted that the stand-alone option was still the preferred way forward. During this winter there were also other issues that contributed to the gradually increasing frictions among some of the members of the Skandia board. Actors who were invited to attend board meetings noted that there seemed to be tension between, on the other side, Johansson-Hedberg and Lindståhl, and, on the other, Magnusson and Björnsson.

Skandia CEO Andersson travelled to London in March, where he spoke with people at the Morgan Stanley office, and complained that things were getting out of (his) control. He told the investment bank's team leader Paulo Pereira that he felt that the process had reached a point of no return. Pereira said he agreed. That same month, Andersson also spoke with Kajsa Lindståhl, stating that the stand-alone path was not going to work much longer, since so much was happening outside the board. Andersson had continued his reasoning by handing Lindståhl the 23 December 2004 letter from Old Mutual. Lindståhl spoke to Hammarkvist, who shared her concern about the consequences of the renewed Morgan Stanley advisery agreement. Lindståhl suggested that she and the Skandia director jointly express their distrust in how the Skandia board was being run by resigning their respective board positions at the upcoming AGM in April. Hammarkvist agreed in principle, but not in action. His argument was that there was still too much to sort out within Skandia, and the Ramqvist settlement was very time-consuming for everybody. At this stage, he said, Skandia did not need any more trouble.

Lindståhl also asked Birgitta Johansson-Hedberg to join a group that opposed the chair's way of running the board's activities; however, like Hammarkvist, she agreed only 'in principle'. She was too involved in a trying transformation of Lantmännen, the Swedish agricultural company of which she was CEO, to get involved in a board conflict. The growing tension on the board did not reach the press; neither did the increasingly strained relationship between the chair and the CEO. On the contrary, a consultancy report from late autumn 2004 described the Skandia board as a well-functioning unit, listed as being among the best company boards of all those they had analysed.[20] In Skandia's 2004 annual report (published in March 2005), Magnusson wrote the following text in the chair's corporate governance commentary:

> It is also the board and management's duty to be observant and monitor structural changes in the industry and to be open for changes if opportunities are created to strengthen Skandia's structure . . . In order for Skandia's board and management to be able to work with a future business focus, the Board has given its deputy chair, Björn Björnsson, special responsibility for handling the disputes stemming from previous years' operations . . . The CEO and Executive Management Board have a clear assignment to focus on the group's operations and development, with customer and shareholder value as the prime criteria. This is where Skandia's focus is today – on its business moving forward.[21]

11.7 ICELANDIC SUPPORT FOR CEVIAN

In the first months of 2005, Christer Gardell and Lars Förberg, his partner at the activist fund Cevian, marketed their analysis of Skandia. They believed that Skandia could well be valued at over 60 SEK per share (even up to 70 SEK if Skandia Liv were demutualized and its full potential explored). Investors in both Stockholm and London heard about this analysis. In January, Gardell had travelled to Reykjavik, Iceland, where he met billionaire investor, Thor Björgólfsson.[22] Björgólfsson and his investment manager, Ragnar Thórisson, listened to Gardell's stories about Intrum Justitia, Lindex and Skandia. Thórisson's view was that, in three to four years, the Skandia share could be valued at 55–60 SEK. This was more or less in line with what Gardell had put forward. Thórisson also fully shared Gardell's conclusion that the Nordic insurance industry was up for consolidation, and that Skandia was the most obvious target. Björgólfsson began to use his investment vehicle Burdarás to buy Skandia stock, beginning with a small investment of 0.2 per cent. In mid-March 2005, Burdarás publicly announced an investment of 3.5 per cent of the Skandia shares. The average price per share was 28 SEK. The Icelanders regarded themselves as co-investors with Cevian, planning to support Gardell as a new director on the Skandia board. After the April 2005 AGM, Burdarás continued to buy shares; by mid-May, the investment amounted to 4.5 per cent.

In mid-March, another Icelandic bank started to support Cevian's plan. Kaupthing – the bank that, in a surprise move, had taken control of and merged two Swedish private investment banks[23] – was reported to control 2.5 per cent of Skandia. For almost a year, it had been rumoured that Kaupthing was interested in buying Skandia's Internet bank, Skandiabanken. In a 17 March press release, Kaupthing wrote that the investment, for the time being, was a financial placement. Kaupthing planned to support Gardell as new director of the Skandia board, just as Burdarás also intended.

Several actors in the financial cities of Stockholm and London met the Cevian case with scepticism. This was especially true when it came to the valuation of Skandia's mutual arm Skandia Liv. Andersson and investor relations officer, Harry Vos, were asked by analysts to check the valuation of Skandia Liv. Was it really worth 25 billion SEK? Andersson and Vos certainly did not agree. In a theoretical sense, yes, it was possible to demutualize Skandia Liv, but that would probably involve heavy compensation to the policyholders – perhaps to the amount of 10 billion SEK or more. Furthermore, Skandia Liv was not just any mutual company – it was one of the oldest mutually operated ones in Sweden. For most financial analysts and investors who were covering Skandia, all these talks ended in scepticism when it came to Cevian's valuation of the company. At the time, the Skandia share was, once again, trading in the high twenties, having fallen back after the initial rally when the Cevian position was announced in December 2004. Skandia's past problems were still keeping the stock valuations low, and no exciting split-up of the company had yet been announced. Financial analysts' reports also mentioned both a possible writedown of the 3 billion SEK investments in the financial adviser Bankhall, and the forthcoming possibly costly settlement with Prudential.

11.8 SETTLEMENT WITH FORMER CHAIR LARS RAMQVIST

In the winter of 2005, the possible settlement with former Skandia Chair Lars Ramqvist remained the top issue on the board's agenda. When Deutsche Bank had pushed for a clearer time plan for the Old Mutual offer, Magnusson berated them, replying that he might not even be the chair after the AGM. It was becoming obvious to the Skandia board that it was more difficult than expected to get shareholder support for a settlement with Ramqvist. The Church of Sweden, a minor but symbolically important investor in Skandia (owner of 1.1 million shares), wanted to see the case go to court; the US advisory agency International Shareholders' Services (ISS) concurred. Swedish institutional investors such as Robur, AP4 and Alecta, however, kept postponing the announcement of their decisions. The CEO at AP3,[24] Kerstin Hessius, complained that the shareholders did not receive sufficient information concerning the board's suggestion to settle the dispute.[25]

On 10 March 2005, a group of major shareholders gathered at Björn Lind's office at SEB Funds. Magnusson and Björnsson were both present, seeking shareholder support for the Ramqvist settlement. They communicated their thoughts on Skandia's present and expected future situations. Magnusson showed images portraying Skandia's diminished market value, and how its overall position had also weakened. These were the slides that Morgan Stanley had shown to the Skandia board back in June 2004 when Magnusson had sought support for opening up the possibility of a structural deal for Skandia. His current message was that there was no more time to lose. Skandia needed to rid itself of the Ramqvist issue in order to move forward. For that, the board needed the support from its shareholders.

SEB Funds and AP2 were two of the institutional investors that were quick to side with the board. Idermark at AP2 pushed for a settlement, declaring that he would like to see a partner from the industry investing in the haunted company. Moreover, he wanted to see Gardell as a new board member. Representatives of Handelsbanken, Robur and Alecta were more sceptical to the suggested settlement. They wanted to consult their own expertise for a second opinion. Thomas Nicolin at Alecta tried to get Skandia to back down from the settlement and seek a court ruling instead. Björnsson then replied that Alecta was most welcome to sue Ramqvist himself, and offered Nicolin all of Skandia's files. He then added that Alecta should be prepared to pay a start-up cost of approximately 25 million SEK. Nicolin declined Björnsson's offer. In the end, Magnusson and Björnsson made their point clear: if they did not get owner support for the settlement (it needed a backing from 90 per cent of the shareholders), then they expected that there would be a shareholder vote of distrust at the AGM.

Chair Magnusson was on holiday in Spain in March 2005 when Nicolin called to inform him that Alecta had sold all of its shares in Skandia; it was one month before the AGM. On 19 March, *Dagens Nyheter* ran an 'Alecta Sellout' story, quoting Nicolin as saying: 'This is a decision made within our capital management . . . Alecta has sold its Skandia shares on a number or occasions since the second half of 2003 . . . And this week was a good opportunity to sell the last part. [Our capital management] thinks that there are better alternatives . . . .'[26]

On 17 March, the Skandia board invited its shareholders to the company AGM; the agenda included the suggestion to settle with former chair, Ramqvist. The same day, the two Icelandic banks – Kaupthing and Straumar–Burdarás – gave their support both for the settlement with Ramqvist and for Gardell's seat on the board. Kaupthing wrote in a press release that the chances of success for a value-enhancing strategy would increase if the board and management pursued a more shareholder-positive strategy and focused on the right matters. As a result, Kaupthing supported the board's wish to settle with the former chair.

In the latter part of March, Magnusson and Gardell (not yet a board member), who supported a settlement with Ramqvist, went to London to meet investors in Skandia; the company's secretary-general, Jan-Mikael Bexhed, went along as well. On 30 March, Magnusson, Bexhed and Gardell met with representatives of Fidelity Funds. At the time, Fidelity was Skandia's largest shareholder with a holding of approximately 8–9 per cent allocated in various funds. The proposed settlement with Ramqvist was on the table that day, as was Skandia's overall future. Director of corporate governance at Fidelity International, Trelawny Williams, expressed his support for both the Ramqvist settlement and Gardell's appointment to the board. Williams also communicated Fidelity's positive view regarding the Skandia board's ambition to investigate structural solutions.

But there were other foreign investors that opposed a Ramqvist settlement. The same day, Institutional Shareholders' Services (ISS) presented an analysis of the proposed settlement, claiming that the general opinion was that Skandia was already involved in public litigation over the former CEO (Petersson), and that negative media attention could hardly be avoided. Through its chief lawyer, Lars Millberg, the Swedish Shareholders' Association applauded the declaration from the international investor community. The opposition to the settlement, however, was quickly dwindling. Cevian publicly stated that, for business reasons, they would go along with the board. On 8 April, Robur yielded when its 'governor general', Marianne Nilsson, officially concluded that there did not seem to be enough opposition to the board's proposal to settle with the former chair. Robur had learned that Fidelity had not posed any objection to Magnusson's suggestion when they had met, and Alecta had already sold out its holdings in Skandia.

The Skandia AGM on 14 April 2005 raised considerable media attention. One reason for this was that Gardell was to be elected as a new board member. He made a point of making this known, and Cevian had bought additional shares in Skandia a few weeks before the AGM (0.4 per cent of the stock). But his election was not the biggest issue at the meeting, and neither was the billion-dollar guarantee to Prudential Financial concerning American Skandia's involvement in the US market-timing scandal (although Björnsson had brought it up during his presentation of ongoing litigations). But the most important issue in the eyes of the media and the general public was the suggested settlement with Ramqvist. Lars-Erik Forsgårdh, CEO of the Swedish Shareholders' Association, did not want to see such a settlement at all. Therefore he strongly opposed voting on the Ramqvist issue before the election of the new board. This would send a clear message to institutional investors: the board might resign if shareholders voted against the suggested settlement. According to Forsgårdh, it would be fairer to first vote for the election of the new board, and then, in a second vote, address the proposed Ramqvist settlement. Forsgårdh and Magnusson engaged in a heated debate on this procedural issue. The latter argued that the suggested settlement with the former chair was not a matter of great importance.

There was a preliminary vote regarding which procedure to use. The actors asked to give their votes on this formality were Cevian, Robur, SEB Funds, SEB Trygg Liv, AP2, Kaupthing and Burdarás. They all expressed support for the board's proposal, and due to their dominant standing at the AGM, there was then no need for a time-consuming full voting procedure involving all present shareholders. During the proceedings, Fidelity International voted only for its own 5 per cent holding in Skandia. Its US affiliate, and owner of an additional 5 per cent, did not vote at all. This was the usual procedure by foreign investors, since registering shares before an AGM in Sweden was a complicated process that they seldom wanted to endure.

Lars-Erik Forsgårdh raised his voice after the vote. He spoke about 'betrayal' and 'bad decisions', criticizing the suggested appointment of Cevian's Christer Gardell as a new Skandia board member. Forsgårdh questioned whether Gardell really stood for a long-term perspective and if he worked for the best interests of all shareholders. He specifically addressed Magnusson, claiming that it was uncertain if Gardell was what the company really needed, especially given the fact that what Magnusson had said in public was actually correct: the Skandia board functioned well. The chair answered by referring to a board evaluation conducted by the consultancy firm Michaël Berglund (see Section 11.6), which was based on information received from interviews with all of the board members in the autumn of 2004. Forsgårdh also asked Magnusson to comment on the rumours that the board of Skandia was planning to (break up and) sell the company. The chair answered that such talks were groundless, but he added that this did not mean that the current business structure was necessarily the best option for Skandia's future.

Despite a heated debate, Cevian's Christer Gardell was appointed new director of the Skandia board in accordance with the nomination committee. Cevian's own representative at the AGM, Lars Förberg, voted for 13 per cent of the shares, although the company itself had direct control of 'only' 3.4 per cent.[27] In conjunction with the decision about board composition, the extra compensation packages to Magnusson and Björnsson were cut in half, which amounted to 500 000 SEK. This signalled that the nomination committee's expectations that the extra workload for the chair and deputy chair would begin to decrease. Still, the nomination committee, which was led by SEB Funds and AP2, decided that extra money was required 'as a compensation for the extensive work that these persons were expected to perform for Skandia in the coming year: something that was above and beyond their ordinary board duty'.[28]

As one of the last topics at the AGM, Magnusson presented the new incentive programme for Skandia, which was very modest compared to what had previously been the case. He asked shareholders rhetorically how much more they would be willing to invest in dealing with the old problems in the company. The cost thus far was roughly 200 million SEK, which Magnusson proposed was perhaps enough. However, Björnsson was to keep his previous assignment, in which he was in charge of handling these old disputes.

A dinner was planned for the newly formed board to take place the following evening, but three directors (Jeansson, Johansson-Hedberg and Ullberg) could not participate. At the dinner, Magnusson asked the present directors to formulate what would be Skandia's future path. Hammarkvist was the first to speak, saying that he expected 'peace and quiet' for the company so that its staff could do the necessary work to get Skandia back on track again. Gardell responded rather harshly. When outlining his picture, he supported Magnusson's position and promoted a more clear-cut shareholder-value perspective.

11.9 OLD MUTUAL PREPARES A BID

In the early spring of 2005, Old Mutual's two-year-old acquisition strategy had not delivered any results. Some financial analysts argued that Old Mutual simply could not afford the price that was required to bid for a UK life portfolio; the competition was too stiff. Moreover, as the analyst Greig Paterson at Keefe, Bruyette & Woods already had noted in an analysis of Old Mutual dated 15 February, Old Mutual's heavy stock exposure to the volatile South African rand was also a problem.[29] He claimed that if the rand fell back, it might prove to be an expensive strategy to finance a bid through loans. Old Mutual management had put itself in a bit of a bind: on the one hand, buying nothing and, therefore, being under pressure to return money to the shareholders would counter its growth strategy; on the other hand, being perceived to pay too much for a UK life portfolio would perhaps make shareholders just as worried. For Keefe, Bruyette & Woods, Old Mutual was a clear sell at a share price of approximately 130 pence and a market capitalization of €7 billion. At the time, many other financial analysts shared that view.

The investment bankers at Deutsche Bank were pressured to come up with a suggested deal for Old Mutual. Jan Olsson, head of Nordic corporate finance for the company, attempted to raise support from the local shareholder community in Sweden. He had asked Lars Lenner at Lenner & Partners to join the Old Mutual team in March. As mentioned earlier, Lenner had spent several months scouting for potential buyers of Skandia, yet he had not been able to come up with a single prospect. Therefore he accepted the task of acting as a 'door opener' for Old Mutual in the Swedish institutional investors' market. A few days before Skandia's April AGM, Old Mutual's CEO went to Stockholm to meet with Lenner. Sutcliffe then mentioned that he had positive contacts with members on the Skandia board, and revealed to Lenner that, in a matter of weeks, he planned to formulate a 'proposal' to Skandia. However, Skandia's April AGM passed without any talk of a structural deal. There was no mention of Old Mutual or any other of the interested parties. Therefore the Deutsche Bank team concluded that Old Mutual needed to take more action, arguing that nothing would happen unless it clearly revealed its cards.

Eleven days after the AGM, Deutsche Bank's Jan Olsson and Tony Burgess met Christer Gardell for dinner in Stockholm. They presented their plans to him. Olsson and Burgess also informed him about the letter that Old Mutual had sent to Skandia early in February, outlining an indicative bid of 40 SEK per share. They also told Gardell about their growing frustration with the process, and how the chair had just turned them down. Gardell stressed that the letter with the indicative price for the Skandia share must be taken seriously, although he added that he thought the figure needed to be much higher. If Old Mutual could present something more attractive for Skandia's shareholders, then Gardell assured the dinner guests that he would personally ensure that their proposal landed on the board's table. He also said that he preferred Olsson and Burgess contact him before presenting such an offer to the board.

Deutsche Bank put together a team of about 30 people, designating Tony Burgess and James Agnew as the team leaders.[30] Burgess had the task of getting Old Mutual's board to accept its bid on Skandia. Agnew was to work out in detail different bid proposals, including calculating the required capital structures and the risks associated with the ongoing litigations. It was also time to work out what was needed to make incumbent Skandia shareholders accept Old Mutual shares as part of the payment. Old Mutual appointed its corporate development director John Deane to be responsible for the entire process.

NOTES

1. Otto Rydbeck tragically lost his life shortly thereafter.
2. On behalf of the Skandia board, Björnsson kept the running contacts with Morgan Stanley.
3. Some board members, however, heard rumours during Christmas saying that Magnusson and Björnsson had talked with Morgan Stanley during the autumn, but that Jungkvist at Skandia HQ, who was in charge of financial strategy and M&A, was not involved. This was not in line with the standard procedure when Skandia dealt with investment banks. Jungkvist's colleagues had heard him complain about this in the corridors.
4. The planned project at Old Mutual received the code name 'Jacaranda'.
5. However, Old Mutual was mentioned as one of many interested parties in board material that was handed out at its meeting in February 2005.
6. In October 2005, Old Mutual mentioned in the prospectus for Skandia that in December 2004 discussions had already been initiated between Old Mutual and Skandia to investigate the potential benefits arising from some kind of combination of the two companies.

7. *Dagens Industri*, 27 December 2004, 'Gardell's hemliga plan för Skandia', Gustaf Tapper.
8. This was all in accordance with a contemporary governance ideal that encouraged board members to align their interests with those of the shareholders. Quite a few Swedish board members did just that.
9. In the 2004 Skandia *Annual Report*, the shareholdings were reported as follows: Magnusson 84 000, Björnsson 25 000, Hammarkvist 10 000, Jeansson 20 000, Johansson-Hedberg 13 200, Lindståhl 5 000 and Ullberg 25 000.
10. When the 2004 results were published on 28 February 2005, Skandia reported a net loss of 1.2 billion SEK.
11. On 17 June 2005, Skandia settled with the US Securities and Exchange Commission concerning the market-timing irregularities carried out at American Skandia; it cost Skandia $95 million.
12. The word 'turbo' was introduced by the motor-interested CEO. Hereafter referred to as the 'Turbo plan'.
13. Alfred Berg became part of Dutch ABN Amro 1995 and used that name after 2003. When ABN Amro was broken up in 2007, the old Swedish investment bank was split between the Royal Bank of Scotland and the Belgian–Dutch bank and insurance company Fortis, which was eventually dismantled and nationalized in 2008.
14. Known for his critical stand on the Skandia valuations made at the height of the IT bubble in January 2000.
15. There were also other such meetings during this period (e.g. with AXA and Storebrand).
16. Fredrik Lindqvist was according to the weekly magazine *Legal Week* the second most used adviser in M&A in Europe during 2006, the year the Old Mutual–Skandia deal was closed.
17. Credit Suisse First Boston. The name of this global banking group was changed in 2006 to Credit Suisse.
18. This was the third Skandia board meeting in 2005. The first was on 14 January and the second on 31 January. (The latter meeting dealt exclusively with the settlement issue with former Skandia chair Lars Ramqvist.)
19. Discounted cash flow is a theoretical valuation model commonly used by financial analysts.
20. Michaël Berglund Executive Search works with recruitment of top management and board members and is also used for board evaluations in Sweden.
21. Skandia 2004 *Annual Report*, p. 60.
22. Björgólfsson worked through the investment company Straumar-c, which cooperated closely with the Icelandic bank Landsbanki where his father Björgólfur Guðmundsson was CEO. Björgólfsson was the first among a group of successful Icelandic financiers to expand in the Nordic countries and the UK during the years 2003–07.
23. See note 10 in Chapter 8.
24. For three years, Hessius was CEO of the Swedish Stock Exchange/OMX and one of the deputy governors of the Swedish Central Bank. In 2004, she became CEO of AP3 after Tomas Nicolin, who had left for a position as CEO of Alecta.
25. The settlement was described in a one-page press release from the board dated 1 February 2005.
26. *Dagens Nyheter*, 19 March 2005, 'Alecta har sålt alla sina Skandiaaktier', Bengt Carlsson.
27. Förberg also voted for Icelandic Kaupthing and Burdarás.
28. Quoted from the press release from the AGM.
29. In spring 2005, the currency exchange rate was SEK100 = £7.4 and SEK100 = R114. Source: the Swedish Central Bank.
30. James Agnew had been working with Old Mutual's listing on LSE in 1999 while he was at Merrill Lynch.

12. An indicative bid leaks out

12.1 NEW ATTEMPTS TO CONTROL THE BUSINESSES IN THE UK

The already strained relationship between Skandia chair Bernt Magnusson and CEO Hans-Erik Andersson continued to worsen. Following the AGM in April, the CEO complained that the chair no longer seemed whole-heartedly to support his and management's efforts to integrate and coordinate the different regions. However, Andersson continued to work and argue for the need to close the gap between Skandia Life UK and the HQ in Stockholm. He wanted to implement the Turbo project's plans for substantial savings in the UK as well. Andersson made a list of 20 candidates ready to take positions in Skandia Life UK, including a candidate who could replace Nick Poyntz-Wright as CEO, in the event Andersson's efforts were met with resistance. Magnusson and his deputy chair Björnsson met the potential candidate, but concluded that he was not the right person for the job. However, the back-up process brought with it a renewed discussion regarding Andersson's ideas and plans both for Skandia Life UK and for Skandia as a whole. Even if the 'stand-alone' option remained the board's main way forward for Skandia, Magnusson wanted top management to work with other alternatives too; he argued that a structural solution represented both a possible and interesting path. He gradually began to regard the 'stand-alone' answer as more of a 'fall-back' solution for Skandia, necessary to explore if an attractive deal did not turn up. Institutional investors, as well as Skandia managers close to Magnusson, heard him describe the 'stand-alone' option as a rather weak case that was difficult for Skandia to develop successfully on its own. At the same time, however, Skandia managers also heard Andersson defend the stand-alone path, claiming it to be the best possible way forward.

As a newly elected board member, Christer Gardell quickly involved himself in vital Skandia matters and positions. For example, shortly after the AGM, he joined the director Karl-Olof Hammarkvist, the CEO Hans-Erik Andersson and the CFO Jan-Erik Back on the board of Skandia UK Holding.[1] Gardell also soon travelled to Southampton for a meeting on 3 May with the management of Skandia Life UK, who had approached

Gardell as a potential saviour of sorts, expecting him to work for a separation between Skandia and Skandia Life UK. However, Gardell found the UK situation troublesome. Once he was back in Stockholm, he spoke to Skandia board members and managers about Skandia Life UK, and stressed its differences. Moreover, he believed the UK management to be unreachable; he was stunned by their 'lack of loyalty' to the mother company. Gardell said that the UK managers did not express respect when he mentioned the name of Skandia CEO Hans-Erik Andersson, chair of the UK holding company.

While in London, Gardell also met with the management of Skandia Life UK's subsidiary, Bankhall. Gardell described Bankhall founders Paul Hogarth and Simon Taylor as seemingly not caring very much about the fact that Skandia had to write off its investment in Bankhall by 2 billion SEK. Instead, the two offered to assist Skandia in selling off Bankhall entirely. Hogarth and Taylor wanted 70 million SEK as a recompense for that contribution. Andersson complained loudly and requested support from Magnusson, who willingly supported the CEO and said a definitive no Hogarth's and Taylor's suggestion. Gardell just shook his head. Back in Stockholm, Gardell agreed with Andersson's suggestion that the greater part of the UK management team had to be dismissed. However, his conclusion was the same as that of Magnusson – the risk of losing sales and 'momentum' was too high to take immediate action.

12.2 OLD MUTUAL ENTERS THE ARENA

When he was in London, Christer Gardell also met with Old Mutual's CEO, Jim Sutcliffe. Sutcliffe had been briefed on Gardell's track record as a successful activist investor on the Swedish market. Now the Old Mutual staff saw Gardell as a potential door opener or catalyst for some kind of 'corporate solution' regarding Skandia. A telephone conference between Bernt Magnusson, Christer Gardell and Hans-Erik Andersson had already been set up for 5 May, Ascension Day, which is traditionally a holiday in Sweden. Gardell conveyed to the others by phone that it was obvious from his meeting with Sutcliffe that Old Mutual was interested in bidding for Skandia as a whole and, at the time, the price range was in 'the upper forties per share'. Gardell added that Sutcliffe had mentioned a price of 48 SEK, to be paid entirely in cash, and to Gardell this was an interesting level.

Following the informal telephone conference on 5 May, Magnusson and representatives from Morgan Stanley returned to Lenner and Deutsche

Bank. Magnusson told them that they had to come up with a written indicative offer. He had informed Sutcliffe by phone that their February proposal of 40 SEK per share was not going to be supported by Skandia's board; Old Mutual needed to put a more attractive figure on the table. At the time, Magnusson, Gardell and Andersson were allocated the task of handling any further contact with Old Mutual, Deutsche Bank and Lenner & Partners.

In early May, Skandia's investment bankers Morgan Stanley had accumulated a long list of interested parties, although Old Mutual was first in line as the sole party that aimed to bid for all of Skandia. There was also a board meeting on 10 May, in which Magnusson informed the other directors about a possible proposition from Old Mutual. One of the board members then asked Magnusson when it was that he had first spoken to the company, and Magnusson replied that it was in late January, at a meeting with its CEO Jim Sutcliffe. He also said that it was a discussion that included Björnsson and Andersson. Then board member Johansson-Hedberg appeared irritated since Magnusson neglected to mention the early letter from Old Mutual (dated 23 December 2004). Magnusson replied that, at the time, there had been so many investment bankers running around presenting cases that he could not be expected to keep track of every single one of them.[2]

Other board members were concerned as well. Anders Ullberg said that the arguments for a structural deal were rather weak – he still preferred the Skandia 'stand-alone' case. At this stage, he said, he was not interested in participating in discussions regarding Old Mutual or any other bidder. Jeansson stated that he supported Ullberg's criticism of the review process that Magnusson wanted Morgan Stanley to conduct. He added that everybody was welcome to present a formal bid for Skandia. If Old Mutual really wanted to talk to Skandia, they should come back with a proposition, Jeansson concluded.

On 12 May, which was the day after Old Mutual's AGM in London, Deutsche Bank invited the trio to Morgan Stanley's office in Stockholm. During the week, the contact had become rather intense between Skandia (Magnusson, Gardell and Andersson), Old Mutual (Sutcliffe, Roberts and Deane), Deutsche Bank (Olsson, Burgess and Agnew) and Lenner & Partners (Lenner).

At the time, the broader business community was once again reminded of Skandia's unstable shareholder base. After the April AGM, eight financial institutions were in control of 25 per cent of the shares: Fidelity, Cevian, the Icelandic investors Kaupthing and Burdarás, AP2, and the Swedish retail funds SEB, Robur and Nordea. All were more or less open supporters of Cevian's conclusion that it could be beneficial for Skandia to participate in a structural deal within the insurance industry. On 4 May, *Dagens Industri* published an article entitled 'Speculators trying to grab what they can of Skandia',[3] which described the entry of several new shareholders in Skandia. Finnish capitalist Björn Wahlroos, along with his financial house Sampo, was back on the Skandia scene again. So was Sven-Olof Johansson, who was renowned in Sweden for a raid on the truck company Scania in the early 1990s. Sheïk al-Ahmoudi and Third Avenue Funds also appeared as investors in Skandia. *Dagens Industri* further reported on rumours of Gardell being on a tour promoting a plan to break up Skandia and sell it off in parts. The media presented Magnusson as prepared to split up the company, whereas Andersson was reported to be holding back such plans. The article in *Dagens Industri* ended with the claim that many financial analysts following the Skandia case thought the ongoing legal disputes might curb any and all attempts to change the company's strategy for the time being.

12.3 STRUCTURING A CROSS-BORDER BID

In early May, Magnusson invited Sutcliffe in amicable terms to present a 'Letter of interest' in Skandia. As a listed company on the LSE, Old Mutual was keen to comply with UK takeover recommendations. The difficult task was to design an indicative bid that was attractive to both its own shareholders and to those at Skandia. Moreover, a bid from Old Mutual for Skandia would represent a European cross-border takeover attempt, and there were often problems associated with such mergers. For example, there were complications connected with the different shareholder bases that, from a financial perspective, often built on local and regional stock markets. This would reduce the interest of accepting a bid from a foreign actor. As over 50 per cent of the Skandia shareholders were of Swedish origin, an Old Mutual–Skandia deal would represent such a takeover attempt. The UK company, of course, was well versed in all these difficulties, which would be exacerbated as Old Mutual had a large South African shareholder base that made up 50 per cent of its ownership. This would have implications for Old Mutual's ability to finance the bid through a rights issue, for example, since South Africa had a currency regulation. Therefore Old Mutual's bankers from Deutsche Bank and Merrill Lynch had to tread carefully when designing a bid that was attractive and would create positive momentum around the Old Mutual stock, so that its market capital would rise and make the bid even more attractive to both Skandia's shareholders and incumbent Old Mutual shareholders.

To achieve positive momentum, Merrill Lynch's investment banker

Michael Findlay claimed that the bid had to attract arbitrageurs, such as hedge funds and a broader group of European investors. The former path would enable incumbent Skandia shareholders (who were not interested in owning Old Mutual shares) to sell their Skandia shares at a good price to hedge funds that were willing to exchange their Skandia shares for Old Mutual stocks. The latter path implied making the Old Mutual share rise through an intensive marketing of the 'technical matter', that a merged Old Mutual–Skandia stock would represent an increased market capital, and therefore be switched to another stock market index. That would make the share attractive to a broader group of European investors than had previously been the case.

Merrill Lynch had worked on similar cross-border deals before; for example when in 1999 British/American Tobacco merged its financial services business with Zurich, a Swiss-based financial conglomerate. But that was in 1999, and this was before the hedge funds had emerged as 'lubricants' on the stock market. Another more recent example was from mid-2004, when Banco Santander bid for Abbey National. The investment bankers had then changed their way of designing a bid in order to make use of the substantial resources controlled by hedge funds. The Spanish bank offered €8.5 billion for the UK bank in what was then regarded as the largest ever cross-border banking deal in Europe. The bid process dragged on with 'long only' shareholders in Abbey National eventually selling off their shares. The buyers were predominantly hedge funds, trading at the valuation gap between the two companies. They bought the Abbey National stock and short sold Banco Santander shares. Just before the deal closed, about 40 per cent of the Abbey National shares were in the hands of hedge funds. With the experience gained from working on this deal, Merrill Lynch argued that the bid for Skandia should be financed largely by an issue to Skandia shareholders of new Old Mutual shares. With such a design, it would be easier to attract the hedge funds as takers of the Old Mutual stocks in which the Swedes were not interested in investing, and were thus expected to sell.

For the Old Mutual camp, the financing of a bid was a crucial matter. In May, its market capitalization was €7 billion. A bid for Skandia amounting to approximately €4.2 billion would be dilutive to Old Mutual's shareholders. If fully financed through a rights issue, this would lead to an approximate 36 per cent reduction in statutory profit per share, a 19 per cent reduction in embedded-value profit per share and a 10 per cent fall in embedded value per share.[4] A bid financed by debt was just as difficult for Old Mutual; it had only €250 million in cash outside South Africa. Management had estimated that it could raise a further €750 million without triggering a negative reaction from the credit-rating institutes.

However, incurring more debt than that was simply out of the question. Because of South Africa's exchange control regulations, it was also difficult to forecast how much money Old Mutual could transfer out of its business in that country. Old Mutual was also already transferring capital to its US Life operations. Acting in a way that would worry credit-rating institutes Moody's and Fitch – and risk a downgrade – could severely hurt the business. Thus the main goal for Old Mutual, Deutsche Bank and Merrill Lynch was to find the right balance between cash and shares.

The investment bankers also worked hard with the index question. In May 2005, Old Mutual's exposure to UK investors was still quite small, since 50 per cent of its shareholder base was situated in South Africa, and was trading shares on the Johannesburg Stock Exchange. Old Mutual in London was included in the Morgan Stanley Capital International Emerging Markets Index, where the UK institutional investors were underweight in shareholding in Old Mutual. With Skandia on board, however, the Old Mutual share would be switched to Morgan Stanley's Life Insurance Index. In such a case, Old Mutual would be traded against European top insurers, with the UK institutions 'automatically' increasing their exposure (to achieve a neutral exposure[5]). The investment bankers further argued that an acquisition of Skandia might increase the investor community's general interest in Old Mutual. Despite fund supermarket awards, its UK franchise for unit-linked products Selestia was too small to have an impact on investors' and financial analysts' valuation of the Old Mutual stock. Thus they speculated that Skandia's fast-growing life portfolio could attract new investors to Old Mutual and narrow the 'valuation gap' between Old Mutual and the rest of the European life insurers. Moreover, for Old Mutual shareholders, an expected re-rating of its share could, in part, compensate for a dilution.

The Old Mutual team also had plans for how to attract Skandia's shareholder base. For some time, Merrill Lynch had marketed Old Mutual to European investors, which included many Swedish prospects. The outcome of that effort created some optimism that there might be an interest among Swedish investors in becoming Old Mutual shareholders, albeit most of them would probably sell anyway. Skandia's shareholders, of whom at least half were Swedish, were not 'natural' holders of Old Mutual shares. Therefore the risk of issued Old Mutual shares flowing back into the London market might worry many of its existing investors and put further pressure on the Old Mutual share. Thus it was important to come up with a bid that was so attractive that these Swedish investors remained shareholders while, at the same time, making it possible for them to exit if necessary. That would shift the Skandia shareholder base in favour of an offer.

12.4 OLD MUTUAL'S PROPOSAL LEAKS OUT

Deutsche Bank had put Old Mutual in touch with the Swedish PR firm Kreab, a communication consultancy firm known for its political contacts.[6] Kreab's senior adviser Göran Riegnell was assigned to assist Old Mutual in connection with its Skandia proposal. On 10 May 2005 James Poole, director of investor relations at Old Mutual, invited him to London. There, Riegnell met CEO Sutcliffe, who informed him about Old Mutual's interest in buying the whole of Skandia. Sutcliffe declared that Old Mutual intended to present a tentative bid, and then wait for the board's evaluation of it. The Skandia board was expected to come with a recommendation to its shareholders. If it were positive, Old Mutual would proceed and make a formal and public offer. Old Mutual's stated ambition was to bring forth a friendly bid, as it was what the board had wished, and believed to be best for the development of the company's share price (it also complied with the Anglo-Saxon tradition). In the meantime, Kreab's task was both to make Old Mutual known to the Swedish public, and to promote the intended offer.

Riegnell remained in London the following day to attend the Old Mutual AGM on Wednesday 11 May. The plan for a Skandia bid, however, was not mentioned at that meeting. Old Mutual's official message was that a deal in the UK was 'not paramount' as its businesses in the UK and the USA were performing well. On the morning of 12 May, Skandia's director and CEO met with Sutcliffe and Old Mutual's group finance director Julian Roberts at Morgan Stanley's office in Stockholm. There, Gardell and Andersson received a paper with a confidential indicative bid (Old Mutual was named 'Opal' and Skandia 'Stone'). Two options were presented: 48 SEK in Old Mutual shares or 45 SEK in cash. The possibility of a split between the cash and the share component, where the former would land between 50 and 66.7 per cent of the total offer, was added to these figures. Skandia was trading that day at 33 SEK per share, so the premium was approximately 40 per cent. The proposal also included two provisions: the right to start exclusive talks with Skandia, and the opportunity to conduct a due diligence. The Skandia group was asked to reply to the Old Mutual team. Both Gardell and Andersson were given a copy of the indicative bid, and both expressed the view that the 45 SEK cash bid was too low. There was also disappointment with the 48 SEK offering, having turned into an all share offer. They left without making any further comment.

Andersson returned to Skandia after lunch, where he received a call from an actor in the financial community who wanted to confirm a rumour he had heard about a bid from Old Mutual. About that time, *Dagens*

Industri received information about a forthcoming bid from Old Mutual for the whole of Skandia.[7] A reporter from the paper phoned Magnusson to see what his reaction would be to the name 'Old Mutual'. Magnusson responded by saying that it was a South African insurance company, which indicated that he was not particularly well informed about it. Early in the afternoon of 12 May Magnusson summoned a telephone conference about Old Mutual's bid plans. These talks involved Björnsson, Gardell, Andersson and Jungkvist. The participants concluded that the indicative price of SEK 47–48 was lower than what had been stated on 5 May. A full board telephone conference was set for the following morning. It was also a discussion about other possible offerors on Skandia. Magnusson should contact Nordea, AXA and Friends Provident, and Björnsson Swedbank, DnB, and Storebrand. Magnusson also made a courtesy call to Sutcliffe, who asked him to try and obtain a clearance from the board for a due diligence.

That same evening, other actors in Stockholm told another reporter at *Dagens Industri* the same story about Old Mutual, but the newspaper decided not to publish it. Several actors on the financial markets had also heard the story during their late-evening flights. The *Financial Times* also picked up the story, but it was too late for it to go out in the paper edition, so the UK daily published the article on its website early the following morning (13 May). This spurred *Dagens Industri* to go ahead and published its own article on the online web edition as well. It stated that Old Mutual's bid was expected to value Skandia at 50 SEK per share. The *Dagens Industri* article also suggested that Skandia had opened its books for Old Mutual to conduct a due diligence, and that Morgan Stanley was assigned to plan an auction to invite other bidders.

In the London morning trade on 13 May, the Old Mutual share lost almost 3 per cent on a stock market that was, for the most part, static. In Stockholm, trading in Skandia shares was suspended until the stock markets received statements from Skandia and Old Mutual. The early Skandia board (telephone) meeting was very crowded, since it included certain members of top management and advisers such as Morgan Stanley, as well as lawyers who were called in to listen. The Old Mutual indicative offer was communicated as a 'friendly' one; the South African company wanted to strike a deal only if the Skandia board supported it.

Old Mutual's indicative offer for Skandia was subject to several conditions. First, Old Mutual should be allowed to perform limited due diligence on Skandia, since its indicative bid was based solely on public information. The accounting in a life insurance company can be complicated and not very transparent, since estimates are based on assumptions that are difficult to evaluate from public information alone. Therefore such material was argued not to be sufficient. Second, there had been ongoing litigations and investigation in Skandia. Hence Old Mutual management believed that it was necessary to conduct a due diligence. However, this was a controversial issue for Skandia since it meant opening up the books to a competitor.

During the aforementioned phone conference, lawyers Robert Ohlsson and Gunnar Nordh of FöretagsJuridik Nord & Co. provided a legal analysis. Ohlsson had continuously conducted such work for Skandia, concluding that Swedish legislation did not provide any obstacles for a board to approve a due diligence process. However, several board members were still reluctant to accept such a procedure in Skandia. Lennart Jeansson stated that he did not want Skandia to open its books at all. He argued that Old Mutual – if it were seriously interested in Skandia – should first present a formal bid to the shareholders. The directors believed that providing such exclusivity to one particular competitor was most inappropriate. The board concluded that it was too early for Skandia to give Old Mutual (or any other party) clearance to conduct a due diligence. Instead, the board asked Morgan Stanley to oversee a structured process where other actors were also invited to present their indicative bids. The delicate question of due diligence was to be dealt with all through May (although a first decision in the process had already been taken at the board meeting on 13 May).

The public confirmation that 'something was going on' came early on 13 May, when official statements confirmed that Old Mutual and Skandia were, indeed, in preliminary discussions that might or might not lead to an Old Mutual offer. When the trade in Skandia shares resumed, the price rose by 7 SEK to 41.6 SEK – 20 per cent – in only two minutes. Conversely, Old Mutual's share continued to slide, losing 5 per cent of its market capitalization during the day, and closing at 122 pence (the LSE indices did not move that day).

In a brief interview published on the *Dagens Industri* website that afternoon, Magnusson did not acknowledge Old Mutual as an interested party at all. Rather, he emphasized that Skandia was a 'beautiful bride with many parties interested in dancing' and that 'there had been many contacts throughout the year'. Magnusson was also quoted as saying: 'It takes two to tango.' Furthermore, he said, there was no disagreement among board members: 'There has been complete unity in the board from day one.'[8]

The leaking to the press continued.[9] The following day, *Dagens Nyheter* ran a lengthy story on the bid,[10] which proposed that Old Mutual could actually bid as much as 48 SEK per share, but could end up buying only

Skandia Life UK. Magnusson was said to be pushing hard for a solution in which Skandia participated in the consolidation of the European financial sector. It was assumed that he kept a rather tight grip on the process. The article also stated that there were opposing sides within the Skandia board, and that Morgan Stanley was contracted to find alternative buyers of the company, although Old Mutual had already initiated a due diligence (that, however, was not correct – it started in June). The *Dagens Nyheter* article also listed the companies that it speculated might want to get involved in a bidding process as well. Nordea was mentioned as the most likely buyer of Skandia's Nordic business, while Hartford Financial, American AIG, French AXA and Swiss Zurich Financial Services were all considered possible bidders for Skandia Life UK. Other newspapers ran similar stories. On 14 and 15 May, *Dagens Nyheter*'s stock market commentator Bengt Carlsson claimed that Old Mutual's leaked indicative bid was too low, lamenting that actors looking for a quick profit from selling the entire Skandia group – or parts of it – surrounded the company. His conviction was that, even without a strong owner, Skandia could have conquered the world.[11]

12.5 SCEPTICAL MEDIA

In London, intensified investor scrutiny and negative media coverage reflected the drop in the Old Mutual share price. On 14 May, the *Financial Times* commented on rumours of a possible deal between Old Mutual and Skandia. A paragraph of the Lex column[12] read:

> One week is a long time in politics. Two days, it appears, is a long time in insurance. At Wednesday's annual meeting and after several years on the deal trail, Old Mutual gave the impression that a UK acquisition was no longer of paramount importance. Therefore, the news on Friday [two days later] that the South African financial services group was in early negotiations with Swedish insurance company Skandia was quite a surprise.

The Lex column concluded by commenting that a purchase of the whole of Skandia at a rumoured cost of around £3.5 billion 'would be a difficult morsel to digest'. If so, the column continued, Old Mutual could pay about £1 billion in cash, but would probably have to raise fresh capital. At Friday's closing of 122 pence, this meant issuing stock 10 per cent below embedded value, the Lex column commented. Meanwhile, Skandia (after having jumped almost 20 per cent) traded at a 50 per cent premium to embedded value. The Lex column concluded that the deal did have some strategic merits, but not sufficient to justify such challenging arithmetic.

A bid for the UK business alone would financially and strategically make more sense. If Skandia was intent on selling itself in one piece, the article surmised that Old Mutual was not the most obvious suitor.[13]

In an analyst note, Citigroup's South African branch warned shareholders both of an immediate dilution of about 20 per cent in Old Mutual's embedded value per share, and a dilution between 3 and 14 per cent of embedded-value earnings per share if it was forced to pay more than 45 SEK. On the other hand, Citigroup analyst Johny Lambridis was generally negative about the future of Skandia.[14] Some of Old Mutual's shareholders[15] in both South Africa and the UK immediately expressed reservations regarding the bid. Fund manager at Jupiter Asset Management[16] Philip Gibbs, who held 2 per cent of Old Mutual at the time of the leak, said, 'these talks look very difficult to justify for Old Mutual'.[17] Based upon stock market rumours, Gibbs regarded the planned deal as a very adventurous one. To him, the whole issue was built on Old Mutual's ambition to rid itself of its heavy South African exposure. On 19 May, *Svenska Dagbladet* quoted Gibbs as saying that Old Mutual should get out of the deal and, that if its CEO Sutcliffe continued to push for it, he would have to go.[18]

Euan Stirling of Standard Life Investments[19] – a company that controlled 1 per cent of the Old Mutual shares – was negative, as were actors from Morley Fund Management.[20] Due to the limited financial resources at Sanlam Investments[21] (Old Mutual's largest private shareholder with 4.2 per cent of the capital), its analysts were also sceptical. Hendrik du Toit, CEO of Investec Asset Management[22] – a company that owned less than 1 per cent of Old Mutual – was also circumspect, while awaiting more information. Mark Webster of State Street Global Advisors,[23] also a shareholder in Old Mutual, commented to the media that he thought a forthcoming deal was unlikely.

Some of Old Mutual's shareholders also expressed worry that its management would end up in a bidding war for Skandia, and then greatly overpay for its portfolio of life contracts. They confirmed, however, that there was synergy in the UK, although there was not in the Nordic and continental businesses. The South African investors were particularly concerned about the financing of the bid. With the exchange control regulations, the Reserve Bank might restrict South African participation in a share issue. Given the fact that Old Mutual was trading at a discount to embedded value, and considering Skandia's current valuation, the dilution for the South African shareholder base might turn out to be quite substantial.

Rodney Alfvén, head of equities research at CAI Cheuvreux Nordic,[24] did not yet believe in a structural deal, explaining to the *Financial Times*:

'Skandia has legal issues in US, plus an arbitration procedure with Skandia Liv in Sweden. And, although these items probably do not involve any large sums of money, I think that Skandia would like to get them out of the way before a structural deal can happen.'[25] Andrew McNulty of UBS in South Africa was quoted in the Swedish press as saying: 'they'll buy the whole of Skandia because it's the chance they have. But as time goes by, they will probably sell off [its] Nordic [business] since they lack experience over there.'[26] Other analysts conveyed more supportive views: Greig Paterson of Keefe, Bruyette & Woods in London was quoted in the South African press, claiming that Old Mutual could acquire Skandia without raising too much new capital. Anonymous analysts were referred to as speaking about Skandia Life UK as 'the jewel in the crown' and the supposed disinterest of Skandia in selling off only that part.[27]

With the exception of the analysts' reports, in mid-May the media was the only other actor category that focused on Old Mutual. This coverage introduced the previously unknown company to the large population of small investors. The voices of the information officers of the company were the first to be heard. *Dagens Industri* interviewed James Poole, head of investor relations at Old Mutual on 17 May, who described the company's interest as sincere. He further projected an image of a future Skandia that would be run with marginal improvements, rather than being the target for numerous split-ups. Poole also mentioned that Old Mutual planned for Skandia to continue as some kind of listed company. In the same article, references were also made to information from UK newspapers, which stated that Old Mutual had difficulties with some of its shareholders regarding how to finance a deal. The two companies were almost equal in size, so Skandia was a 'big bite' for Old Mutual to swallow.

Dagens Industri reported further details of the discussions within the Skandia board in its 17 May edition. According to the newspaper, a work committee had been formed with the purpose of handling Old Mutual's proposal. It consisted of Chair Bernt Magnusson (speaker of the group), Deputy Chair Björn Björnsson and Director Lennart Jeansson. The media further reported that Old Mutual's CEO had been at Skandia's HQ the previous Thursday.[28] Deutsche Bank was mentioned as Old Mutual's adviser, and Morgan Stanley was reported to have been leading a team of advisers who were preparing to go through Old Mutual's economic standing in order to provide Skandia's board with a better platform upon which to showcase its analyses of the offering (and for its recommendation to the shareholders).

On 18 May, Burdarás reported an increase in its holding in Skandia by roughly one percentage point, ending up with a 4.4 per cent stake. Burdarás's CEO, Fridrik Johansson, refrained from discussing Skandia in the media, although he admitted to the press that he did not think that the company was valued properly. Three days after the *Dagens Industri* article featuring Old Mutual manager James Poole, its CFO Julian Roberts gave his first interview to the Swedish press. The interview was published in *Dagens Nyheter* and included a short presentation of the company. Roberts also stated the arguments behind the proposal – namely growth and risk diversification – and diminished dependence upon South Africa.[29]

Business journalist Bengt Carlsson ran a lengthy article in *Dagens Nyheter* on 22 May, where he discussed different kinds of valuations of Skandia. Christer Gardell's rumoured evaluation from the autumn of 2004, which indicated a price between 60 and 70 SEK was one of those listed. Another valuation was reported to supposedly come from ABN Amro.[30] It suggested a much lower price: approximately 48 SEK. Carlsson further reported that one Skandia director had said that the latter value 'sounded reasonable', which was in accordance with the rumoured Old Mutual offer. Carlsson presented Gardell's higher valuation (especially that addressing its life arm) to be very uncertain.[31] A few days later, the 25 May edition of the *Financial Times* reported that Morgan Stanley had received a mandate to invite companies to also bid for parts of Skandia.[32]

A new and cautiously interested party appeared on the scene on 31 May: Nordea. Its CEO Lars G. Nordström stated in a *Dagens Industri* article[33] that the bank was looking at Skandia. However, he clarified that Nordea was still far from presenting some kind of bid for Skandia (or parts of it). In Nordström's eyes, Skandia was not the 'beautiful bride' about whom Magnusson had spoken. More than six months had passed since Nordea had started working seriously on the Skandia case. The bank had done a feasibility study that addressed the potential acquisition of the Nordic and UK parts of the company, which had been presented at an executive management meeting back in March. But at the time, it was too risky to bid for all of Skandia with the aim to sell off parts afterwards. Therefore it quickly became obvious to Nordea that the best strategy was to wait until Skandia came up with an offer to buy only its Nordic arm. Once the rumours about the bid became widely known on 13 May, Nordea's managers expressed almost shock at the price: close to 50 billion SEK. They did not believe that anyone wanted to pay that much for the troubled Skandia.

12.6 A BOARD AGREEMENT ON THE TURBO PLAN

During the entire spring of 2005, Skandia's CEO and his management team had worked on making the company capable of 'standing alone'. The Skandia board had asked the team to present a revised Turbo plan at the board meeting scheduled for August (i.e. after the summer holidays). However, the date was changed to 30 May as a consequence of the leak of Old Mutual's serious interest in purchasing the company and the rising Skandia share. Therefore Magnusson asked Andersson to have the Turbo plan prepared for presentation at that upcoming board meeting. This meant that those involved in preparing the Q1 figures, to be published on 31 May, had to speed up the work on the Turbo plan.

At the 30 May board meeting, CEO Hans-Erik Andersson and CFO Jan-Erik Back described the Turbo plan in a 15-page slide show based on material that Skandia had compiled with the assistance of the consultancy firm, Monitor. The Turbo plan indicated cost and revenue savings estimated at a total of approximately 1.2 billion SEK. The effects of the plan were expected to be seen in 2006 and 2007. Once again, however, the management of Skandia Life UK objected. Before the meeting they had sent a letter to the board expressing their negativity to the plan, arguing that the Turbo plan was nothing more than a revised version of McKinsey's Glue plan. The latter contained projected cost reductions of 600–900 million SEK, and revenue increases of 200–300 million SEK. Thus the Glue plan added up to 0.8–1.2 billion SEK, which was not very far off the estimated Turbo plan mark. The UK managers still argued these cost reductions were not realizable.

The negative views of the Skandia Life UK management worried its board of directors. One of its independent directors, Ashok Gupta, expressed his concern to Skandia's chair, arguing that the small HQ in Stockholm was not equipped to fulfil its ambition of gaining control over its UK operations. The Skandia board discussed the UK problem at the 30 May meeting, where the deputy chair said that he lacked confidence in the Skandia Life UK management in general, and the Bankhall staff in particular. In this case, he claimed, the Turbo plan was unachievable. Magnusson was also hesitant about some of the specifics of the plan. The material and handouts from the Morgan Stanley advisers supported a similarly pessimistic view, indicating that most of the effects of the Turbo plan would probably not show up in Skandia's bottom line and stock market price until after 2010. The advisers added that the financial community would appreciate such a plan only if (and when) it materialized in the hard work of the Skandia management. In the eyes of investors, it is action that creates value for a company, they claimed.

The Morgan Stanley material also included calculations of Skandia's value: both the FTV from February 2005 at 34–38 SEK, and the takeover break-up value at 43–48 SEK. The board also tried to estimate the 'Cevian effect' on the Skandia share price. Before the Old Mutual leak in May, Skandia was trading at around 36 SEK. If one were to consider the

'Cevian effect' from December 2004 and the stock market development since then, Skandia's share price would most likely have been around 31 SEK in early May 2005.

The other board members elected at the AGM – Christer Gardell, Karl-Olov Hammarkvist, Lennart Jeansson, Birgitta Johansson-Hedberg, Kajsa Lindståhl and Anders Ullberg – were all positive when it came to the Turbo plan, and offered their full support. By the end of the meeting, Magnusson had also agreed to it and concluded by saying that the plan should be put into practice. The board decided unanimously to endorse it. Then they turned their attention to the delicate issue of whether Skandia should open its books, so that (serious) potential bidders could conduct a limited due diligence.

NOTES

1. In 2005, it was unusual for a listed company in Sweden to have its directors on its subsidiaries' boards.
2. Old Mutual's name had figured in Morgan Stanley's board material as of 14 January and 22 February, but was not specifically highlighted. The name of Old Mutual had not been discussed.
3. *Dagens Industri*, 4 May 2005, 'Spekulanter i huggsexa om Skandia', Karin Svensson. Several other papers ran similar stories.
4. All according to an analysis by Keefe, Bruyette & Woods on 13 May, the day the bid was leaked.
5. On the stock market, the performance of most fund managers is evaluated by an index composed of a group of stocks, which makes the choice of index extremely important for the investments made. Also, many pure index-tracking funds buy all the stocks included in the relevant index.
6. With the conservative party (Moderata Samlingspartiet).
7. On 29 March 2009, six people were prosecuted by the state attorney in Stockholm in what has been described as the largest ever insider-trading network on the Nordic stock market. Through 60 insider deals during 2004–06, mostly on the SSE, some 5 million SEK grew to 150 million SEK. One of the trades involved Skandia and the press leak on 12 May. In the winter of 2008, it was revealed that one of the employees at Cevian had called *Dagens Industri* and the *Financial Times* in the afternoon of 12 May about a possible Old Mutual bid. The Cevian employee then emerged as the central actor in the net. When the investigation began Gardell immediately fired his employee, denying any knowledge of insider trading. In the summer of 2008, a Morgan Stanley employee was also included in the investigation, on the grounds that he might have leaked information to the Cevian employee (a close friend) concerning work that Morgan Stanley was pursuing on bids. One of the leaks involved Morgan Stanley's work with Skandia in May 2005.
8. *Dagens Industri*, 14 May 2005, 'Magnusson: Det finns många friare', Karin Svensson and Jan Wäingelin.
9. There was a great deal of speculation about Skandia during May and June; at that time, it was the most publicized company in Sweden (source: Affärsdata).
10. *Dagens Nyheter*, 14 May 2005, '50 kronor per aktie räcker inte', Bengt Carlsson.
11. *Dagens Nyheter*, 15 May 2005, 'Skandia kunde erövrat världen utan stark ägare', Bengt Carlsson.

12. The *Financial Times*'s daily column with three or four unsigned short commentaries on occurrences in listed companies around the world.
13. *Financial Times*, 'Lex column: Old Mutual/Skandia', 14 May 2005.
14. *Citigroup*, 31 August 2005, 'Old Mutual: Skandia Negotiations Drawing to a Close', Johny Lambridis.
15. As of 28 February 2005, Public Investment Commissioners of the Republic of South Africa (PIC), part of the South African public pension system, was the largest investor in Old Mutual with 13.3 per cent; Old Mutual Life Assurance Corporation with 7.1 per cent; Barclays with 4.2 per cent; and, Legal & General Investment with 3.4 per cent (source: *Old Mutual's Annual Report* 2004). At this time, UK-based institutional investors held 41 per cent of the Old Mutual shares, and (mainly) South Africans controlled 59 per cent.
16. The Bloomberg News quoted one of the UK's leading fund management groups, along with other investors, in its 17 May 2005 edition.
17. *Financial Times*, 14 May 2005, 'Old Mutual confirms it is in talks to buy Skandia', Lina Saigol and Rupini Bergström.
18. *Svenska Dagbladet*, 19 May 2005, 'Kritik i Old Mutual mot Skandia-bud', Jan Almgren.
19. A globally active network of investment companies, affiliated with the Scottish Standard Life Group.
20. A UK-based asset management company and part of the Aviva group.
21. Sanlam Investments consisted of some of South Africa's leading private investment and wealth management businesses.
22. A listed UK–South African specialist investment bank and investment manager.
23. State Street Global Advisors is an institutional US-based investor with $1.9 trillion in assets under management.
24. A full-service broker within the French Crédit Agricole group and a wholly owned subsidiary of Calyon. The Nordic arm is present mainly in Sweden and Norway.
25. *Financial Times*, 14 May 2005, 'Old Mutual confirms it is in talks to buy Skandia', Lina Saigol and Rupini Bergström.
26. *Dagens Industri*, 19 May 2005, 'Budet möter motstånd', Joakim Adler.
27. *Business Day*, 16 May 2005, 'Old Mutual targets Swedish assurer Skandia', Stephen Gunnion.
28. Possibly referring to the meeting at Morgan Stanley's office on 12 May.
29. *Dagens Nyheter*, 20 May 2005, 'Old Mutual vill växa med Skandia', Bengt Carlsson.
30. The analysis referred to by *Dagens Nyheter* was ABG Sundal Collier, 16 May 2005.
31. *Dagens Nyheter*, 22 May 2005, 'Kontroversiella siffror i plan för styckat Skandia', Bengt Carlsson.
32. *Financial Times*, 25 May 2005, 'Suitors circle Skandia in hope for a break-up', Lina Saigol and Andrea Felsted.
33. *Dagens Industri*, 31 May 2005, 'Vi tittar på Skandia', Kim Lundin.

13. Summer of due diligence

13.1 DIFFERENT OPINIONS REGARDING OLD MUTUAL'S INDICATIVE BID

In May 2005, Morgan Stanley had a list of at least 20 different financial houses that had knocked on Skandia's door. Thus Old Mutual was far from being the only company that had written letters to the chair of the board, although it was the only one that had thus far showed an interest in bidding for Skandia as a whole. Analyst reports supported the rumour that Skandia was the target of a bidding contest. Analysts from ABG Sundal Collier,[1] Espen Bruu Syversen and Sigmund Håland, released a report on 16 May; in their analysis, Skandia as a stand-alone company was valued at 39 SEK per share. Their break-up value added up to 47 SEK per share. However, the ABG analysts wrote: 'this could prove conservative if other bidders enter the field . . . we cannot see it being valued at much less than SEK 50 per share in a takeover/break-up scenario'.[2]

On 13 May the board reconvened at Skandia's HQ. Bernt Magnusson had talked to Old Mutual's CEO the day before, and had been asked to try to obtain clearance from the board for Old Mutual to go ahead with conducting a due diligence. Magnusson had promised to raise that issue at the meeting. The board discussed the current situation of a structural deal becoming more and more of a reality. However, Birgitta Johansson-Hedberg saw no such fit between Old Mutual and Skandia. Karl-Olof Hammarkvist and Kajsa Lindståhl expressed scepticism regarding the due diligence proposal, and Anders Ullberg foresaw problems if Skandia were to give information to a competitor that, in the end, did not buy the company. Lennart Jeansson shared Ullberg's view, adding that he had nothing against Old Mutual, but wanted a 'binding offer in the market' before Skandia could open its books to them. Moreover, there was already a great deal of available information since Skandia was a listed company that had been continuously scrutinized by market actors.

However, Magnusson argued in favour of a due diligence. He claimed that because there was a written indicative bid at 48–50 SEK per share when it had been traded at 33 SEK, which had suddenly rushed up to

41.60 SEK on the day of the leak, this should motivate the board to let prospective buyers look into Skandia. He (and other board members) stressed that it was the board's duty to find out if there were structural deals that might generate a higher total value for the current shareholders. He thought that Skandia could probably expect other bidders besides Old Mutual. Thus it was appropriate to invite them, as well as other interested buyers, to take a closer look at Skandia and conduct a due diligence (a decent price presupposes competition). The other board members agreed. Magnusson was of the opinion that Morgan Stanley's calculations indicated that Skandia – with the right bidder – could be valued quite a bit higher than 50 SEK.

The board meeting that took place on 30 and 31 May gave Andersson the green light to carry on with his Turbo plan. Old Mutual's due diligence request was again cautiously discussed. Morgan Stanley flew in its own leading expert in takeover processes to that meeting: its partner Paulo Pereira, who explained to the board that due diligence was standard practice in international deals of this kind.[3] However, Lennart Jeansson was not convinced by his presentation. He said that he had never heard of a bidder conducting a limited due diligence on a listed company, and that he had vast experience of buying listed companies from his time at Volvo. Anders Ullberg also argued against it, saying that he did not understand the rationale behind putting Skandia – a company that was in the midst of a turnaround – up for sale. Birgitta Johansson-Hedberg agreed, but Christer Gardell was of a different opinion. He argued that, with a bid premium of 25 per cent, it was the board's duty to open the books. As he saw it, the board also had to consider the legal repercussions; there could be a danger of further lawsuits if Old Mutual's request were not handled properly, since a board's refusal might result in shareholders becoming stuck with a value of the company that is too low.

As a result, the due diligence issue was a difficult one to solve.[4] Old Mutual had informed the board that the company would walk away if it were not allowed to carry out such a procedure. Legal adviser Robert Ohlsson was called in on the matter, but he did not make any decisive recommendation. He primarily argued that both alternatives were legitimate.[5] The veritable risk of a dramatic drop in the Skandia share price if Old Mutual should withdraw its indicative bid was a main theme in the discussions that ensued. As the leak on 12 May had sent the share up above 40 SEK, one could assume that many shareholders preferred a 'safe haven' for Skandia; in other words, a sale, as Morgan Stanley described it during its May 31 presentation. Many analysts' reports supported Morgan Stanley advisers in their concern for the Skandia share. For example, Greig Paterson at Keefe, Bruyette & Woods[6] argued that the share would fall, possibly as far back as below 30 SEK.

After some hesitation the sceptical board members, Hammarkvist, Jeansson, Johansson-Hedberg, Lindståhl and Ullberg, decided to accept a due diligence. As a consequence – at the end of May – a united board decided that Morgan Stanley should invite relevant and interested parties to come up with indicative 'bids'[7] for Skandia: in whole or in part. In addition to Old Mutual, there were approximately 20 prospective buyers that would be granted the right to conduct a limited due diligence. The board also asked Morgan Stanley to establish an 'auction' where constructed consortia, too, would be given the opportunity to present bids for the whole or parts of Skandia. The board's instructions were firm: it did not want to end up with a Skandia that did not include its UK business, and management concurred with this view. Moreover, Morgan Stanley would be required to put together an information package that included the company's business plan, the old 'Glue' documentation and a copy of the Turbo plan, including the fresh valuation of Skandia's embedded value that the consultancy firm Tillinghast had prepared. Therefore Morgan Stanley's retainer agreement from December 2004 was revised, the signing of which this time involved the entire board. A special committee was formed in order to handle the differences of opinion among the directors regarding the upcoming deal process; Magnusson, Björnsson, Jeansson and Andersson formed this committee.

Andersson informed Magnusson about his thoughts on the auction process, saying that he did not believe Morgan Stanley would be able to bundle together groups of bidders in different consortia. He told Magnusson that it was too early to sell Skandia, that the company should be properly turned around first, and that any talks of structural affairs made the company lose momentum. Andersson further argued that it was almost impossible to construct a bidding situation for different parts of a company in only a few short months. He believed that Skandia could not be split up that fast, especially since its operational structure differed significantly from its legal structure. Furthermore, there were no separate balance sheets for the different units, and it was difficult to identify which unit would have to cover the costs such as those that had been incurred by the ongoing litigation issues (note: at the time, they were ascribed to the HQ in Stockholm). However, regardless of his opposition, Andersson did not convince Magnusson that these problems were big enough to change the decision.

When the Q1 report was published on 1 June, the CEO did his best to portray a confident leader. *Dagens Industri* quoted him as saying at the press conference following the two-day board meeting:

> We have a good strategy and can manage [Skandia] on our own but when structural proposals emerge, it is the board's duty to evaluate them. Many interested parties have showed up, but we hope this situation [of uncertainty] will not last much longer. In the end, it is up to the shareholders to evaluate all the alternatives. If there will be a deal, I wish that it will be one that [also] benefits both customers and employees.[8]

Andersson also expressed confidence in Skandia, saying that the company was doing better. The Q1 report conveyed a profit before tax of 386 million SEK: twice as much as the same period a year before. Premiums were up 7 per cent to 27 billion SEK, and new sales of unit-linked policies were up 15 per cent. The trend was up on most markets, including in the Nordic region; however, the Swedish market was still lagging. The market share for new policies had fallen to 14 per cent compared to 16 per cent a year earlier.

13.2 THE SUITORS

The assignment of the Morgan Stanley team was to construct a market for indicative 'bids' for parts or the whole of Skandia. Judging from the media reports and analysts' notes, the list of contact names was quite extensive.[9] For Morgan Stanley advisers, there was a very real possibility that, in the end, Old Mutual would be the only actor interested in bidding for Skandia as a whole. However, they also argued that they could construct consortia of companies that would bid for different parts of the company. They saw the most reasonable idea as splitting Skandia into three distinct parts: the UK, the Nordic region, and the rest of the world (which included continental Europe and Latin America). Then, each potential bidder could look at the part (or parts) of the company in which it was interested, without collaborating with other companies in the quest for Skandia. This first phase of the auction process was based mainly on public information, with some assistance from the company. The procedure was complicated and the outcome was unsure; however, it would at least give the Skandia board a reference value of the company: a 'second opinion' regarding its estimated FTV of 34–38 SEK.

Morgan Stanley sent a letter on 9 June to all potential Skandia owners, asking each bidder to submit confidential, indicative and non-binding initial proposals including information regarding how each of the bids would be financed. They were also asked to provide the board's confirmation of the proposed acquisition(s), with a submission deadline of 16 June 2005. All the proposals were to be addressed to Jakob Lindquist, c/o Morgan Stanley's London offices. Approximately ten actors responded in writing. Several of the responses said 'no, thank you'; others expressed various more or less distinctly formulated preferences for buying certain parts of the company.

Some of the actors that expressed serious interest also attached specific reservations. The private equity firm 3i[10] particularly eyed Skandia's UK business, yet expressed some concern about future competition in the UK savings market. The firm also voiced worry regarding the need for additional investment required to support Skandia's future growth. Therefore 3i provided only an indicative price that included a discount to the trading value in mid-June (around 40 SEK). The Wallenberg-controlled private equity firm EQT displayed its interest through its EQT IV fund; however, it said that it was too early to indicate a price, given the particular circumstances surrounding a private equity firm when it considers bidding for an insurance company. The company requested to remain as a bid candidate and later – if eligible – be given an opportunity to explore possible partnerships with other potential buyers.

Several other candidates stated a more dedicated interest in bidding for the whole of Skandia or various parts of it. The Norwegian (partly) state-controlled bank DnB Nor – advised by JP Morgan – indicated its interest in Skandia's Nordic division, and added that it might also consider buying Skandia's banking business, its mutual funds business, and its Nordic division's business distribution rights. Nordea, with HSBC's assistance, also eyed Skandia's Nordic division; however, its six-page reply was littered with reservations. The bank found the planned process of a Skandia being spilt up and sold in various parts especially 'complex', particularly when it was uncertain whether Skandia Nordic would ultimately be available at all. In spite of this, Nordea still put forth an indicative price between 10 billion SEK and 14.5 billion SEK, which was to be paid entirely in cash.

Another candidate particularly eyeing Skandia's Nordic business was Storebrand, the Norwegian-listed life and savings group,[11] which expressed some enthusiasm concerning the entire Nordic division. The company also displayed interest in both Skandia Life UK's Norwegian and Finnish operations, indicating that it might consider a transaction that involved solely the Nordic division's life insurance operations. Storebrand valued Skandia's Nordic division at 15.7 billion SEK, with Sweden and Denmark alone being valued at 12.7 billion SEK, and Skandiabanken at 3 billion SEK. Central costs, tax shields and legal disputes were to be subtracted from the offer, thus shaving off 2.8 billion SEK. The main issue, however, was Storebrand's ability to finance the bid. The company presented three alternatives: shares in a combined Storebrand/Skandia Nordic division; cash; or a mixture of cash and shares. A cash offer would, therefore, include a rights issue for Storebrand shareholders; investment banks ABG Sundal Collier and UBS were to aid Storebrand in that process.

Four bidders focused their June work on three specific Skandia entities: Skandia Life UK, Asia Pacific and the offshore segments. All four companies experienced difficulty in defining their respective interests and implications of their indicative offers. Dutch Aegon[12] stated its indicative value for Skandia Life UK at approximately £1.1 billion, excluding the Swiss, Australian and Chinese businesses. According to its advisers (UBS), these three businesses could be worth close to SEK 1.4 billion – if they were sold separately. Aegon refrained from pricing costs attributed to the joint group activities at the Skandia HQ. Friends Provident[13] of the UK also put in a bid for the same UK, Asia Pacific and offshore segments, with an indicative price of £2.2 billion. The bid would then be split between Skandia Life UK, Royal Skandia and Asia Pacific, which were valued at £1.15 billion (1.5 times its embedded value); Switzerland was valued at £700 million (1.0 times its embedded value). Friends Provident did not plan to keep the Norwegian and Finnish businesses, and was likely to sell the Swiss business as well. It referred to its adviser Merrill Lynch for any further discussion. The bid would be financed by a combination of cash and a rights issue to shareholders in Friends Provident.

Great-West Lifeco (Great-West[14]) from Canada was the dark horse in the contest. It never figured in the speculations but became one of the keener suitors. Great-West's proposition was twofold: one part referred to the UK, Asia Pacific and offshore segments (with a combined valued of 16–18 billion SEK); the other concerned the German and Austrian operations (with a combined valued of 3–5 billion SEK). But the bid also included several reservations: Bankhall's debt, which amounted to 2.6 billion SEK, was to be absorbed by the mother company, and legal costs, as well as synergies, had yet to be considered. The company engaged HSBC as its adviser (which now meant that HSBC was working for both Nordea and Great-West Lifeco on this matter). French AXA, assisted by its adviser Goldman Sachs, came up with two proposals. The main one involved the Europe and Latin America segment, which included the UK, the Asia Pacific and the offshore segments (its total value was estimated at 27.3 billion SEK, of which the UK made up 70–75 per cent). The other concerned the UK and Bankhall businesses, which had an indicative value of 14.6 billion SEK. Both bids excluded costs that stemmed from joint group activities that took place at Skandia's HQ. AXA stated that a possible offer would be made in cash, and that it wanted to keep the Skandia brand for at least two years.

Almost all potential bidders expressed some reservations in their letters. They found the auction process confusing, and did not understand whether or not the sales process was a serious one. For example, Lindquist paid a visit to Nordea in early May to ask whether Nordea wanted to make a proposal. Jakob Grinbaum said that Nordea was going to submit an indicative bid only if the process was a serious one. He was not interested in participating in the process if Old Mutual was already destined to win; nor was Nordea interested in delivering a free fairness opinion regarding Old Mutual's bid. Therefore Nordea suggested to Lindquist that its costs for putting a bid together should be partly paid by Skandia itself, a procedure sometimes applied when investment bankers want to ensure that a sufficient number of actors participate in an auction. Lindquist spoke to Skandia about Nordea's suggestion; however, Skandia rejected it.

Old Mutual was the only actor that came up with an indicative bid to buy the whole of Skandia. Its CEO Sutcliffe sent the offer on 16 June 2004. He was the only bidder who addressed the letter directly to Skandia's chair. Sutcliffe outlined in his letter a common future for the two companies, with the same proposal as that of 12 May; the total offering was composed of two-thirds cash and one-third new shares. The cash part was to be financed through internal sources, new loans and an underwritten marketed equity offer to Old Mutual's shareholders. Synergies were identified as 'over' £100 million. The net present value of these cost savings was estimated to be approximately £570 million, the equivalent of 21 per cent of Skandia's market capitalization at the time. Half of the savings were expected to be realized during the first year (2006), with the full effect on earnings in 2007. These estimates, however, were subject to a further due diligence process.

Sutcliffe also wrote that Old Mutual had no plans to divest any of the Skandia businesses, and that it planned to offer Skandia's management continuous positions within the combined company. He also said that there was a need for approval from South African authorities in order to raise share capital, mentioning that, immediately before the announcement of a formal offer, the company would seek acceptance of the offering (that is to say, irrevocable undertakings from shareholders representing at least 30 per cent of Skandia's stock). Old Mutual's plan was to announce its formal bid on 22 July. An initial three- to four-week acceptance period for Skandia shareholders would then follow, with a final acceptance day set for late August (a possible extended acceptance period would delay announcing the acquisition of Skandia until September). Sutcliffe added that, in his opinion, the merits for Skandia's shareholders, policyholders, management and other stakeholders were compelling. He further expressed an interest in being given the opportunity to present his vision and all the benefits of a combined company to the Skandia board, and address any of its concerns. He said he looked forward to hearing from

Magnusson after Skandia's 21 June board meeting, and to moving to the more detailed second phase of the process.

Several letters that had been sent before 16 June indicated the potential bidders' difficulty in understanding exactly what parts of Skandia had been included in their proposals. The operational structure of Skandia matched neither its juridical construction nor its accounting procedures. Another problem was how to treat Skandia's HQ. None of the bidders was able to determine which bidder would take responsibility for these costs: who would foot the bill for all of Skandia's liabilities? There was also the uncertainty associated with the mutual society Skandia Liv, and how to evaluate all the ongoing changes in its relationship with Skandia. Moreover, there were tax issues that made it difficult to separate Skandia's Nordic business from its HQ. Another kind of complication arose when it became apparent to the actors that the lead bidder in any consortium would have to take responsibility for the HQ in Stockholm, which was troublesome since the Nordic region was connected to Stockholm. The bulk of the company was Skandia Life UK, so the expected consortium leader would be whichever company bid on that large UK business – and probably, the actor would not be interested in having the HQ in Stockholm. Irritation among bidders also grew as Morgan Stanley asked triple A[15] financial players, such as Nordea, to submit written letters of intent that were to be signed by their respective CEOs stating: 'x has a sincere interest in Skandia and the financial and managerial capability to finance a bid.'

13.3 A DIFFICULT BOARD MEETING

Before the board meeting on 21 June, Magnusson had invited the nomination committee chair, Björn Lind of SEB Funds, to express his views regarding Skandia's future to the other directors. Long before, Magnusson had asked Lind to collect information from other influential shareholders, from members of the nomination committee as well as several others. Magnusson wanted Lind to find out their interest in participating in a structural deal, and issues related to such a path (i.e. preferences regarding stock or cash payments, attitudes to foreign shareholding etc.). In May and June Lind broached the issue in meetings with many of the larger shareholders. He also received some information from those at Morgan Stanley. Lind then met the Skandia directors just before the formal board meeting, and told them that the market did not believe in a stand-alone case for Skandia, and that market actors worried about Skandia's decreasing market share in Sweden. His conclusion was that investors in general wanted Skandia's participation in a structural deal, and that investors had expressed full confidence in the board's work. Björnsson and Gardell both expressed discontent about many of the other board members' continuously negative attitude towards a due diligence process. Magnusson did not comment on the issue. Some of the 'negative' board members said that they could not help but notice how worried he looked when it came to their lack of understanding about this new opportunity that might, as he believed, benefit both Skandia and its shareholders.

Morgan Stanley made a presentation of the indicative bids to the Skandia board at the 21 June meeting. Skandia Life UK received a high value, with AXA offering the highest bid. Allianz offered to pay the most for Skandia's European business. However, the bidders on the Nordic business dashed the hopes of both the Skandia board and Morgan Stanley. Nordea mentioned 10 billion SEK in its offer, revealing a multiple of approximately 1.2 times book value, which was less than Storebrand's 12.7 billion SEK. Those who knew Skandia best, it seemed, offered the lowest price. The Morgan Stanley team noted in its discussions with Skandia directors that both Nordea and Storebrand put a low value on Skandia's Nordic operations; perhaps this was done with the intention of conveying a picture of a weak Skandia. Moreover, it appeared to them that Storebrand lacked the sufficient funds to make a full bid.

The combined offer from Nordea and Great-West came to 34–38 billion SEK, while the combined offer from AXA and Storebrand totalled a gross value of 49 SEK and a net value of almost 45 SEK. Thus the best-constructed total price offered by these 'bidders' for a split Skandia did not outdo the price that Old Mutual had indicated that it was willing to pay for the whole company. Lindquist assured the Skandia board members that he and the adviser firm were still confident about the process. Some board members, however, expressed growing scepticism.

The board discussed revising the Morgan Stanley engagement letter at the same meeting. The mandate for Morgan Stanley became to sell Skandia, topped with a transaction fee according to the value of a future structural deal. On behalf of the Skandia board, Björnsson prepared the agreement with Morgan Stanley, which stated that Morgan Stanley this time should receive compensation for advisory service and announcement fee for its work in the auction process.[16] If a deal were struck to sell Skandia, Morgan Stanley would receive 20 basis points[17] – up to 36 SEK. The latter figure was the FTV that was presented to the board back in February 2005. As a consequence, Morgan Stanley would receive 72 million SEK if there were a bid in the amount of 36 billion SEK. For every extra SEK over and above this number, Morgan Stanley would receive one additional basis point: that is to say, another 10 million SEK. The transaction fee was capped at 250 million SEK.

Jeansson noted that this agreement was expensive and, as Hammarkvist had said, he complained that the process had been concluded without competition. Gardell said that it was a ridiculous amount to pay to Morgan Stanley. Jeansson continued his criticism, stating that it was not acceptable for Morgan Stanley to receive a transaction fee starting already at the level of 36 SEK per share when the Skandia share was trading above that level (close to 40 SEK). Instead, Jeansson suggested that an extra fee should be paid to Morgan Stanley if a bid were to come in above 40 SEK per share. Two Swedish financial advisers, Stefan Erneholm and Stefan Haskel, were called in to deliver a second opinion on the Morgan Stanley engagement letter. They said that the pricing structure in the letter was in accordance with standard practice; Skandia's own M&A expert Per Jungkvist said roughly the same thing. However, Jungkvist added that he was not satisfied with the work that had been done by the adviser. As a consequence, Morgan Stanley devoted more people to its Skandia project. The minutes from 21 June meeting showed that the board intended to continue with its engagement of Morgan Stanley, but with a few amendments. Morgan Stanley was to receive an extra fee only if a bid came in above Skandia's current share price: 40 SEK. The board gave Björnsson the mandate to return to Morgan Stanley to try to make the proposed changes to part of the contract.

A story broke the board meeting day that Robur, Swedbank's retail funds, had sold almost one quarter of its holding, following the leak of Old Mutual's interest to the *Financial Times* and the subsequent rise in the Skandia share. Marianne Nilsson, head of corporate governance at Robur, was interviewed in *Dagens Industri*[18] saying the transactions were a 'capital management decision', referring to Robur's large exposure in Skandia (its stock had risen in comparison to other financial stocks listed on the SSE).[19] Nordea's retail funds were also reported to be among those selling off Skandia shares; these made substantial gains from the rally subsequent to the short suspension of trade in Skandia shares on 13 May 2005.

On 27 June, *Affärsvärlden*[20] ran a story about Skandia's Turbo Plan on its website, stating: 'Skandia management has put forth an ambitious growth strategy for Skandia called the Turbo plan'.

> However, the Skandia board had chosen instead to pursue the plans of selling or splitting the company. The Turbo plan has been operational for at least two months, and includes ideas about how the company should get rid of its old federative-like structure with highly independent subsidiaries, as well as tools for a tighter relationship between Skandia's HQ and the management at Skandia Life UK. The Skandia management, however, still lacks clearance from the board to implement the plan. Instead, the priority of the board

> presidium,[21] including Chair Magnusson and Deputy Chair Björnsson, is to carry on, with the help of the investment bank Morgan Stanley the initiated sales process. South African Old Mutual is in Stockholm this week to meet institutional investors in an attempt to gain support for its position as a future serious and trustworthy owner of Skandia as a whole – or in part. During the Midsummer holiday, *Affärsvärlden* has spoken with a number of people close to Skandia who all give the same picture of a management that lacks support from its board to pursue a strategy for an independent growth company, if needed flavoured with the Turbo plan.

The piece ended with a note that the reporter had spoken to actors who ascribed much more value to Skandia than was reflected in the share price. Former CEO Björn Wolrath was quoted, among others, as saying, 'In my world, Skandia should be trading around 100 SEK a share. But then, Skandia's shareholders must be ready to wait a while.'

13.4 A LETTER FROM FIDELITY

Towards the end of June 2005, most actors close to the bidding process recognized that Old Mutual was the most serious contender, and the only one with genuine interest in buying the whole of Skandia. On 27 June, Old Mutual's managers went on a 'road show' to Sweden, organized by Deutsche Bank and Lenner & Partners. This involved the CEO, his staff and his advisers travelling round to various companies and presenting Old Mutual to prospective Swedish investors. Sutcliffe stated that he wanted the Swedish shareholders, who held 54 per cent of Skandia's stock, to also become shareholders of the 'new' Old Mutual. Therefore he planned for Old Mutual to have a secondary listing on the SSE with the intention of making it easy for Swedes to retain their shares. For example, the CEO and CFO presented their case to representatives from AP2 over lunch at Deutsche Bank's office in Stockholm. AP2's CIO Petter Odhnoff, and Carl Rosén, who was responsible for its corporate governance activities, concluded in their analyses that Skandia needed an industrial partner. Therefore they expressed their support of Old Mutual's effort.

Deutsche Bank's team saw that Old Mutual's plan was running smoothly. Actors from several insurance companies and banks colonized Skandia's 'data room', which had been formally set up to facilitate the limited due diligence process. Both Old Mutual and Deutsche Bank actors, however, concluded that most of these activities only represented attempts to establish an impression of fierce competition. After a while, the Old Mutual camp, which included Jim Sutcliffe, Julian Roberts, Lars Lenner, Jan Olsson and several others, concluded that the company was rather alone in the Skandia contest. Sutcliffe and Roberts began to talk about offering Skandia's CEO the position of running the company's integration into Old Mutual. Old Mutual was ready to provide a binding bid; however, the due diligence process dragged on.[22] Old Mutual believed that the delay had to do with the differing opinions on the Skandia board. That was partly true, but the suggested (complicated) auction process also contributed to the delay. Therefore the early summer passed without any positive sign from the board regarding an Old Mutual solution.

Morgan Stanley prepared for the delivery of a fairness opinion during the first week of July.[23] This regarded the various valuations of (parts of) Skandia that had been received. The adviser continuously kept this information updated. Since the adviser had a vested interest in the sales process, the Skandia board terminated Morgan Stanley's mandate pertaining to the fairness opinion. However, engaging another investment bank in order to deliver a second opinion proved difficult. All interested parties had already engaged most of the qualified investment banks. In the end, ABN Amro signed up. The mandate was formally addressed at the 5 July board meeting, when the board also decided that this information should be kept confidential.

Dagens Industri interviewed Magnusson on 9 July. He concluded that 'nothing can force us (Skandia) into a structural deal'. He also told the reporter that he was in continuous talks with some of Skandia's largest shareholders, and that there was also a good dialogue between the members on the board.[24] However, it was known within Skandia that Magnusson, Björnsson and Gardell had run into trouble in their quest to sell Skandia, since Old Mutual's interest was conditioned on a Skandia board recommendation. Magnusson tried to encourage Jeansson and Ullberg, in particular, to change their sceptical views on the merits of the proposed bid. However, Jeansson became even more negative as time passed, delivering increasingly harsh comments to Morgan Stanley regarding the limited due diligence process. At the same time, some board members suggested that Skandia, in turn, ought to perform a counter due diligence on Old Mutual, as its share were (part of the) payment in the bid. But Gardell did not support this idea, saying that he did not want Skandia's time and resources spent on such an effort. Other board members talked among themselves about how they found this position strange, considering Gardell's strong support for Old Mutual's due diligence on Skandia.

In early July, Gardell contacted Skandia's largest shareholder, Fidelity International, and spoke with Trelawny Williams, who was responsible for Fidelity's corporate governance activities. Fidelity had supported Gardell's membership on the Skandia board. Gardell now conveyed to Williams that Fidelity's view of Skandia's future would be a valuable input into the process. On 12 July, the chair of the nomination committee called Williams with the same request. Björn Lind's impression from what he had heard in the public, read in the papers and learned from Magnusson was that it would be very helpful for the Skandia board if its largest shareholder expressed its view on the case. Lind asked Williams if Fidelity could state its opinion.

Later that day, Williams called Magnusson and expressed his concern about the development of the Skandia case. Williams also asked him for advice on the matter. Magnusson suggested that Williams write him a letter in which he expressed his views and concerns so that Magnusson could share it with the board. Later that day, Magnusson received a fax from Williams stating that Fidelity International believed Skandia lacked the scale and critical mass to play a leading role in the future insurance industry. Magnusson read the letter to the board members on a conference call the following Monday. Magnusson's conclusion from his communication with Fidelity was that Skandia's largest shareholder would support a sale of the company. He also told the board that Fidelity would support Old Mutual as a buyer. Magnusson regarded the letter from Fidelity as important since it came from one of the largest mutual fund managers in the world.

Fidelity's role in Swedish companies had historically been that of a passive investor, supporting the managements of the companies in which it invested, or voting with its feet if there happened to be a dispute about the strategic direction or other similar matters. However, Williams concluded in July 2005 that it was justified to support the path that Skandia's chair and others had advocated. He had already done that at the AGM in April, when Fidelity supported the board membership for Christer Gardell.

Fidelity's written support gave Magnusson the strong backing he was seeking in his ongoing attempt to attract more public bids for Skandia. SEB Funds, Cevian and Fidelity were in control of approximately 16 per cent of the Skandia shares. If Burdarás and AP2 were added to that figure, the shareholders that supported the sale of the company would be more than 20 per cent. The letter from Fidelity, however, did not alter the position of those board members who were sceptical.

13.5 LENGTHY DUE DILIGENCE

The second phase of the auction process took place in July, vacation time in Sweden. During this time, however, those companies that were actively participating in the Skandia bid were invited to obtain certain privileged information. There were also presentations on a management-to-management level, which became quite time-consuming. Lawyers, accountants, consultants and investment bankers all gathered in the data room at the offices of Gernandt & Danielsson, a law firm situated a few blocks from the Skandia HQ. All were invited to go through any information that Skandia and Morgan Stanley had provided. Such an arrangement is known in the industry to last usually no more than two weeks. In this case, the room stayed open for well over a month.

Skandia's top management, which included Andersson, Jungkvist, Back, Vos and Bexhed, spent a great deal of time handling the delicate due diligence process and setting the limits on what information should be made available to the bidders. After all, most of the companies that were given access to Skandia's data room were competitors. The problem was that most firms just kept asking for more and more information. Andersson protested the detailed level of these requests, and did not like relinquishing that much information to competitors – particularly when no deal was certain. Furthermore, he argued that information overload could have an adverse effect on the potential buyers. Andersson also disliked the fact that the process dragged on for so long, which he found to be both time-consuming and potentially disastrous for the company.[25] Moreover, Andersson claimed that such a long due diligence might actually become a self-fulfilling sales process. Andersson informed Magnusson of his numerous concerns. Magnusson agreed that the procedure was problematic and asked him to be very cautious – but not so cautious that serious parties decided to walk away.[26]

The entire summer passed, with Skandia top management keeping its eye on the bidding process and worrying about its consequences. This took much of the team's focus away from the company's day-to-day matters, which meant, for example, that Gert Engman was left running the Nordic region on his own, having very little contact with Andersson.

13.6 ATTEMPTING TO SELL PARTS OF SKANDIA

Bernt Magnusson adopted a particular routine as a way of involving board members in the second phase of the bid process that ran during the summer vacation. Every Monday morning, there was a one-hour telephone conference that involved all members of the board as well as all invited investment bankers and lawyers – approximately 25 actors. Magnusson, Björnsson and Jeansson attended every meeting. Several other board members participated less regularly (one director did not participate at all).

This second phase of the bidding process was even more complex. After analysing the outcomes of the first tentative round, Morgan Stanley began to organize the bidders in 'synthetic' consortia. A problem then was that the members in the consortia did not know who the others were. For example, Nordea was never informed about the other members in 'its' consortium, although its investment bankers from HSBC had figured out that Nordea was originally put in a consortium with German Allianz. However, Allianz soon backed out of the race; therefore Nordea was put in a consortium with AXA close to the end of the process. Nordea's CFO Arne Liljedahl told people around him that he disliked this process, which he likened to a blind date. As was already apparent in the preliminary round back in early June, none of the potential bidders in these 'blind' consortia wanted to take on the costs of the Skandia HQ, or even share them. The information provided in the data room did not eliminate that uncertainty either.

Nordea representatives met some of the Skandia's Swedish management at the Morgan Stanley offices in mid-July. Skandia's CFO Jan-Erik Back attempted to present an intelligible picture of Skandia's rather complicated federative-like structure, with a Skandia Life UK partly interconnected to the HQ in Stockholm. For Nordea's representatives, however, this presentation only added to the bid's uncertainty. They also saw Gert Engman, Head of Skandia's Nordic region, as an opponent rather than an ally.

Skandia Life UK was the jewel in Skandia's crown. Analysts, including those at Deutsche Bank and Morgan Stanley (whose coverage was suspended since the firms were on active mandates with Old Mutual and Skandia), had been unequivocal in pointing to the UK operations as the most attractive part of Skandia. In their analyses, Skandia Life UK was valued at approximately 20 billion SEK: half of Skandia's total value. In late July, at least four interested parties met with representatives from Skandia Life UK in London and Skandia in Stockholm.

Old Mutual invited Skandia Life UK's management to its London office in an attempt to show that Old Mutual was a company run by actors as professional as those at Skandia Life UK. Old Mutual's head of corporate development, John Deane, spoke to the CEO of Skandia Life UK, Nick Poyntz-Wright, underlining the fact that Old Mutual was listed in the UK, that it had access to capital, and that it had a well-qualified UK-based management team. Above all, Old Mutual had the Selestia platform (a Skandia Life UK copy); their core platforms complemented each other. When summarizing, Old Mutual's actors judged these talks as successful. Similar comments could also be made about Great-West, whose management team visited the Skandia HQ in Stockholm. Morgan Stanley later grouped Great-West with Nordea and, on 18 August, confirmed one of the final bid constellations.

Friends Provident, another competitor for Skandia Life UK, also met with the company's management. These two UK companies knew each other well. Friends Provident had considered bidding for Skandia Life UK, thus becoming part of an initial theoretical consortium. Initially the bidder that considered paying the most for Skandia, Friends Provident now suddenly walked away. A final binding bid was never to appear.

AXA was a fourth potential bidder that also met with Skandia Life UK, appearing with a massive team of lawyers, accountants and investment bankers. They heavily outnumbered the Brits, who only showed up with a management team of six people (and one lawyer). Morgan Stanley hosted the meeting, represented by three advisers. According to the French delegation, the most 'junior' member of Morgan Stanley's staff did most of the talking. The AXA delegation (including its CFO Denis Duverne) was surprised – if not downright insulted – by the meagre representation from Morgan Stanley. The UK management team had predicted that AXA would be the end for a semi-autonomous Skandia Life UK and cut their staff (around 2000 employees) substantially. As they listened to the French presentation, their suspicions were confirmed. AXA's managers delivered long speeches about how the company had been catapulted from nowhere to becoming a success. They also presented plans for a possible takeover of Skandia Life UK. Their ideas, however, did not sit at all well with the UK management, who made their opinions clear (to what they perceived to be a group of arrogant Frenchmen). AXA had intended to take the UK business model, to which it would add its distribution power. The UK response was: 'What distribution power?' The Brits looked at AXA's plan as an intention to 'destroy and integrate'. AXA walked away from the whole bid process immediately following these discussions, completely put off by the disrespectful attitude they perceived. AXA's CFO Denis Duverne contacted Skandia's chair to confirm this exit. Morgan Stanley kept calling AXA, but the company never returned the calls.

During this second phase of the due diligence process, the European part received a rather low value. The bidders found it very difficult to evaluate the many start-ups in Europe. Therefore there didn't appear to be anyone interested in purchasing Skandia's continental European operations.

NOTES

1. A Norwegian listed investment bank that focuses on equity research and corporate finance.
2. ABG Sundal Collier, 16 May 2005, 'Skandia; Old Mutual's flirt just the beginning?' Espeen Bruu Syversen and Sigmund Håland.

3. Some sceptical directors later complained that the Morgan Stanley expert had talked to them as if they were 'cousins from the countryside', understanding nothing of what was going on outside Sweden. They even felt insulted.
4. See, www.naringslivetsborskommitte.se. These rules were in place in 2003.
5. No Swedish rules could, however, force Skandia to open its books since they allowed plenty of room for the board to decide for itself. Swedish takeover rules regarded due diligence as exceptional action, so a decision not to accord a due diligence was probably more common in that country. At the same time, however, takeover rules in Sweden stipulated that a board should accept it if a bid seemed interesting enough for the shareholders to take part in – also because a refusal might worsen the conditions for making an offer. Such a decision could, therefore, sometimes be regarded as an illegitimate measure. This somewhat inconsistent description of the regulatory situation did not clarify the issue for the sceptical directors, so they did not know where to turn. Sorting out what the board considered to be best for the company's (divided) shareholders proved a delicate matter. The Skandia board was situated in a squeezed position between a bidder requesting due diligence, and the unknown will of the majority of the company's shareholders (that might or might not prefer business to be conducted as usual).
6. Keefe, Bruyette & Woods, 13 May 2005, 'Old Mutual's talk with Skandia: beginning the end game?', Greig Paterson and William Hawkins.
7. The word 'bid' will be used although these offerings represent informal price indications rather than formal bids.
8. *Dagens Industri*, 1 June 2005, 'Skandiachefen hoppas på snar strukturaffär', Martin Hammarström.
9. A listing that is based upon what was communicated in analysts' reports and media speculation includes many (potential) actors. Some of the mentioned insurance companies were:

    - AXA, the French insurer and, according to the investment bank Keefe, Bruyette & Woods, the most obvious counter-bidder for the entire group. On the positive side, AXA seemed to favour greater scale in unit-linked business. On the negative side, there was the possible cultural clash between the French and the UK management.
    - ZFS, Zurich Financial Services, had recently highlighted strategic orientation to unit-linked business in Europe.
    - Friends Provident, a UK financial services group that might be interested in Skandia Life UK. There would be a good fit both operationally and culturally; however, there might be a problem with financing.
    - Prudential, an UK group, might be interested in a global player or just the UK part. Analysts thought that this suggested merger might not work culturally.
    - Legal & General was thought to look at Skandia's UK business, but analysts deemed it to be a less likely buyer since the company had already invested money in linking up with a co-funds multi-manager platform that had a similar offering as Skandia Life UK.
    - Aviva, a UK life and insurance company that was interested in pan-European growth.
    - Storebrand, the Norwegian life insurer that was looking for expansion abroad. The problem was probably a lack of financial strength.
    - Allianz, one of the world's largest life and insurance companies located in Germany with previous Skandia manager Carendi in charge of its unit-linked division.
    - AMB-Generali, a German insurance group.
    - Mediolanum, a leading Italian financial and insurance group partly owned by Finivest, an investment group controlled by the Silvio Berlusconi family.

Possible banks included:

- Nordea, certainly an obvious candidate for the Nordic business, given its well-known interest in the Swedish life market. It also had the financial strength to deploy money into a new growth area.
- DnB Nor, among the other Nordic banks known to be looking for growth opportunities in Sweden; it had even bought a small shareholding in Skandia during the spring.
- Swedbank, a Swedish bank that had been looking at Skandia before.
- Danske Bank, a Danish bank expanding in Sweden.
- Kaupthing, the Icelandic bank had showed interest for Skandia and bought a few per cent of its shares. The general view was that it was eyeing Skandiabanken, Skandia's successful Internet bank valued at approximately 4 billion SEK. Kaupthing's shareholding was sold during the first week of July.

10. At the time, one of the leading global private equity firms focusing on everything from buyouts to growth capital to venture capital.
11. Storebrand had a history of deals with Skandia: bidding for the group in a highly publicized and hostile affair in 1990, as well as a part owner of the joint P&C division, If Insurance: sold to Sampo in 2004.
12. One of the world's largest insurance companies and the sixth largest in the UK.
13. A life assurance business mainly based in the UK.
14. Great-West was one of the leading Canada-based life insurance companies with a market capitalization of US$19.5 billion. It had acquired London Insurance Group in 1997 and Canada Life Financial Corporation, with a presence in Germany, in 2003.
15. 'Triple A' denotes the highest available rating for commercial debt issuers.
16. Morgan Stanley had several different engagements with Skandia during these years.
17. A basis point is a rather commonly used term for a tenth of 1 per cent.
18. *Dagens Industri*, 21 June 2005, 'Robur säljer efter Skandias uppgång', Karin Svensson.
19. Robur's sale was a classic fund reallocation decision since, during this period, it decided to reduce its exposure to the financial sector, and since Skandia was the only performing stock in that category and valued with a premium it was sold off first.
20. The article was written on 27 June 2005 by one of the authors of this book, Sophie Nachemson-Ekwall.
21. *Affärsvärlden* may have made a mistake and referred to information about the committee that had been formed to deal with the auction process.
22. Old Mutual due diligence was to be conducted under the supervision of Skandia's own M&A specialist Per Jungkvist.
23. A fairness opinion is a statement regarding the reasonableness of an offer from a financial viewpoint for shareholders in a target company. According to Swedish takeover rules, the target company must obtain a valuation opinion from an independent expert regarding the company's shares.
24. *Dagens Industri*, 9 July 2005, 'Inget tvingar oss till strukturåtgärder', Jan Wäingelin.
25. There was no formal limited time frame for a company to conduct due diligence in Sweden; therefore such a process could last for months.
26. This kind of concern was eventually taken care of in a particular statement (2005: 47) dated 6 November issued by the Swedish securities council (Aktiemarknadsnämnden). It is a self-regulatory body that ensures that listed companies and bidders on companies listed on the SSE follow the regulations set up by the takeover rules included in the contract of a listed company. The statement says that a target company is not obliged to take active measures to simplify the making of an offer (a due diligence process). Consequently, it also states that a refusal to take part in the making of an offer is not to be regarded as an unacceptable countermeasure.

14. Old Mutual's friendly bid

14.1 TROUBLE WITH FINANCING THE BID

Two options were presented in Old Mutual's original indicative bid, compiled by Deutsche Bank on 12 May 2005: either 48 billion SEK in Old Mutual shares or 45 billion SEK in cash and shares (where the cash component could be in the range of 50 to 66 per cent of the offer). Old Mutual's board decided during the early summer that the company should offer a 50–50 allocation of cash and shares. The plan was that Deutsche Bank would help Old Mutual raise the required cash in the market, but the possibility of a large rights issue was ruled out very early in the process. With the initial negative stock market reaction, it was argued that a rights issue would be difficult to combine with a share offer (since the former was likely to depress the value of the latter). Old Mutual board adviser Lazard[1] warned about such a drop in the share price. The South African exchange control regulations also made it difficult for the South African shareholders to participate.

While preparing the bid financing, Old Mutual instead asked Deutsche Bank to stretch the debt issue to the maximum that might be accepted by credit-rating agencies Moody's and Fitch.[2] The financial and treasury team at Old Mutual had decided not to talk to Moody's and Fitch until a relatively late stage, arguing that it was best not to worry the credit-rating institutes. Old Mutual management had publicly stated that it targeted a high A-rating. The ratings for its senior debt that summer were A− (with a stable outlook) at Fitch, and A3 (with a negative outlook) at Moody's. The last time Old Mutual's credit ratings were downgraded was in May–June 2004.

Old Mutual did not want to risk being downgraded, something that would have negative implications for its US business. Therefore Deutsche Bank had to suggest a plausible financial package. The company came up with a package that included the debt of £1.5 billion. However, the Old Mutual board went back to Deutsche Bank with the message that they preferred a more debt-financed deal.

When Old Mutual finally contacted the credit-rating institutes in late June/early July and presented its plan for financing a bid for Skandia, the reaction was that of hesitation. Old Mutual's balance sheet, gearing, hard currency interest coverage and thus credit rating were all problematic issues. Moody's credit analyst, Stephen Hunnisett, gave Old Mutual a preliminary warning – Old Mutual's financial position would be stretched too far by an acquisition of Skandia financed the way Deutsche Bank had suggested; Old Mutual would be downgraded. In Moody's analysis, a substantial UK and Swedish business together would leave the Old Mutual Group geographically well balanced. However, that balance was not enough to allay Moody's concerns regarding the destabilizing effect of the volatile rand, since South Africa was still the home of 70 per cent of Old Mutual's assets.

Old Mutual considered its South African business mature and open to fierce competition from new entrants. The acquisition of Skandia would substantially increase the amount of goodwill on Old Mutual's balance sheet. In sum, taking up loans in South Africa raised against South African assets to pay for Skandia was not risk-free. There was no way Moody's would subscribe to a gearing above 30 per cent. Moody's current credit rating was based on Old Mutual's aim to keep a core financial leverage below 30 per cent with hard currency interest coverage above three times. With the additional debt of £1.5 billion, gearing would be above 35 per cent. Thus there needed to be some reallocation of the split between equity and loans.

14.2 THE MORGAN STANLEY AGREEMENT

In July, Deputy Chair Björn Björnsson contacted Per Hillström at Morgan Stanley to discuss the board's request to make a change in the letter of engagement. The earlier draft stated that Morgan Stanley was to receive 0.20 per cent of the transaction value if the bid for Skandia came in below 36 SEK per share. For each 1 SEK above 36, there was an increase in fee paid by 0.01 per cent of the base value. Morgan Stanley, however, refused to accept an amendment to the contract to the effect that it would receive only the transaction fee if a bid landed above 40 SEK per share. At the board meeting on 20 July, Björnsson informed the board of directors that he had not been able to persuade Morgan Stanley to accept their new wording in the final letter: 36 SEK per share remained the striking price. There was also a fixed announcement fee of $2 million and a monthly pay of $120 000. A letter from the board also stated that if a transaction were completed with a bidder acquiring more than 50 per cent of all outstanding Skandia shares, there would be a transaction fee to Morgan Stanley. On 11 August, the agreement was formally signed.

14.3 AN ERODING SKANDIA CONTEST

During July, Magnusson continued to keep track of the largest shareholders' views. For example, during the board meeting on 20 July, SEB Fund's Björn Lind was invited to call on the phone to talk during one of the breaks. Lind had once again discussed Skandia matters with several other shareholders, in particular with those who represented various Swedish institutions. Lind told the board that the shareholders would take a stance on a proposal if, and when, there was a bid on the table. At the same meeting, the Skandia chair reminded the board members of Fidelity's view that had been expressed a week earlier (on 12 July).

In early August, it became clear to actors who were involved in the bidding process that the decision to let Morgan Stanley construct an auction for Skandia had run into trouble. The idea was that use of constructed consortia would result in a bidding situation that provided a higher sales price for Skandia – higher than Old Mutual's indicative bid of 48 SEK per share. However, this did not turn out to be the case. The only realistic consortium, which was led by Great-West, and included Storebrand as the bidder for Skandia's Nordic part, came up with a price of 39.70 SEK per share. This was 30 per cent below Old Mutual's indicative bid from 13 May. Thus, by the time mid-August rolled around, Old Mutual's indicative bid from May was the only one left on the table.

Taking vacation in July was not an Old Mutual tradition; therefore frustrations had mounted in the office by the time August came round: there had not been any resolute response from Skandia. There were many actors involved in this process: for example, Deutsche Bank had involved 60–70 people; the law firm Linklaters had assigned 20 to work on a team the entire summer, with an additional 70 on such matters as due diligence, regulatory and tax issues, and contacts with the LSE. At the time, Old Mutual became aware that it was the only bidder left that was interested in Skandia as a whole. Therefore its intention was to present a complete bid to the Skandia board. There were other things that seemed to weigh in Old Mutual's favour. Its share had regained the 6 per cent it had lost in May, and the public attitude in Sweden regarding selling Skandia was becoming less negative as the media appeared to become more neutral.[3]

With only Old Mutual left on the table, Skandia's management expressed deepening concerns about the sales process. As the team's knowledge of Old Mutual increased, its impression of Old Mutual and its management had been lowered. From having had a more or less neutral attitude towards Old Mutual as late as mid-June, Hans-Erik Andersson was from August downright negative, a view that was also expressed in board meetings that month.

Over the summer, the media was silent when it came to Skandia. Starting in mid-August, however, *Dagens Nyheter*'s business journalist Bengt Carlsson published several articles over the course of two weeks addressing Skandia's dealings.[4] For the broader public, his articles were probably the most important source of information about what was going on within the company. On 14 August, he published that the final deadline for bids was 22 August (in fact, it was 17 August), and that it was the consortium that contained AXA and Nordea that had needed a great deal of time to decide how to present a bid (in fact, it was not AXA; it was Great-West).

Carlsson further claimed that the (limited) due diligence process was still ongoing, and that it was disturbing management of daily duties. He also wrote that many larger institutional shareholders were frustrated by a lack of information about an awaited bid from Old Mutual, arguing that the outcome might be no bid at all. As he saw it, Skandia did not necessarily have to be sold. Carlsson contrasted that conclusion by citing when American Skandia had been sold to Prudential in December 2003 (at that time, Skandia was in a financial squeeze and was forced to sell even at a low price). He also discussed a possible price for Skandia. To him it was obvious that the price from Old Mutual was higher than the indications from the supposed AXA–Nordea consortium (in fact, as mentioned above, it was Great-West–Nordea). However, it was still far from Christer Gardell's estimated 60–70 SEK. Moreover, Carlsson believed that large shareholders wanted cash rather than newly issued shares in Old Mutual. He ended the article by speculating that a bid from Old Mutual would result in 46–48 SEK per share with two-thirds cash and one-third stock to be quoted on the SSE.

14.4 A FORMAL BID FROM OLD MUTUAL

Frustration grew on the Skandia board. Directors told Morgan Stanley of their disappointment that the promised bid had not yet materialized, and they had also noticed that everybody on the stock market behaved as if they were informed about the unsuccessful dealings. To top it all, the Skandia share had fallen. In August, it was trading slightly above 40 SEK, which was far from the 50 SEK that was talked about in the board when the Old Mutual bid had been leaked back in May. Lennart Jeansson became more and more vocal as the summer went on. He was tired of all the wheeling and dealing with Morgan Stanley and the board members' differing agendas. He repeated at a number of board meetings that it was time for Old Mutual to come forth with a formal bid.

At this delicate stage of the process, it was difficult – but important – to hide Old Mutual's (tall) CEO Jim Sutcliffe from view. Therefore the manor house of Almare Stäket, situated several miles outside Stockholm, was the chosen venue for a meeting between the Skandia board's special committee and those representing Old Mutual. The manor was close to Arlanda Airport, which was convenient for those who were participating: Skandia Chair Bernt Magnusson, Deputy Chair Björn Björnsson and Director Lennart Jeansson, as well as Skandia's top management, consisting of CEO Hans-Erik Andersson, CFO Jan-Erik Back, and head of strategy Per Jungkvist; Jim Sutcliffe and Julian Roberts and his team from Old Mutual, as well as investment bankers from Morgan Stanley and Deutsche Bank.

The overhead slides used by Old Mutual were the same as it had used on earlier occasions to present the company. The CEO dwelt in particular on the management consequences of an acquisition: Andersson would stay on as CEO of Skandia with a position as a member of the Old Mutual executive team. In his part of the presentation, the CFO went through the financial details of such a takeover, and presented what Old Mutual had found in its limited due diligence. In essence, Skandia looked as it had before the opening of any books. There were no skeletons in the closet, and the house was in order. This was also what all other potential bidders had noted. However, following these initial comments, Roberts's tone changed. He claimed that the reported profit margin on the new sales in the Nordic region was overestimated. He also pointed to the calculations that Old Mutual had to do to get Skandia's embedded value more in line with European principles. Such a restatement would, according to Roberts, have an effect on the rating institutes. It took him well over an hour to get to the slide that stated the actual bid, which included two specific components. The first was the sale of Skandiabanken for a specified price. When Old Mutual management had met with Skandia representatives, the bank had been described so that Old Mutual's staff got the impression that the bank could easily be separated out and sold. They estimated that Skandiabanken could be sold for at least 4 billion SEK, thereby strengthening Old Mutual's balance sheet. The second component was the presentation of 42 billion SEK as the bid price, paid 60 per cent in shares.

Most Skandia board members present expressed surprise and disappointment. Magnusson said that it seemed to be a bit on the cheap side. Merrill Lynch, however, argued that this was a reasonable price given that Old Mutual's stock was going to be revalued (once it became clear that it was to be the buyer of Skandia). Tony Burgess at Deutsche Bank showed similar calculations, arguing that Skandia shareholders, who would receive Old Mutual shares, were investing in a good currency. During the presentation, Lennart Jeansson asked quite a few questions, particularly several cash-related ones. Old Mutual had more cash than Skandia did, so it was likely that it could finance Skandia's growth plans much more easily. Therefore Old Mutual's team believed that Jeansson was on the Old Mutual side of the table – even with a bid of 42 billion SEK. The meeting ended rather abruptly, with Magnusson adding as a final comment that the investment bankers would have to continue talking. Everybody present at the meeting, including the board, management and most of the investment bankers, returned to their respective offices telling colleagues that they expected Old Mutual to drop out of the entire affair.

Later, on 16 August, Jim Sutcliffe told the Deutsche Bank team that it was time to walk away. Tony Burgess's team spent the entire day on 17 August preparing a facsimile declaring Old Mutual's loss of interest in bidding for Skandia. The fax was to go public at 7:00 am London time the following day; however, it was postponed (many people had to vet the document first). In the end, it was never sent. Instead, Sutcliffe called Magnusson to tell him that the bid process was terminated, and that Old Mutual had lost interest in buying Skandia.

Therefore Old Mutual's decision to continue the process came as a complete surprise to most of the actors, including advisers. Some of the investment bankers, for example, had already left on summer holiday (in London, bankers take their vacation in August). They were called back to the office; other actors were forced to postpone their vacations. Some Skandia board members speculated that Bernt Magnusson had talked Old Mutual into coming back, but Magnusson himself made clear that he only encouraged Sutcliffe in his turnaround. Magnusson saw two plausible reasons for the sudden change: first, that Old Mutual had pleased Moody's with a new bid-financing construct; second, that renewed talks with some of Old Mutual's main shareholders in South Africa initiated a revised bid attempt.

During the week after the Almare Stäket meeting, the investment bankers met to sort out this new situation. Morgan Stanley's people tried to increase the bid by a Swedish crown or two, but the message from Deutsche Bank to Morgan Stanley was that the bid had not changed. This was as high as Old Mutual could go, given the position of the credit-rating institutes. Hence Morgan Stanley had to return to Old Mutual once again with the message that the Skandia board was not ready to make a positive recommendation. It was not just the price that mattered: the proposition that Skandia should first sell off Skandiabanken had not been well received. Both the Skandia board and its executive management firmly rejected that suggestion. Skandiabanken was a vital part of Skandia's Swedish strategy.

Moreover, the idea that Skandiabanken should be sold by the board to make possible the success of a bid was actually legally questionable in Swedish law. A company cannot be bought by its own money.[5]

During late August, the Skandia board discussed the question of Skandiabanken's standing. Union representatives on the Skandia board had initially been neutral regarding the sale to Old Mutual. The only thing they did not want to happen was a sale of Skandia to Nordea, which would lead to substantial personnel reductions in Sweden. The proposed sale of Skandiabanken, however, swayed their opinion of Old Mutual. They were now negative about the bid, thus siding with those directors who were critical of the sales process. For Old Mutual, this lack of support from the Skandia board was problematic. Old Mutual's board still demanded a positive recommendation from the Skandia board before a public bid (in compliance with demands from Old Mutual's South African's shareholders). At the time, it was difficult for Old Mutual to sort out whether or not the Skandia board had given its 'blessing'.

Following the meeting at Almare Stäket, several of the directors expressed concern about the tension and disagreements between members on the Skandia board regarding the company's way forward. At the board meeting on Saturday 20 August, Bernt Magnusson, Björn Björnsson and Christer Gardell all took a clear stand in favour of continuing the sales process, while the other directors remained sceptical. According to Morgan Stanley's Jakob Lindquist, there were two bids on the table, and both were lower than the indicative bids from June. There was the bid from the theoretical consortium, which included Great-West and Nordea at 39.70 SEK. The preliminary bid from late June with AXA and Nordea had indicated 44 SEK. Old Mutual's bid had gone down from the indication of 45–48 SEK in May to 42–43 SEK. Board members concluded from the presentation that Morgan Stanley saw Old Mutual's bid as a fair price for the whole company to be sold as one entity. The price of 42–43 SEK was still a premium compared to the fair trading value of 34–38 SEK that Morgan Stanley had presented in February 2005, and to which it had returned several times (including at the end of May). Morgan Stanley had also provided material that could be used in support of the re-rating argument Deutsche Bank and Merrill Lynch had presented (i.e. for a lower bid). The Morgan Stanley material seriously questioned the effects of the Turbo Plan from May, in which Tillinghast's consultants had presented new embedded-value calculations.

Some of the board members, however, were disappointed by the Morgan Stanley presentation. Many felt that their adviser did not really address their basic scepticism about whether a sale was at all possible and, if so, not problematizing Old Mutual as a buyer. Christer Gardell, however, found merit in the presented revaluation of Old Mutual. He argued that Old Mutual would probably have a better chance of realizing the Skandia stand-alone case. After all, in his eyes, the Turbo Plan was nothing more than a 'power-point presentation'. Gardell also claimed that it would be much easier for Old Mutual to handle the management risk than for Skandia to face it on its own. Björnsson had made his own calculations after the Almare Stäket meeting, from which he concluded that Old Mutual might be right: perhaps Skandia was not as valuable as they had all thought. After all, there were no other bidders around. Björnsson also expressed doubts about the Tillinghast embedded-value calculations in the Turbo Plan, and concluded that the bid around 42 SEK was good enough for him.

Before the board meeting on Saturday 20 August, Magnusson had once again contacted Björn Lind from SEB Funds. This time, he wanted Lind to find out the views of the other institutions that had major holdings in Skandia on a bid price of approximately 42–44 SEK per Skandia share. Lind got hold of seven of these institutional shareholders, and five of them – SEB, AP1, AP2, AP4 and Nordea – were positive to such a bid, although they did find the price indication a bit low. The other two institutions – Robur and Handelsbanken – were not ready to make a decision. Lind presented this information about the shareholders' views at the aforementioned 20 August Skandia board meeting. Lind's overall message was that Skandia's Swedish institutional shareholders would base their actions on the board's recommendation, and would act only if such a statement were given. Once again, Lind added that they all had confidence in the board's handling of the situation. Birgitta Johansson-Hedberg, however, expressed some concern that Lind, as the chair of the nomination committee, had, in her view, almost instructed the board what to do. Lind replied that he had been invited by the chair to present to the board the views of the institutional shareholders; he said that this was precisely what he had done. Then, one of the union representatives asked Lind if it mattered to him – or them – whether Skandia was sold to a Swedish or a foreign buyer. Lind said that that aspect did not matter at all for the institutional investors.

During the 20 August board meeting, all board members besides Magnusson, Björnsson and Gardell made it clear that they thought the indicated price of 42–44 SEK was too low. Lennart Jeansson and Anders Ullberg based their positions on their own calculations. They also claimed that Skandia's management could very well pursue the Turbo plan in a stand-alone Skandia. Directors Karl-Olov Hammarkvist and Kajsa Lindståhl agreed. Johansson-Hedberg added to the scepticism, arguing against a Skandia owned by a foreign company. Jeansson concluded that, given this disagreement within the board, it was time for Old Mutual to present its bid straight to the shareholders. After all, it was up to them to decide which path Skandia should follow.

Bernt Magnusson called Jim Sutcliffe following the board meeting to inform him that there would be no positive board recommendation. The bid was simply too low. Old Mutual was still not willing to present a bid that did not receive support from the board. Old Mutual's CEO Sutcliffe learned that the board was too split for this to happen. Magnusson also discussed the situation with Deutsche Bank and Lars Lenner at Lenner & Partners, suggesting that Old Mutual and the investment bankers should contact the institutional shareholders directly to find out their positions. On the following day (21 August), *Dagens Nyheter* published yet another Skandia article. The main message was that there might not be a bid after all. Moreover, the article reported the rumour that a listing of Skandia Life UK had been turned down, the reason being that Skandia shareholders would then be stuck with shares in a UK life insurer.[6]

Skandia presented its second-quarter report on 22 August. The results were poorer than expected by analysts and investors, partly because of tax issues in Germany and partly due to a drop from the high sales level in 2004. Many businesses, however, were actually performing better. During the last two weeks in August, Skandia's share price dropped somewhat more than the SSE index.[7] At the time, Skandia's CEO did not say much in public about the bid.

14.5 MEETING WITH SKANDIA'S LARGER INSTITUTIONAL SHAREHOLDERS

On Tuesday 23 August 2005, a large number of Skandia's institutional shareholders were present at a meeting at Morgan Stanley's Stockholm office. Around 35 per cent of outstanding shares in Skandia were represented through AP1, AP2, AP4, SEB Funds, Robur, Burdarás and Cevian. All in all, they represented slightly more than the 30 per cent threshold about which Jim Sutcliffe had written in his letter to Magnusson three months earlier (in May).[8] Bernt Magnusson, Hans-Erik Andersson and Christer Gardell attended in person, while Lennart Jeansson listened over the phone. Morgan Stanley advisers were also present.

Magnusson opened the meeting by pointing out that everyone in the room had become insiders, and that a logbook must be kept.[9] Andersson then made a presentation about Skandia's future plans, focusing on the Turbo Plan. For the first time, shareholders could also review part of the material that Morgan Stanley had put together during the summer for the benefit of all those who were seriously considering a bid for Skandia. Morgan Stanley's representatives said that they had initially expected a bidding contest. However, that never materialized, so what was left on the table was merely Old Mutual's offering: 42 SEK per share. In the eyes of the representatives who attended the meeting, that was a bit low.

Morgan Stanley then presented the Skandia case, at the time also commenting with some scepticism on management's Turbo plan. They stated their belief that, if a bid were not brought forth, the Skandia stock would significantly drop from its present level in the low 40s. The Morgan Stanley team had argued in such a way that a number of the representatives from the institutions concluded that Morgan Stanley did not appreciate the Skandia stand-alone case. Some of them interpreted Magnusson and Björnsson's body language as supporting the Morgan Stanley presentation, while they took Andersson's facial expression as a sign of repudiation. Andersson then criticized those parts of their presentation that questioned his Turbo plan and ambitions for Skandia. As a reply to that, Magnusson expressed his scepticism regarding some of Andersson's arguments, claiming that the Turbo plan might be of less importance for the valuation of the company than Skandia's CEO both thought and hoped. Magnusson concluded that, if one considered all the known circumstances, it seemed that Old Mutual's proposed bid was the best available option for Skandia.

The chair of Skandia then concluded that it was up to the representatives from the shareholding institutions to evaluate the information they had, and then decide which path Skandia should follow. The representatives from the institutions also had the impression that Director Christer Gardell (i.e. Cevian) also stood behind the Morgan Stanley analysis and supported a bid from Old Mutual. However, it was unclear which positions the other board members took. Lennart Jeansson argued by phone that the best option was probably for Old Mutual to come up with a public offer so that Skandia's shareholders could make up their minds about what they wanted to do. He further said that he wanted to know the shareholders' thoughts about a possible structural deal. Thomas Halvorsen from AP4 stated his disappointment with the way the meeting had been conducted. He complained that the presentation that had been given to shareholders was an unprofessional way of providing a basis for a valuation of a bid (then he left). Halvorsen's speech made it apparent to the participants that not all shareholders would applaud an Old Mutual bid. Marianne Nilsson from Robur asked what position the board as a whole took on the matter. Magnusson answered that it still had to be sorted out.

When leaving the meeting, several shareholders expressed to each other their ongoing confusion. Many of them had previously heard Christer

Gardell argue that Skandia was worth as much as SEK 60 per share. This time, however, it appeared that he seemed willing to accept a bid at a low 40 SEK. To them, this did not make any sense, so the undecided shareholders were unable to see a coherent picture. What further complicated the matter was that this meeting had been the first time that they had received any insight in the Turbo plan. To those who were not members of the Skandia nomination committee, this was new and interesting information. They also expressed surprise that Magnusson and Björnsson seemed to be so pessimistic about Skandia's future as a stand-alone company.

On 24 and 25 August, Lars Lenner arranged individual meetings with the institutional representatives that had attended the shareholders' meeting the day before. This time, however, Old Mutual actors and its adviser Deutsche Bank were present as well. They met with representatives from AP1, AP2, Burdarás, Cevian, Handelsbanken, Robur and SEB Funds. They did not, however, meet any representatives from AP4, which had simply returned the invitation, saying it was busy with other matters.

NOTES

1. Lazard is one of the world's largest financial advisory and asset management firms. It is listed on the New York Stock Exchange.
2. Four credit agencies dominate the world's commercial loan market, namely Standard & Poor's, Moody's, Fitch and DBRS. The agencies rate commercial paper and corporate bonds on different scales from top prime rate to default. Moody's uses the scale for loans: short-term P-1 to P-3, and long-term Aaa to Baa3. Fitch uses the scale for loans: junior F1+ to F3, and loans senior AAA to D.
3. The Swedish PR and lobbying group Kreab prepared continuous updates on Swedish public opinion.
4. *Dagens Nyheter*, 14 August 2005, 'Oväntat svagt intresse för att lägga bud på Skandia'; *Dagens Nyheter*, 17 August 2005, 'Skandia har två val för att rädda kursen'; *Dagens Nyheter*, 21 August 2005, 'Oklart om det blir något bud på Skandia'; and *Dagens Nyheter*, 23 August 2005, 'Nu hoppas man att de dåliga nyheterna är bortsopade' (all articles written by Bengt Carlsson).
5. The Swedish Companies Act (SFS 2005: 551), chapter 19 forbids the acquisition of the company's share paid for with the company's own means, unless in specified circumstances.
6. *Dagens Nyheter*, 21 August 2005, 'Oklart om det blir något bud på Skandia', Bengt Carlsson.
7. The Skandia share price dropped approximately 4.5 per cent, and the SOX 30 index dropped approximately 1.5 per cent.
8. He wrote that Old Mutual would ask for support from at least 30 per cent of the shareholders before presenting a bid.
9. The opportunity to benefit from privileged information from the company would be noted and available to authorities. Any trading in Skandia shares based upon that information would be illegal until the same information had been made publicly available.

PART VI

Old Mutual acquires Skandia (Summer 2005 to Spring 2006)

15. A divided board

The Swedish media had been haunting Skandia directors and executives since 2002. From June 2005, however, the tone among many media slowly began to change. Around the same time, the focus turned towards the company as such – that is, to its current position and strategic options. Some media reports addressed the issue of a possible bid for Skandia from a 'saviour', and there was also speculation that a Nordic suitor, such as Nordea or Storebrand, would go for a part of Skandia. In August, this kind of discussion was replaced by a debate about whether it was right to sell Skandia at all. Things were also written about the stand-alone plan, and about suitors turning their back on Skandia. Most of these reports reflected material and views that had been provided by various Swedish institutional investors.[1]

15.1 THE FOURTH NATIONAL PENSION FUND STATES ITS POSITION

In the last week of August 2005, both Old Mutual and Skandia received a first impression of how Skandia shareholders really looked upon an Old Mutual bid. They also became aware that many Swedish institutional investors actually opposed such a proposal. The first shareholder to openly state its position was the Fourth National Pension Fund (AP4). During a meeting between institutional shareholders and some of Skandia's directors and its CEO in Stockholm on 23 August, Thomas Halvorsen, having been the CEO of AP4 since 1993, had asked critical questions and demonstrated his dislike both of the auction process and of Old Mutual as an indicative bidder. In August, AP4 owned 1 per cent of the shares in Skandia, making it one of the 10–15 largest shareholders. However, AP4 had an interesting history as investor on the SSE, where it had previously taken a controversial stance regarding several governance issues.

AP4 was founded in 1974 as one of the four original Swedish state-owned pension funds. Of the four, it was the only one that was eligible to invest in stocks from the very beginning; the others were forced to invest in fixed-income securities. For a long time, AP4 had been one of the larger institutional investors on the Swedish stock market. Back in 2000, it was actually the largest, owning shares worth 120 billion SEK. Skandia, then at its height with a market capital of 250 billion SEK, was one of its investments; the shareholding amounted to 2.2 per cent of the fund's capital. CEO Halvorsen had adopted an investment policy that often corresponded with the interest of the management of the company in which AP4 had invested. The Renault–Volvo merger attempt from 1993 was perhaps the best example of this kind of rationale.[2]

The conditions for AP4 were radically altered in 2001 when a large reform of the Swedish public pension system was implemented. The assets of the original four AP funds were redistributed, and each received 134 billion SEK, divided 70 to 30 between fixed-income securities and equities. Since then, the fund boards were to consist of nine members, all government-appointed. However, employer and employee organizations suggested two of the candidates for each board.

The new AP funds were permitted on paper a high degree of flexibility to allow investments in a variety of assets. In reality, though, a tough set of rules was enforced to control performance. For example, a maximum of 10 per cent of a fund's assets could be exposed to a single issuer or a group of issuers. Moreover, each fund could only have a shareholding that added up to 10 per cent of the votes in a single listed company. These regulations and procedures worked to ensure that state capital and democratic politics were kept at some distance from the governance of otherwise private listed companies.[3]

Ultimately, the AP funds' performance was evaluated annually against a benchmark index by the Finance Department. Thus these long-term pension funds started to act as any other mutual fund that evaluated its performance against an index of some kind. This index tracking encouraged conformity, as the easiest way to avoid criticism for bad results was to keep investments as close to a given index as possible. AP4's CEO Thomas Halvorsen was critical of that development, as was the fund's deputy CEO Björn Franzon.[4] Halvorsen, however, soon adjusted the fund's investment portfolio to these rules.

During the first years following the millennium, there was an open debate in Sweden concerning the lack of domestic capital formation[5], and the possible role that capital from (for example) the four AP funds could play if investing in Swedish companies. One of those concerned was AP4 board member Göran Johnson, head of IF Metall (a merged Swedish Industrial Workers' and Swedish Metalworkers' Union) and a member of the executive committee of Sweden's Social Democratic Party (Sveriges Socialdemokratiska Arbetareparti). The CEO of the Swedish Shareholders' Association, Lars-Erik Forsgårdh, was also worried about this lack of a long-term commitment from Swedish institutional and private investors, as well as the resulting continuous sellout of Swedish companies to foreign investors. In the winter of 2005, these two actors came together in an 'alliance' to reform the AP funds' investment policy. A letter was sent to Per Nuder, current Swedish minister of finance, requesting a discussion about the need for long-term capital investing on the Swedish stock market. Johnson's prime interest was that of all future employment in Sweden, whereas Forsgårdh was keen to keep enough blue chips listed on the SSE.

Forsgårdh and Johnson claimed that the AP funds could take more responsibility for governance matters if they had a more flexible investment policy, as well as a mandate to invest more capital on the home market. Both Nuder and his deputy responsible for capital markets and AP funds, Sven-Erik Österberg, had reacted positively to these suggestions.

In the summer of 2005, AP4 found itself in a delicate situation as an investor in Skandia. Three of its board members (Göran Johnsson, Kajsa Lindståhl and Karl-Olof Hammarkvist) favoured the idea of Skandia remaining an independent Swedish company. The latter two directors were also, at the same time, members of Skandia's board.[6] Moreover, AP4 had a CEO (Thomas Halvorsen) who had a track record of often siding with top management. The fund, however, was far from the largest shareholder in Skandia. In the spring of 2005, it controlled 1 per cent of the stock. This number was close to an index-neutral exposure. When Skandia rallied following the leak in May, AP4's exposure weakened to just below such a holding.

By coincidence, Thomas Halvorsen met Birgitta Johansson-Hedberg at a cocktail party during the first week of July. He told her that he disliked Skandia's ongoing auction process, pursued by Morgan Stanley. Halvorsen also mentioned that he did not like the fact that Old Mutual had its sights on Skandia. Consequently, AP4 had declined to meet with Old Mutual's CEO Jim Sutcliffe on his tour in Sweden during the last week of June. Halvorsen, however, was very interested to hear more about the 'Turbo plan' – something he had understood to be a Skandia stand-alone case, advocated by the company's top management. Johansson-Hedberg understood from their conversation that AP4 would support such a strategy.

After the 23 August meeting in Stockholm between the larger Swedish institutional shareholders and some of Skandia's directors and its CEO (see Section 14.5), the Skandia board asked the shareholders who had participated (and who had, therefore, become insiders) to submit their views in writing on a possible bid from Old Mutual for the whole of Skandia. Together, they represented approximately 25 per cent of the shares and votes in Skandia and included, among others, AP2, AP4, Burdarás, Cevian, Nordea, Robur and SEB Funds. The shareholders were asked to respond in a few days, that is, before the upcoming Skandia board meeting scheduled for 27–28 August. AP4's CEO answered in a letter sent to the Skandia board on 26 August that started by reminding the board of the fund's standing during the Renault–Volvo merger attempt. AP4 had first supported the Volvo board, but later changed its mind when new information had been presented.[7] He then concluded:

> AP4 has never, in a bid situation, acted against the recommendation of a united board . . . My answer is that it can, with almost full certainty, be assumed that the fund will support a position taken by a united board, no matter what decision is being made – as long as it is clearly motivated. According to best practice in Swedish governance, the board first presents its view to the shareholders, who come up with their own decisions afterwards.[8]

Halvorsen concluded his letter with the comment that he had great confidence in the Skandia board.

15.2 DIFFERENT OPINIONS ON OLD MUTUAL'S QUALITIES

In late August 2005, Skandia's CEO Hans-Erik Andersson was disillusioned with all the Old Mutual talks. He expressed to his management team his disapproval of the limited due diligence process that had been going on during the summer. He told the executive management board that he was going to work against a sale, and that he expected them all to do the same. And most of them did just that – including Michael Wolf, who, along with Gert Engman, was in charge of the initial implementation of the Turbo plan. Andersson and his team argued to the chair, deputy chair and several of the board members that, over the summer, the bid had been significantly reduced in value, and that impressions from the management-to-management meetings with Old Mutual led them to believe there was little to be gained from working together (albeit he spoke of its CEO with respect).

The confidence of Skandia management also grew as the company's results improved. The second quarter (announced on 22 August) was stronger than the first, which had made parts of the board more and more convinced that Skandia would be able to finance its own growth plans. This made a merger with Old Mutual look risky by comparison.

The plan was to let management present its views about a possible merger with Old Mutual in front of the Skandia board during the weekend meeting of 27–28 August. Before that, management had conducted its own limited due diligence on Old Mutual, and was to present the results as a slide show at the board meeting. The report included, among other things, a sensitivity analysis of Old Mutual's embedded value. The financial consultant firm Tillinghast, under the supervision of Skandia's head of strategy, Per Jungkvist, and actuary, Steve Hardwick, conducted this analysis, which showed that – with a more conservative presentation – Old Mutual's embedded value could be viewed as unstable (particularly with regard to the US market exposure).

Late in the afternoon on Friday 26 August, the day before the board meeting, Chair Magnusson sent CEO Andersson's Old Mutual due diligence report to Morgan Stanley. The material included the slides outlining Tillinghast's calculations of Old Mutual's embedded value. These came as a surprise to Jakob Lindquist, who ended up talking to Andersson for hours on the phone that evening. Lindquist argued that there was nothing wrong with the analysis, but it had to be clarified that Tillinghast had made the calculations based upon specific instructions from Skandia's management. Lindquist believed that Skandia's management intended to present the analysis as if it expressed Tillinghast's opinion – and this was not correct. Andersson's impression was that Lindquist attempted to persuade him not to present the new embedded-value calculations to the board.

As for Tillinghast, the issue was delicate since the company had already done work for Old Mutual that actually supported that company's own embedded-value calculations. Tillinghast conveyed this problem in a letter to the Skandia board dated 27 August.[9] The message was repeated in further correspondence with the Skandia board in the following weeks. Andersson argued that the board needed to see the full picture of the bidding company, which included the calculations that Skandia had asked Tillinghast to make (that incidentally addressed the uncertainty of the Old Mutual embedded-value accounting).

When the board met on the morning of Saturday 27 August, the Morgan Stanley team was present during certain sessions; as was Paulo Pereira, Head of Morgan Stanley Europe M&A; Gunnar Nordh of FöretagsJuridik Nord & Co.; other legal advisers; and, on behalf of the shareholders, Björn Lind, chair of the nomination committee. Skandia's CEO started the board meeting by presenting his (and management's) view. This included a thorough analysis of Old Mutual, stressing the particular risks revolving around the company's dependence upon South Africa, its currency and US life issues. It also included concerns regarding Old Mutual's ongoing dealings with Moody's. Andersson summarized his presentation, describing Old Mutual as a financial conglomerate. He also claimed that the UK company's strategy in asset management was not compatible with Skandia. Old Mutual, however, was regarded to be financially robust with a high rating and a high dividend yield, although its intention to sell Skandiabanken would weaken Skandia's position in Sweden and constitute a threat to Skandia's strategic plan. Andersson then presented Tillinghast's embedded-value calculations in the same way as he had described them in the board material (the talks with Morgan Stanley did not bring about any changes). His message: Skandia's shareholders should not accept shares in a merged company as (part of) its payment.

Per Jungkvist also presented the material on Old Mutual to the Skandia board. He claimed that that there were risks associated with its South African exposure, the volatile rand and the South African currency regulations. He added that the Old Mutual embedded-value calculations were uncertain for the US-based business, and that it still ran with a cash-flow deficit. As he saw it, all of this pointed to the possibility that, if Old Mutual took over Skandia, then an internal competition of capital might emerge. There were no guarantees that Skandia would get capital from Old Mutual to pursue a growth strategy beyond what Skandia could finance on its own. His presentation of Old Mutual also included the issue of its business in the troubled country Zimbabwe, since Old Mutual owned a newspaper there as well. Jungkvist argued that buying shares in a company that was present in such a country was unattractive to most Skandia investors.

When the management presentation was over, actors from Morgan Stanley entered the boardroom and presented (once again) what could be expected from Old Mutual's offer. Paulo Pereira concluded by saying that he believed Old Mutual would stand by the bid, even if it did not gain control of 90 per cent of the Skandia shares. According to the Swedish Companies' Act, reaching that threshold made it possible to force the minority shareholders to sell in order to gain full control. Therefore, what Old Mutual currently needed was the Skandia board's support for a deal. Lennart Jeansson complained that the discussions about the Old Mutual bid took attention away from more important issues, such as the management problems in the UK business. He believed that Skandia needed peace and quiet so that all could work with efficiency. Karl-Olof Hammarkvist agreed, as did Anders Ullberg, who added that what Skandia needed was a new start.

15.3 TWO CAMPS EMERGE ON THE SKANDIA BOARD

On Sunday 28 August, the board continued its weekend meeting by making a detailed analysis of Old Mutual's tentative bid. Bernt Magnusson described the situation as a complicated one, saying there were some 'soft parameters' that were difficult to evaluate and that there were also disagreements among key actors: Skandia's management believed in the Turbo plan; the UK management had its own agenda; shareholders were of different opinions; board directors disagreed with each other; politicians had certain views, and so on. He concluded his introduction to the discussion by saying that it would of course be favourable for Skandia to have both board and shareholder unity, and that perhaps a strong owner was needed to accomplish this. He later asked the board members what they would say if they were asked to 'informally' cast their votes for or against the Old Mutual offer. Thus, at this stage he wanted each board member to state whether or not they supported Old Mutual's bid for Skandia.

Karl-Olof Hammarkvist said that he was sure that Old Mutual would not get 90 per cent acceptance from the Skandia shareholders. He still could not understand the industrial rationale behind such a merger. To him, continuing to run Skandia as a stand-alone company 'was not rocket science'. He further argued that it was not acceptable to sell all of Skandia simply because there were management problems in the UK. He concluded that the stand-alone case was strong and the industry was not yet in a consolidation phase. He preferred that the structural ideas should be revisited after two to three years. His answer was no to Old Mutual's bid.

Birgitta Johansson-Hedberg started by stating that she disliked the entire bid process. Before the meeting, she had written a firm 'no' with a circle around it on her papers. Below that, she had added 10–15 lines of arguments against an Old Mutual deal. Johansson-Hedberg fully backed Hammarkvist's position, as she supported the stand-alone case and believed that it was important to hold on to Skandiabanken. She also said that she could not see the industrial rationale in combining the two companies. Besides, she said, Old Mutual's shareholder base (with South African institutional investors as the dominant part) was just as unpredictable as Skandia's shareholder base. Thus, selling Skandia to Old Mutual would not solve the problem of the lack of strong long-term shareholders, which was something for which Magnusson had originally argued. Therefore Johansson-Hedberg said 'no'.

Lennart Jeansson also answered 'no', stressing Morgan Stanley's work with the bid process. Jeansson said that the more work that had been put into the process, the longer it had dragged on and, as a result, the lower the bid level had dropped. He was also negative about Old Mutual's idea of selling off Skandiabanken. Jeansson concluded that the best solution was for Old Mutual to publicly present its bid.

Christer Gardell did not find the tentative bid to be generous and, similar to Jeansson, did not like the idea of selling Skandiabanken.

However, Gardell warned that if the board went against a (tentative) bid and, as an effect, it fell through, then the board might face a legal responsibility. This remark irritated Jeansson, who added that management's presentation had been critical of Old Mutual as a buyer, so he supported the stand-alone case, as he could not see any industrial merits emerging from a merger. Gardell replied that, in the long run, the stand-alone case was too uncertain. Johansson-Hedberg then turned to Gardell and asked him how long-term was his investment horizon. He answered that he did not plan to sell off his Old Mutual shares.[10] Gardell stuck to his position that it was worth considering a bid presented at 30 per cent above the fair trading value, and said that the stand-alone case ought to be implemented in both instances. In addition to expressing worry about Skandia's capital situation, Gardell was also concerned about Skandia's compensation packages to the management teams outside Sweden, which were not competitive. In the end, Gardell found a 'yes' better for Skandia than a 'no'.

Anders Ullberg said 'no'. He did not find the bid impressive enough and was not worried about the stand-alone case. He had apt experience from his position as CEO of SSAB, where he had developed a niche-oriented company. Kajsa Lindståhl supported Birgitta Johansson-Hedberg's view regarding the unstable shareholder base of Old Mutual, expressing her support of Skandia's ability to obtain economies of scale on its own. Her stance was 'no'. Björn Björnsson talked first about numbers, stressing that the fair trading value of Skandia remained around 35 SEK (with the parts valued separately, it was around 40 SEK). Old Mutual could pay a price above 40 SEK as an effect of its lower cost of capital. He stressed that most actors were aware that Skandia UK management wanted to garner support for a management buyout. With some reluctance, Björnsson voted 'yes'; the price, although not ideal, was acceptable. His view was that a putting aside of all personal ideals and feelings, making a rational decision based upon analyses and figures, would support such a conclusion.

The three board representatives from Skandia's trade unions also cast their votes and all said 'no'. This left Chair Bernt Magnusson to state his vote. He believed that Skandia would develop better within a big organization even if the initial synergies were not overwhelming. The Old Mutual offering was also better than all constructed consortia. Therefore he was positive to Old Mutual as a buyer.

By the time the boardroom discussion had finished, the directors could not deny the fact that the board was split into two groups. It was obvious that a recommendation to the shareholders to accept Old Mutual's tentative bid would not be possible. Eight board members, including the three union representatives, stated that they would vote against supporting Old Mutual's tentative bid. The other three board members stated that they would support it. Jeansson then added, as he had done several times before, that Old Mutual had been discussed on the board, and that it was now up to the shareholders to decide. That was something that the other directors could agree on. Therefore, the board meeting ended with the decision that a letter should be sent out as a stock exchange announcement the following morning (Monday 29 August).

The board members reviewed the minutes of the meeting on Sunday afternoon, noticing that the text indicated that the board had decided not to recommend the Skandia shareholders to accept the tentative bid from Old Mutual (as per letters to the board dated 19 and 23 August 2005). Thus the eight board members who opposed the Old Mutual deal left the Sunday meeting feeling confident that the struggle was over. Chair Magnusson then called the larger shareholders (who were still insiders from the meeting the previous weekend) and informed them of the board's stance. He scheduled a new meeting with them later that same Sunday afternoon.

15.4 A SECOND SHAREHOLDER MEETING

During the weekend of 27–28 August 2005, it became known in certain circles throughout Stockholm that the Skandia board could not come to an agreement, and that Old Mutual had carefully analysed the outcome, and had asked several of Skandia's shareholders, as well as a few of its board members, for assistance. Old Mutual still sought a friendly bid, arguing (internally) that a hostile bid would increase the risk of Skandia's shareholders not accepting Old Mutual shares as payment. Moreover, if they sold out, the Old Mutual share might fall, which would surely not be in the best interests of the company's shareholders.

On the evening of Saturday 27 August, journalist Bengt Carlsson had already written a story about the board meeting in *Dagens Nyheter* (web edition).[11] The text included a description of how board members and advisers had arrived at Skandia early the same day. The text implied that the discussions between the Skandia board, Old Mutual and Skandia's large shareholders were approaching an end. The story included new public bid information as well. According to Carlsson, it had dropped slightly to 41.20 SEK. The bid (mostly in stocks) had been presented to larger shareholders earlier in the week, who were expected to come forward with their opinions regarding the price before noon on Friday. However, Carlsson wrote that the process had run into trouble and, as the weekend approached, no one knew what was going to happen.

On Sunday 28 August Old Mutual's CEO spent the afternoon and evening at a wedding outside London. He kept walking in and out of the ceremony, answering phone calls from Sweden. Magnusson called to tell him that Old Mutual had to raise the bid if it wanted the board to give a positive recommendation to its shareholders. By late afternoon, there was a new meeting in Stockholm, this time involving Skandia's main shareholders. By that time, Old Mutual's tentative bid was on the table, albeit not yet made public. As chair of the nomination committee, Björn Lind was well informed of the division on the Skandia board. Johansson-Hedberg had even called him before the meeting to ask if he thought the directors should resign. Lind had advised her to stay and not create any more turmoil.

On the evening of Sunday 28 August, a meeting occurred at Morgan Stanley's office in Stockholm between invited (institutional) shareholders and the five members of the Skandia board committee that was established to conduct the Old Mutual talks: Chair Bernt Magnusson; Deputy Chair Björn Björnsson; Directors Lennart Jeansson, who participated by phone, and Christer Gardell; and CEO Hans-Erik Andersson. Magnusson informed the shareholders that the Skandia board held opposing views on the Old Mutual bid: three directors were in favour and five directors and three union representatives were against. Therefore it was not possible to present a unanimous board recommendation at the meeting.

Thus the institutional investors were left on their own to cope with the unusual situation of deciding Skandia's future themselves. This led to the emergence of different camps among the institutions. During the meeting it was said that actors representing approximately 25 per cent of the Skandia stock had already declared a positive stance to Old Mutual's tentative bid. Cevian was one of the supporters, as was SEB Funds. Petter Odhnoff of AP2 had joined in the meeting by phone, and was hesitant; he found the proposed bid a bit low. AP4 was negative. Deputy CEO Björn Franzon, who also participated by phone, argued that the industrial rationale in the proposed deal was poor. He also expressed scepticism about Skandia doing business with South Africa. Marianne Nilsson of Swedbank's Robur funds was negative as well. She was concerned with the board's lack of unanimity, which most certainly had to be resolved.

The shareholder representatives argued back and forth, attempting to determine whether or not it was possible to obtain a board recommendation for (or against) Old Mutual's bid. They wanted the board to solve this problem. Was there a way Old Mutual could come up with a bid that Lennart Jeansson would accept? Jeansson, who also participated by phone, clarified that he thought Old Mutual's valuation of Skandia was too low, and that he did not accept Old Mutual's structural proposal (including selling Skandiabanken). He also confirmed that the board, as a whole, would not recommend the tentative bid. Cevian's Lars Förberg harshly criticized Jeansson, and questioned whether his views were really in line with the board's duties. Förberg also talked about possible legal consequences following the board's treatment of the bid process. Jeansson answered that the board saw it as important that Skandia shareholders were given the opportunity to state their preferences, saying that he wanted Old Mutual to make its bid public, so that shareholders could decide for themselves.

As the debate at Morgan Stanley's office in Stockholm continued, Jim Sutcliffe called Bernt Magnusson's mobile phone; a Deutsche Bank representative listened in on the line. Sutcliffe wanted to speak with the chair of the nomination committee, since the two of them had had quite a bit of contact earlier in the process. Lind then informed Sutcliffe that most shareholders found the bid to be on the low side, but also that most of them were generally positive. Sutcliffe said that he felt the process was becoming a bit stuck, and asked for Lind's advice regarding a way forward. He stated that Old Mutual really wanted to place a bid, and asked if Lind still thought there was support from the shareholders. Lind said that there was some support, but added that most shareholders thought the tentative bid was too low. Lind told Sutcliffe that, given the current situation, Old Mutual's best move was probably to make a public bid. Lind referred to his own father's wisdom, and said: 'If you want something, you have to be polite and explain what it is.'

The conclusion from the 28 August meeting was that it was up to Old Mutual whether or not it wanted to make a bid without the guarantee of a positive board recommendation. Magnusson assured Sutcliffe that he would continue to work for a board approval. At Deutsche Bank, actors involved in the deal were informed that the bid was soon to be made public. The following morning, *Dagens Nyheter* wrote that the majority of the Skandia board was against the Old Mutual deal. However, the newspaper added that the response from the South African company could very well result in a bid for Skandia without the board's recommendation.[12]

15.5 A WEEK OF MEDIA SPECULATION

The Skandia board decided during its Sunday meeting to issue a press release before the stock market opened on Monday morning. However, in the end the message was postponed. Instead, Bernt Magnusson had returned to the board members after the meeting with the institutional investors, suggesting a new phrasing stating that the board had not yet decided, and as a result, talks with Old Mutual would continue. Birgitta

Johansson-Hedberg complained about this, as did Karl-Olof Hammarkvist and Kajsa Lindståhl. It was obvious to the directors opposing the tentative bid that the board had made its decision. To them, it was yet another attempt by the chair to try to bring about a united board.

Late on Monday afternoon on 29 August, Old Mutual finally publicly declared its interest and position in a press release:

> Old Mutual notes the recent press speculation concerning a possible offer for Skandia. Old Mutual confirms that it has held discussions with Skandia and a number of Skandia's major shareholders during the course of the past week concerning a possible offer: at a price of approximately SEK 42 per share, comprising 40 per cent in cash and 60 per cent in Old Mutual shares. Old Mutual believes that, after discussions with these large shareholders, a majority of them will welcome such a proposal. Old Mutual is keen to secure a recommendation from the Board of Skandia and is considering selected modifications to the proposal in order to address issues raised by the Skandia Board. A further announcement will be made as soon as possible.[13]

The reply from the Skandia board came at six o'clock the same evening:

> In relation to the statement made by Old Mutual today concerning a possible offer for Skandia, the board of Skandia makes the following comments: Discussions with Old Mutual are continuing. The board will evaluate an offer if and when a formal offer is presented. A further announcement will be made when necessary. For further information, please contact board chair, Bernt Magnusson.[14]

The naysayers on the Skandia board were disappointed with the press release. From this point, director Anders Ullberg initiated e-mail correspondence with the other naysayers. This was a clear indication that a 'no' camp had been formed of board members who shared a common view and agenda.

Old Mutual's forthcoming bid for Skandia had started to leak to the public near the end of August and beginning of September. Skandia's major shareholders expressed different views regarding the bid; some were positive, others more sceptical of the proposed compensation. The press reported a new Skandia story almost daily. On 30 August, *Dagens Industri* published a critical commentary on Magnusson's work. As board chair he had not been able to fulfil what the paper regarded as one of his most important tasks: to keep the Skandia board united.[15] The same day *Svenska Dagbladet* wrote that the board's naysayers might soon have to resign, given the assumed support among most shareholders.[16] Jim Sutcliffe came to Stockholm and stayed for a whole week. As Old Mutual's CEO, he met with investors in meetings set up by Lars

Lenner, and he met important official people in appointments set up by the public relations firm Kreab. At least a dozen meetings were held, including some with representatives from the media. However, Sutcliffe did not meet anybody from AP4. Thomas Halvorsen, who, on behalf of the fund, had expressed his scepsis regarding the South African suitor at the 23 August major shareholders' meeting, did not alter his negative stance. So, once again, AP4 turned down Old Mutual's invitation for a meeting.

Tidningarnas Telegrambyrå (TT), a newswire in Sweden, also wrote on 30 August that a large number of shareholders were positive. TT had even quoted Petter Odhnoff, CIO at AP2 as saying: 'We welcome a new bid from Old Mutual. We view it as a high quality company.' He also stated that the fund would make its own decision regardless of the board's decision, and that the fund had no problem with accepting shares in Old Mutual. The way in which to value Old Mutual's exposure in the South African market was of crucial importance to him. SEB Funds were also reported positive to the bid. TT quoted Björn Lind: 'We met them [Old Mutual] last week and, considering the information we have, we look upon Skandia and Old Mutual as a good combination.' However, he did not comment on the proposed bid level at 42 SEK. Lars Förberg, partner at Cevian, was even more positive: 'It is a solid, robust company with a fantastic cash flow . . . We do not view this as a takeover; rather as an industrial merger where Old Mutual's strong cash flow can be used to enhance growth in Skandia.' All others who were interviewed in this report (including Joachim Spetz of Handelsbanken and Lars-Erik Forsgårdh of the Swedish Shareholders' Association) were critical of the snail-like pace of the process. They argued that it was either bad for Skandia or bad in general.[17]

Some members of the Swedish business elite began publicly to question the merits of an Old Mutual–Skandia deal as well. On 30 August 2005, *Dagens Industri* quoted several prominent businessmen as saying that it would be a great mistake to sell Skandia since 'it would result in a move of the head office and a competence drain'. Gustaf Douglas, investor in both the service company Securitas and the lock company Assa Abloy, said: 'It is of great value to keep a certain type of jobs within the country.' One of Sweden's richest industrialists, who did not want to be named, supported Douglas by saying: 'Skandia's shareholders should say no to a bid on the company. A sale to South African Old Mutual is bad for Sweden and the Swedish capital market.' Both Douglas and the anonymous industrialist pointed to the current buying spree among listed companies: many good ones were sold without a real cause. Douglas was quoted as saying: 'Three out of four deals lack industrial motives; instead, they are initiated by short term financial motives.'[18]

The *Financial Times* also published articles about the Old Mutual–Skandia issue. The Lex column noted on 30 August that the suggested bid of 43 billion SEK was probably on the low side. This was a 20 per cent premium on Skandia's share price in May, that is, before serious talks began. However, the Lex column wrote that insurance stocks had since risen, eroding that premium. It added that an increase of the 40 per cent cash component would help prevent a back-flow from Swedish retail shareholders. The column further stated that Old Mutual could not go too high, however, given the limited synergies of perhaps £60 million, and the fact that Skandia was a big bite corresponding to 60 per cent of (Old Mutual's) own market value. The Lex column concluded that a 5–10 per cent increase should 'turn this hug into a mutual cuddle'.[19] On 31 August the *Financial Times* quoted Fridrik Johannsson, CEO of Burdarás, who, incidentally, had a 3.5 per cent stake in Skandia and who had been seen all along as an ally of Cevian: 'I think the deal makes sense from an industrial and financial perspective and I am actually awaiting a formal offer later this afternoon.'[20]

On Wednesday 31 August, *Dagens Nyheter* published a survey of the positions taken by major Swedish shareholders. This was the first time that AP4's negative stance had been publicized and that an institutional investor had spoken out in public against Old Mutual's bid. Thomas Halvorsen was quoted as saying:

> Skandia can make it on its own . . . without major changes in the bid proposal, the Skandia board must call it off . . . This has already been going on for too long and we have reached the end of the road. It is time for the board to stand up behind 'the stand-alone alternative'; that is to say, Skandia can develop on its own, and I believe in its so called 'Turbo Plan'.[21]

The following day (1 September), *Svenska Dagbladet*'s reporter Jan Almgren did his best to sort out the pros and cons of an Old Mutual bid: 'A management set for combat speaks against a sale. The insurance company's weak cash flow speaks for a deal with Old Mutual.' According to Almgren, some circumstances spoke against a deal with Old Mutual:

> Judging from its Q2 report, Skandia's growth was strong and its business was performing well. Skandia was gaining a market share in Sweden again. However, it was likely that Old Mutual's sole interest was in Skandia's British business, creating a risk that its Nordic business would be resold or not given enough attention.

Almgren further claimed that there was a nationalistic issue involved that could not be ignored – yet another cherished Swedish company was in a selling situation. He also regarded the bid at 42 SEK per share as low, particularly as it was to be partly paid in Old Mutual shares. He also saw elements in favour of Old Mutual's ambition. One such item was that Skandia's cash flow remained weak; during the second quarter, the company spent an additional 600 million SEK. He continued by writing: 'A negative cash flow makes a company vulnerable, particularly when it has growth needs or ambitions.' According to Almgren, Old Mutual had the cash flow that Skandia needed. He added that the impact of scale could not be overlooked – it reduces risk and, in the eyes of the rating institutes, would strengthen the constellation. Almgren concluded by stating that 42 SEK was a fair price for Skandia, given the risk of a drop to 35 SEK in share price if Old Mutual suddenly decided to walk away.[22]

On Thursday 1 September, Old Mutual's CEO was still in Stockholm broadening his 'sales meetings' to include both some smaller shareholders and the media. That day the CEO of the Swedish Shareholders' Association, Lars-Erik Forsgårdh, met Jim Sutcliffe at Skandia's offices. Lars Lenner, who had set up the meeting, joined in as well. From the very beginning, Forsgårdh made it clear to Sutcliffe that the association would vote against a deal. In a signed commentary published in *Svenska Dagbladet* (on 2 September), Forsgårdh demanded that Skandia's chair Bernt Magnusson call off the bid process with Old Mutual, since it had become known that a majority of the board members were against it: 'A major service company, and one of particular importance for the Swedish capital market, must not be sacrificed for a few SEK on top of the stock price, simply because it suits a group of speculators led by Christer Gardell.'[23] According to the management at the Swedish Shareholders' Association, most of the small shareholders shared the view of the majority of the Skandia board.

Dagens Nyheter published an interview with the CEO of Old Mutual on Friday 2 September 2005. Jim Sutcliffe was quoted as saying that his ambition was to present a bid within days. He reaffirmed that the modifications to the bid proposal, which the Skandia board had demanded, had been processed. Sutcliffe also confirmed that a sale of Skandiabanken was an alternative in order to reduce the level of indebtedness, and that this idea had met with objections from the Skandia board. The article also addressed a government-friendly newspaper in Zimbabwe in which Old Mutual had shares. The question was why this involvement, to which Sutcliffe answered:

> It is not Old Mutual that owns the shares, but our clients whose money we are managing. However, it is a very complicated situation in that country and, consequently, a difficult situation for us. It is simply not possible to sell the

shares because there are no buyers on the country's small stock exchange. This, however, is not something that the Skandia board has brought up.[24]

15.6 SOFT IRREVOCABLES FROM SHAREHOLDERS

Without a board recommendation, Old Mutual sought other ways to go ahead and present a public bid. Their case should then be based on letters of intent from supporting shareholders. Such letters came in a variety of forms, ranging from 'irrevocables' to non-committing formulas called 'soft irrevocables'. Lars Lenner worked to get the Swedish institutional shareholders who were now insiders (since the 23 August meeting) to sign the documents, but it was a difficult task. Hardly any of them wanted to commit themselves at this stage, and those who had expressed passive support could not make such a binding promise.[25] The foreign institutional investors were just as difficult to manage. But Fidelity, which controlled 10–11 per cent of the Skandia shares (including American Fidelity), responded positively when Deutsche Bank approached its office, although it refused to sign a written commitment (as it was against the fund's policy). Fidelity International's interest in an Old Mutual–Skandia deal had increased, since it had built up a holding in Old Mutual during July and August, amounting to 2–3 per cent. Thus Fidelity's fund managers were confident that Old Mutual's stock would rise following a successful Skandia takeover.

In the last week of August, AP2's board of directors, who had a shareholding of 3 per cent in Skandia, discussed the Old Mutual case and the possibility of signing a letter of intent. CEO Lars Idermark had decided to leave the fund in October, so CIO Petter Odhnoff was asked to be acting CEO while the board searched for a successor. Both Idermark and Odhnoff had told the board that they regarded a coming bid from Old Mutual as positive since it would end a long period of market speculation. The current expected price level – around 41 SEK – was described to AP2's board members as somewhat low. However, both managers argued that AP2 should sign a letter of intent for two reasons: once a bid was on the table, it would probably be easy for the institutional investors to either turn it down or get Old Mutual to increase the bid; AP2 should, thereby, get out of the insider position into which it had entered at the shareholder meeting on 23 August. The whole affair had already dragged on far too long. In their view, it was high time for AP2 to be able to trade in the share again. AP2's board decided to back Idermark, and that also included the signing of a binding irrevocable that supported a bid.

Regarding the fund's signing of a letter of intent, there was a fair amount of discussion between Idermark and Odhnoff, and Lenner. On Thursday 1 September, Lenner returned several times to ask for modifications of some of their formulations in the document. However, Idermark and Odhnoff made it clear that AP2 did not want to make a full-fledged commitment to accept a bid. They also talked to Björn Lind, who did not want to sign anything without AP2's support. Late on 1 September AP2 gave Lenner clearance. The fund would sign a document early the following morning (Friday 2 September). Lenner suggested that Old Mutual made a stock exchange announcement of this shareholder support before trade opened. However, by the time morning had arrived, AP2 had changed its mind, deciding not to sign the irrevocable at all. Idermark and Odhnoff called Lenner early that following morning to inform him of the fund's turnaround.

Lenner said that he had already told Old Mutual that AP2 and SEB Funds were to sign letters of intent; therefore he protested firmly. He argued that Idermark and Odhnoff had promised, and without the cooperation of AP2, the bid would not be presented at all. Old Mutual had to walk away. By eleven o'clock on Friday morning, Old Mutual had received letters of intent to accept its offer from shareholders, who represented 15.6 per cent of Skandia's shares. AP2 ultimately gave in, and SEB Funds soon followed suit. Cevian and Burdarás were among those who had signed the irrevocables, but the names of the other signing institutions were not revealed at the time. The press revealed a little later that SEB Funds was one of those institutions (never publically confirmed). The other – AP2 – remained unknown for quite some time. The letters of intent from SEB Funds and AP2 were both of a non-committing nature. These were referred to as 'soft' irrevocables, simply stating that they welcomed a bid for Skandia. However, these differences in the levels of commitment among the actors that made up the supporting 15.6 per cent were never made public.

15.7 THE PUBLIC BID

Jim Sutcliffe had invested much of his time and prestige in carrying through a Skandia deal. As Old Mutual's CEO, he had employed substantial company resources for that purpose. Therefore many observers expected that he would be pressured to resign if, at this late stage in the process, the deal turned sour. His plan had been to spend a week speaking to investors in Stockholm and not present a public bid until the following week. By Thursday night, however, he had had enough of those talks, so he changed his mind and decided to present a complete bid to the public the following day (Friday 2 September). The press conference was set for 5 p.m. and was to be hosted in Stockholm by the Swedish PR firm Kreab.

The press conference was held late in the evening, and it attracted quite a few journalists and analysts. Old Mutual's CEO Jim Sutcliffe and CFO Julian Roberts both spoke during the presentation. The audience received a 25-page handout, entitled 'Old Mutual bid on Skandia at 43.60 SEK'. Old Mutual and Skandia – a powerful combination.[26] The price, at 43.60 SEK, was a bit higher than was previously announced. It was composed of 16.50 SEK in cash and 1.372 Old Mutual shares per Skandia share. The difference from the previously indicated price at 42 SEK was due to a rise in the Old Mutual share during the week. Old Mutual's managers stated that the two companies would together make up an insurance and life group with a market capitalization of £7.9 billion. The Skandia shareholders' part of the new group would be 26 per cent and a Swedish listing was to follow. Old Mutual further argued that the bid was generous: 25 per cent above the stock price from 12 May, the day before its interest in buying Skandia had been leaked.

Roberts presented expected synergies of £70 million emerging from lower HQ costs both in Sweden and in the UK (£60 million), and from a better tax position in the UK with substantial unrelieved taxable expenses (£10 million). Added to this should be general synergies between Old Mutual's Selestia offer and the Skandia Life UK open architecture platform. Old Mutual's CFO stated that his respect had grown for Skandia management's competence and that CEO Hans-Erik Andersson had been invited to join the Old Mutual executive team. He talked about a strong combined senior management with little overlap.

The bid was conditional on a public recommendation from the Skandia board. The final date for that board statement was set for 23 September 2005. Old Mutual management claimed that it had made this public bid in accordance with certain requests that had been expressed by the Skandia board and that they had, therefore, expected its support (a cooperation agreement was demanded[27]). Old Mutual's bid, however, was subject to several other conditions as well.[28] These included that Old Mutual's shareholders would vote in favour of a share issue to finance part of the bid. There was also the condition that, in order for the bid to be binding, 90 per cent of the Skandia shareholders had to accept the offer by 21 November. The acceptance level of 90 per cent was more or less standard Swedish procedure given the Swedish minority rights, and needed to gain effective control of the cash flow in a Swedish listed company. The bid was also dependent on Old Mutual's ability to raise new debt in order to finance the cash part of the offering. Old Mutual stated that, given the fulfilment or waiver of all conditions, it expected full settlement in January 2006. There was also a more general reservation that all the conditions could be waived, if circumstances changed. The press release announcing the bid included a statement that there were letters of intent from shareholders representing 15.6 per cent of the Skandia stock who accepted the offer. However, it gave no indication that these letters of intent also included the 'soft' irrevocables.

Skandia distributed a press release late on Friday evening, 2 September, confirming that the board had received a public bid for the company. The press release included the same sentences used earlier in the week: the board would evaluate the bid and return with a recommendation to Skandia's shareholders.

NOTES

1. *Dagens Nyheter*, 1 June 2005, 'Starkt framåt för Skandia som håller tyst om friare', Anders Olsson; *Dagens Industri*, 1 June 2005, 'Skandiachefen hoppas på snar strukturaffär', Martin Hammarström; *Dagens Nyheter*, 11 June 2005, 'Skandia klarar sig bra på egen hand, säger Skandiachefen', Bengt Carlsson; *Dagens Industri*, 18 June 2005, 'Ny spekulant redo ta upp kampen', Karin Svensson; *Dagens Nyheter*, 28 June 2005, 'Old Mutual kritiseras av Skandiaägare', Pia Gripenberg and Olof Sandström; and *Dagens Industri*, 1 July 2005, 'Cheferna flyr Skandia', Cecilia Aronsson.
2. Following the management revolt, AP4 had led Swedish institutional investors in a search for a new Volvo board of directors.
3. Sweden had a heated political and public debate in the early 1980s when its Social Democratic government introduced what was known as Wage-earner funds (Löntagarfonder) with the aim to invest in large stakes in Swedish listed companies, thereby sometimes gaining strong positions.
4. *Finanstidningen*, 12 December 2000, 'Vi abdikerar inte från ägaransvaret', Caroline Sundewall.
5. See, Brodin et al. (2000), Henrekson and Jakobsson (2002), and Jonung (2002).
6. Neither Hammarkvist nor Lindståhl participated in AP4 board discussions concerning AP4's stance on Skandia.
7. AP4's actions in the Renault–Volvo merger attempt are described in, for example, Sundqvist (1994).
8. A letter dated 26 August 2005 from AP4 and addressed to the Skandia board.
9. Tillinghast also phoned one or two Skandia directors and informed them about the current situation.
10. Cevian eventually sold all shares in Old Mutual shortly before Easter 2006, having then more than doubled the value of the fund's investment in a little more than a year.
11. DN.se, 27 August 2005, 'Aktier som köpeskilling problem i Skandiaaffär', Bengt Carlsson; and DN.se, 28 August 2005, 'Oenigt Skandia nobbar OM', Bengt Carlsson.
12. *Dagens Nyheter*, 29 August 2005, 'Skandiastyrelsen säger nej till OM', Bengt Carlsson.
13. Old Mutual, 29 August 2005, Discussions with Skandia, press release.
14. *Waymaker*, 29 August 2005, 'Skandia: Skandias styrelse kommenterar Old Mutuals underhandsbesked'.
15. di.se, 30 August 2005, 'Skärpning, Skandia', Karin Svensson and Jan Wäingelin.

16. *Svenska Dagbladet*, 30 August 2005, 'Styrelsen gick emot storägarna', Jan Almgren, Erik Bergin, Anna-Karin Storwall and Erik Wahlin.
17. TT, 30 August 2005, 'Storägare positiva till Skandiaaffär', Johan Andersson. Tidningarnas Telegrambyrå (TT) is the largest news agency in Scandinavia, and the only nationwide Swedish agency with a complete news service. Most of Sweden's 100 largest newspapers and media groups subscribe to TT's database.
18. di.se, 30 August 2005, 'Näringslivet sågar försäljning', Henrik Huldschiner and Gerhard Larsson.
19. *Financial Times*, 30 August 2005, 'Lex: Skandia/Old Mutual'.
20. *Financial Times*, 31 August 2005, 'Old Mutual in talks over Skandia', Rupini Bergström and Andrea Felsted.
21. *Dagens Nyheter*, 31 August 2005, 'Flera storägare stödjer Old Mutual', Bengt Carlsson.
22. *Svenska Dagbladet*, 1 September 2005, 'Kommentar: Försäljningen av Skandia – Tuppfäktningen kring bolaget trappas upp', Jan Almgren.
23. *Svenska Dagbladet*, 2 September 2005, 'Rädda Skandia från spekulanterna', Lars-Erik Forsgårdh.
24. *Dagens Nyheter*, 2 September 2005, 'Skandia blir prestigemärket', Bengt Carlsson.
25. Due to certain regulations regarding mutual funds.
26. Press and stock market material from Old Mutual, 2 September 2005 (not for distribution in the USA, Cananda, Australia or Japan), 'Old Mutual plc: SEK 43,60 Offer for Skandia, Old Mutual and Skandia – a powerful combination'.
27. The 'Proposed Co-operation Agreement' included a request that Skandia *inter alia* would agree 'not to solicit, encourage or facilitate any alternative acquisition for Skandia . . . that it will neither directly nor indirectly underake any other action that may prevent or frustrate the Offer . . . and that it will co-operate in general with and assist Old Mutual in the preparation of the prospectus'.
28. The completion of the offer as presented on 2 September 2005 was conditional on 12 stipulations. Three of these should be highlighted: (i) the offer being accepted to such an extent that Old Mutual would become owner of more than 90 per cent of the Skandia shares; (ii) the Skandia board would make public a favourable recommendation of the offer no later than 23 September 2005, and not subsequently withdraw that recommendation; (iii) Skandia would sign the proposed Co-operation Agreement no later than 23 September 2005. At the same time, Old Mutual reserved 'the right to withdraw the Offer in the event that it was clear that any of the 12 conditions were not fulfilled or could not be fulfilled'. Also, Old Mutual reserved the right to waive, 'in whole or in part, any or all of the conditions and with respect to condition (ii) above, to complete the Offer at a lower level of acceptance' (source: see, note 26).

16. A controversial bid

16.1 OLD MUTUAL'S BID FOR SKANDIA

Old Mutual's Friday evening press conference in Stockholm on 2 September marked a turning point for a Skandia that, since the spring of 2003, had been subject to various takeover speculations. The same day, a public binding bid was presented to Old Mutual and Skandia shareholders as well as to the general public in Sweden, the UK and South Africa. This procedure ensured that all were given access to the same official documentation at the same time (the writings and handouts from 2 September 2005).

On the previous Monday afternoon (29 August 2005), Old Mutual had confirmed that, for some time, it had held discussions with Skandia and a number of the company's major shareholders concerning a possible offer where Skandia was valued at approximately 42 SEK per share. When the bid was formally announced, Old Mutual presented a value of 43.6 SEK per share: the difference reflecting a rise in Old Mutual's share price during the week. On that Friday, the Skandia share was trading at 41.5 SEK. It continued to lose ground by a few öre[1] each day. By 15 September, Skandia was trading at 40 SEK. This was far from the expectations marketed by Skandia Director Christer Gardell, and also far from the price indications that appeared when the Old Mutual bid speculations were confirmed on 13 May 2005. That day, Skandia rose to 42 SEK.[2] Four months later, the Stockholm stock market had risen by 12 per cent and the Morgan Stanley insurance index rose with it. Simply keeping up with a development such as that would have set the value at 47 SEK per share.

Skandia's share price fell following Old Mutual's bid announcement. Given the fact that 60 per cent of the bid was to be paid in Old Mutual shares, a falling Old Mutual stock meant that the value of the bid to Skandia's shareholders fell substantially. However, the Skandia share slid even further, widening the gap between the value of the Old Mutual bid and the Skandia share price. At the time of the announcement of the bid, the spread was 3 per cent. By mid-September, it had grown to 5 per cent.

For financial analysts following the Skandia case, the Old Mutual offer was complicated. Most of them viewed the bid as a fair stand-alone calculation. For them, the main question was whether or not Skandia's shareholders would profit from becoming Old Mutual shareholders as well. For most Swedish investors – both institutional and retail – Old Mutual was a non-issue. Hardly any of them had the incentive to become, or to remain, Old Mutual shareholders. Swedish institutional investors mostly owned shares in Skandia because the company was listed on the SSE and was part of the OMX index (which most of them were tracking for their funds' performance). They were all 'natural sellers' of Old Mutual shares, just as its shareholders feared. This was a concern that Old Mutual's corporate broker Merrill Lynch tried to dampen.

Furthermore, many of the institutional investors in Skandia had been insiders during the two-week period before the public bid (23 August–2 September) and were, thus, not permitted to trade in the Skandia share. Once the bid was announced, they could do business once again. All in all, one-third of Skandia's shares changed hands during the first two business days following the announcement of the bid. Less than a week later, Swedish institutional investors had reduced their total shareholding by ten percentage points; the share fell under intensive trading. At the same time, international hedge funds bought heavily into the stock as the wide spread between the value of the Old Mutual bid and the Skandia share turned Skandia into a lucrative place for short-term gamblers: activist funds, arbitrage funds, special situations funds and so on.

On 3 September (the day after the formal pubic bid), *Dagens Nyheter* ran an article on the unusual condition of a board approval of the bid (by Swedish standards).[3] Fredrik Lindqvist from Linklaters (which had been Old Mutual's legal adviser before the bid) had approached the Swedish Securities Council about this condition. Chair Johan Munck had told Linklaters that such a condition was not in accordance with Swedish takeover regulations. The Council was also in contact with the British Takeovers and Merger Panel, from which it had understood that such a condition was not in accordance with UK practices either.[4]

The reason for the condition was that Old Mutual's South African shareholders had signalled to Old Mutual's board of directors that they would participate in a rights issue only if they were presented with a friendly bid. A hostile bid was expected to trigger a massive sellout by former Skandia shareholders who were not interested in owning Old Mutual's shares, thus pressing its price. In its advice to Old Mutual, Linklaters maintained that the condition was acceptable, claiming that the decision of the Swedish Securities Council was inconclusive. Munck was quoted in *Dagens Nyheter* expressing surprise at the fact that, despite Swedish Securities Council's view, Old Mutual had kept the condition. The condition was simply unheard of on the Swedish stock market.

16.2 EARLY REACTIONS TO THE BID

Old Mutual's bid for Skandia triggered several prominent Swedish business people to make their voices heard both through the media and in various collegial circles. On Saturday 3 September 2005, the day after Old Mutual's bid for Skandia, *Dagens Industri* published the views of Gustaf Douglas and Carl Bennet (well-known controlling shareholders in large listed and unlisted companies), and of Bengt Rydén (former head of the SSE).[5] Both Douglas and Bennet had, in addition to their business networks, connections with Sweden's political establishment: for Douglas, the Conservative Party (Moderata Samlingspartiet), and, for Bennet, the Swedish Social Democratic Party (Sveriges Socialdemokratiska Arbetareparti). Douglas had initiated what appeared to be a campaign to keep Skandia Swedish, and Bennet had joined in this effort. The newspaper encapsulated their stance: 'It is important that Skandia remains Swedish with a Swedish controlling shareholder. Skandia has a leading position in a business with a promising future. It is just the type of company that is especially important to keep in Sweden.' Rydén expressed similar resentment towards the ambition of some of Skandia's larger shareholders to sell the company to South African Old Mutual. He said:

> It would be bad for Sweden if Skandia had owners that moved all its decision-making out of Sweden. Skandia is an important part of the Swedish capital market, both as an investor on the stock exchange and as a seller of savings products. I do not think anyone should consider Old Mutual's bid before the Skandia board has presented management's stand-alone plan: the so-called Turbo plan. That is important for everybody to take part in.

The following day business journalist Bengt Carlsson ran a column in *Dagens Nyheter* where he argued that Old Mutual's bid presentation was particularly unclear regarding Skandiabanken – something he believed was a major source of the differing opinions within the Skandia board. Carlsson also described the board as under pressure from several major shareholders that wanted to see a deal done with Old Mutual.[6]

Dagens Industri published an interview with Old Mutual's CEO on Monday 5 September. Jim Sutcliffe explained: 'It is important for our shareholders that the bid is not perceived as hostile.' Sutcliffe denied that the condition of board approval was against Swedish takeover regulations. The article also reported that Old Mutual's advisers believed that the company would be revaluated after an acquisition of Skandia, since doing so would diminish its massive dependence on the South African home market. There was also a commentary that presented several arguments against the deal. *Inter alia* it was presumed that Skandia's shareholders would not be offered a seat in Old Mutual's boardroom, and that Skandia did not need to become much bigger to survive. Moreover, the (still not public) Turbo plan was said to match the cost reduction that Old Mutual had projected for the merged company. The commentary argued: 'A clear no to Old Mutual from the Skandia board and management is a precondition for giving shareholders the courage to say no to an acquisition. The fear of ending up in a lengthy struggle with a part of the shareholders is not reason enough to say yes.'[7]

Certain international media also reacted with hesitation when addressing the Old Mutual bid. On 3 September, *The Times* in the UK wrote that many Old Mutual shareholders were sceptical to the bid and might try to disrupt it through a massive sellout of Old Mutual shares. According to the paper, institutional shareholders had confronted Old Mutual's CEO with their worries and views that the company might have to reconsider the bid.[8] In a comment to the *Financial Times* on 3 September, an institutional investor with a holding of 1 per cent in Old Mutual described the synergies as 'lukewarm'.[9] On 4 September, *The Observer* published a commentary stating that the bid was clearly good for Skandia's shareholders, but to many observers, Old Mutual appeared so desperate to do a deal that it had ignored the risks. The commentary concluded by saying: 'admittedly it had recouped some of the outlay from other disposals along the way but, all in all, those who doubt whether the Old Mutual–Skandia deal is an unreservedly good thing may be justified in resisting the persuader's [that is, Sutcliffe's] charm.'[10]

On Monday 5 September 2005, the Old Mutual share fell slightly on the stock market in Johannesburg and London (trading at 141.50 pence on the LSE). The Old Mutual share was in a sliding mode the entire week, as quite a few Old Mutual shareholders seemed to be sceptical about the intended merge. The Skandia bid was supposed to result in a revaluation of Old Mutual. However, during the first weeks of September, some Old Mutual shareholders quoted in the South African press appeared to be more worried that the Old Mutual board would end up having to sweeten the bid.[11] To make matters worse, Old Mutual needed shareholder approval for a rights issue directed to Skandia's shareholders. The company was expected to issue new shares amounting to 30–35 per cent of the current ones. Thus, in order for the bid to go through, the support from Old Mutual's shareholders was as important as that of Skandia's. Old Mutual's management had, therefore, been in close contact with its largest shareholders since mid-August.

A week following the bid announcement CEO Jim Sutcliffe, while on a road show in South Africa, stated officially that Old Mutual shareholders were generally supportive of the bid. However, it seemed difficult to find analysts who were impressed by the synergies of £70 million that CFO Julian Roberts said he had identified. Chris Steward, portfolio manager at Investec Asset Management, told the South African newspaper, *Business Day*:[12] 'Strategically, we see some merit in the deal – particularly between Skandia's UK operations and Old Mutual's fledgling operation in the UK.' However, he added that he was worried that Skandia's shareholders would be sellers of Old Mutual shares for a long period of time, thus creating the risk of an overhang in the stock. Public Investment Corporation (PIC)[13] (Old Mutual's largest shareholder with about 7.3 per cent of the stock) said in the same article that it still was too early to make a commitment.[14]

The reaction among the South African financial analysts covering Old Mutual split them into two camps. Three days after the publication of the bid, Fox-Pitt Kelton restated its 'outperform' rating, entitling its analysis 'Full steam ahead'. They expected the bid to come through with an explicit support of 15 per cent of Skandia's shareholders, including 'key investors' such as Cevian and Burdarás. The low valuation of Old Mutual's share was judged to be due to arbitrage trading rather than to negative views on the fundamentals of the proposed combined group. Despite that, the industrial rationale was debatable. A size increase and lessened dependence on South Africa would make the stock much more attractive to investors worldwide. A 'fair value' of 185 pence per share was ascribed to the combined group, compared to its current trading at 141 pence. The 'new' Old Mutual share was also expected to outperform its competitors.[15]

Johny Lambridis, at Citigroup in South Africa, took the opposite stand. He viewed the deal as risky business with a Skandia that still had outstanding litigation and recent brand damage in its home market – this was alongside the stiff competition both in the UK and Sweden. Old Mutual was expected to stand by the offer – or else leave the scene. A hostile bid or some kind of bid war was seen as unattractive. Citigroup also rejected the possibility of re-rating Old Mutual (it believed it would happen anyway). As for Skandia, Citigroup still believed that the sums of its parts (calculated at 52 SEK) would be valued higher than a bid on the whole company.[16]

During the following days, there were also news stories about Old Mutual's problematic exposure to Zimbabwe (controversial because of its regime). Swedish public service radio (Sveriges Radio) reported that Old Mutual held investments on the Zimbabwe Stock Exchange worth approximately 16 per cent of the Zimbabwe market's total capitalization.[17] The same radio station reported that several of Skandia's board members were worried about this exposure, albeit it made up just a fraction of Old Mutual's assets. Jim Sutcliffe explained the situation in an interview in the *Financial Times*: 'The issue of our stake in Zimbabwe Newspapers has never been raised with me by the company [Skandia], but I am quite comfortable that our business practices would stand up to a test and follow the standards that Swedes expect.' Sutcliffe added that Zimbabwe's business and political environment was complicated; however, he would be prepared to sell Old Mutual's stake in the newspaper group worth about $1 million if the opportunity presented itself. He rhetorically asked the journalist: 'It could be sold, sure, but who do you think would buy it?'[18]

16.3 INITIATING A BOARD DOCUMENT

At a meeting on 5 September, the Skandia board decided on the process for the production of the board's statement on the Old Mutual bid. The bid letter from Old Mutual to Skandia had just arrived. Bernt Magnusson said that the situation was both delicate and unusual and, to complicate matters, that there had been some turmoil both inside and outside Skandia. He exemplified the latter with the big trade in the Skandia share and the differing press comments regarding the merits of an Old Mutual deal. He said that the media had been mainly negative in Sweden, but had been predominantly neutral to positive abroad. Magnusson continued by stating that, regarding the bid, the board had agreed to disagree; in other words, they were divided on the issue. This meant that it would not be sufficient to state just one opinion in the board document. Two were needed: one advocated by the board members who were against the bid (the five directors Kajsa Lindståhl, Birgitta Johansson-Hedberg, Lennart Jeansson and Anders Ullberg, along with the three union representatives), and one supported by those who were in favour of the bid (the three board members Bernt Magnusson, Björn Björnsson and Christer Gardell).

In a situation with a divided board there was a particular need for a process that worked. Magnusson said that this was the task for the board to set up and manage. Consultant firm Erneholm and Haskel, in cooperation with Skandia's secretary-general Jan-Mikael Bexhed, were suggested to produce the document to be presented in connection with the board's 23 September decision. The important thing with this document was that both positions – a 'yes' and a 'no' to the bid – had to be well motivated.

16.4 EMERGING SHAREHOLDER ACTIVITY

On 6 September 2005, the *Financial Times* wrote that Fidelity had sent a supportive letter to Old Mutual's board saying that it was in favour of the Skandia acquisition.[19] The letter was dated 2 September, the same day as the bid press conference. Another letter was sent to Old Mutual's board on 9 September stating that Fidelity had bought additional shares in Skandia to support Old Mutual's bid. For Old Mutual, this support could be counted twice. Fidelity International was both a large Skandia shareholder with officially approximately 5 per cent of the shares, as well as an Old Mutual shareholder in control of close to 2 per cent. However, Fidelity never confirmed the two letters in public.

On Friday 9 September, the Swedish Shareholders' Association counteracted the rumoured letter from Fidelity. The CEO Lars-Erik Forsgårdh sent a letter to the Skandia board before its planned meeting (for Sunday 11 September), in which he asked the board members not to support Old Mutual's offer. This request was made public the same morning. The main argument was that Skandia represented more than just a listed company. According to the Swedish Shareholders' Association, a buyer would also control Skandia Liv, in which about half of all Swedes had an interest: either directly through pension savings, or indirectly through the investments that Skandia had in other Swedish listed corporations. The Association argued that it was not a good idea to entrust a large part of the nation's savings to a foreign company. In its letter to the Skandia board, it expressed the hope that the directors would be brave enough to say 'no' to the proposed deal. The Association wanted the Skandia group to continue standing on its own, something that in its view would be in the best interests of the Swedish people.

Following the announcement of the bid, it took a week for the first article about the institutional selloff to appear in the Swedish media. On Friday 9 September, *Dagens Industri* addressed the Swedish institutional and retail investors' dilemma:

> The proposition with a mix of shares and cash seems unattractive. Who wants to have stocks in Old Mutual that are traded on the Stockholm Stock Exchange? In the new Old Mutual, Skandia shareholders will get 25 per cent of the shares, and foreign capital already accounts for almost 50 per cent. In the future, these investors have no reason to trade Old Mutual shares through the Stockholm Stock Exchange. With only 14 per cent of the new Old Mutual's shares in Swedish hands, the trading in that market place will be unattractive – and the sell-out has already started. During the past week, 18 per cent of the shares in Skandia have changed hands. Rumours point to Cevian friends as being on the buying side. It is interesting to note that, at the same time, British analysts are taking a cautious stand on the Old Mutual share. No one has a clear buying recommendation.[20]

On Friday evening, 9 September 2005, Deutsche Bank held a reception to celebrate the opening of its Stockholm investment banking office. Jan Olsson was presented as the new director in Sweden, responsible for the

Nordic region. Deutsche Bank's CEO Josef Ackerman was the host of the event. Many actors involved in the Skandia affair were present, including Jim Sutcliffe. Hans-Erik Andersson was also among those invited. During a conversation with Andersson, Ackerman said that he thought the suggested deal was marvellous – although perhaps not for the CEO of the target company.

Thomas Halvorsen of AP4 was at the Deutsche Bank reception as well, talking both to Nordea's CFO Arne Liljedahl and its chief strategic officer, Jakob Grinbaum. Halvorsen had received a mandate from his board to organize a possible Swedish opposition to Old Mutual's bid that included a search for a 'white knight'. Therefore he wanted to learn more, for instance, about Nordea's views on Skandia. Halvorsen tried to get Nordea's management to understand that it was time for them to act, and asked if they planned to take a closer look at Skandia. Liljedahl and Grinbaum listened, but made no statements. Later that evening, Jan Olsson introduced Liljedahl and Grinbaum to Jim Sutcliffe. The three of them talked about Nordea's possible interest in Skandia's Nordic franchise. Later in the autumn, the discussions continued between Old Mutual and Nordea; however, Old Mutual never returned with any proposition. Nordea also maintained its scepticism when it came to Skandia's business model, so it was certainly not going to bid for all of the company.

16.5 OLD MUTUAL TOP MANAGEMENT MEETS THE SKANDIA BOARD

A week after the bid had been presented, the Skandia board's position was still unclear to the general public, as was what had really happened in the talks between Old Mutual, Skandia and the group of larger institutional investors involved in the discussions. However, details of the proposed Old Mutual–Skandia deal began to leak throughout the media. On 9 September, Bengt Carlsson referred in *Dagens Nyheter* to an internal presentation made earlier that week by Skandia's head of Nordic operations, Gert Engman. The message was that Skandiabanken was going to become more integrated in Skandia. Carlsson also expected that competitors for Skandiabanken would be happy to see it lose momentum as a consequence of a deal.[21] The same day, *Dagens Industri* published details of the 28 August meeting with major institutional investors, and Lennart Jeansson talking on behalf of the sceptical board members. In the article, it was further claimed that Skandia director Christer Gardell's vested interest in selling his fund's Skandia shares meant that it was questionable whether or not he should participate in voting on the matter.[22]

On Sunday morning, 11 September 2005, the day of the Skandia board meeting, Carlsson wrote another *Dagens Nyheter* piece stating that it was unlikely the Skandia board would choose to vote either for or against the Old Mutual bid, and that Old Mutual would not retract the bid regardless of what the board decided. He also thought that, given the fact that the South African currency control influenced Old Mutual's ability to move money out of South Africa in order to finance Skandia's expansion, board members worried about Old Mutual's cash flow. He further speculated about a possible board split, which would result in some of the members resigning. This would create an unusual situation in the company, with the board against a bid and a group of larger active shareholders supporting it. Moreover, the infectious question of Skandiabanken spread throughout the agenda. Jim Sutcliffe said: 'All options are open. We are in talks with the Skandia management. We are very cautious with regards to our capital.' He also pointed to the possibility of selling Skandiabanken in order to reduce debt.[23]

At the Skandia board meeting on 11 September, Jim Sutcliffe was given the opportunity to present his company's case to the Skandia directors. He had looked forward to the meeting, as it was the first time that he would meet all the board members. He told people around him that he was going to sell Old Mutual's position to Skandia's decision-makers. He was given 60 minutes to present his case. However, the meeting was a disappointment for Sutcliffe; he was not prepared for a split board. His impression was that all of them – with the exception of Bernt Magnusson, Björn Björnsson and Christer Gardell – had 'no' written all over their faces. Sutcliffe told his colleagues on the way back to London that there was no way this transaction could be carried out as a friendly bid and obtain the board's full support.

At the meeting, the board revisited the decision that had been made a week earlier regarding how to run the process that would produce the board's documentation addressing the bid. The preferred consultant Erneholm and Haskel had been contracted for the task, and it was reported that the firm had begun working with Skandia's secretary-general Jan-Mikael Bexed, as requested. The board then discussed how the process should continue, and it was decided that each director should give their views on the matter to Bexhed and to Erneholm and Haskel as soon as possible. The advisers were asked to report to the entire board and to have a full prototype ready the coming weekend for the directors' revision (that is, around 16–17 September). It was decided that the final version should be sent to all members of the board on 22 September for their approval and signatures.

16.6 A CASCADE OF ARGUMENTS

The media reports that followed the board meeting on Sunday 11 September wrote that Old Mutual was beginning to change its attitude towards the value of a friendly bid. In the 12 September edition of South African newspaper *Business Day*, Old Mutual's spokesman Alex Sandberg was quoted as saying:

> We have said that we would like this board's recommendation and we continue to seek it, and we are hopeful we are going to achieve it . . . We have had a long dialogue with this company that has stretched over many months and, during that process, the board has allowed us to conduct due diligence, which is a deep and broad exercise; we have worked with their management closely on this. It has encouraged us, inviting us to speak to its major shareholders, which we have done. The majority of them are in favour of our offer.[24]

An Old Mutual source also said that the shareholders who supported the deal with Skandia had doubled from 15 per cent to approximately 30 per cent. There were also speculators who were assumed to hold 15 to 20 per cent in Skandia shares, anticipating that the deal would go through. The source said: 'There is pretty significant momentum building here. The majority of the voting stock seems to indicate they want the deal to happen.' Old Mutual's spokesman Alex Sandberg said, 'Old Mutual will continue its dialogue with Skandia and I am hopeful of a favourable response.'[25]

Eduardo D'Almeida, head of asset management at South African Sanlam Asset Management (which owned about 3.5 per cent of the shares in Old Mutual), said to *Dagens Industri* on 13 September: 'We respect the Swedish takeover rules demanding that a bid is directed at shareholders, but for us it still remains important that the board and management stand behind a bid . . . The deal is risky as we see it, Old Mutual's profit will be diluted in the short run. It is important that the acquisition can be cleared without trouble . . .'. Errol Shear, head of equities at life insurer Stanlib Asset Management (which owned about 4 per cent of the shares in Old Mutual), expressed a similar view in the same article: 'We do not expect all to be positive, but it is absolutely essential that a majority of the board members and management supports it. We will make careful calculations and evaluate who says no.'[26]

Meanwhile, the debate for and against the Old Mutual bid continued in the Swedish media. On 12 September, business journalist Tommy Borglund in the Swedish weekly business magazine *Veckans Affärer* published an article in which he described Skandia as a prime example of corporate disarray, a 'just cause' for moral outrage and shareholder revolt. He described the burial of the company as long overdue or, at least, that it should be brought under the control of some other force. He welcomed the bid for Skandia and described Sweden as a country with a poorly developed market for corporate control. Borglund saw the only possible alternative path to the future as paved with sophisticated ethical codes, strong leadership, and shareholders in charge. He also claimed that acquired companies paid higher salaries, invested more, and were more efficient than others.[27] In the same edition of *Veckans Affärer*, journalist Anders Haskel argued quite differently, writing that the recent revaluation of the Skandia share should not be interpreted as a reaction to the bid. Haskel assumed that Skandia was simply doing well and this was reflected in its share price. If the bid fell through, the Skandia share might not be hurt that much, not even in the short term.[28]

The negative sentiment around Old Mutual's stock remained. *Dagens Nyheter* quoted an analysis from the investment bank UBS on Thursday 15 September that criticized the intended deal, stressing that Old Mutual's shareholders would face a heavy dilution if the Skandia deal were closed. Furthermore, UBS did not believe in the presented synergies of £70 million, estimating that only half of them would hit the bottom line.[29] That day, the Old Mutual stock traded at 137 pence, having fallen by 5 per cent since the bid was announced on 2 September. The FTSE index on the LSE also fell during this period, but only half as much.

Journalists for both *Dagens Nyheter* and *Dagens Industri* published more arguments against a sale of Skandia during the following week.[30] One was that Old Mutual would have difficulty getting cash out of South Africa because of currency regulations. This was something Jim Sutcliffe had previously described as not important in relation to the Skandia bid. The papers also reported negative views from investments banks and analysts, most of whom focused on Old Mutual's proposed overstatements regarding the economies of scale involved, and the possible financial strain that a deal might imply for Old Mutual's shareholders. The whole affair was described as a propaganda war with a well-organized and well-remunerated team on the yes side that faced a rather disorganized body of naysayers. There were also articles about how the owner base of Skandia was shifting to a non-Swedish one. Several institutional investors were suggested to be rather flexible in their positions. Some of those who had changed their initial stance were named; among them were AP1, AP2, Fidelity and SEB Funds.

The *Financial Times* reported that the bid resistance was criticized as an 'emotive response'. Former Trade Minister Anders Sundström was quoted as saying that 'to sell Skandia would damage Sweden'. Lars Milberg from the Swedish Shareholders' Association was quoted as dubbing Skandia 'one of the [Swedish] crown jewels'. The *Financial Times* reporter Päivi Munter described the situation in the following way:

> The outcry surrounding Skandia comes at a time when globalisation is undermining many Swedes' sense of security. Large numbers of manufacturing jobs are being moved from high-tax Sweden to low-cost countries in Asia and Eastern Europe, raising the unemployment rate to a historically high level of about 7 per cent. This has become a key theme before the general elections. Still, some market participants professed their surprise at the nationalistic response to Old Mutual's bid for the oldest listed company on the Stockholm bourse.[31]

NOTES

1. 1 SEK = 100 öre.
2. Before Old Mutual had entered the scene in May most of the analysts had a trading value for Skandia of approximately 35 SEK. After the bid was announced, they landed at 42 SEK on average. Most actors calculated that the Skandia share price would collapse – in the short term – if Old Mutual walked away.
3. *Dagens Nyheter*, 3 September 2005, 'Budet bryter mot regler', Bengt Carlsson.
4. Aktiemarknadsnämnden, 1 September 2005, AMN 2005: 33, 'Concerning certain conditions of withdrawal of a public offer (Old Mutal/Skandia)'. The document was not made official until a few weeks later.
5. *Dagens Industri*, 3 September 2005, 'De vill att Skandia förblir svenskt', Henrik Huldschiner.
6. *Dagens Nyheter*, 4 September 2005, 'Old Mutual riskerar skjuta sig själv i foten', Bengt Carlsson.
7. *Dagens Industri*, 5 September 2005, 'Skandiaägare beredd att avstå kontanter'; and *Dagens Industri*, 5 September 2005, 'Tveksamheter i budet från Old Mutual', Sophie Nachemson-Ekwall.
8. *The Times*, 3 September 2005, reported by newswires Bloomberg News and Direkt, 5 September 2005.
9. *Financial Times*, 3 September, 'Old Mutual in bid for Skandia'. Rupini Bergström and Henry Tricks.
10. *The Observer*, 4 September 2005, 'Old Mutual's risky Swedish connection', Heather Connon.
11. *Business Day*, 7 September 2005, 'Old Mutual's big bid'.
12. *Business Day*, 5 September 2005, 'Old Mutual woos shareholders to put Skandia purchase in motion', Stephen Gunnion.
13. Part of the South African public pension system. In February 2005 its shareholding had been 13 per cent.
14. See note 12.
15. Fox-Pitt, Kelton, 5 September 2005, 'Old Mutual: Full Steam Ahead', Mikir Shah and Johnny Vo.
16. Citigroup, 31 August 2005, 'Old Mutual; Skandia Negotiations Drawing to a Close', Johny Lambridis.
17. *Sveriges Radio, Kanal 1, Ekot*, 2 September 2005, 'OM lägger bud på Skandia', Magnus Thoren and Patrik Holmström.
18. *Financial Times*, 5 September 2005, 'Skandia grills Old Mutual on Zimbabwe holdings', John Reed.
19. *Financial Times*, 6 September 2005, 'Fidelity supports 3.3bn Old Mutual offer for Skandia', Andrea Felsted and Rupini Bergström.

20. *Dagens Industri*, 9 September 2005, 'Budprocessen stinker', Sophie Nachemson-Ekwall.
21. *Dagens Nyheter*, 9 September 2005, 'Skandias styrelse fortfarande oening till OM:s bud', Bengt Carlsson.
22. See note 20.
23. *Dagens Nyheter*, 11 September 2005, 'Skandiastyrelsen ger inte klart besked om OM', Bengt Carlsson.
24. *Business Day*, 12 September 2005, 'Old Mutual chiefs take merger case to Skandia board', Stephen Gunnion.
25. See previous note.
26. *Dagens Industri*, 13 September 2005, '. . . och ledningens trovärdighet analyseras', Sophie Nachemson-Ekwall.
27. *Veckans Affärer*, 12 September 2005, 'Äntligen, Skandia', Tommy Borglund.
28. *Veckans Affärer*, 12 September 2005, 'Skandia säljs för billigt', Anders Haskel.
29. UBS, 5 September 2005, 'Old Mutual Plc; The Skandia Offer', Andrew McNulty and Roger Hill.
30. *Dagens Industri*, 12 September 2005, 'Nej-sägare i Skandia står fast', Sophie Nachemson-Ekwall; *Dagens Industri*, 13 September 2005, 'och ledningens trovärdighet analyseras', Sophie Nachemson-Ekwall; *Dagens Industri*, 14 September 2005, 'De kan rädda Skandia', Sophie Nachemson-Ekwall; *Dagens Nyheter*, 15 September 2005, 'Skandiabudet döms ut', Bengt Carlsson; *Dagens Industri*, 15 September 2005, 'Han beställde ny analys', Gustaf Tapper; *Dagens Nyheter*, 16 September 2005, 'Skandias styrelse enhälligt för 'turboplanen', Bengt Carlsson; and *Dagens Nyheter*, 18 September 2005, 'Propagandakriget ännu en sida av Skandia', Bengt Carlsson.
31. *Financial Times*, 19 September 2005, 'Bid for Skandia meets emotive response', Päivi Munter.

17. Trying to keep Skandia independent

17.1 ACTIVITIES IN AND AROUND THE SWEDISH AP FUNDS

The deal opposition continued to grow. Leading Swedish business actors discussed Skandia's future standing among themselves, and with advisers, analysts, journalists, politicians and so on. A kind of social movement arose, composed of loosely coupled business people who all tried to persuade the larger Swedish retail and pension funds that had shareholdings in Skandia to turn down Old Mutual's bid. Sven-Eric Österberg, deputy minister of finance in Sweden's Social Democratic government (and who had a particular responsibility for the financial markets and pension funds) also carefully monitored what happened in and around Skandia. Österberg had been a member of parliament since the mid-1990s, and had been mostly engaged on its finance committee. He had also been involved in the reformation of the Swedish pension system and the remodelling of the four AP funds in the 1990s. Österberg had debated many times with Lars-Erik Forsgårdh of the Swedish Shareholders' Association and Göran Johnsson, chair of the Metalworkers' Union, in an attempt to get the four fund chairs to come up with a suggestion for how to reform the funds' investment policies in order to become more 'long-term'.

The deputy finance minister liked the idea of AP funds becoming substantial stakeholders in Swedish blue chips. He said in a press comment in the spring of 2005 that it would be preferable if the AP funds were allowed to increase their stake in a single company, above the currently stipulated 10 per cent.[1] This was both a delicate and complex matter, since few politicians in Sweden wanted to arouse the old debate from the 1970s and 1980s concerning substantial union ownership in the private corporate sector. Österberg had spoken to the four chairs of the AP funds after Old Mutual's bid on Skandia had been announced. He expressed his support for a possible joint action from the AP-funds to stop Old Mutual's takeover of Skandia, although he (like many others in this process) preferred to work without going public.[2]

AP2 funds' CEO Lars Idermark and CIO Petter Odhnoff obtained board support in late August 2005 for Old Mutual's request of a signed 'soft irrevocable'. It stated that AP2 (as one of the anonymous actors) was inclined to sell its Skandia shares (3.2 per cent of the stock) to Old Mutual. Idermark and Odhnoff thought that the price of the Skandia stock would rise after the bid was announced. In their view, Skandia was worth close to 50 SEK. Instead, the share slid downwards, trading at approximately 40–41 SEK. The split on the Skandia board and insight into the discussions regarding the stand-alone plan presented new information to AP2's executives and directors. Idermark and Odhnoff had second thoughts about its support. So did the AP2 board.

Similar to the other AP funds, AP2 included several directors who were connected to both the political elite and to Skandia's sceptical board members. For example, AP2 chair Gunnar Larsson was a member of the Social Democratic Party and former municipal commissioner for the city of Gothenburg. He knew former Volvo manager and current Skandia director Lennart Jeansson, who also served as board member for AP6 (a Gothenburg-based fund with directives to invest exclusively in unlisted companies). Two other AP2 board members also had backgrounds in Gothenburg and Volvo: Eva Persson, who was secretary-general of the Volvo board and member of the executive team alongside Lennart Jeansson; and Anders Jonsson, former head of Volvo Group Finance, who had also been CEO of Stena Metal in 2005 (part of the private Gothenburg shipping group where Jeansson was chair).

Another AP2 board member was Bo Dockered, who belonged to Sweden's Centre Party (Centerpartiet). Dockered was also well connected to Sweden's Social Democratic government. He was former chair of the Swedish Farmers' Association and chair of the state-owned companies Sveaskog (forest industry) and Trav & Galopp (gambling business). Moreover, he knew Skandia director Birgitta Johansson-Hedberg quite well, given her background both as director and CEO of Swedbank, a bank that had incorporated the farmers' main banking partner Föreningsbanken which Dockered had once chaired. Dockered also had Johansson-Hedberg as a board member of Sveaskog and, in her current position as CEO of Lantmännen (which represented 44 000 Swedish farmers), she and Dockered met regularly. Dockered also knew AP2's CEO Lars Idermark, who, like him, had a background from the board of Lantmännen. AP2's board also included independent adviser Märtha Josefsson, who was also the former director at Skandia Asset Management and founder of Carlsson Investment Management, which Skandia had bought in late 1990s.[3] Thus Josefsson knew Skandia and claimed to understand the dynamics of the management's Turbo plan.

During the first weeks of September, AP2's view of Old Mutual's bid for Skandia was under intense review. AP4 had by then already revealed its negative standing to the bid. Chair Gunnar Larsson held a rather low profile in the discussions, while Bo Dockered supported a Skandia that was kept under Swedish control. Märtha Josefsson argued that the asset management of Skandia Life ought to remain Swedish, and she found the stand-alone case appealing. Given AP2 management's disappointment with the bid price, the discussions at the AP2 board during the early weeks of September ended with a shared view: the fund should work for an independent Skandia. AP2 was, at the end of September, in control of 3 per cent of Skandia's shares. Two of the fund's financial analysts were allotted the task of preparing an internal in-depth analysis of Skandia. The aim was to give a board presentation well before 23 September, the date when Skandia's board had promised to come up with its own recommendation.

Dagens Industri reported on 14 September 2005 that AP funds considered withdrawing its support for Christer Gardell's (i.e. Cevian's) position in Skandia. Two of the AP funds (AP1 and AP2) had been co-investors in Cevian, and such a development could possibly precipitate the stop of a Skandia sale, since AP4 had also expressed its negative standing. The three AP funds owned a total of 5.5 per cent of the Skandia shares. AP1's and AP2's situations were extraordinary, since their investments in Cevian (which amounted to more than 600 million SEK) represented 44 per cent of its capital (1.4 billion SEK in assets). Cevian owned 3.4 per cent of the shares in Skandia.[4]

The same article reported that board members of the three AP funds anonymously expressed surprise and disappointment regarding Cevian's activity in Skandia. One director said the fund's belief was that Cevian invested in mismanaged listed companies and, as he understood it, Skandia did not belong to that category. The director also saw it as important for the AP funds' reputation to know what kind of fund it was working through. Another board member was quoted saying that it would be a surprise if Cevian did not choose to support the view of the majority of the directors on the Skandia board. The board member in question saw that a long-term investor (such as an AP fund) would not worry if the Skandia share lost a few SEK in the short term. A third director was concerned about rumours, saying that Christer Gardell had made the Skandia board members uneasy by bringing up the risk of legal processes. As this AP fund director saw it, AP funds could – and should – exercise control over Gardell's way of using the capital invested in Cevian. Deputy Finance Minister Sven-Eric Österberg said:

> If AP funds' requirement of long-term return on investments can be matched with an ambition to own shares in a company, then there is nothing that

> prevents it from cooperating as owners . . . It is an important question. I cannot influence the activities of AP funds, but it would be a strength for Sweden and for the financial marketplace of Stockholm if Skandia remained Swedish.

Dagens Industri wrote that, in order to stop the bid, an opposition would require support from 10 per cent of the shareholders.[5] This meant that the three AP funds needed support from others, which would not be impossible given the fact that, at the end of August, half of Skandia's shares were in Swedish hands. However, the article concluded that the impression was that at least half the Skandia shares were in the hands of short-term investors.

17.2 A CRITIQUE OF MORGAN STANLEY

In September and early October the Skandia board dealt with the workings of Morgan Stanley. On 15 September both *Dagens Industri* and *Dagens Nyheter* wrote about the adviser's valuation of Skandia.[6] The newspapers pointed to an analysis that should have been done around Christmas 2004, when the adviser was supposed to have calculated a fair trading value of 47 SEK (according to the journalists, this figure was not based on a break-up calculation). The papers also wrote that Morgan Stanley had come back in August 2005 with a new calculation indicating a Fair Trade Value (FTV) of 36 SEK.

These press reports produced strong reactions among directors at both the Skandia board and within Morgan Stanley, as much of what had been written in the articles was wrong. Board directors and advisers were upset by the leakage of confidential material, which seemed to have been aimed at discrediting the work of Morgan Stanley. During its retainer agreement with Skandia, the investment bank had on a continuous basis presented FTV analyses to the board. Moreover, the particular figure mentioned in the reports that was supposed to be valid for December 2004, 47 SEK, was instead an average figure based on seven different valuations, presented to the Skandia board on 25 February 2005. The adviser actually provided a large span of values – ranging from around 34 SEK up to about 57 SEK – which the Skandia directors had to consider when forming their views on this crucial matter.

At this time, the naysayers in the Skandia board proposed that the Morgan Stanley agreement should be revoked, as in their eyes the adviser had generally supported material that favoured a sale of Skandia. In the end, all the other board members accepted their suggestion, so the board decided to give CEO Hans-Erik Andersson the mandate to terminate the agreement with Morgan Stanley. The other investment bank engaged by the Skandia board, ABN Amro, which had been working on a fairness opinion since the middle of July, was to continue.

17.3 THE CONFLICT WITH THE BRITS CONTINUES

For Skandia's CEO, the problem of dealing with the board's split and the Skandia shareholders was exacerbated by the continuous conflict with the management of Skandia Life UK. The relations with its CEO Nick Poyntz-Wright continued to be characterized by tension. Skandia held its annual management conference on 13 September in Italy. The event had always been a grand happening, at which 50 of Skandia's top managers discussed the company's future. Half a dozen of the Skandia Life UK managers were expected to join this top management conference, but a few days before the meeting, they all cancelled their flights. Their reason was that they were all tired of discussing the stand-alone path and Turbo plan with the Swedish executives. For Poyntz-Wright and his management team, there was no point in continuing discussing those topics. The UK management told those in Stockholm that the outcome was predetermined: Skandia would be sold. As a consequence, Poyntz-Wright said that he and his team refused to participate in the upcoming meeting in Italy. He had already opposed the conference theme, well before the discussion of the Turbo plan at the Skandia board meeting at the end of May.

Andersson could not accept this behaviour. So he turned to members of the Skandia Life UK board and obtained their support for a tough approach. He decided to warn Poyntz-Wright that he would lose his job if he did not show up in Italy. The Skandia Holding UK board member Ashok Gupta tried to act as some sort of mediator, and Morgan Stanley's Jakob Lindquist flew to Southampton in an attempt to persuade Poyntz-Wright and his people to attend the meeting. In the end, Poyntz-Wright obtained legal advice, which told him to go or else he would be in danger of being discharged on formal grounds. So Poyntz-Wright and two other members of the executive team turned up unannounced for breakfast on the first day.

The distance between Skandia Life UK and the rest of the group during the conference proceedings was striking. This became clearly visible on various occasions: for example, when one country manager in an open session asked the Skandia Life UK representatives to stop sabotaging the debate by constantly talking about Old Mutual's bid. Applause erupted in support of the country manager – by everyone but the UK participants.

17.4 PUBLISHING THE TURBO PLAN

Skandia was tearing itself into pieces. There was a split board, conflicts among Skandia and its UK subsidiaries, and a whole host of divided shareholders. In this complicated situation, however, it became possible for the CEO to talk more openly about his plans for the stand-alone case to those on the board who did not support the bid. Hans-Erik Andersson said he wanted to work against the Old Mutual bid. However, Björnsson (one of Skandia's directors who supported the bid) claimed that it would be a mistake for the board and management to act against the wishes of a majority of the shareholders.

On the morning of 15 September, the Skandia board released the information given to potential bidders in the limited due diligence process.[7] The purpose was to enable the shareholders to make up their minds ahead of the board's decision on 23 September. This came in the form of an eight-page presentation of the Turbo plan, with estimated cost savings for the years 2005–07. It also included management's own sales prognoses as far away as 2009. Tillinghast's updated valuation of the embedded value, calculated at 34.4 billion SEK, was also enclosed. The presentation revealed very strong growth for both sales and profit, compared to the previously reported figures; this was a document with a multitude of figures and arguments. The Turbo plan was expected to deliver increased efficiency through improved cost and revenue synergies across the Skandia group; the estimated total came to 1.2 billion SEK for 2009. Skandia's pre-tax profit was projected to be 2.9 billion SEK for 2005, 5.4 billion SEK for 2006 and 6.5 billion SEK for 2007. The figures were 20 to 30 per cent higher than what most analysts following the Skandia story had forecast.

By calculating backwards, those who believed in the forecasts could value Skandia at about 50 billion SEK – that is, to 50 SEK per share. Apparently very few investors did so, since the Skandia stock did not move, trading at around 40 SEK. The main reason for the market's reserved reaction could be found on page five of the document:

> It should be noted that the Turbo plan reflects the executive management's best judgement with regards to the high degree of uncertainty that exists with this kind of group efficiency programmes. Here, it shall be noted that the management of Skandia Life UK, through Deputy Head for UK, Asia Pacific & Offshore, Nick Poyntz-Wright, has presented a diverging view to the board, and dissociated itself from both the direction in the plan and the possibility to achieve the presented effects.[8]

Chair Bernt Magnusson (along with Directors Björn Björnsson and Christer Gardell) demanded a publication of the UK management's reservation: a position based on advice from Skandia's legal adviser, Robert Ohlsson at FöretagsJuridik Nord & Co. According to Ohlsson, it should also be included in the forthcoming board statement planned for 23 September regarding Old Mutual's bid.

When the UK management's reservation hit the wire services on 15 September, some traders in London shook their heads. In their opinion, Nick Poyntz-Wright was a sensible guy, representing 50 per cent of the market value for the company, and had obviously turned down the Turbo plan. The media was quick to pick up these UK sentiments. The next day, the press reported that none of the bidders who had read through the Turbo plan during due diligence had credited it any particular value. The calculations were just too uncertain and, in essence, they boiled down merely to a reduction of head-office staff in both Stockholm and Southampton. Since the board had agreed not to make any comments on the released text (or related matters) before the press conference that was scheduled for 23 September (i.e. immediately following the board's decision and final statements about the bid), the individual directors' possibly differing views regarding various ingredients in the document were not publicly expressed.

Meeting the press on 15 September, CEO Hans-Erik Andersson (flanked by CFO Jan-Erik Back) claimed to be in charge of a company that worked according to the plans approved by the board back in January 2005. In an interview published in *Dagens Industri*, the Turbo plan, although decided upon, was described to be somewhat on ice since most of the focus during the summer had been directed on bid-related processes. Andersson had not commented on that issue in the boardroom; he had said only that it was good that all shareholders and Old Mutual had access to the same information. Andersson avoided answering the question that addressed rumoured attacks from Director Björn Björnsson on the credibility of the Turbo plan, as well as the one that asked for his opinion of Old Mutual as a prospective owner. However, he was firm regarding Skandia Life UK's CEO. If Nick Poyntz-Wright did not support the planned changes – including those in the UK operations – there would be changes in the UK staff. Andersson further underlined the importance of Skandiabanken to the overall Skandia concept. He added that he did not expect Skandia to split up if Old Mutual's bid fell through.[9]

17.5 A DELICATE POLITICAL ISSUE

The Swedish opposition to Old Mutual's bid continued to be heard. On 16 September, Anders Sundström got involved in the debate; he was the former minister of industry in Sweden's Social Democratic Party and current CEO of Folksam (one of the insurance companies with close relationships to the Worker's Union, the Consumer Cooperation and the Social Democratic Party). In a full-page commentary in *Dagens Industri*,[10] he encouraged the Swedish institutional shareholders not to sell their Skandia shares. The reason was predominantly nationalistic. His concern was to keep Swedish control of one of the larger pension managers on the capital market. That same day, incumbent Minister of Industry Thomas Östros was quoted in *Dagens Industri* as saying that he wanted Skandia to remain Swedish:

> I cannot interfere with the Skandia deal directly. That would be inappropriate. But I have continuous contact with the large owners and I have presented my view to them. I hope that the owners' decisions are not determined by short-term profit taking, but that the long-term effects are considered. . . . They must ask themselves how a sale would impact Stockholm as a financial centre.[11]

This was a particularly delicate situation, as Minister of Industry Thomas Östros was visiting Saab, the Swedish weapon systems company that was about to deliver JAS Gripen fighter planes to South Africa. He was to host a meeting with the South African minister of trade and industry, Mandisi Mpahwla, and a delegation of South African business people. The minister had answered the journalist's questions politely, trying to calm the concern over the country's currency restriction. It was planned that Swedish Prime Minister Göran Persson would travel to South Africa in the beginning of October with the purpose of increasing trade between the two countries. So the autumn of 2005 was certainly not a good time for any diplomatic dispute about a possible South African control over a large financial player in the Swedish capital market.

NOTES

1. *Dagens Industri*, 16 June 2005, 'Men Österberg oroar sig för AP-fonderna', Karin Svensson.
2. Usually such processes are carried out in ways not visible to the general public. See, e.g., Sjöstrand et al. (2001).
3. When Skandia Asset Management was sold to DnB 2004, Skandia mutual funds (previously Carlsson funds) remained at Skandia Liv.
4. *Dagens Industri*, 14 September 2005, 'De kan rädda Skandia', Sophie Nachemson-Ekwall.
5. The right to squeeze out the minority shareholders under the Swedish Companies' Act requires control of more than 90 per cent of the shares and voting rights in the target company.
6. *Dagens Industri*, 15 September 2005, 'Han beställde ny analys', Gustaf Tapper;

Dagens Nyheter, 16 September 2005, 'Bank tjänar millioner om Skandia säljs', Bengt Carlsson.

7. Press release, 15 September 2005, 'Skandias styrelse informerar – icke publik information som lämnats till Old Mutual i due diligence processen', Skandia.
8. Ibid.
9. *Dagens Industri*, 16 September 2005, 'Skandias VD träder fram', Sophie Nachemson-Ekwall.
10. *Dagens Industri*, 16 September 2005, 'Sälja ut Skandia skadar Sverige', Anders Sundström.
11. *Dagens Industri*, 16 September 2005, 'Kamp om Skandia – på ministernivå', Ola Hellbom.

18. A hostile bid

18.1 PUBLIC RELATIONS PROBLEMS

Actors close to Old Mutual's CEO heard Jim Sutcliffe express doubts about the entire Skandia deal two weeks after it was announced publicly. One Swedish investor startled him by asking what Old Mutual might do if 'they' – a group of opposing Swedish investors – gained control of 10 per cent of the shares. Similar questions indicated that Old Mutual's marketing in Sweden had begun to lose momentum. Sutcliffe and CFO Julian Roberts complained about the performance of the Swedish PR team Kreab, which they thought was acting too passively, and had not tried hard enough to influence what the press had been writing.

In mid-September, Kreab's staff found itself caught in a difficult situation. From the very beginning (back in May) they had been informed that Old Mutual's plan was quite straightforward: the Skandia board would recommend a public bid, and then the majority of the shareholders would accept it. While preparing for the deal, Kreab focused on its role as gatekeeper for Old Mutual. The PR firm arranged courteous meetings with 'important people' in Sweden (such as government officials, representatives of the Wallenberg family, leading opinion-makers and so on). During the summer, Kreab had the impression that Old Mutual and its investment banks were in control of the bid process and, according to its public opinion analyses, Skandia was not a company of national concern. Therefore the PR firm acted on that premise.[1]

Information personnel at Old Mutual's office in London witnessed a heated debate in the media in the first weeks of September 2005, for which they were unprepared. The stories that were popping up in the news appeared to be out of Kreab's control. The Old Mutual actors were surprised, and complained about the dynamics of the media coverage in Sweden. From their experience, UK business journalists usually listened more to the information that PR firms transmitted, and accurately reported it by sticking to a specific perspective throughout an entire (deal) process. The media in Sweden, however, appeared to be less predictable. The Swedish business reporters involved did not seem to fully trust the information that PR managers were putting out – in this particular case,

Kreab's messages regarding the Old Mutual–Skandia affair. To Old Mutual's distress a Swedish reporter could change his or her opinion at the drop of a hat. Moreover, one paper's commentaries and reports could present differing views – sometimes even in the same edition of the publication. Meanwhile, the whole Old Mutual process had become more complicated to handle, since the question of a hostile bid became an issue.

For Old Mutual, the media situation was complicated by the fact that the company was in the midst of changing its head of communications. James Poole had reached retirement age, and Katie Bell (who had formerly worked with Brunswick[2]) was to take over as Old Mutual's new director of corporate affairs, responsible for the company's worldwide communications. She formally assumed the role on 12 September. As a professional, Katie Bell had experience of hostile takeover battles; this time, she landed in the middle of a complicated one with many information-related challenges. One of her first strategies was to strengthen Old Mutual's PR team by bringing with her colleagues from her former employer.

18.2 SHORT SELLING SKANDIA SHARES

Speculators took a stance before the Skandia board's 23 September public recommendation regarding the bid. With a board apparently split into two groups and with the possibility that as much as 10 per cent of its shareholders would turn down Old Mutual's offer, people began to calculate what the effects on Skandia's share price would be if Old Mutual suddenly decided to walk away. Several investors began short selling Skandia stocks. During the weeks of 15 September and 23 September, 34.5 million stocks were short sold.[3] This amounted to 3.5 per cent of the Skandia shares.

Meanwhile, Old Mutual lost ground on the LSE. During the three-week period between the bid announcement and 23 September, the share fell almost 7 per cent from 141.5 pence to 134.5 pence, slightly more than the FTSE index.[4] However, the UK pound became stronger versus the Swedish krona (SEK), so the actual drop in the value for Skandia shareholders stopped at 2 per cent. On 26 September, the value of the Old Mutual bid to Skandia shareholders amounted to 42.7 SEK per share; however, Skandia was trading at around 40 SEK. The spread of about 6 per cent between the bid value and the traded value was an indication of some market uncertainty regarding the suggested deal.

Several Swedish investors sold off their Skandia shares during this time. According to statistics from VPC[5] and SIS Ägarservice,[6] foreign investors controlled 47.4 per cent of the Skandia stock on 31 August. By 30 September, 13 per cent of the shares had left the country, thus increasing the foreign presence to 59.8 per cent of the shares. Old Mutual's press spokesperson, Alex Sandberg, was quoted in *Dagens Industri* on 20 September:[7] 'As we see it, we have control over 50 per cent of the shares in Skandia. Of these, 30 per cent are in the hands of long-term investors and an additional 20 per cent are in the hands of short-term speculators.' (This statement was dubious with regard to the City Code in London, but not to the Stockholm rules).[8]

Svenska Dagbladet published an article on 22 September about a letter that, according to its sources, had been sent by Fidelity to the Skandia board a day before they were supposed to meet.[9] In the letter, Fidelity apparently wrote that it supported a merger between Old Mutual and Skandia, and that it controlled 9 per cent of the shares in Skandia: four percentage points more than what had been revealed to the public. This implied that almost 25 per cent of the shareholders in Skandia supported the deal. The story of this Fidelity letter was probably both a leak and some kind of misinformation from Skandia's 'sell side'. Fidelity did, in fact, send two letters to Old Mutual; however, none during this period.

18.3 PLANNING FOR A BLOCKING MINORITY

Before the Skandia board's announcement on 23 September 2005, the financial analysts at AP2 had ready their calculations regarding Skandia, concluding that Skandia was worth more than Old Mutual was offering. AP2's chair Gunnar Larsson contacted Skandia director Lennart Jeansson and informed him about the fund's view. Meanwhile, Carl Rosén, who was in charge for AP2's governance policy, prepared a press release stating its support for Skandia as a stand-alone company. The fund was ready to act as soon as the board had issued its public statement. Larsson also had AP2's board of directors on alert for a telephone conference set for the following morning.

AP4 was working much in the same way as AP2 was operating. On 21 September, its CEO Thomas Halvorsen wrote a letter to the fund's board members asking them to back a public statement that supported the expected negative view of the majority of the Skandia board. Halvorsen also wanted to have their support in order to block Old Mutual's bid by letting AP4 lead the formation of a group of core Swedish institutional investors, who owned at least 10 per cent of the total capital in Skandia. He further wrote in the letter that, during the coming week, it was most likely that the Old Mutual–Skandia struggle would be heavily covered in the media, thus making a swift process necessary. He also added that an attempt to create a blocking minority could be successful. To Halvorsen, the expected 10 per cent for a 'no' would also be a good start to get further support. He hoped that one-third of the shareholders would eventually turn against Old Mutual's bid. This could also force Old Mutual to raise its bid so there would be a new, more 'decent', bid premium.

18.4 BOARD VOTE AND PRESS CONFERENCE

The Skandia board voted on Old Mutual's bid late on Thursday 22 September 2005. The board members' positions had not changed during September, so eight directors voted in favour of a negative recommendation (i.e. for a 'no' to the bid); three directors voted against that conclusion (i.e. for a 'yes' to the bid). The board majority was composed of five directors who had been elected at the AGM: Karl-Olov Hammarkvist, Birgitta Johansson-Hedberg, Lennart Jeansson, Kajsa Lindståhl and Anders Ullberg; as well as the three directors the unions had chosen: Anne Andersson, Mia Garren and Ingolf Lundin. The board minority was composed of three directors who had been elected at the AGM: Bernt Magnusson, Björn Björnsson and Christer Gardell.

Both Chair Magnusson and Deputy Chair Björnsson argued that the board should refrain from making any recommendation. Magnusson tried to keep a neutral position, pledging the board members to a mild formulation stating that the board remained undecided. The naysayers' impression was that Magnusson still did not want to have to go public with a 'no' vote, thereby forcing Old Mutual into a hostile bid position. However, the naysayers insisted on it, so Magnusson and Björnsson finally agreed. The board ultimately made its 'no' recommendation. Meanwhile, as it was clear that the majority's decision was no, it was also decided that Old Mutual, which was busy preparing the bid document, would no longer have access to Skandia's financial information or support from its management. Thus the board closed the Skandia books. It also (unanimously) decided to support and undersign a 12-page statement – dated and released to the press the following day.

Soon after that the board meeting had ended, reporters from *Dagens Industri* got wind of what had happened. The newspaper interviewed Old Mutual's spokesperson Alex Sandberg late the same evening (22 September). Following the rules of Old Mutual's governance policy, he refused to describe the bid as being hostile. His statement was published the following morning, along with that of another well-informed source that instead had asserted: 'From now on, Old Mutual's bid for Skandia is hostile.'[10]

The Skandia board published its view on the bid in a press release and at a press conference the following morning.[11] This was a big Stockholm event with London (UK) and Johannesburg (South Africa) connected as well. Bernt Magnusson (belonging to the minority) and Lennart Jeansson (belonging to the majority) both sat on the podium and jointly led the meeting. Magnusson began the press conference by informing the participants that there would be no 'one-on-one' press interviews afterwards; all questions had to be asked at the meeting.

He continued by informing the audience that comparing Skandia's two future paths had been a difficult task for the board – the stand-alone alternative and the sale to Old Mutual – so it was not that remarkable that, over time, two different views had emerged. The majority of the board had decided not to recommend to shareholders to accept Old Mutual's offer; however, there was also a minority supporting the bid. Magnusson stressed at the end of his short speech that it was up to the shareholders to make the final decision. The 12-page document had been produced with the aim of facilitating such a task. Journalists then asked Magnusson if he could remain chair of a split board even though he was in a minority position. Magnusson answered that it would be possible only for a limited time.

The written 12-page board statement began with its advice to Skandia shareholders: 'Skandia's board is of the opinion that the offer is not attractive for Skandia's shareholders. The board, therefore, advises the shareholders of Skandia against accepting the offer – a more detailed report is provided on pages 7–9.' This was followed with a second statement: 'A minority within the board has a dissenting opinion and recommends that the shareholders accept Old Mutual's offer – a more detailed report is provided on pages 9–11.'[12] Therefore the recommendation was composed of two parts: the one supported by the majority (not to accept the Old Mutual bid), and the other supported by the minority (to accept the bid). In both cases, the document contained notes clarifying the individual votes.

A general overview of Old Mutual's bid then followed. Old Mutual offered 1.650 SEK in cash and 137 new Old Mutual shares for every 100 Skandia shares. Based upon Old Mutual's closing share price on the LSE on 22 September of £1.3775 and an SEK/£ (pounds sterling) exchange rate of 13.78 SEK/£1, the offer was worth 42.54 SEK per Skandia share. The proposal was also subject to certain listed conditions included in the board's statement (e.g. 90 per cent acceptance with a right to pursue the offer at a lower acceptance rate).

Following the presentation of the basic bid figures on the first pages of the board statement, the document then included several pages that addressed Skandia's current business model and the company's development from 2003 to September 2005. The various strategic alternatives for Skandia were also evaluated in the text. Then the board's statement included a long list of arguments against the Old Mutual bid, which included price and a critical stance on Old Mutual's financial position. The board statement also included ABN Amro's independent fairness opinion. From a strict financial perspective it supported Old Mutual's bid. However, the adviser was never asked to evaluate the industrial rationale for an acquisition, and ABN Amro also dealt very little with the new plans proposed by Skandia's management. Consequently, the board wrote: 'In the board's view, the fairness opinion issued by ABN Amro takes insufficient account of Skandia's potential and future business opportunities.'

A large part of the statement contained the considerations of the board majority that, to a large extent, consisted of arguments that supported the stand-alone case and analyses proposing that the bid was too low. Skandia's future was seen as stronger than currently reflected in its share price, and Old Mutual's future was regarded as more risky than its current share price indicated (due predominantly to South African regulations, South Africa's economic uncertainty, the shaky rand and Old Mutual's lack of a principal owner). The board document further underlined that Skandia had presented good financial statements since Old Mutual's indicative bid in May. The report also showed that the price of insurance stocks had risen during the summer months. Adding all of this together meant that the value of the offer had fallen. According to the document, the premium over current share price had become 5 per cent, regarded as far too low. Average takeover premiums were argued to be somewhere around 25 per cent.

The document also included a reservation from the minority of the board members. They argued in support of Old Mutual's proposal: the price included a reasonable premium if it related to an estimated Skandia share price that was not influenced by bid discussions. They also claimed that the bid value both exceeded estimated aggregated values of Skandia's various businesses and the value indications that had been expressed by other interested parties in connection with the due-diligence-based analysis of Skandia. Those in the minority camp emphasized that these other actors also had information on Skandia's business plans, including the Turbo one. They also highlighted the favourable effects of a combination of Skandia's capital-intensive growth potential and Old Mutual's strong cash flow. They further claimed that Skandia would benefit from a larger capital base, making it possible to broaden the product range and meet future more rigorous capital adequacy rules; and they emphasized that the low degree of geographical overlap between the companies would facilitate integration.

Moreover, the board document stressed that a public offer in Sweden could not be made conditional upon a recommendation from the target company's board. The report noted an earlier press release from 15 September stating that Old Mutual had declared it had abandoned this bid condition.

The shift in power to the board majority meant that Hans-Erik Andersson had his hands free to search for a new investment bank to replace Morgan Stanley, and to work on a defence programme that would present the stand-alone alternative. Therefore a so-called 'beauty contest' was arranged. This would be carried out quickly since time was running short. One thing was important: the winner had to be an independent investment bank that only worked for the board, and with no interest other than to present a strong defence.

18.5 SWEDISH INSTITUTIONS ACTING IN CONCERT

In a short press release dated 23 September, AP2 proclaimed that its board had decided to reject Old Mutual's offer: 'The Second Swedish National Pension Fund sees its interest in Skandia as a long term investment, and trusts that the entire board of directors will now actively strive to strengthen the company's position.'[13] AP2's CEO Lars Idermark was quoted as saying: 'AP2 has been an owner for a few years and also been involved in the nomination committee. Our standing is that Skandia once again needs to focus on daily matters.'[14] The Swedish Shareholders' Association also acted the same day, announcing that it would summon proxies from Skandia's 119 000 private shareholders to be prepared to vote in the case of an upcoming EGM (extraordinary general meeting). These private investors controlled approximately 4 per cent of the share capital in Skandia. Swedish Shareholders' Association CEO Lars-Erik Forsgårdh said: 'We want to be prepared for the defence of our standing and the position taken by the board.' Meanwhile, he demanded that Bernt Magnusson leave his position as Skandia chair.[15]

AP4 issued its public statement in a press release dated 27 September. The fund's message was that since the board had turned down the bid, it was to be seen as hostile. AP4 also added: 'since the major part of that company's cash flow and profits are generated in South Africa, the currency risk and political risk inherent in the offer appears to be abnormally high'.[16] AP1 declared its position on 30 September. The fund's CEO William af Sandeberg was open to cooperation with other naysayers: 'Before we move on, everyone has to speak their mind. Then, when we know the views of the others and who says no, we can think about how to act. If there exists a group of naysayers, we shall of course talk to each other before we act.'[17]

So the naysayers slowly moved forward. AP1, AP2 and AP4, representing 5.5 per cent of the shares, took a stand against the Old Mutual offer, and there were speculations in the media that Robur, Handelsbanken and Skandia's own funds were to join into a concerted 'no' to the bid. However, they all preferred to wait with an official stand until the complete Old Mutual prospectus was made public. The three were in control of an additional 5 per cent of the shares – just enough to push the naysayers over the 10 per cent hurdle needed for the formation of a 'blocking minority'. Several investors, advisers to different parties, analysts and journalists apparently thought that a bit over 10 per cent would be enough to provoke Old Mutual to walk away. Lennart Jeansson argued that Old Mutual's credit rating would be lowered if it did not get full control right away of Skandia's cash flow. He believed that this would force Old Mutual to think twice.

Deputy Finance Minister Sven-Eric Österberg talked to the AP funds, and suggested that they coordinate their activities. He also spoke with Gunnar Larsson at AP2; however, it was not going to be an easy task, as they all were autonomous units acting independently of each other. AP2 also had its own problem, since it had been perceived by several actors to have done a complete about-turn – something to which Skandia director Christer Gardell was keen to draw attention. Petter Odhnoff (who was in charge of AP2's investment in the Cevian fund) attempted to talk with Gardell. Odhnoff presented his analysis and said that Skandia needed two more years. But Gardell did not change his mind and told Odhnoff that he was sure that the deal would go through.

18.6 LOWERING THE ACCEPTANCE HURDLE?

The date was 24 September, the day after the Skandia board had publicly rejected the Old Mutual bid. Business journalists began to speculate about the possibility of Old Mutual deciding to remain with its bid and settle for a holding equivalent to 60–70 per cent of the Skandia shares. This would 'starve out' the rest by acting in such a way that the remaining shareholders would be left to suffer. People working closely with Old Mutual's CEO heard him talking the following week about lowering the acceptance rate from 90 per cent to 50 per cent. Jim Sutcliffe was looking for arguments regarding how to present a friendly bid that was conditioned to a 50 per cent acceptance.

Dagens Industri wrote that Old Mutual's investment bankers were preparing for a possible outcome of an acceptance rate below 90 per cent. Investors on the stock market were speculating about the probability of Old Mutual continuing its quest, given that it lacked the financial resourses to commit to a substantial long-term investment in Skandia shares. The newspaper also wrote about anonymous investors, emphasizing that Skandia's financial statements were better than expected, which made it possible for the rating institutes to accept Old Mutual's shareholding in Skandia, rather than a full-fledged takeover.[18]

The three board members supporting Old Mutual's bid remained on the board and Bernt Magnusson continued as its chair. The Swedish Shareholders' Association's demand that he should resign, however, received very little support and not a single shareholder in Skandia called for an EGM to replace the board minority.[19] Instead, they were waiting for September to become October, so they could see the upcoming new shareholders list and what actors had bought and sold shares in September. The new list would also influence the nomination committee's composition. As before, Skandia's four largest shareholders would form the nomination committee; in early October, that was Cevian, Burdarás, Fidelity and AP2. There was the possibility that the first three of these would try to replace some of the board members who opposed Old Mutual's bid.

18.7 THE QUESTION OF NATIONAL INTEREST

AP4 had opposed Old Mutual as Skandia's new owner because of its South African base and dependence. This stance soon backfired. Deal supporters informed Old Mutual and its followers about the negative comments AP4's Deputy CEO Björn Franzon had made at the shareholder meeting on 28 August (he had questioned if it was really a good idea to do business with a company from South Africa). Additionally, AP4 had issued a press release that contained similar content, which had reached the 'general public' in South Africa. On 5 October, South African ambassador Sonto Kudjoe sent a letter to the Swedish government complaining of the 'slanted impression' that the AP4 press release was creating, which was (more or less) a copy of what the Skandia board had written in its own press release from 23 September. Kudjoe, however, did not believe that the board's press release had the same impact as that of AP4, since he saw AP4 as an official representative of Sweden. The ambassador also contacted Sweden's Deputy Minister of Finance Sven-Erik Österberg, complaining that Österberg had said in public that he would prefer Skandia to remain Swedish. This only added to the Swedish government's reluctance to make further public comments about the Old Mutual–Skandia case. Later in

October, a Skandia representative visited Österberg and presented the company's stand-alone case. The deputy minister of finance listened politely, but made no statement. With the Swedish prime minister's upcoming trip to South Africa, it was not the right time to make almost any statement regarding Skandia.

Old Mutual's advisers at Kreab were happy to see that the political side of the process had come to an end. Kreab's optimism increased when they noted that the Swedish public had remained rather passive to Old Mutual's hostile takeover attempt. Skandia, however, remained a hot topic for financial actors and business journalists in Stockholm. AP4's bid refusal aroused an interest in its investment policy and allocation of capital. Christer Gardell drew attention to the fact that AP4 was slightly underweighted in Skandia when he spoke with fellow institutional investors, arguing that in its portfolio allocation, AP4 had acted as if it did not believe in the Skandia stand-alone case ('Why all this resistance when there is a lucrative offer on the table?').

On 3 October, Robur's Marianne Nilsson declared the fund's 'no' to the bid and referred to the board recommendation as a decisive factor for the decision.[20] Handelsbanken joined in on 5 October, which meant a 'blocking minority' was in place.[21] AP4's Thomas Halvorsen counted the naysayers and told people around him that the blocking minority might soon grow to 20 per cent of Skandia's shareholders. The proxy votes of the Swedish Shareholders' Association would add to that.

Investment bank Merrill Lynch held its annual conference for investors in London on 5 October. Skandia's CEO Hans-Erik Andersson was there, as was Old Mutual's CEO Jim Sutcliffe and company spokesperson Alex Sandberg. The latter two refused to talk about any hostile bid, claimed to be resilient and referred to the support from a majority of the shareholders they had met. Andersson appeared to be in a good mood when he explained to conference participants why Old Mutual's bid was interpreted as a hostile one. He also described Skandia as a company with a bright stand-alone future, with a management team that was happy to stick to such a strategy. Andersson further said that Old Mutual should let its hostile bid drop, and that a continuation of the bid process would probably only destroy values. He added that he expected Old Mutual would discharge him if they were to be majority shareholders in Skandia. He also said that Skandia had changed investment banks from Morgan Stanley to Goldman Sachs, which had already worked for Skandia in the past (Andersson also knew its partner, John Rafter). Goldman Sachs signed a retainer contract that potentially ran to the middle of 2006.

John Rafter was going to work with Goldman Sachs Nordic head, Greger Hamilton. Hamilton had been assigned the planning of a major road show to promote Skandia as an independent (stand-alone) company. The Old Mutual camp, however, criticized this assignment, since this meant that Goldman Sachs would actually be working against a major group of Skandia's shareholders – and this with the risk of soon being replaced at an EGM. Moreover, it was problematic that Skandia intended to spend a substantial amount of money on a defence strategy that had such an uncertain future. The Old Mutual camp further noted that, two months earlier, the same investment bank had acted as an adviser for AXA, putting together a bid on Skandia that valued the company at no more than 35 SEK. Now, Goldman Sachs would have to argue that Skandia was worth more than Old Mutual's bid at 42–43 SEK. The Old Mutual camp also remarked that Goldman Sachs already assisted several of the global hedge funds that were active in the trading of the Skandia stock. Skandia's CEO shook off these criticisms.

The next day (6 October), *Svenska Dagbladet* published an interview with Skandia's CEO, presenting what appeared to be a revitalized Hans-Erik Andersson. He commented on a possible upcoming change in the bid conditions from Old Mutual's side. The journalist: 'Jim Sutcliffe has indicated that he might complete the deal even with only 70–80 per cent of the shares. Comment?' Andersson: 'It will not be easy in that case. I will not stay on, and most importantly it will (then) be very difficult to realise the major synergies . . . .'[22]

NOTES

1. Kreab pursued continuous public surveys and the Old Mutual bid on Skandia never became an important question for the broader Swedish public. The bid remained an issue for the financial market, the media and politicians during the entire period.
2. A global corporate communications group run as a private partnership.
3. Short positions in listed companies on the SSE (i.e. outstanding loans of shares) are registered and made public on a weekly basis.
4. The leading all-share index on the LSE.
5. Värdepapperscentralen, NCSD – Nordic Central Securities Depository. A compulsory shareholding clearance organization.
6. SIS Ägarservice AB. A private company compiling Swedish shareholder statistics.
7. *Dagens Industri*, 20 September 2005, 'Skandias öde i hans händer', Sophie Nachemson-Ekwall.
8. See Rule 19.3 'Unacceptable statements'.
9. *Svenska Dagbladet*, 22 September 2005, 'Fidelity trycker på för affär', Jan Almgren.
10. di.se, 23 September 2005, 'Skandia nobbar Old Mutual', Sophie Nachemson-Ekwall and Jan Wängelin.
11. *Statement by the board of Skandia with respect to Old Mutual's public offer*, dated 23 September 2005.
12. Press release from the Skandia board, dated 23 September 2005.
13. AP2, 23 September 2005, 'Statement by *AP2* concerning Old Mutual's offer for Skandia'.

14. Ticker, 23 September 2005, 'Skandia: Andra AP-fonden säger nej till Old Mutuals bud', Henrik Öhlin.
15. Ticker, 23 September 2005, 'Skandia: Aktiespararna avvisar bud, avgå Gardell & Co', Mats Hård.'
16. 'AP4 rejects Old Mutual's offer for Skandia', AP4 English press information issued 27 September 2005.
17. *Dagens Industri*, 1 October 2005, 'Skandiaägare byter sida inför slutstriden', Sophie Nachemson-Ekwall and Karin Svensson.
18. *Dagens Industri*, 24 September 2005, 'Svälta-räv-spelet har just börjat', Sophie Nachemson-Ekwall.
19. TT Nyhetsbanken, 23 September 2005, 'Ägarstriden i Skandia hettar till', Joakim Goksör.
20. Banknytt Online, 4 October 2005, 'Robur tackar nej till old Mutuals bud'.
21. Ticker, 5 October 2005, 'Skandia: SHB Fonder tackar nej till budet från Old Mutual', Mats Hård.
22. *Svenska Dagbladet*, 6 October 2005, 'Budet bör dras tillbaka', Jan Almgren.

19. Hedge funds intervene

19.1 PAULSON & CO. TAKES A STRONG POSITION IN SKANDIA

Old Mutual's CEO Jim Sutcliffe and CFO Julian Roberts returned to London following the bid presentation on 2 September in Stockholm. A week later, Old Mutual hosted a lunch for institutional investors. The room was crowded and many investors, unknown to the company, showed up. Most participants were young men from the UK and American hedge fund industry. In fact, there were more than 50 of them. Several of them returned, called and traded heavily in the Old Mutual and Skandia stocks during the following weeks.

In the autumn of 2005 Paulson & Co.[1] was one of the hedge funds that eyed Skandia, at that time controlling approximately $4.2 billion in assets. The company had been involved in one other European deal, namely Swedish Hexagon's[2] bid for Swiss Leica[3] in spring 2005. Paulson & Co. took a large position in Leica Geosystems and successfully blocked Hexagon from gaining control. In the end, Paulson & Co. forced Hexagon to raise its bid. Founder John Paulson and Manager, Paolo Pellegrini were familiar with the activities of Cevian and Christer Gardell. They had actually also met him during one of his visits to New York (in late autumn 2004).

A year later, Paulson evidently shared Gardell's view that a combined Old Mutual–Skandia would allow the two firms to compete more effectively on a global scale. They both thought Skandia was too small by itself and Old Mutual, although larger, would benefit from a geographical spread beyond its South African and US presence. This would make Old Mutual's share rise, reflecting the combined company's larger scale and lesser country risk. Such a scenario would then result in a double win for Skandia shareholders: a takeover premium plus a re-rating of the acquirer's stock.

Rumours began circulating in early October that one hedge fund in particular was accumulating a strong position in Skandia. On 6 October *Svenska Dagbladet* claimed that someone had gained control of almost 5 per cent of the Skandia stocks, investing 2 billion SEK and attaining the position of the second largest shareholder after Fidelity.[4] Along with Cevian, Fidelity and Burdarás, Skandia's four largest shareholders would then control 21 per cent of the shares. These holdings also gave them control of Skandia's nomination committee, thereby in the position to suggest its next set of directors. The following day, it became known that Paulson & Co. had written a letter to the Skandia board a few weeks earlier revealing its shareholding and support of the Old Mutual bid.[5] Hedge fund actors in London said that Paulson & Co. tried to persuade Old Mutual to either raise the Skandia bid or drop the 90 per cent hurdle. Meanwhile, the media reports both in South Africa and the UK indicated that Old Mutual, if necessary, would stand by the bid at a lower level of acceptance (and live with a minority).[6]

19.2 SKANDIA'S CHAIR BERNT MAGNUSSON RESIGNS

Skandia's chair Bernt Magnusson announced on Friday 7 October 2005 that he was resigning. The decision to leave and when to do so was Magnusson's own, although several institutional investors who had been negative to Old Mutual's bid had stated in public that they expected such a development.[7] Magnusson had contacted Gunilla Svensson, director of press relations at Skandia, on the afternoon on 6 October. He asked her to prepare a press release outlining the message that he would be resigning as Skandia chair. That evening, he informed Directors Björn Björnsson and Christer Gardell. He also called Director Lennart Jeansson to ask him if he was ready to take over as chair of the Skandia board.

On Friday morning Bernt Magnusson summoned all directors to a board meeting at Skandia's HQ. Several of them (Anne Andersson, Björn Björnsson, Christer Gardell, Mia Garren and Lennart Jeansson) participated by phone. Magnusson began by informing the other directors that he had decided to leave the Skandia board promptly. He then expounded on his reasons by saying that, in the end, it was not possible to chair a divided board. In the circumstances, he felt that his role on the board had turned into that of a 'caretaker government'. He added that the turbulence among Skandia's shareholders made it difficult for him and the board to know – with reasonable certainty – each other's views on various matters; it was not possible to hold 'daily EGMs'. Magnusson added that he did not want to continue attempting to manage the balance between various kinds of shareholders. As chair, he had been careful not to discriminate between different kinds (short-/long-term, Swedish/foreign and so on). Therefore he concluded that the chair's gavel ought to be swung by someone from the board majority – not the minority. He suggested Lennart Jeansson, who had already been serving as spokesperson for the majority rejecting Old Mutual's bid. The board also decided to elect Jeansson as Skandia's new chair.

Jim Sutcliffe became upset when he heard Bernt Magnusson's voice over the phone saying that he had resigned. Julian Roberts complained, too, when he heard the news. Sutcliffe asked Magnusson if he would reconsider, but Magnusson said 'no'. With Magnusson gone, it would be difficult to persuade Old Mutual's board to agree that the bid was no longer hostile. This was a problem for Sutcliffe since he still had a mandate to pursue only a friendly bid. Not all Old Mutual's advisers were confident that the company would indeed stand by the offer. Some of them began preparing themselves for phone calls with the message that the takeover process was over.

19.3 ACTIVE HEDGE FUNDS

The Swede Lars Bane at the US hedge fund Noonday closely monitored Old Mutual's bid for Skandia during September. Back in the winter of 2004–05, he had been sceptical of Christer Gardell's plans. But with Old Mutual on the scene, he had to admit that his old friend might have been right. Bane had already begun buying shares back in early September; that is during the week when the bid was made public. He tried to build up a position of a few per cent. Bane was among those hedge fund managers who had been in constant contact with Old Mutual and its advisers at Deutsche Bank and Merrill Lynch, arguing for a drop in the required acceptance level from 90 to 50 per cent. Bane promised Jim Sutcliffe that, providing Old Mutual delivered on that, his fund would buy more Skandia shares.

The 388-page prospectus from Old Mutual to its shareholders was posted on Old Mutual's website on the evening of 7 October. It included comprehensive financial information on Old Mutual and the motivation for the share issue that was needed to finance the Skandia bid. An EGM was set up for 14 November. Lars Bane at Noonday, John Paulson at Paulson & Co. and other hedge fund managers who had eagerly awaited the prospectus could see that the 90 per cent requirement was still included. The Skandia share traded at 39.80 SEK when the stock market closed, 9 per cent below Old Mutual's bid of 43.6 SEK. Old Mutual's CEO spoke to several hedge fund managers asking them to remain calm, and stating that the company was not about to give up on Skandia. The company also sent a letter regarding the matter to the most active of the funds: Paulson & Co.

Thus Old Mutual still kept its doors open, which was also expressed in the prospectus, since it included, for example, a reservation that the 90 per cent requirement might later be waived. The prospectus also contained a statement that Old Mutual would dominate the board, even if it decided to settle for an amount that was between 50 and 90 per cent of the shares. Old Mutual also stated that, at a later stage, it might work towards delisting the company from the SSE. The company reiterated the claims of a powerful industrial rationale for the affair, with strong growth potential for the combined group. Old Mutual would also provide management systems and bring stability to Skandia. Demographic changes, and the relationship between these changes and the development of private savings markets were accentuated, and a continuous use of open architecture business models was deemed promising. It was also mentioned that the increase in size was directly linked to distribution capability, thereby improving the capacity to attract customers. Other important arguments for the deal addressed the balancing of currency risk and other market risks. Finally, future-oriented calculations were provided to show how the takeover would create shareholder value.

19.4 SWEDISH INSTITUTIONAL INVESTORS SELL OUT

On 10 October, Skandia published the list of its shareholders as of 30 September 2005. This offered a picture of the activities of the Swedish institutional investors during the four weeks of September. The list reflected that a net of almost 10 per cent of the Skandia shares had moved from Swedish institutional investors to non-Swedish actors, thus bringing the foreign holdings to close to 60 per cent during this period. Almost all Swedish institutional investors had sold Skandia shares during that month, such as Robur (−1.3 per cent), Nordea (−0.8 per cent), SEB Funds (−2 per cent) and Handelsbanken (−0.4 per cent). AP2 had also sold, albeit only a small piece of its holding (−0.2 per cent). Skandia's own mutual funds had also reduced its share (−0.3 per cent).

This general institutional selling was partly a technical issue. The majority of the fund managers had sold shares before their own boards had presented any views regarding Old Mutual's bid for Skandia. The sales occurred because most Swedish institutional investors closely tracked the Swedish stock market indices, and many of them were rebalancing their portfolios from the financial sector to the industrial and engineering ones at the time. Skandia was the sole insurance company included in the financial group. It had performed well during the last six months compared to its index peers (other Swedish banks). Therefore it was logical to sell part of the well-performing Skandia stock even before the board published its recommendation on 23 September. As an example, an enrolled external fund manager sold AP2's Skandia holding. This particular manager had sold the Skandia shares without consulting AP2. For AP2, this was (in retrospect) an administrative mishap; however, nobody at the fund had realized that such a thing could happen until it was too late. Nordea, the institution with the largest investment in Skandia (3.5 per cent as late as August), reduced its overall fund exposure to Skandia in small steps throughout the autumn. However, most of the other funds (e.g. Robur and Handelsbanken) stopped their sale of Skandia shares after 23 September. The crucial matter then had to do with the kind of connection that existed (or did not exist) between an institution's portfolio management and its governance considerations. In some London quarters, the Swedish idea of separating governance issues from daily asset management was seen as peculiar.

AP2 supported Skandia's new chair, Lennart Jeansson. AP2's chair, Gunnar Larsson, made his first public statement in *Dagens Industri* on 8 October: 'Now it is time to consider if we shall increase our stake in Skandia. It is important to support a development where the company can focus on its business.' AP2's CEO Lars Idemark added: 'We, the larger Swedish shareholders [in Skandia], must be taken seriously. It would be very stupid not to co-opt one of us to the nomination committee.'[8]

On 11 October, Larsson once again commented on the Old Mutual–Skandia matter to *Dagens Industri*,[9] this time with a message particularly addressing Cevian and Christer Gardell:

> If we say a distinct no and yet someone uses our money to pursue a sales manoeuvre that is against our will, it becomes all wrong. My board must get a presentation of how our dealings with the Cevian fund works. We want to be able to immediately terminate our obligation with Cevian now . . . In the future we have to guard ourselves against this kind of situation where we and Cevian are directly opposed.

The legal possibilities for AP2 to demand a repayment of its investment in Cevian with short notice were limited. Larsson was informed about this fact; however, he had apparently wanted to make the rules of the game visible to everyone – particularly to Cevian. After all, AP1 and AP2 had together invested 44 per cent of the 4 billion SEK that made up the Cevian fund. In the afternoon on that same day, AP2 increased its shareholding in Skandia from 3 per cent to 3.5 per cent, just above Cevian's 3.4 per cent. Approximately 40 SEK per share was paid with the aim of putting some more muscle behind its position. AP2's CEO Lars Idermark was quoted as saying: 'Old Mutual should understand that it is time to say farewell.

The bid is too low and it is hostile. Old Mutual's shareholders should know that this is not how one acquires a service company.' He hoped that Cevian would change its position.[10]

19.5 PLAYING BY A NEW SET OF RULES

Old Mutual had dropped its stipulation of a positive board recommendation by early October. The Swedish Securities Council had made it clear that such a condition was not in accordance with Sweden's takeover rules anyhow. CEO Jim Sutcliffe dropped the requested Skandia management support as well. Following the Merrill Lynch conference, it was also evident that Skandia CEO Hans-Erik Andersson would resign if Old Mutual were to take over.

By mid-October, Old Mutual's team had worked to secure continued support from the hedge funds that had bought into Skandia (and that later might be willing to buy more shares). The third stipulation was also reconsidered: the need to obtain Skandia's shareholders' 90 per cent acceptance. Old Mutual, with the help of Deutsche Bank and Merrill Lynch, analysed the various costs and benefits it could achieve at various levels of acceptance. By this time it was obvious to decision-makers at Old Mutual that it was unlikely to obtain a 90 per cent acceptance. However, at 75 per cent, Old Mutual still qualified to receive certain UK tax benefits that might make the deal worthwhile. At 66 per cent acceptance, there was a central section in UK takeover rules called 'merger accounting' that benefited the acquiring company financially. More than 50 per cent would at least leave Old Mutual with basic control of the acquired company.

Old Mutual presented the Swedish version of the prospectus on 12 October. This took the form of a short summary of the original English one: merely a few pages. However, it was supposed to be read alongside the other. Jim Sutcliffe had travelled to Stockholm the day before to market the company's bid for Skandia. He had held a press lunch at which the Swede Anders Fogel from Brunswick was present to support Old Mutual and Kreab in their communication to the Swedish public. Brunswick was assigned to take care of the contacts with the media, while Kreab focused on backstage efforts, preparing full-page advertisements that contained a personal message from Sutcliffe. These were run in most of Sweden's leading news publications. Sutcliffe still refused to talk about the bid as being a hostile one; he preferred instead to bring up the issue of possible synergies between the two companies. Sutcliffe claimed that when Old Mutual controlled 50+ per cent of the Skandia shares, they were substantial. He added that with a two-thirds majority, and through board control,

Old Mutual could force major changes in Skandia's businesses, and this could include a sale of Skandia Life UK to Old Mutual.

The Swedish Shareholders' Association, opposing Old Mutual's bid, complained to the Swedish Securities Council on 13 October saying that the company was breaching Swedish takeover rules in three crucial ways: (i) the Skandia board's recommendation to its shareholders to decline Old Mutual's offer was excluded from the information in the 2 September Swedish bid prospectus; (ii) the 15 per cent of shareholders supporting the bid had not been lowered despite the fact that AP2 no longer supported it; and (iii) the clause stipulating that Old Mutual, if settling for between 51 and 90 per cent of the shares, might be working for delisting Skandia was an inappropriate threat to shareholders. On 27 October, the Swedish Securities Council would give the critics right on points (i) and (ii) and expressed some concerns regarding (iii).[11] For Old Mutual, the critique was a setback. After a successful bid, the company had planned to list its own shares on the SSE (and was, therefore, obliged to follow the Swedish Takeover Code). But as it was not listed in Stockholm, that rule breaking carried no formal sanction.

However, there were other formulations in Old Mutual's UK prospectus that were of more concern to several Swedish shareholders. While reading through them, several Skandia shareholders and board members became aware of some novel wordings with regard to Swedish minority rights. In Old Mutual's UK prospectus, these reservations appeared on page 21:

> Upon acquiring 90 per cent of the Skandia shares, Old Mutual would be able to compulsorily acquire the remaining Skandia shares, which it does not own. However, if Old Mutual waives the acceptance condition having received acceptances of less than 90 per cent of the Skandia shares, it could not be certain of obtaining in excess of 90 per cent acceptances in due course. If Old Mutual were to complete the Transaction at a level of acceptances below 90 per cent, the impact would depend upon the level of shareholding that Old Mutual ultimately achieves. With an Old Mutual shareholding of between 50 per cent and 90 per cent in Skandia, the following would occur:
>
> - Old Mutual would not be able to compulsorily acquire the remaining Skandia shares, although it would be able to increase its shareholding in the market.
> - Old Mutual would be entitled to appoint the majority of the board of directors of Skandia; Skandia could remain a listed company although Old Mutual might be able to commence discussions for moving Skandia from the A-list on the SSE to a lesser list, and delist Skandia from the LSE.
> - Any transaction carried out by Skandia would have to be in the best interests of all Skandia shareholders, and although Old Mutual would

be entitled to vote for its Skandia Shares, any transaction regarding the sale or purchase of subsidiaries or businesses between Old Mutual and Skandia would require approval from holders of Skandia shares.

- The full amount of the cost savings identified for the Transaction referred to in Part IV of this document (other part of text detailing operative synergies and tax efficiencies) may not be obtained or may only be obtained over a longer period of time.

The Swedish Shareholders' Association was the first organization to react publicly to this part of the prospectus. They could not recall anything similar ever being done in a bid for a Swedish listed company; in fact, it was not included in the Swedish version of the document. Reading between the lines revealed that Old Mutual's advisers had prepared Old Mutual for a loophole in the new Swedish Companies Act that dated back to early 2005. The current legislation made it possible for bidders in control of 66 per cent of capital and votes to force through a full-fledged merger.[12] This rule was controversial and had already resulted in strong shareholder protests in companies where it had been applied. It made it possible to de-list a target company, and then allow the new major shareholder to starve out the minority shareholders. The Swedish Shareholders' Association had previously pointed out the problems with this regulation for the Swedish Securities Council. As yet, it had been tested only on smaller companies.[13] Suddenly it became evident that Skandia might become the first case to show how the law could be used in connection with hostile takeovers of large Swedish listed corporations.

In the second week of October Jim Sutcliffe met with many actors who had been, in one way or another, linked to the bid process. Kreab had conducted surveys since the end of May regarding public opinion. The impression the entire time had been that Skandia was not of particular interest to most people in Sweden; the company was a concern mainly for the financial and political community in Stockholm. The strategy was to keep it that way, as this would make the situation less risky if difficulties arose in a hostile process. Sutcliffe succeeded in getting the message across that Old Mutual was, indeed, prepared to live with a minority of naysayers. He told Swedish institutional investors that Old Mutual was prepared to continue with only 60–70 per cent of Skandia under control. Based on that very premise, Old Mutual's advisers (including Kreab) began preparing for a Skandia board composition process by mid-October. The market would be informed about the new nomination committee at the time of the nine-month report that was to be published on 31 October.[14]

Fidelity International was Skandia's largest shareholder on 30 September, with its 5 per cent. Fidelity's total holding – including both Fidelity International and its Boston-based affiliate – was approximately 9 per cent. Burdarás controlled 3.2 per cent and Cevian remained at 3.4 per cent. Burdarás' shareholding had increased in October to 4.6 per cent, and the hedge fund supporter Paulson & Co. was said to be in control of 5 per cent. AP2 had increased its holding to 3.4 per cent. Due to this ownership and the newly established nomination committee procedure, this would be the first time international investors participated and took an active role in the formation of a board in a large company listed at the SSE. This would also be the first time investors such as international hedge funds were to participate as well.

International investors wanting to take an active stand had to take a 'crash course' in Swedish corporate governance regulation and custom. This included Fidelity, which, even though it had been a long-term investor on the Swedish stock market, had never before participated in composing a board of directors (neither directly nor indirectly through a nomination committee). Lars Förberg of Cevian had said on 11 October that he was willing to run Skandia impartially, and participate in the creation of a new nomination committee. This would be the starting point for a new board that reflected the company's changed shareholding.[15]

At the end of October, Linklaters, on behalf of Old Mutual, made a formal request to the SEC; Old Mutual received exemption from the US regulations and was given clearance to acquire shares in Skandia in the midst of the bid period.[16]

19.6 THE DEFENCE DOCUMENT

Skandia CEO Hans-Erik Andersson spent time in mid-October trying to terminate Skandia's contract with Morgan Stanley. The agreement stated that the adviser should get a transaction fee if a bid exceeded 36 SEK, and that it was sufficient if the bidder acquired more than 50 per cent of Skandia's shares. Late in the autumn of 2005, this was precisely the case. Andersson had told the Morgan Stanley team that it would not get any further compensation, arguing that the board had not been completely satisfied with the work it had done thus far. When Andersson told this to Morgan Stanley's Per Hillström, the adviser was firm in his opposition. Terminating Morgan Stanley's work was one thing; not paying for services that had already been provided was something else. Hillström returned with the contract that had been signed by Deputy Chair Björn Björnsson on 11 August 2005 on behalf of Skandia. Skandia's legal advisers recommended that the company fulfil its agreement since the contract had already been discussed and approved by the board.

In the weeks following the divided board's decision, Skandia's management team went into overdrive. With the assistance of its new advisers, Goldman Sachs, work was done to prepare the arguments opposing the offer. This entailed accounting measures, checking legal conditions for giving various kinds of information to the markets, and formulating the strategic and operative plans of the Turbo plan in language suitable for publication.

Old Mutual's offer period for Skandia began on 17 October 2005. Two days later, Skandia chair Lennart Jeansson and CEO Hans-Erik Andersson presented the 44-page defence document[17] ('Skandia – a strong business with an exciting stand-alone future') outlining Old Mutual's offer, the arguments against it, and detailed plans for Skandia's future as a stand-alone company based upon the Turbo plan.[18] The board wrote on the second page of the document that it advised Skandia shareholders not to accept Old Mutual's offer, which meant that they should take no action. The prospectus included five main points:

1. Skandia's board of directors advises shareholders to reject the offer from Old Mutual;
2. The Offer represents an inadequate premium for Skandia shareholders (with the takeover premium estimated at only 5 per cent[19]);
3. There is no industrial logic to a merged Skandia–Old Mutual;
4. Skandia has a compelling stand-alone future driven by growth and improving profitability; and
5. The Turbo plan offers significant additional value for Skandia shareholders.[20]

Chair Lennart Jeansson wrote in the document that it was the wrong time to sell Skandia. A board conclusion appeared on page 5: 'The Board is prepared to consider compelling proposals. The Offer is not a compelling proposal. The Board believes Skandia is worth more. Hence, the Board determined on 3 September to recommend to shareholders that they reject the Offer.'

The 'no' camp at this stage counted 15 per cent, including both Nordea and Handelsbanken. Lennart Jeansson and Hans-Erik Andersson claimed that several foreign investors had also expressed supporting a 'no'. For example, US Third Avenue Funds, with a 0.6 per cent holding in Skandia, announced on 12 October that it declined Old Mutual's offer.[21] Its holding was rather small, but it was symbolically important as it created the possibility for Skandia to claim there were also non-Swedes who supported the stand-alone case. Third Avenue Funds later increased its holding by 0.3 per cent to 0.9 per cent. However, the hedge funds that had taken positions were still very active. The Skandia share price fell on 20 October to

38.7 SEK. This was quite a long way from the 2 September bid, when the exchange between Old Mutual and Skandia shares reflected a value of 43.6 SEK. On 31 October, the spread between Skandia's shares and Old Mutual's offer reached its widest: 9 per cent.

Goldman Sachs met with Petter Odhnoff of AP2, Lennart Jeansson and Hans-Erik Andersson during the last week of October to plan the forthcoming 'road show' and connected activities. Jeansson expressed confidence that Old Mutual would end up by withdrawing its bid.

19.7 BID REACTIONS IN SOUTH AFRICA

Scepticism regarding Old Mutual's bid for Skandia had reached South Africa. Old Mutual's share had traded sluggishly for weeks, plummeting to its lowest mark on 21 October 2005. In London, it settled at 129 pence that day, its lowest level since early August. The Johannesburg Stock Exchange all-share index had risen approximately 20 per cent, the S&P 500 had gone up 7 per cent and Nedcore, which was partly owned by Old Mutual, was up 13 per cent since the rumours of the deal leaked in May. For analyst Mark Salmon at Investec, it was reasonable to assume that Old Mutual would be noted at least 10 per cent higher than its current price, were it not for the expected Skandia transaction.[22] There were rumours on the stock market that investors were worried that Old Mutual might up the bid before its EGM on 14 November.[23] It would be enough if 50 per cent of the shareholders voted in favour of the rights issue. Old Mutual's management, however, attempted to secure much stronger support than this.

Many of the South African financial analysts following Old Mutual suggested that shareholders should vote against Old Mutual issuing new shares. Investec[24] argued that the transaction would not add value to Old Mutual's shareholders at all. The message from the firm Barnard Jacobs Mellet[25] was to vote 'no' to preserve capital, suggesting that it would be a much better decision for Old Mutual's shareholders to let its management carry through a cost savings programme within its South African group, rather than spend money and time on buying Skandia. Old Mutual's calculated embedded value was stated at £5.3 billion, which was pretty much in line with its market capitalization.[26] Both analysts argued that since Skandia was trading with a premium, a bid financed by issuing new stocks could bring about a dilution for Old Mutual's shareholders of approximately 10 per cent per share.

UBS focused on the debt ratio of a combined Old Mutual–Skandia group at 64 per cent, which was much higher than for any other European insurance company. Selling Skandiabanken would solve only part of the problem.[27] Keefe, Bruyette & Woods expressed some concerns about Old Mutual's South African exposure, which was not going away simply because of a Skandia takeover. Through the partial listing of Nedbank, one-third of Old Mutual's market capital was directly exposed to the Johannesburg Stock Exchange. The rand exposure was added to this. According to Keefe, Bruyette & Woods, a 10 per cent currency change between the rand and the UK pound sterling could be translated to a 40–50 per cent change in the value of Old Mutual's stock. That risk would not cease just because of a Skandia takeover.[28]

The Skandia board majority had claimed (at least) twice[29] that the market-adjusted premium of Skandia was just above 5 per cent if one considered the market movements that had occurred since the news of talks between the two companies broke in May. Investec's Mark Salmon argued in a note to investors on 27 October that the logic of this was 'probably sound'; however, it actually constituted a good argument for Old Mutual's shareholders to approve of the offer instead.

> The biggest flaw in it is that it is too big for Old Mutual to complete without issuing stocks, and its own stock does not enjoy the rating we believe it deserves. . . . Like Skandia, we cannot see the industrial logic that Old Mutual believes it will enjoy from the transaction. . . . Should Old Mutual shareholders, in aggregate, not grant the necessary approvals, this will be a no confidence vote in management and, indeed, the board that will hopefully not prove to be too disruptive.[30]

There were also rumours that some South African shareholders tried to persuade Old Mutual's management to guarantee that the bid would fall if less than 75 per cent of the shareholders of Skandia accepted Old Mutual's bid.[31] Thus there were many conflicting views of the whole affair – in Sweden, in the UK, and in South Africa.

NOTES

1. Founded in 1994, Paulson & Co. is a hedge fund sponsor controlled by John Paulson. The different funds invest in equity across the globe and are involved in ordinary long–short positions-taking usually based upon fundamental inhouse analyses. Some Paulson funds pursue merger arbitrage; others follow event-driven strategies (the Skandia bid may be seen as an example of both). In late 2008 its assets under management amounted to approximately $36 billion (*Business Week*, 7 March, 2004; see also www.wikipedia.com).
2. Hexagon was an object-measurement technology group formed in the 1990s, based in Sweden and controlled by major investor and chair, Melker Schörling.
3. Leica Geosystems was a 200-year-old Swiss measurement-technology company.

4. *Svenska Dagbladet*, 6 October 2005, 'Ny storägare ger sig in i Skandiastriden', Jan Almgren. *Business Day*, 7 October 2005, 'Stery shareholder boosts Old Mutual bid', Rob Rose.
5. *Svenska Dagbladet*, 7 October 2005, 'Paulson ny storägare i Skandia', Jan Almgren.
6. *Business Day*, 4 October 2005, 'How low will Old Mutual go in its bid for Skandia?', Neels Blom.
7. E.g. *Dagens Industri*, 16 September 2005, 'Total splittring i Skandia', Karin Svensson; *Dagens Industri*, 17 September 2005, 'Skandias ägare oroade', Karin Svensson; and TT Nyhetsbanken, 23 September 2005, 'Ägarstriden i Skandia hettar till', Joakim Göksör.
8. *Dagens Industri*, 8 October 2005, 'Han vill samla nej-sägarna', Sophie Nachemson-Ekwall.
9. *Dagens Industri*, 11 October 2005, 'Gardell under hård press', Sophie Nachemson-Ekwall.
10. *Dagens Industri*, 12 October 2005, '*AP-fond*: Det är dags att dra sig ur', Sophie Nachemson-Ekwall.
11. *Aktiemarknadsnämnden*, 27 October 2005, 'Frågor om Old Mutuals bud på Skandia', Aktiemarknadsnämndens uttalande 2005: 46.
12. A statutory merger enables the bidding company (the offeree) to buy out – i.e. 'to force a merger' on – the minority shareholdings when it controls two-thirds of the shares and voting rights in the target company. This stipulation was in conflict with the idea of minority protection rights at ≥ 10 per cent, and was later changed.
13. This legislation regarding forced mergers was general; however, it had not really been aimed at listed companies.
14. At Skandia's AGM in April 2004 it was decided that Skandia's nomination committee should be composed of five representatives: one for each of the four largest shareholders and one more representing the smaller investors. In 2005, the nomination committee consisted of SEB Funds, AP2, Robur, Nordea and Skandia's Shareholders' Association. Bernt Magnusson acted as chair and Christer Gardell was co-opted to the committee.
15. *Dagens Industri*, 11 October 2005, 'Gardell under hård press', Sophie Nachemson-Ekwall.
16. Linklaters, 25 October 2005, Letter to the SEC, 'Tender offer by Old Mutual plc for Försäkringsaktiebolaget Skandia (publ)', Brigid Rentoul. 'US Securities and Exchange Commission, 26 October 2005, 'Tender Offer by Old Mutual PLC for Försäkringsaktiebolaget Skandia (publ)', James A. Brigagliano.
17. Skandia, 19 October 2005, 'Skandia – a strong business with an exciting standalone future', important information for shareholders, Handelsbanken Capital Markets (Skandia's brokerage firm for the event).
18. The defence prospectus also included the calculations from the Turbo plan, projecting Skandia's profit expectations from 2005 to 2010. Profits were shown to increase from 95 million SEK in 2005 to 515 million SEK in 2006, 870 million SEK in 2007, 1150 million SEK in 2008, 1170 million SEK in 2009 and 1215 million SEK in 2010. Implementation costs for the Turbo plan over the period was summarized to be 1215 million SEK, with the bulk of costs to be taken in 2006–08. The board wrote: added together, these expectations made the Old Mutual offer both 'inadequate and unattractive'.
19. This was compounded by some adjusted valuations of Skandia's current operations, and the fact that Old Mutual itself contained important elements of risk with its exposure to the rand.
20. See note 18.
21. *Business Day*, 13 October 2005, 'In Brief – Company News', Ron Derby. *Dagens Industri*, 14 October 2005, 'Utländskt nej till Old Mutual', Cecilia Aronsson and Sophie Nachemson-Ekwall.
22. Investec, 27 October 2005, 'Old Mutual; A hop, a skip and a jump too far', Mark Salmon.
23. Skandia, 19 October 2005, 'Skandia – a strong business with an exciting standalone

future', important information for shareholders, issued by Handelsbanken Capital Markets (Skandia's brokerage firm for the event).
24. See note 20.
25. Africa's largest independent brokerage firm with offices in, for example, Johannesburg.
26. Barnard Jacobs Mellet, 14 October 2005, 'Old Mutual Ltd; Vote No to Preserve Capital', Marius Strydom.
27. UBS, 21 September 2005, 'Old Mutual; A fair valuation for the combined group', Andrew McNulty.
28. *Dagens Industri*, 20 October 2005, 'Affären som ingen vill ha', Sophie Nachemson-Ekwall.
29. Both at the press conference on 23 September and again in the defence document from 19 October.
30. Investec, 27 October 2005, 'Old Mutual; A hop, a skip and a jump too far', Mark Salmon, p. 14.
31. *Business Day* (South Africa), 4 October 2005, 'Old Mutual's offer for Skandia hits new hitch', Rob Rose.

20. Facing a new reality

20.1 IN SEARCH OF A 'WHITE KNIGHT'

As new chair of the Skandia board, Lennart Jeansson went to London to meet his counterpart at Old Mutual, Christopher Collins. Jeansson explained to Collins the Skandia board's new and negative position regarding the bid. He expressed confidence after the meeting that Collins had understood the purport of what he had said. Jeansson told his fellow directors on the Skandia board that Old Mutual would soon withdraw its bid. However, Lennart Jeansson was mistaken. Collins's role as chair and board member of the South-African-dominated (and London-listed) Old Mutual differed somewhat from the chair's authority as stipulated by Swedish governance practice. For example, Collins presided over a board with ten directors,[1] of which four were either executives or closely related to Old Mutual. For Collins and the non-executive directors, it would also be very risky to challenge the will of Jim Sutcliffe, since he was both the architect of Old Mutual's international expansion and a very respected leader among Old Mutual's investors – especially its South African shareholders.

AP2's quest for stand-alone supporters on the buyer side remained unanswered. Almost all Swedish institutional investors were more or less index trackers. The large Nordic bank-controlled mutual funds – that is to say, those linked to Handelsbanken, Swedbank and Nordea (that were all negative to the bid) – did not want to increase their investments. SEB Funds (a supporter of the bid) was a seller and when traders called round to potential investors, there was no one in Sweden ready to pick up its block of shares. Nordea expressed no interest in the whole of Skandia, although it had previously expressed interest in parts of it. The Handelsbanken sphere had since long taken its hand from Skandia and Swedbank had not even participated in the foregoing auction process. Moreover, the four state-controlled AP funds did not cooperate. Not even the openly negative Thomas Halvorsen of AP4 bought additional Skandia shares. AP4's portfolio managers thought that buying more Skandia shares from a portfolio perspective was too risky. As Halvorsen put it, the case for success was just not good enough to deviate from the index. AP2's Gunnar Larsson and Petter Odhnoff complained in limited circles about all this passivity or negativity. Thus the naysayers, without further external support, might be too weak to force Old Mutual to give up.

The Swedish business elite looked for a 'white knight' or 'white squire'.[2] That was seen as a possibility, with Lennart Jeansson as chair supporting the stand-alone case. In his 'home town' of Gothenburg, Jeansson had high standing. Among others things, he was a good friend of Dan Sten Olsson, the main owner of the family-controlled shipping conglomerate Stena, a company Jeansson also chaired.[3] Perhaps Stena could allocate a few billion SEK in Skandia shares? Meanwhile, AP4's Thomas Halvorsen and Björn Franzon scanned the investor interest in Stockholm. Perhaps Alecta would be interested in a Skandia investment? When Lars Otterbeck had been CEO, it had owned shares in the company. Someone also called Fredrik Lundberg at Lundbergföretagen,[4] an estate and industrial owner that had lately invested substantially in Handelsbanken. IKEA[5] was also contacted and asked if any of its investment arms might be prepared to put some money in Skandia. After all, it had entered banking in recent years (through its bank Ikanobanken).

Along the way, the naysayers became aware of Burdarás as a possible seller of quite a large stock of shares; they saw what could be a unique buying opportunity. The holding amounted to 4–5 per cent of the Skandia shares. Brokers contacted Swedbank's Robur, which turned down the offer to increase its holding. Burdarás eventually sold its shares straight into the market. On the 31 October shareholder list, Burdarás had reduced its holding to 1.6 per cent.

20.2 SKANDIA LIV

A possible white knight was Skandia Liv, the Skandia-controlled mutual Swedish insurance company. During the autumn its board had received several appeals from various categories of actors to buy Skandia: politicians, AP funds and business people. The idea was that Skandia Liv would make a counter-bid of approximately SEK 45 billion. The chair of Skandia Liv Bo Eklöf had many talks, and its board seriously looked into the matter. Very little was leaked to the media during this process. Although the idea was tempting, Eklöf hesitated in the end. In such a case Skandia Liv would buy Skandia and later sell it as a 'Swedish' company on the SSE. Many actors praised this rationale, which was also technically possible to put into practice.[6] Eklöf's problem was that such an acquisition was difficult to motivate from a portfolio perspective. In the autumn of 2005, Skandia Liv had 175 billion SEK invested on the stock market.

To use approximately 25 per cent of those funds on a single company was viewed as risky. The board and its CEO concluded that such an act could not be justified.[7]

The idea of Skandia Liv as a potential buyer was also discussed in public. For example, one organization that rallied against Skandia wrote an open letter on 27 October to both the board of directors of Skandia and Skandia Liv, pledging that Old Mutual be stopped from taking over Skandia Liv. This organization, the Class Action against Skandia Association (Föreningen Grupptalan mot Skandia),[8] with some 15 000 members, acted with the sole purpose of obtaining compensation from the 2002 billion SEK DnB deal between Skandia and Skandia Liv. To protect the interest of the policyholders, the group suggested that Skandia Liv should present a competing bid for Skandia. Following a successful takeover, parts of Skandia could then be sold (e.g. Skandia Life UK).[9] Neither the Skandia Liv board, nor its chair Bo Eklöf, ever responded to that suggestion in public.

Old Mutual also openly focused very much on Skandia Liv. In an interview published by *Svenska Dagbladet* on 28 October, Jim Sutcliffe argued that they had no reason to worry about the change of control. The CEO also stated that he might not take a position on its board: 'We might consider a solution where . . . Skandia abstains from nominating candidates to Skandia Liv's board of directors. If that would imply that we, in the case of a Skandia deal, are not on the board of Skandia Liv, then we just have to live with that.' Sutcliffe also said that Old Mutual planned to pursue the deal even if Old Mutual obtained only 60–70 per cent of the Skandia shares.[10]

Skandia Liv's chair Eklöf supported Sutcliffe's view in a comment published on 29 October in *Dagens Industri.* He said that it was very unlikely that a new owner of Skandia Liv would use the policyholders' savings for its own purposes. Eklöf wrote that new legislation, powerful supervision from the Swedish Financial Supervisory Authority, increased transparency and governance would give policyholders adequate protection.[11] The Class Action against Skandia Association replied to Eklöf's comment on 2 November in *Dagens Industri.* The group said that Eklöf was naive to believe that the Swedish Financial Supervisory Authority could protect the interest of the policyholders after the control of the mutual company had been taken over by a foreign actor.[12]

However, the Skandia Liv board did act in line with the policyholders' concerns regarding Old Mutual's takeover plans. Skandia Liv's independent board of directors (excluding Björn Björnsson and Gert Engman) revealed on 15 November a plan to change Skandia Liv's shareholding structure, with the long-term intention of converting Skandia Liv into a *bona fide* mutual company. Skandia Liv's new CEO since August was the internally recruited Bengt-Åke Fagerman; he was among those working with this project. The life assurance policyholders' influence over their savings was, according to the project group's proposition, to be guaranteed by granting them the responsibility of appointing Skandia Liv's board of directors.[13] That idea brought with it some upheaval within the Skandia Liv board, and Director Björn Björnsson resigned in protest.[14] In the end, however, nothing ever came of those 2005 plans involving Skandia Liv. The company never materialized as the white knight for which Skandia was searching, and never turned into a *bona fide* mutual company after the Old Mutual takeover either.

20.3 SWEDISH MINORITY RIGHTS

The issue of minority protection in insurance companies was the focus in October. Christer Gardell brought this to the attention of the Skandia board, discussing it during informal meetings between Skandia's large Swedish institutional investors and representatives of the Skandia board. Nordea, Robur, the Swedish Shareholders' Association, AP1, AP2 and AP7 were among those present at these meetings. The minority protection of the Swedish Companies Act was not going to be applicable to Skandia. The Insurance Companies Act (the law governing Swedish insurance companies) differed from the Swedish Companies Act on this point. The former was about to change, but the preparations made by the government were not yet ready for a bill.

While the Companies Act had developed in recent decades, the Insurance Companies Act had remained relatively unchanged. The Swedish Financial Supervisory Authority[15] had been given the right to enrol an auditor in an insurance firm; however, this auditor's task was limited to strictly supervising the company's accounts in order to protect customers and secure the stability of the financial system. It was not an auditor with a mandate to evaluate business opportunities for a superintended firm. This weaker minority protection in insurance companies, however, was not new to the institutional investors. They had met the issue before – in fact in Skandia – when they had dealt with a request from the Swedish Shareholders' Association to enrol a minority auditor on to the board during the spring of 2003 on their behalf. However, there was an agreement to choose another solution at the time.

In various meetings with Swedish institutional investors, Christer Gardell warned the naysayers of the risk that Old Mutual might be satisfied with the majority shareholder position, and, as such, accept not having achieved full control. However, those opposed did not share his view. Moreover, many Swedish investors argued that Old Mutual, seeking a respectable position in Swedish society, would comply with the rules of Swedish governance and its code of conduct, takeover rules and tradition of self-regulation. They were also confident that Old Mutual's advisers knew that the Swedish Insurance Companies Act was under review. Representatives of AP2 and AP4 were convinced that Old Mutual would be stymied if it ended up with a large minority of negative shareholders. Skandia chair Lennart Jeansson had told some of the institutional investors that Old Mutual had given him the impression that it was worried about ending up in such a situation. He had also told them that he believed Old Mutual would have problems with its credit rating if it ended up with a minority shareholding (this would complicate its access to cash flow). During one meeting, AP2's Petter Odhnoff added that if the naysayers stuck together, then Old Mutual would probably withdraw its bid. However, Gardell refused to give in. He continued to warn the minority shareholders that Old Mutual would carry through with its bid if it received more than 50 per cent acceptance.

20.4 A LETTER FROM SKANDIA CHAIR LENNART JEANSSON

Skandia chair Lennart Jeansson wrote a letter on 2 November to Christopher Collins, his counterpart at Old Mutual. A similar letter addressed to 30 of its larger shareholders was attached to it, focusing on their forthcoming vote on Old Mutual's rights issue that was needed to finance the bid. The letter to Collins said:

> Second, I am deeply concerned about Jim Sutcliffe's statements that Old Mutual may be prepared to go ahead with the Offer at levels well below 90 per cent, possibly going as low as 51 per cent. I see that as a hostile move. The established market practice in Sweden is to achieve 90 per cent acceptance. I am surprised that Old Mutual would contemplate going ahead with the Offer in a manner that is so obviously counter to the accepted norms of corporate behaviour in the Swedish market . . . I know that this, in turn, would be likely to negatively affect the morale and retention levels of key managers and employees . . .

Old Mutual's advisers reacted angrily to this letter, turning to the Swedish Securities Council (Aktiemarknadsnämnden) for a statement.[16] On 6 November the Council addressed a number of complaints from Old Mutual, in which the UK company proposed that Skandia counteract and inhibit Old Mutual's bid and bid-related processes: (i) by not cooperating in administrative and regulatory matters related to the bid; (ii) by not publishing and not providing Old Mutual with the fairness opinions it itself had commissioned (the one from ABN Amro had been published, but not the one that had been rumoured to be from Morgan Stanley); (iii) by spending money on and publishing the 'defence document', not including in it adequate information of the bid, and providing instructions to shareholders on how to revoke their already-established acceptances of the bid; and (iv) by its chair sending a letter to Old Mutual's shareholders warning them to pursue the offer at lower levels of acceptance.

The Council pointed out in its document that the obvious lack of fruitful communication between the parties involved was not a matter for the Council, stating: (i) although it was evident that Skandia was not particularly cooperative in its approach, this was not grounds for formal critique; (ii) Skandia was under no obligation to publish any fairness opinions; (iii) Skandia's activities were in many instances unique to the Swedish market – but not deemed inappropriate – since the target company was fully entitled to publicly argue against a bid that the board had chosen not to recommend to its shareholders; and (iv) Jeansson's letter was again a unique action, containing some inaccurate propositions of what was standard practice in Sweden; however, not entirely inappropriate. In sum, no formal critique was issued.

Meanwhile, the South African media interviewed Lars-Erik Forsgårdh, head of the Swedish Shareholders' Association, asking him why he had acted in such a nationalistic way. However, Forsgårdh did not to regard himself as a 'nationalist'. He just could not see any rationale in a South African company owning a Swedish mutual life company. Old Mutual did everything it could to get out of South Africa. This was its very reason for the bid, so, to Forsgårdh, Old Mutual did not bring anything useful to Skandia's current business.[17]

20.5 SKANDIA ROAD SHOW

During a road show in October and November 2005, Skandia CEO Hans-Erik Andersson, CFO Jan-Erik Back, Investor Relations Manager Harry Vos and their staff met with approximately 45 institutional investors in London, Boston and New York. Goldman Sachs had prepared both the defence package and the tour. Andersson met representatives from long-only funds that were against Old Mutual's bid, among others. These included names such as Viking, K Capital partners, Government of Singapore, Tisbury, Putnam and Citadel. Some of them said that they were rather unhappy with the work of the Skandia board. They were particularly displeased with the fact that the head of the activist fund, Christer Gardell, had obtained a seat and remained on the board. Some of them also bought more Skandia shares in the autumn. However, out of all these and other foreign investors, Third Avenue was the only one to go public with its support.

According to follow-up contact by Goldman Sachs, many of Andersson's presentations to the long-only fund managers were well received, and his vision of a future stand-alone Skandia was generally seen as a trustworthy option. Some fund managers even shook Andersson's hand afterwards and congratulated him. However, this did not imply that they would hang on to their Skandia shares regardless of what happened. Some of them had a trigger price at 45 SEK a share, and would sell if Skandia crossed that line.

Andersson also met with quite a large number of hedge funds that expressed no interest in Skandia as a long-term investment; instead, their interest lay in the probability that Old Mutual would pursue its bid. Andersson's presentation of the Turbo plan, if they accorded it credibility, made it less risky for these hedge funds to bet on the acquisition; these included merger arbitrage funds and activist funds. If the bid was withdrawn, the risk of a heavy fall in the Skandia share price diminished with a successful marketing of the Turbo plan. Andersson complained afterwards that he made his presentations when many of the leading fund managers had already met Christer Gardell and listened to his story. Andersson and his Goldman Sachs advisers recognized that they were working at a rather late stage in the process, with a clear possibility that many shareholders had already made up their minds.

Soon after the preview of the Q3 report became public on 31 October, Andersson spoke to South African investors. His phone call from Stockholm was broadcast and televised in South Africa. He also went to London, where he talked to some of the South African newspaper journalists. By doing so, he could build on the bid opposition among the South African shareholders (although they were – as in Sweden – quite disorganized). Most shareholders, however, were also aware that a 'no' vote at the upcoming 14 November EGM might also be a no-confidence vote in the Old Mutual management team. There were rumours that they wanted to avoid this, since a period of uncertainty regarding its top management team (and strategy) might put further pressure on the share price.

Andersson marketed Skandia to the South African audiences as a stand-alone company that was better off without Old Mutual. He told investors and journalists that the Q3 sales figures from Skandia strengthened its case to remain on its own. Moreover, it also warranted a higher offer price from Old Mutual. The Old Mutual camp, however, counteracted this campaign. As Jim Sutcliffe put it, the rationale behind the merger was to create value for the shareholders by enhancing earnings a share on an embedded-value basis by 2007, at the same time as the return on investment capital would be well in excess of the cost of capital. If they believed in Andersson's plans, then the risk to Old Mutual's shareholders of letting Old Mutual's management pursue the deal could be reduced.[18] Reluctant South African shareholders were calmed – buying Skandia was not to be a risky investment. Skandia's defence strategy had backfired.

20.6 A NEW NOMINATION COMMITTEE

Lars Bane at Noonday had promised Jim Sutcliffe that his fund would buy more shares if Old Mutual dropped the 90 per cent condition of acceptance; the US hedge fund was in control of a few per cent of the shares in Skandia. As Bane saw it, there was only one way forward. He told Old Mutual that the Swedish institutional investors would never hand in their shares. Instead, they were going to vote with their feet, selling off in the market. When that happened, Noonday was going to be on the buying side. Bane further told Sutcliffe that if the 90 per cent hurdle was dropped to 50 per cent, then he could allocate $1 billion to support the bid, equivalent to 15 per cent of the shares in Skandia.

Bane talked to Lennart Jeansson in late October/early November. The Skandia chair argued that the bid was about to be stopped. Bane replied in a rather harsh tone that Old Mutual would take over Skandia, and that it was only a question of price. Bane had received indications from Old Mutual and its advisers that they were considering raising the bid, given the fact that they could get a commitment from the institutional investors in Sweden that they would be willing to tender. Jim Sutcliffe was still walking around London talking about the bid as a friendly one – he kept up the façade and most investors even supported him. For a hedge fund activist such as Lars Bane, this was seen as a window of opportunity, so he came up with a new suggestion of how to structure the offer. The initial bid would remain as it was set on 2 September. If the share relationship between Old Mutual and Skandia increased and amounted to between 47 and 50 SEK, then a cash moment worth 2 or 3 SEK could be added. The technique was a US one known as 'collar'[19] offering protection for both upturn and downturn. Thus the bid would always be worth 50 SEK. The advisers at Goldman Sachs found the idea appealing and thought that it might work to open up the deadlock between Old Mutual and the negative Skandia board.

Meanwhile, back in Stockholm, Skandia's shareholders prepared to have a new nomination committee set up for the spring 2006 AGM. In November, Fidelity, Paulson & Co., Cevian and AP2 accepted the invitation to participate in forming that committee. All but AP2 supported Old Mutual's bid, although neither Fidelity nor Paulson & Co. said so in public. As soon as the nomination committee began rolling in mid-November, Fidelity International wrote yet another letter. This time, it was sent to Jeansson, Skandia's chair, informing him of Fidelity's positive view regarding Old Mutual's bid.

There was still one seat vacant on the nomination committee, namely the one for the small shareholders. The Swedish Shareholders' Association pitched for that position, since its campaign to get voting power had been successful. The association received proxies representing 3.8 per cent of the shares in Skandia (23 000 proxies) and there were more to come. The association's chair, Sten Trolle, told *Dagens Industri*: 'It is a very strong sign that the Swedish shareholders do not want Old Mutual as buyer of Skandia.'[20]

John Paulson made a public statement on 12 November, confirming that his activist fund Paulson & Co. controlled 5 per cent of the Skandia shares. Paulson was quoted in *Svenska Dagbladet* as saying that he thought Old Mutual could settle for a holding just above 50 per cent.[21] Both Fidelity and Paulson & Co. had hired lawyers to represent their respective interests. The other participants pointed out that the nomination committee was a decision-making body. Paulson & Co. adapted to the rules of the game and sent Paulo Pellegrini to attend the committee's first meeting in December. He joined the committee and worked for a board in favour of Old Mutual's bid, consulting with former committee chair, Björn Lind, to become informed about the working rules.

20.7 EMERGING MARKETS' RALLY

In November, the balance in favour for the naysaying Swedish long-only funds had become a balance in favour of the short-sighted foreign hedge funds. The US Federal Reserve decided to raise its funds rate on 1 November by 0.25 per cent to 4 per cent. According to Alan Greenspan (chair of its board of governors), US and global growth would remain buoyant, despite the effects of recent hurricane, 'Katrina' that struck New Orleans on 30 August. Most investors seem to have reached for the buy button following this move. This had implications for an emerging market such as South Africa. From November onwards, foreign investors increased their holdings in emerging-market bonds and equities, pushing valuations towards, and in some cases beyond, the upper end of their historical range. Additionally, an increased appetite for risk, that is, lowering bond spreads, made emerging markets' stocks climb even higher.

The Johannesburg stock market had been trading slightly upwards throughout September and October; by 14 November, it had risen by 8 per cent. Old Mutual followed suit and climbed with 7 per cent. In Sweden, Skandia increased to 43 SEK. A rising stock market that increased Old Mutual's share would automatically mean better compensation for Skandia shareholders who had accepted the bid. For the hedge funds that saw the realization of their bid speculations, the risks were simultaneously reduced. A rising stock price would increase the probability that long-only funds would sell (i.e. the majority of the Swedish institutional investors). Thus the balance among Skandia shareholders in November slowly changed from a slight overweight for the naysaying Swedish long-only funds to a similar predominance for short-sighted foreign funds.

On 14 November, 92 per cent of Old Mutual's shareholders voted in favour of the board's proposal to fulfil its bid on Skandia (worth 45 SEK per share at the time). The company also decided to prolong the acceptance period for Skandia's shareholders from 21 November to 16 December 2005. In Stockholm, Christer Gardell noted Old Mutual's shareholders' clearance for pursuing the takeover attempt. On the evening of 14 November, Gardell attended an investors' meeting, where he talked about a new fund he was planning to set up, this time with SEK 5 billion of assets. The fund would widen its focus away from mid-sized companies to larger conglomerates with a market cap above SEK 50 billion (i.e. to companies bigger than Skandia). Gardell said that he was confident of raising the sum, being able to show an extraordinary track record of having 70 per cent in annual returns in the last three years (Skandia then included). He publicly stated that Skandia would be sold before Christmas.[22]

The Swedish institutional investors who opposed the proposed deal began to admit to themselves that they were losing the battle. The capital management manager at AP2, Petter Odhnoff, went public on 15 November.[23] He lamented that other Swedish institutions were 'weaklings', unwilling to stand firm instead of selling their shares in Skandia. Skandia reported its Q3 results the same morning, two days ahead of schedule. The company reported an underlying profit of 1.136 billion SEK, up from 737 million SEK last year and ahead of market expectations. Skandia was also gaining market share in Sweden. Once again, Skandia's board publicly demanded that Old Mutual give up its hostile bid. Skandia's CEO was quoted as saying to the international media: 'I hope they will drop the offer at some point, so we can get on with building our respective businesses.' Hans-Erik Andersson further said that more than 50 SEK a share would be a more correct value for Skandia,[24] a sum that was well above Old Mutual's offer at 45 SEK. The next day, Andersson spoke about the 25 per cent of the shareholders that were intending to say no to Old Mutual's bid. This figure then included the 15 per cent from the Swedish institutional investors that supported the Skandia board, as well as 3.5 per cent from the Swedish Shareholders' Association. The rest of the estimated 25 per cent were anonymous international investors, apart from the vocal Third Avenue, with 0.9 per cent of the shares.[25]

Andersson was interviewed on 16 November on both Bloomberg[26] and the American business channel CNBC.[27] Andersson was under some intense questioning regarding at what price above 50 he might consider selling.[28] He told the CNBC reporter that he would accept an offer of 50 SEK. The newswires were quick to pick up his words. That day the bid was worth 45.6 SEK, so the suggested 50 SEK was actually a bit away (4.5 billion SEK) from the desired price. Andersson afterwards regretted his statement and admitted to colleagues that his price indication had been a slip of the tongue.

A rise in the Skandia share price in the following two weeks implied that the spread between the value of the Old Mutual bid and the Skandia share was steadily closing. The share was still traded heavily and Swedish institutional investors continued their selloff, albeit at a slower speed than during September and October. High trading volumes and rising share prices in November revealed short-term speculators such as hedge funds betting on the Old Mutual and Skandia deal. A weak Swedish krona (SEK) played its part in this trading activity. When the bid was presented on 2 September, £1 was equivalent to 13.65 SEK. On 16 November the relationship was 14.24 SEK: the pound's increase was slightly more than 4 per cent. Old Mutual's share rose by 5 per cent during the same period. Therefore the actual increase in the value of Old Mutual shares for Skandia's shareholders was 9 per cent.

The trend prevailed, with Swedish brokers doing the selling on behalf of their clients, and foreign houses doing the buying. Eight out of ten of the largest banks acting on the buying side were non-Swedish, the biggest being Dresdner.[29] The bank had bought 188 million Skandia shares and sold 133 million shares since 2 September, thus creating a net holding of 56 million shares. This was equal to 5 per cent of the Skandia stock.[30] About 2 billion stocks in total had changed hands; this was twice the total number of Skandia shares. During the same period, Deutsche Bank had bought 21 million shares. Crédit Suisse First Boston[31] also emerged as a large actor, having bought 5 per cent and sold 4 per cent. Nine out of the ten largest net sellers were Swedish; the tenth was Danish (Danske Bank).[32] The largest seller was Old Mutual's broker, Handelsbanken.

20.8 RAISING THE BID?

Some hedge funds in London were making bets that Old Mutual would raise its bid. If the company were successful in its bidding, then quite a number of institutional and private investors would be left with a 'dead stock', in the sense that Skandia's share on the SSE index would be reduced and index-tracking funds would be forced to sell out their investment just to keep a neutral position. Many of these investors would almost certainly be attracted by a slight increase in the bid. For Old Mutual's part, it would also be valuable to get outright the full control of Skandia. Rumours that were circulating around 20 November indicated that Old Mutual considered paying 48 SEK per share with a collar that a higher price might be paid out if Old Mutual's share rose. However, a positive bid recommendation from Skandia's board would still be required to unsteady the stance of Swedish naysayers and persuade them to accept a bid.

The Goldman Sachs investment bankers John Rafter and Greger Hamilton liked the collar idea. They were frank at the time, claiming that Skandia's chances of remaining independent were, if not completely gone, then at least quickly diminishing. Skandia CEO Andersson was also positive in his comments on the collar idea; however, Chair Jeansson turned it down. Rumours in the financial markets therefore began to emerge indicating that Skandia's board was not ready for that kind of negotiation. Petter Odhnoff of AP2 tried to focus on the possibility of increasing the bid; however, he was not able to gain enough support from the other Swedish institutional investors. Christer Gardell tried to persuade the naysayers on the board to participate in a straight price negotiation. The Old Mutual and Skandia camps were also conducting talks during the weekend of 26–27 November. But these discussions did not result in much, so Skandia's board members remained sceptical to Old Mutual and its bid. They were not inclined to take up further talks with Old Mutual either. However, Sutcliffe and his team felt obliged to take up such discussions with the Skandia board and then (perhaps) come forward with a higher bid. For some reason, however, Old Mutual never did and its investment bankers never returned with a suggestion.

The offer time was quickly running out, and hedge funds were still very active in early December. Neither Noonday nor Paulson & Co. was going to hold on to Skandia shares for very long. These short-term investors wanted to get an assurance from Old Mutual that it would drop the 90 per cent hurdle before 16 December, the final day set for acceptance of the bid. They were convinced that Old Mutual would end up lowering the acceptance level to 75, 66 or even 50+ per cent. Old Mutual's bid was already a win–win game for them since the Skandia share had risen from approximately 40 SEK to 44–45 SEK.

There were arguments for a higher bid. In November, the weakening SEK meant that the cash part of the offer could be sweetened at less cost to Old Mutual, adding at least 3 SEK to the offer. The embedded value disclosed in Skandia's Q3 report, which provided an additional 3 SEK, was added to that figure. However, the Old Mutual team stuck to the original prospectus. Sutcliffe and his advisers expressed confidence that the company's case was getting quite strong, and that Old Mutual eventually would acquire full control of Skandia without altering its bid conditions. Moreover, Old Mutual's share constantly increased in value at the end of November, and Swedish institutions continued to sell their holdings in Skandia. Old Mutual's leading actors internally claimed to know that most investors were positive to the company's bid.

A new worry began to grow among the naysayers. At a meeting in November, Christer Gardell brought up once again the risk associated if Old Mutual were to settle for only 50+ per cent of the shares. This time, he stressed the possibility of Old Mutual slowly increasing its holding to 66 per cent. If such a thing were to happen, Old Mutual could use the forced merger model. The Swedish institutional investors also received a detailed description of how this procedure worked when they attended a meeting with Old Mutual's advisers. Nordea, Robur, the Swedish Shareholders' Association, AP7, AP2 and Handelsbanken were all present at the gathering. The information about the forced merger model was new to most of them in the sense that they had not understood it was also possible to use the model for large listed companies.

NOTES

1. In 2005, Old Mutual's board of directors was made up of: (1) Christopher Collins, non-executive chair since May 2005, having been a non-executive director since March 1999. Collins was formerly chair of Hanson plc from 1998 until April 2005; (2) Warren Clewlow, chair of Nedbank (partly owned by Old Mutual) and previously CEO of South African Barloworld; (3) Russell Edey, chair of Anglogold Ashanti with a background at investment bank Rothschild; (4) Michael Marks, one of the founding partners of New Smith Capital Partners with a background at investment bank Merrill Lynch; (5) Wiseman Nkuhlu, a qualified chartered accountant and former chief executive of the New Partnership for Africa's Development and a former economic adviser to South African president Thabo Mbeki; (6) Jim Sutcliffe, CEO of Old Mutual; (7) Julian Roberts, CFO of Old Mutual; (8) Nigel Andrews, chair of Old Mutual's US business, governor of the London Business School with a background at GE Capital; (9) Rudi Bogni, chair of Medinvest International, Luxembourg and of the international advisory board of Oxford Analytica; and (10) Norman Broadhurst, previously group finance director of Railtrack.
2. A white squire is similar to a white knight, except that it exercises only a significant

minority stake, as opposed to a majority stake. It serves as a figurehead in defence of a hostile takeover. See www.wikipedia.org.

3. A private shipping and property group based in Gothenburg.
4. A listed property and investment company controlled by the Fredrik Lundberg family.
5. IKEA is a large global home equipment company of Swedish origin with a turnover of around 250 billion SEK (2009).
6. Skandia Liv could not buy its own mother company directly; however, it was possible to set up a trust abroad that acted as buyer and used the capital of Skandia Liv as payment.
7. However, it should be noted that other life mutuals have acted differently. For example, in the early twenty-first century, Finnish insurance company Sampo allocated quite a lot of its capital to the Swedish bank Nordea, and the Swedish insurance company Folksam decided to become a large owner in a Swedish bank (Swedbank), which, during the financial crisis in 2008 and 2009, needed to strengthen its capital base.
8. The Class Action against Skandia Association was formed on 22 October 2003 to protect the interest of some 1.2 million life insurance customers in Skandia Liv. In 2005, the association had about 15000 full-paying members, and stood behind a legal examination that should clarify if Skandia had caused the customers in Skandia Liv damage by the way in which the SEK 3.2 billion sale of the capital management company Skandia Asset Management to Den Norske Bank in December 2002 was carried out. Around 2/3 of the capital of Skandia Asset Management emanated from pension funds administered by Skandia Liv. No part of the proceeds of the sale was paid to Skandia Liv. Two billion SEK was demanded in compensation.
9. *Dagens Industri*, 27 October 2005, 'De utmanar Skandia', Mosse Wallén.
10. *Svenska Dagbladet*, 28 October 2005, 'Old Mutual gör eftergift', Jan Almgren.
11. *Dagens Industri*, 29 October 2005, 'Grupptalan målar en skräckbild', commentary by Bo Eklöf.
12. *Dagens Industri*, 2 November 2005, 'Skandia Livs ordförande är alltför godtrogen', comment signed by representatives of Grupptalan mot Skandia.
13. *Svenska Dagbladet*, Brännpunkt, 15 November 2005, comment signed by Bo Eklöf.
14. *Dagens Industri*, 10 December, 'Skandia Liv vill kasta loss från moderbolaget', Bengt Carlsson.
15. The Swedish Financial Authority supervised the insurance companies.
16. Aktiemarknadsnämnden, 6 November 2005, 'Målbolags åtgärder vid offentligt bud (Skandia, bud från Old Mutual)', Aktiemarknadsnämndens uttalande 2005: 47.
17. 'It would not be good for Sweden, it wouldn't be good for the Swedish market and it wouldn't be good for Swedish savers, says Lars-Erik Forsgårdh, CEO of the Swedish Shareholders' Association' in *Business Day*, 23 September 2005, 'OM-marriage raises objections', Lindsay Williams. Also cited in *Business Day*, 20 September, 'Old Mutual stirs Swedish resistance', Simon Johnsson.
18. *Business Day*, 14 November 2005, 'Shareholders vote on Old Mutual green light for Skandia', Stephen Gunnion.
19. 'A collar is an investment strategy that uses options to limit the range of possible positive or negative returns on an investment in an asset to a specific range. To do this, an investor who owns an asset simultaneously buys a put option and sells (writes) a call option on the same asset. The strike price on the call needs to be above the strike price for the put, and the expiration dates should be the same' (Wikipedia). Noonday's idea was 'kind of' a collar.
20. di.se, 15 November 2005, 'Trolles mål: Kicka Gardell', Cecilia Aronsson.
21. *Svenska Dagbladet*, 12 November 2005, 'Doldis säger ja till bud på Skandia', Jan Almgren.
22. *Dagens Industri*, 16 November 2005, 'Gardell på ny pengajakt', Stefan Lundell; and DN.se, 15 November 2005, 'Skandia kan vara sålt innan nyår', Monica Hedlund.

23. *Dagens Industri*, 15 November 2005, 'Ställningskrig i Skandia', Jonas Jonsson and Sophie Nachemson-Ekwall.
24. *Business Day*, 16 November 2005, 'Results boost Skandia's spirits', Stephen Gunnion.
25. *Dagens Industri*, 16 November 2005, 'Utlänningar sågar Old Mutuals bud', Bengt Carlsson and Sophie Nachemson-Ekwall.
26. An information services and media company providing tools for and data on the financial market.
27. A TV channel focused on business news.
28. The news anchor had asked straight up if he would accept a bid starting with a five and ending with a zero. Anderson's short answer had been 'absolutely'. Reported in, e.g., *Dow Jones International News*, 17 November 2005, 'Skandia CEO would accept SEK 50 bid from Old Mutual', Maria Åkerhjelm.
29. One of Europe's largest banks and since 2001 a subsidiary of German insurance company Allianz.
30. On 18 November, it was revealed by *Veckans Affärer* that the German bank Dresdner had traded in Skandia shares amounting to 20 per cent of the total stock during September, October and November.
31. One of the world's leading investment banks, brokerage houses and asset managers working out of Switzerland.
32. The largest bank in Denmark.

21. Old Mutual acquires Skandia

21.1 WAIVING THE 90 PER CENT THRESHOLD

Old Mutual had a board meeting in London on 28 November 2005. The topic discussed was the possible waiving of the bid condition that stipulated a 90 per cent acceptance by Skandia's shareholders. At the meeting, Deutsche Bank presented new calculations for Old Mutual that also took Moody's views into account. Deutsche Bank concluded that, given the outlook that Skandia could solve its own financing, it should be possible for Old Mutual to live with a shareholder minority. However, Deutsche Bank's James Agnew admitted that the risk involved was high.

Jim Sutcliffe was in Stockholm at Lars Lenner's office when the two participated in Old Mutual's board conference call. They all discussed the various thresholds linked to a shareholding in Skandia: 90, 75, 66.7 and 50+ per cent. Lenner explained the rationale behind lowering the acceptance condition all the way to 50+ per cent, without stopping at 66.7 per cent. Once again, the difference between UK and Swedish takeover rules mattered. Lowering from 90 to 50 per cent in UK regulations meant that a new bid was required. In Sweden, however, such a change in a bid condition could be done simply by a stock exchange announcement. Lenner claimed that if one took the current hedge fund activity into account, then Old Mutual was already supported by 50 per cent of the shareholders. Requiring 66.7 per cent would give the hedge funds the possibility not to hand in their shares, thereby providing them with an opportunity to push for a higher price. James Agnew at Deutsche Bank added that, since the hedge funds could then buy shares with confidence that the bid would go through, lowering the threshold straight to 50+ per cent would increase their activities. Moreover, at the same time traditional mutual funds would most certainly sell off their shares. Old Mutual's board members carefully listened to the arguments, along with their investment bank, Lazard. Jim Sutcliffe argued in favour of lowering the bid acceptance level to just above 50 per cent (50+); the board decided to comply. He told them that they should expect the outstanding minority to arrive at approximately 30 per cent of the shares. Since Old Mutual had already dealt with minority shareholders in South Africa, this situation was not new and could, therefore, be handled. As a consequence, CFO Julian Roberts began to draw up plans for Skandia to remain as a listed company. Besides, the alternative to drop the bid and walk away would be much worse.

Old Mutual advisers continually argued that it was pivotal to get hedge funds such as Paulson & Co. to support the bid. With the increasing likelihood of a bid completion, there was the increased probability that Old Mutual would be included in the Morgan Stanley insurance index. With financial markets in a good mood, a rise in the Old Mutual share would also come and, since the bid was paid partly in Old Mutual stocks, it would probably carry Skandia with it. At the same time, a bid withdrawal no longer seemed a realistic alternative for the Old Mutual board and management. This was the downside of drawing in many large hedge funds into the bid process, which also involved them as heavy traders in Old Mutual's stock. If the bid were withdrawn, the investment bankers at Deutsche Bank and Merrill Lynch expressed concern that Old Mutual's share would fall and that hedge funds betting on the bid would experience substantial losses, thus spiralling further sellouts. As a consequence, Old Mutual – with a non-realized strategy, a huge sum of money to spend and a low share price – would turn itself into a takeover target. Thus the advisers warned the Old Mutual board to take the risk and put its own company 'in play'.[1]

Two weeks after Old Mutual's EGM, the company officially announced on 1 December that the board partially waived the condition linked to the level of acceptance required from 90 per cent to more than 50 per cent of the total number of shares and votes in Skandia. If Old Mutual did not receive that support by the closing date of 16 December, then it would withdraw the offer. Skandia rose on the stock market by 2.3 per cent to 45.30 SEK; 3 per cent of the stocks also changed hands in heavy trading. One of Old Mutual's contracted brokers, Dresdner, bought half of the shares. The latest statistics indicated that 30 per cent of the Skandia shares were in control of different arbitrage investors ready to accept the Old Mutual bid.[2] Jim Sutcliffe was quoted as saying that there was support on both sides, and that this move would accelerate the process.[3]

There were rumours that one or two managers, while in closed meetings with investors and analysts, had said much earlier that Old Mutual would settle for 50+ per cent in Skandia. This change of percentage meant that the company was likely to gain control over Skandia and be able to proceed with the takeover. They were also supposed to have added that the other terms of the offer were kept intact – including the price Old Mutual was willing to pay. Some immediate press comments regarding this rumour implied that the decision to lower the threshold came as no surprise, and this meant that the deal was essentially done. Reports referred to named and unnamed sources that explained the (drastic) implications of the lowered acceptance level for institutional investors with Skandia shares who had said 'no' to the deal.[4]

Skandia chair Jeansson said in a public comment the same day that by deciding to settle for 50+ per cent, Old Mutual was expressing a lack of confidence in the level of support it had among the company shareholders. He also claimed that Old Mutual would not achieve even 50+ per cent by the time the offer closed. He added that he was well aware that the decline in Sweden's currency over the past few weeks had lifted the value of the offer to more than 45 SEK per share (from the 43.60 SEK it was worth when the bid was launched in September). Jeansson said: 'We still recommend shareholders not to tender their shares to Old Mutual.'[5]

The Swedish institutional investors that were negative to the bid were somewhat taken off guard by the Old Mutual move. For example, Thomas Halvorsen at AP4 had planned for a situation where Old Mutual lowered the acceptance level to 66.7 per cent.[6] But many other investors reacted differenty, claiming that to them this was not a surprise, and that it meant that the deal was essentially done.

The Swiss investment bank CSFB flagged a 5.4 per cent holding in Skandia on 2 December, thus replacing Paulson & Co. as the largest known owner of Skandia shares. CSFB declared its intention to accept Old Mutual's bid. Foreign shareholdings in Skandia at that time had increased to 63 per cent (up from 47 per cent since 31 August). The latest statistics indicated that 30 per cent of the Skandia shares were controlled by different arbitrage investors ready to accept the Old Mutual bid. (See Figure 21.1)

21.2 A WINNING STRATEGY

When Old Mutual lowered the acceptance rate to 50+ per cent in December, Cevian and its hedge fund supporters viewed the bid for Skandia as a done deal. Skandia shareholders who planned to support the Old Mutual bid focused on the formation of the nomination committee that was to suggest a new board of directors. Among those involved, Old Mutual was expected to get support from 60–70 per cent of the Skandia shares and then live with a powerful minority.

Skandia had an extra board meeting in Stockholm on 7 December. However, part of its management team, including CEO Hans-Erik Andersson, was in London conducting a board meeting at Skandia Life UK Holding and thus had to listen in by phone. New statistics on the shareholdings were presented at the Skandia board meeting. At the end of

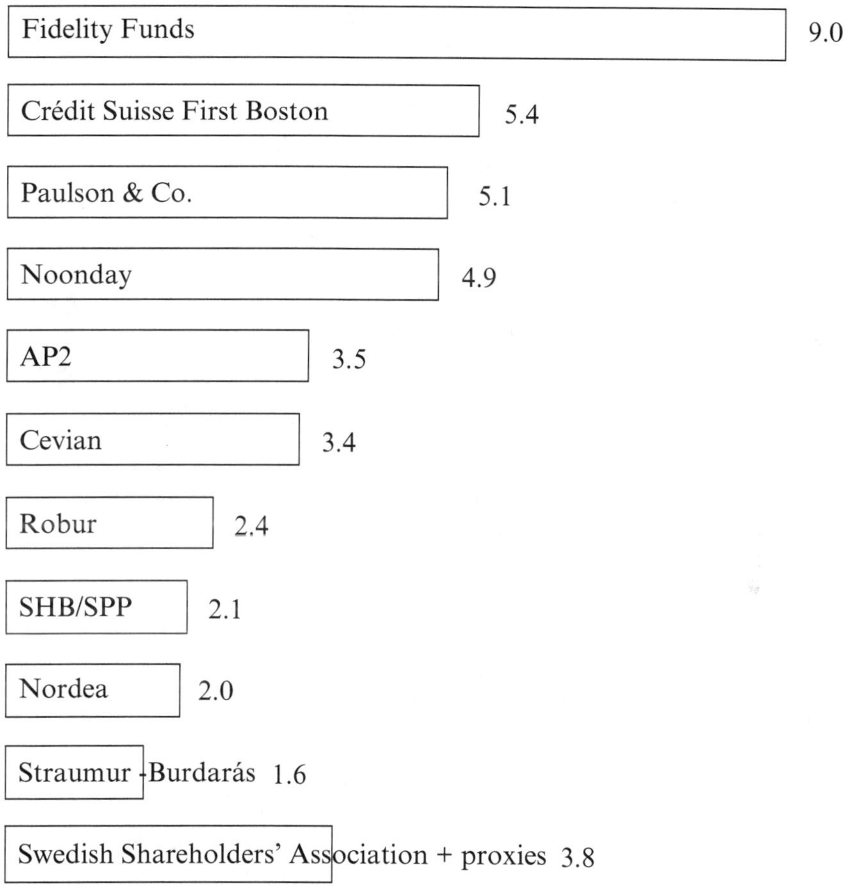

Figure 21.1 Skandia's largest owners as of 1 December 2005 (per cent)[7]

November, it was obvious that close to 70 per cent of Skandia's shares were in the hands of short-term investors who were probably all ready to accept Old Mutual's bid. It seemed as though Old Mutual's lower acceptance hurdle was becoming the winning strategy. Skandia was trading at 46 SEK at this time. Andersson said that he wanted to be straightforward with his board members: there was no stand-alone case left. Andersson said that he saw no possibility of Skandia being controlled by a large shareholder that could pursue its own agenda and business plan. It was also evident that he had to resign as CEO. His conclusion was that Old Mutual had won, although Skandia shareholders still might get a better price. Andersson therefore suggested that the board should go for one or two additional

SEK (particularly since a dialogue had finally materialized between the two companies). However, even trying to accomplish that was an uphill journey. The naysayers on the Skandia board (or at least some of them) still remained firmly against Old Mutual's wish to buy Skandia. Director Kajsa Lindståhl also questioned why Skandia should negotiate a higher bid at all, since such an effort principally favoured the hedge funds.

The next day, *Dagens Industri* ran a story about Skandia's board meeting. The date was 8 December and Skandia's CEO was quoted as saying: 'The war is over.' This implied that Old Mutual had finally won. 'The war is over' headline spread like fire over newswires throughout the world.[8] The *Dagens Industri* article, however, failed to notice that Andersson had also said it was 'still possible to win the battle for price'. The message that the Skandia board had given up effectively punctured its ability to press Old Mutual to increase its bid. Old Mutual's CEO spoke to the media the same day, and said that Old Mutual would not raise its price. Jim Sutcliffe was confident that more than 50 per cent of the Skandia shareholders supported the bid.[9]

Skandia's share rose that day by 1.2 SEK to 46.90 SEK. With Old Mutual trading at 158 pence, the combined stock and cash bid was worth 46.75 SEK. The spread had quickly narrowed to nil, which was considered an indication that the speculators trading in the Skandia stock were confident that the bid would be realized. Event-driven hedge funds had begun leaving the scene in favour of pure arbitrage actors. The fact that Old Mutual's share remained stuck at 158 pence indicated to some actors that there was still some concern that the company might sweeten its bid. AP2 again publicly stated its intention to remain a long-term shareholder. However, others were quick to sell; SEB Funds was among them. Manager Björn Lind was satisfied with the price of 47–48 SEK, so smaller posts were sold off, which totalled 1 per cent by the end of December. Nordea, the Merger Funds (part of Fidelity), Abu Dhabi Invest[10] and the Government of Kuwait[11] also sold their Skandia shares,[12] the latter two of which had been shareholders for the past two years.

Old Mutual's CEO presented his plans for Skandia to the press in mid-December. When a new board was in place, it would take a couple of months for the new regime to work through the company with some of the members of Skandia's management who wanted to stay. He partly supported the Turbo plan, although Old Mutual would handle Skandia's UK business separately. For him, it was unrealistic to start a full-scale centralization of product development – much of that work was better done locally. Sutcliffe added that the minority on the board should prepare for the fact that Skandia, either through a rights issue or by taking up hybrid loans, needed financial support to grow.[13] This was the sort of money

Sutcliffe meant when he said that Old Mutual could provide if it gained full control over the company.[14]

21.3 THE MINORITY ORGANIZES ITS OPPOSITION

The minority opposing Old Mutual's bid formed its team and began to meet in a more organized way. Petter Odhnoff of AP2 did most of the talking on behalf of the largest shareholder in Skandia advocating a 'no' to the bid. AP4 acted as a strong supporter. For example, it helped its Gothenburg-based colleague with meeting space at the AP4 head office in Stockholm (close to Skandia's HQ). These organized naysaying investors had many contacts with Skandia's chair, Lennart Jeansson and its CEO, Hans-Erik Andersson. Jeansson claimed in those talks that Old Mutual was afraid of ending up having to deal with a large minority of naysaying shareholders, which would result in difficulties with its credit rating. He said that if they all stuck to their 'no' vote, then Old Mutual would probably retract its offering.

Carl Rosén of AP2, a member of Skandia's nomination committee, flew into London in early December to talk to some of the shareholders. He would later convey that it was an overwhelming experience for him to realize that neither he nor his colleagues in Stockholm had grasped the full implications of the drastic changes in the Skandia shareholder base. The short-term investors had become so strong. Moreover, they differed sharply from, for example, traditional long-only funds. They were prepared to make massive bets on single events and they borrowed large sums of money to do so. For instance, Noonday made it clear to Rosén that it was betting on the possibility of Old Mutual going through with the deal. This had nothing to do with operational considerations, such as company synergies or business recipes; it had to do with the difference between the price of acquiring Skandia shares and the value of the Old Mutual bid. Trelawny Williams of Fidelity confirmed to Rosén in a phone call that Fidelity maintained its stance that a merger between Old Mutual and Skandia would be a good thing. This position had already been firmly established back in August 2005. Williams suggested that the nomination committee should defer its work, since the affair seemed to be drawing to a close. He argued that the composition of the Skandia board must be based on the new shareholder situation.

Shortly after the Swedish celebration of Lucia on 13 December, the 'no' side, led by AP2 and AP4, met with other shareholders that supported their position. William af Sandeberg (AP1), Carl Rosén (AP2), Thomas Halvorsen (AP4), Peter Norman (AP7), Joachim Spetz (Handelsbanken

Funds), Peter Rudman (Nordea) and Marianne Nilsson (Robur) all attended the meeting at AP4's HQ. These seven institutions represented the 'hard core' of the organizations that did not intend to accept Old Mutual's bid; they controlled a total of 15 per cent of Skandia's shares. The assembled shareholder representatives all received a list of three proposals from the Skandia board that Lennart Jeansson would hand over to Old Mutual. The Skandia board demanded a number of conditions to support the offer: a higher bid (one with an appropriate premium), a guarantee that Skandia Liv would be left alone and a promise that Skandiabanken would not be sold. Jeansson received full support for the board's proposals. When meeting with Old Mutual, however, the naysayers addressed only the first item of the board's list. Equipped with a mandate from his board, Odhnoff (AP2) led the naysayers' efforts to get Old Mutual to raise its bid by a few SEK.

Jim Sutcliffe showed little interest in changing the bid. He repeated to Petter Odhnoff (AP2) in a number of different meetings that Old Mutual, with its various businesses, was well versed in the art of living with minority shareholders. He did, however, offer some increase in the bid, but then such a rise was subject to certain specific conditions (e.g. a board recommendation from Skandia to its shareholders to accept the bid).

The naysaying minority in Sweden hung on to their plan. They wanted to ensure that Old Mutual would end up having to accept a minority auditor and other restrictions. This was something that made it difficult for Old Mutual to rearrange Skandia according to its own preferences.[15] On 16 December 2005 (the day Old Mutual's bid was to close) several of the naysaying institutional investors in Sweden were interviewed in *Svenska Dagbladet*.[16] William af Sandeberg of AP1 said: 'We have said no and we will stick to that.' Björn Franzon of AP4 claimed that '(I)t is not just any minority that Old Mutual will have to cope with . . . . We are large Swedish institutional investors and [represent] thousands of private shareholders. . . . We expect that Jim Sutcliffe respects the minority rights [linked to Swedish companies], and they are, in fact, very strong.' Carl Rosén of AP2 was also quoted as saying: 'We have told Old Mutual that we are used to long cold winters. We have no plans to sell our shares. We still do not understand why [Old Mutual] wants to pursue a deal when they cannot get 90 per cent acceptance. The major synergies will then not be there.'

21.4 OLD MUTUAL'S FINAL PLAN

Skandia's new nomination committee held its first meeting on 19 December. Paolo Pellegrini of the hedge fund group Paulson & Co. was chair. A press release Skandia issued that day stated that the composition of the nomination committee might be changed to reflect a future changed shareholder base.[17] The nomination committee was split, with Pellegrini fully committed to selling the fund's shares to Old Mutual, and Carl Rosén (AP2) decisive in his own mandate to hang on. During the meetings Pellegrini attempted to discuss Skandia's future strategic outlook; however, Rosén kept informing him that this was not the task of a Swedish nomination committee. Pellegrini and Rosén focused instead on how to coordinate work to persuade Old Mutual to increase its bid.

The *Financial Times* published a report on 20 December that said Old Mutual was in control of 62.5 per cent of the shares in Skandia.[18] The media comments around the world announced the end of this long affair and Jim Sutcliffe proudly announced that Europe's eighth-largest[19] insurance company (and the UK's number three) would soon be formed. The market capitalization of the new entity was estimated to be approximately £8 billion and assets under management were thought to be £190 billion. South African shareholders were expected to hold 42 per cent of the shares in the enlarged group, and Skandia shareholders would take 26 per cent. That same day, Old Mutual extended the final closure of its offer to 12 January 2006, and expected to receive full UK regulatory approval to acquire Skandia by then (i.e. clearance from the UK Financial Services Authority).

During a telephone conference with analysts and the media, Old Mutual's CEO Jim Sutcliffe stated that the focus was on delivering the takeover benefits. An integration plan, with Old Mutual's management framework as the basis, would be introduced. The two companies were to operate as one entity in Sweden as of 1 February 2006. The new group would concentrate on regaining Skandia's Swedish market share by winning back the trust of its customers. In an attempt to reduce costs, Old Mutual planned to merge Skandia's portfolio in the UK with its own supermarket platform, Selestia. CFO Julian Roberts stated that Old Mutual's top management would initially focus on getting full regulatory approval. He also expressed hopes that more shareholders would accept the offer before the (new) deadline on 12 January 2006. He said that Old Mutual would wait to see if it got 75 per cent, a level at which the company would get an extra £10 million of tax synergies. He also mentioned that Old Mutual planned to retain Skandia's brand in Sweden and take a secondary listing of Old Mutual on the SSE, so that Swedish shareholders could easily trade in its shares.

Old Mutual's official message was that the company was comfortable with the level of acceptances it had already received, and that it had experience in working with companies in which it did not own 100 per cent of the shares. In private talks, Old Mutual mangers told investors that the final goal was still to buy at least 90 per cent, so that the remaining minority investors would be forced to sell, and eventually the Skandia stock would be de-listed.

On 21 December Skandia's board issued a long statement in response to Old Mutual's message that it had control of over 60 per cent of the shares: 'Yesterday's announcement by Old Mutual entails that Skandia has a large number of shareholders who have not accepted the offer. Thus it is evident that Skandia will continue to be a listed company.' The board also said that minority shareholders would retain a number of important rights. Skandia's board added: 'Naturally, the forms of co-operation must be characterised by respect for Skandia as an independently listed company and, thus, show the same respect for all of the company's shareholders.' The board further stated that it would discuss the future cooperation between the two groups, within Old Mutual following the change of control. A quote from Skandia chair Lennart Jeansson was included in the board's message:

> The fact that Skandia has obtained a new principal owner in Old Mutual, with more than 50 per cent of the shares, is not without precedent on the Swedish stock market . . . We understand that Old Mutual is familiar with the principles that have been established for how large shareholders exercise their influence, while maintaining respect for the rights of other shareholders . . . The offer process has been lengthy. Clarity about the shareholder status is essential, so that Skandia and Old Mutual can concentrate on their businesses and their customers.[20]

However, Old Mutual's agenda going forward was not in accordance with Jeansson's wishes. Management and advisers were preparing an EGM to replace the majority of the Skandia board members (the naysayers) and take control of six of the eight seats on the new board. With 66.7 per cent shareholding, a proposed option was for a forced merger between Old Mutual and Skandia, which the loophole in the new Swedish Companies Act facilitated.[21] In January, when the nomination committee was summoned, the fund managers in Nordea and Robur refused to participate any longer in the naysayers' discussions. Meanwhile, the media speculated about a change in Skandia's CEO.[22]

21.5 OLD MUTUAL IN CONTROL

When the Skandia board met on 20 December 2005, the naysayers on the board were ready to face the only remaining option worth working for:

to fight for a higher bid. Lennart Jeansson was to talk to Old Mutual and argue for a bid increase of a few SEK. AP2, Noonday and Third Avenue were also involved. Lars Förberg announced on 21 December that Cevian had accepted the Old Mutual offer and handed in its holding of 3.4 per cent.[23] The Swedish FSA stated at the same time that Björn Björnsson had sold his shareholding in Skandia, which amounted to 25 000 shares.

Old Mutual's bid for Skandia took an unexpected turn a few days before Christmas. Noonday called back its Skandia shares – the entire 5 per cent block. This could be done as long as Old Mutual had not received full legal approval of its bid (such a clearance was not due until 20 January). Noonday's call-back made the support for the bid suddenly drop below 60 per cent, which could be tipped even further. James Agnew of Deutsche Bank called Lars Bane and complained. This was not proper play in Agnew's eyes.

However, Noonday officially declared its 5 per cent shareholding in Skandia on 27 December.[24] Four days later, statistics showed that 74.5 per cent of Skandia's stock was in the hands of foreign investors. Hedge funds such as Paulson & Co. and Noonday were intense in their efforts to persuade the resistant fund managers to throw in the proverbial towel. Fronting for different hedge funds and traders, CSFB flagged again; this time, it was in control of 9.9 per cent of the shares.[25]

After the New Year, AP2 coordinated yet another meeting with the institutional investors that opposed the bid. Lennart Jeansson flew to Stockholm to participate in the discussions. A few more meetings were planned for the first weeks of January. At this stage of the process, the majority of the naysayers just wanted to get a better price. Lars Lenner had told Petter Odhnoff that Old Mutual would consider increasing the bid by a few SEK if AP2 could get support from all Swedish institutions, a positive statement from the board of directors, and a blessing from the Swedish Shareholders' Association. Those opposed, however, had very different views about how much higher Old Mutual's bid had to go in order to be accepted. A group of AP funds stood behind the idea to get Old Mutual to raise its bid by 1–1.5 SEK but to some of the other naysayers this was not enough (Handelsbanken, Nordea and Robur). They expressed no intention of hanging on to their Skandia shares – particularly since there was a possibility that Old Mutual would move Skandia off the SSE's 'A-list' (this would remove Skandia from the index against which these institutional investors were measured).

Robur was not going to remain a shareholder if and when Old Mutual gained control of more than 50 per cent of the Skandia stock. Being overexposed to Skandia on the SSE was not in its customers' interest. Robur maintained its guiding principles of letting the portfolio managers make their own investment decisions. Handelsbanken acted in a similar way, not able to guarantee that its funds remain long-term Skandia shareholders. Nordea had become overexposed in Skandia when Old Mutual made its offering; due to the uncertainty that then arose they decided to lower its large exposure. Nordea had actually been one of the the biggest shareholders in Skandia at the time of the bid (3.3 per cent); the company eventually sold half of its holding, arriving at approximately 1.5 per cent in December (still a significant position). However, to ask for an additional 1–2 SEK in January 2006 was not particularly interesting to Nordea. Peter Rudman, head of corporate governance, rather wished that the group of naysayers should beg for much more. His main reason for this stance was that Old Mutual ought to be squeezed to compensate Skandia shareholders for the risk they would incur waiting for the part-payment in Old Mutual shares. He also meant that 1–2 SEK would hardly make a difference, since share price fluctuations often – even on a daily basis – matched that figure. Odhnoff tried to talk Rudman back to support the share price demand that the others in the naysaying group had raised, but Rudman hung on to his view.

21.6 FURTHER SELLING OF SKANDIA SHARES

The rally on the world stock market gained momentum in January 2006, particularly on emerging markets. By the time the New Year had rolled around, Skandia closed at 47 SEK (close to the share price discussed back in May 2005). Skandia was trading at 10 per cent higher, at 52 SEK towards the end of the month. The incentive to sell off Skandia shares for institutional investors in Sweden increased as its share price rose. They had their trigger prices to watch, which made most of them sellers at (and above) 50 SEK. Also, when they sold to a controlling shareholder such as Old Mutual, Skandia's fraction of the SSE index would be reduced. Therefore the Swedish institutions had to sell to avoid becoming overexposed to the Skandia share. Noonday, however, which already had 5 per cent, continued to buy Skandia shares instead.

Old Mutual had control of 69.7 per cent of the shares in Skandia on 17 January 2006.[26] Nine days later, the company declared holding 72.3 per cent of the stock, and CEO Jim Sutcliffe announced the bid unconditional and, once again, prolonged the acceptance period: this time to 9 February.[27]

Old Mutual's CFO Julian Roberts had turned down the naysayers' demand of three seats for independent directors on the new Skandia board. According to Roberts, two independent board members were sufficient. Deputy Chair Björn Björnsson was suggested as independent from Old Mutual; this was correct in a strict sense. In the eyes of the naysayers, however, he was not. Yet he still received support from all parties – including the AP funds. The second candidate was Lars Otterbeck, retired CEO of Alecta who had contributed to the election of Bengt Braun as Skandia chair back in 2003.[28]

Thor Björgólfsson, the owner of Burdarás, was interviewed in *Dagens Industri* on 4 February. The investor had again bought Skandia shares, ending up with a total of 6 per cent of the stock towards the end of the takeover process. This gave Burdarás approximately 1.1 per cent of the shareholding in Old Mutual. Björgólfsson discussed Burdarás remaining a long-term shareholder in Old Mutual: 'We plan to remain shareholders in Old Mutual. The combination with Skandia offers exiting business opportunities.' He also planned to support Christer Gardell as new board member of Old Mutual.[29]

Petter Odhnoff of AP2 had a meeting with Jim Sutcliffe at Lenner and partner's office in Stockholm on 6 February. Odhnoff then frankly admitted that the remaining minority on the board would be too weak to stop a split-up of Skandia. This was something that could favour one group of shareholders more than others (i.e. Old Mutual). Sutcliffe stated that it would be much better for the company not having to live with a group of minority shareholders. He wanted control of 90 per cent of the shares. Old Mutual, however, had no plans to offer anything extra to AP2 or anybody else. The bid remained as before.

AP2 distributed a press release on 8 February stating that it would sell its shares in Skandia, and that Carl Rosén had resigned from the nomination committee. AP2's chair, Gunnar Larsson, was disappointed by the decision to sell. He had long argued that the takeover could have been stopped if the Swedish institutional investors had kept their shares along the way. Odhnoff explained how the sales were a consequence of a lack of belief in the way in which Old Mutual had decided to run the company. He added that Old Mutual also seemed reluctant to comply with some of the suggestions from the minority of shareholders. However, AP2 made a profit of 1 billion SEK on the sale. The same day, the chair of the Swedish Shareholders' Association, Sten Trolle, publicly regretted AP2's decision. At the same time, however, he recommended that its members sell their Skandia shares.[30] Other investors, such as AP1, followed suit.

Once again Noonday acted as an intermediary between the Swedish sellers and the foreign buyers. In the two-week period following the AP2 walk-off, the Noonday fund acquired another 4.8 per cent of the Skandia shares. In total Noonday then controlled 11.8 per cent. Eventually the stake was sold for 190–200 pence. The profit amounted to 1 billion SEK.

Old Mutual declared on 9 February that it had received acceptances for more than 88 per cent of the shareholders in Skandia. The acceptance period was yet again prolonged – this time to 14 March.[31] Virtually all of the Swedish institutional investors had sold their shares on the market (predominantly to short-term investors such as hedge funds). Supporters of the Old Mutual bid mockingly noted that Swedish institutional investors had decided to sell (at a lower price) rather than be caught in public having to hand in their shares to Old Mutual (at a higher price).

21.7 EPILOGUE

Hans-Erik Andersson was asked to step down as CEO of Skandia on 14 February, and he left the company a week later at the EGM. Old Mutual's CFO Julian Roberts stepped in and replaced him. During the following months, many of the other members of Skandia's executive team left the company as well. These included Michael Wolf, head of Europe; Jennifer Ruhle, director of human relations; Jan-Michael Bexhed, head of legal affairs; and Gunilla Forsmark-Karlsson, head of Skandiabanken. CFO Jan-Erik Back left the company soon afterwards. Director of Skandia's Nordic region, Gert Engman, stayed on until November 2006. Skandia Life UK experienced a similar walk-out. A year after the merger, its CEO Nick Poyntz-Wright was more or less the only top manager left from the 'Skandia days'.

In the end, Christer Gardell never did obtain a seat on Old Mutual's board. He decided to sell all his Old Mutual shares once the global stock market rally, which had begun in late 2005, reached its high shortly before Easter 2006. By that time, Gardell's Cevian fund had earned 800 million SEK on its Skandia investment, a return of almost 100 per cent in slightly more than a year. Burdarás followed suit and realized a handsome profit as well. In an interview about the Skandia deal on 22 February, Gardell concluded: 'Many claimed that the bid was too low but, in the end, everyone got over 50 SEK. Hans-Erik [Andersson] said he would have sold at 50 and now the bid is worth 53. Everybody should be happy.'[32]

Old Mutual's Skandia takeover got a head start and its CEO Jim Sutcliffe conveyed to investors back in the summer of 2006 that the acquired company had been a better buy than expected, its quality and numbers turning out ahead of plans. Old Mutual carried out thorough programmes of restructuring in both Sweden and the UK. This work, which included ideas from the Turbo plan, was still being implemented in 2008. Skandia Nordic performed rather poorly in its first two years; however, Skandia won market shares again in the autumn of 2008.

Skandia Life UK developed largely according to plan, and continental Europe performed better than expected between 2006 and 2008. However, the Skandia takeover did not change Old Mutual's fortunes as a group. During its first two years following the close of the deal, it remained the cheapest insurance stock in Europe. This could partly be blamed on currency matters. The South African rand had depreciated 30 per cent since the spring of 2006; half of Old Mutual's embedded value was still denominated in rand. Financial analysts following the stock also complained about its conglomerate kind of structure, with life and savings business on different markets lacking synergies.[33]

As promised, Old Mutual pursued the secondary listing of its stock on the SSE. However, the activity in the share was low from the start; in 2007, it was virtually dead. SEB Funds held only 3 per cent of the Old Mutual shares in custody during that summer. Old Mutual was finally de-listed in Stockholm in September 2007. Julian Roberts then returned to England, having spent a year and a half travelling back and forth between London and Stockholm. He remained CEO of the Skandia group.

In 2007 Old Mutual also began to reveal problems with its US expansion. Losses were reported in the 2008 Q2 report. The US financial sub-prime crisis had exploded at the time and a financial meltdown wreaked havoc throughout the world.[34] Old Mutual announced a loss of $135 million on 10 September 2008, which it attributed to the slump in the value of the preferred shares it held in Fannie Mae and Freddie Mac, the US home mortgage giants that had been nationalized the same week. All in all, a capital amounting to roughly $500 million would have to be injected into Old Mutual's US and Bermuda life businesses.[35] CEO Jim Sutcliffe then resigned and Julian Roberts took his place.[36]

In October 2008, shortly before leaders from Europe, the USA and Asia announced their financial aid packages to save the global financial system from collapsing, Old Mutual was trading at 64 pence, about 50 per cent below the introductory price on the LSE from 1999. The main LSE index was unchanged at the same period. For South African investors the development was just as bad. The Old Mutual stock had remained unchanged during the ten-year period, while the Johannesburg Stock Exchange index had increased 265 per cent (during these years the rand had lost almost 40 per cent of its value against the pound sterling). In March 2009, Old Mutual including Skandia was trading around 50 pence per share (on 6 March it even went as low as 30 pence). Thus the company was then worth less than what it had paid for Skandia alone.[37]

NOTES

1. *Business Day*, 2 December 2005, 'Old Mutual cuts Skandia acceptance level to 50%', Stephen Gunnion.
2. *Dagens Industri*, 2 December 2005, 'Old Mutuals VD lovar hårda tag', Sophie Nachemson-Ekwall.
3. Old Mutual, 1 December 2005, 'Update on offer for Skandia', press release.
4. E.g., Dow Jones Newswires, 1 December 2005, 'Update: Old Mutual Cuts Skandia Acceptance Level', Sarah Spikes.
5. Skandia, 1 December 2005, 'Skandia comments on Old Mutual's Offer for Skandia', press release.
6. See note 4.
7. SIS Ägarservice and research conducted by the authors.
8. *Dagens Industri*, 8 December 2005, 'Striden är över', Sophie Nachemson-Ekwall and Jan Wäingelin.
9. Dn.se, 8 December 2005, 'Old Mutual: Majoritet för budet'.
10. A sovereign wealth fund.
11. See note 10.
12. SIS Ägarservice, 30 November 2005.
13. Hybrid loans represent alternative loan programmes designed to fill particular needs that the more straightforward fixed rate loans do not address. Many of these loans have more liberal qualifying standards than traditional loans. The conditions are often constructed in such a way that they may be classified as equity capital by the bank.
14. *Dagens Industri*, 9 December 2005, 'Marknaden tror på seger för Old Mutual', Sophie Nachemson-Ekwall.
15. A 10 per cent minority have, for example, the right to demand an EGM, appoint an extra auditor, demand a certain dividend (i.e. a kind of 'starvation prohibition'), and be bought off. It could also oppose adoption of the report and accounts, and then sue directors of the board for damages.
16. *Svenska Dagbladet*, 16 December 2005, 'Old Mutual möter kompakt motstånd', Jan Almgren.
17. Waymaker, 19 December 2005, 'Skandia: Skandias nomineringskommite (sic!)', press release.
18. *Financial Times*, 20 December 2005, 'Old Mutual wins control of Skandia', Andrea Felsted and Rupini Bergström.
19. Measured by market capitalization.
20. Hugin, 21 December 2005, 'Statement by Skandia's board', press release.
21. The loophole was closed one year later, after intensive lobbying from AP2 and the Swedish Shareholders' Association (among others).
22. *Dagens Industri*, 21 December 2005, 'Michael Wolf kan bli ny Skandia-VD', Bengt Carlsson and Sophie Nachemson-Ekwall.
23. Ibid.
24. Ticker (news agency), 28 December 2005, 'Skandia: Noonday ökar till 5 procent av kapitalet', Mats Hård.
25. SSE announcement, 2 December 2005.
26. Old Mutual, 17 January 2006, 'Old Mutual's offer for Skandia – Updated Acceptance level', press release.
27. Old Mutual, 26 January 2006, 'Old Mutual's Offer for Skandia now wholly unconditional', press release.
28. Lars Otterbeck was later to stay on as board member of Old Mutual and become chair of Skandia's Nordic region. Otterbeck had completed a doctorate at the Stockholm School of Economics, where he also had worked for several years as associate professor in business administration.
29. *Dagens Industri*, 4 February 2006, 'Han står bakom Gardell', Sophie Nachemson-Ekwall.

30. *Svenska Dagbladet*, 9 February 2006, 'Sälj Skandia innan aktien är helt död', Jan Almgren.
31. Old Mutual: 'Update on acceptances of Skandia offer and extension of final closing date to 14 March 2006', press release.
32. *Dagens Industri*, 22 February 2006, 'Ingen tycker att Skandia är fint', Gustaf Tapper.
33. Old Mutual's investor conference 20 June 2006; also Citigroup, 21 June 2006, 'Skandia integration update 2', Johny Lambridis.
34. Old Mutual, 6 August 2008, 'Old Mutual plc Interim Results for the six months ended 30 June 2008', press release.
35. Old Mutual, 10 September 2006, 'Update on Old Mutual US Life', press release.
36. Old Mutual, 10 September 2006, 'New Chief Executive Appointed', press release.
37. Old Mutual's preliminary results for 2008 were released on 4 March, stating a profit of £641 million before tax compared to £1624 the previous year. However, the report also revealed great progress in the Nordic region. The report further stated that the Skandia group had been gaining market share across Europe, yet it had performed less well on the UK market. In a comment to the report, CEO Julian Roberts wrote that the board and management had realized that the Old Mutual portfolio of business was too broad and needed more focus: 'We operate in too many countries and have too many lines of business, a number of which are sub-scale in their different markets. This makes the group complex and difficult to manage in a decentralised manner as we have done in the past. It therefore requires simplification' (Old Mutual press release; 12-month preliminary results 2008, 4 March 2009).

PART VII

Conclusions

22. Some conclusions on corporate control and governance processes in financial capitalism

22.1 CHAPTER OVERVIEW

In this final chapter, we shall analyse a selection of the topics that the extensive empirical investigation (see Chapters 2–21) and theoretical platform (see Chapter 1) has made it possible for us to address. We then claim to have chosen the more important themes that are intimately linked to the stated purposes of the study. As described in Chapter 1, the theoretical ambition has been to try to improve socioeconomic theories that address corporate control and corporate governance processes. The empirical aim has been to provide an extensive case study of a hostile cross-border takeover process. This enables a better understanding of corporate control struggles in early financial capitalism. This combined theoretical and empirical ambition could also be phrased as a more specific research question: how are changes of corporate control achieved in the emerging global financial capitalism of the early twenty-first century?

The rest of this chapter is divided into six sections (22.2–22.7): the first one addresses more general issues related to contextual conditions (financial capitalism), and contains a discussion regarding both the relevance and possible idiosyncrasies of the Old Mutual–Skandia case.

We analyse the empirical material in the following four sections (22.3–22.6), and draw some conclusions from the study, based upon the basic concepts and theories elaborated in Chapter 1. We begin this analysis by bringing to the forefront the differing value bases that the main actors have expressed (and professed themselves to hold) in their activities in the hostile takeover process. When defining their company's mission and their own mandates, some of the actors express more of a short-term shareholder-value perspective; others foster long-term conceptions that are sometimes also related to a stakeholder-value view. We try to show how these often well-developed perspectives on the *raison d'être* of (limited) companies have been used, more or less explicitly, as a basis for the considerations and standpoints of the different main actors in the Old

Mutual–Skandia takeover process and may, therefore, serve as one of the more important explanations for why, in the end, Old Mutual succeeded in acquiring the whole of Skandia.

In the third section, we discuss the connection between such general understandings (shareholder value and stakeholder-value views), and the relative emphasis that was given to each of the two fundamental dimensions of corporate governance as described in Chapter 1 – that is, how the financial (capital-based) and operational (business-based) perspectives have worked during Old Mutual's takeover of Skandia. In this context, the activities of the more leading actors within these two governance flows are discussed and explored. Additionally, there is an analysis in terms of human risk-taking regarding the kinds of risks that various (categories of) actors have been inclined to take in the Old Mutual–Skandia takeover struggle.

We address the basic agencies and positions inside and outside the focal organization (the target company Skandia) in the fourth section, and analyse how they have been enacted during the acquisition process. There is a particular focus upon the Skandia board in this analysis, particularly its composition and assignments, as well as the various ways in which the directors have worked when trying to outline a common future path for the company. Both Old Mutual's and Skandia's top management teams are in the spotlight, especially the activities of both CEOs. When we analyse the Skandia board more carefully, not limiting ourselves to its internal processes; the directors' relationships to outside actors are also addressed, particularly their linkages to those actors that are more directly involved in the struggle for control over Skandia: the (potential) bidders, the company's (changing) shareholders and the various advisers.

Actor activities are elaborated upon in the fifth section, starting from an understanding of the human being as interactive and multi-rational – that is, corresponding to the *homo complexicus* construct presented in Chapter 1. We attempt to show how various actors deal with genuine uncertainty, a condition that is always present when actors think about a company's future. The main actors are described as being embedded in networks of different kinds, including both those that build upon strong and rather permanent ties between them (e.g. circles) and those that express weaker and more temporary interpersonal ties (e.g. coalitions). We also discuss actors' relationships to the surrounding institutions, particularly those that represent systems of enforced norms regarding corporate governance and control issues in financial capitalism. We even discuss the possible varying degrees of actor awareness about these ruling constructs: legislation, regulations, custom, codes of conduct, habits and so on, as well as the differences regarding their knowledge about, and attitudes towards, these institutions: for example, the inclination to actively promote or comply with a certain norm.

Based on our conclusions from this theoretically based extensive empirical research effort, we raise a few questions in the brief final section of this chapter that we believe will be particularly important in the coming decade. These questions link to corporate control and governance processes, particularly how such processes are shaped by the changing rationales as expressed by actors in contemporary financial capitalism.

22.2 GENERAL OBSERVATIONS

We claim that Old Mutual's takeover of Skandia took place in a context that corresponds, to a large extent, to the description of the setting we denoted in Chapter 1 as globalizing financial capitalism. From the case description, one can easily recognize that financial motives have played a crucial role in the studied takeover process, as have the institutional forces that regulate the financial markets, particularly those that monitor the actions that were taken to achieve corporate control on the market, as well as those that provide guidelines for corporate governance processes. We have also made explicit some of the crucial cross-national institutional differences in these regulations, and have discussed this variation and its different effects upon the actor activities in the focused takeover struggle. In the Old Mutual–Skandia case there is actually a 'clash' between such (competing) institutional solutions (basically between a Nordic/ Swedish regulation and practice, and a corresponding UK Anglo-Saxon tradition).

The success of the hostile bid from the UK/South African company Old Mutual for Swedish Skandia illustrates some of the effects of the diffusion of actor experiences that were previously enshrined in more local or regional legislation, codes of conduct and customs. This also shows some of the consequences of such institutional export on a bid process. The opening up of (predominantly) national corporate control markets late in the twentieth century further indicates that the previous implicit competition between national institutional systems may be replaced in early twenty-first-century financial capitalism by demands for changes both at the local level (in this case study, perhaps particularly visible for Sweden) and on a more regional or even global scene (i.e. US and EU ambitions to both change and harmonize corporate and financial legislation/regulations on the global scene).

We also believe that a closer look at the contextual aspects of the empirical material presented in this volume makes it rather plausible that the case of Old Mutual's hostile takeover of Skandia functions as a kind of 'enlightening' narrative, making detectable some of the new, more important conditions and processes that are emerging on the increasingly global market for corporate control. Looking at the material, one would predict that such hostile bids become more frequent in the future, as in the new era of financial capitalism where any capital accumulated around the world could (at least potentially) be used for any acquisition attempt anywhere. At the same time, such efforts could attract investment banks, financially strong institutional investors, as well as various kinds of hedge or activist funds to act as facilitators or lubricants in takeover processes on any stock market around the world. Previously, the closeness between the actors (i.e. local markets) and their more common interactions (everybody knew each other quite well) created a disposition for the application of more 'friendly' approaches. Takeovers were often decided inside rather narrow and specific business spheres or actor circles. Thus we regard Old Mutual's cross-border hostile takeover of Skandia as far from an exceptional process; on the contrary, based on our material, one would expect an increasing share of similar acquisition attempts in the future.[1]

We have also determined that corporations lacking a dominating, controlling or cooperating group of shareholders is more exposed to radical changes in their shareholder bases than in the past (at least this is the case for the Nordic region). The studied takeover process would not have been possible if the target company had kept its voting restrictions from the twentieth century. It can also be noted that the control of Skandia as late as in 2004 as regards the voting rights lay mainly in the hands of Swedish institutional investors, since most of the foreign shareholders refrained from participating in the governance processes (few of them voted at the AGMs and few suggested candidates for the board). Moreover, some of the Swedish institutions were competitors to Skandia at the time (Alecta, Robur and SEB Funds). Alecta, however, decided to leave as shareholder in the company for this very reason, and neither Swedbank (cf. Robur), Nordea nor SEB acted overtly in the process. All in all, not only the distribution of the shareholding in the early years of the twenty-first century, but also the kind of shareholding that was involved, made Skandia vulnerable to almost any effort to take control of the company.

We also described in Chapter 1 how, at the turn of the millennium with the financialization of the economic systems around the world, many institutional shareholders changed their approach to governance and became ready to take active part not only in domestically based governance processes, but also in cross-border takeover attempts that involved foreign as well as transnational corporations. In Chapters 3–21, we have showed how pension funds, retail funds and different kinds of hedge funds and activist funds together took positions in the two focal companies, and that their acting mattered for the final outcome of the takeover process. The Old Mutual–Skandia case demonstrates how uncertainty is a dominating, ever-present triggering force for such investor actions, and how these actors tried in different ways to reduce and control some of that ambiguity – both in terms of institutional forces and with respect to the (expected) actions of others involved in the struggle for control. This is apparent in the emergence of actor coalitions, in the activation of latent networks, and in most of the private small talk that centred on the Old Mutual–Skandia struggle.

All of this, along with the emerging global market for corporate control, made Skandia an interesting target for almost all those actors around the world that could raise (or already controlled) substantial amounts of capital suitable for risk-taking. The abundance of cheap money in the world economy was, at the time, another particularly favourable condition for attracting the potential interest of various kinds of short-term investors (e.g. ready to arbitrage in the Old Mutual–Skandia struggle). The emerging-markets rally in the autumn of 2005 was the perfect time for launching such a takeover process.

Perhaps the fact that Skandia had grown so dramatically outside the Nordic countries (especially in the UK and the USA) and had, therefore, become more internationally visible, played a role in the company gradually becoming an attractive global target. Maybe the same could also be supposed regarding its tremendous success in the 1990s, when its internationally well-reputed unit-linked-business brought about its skyrocketing share price. Even the Skandia scandal that erupted in Sweden in 2003 contributed to the general interest in the company. However, as described in the case, this interest may have also worked against the company, actually making some external actors more reluctant to get involved. Also, it appears likely that its generally greater vulnerability (i.e. its [potential] involvement in legal procedures) and reputational problems increased its exposure to potential and dramatic control changes.

One important and obvious consequence of the company's reputational problems and general business crisis in Sweden was a change of both its board composition and its CEO, which was based on the organized activity of some previously more passive institutional shareholders. These changes in the executive agencies represented a break with many of the long traditions that had been associated with Skandia. Judging from the case material, the new executives were less inclined to defend what had happened in previous years – they wanted to get rid of Skandia's old problems and start afresh. At the same time, however, this change of executives also brought several new actors to the Skandia scene, who were less familiar with the company's culture and work procedures.

Moreover, it may have been important for the materialization of this particular takeover process that the target Skandia was a company that was not particularly well integrated; its structure is often referred to as 'federative-like' (this expression indicates the presence of a very decentralized organizational structure), and there was also continuous friction between the Skandia HQ and the UK management team that was never resolved during the acquisition process. The described design and working of the systems for economic control in the target company was also an indication of the strong autonomy of certain sizeable parts of Skandia (particularly for its UK business).

The case description further indicates that a hostile takeover process may be difficult for any actor to control. We can see from the empirical material that, in the process, the acquiring company has problems getting into the driver's seat – and also staying there (there were times when Old Mutual even indicated that it considered giving up the entire project). Moreover, the active chair in the target company also had increasing difficulty in taking charge and leading the strategic process. A divided board thus emerged. The same is valid for some of the leading actors that were active in the different shareholder coalitions. In the end, however, Old Mutual acquired Skandia (in practice in late 2005, and legally in early 2006). Our interpretation is that this completed process could be understood as the gradually intended result of the agency of a dominant coalition of actors: in the end, it comprised Old Mutual's top management, a host of activist and hedge funds, several global investment banks, a number of Old Mutual and Skandia shareholders, and three of Skandia's board members. This agency was characterized by its systematic reference to the rationale of a 'radical' version of the shareholder-value view, based on a short-term perspective, according to which maximization of market capitalization should, at any given time, be persistently at the forefront in any corporate governance processes (see, Section 22.3).

The agency of the dominant coalition was expressed in a multitude of forms, ranging from various forms of calculation (valuation of companies, predictions of index reshuffling, financial engineering and so on) and rhetorical arguments ('rational' thinking, and what is known as 'fiduciary obligations') to a creative use of a situation of ambiguity regarding legitimate and acceptable forms for corporate governance and control processes (with a focus on the Swedish scene). This also included ingredients that were relatively new and less well known to several actors: for example, soft irrevocables, the functioning of the nomination committees, and the use of due diligence procedures. In our opinion, the dominant coalition was, for the most part, on the offensive from the very beginning, was generally better informed about what was going on as the process moved on, became more familiar with the distinguishing features of the new era of financial capitalism, and had more elaborate networks on the global scene.

22.3 DIFFERING VIEWS OF THE PURPOSE OF A LIMITED COMPANY

Several views exist regarding the *raison-d'être* or purpose for limited companies as described in Chapter 1. The basic dividing line was between the shareholder value and the stakeholder-value views, although it was suggested that the more important differences were linked to the time perspectives used, and predominantly located inside the shareholder-value perspective. Thus some of the promoters of shareholder value focus on the current shareholders in a company, basically acting in a short-run perspective. In such cases, there is rather seldom an evaluation of the various qualities – values, ambitions, experiences and competencies – associated with the shareholders and the shareholding (no 'discrimination'). Other advocates of the shareholder-value view instead put the emphasis on the value created for all shareholders, current as well as future ones, and basically in their actions apply a long-term perspective. Their ambition is to bring about a successful (re)production of 'sustainable business structures', providing wealth to all shareholders over time.

Starting from the nexus of the case – the Skandia board – one could easily identify variations in the short-term/long-term shareholder-value dimension; it is also evident that this difference in the basic understanding of the ultimate purpose of a large listed limited company played a role in the directors' understandings about which strategic path Skandia ought to follow. These differences in perspectives could be interpreted as important for the entire takeover process, thus contributing to the emergence of a divided Skandia board, where two opposing 'camps' were gradually formed. One of the camps embraced a shareholder-value view, which more closely resembled the short-term financial perspective: they were more inclined from the very beginning of the process to support a Skandia development that would include rather immediate structural changes and the entry of new controlling shareholders. The other camp supported a more long-term shareholder view, which (also) stressed the operational dimension, proposing a Skandia that would develop on its own (at least for a few years) in order to create a sustainable business structure. Later in the process, when Old Mutual was regarded as a potential buyer of Skandia, there were also some directors who expressed positions of a stakeholder kind (e.g. they talked about the importance of Skandia for Sweden).

The short-term kind of shareholder position was to a large extent based on various calculations of Skandia's and Old Mutual's shares prices, and on the expected benefits for their current shareholders, regardless of who they were and what their ambitions were for their respective companies. Chair Magnusson expressed a rather complex rationale in his actions. He leaned towards a short-term shareholder perspective when he claimed several times that he did not discriminate between various categories of shareholders; he saw it as his duty to work for the current shareholders in the company, and listened carefully to what they said. Nor was he particularly distressed by the fact that the operations and business synergies were low between Old Mutual and Skandia, something that those who promoted a long-term shareholder view usually found most troublesome, and made them reject the proposed deal/merger.

However, Magnusson's actions also indicated that he, too, applied a long-term horizon. His search for a new 'strong' controlling shareholder to sort out the messy situation in the company could be interpreted in that way; he actually regarded such a development necessary for the company to be able to prosper in the long run (and the sooner that restructuring path was put into practice the better for Skandia). Thus he had gradually become convinced that a Skandia 'on its own' was not capable of clearing up the troubled situation. One possible conclusion regarding this action of Chair Magnusson is therefore that he expressed a somewhat mixed rationale, doing things very much in the spirit of a short-term shareholder-value view, but applying a long-term perspective at the same time. He appeared with this dual or Janusian[2] rationale quite consistent throughout the entire takeover process (April 2004 to October 2005). To give just one concrete example of this duality: when Magnusson (and the other directors) decided to keep the recently recruited CEO at his post, it was motivated both by securing organizational stability (providing an opportunity to have an in-depth analysis of Skandia's strategic situation and a long-term outlook for the company), and by a wish to avoid further uncertainties that could produce short-term negative reactions on the stock market.

Magnusson's rationale was not uncontroversial at the time, since this kind of more complex (dual) acting had not been a tradition in Sweden, particularly not in the era of industrial capitalism, when the chair and the board in its entirety had been primarily regarded as responsible for the well-being of the company (rather than of the shareholders). Hence, Magnusson's combination of a long-term perspective with a short-term shareholder-value view was difficult for some actors to grasp and fully appreciate. The fact that much of the support for his strategic action came from actors whose rationales were more associated with clear-cut short-term shareholder values, and not at all connected to a long-term perspective, was probably instrumental in complicating his position even more.

Old Mutual's leading actors (CEO Jim Sutcliffe and CFO Julian Roberts) foremost argued in the interest of their company's current shareholders throughout the takeover process. Management essentially had the choice between a large cash dividend to Old Mutual's shareholders or a takeover that would rather lead to a positive revaluation of the share. Our interpretation is that they supposedly consistently applied a short-term shareholder-value perspective in their acquisition ambitions (even though they also spoke about more long-term goals (e.g. expand outside South Africa)). For example, this can be seen in the preparatory works within the company that were conducted with its investment bank advisers. This work revolved much around how shareholder value was to be created in the short term. This was considered as a question of how institutional investors of various kinds – including current shareholders of both the companies directly involved – would react to a bid proposal in terms of selling or buying shares; and how arbitrage shareholders (hedge funds) would be encouraged to take positions to counteract the fall of the share price due to selloffs. The financial engineering of it enabled the bid to go through as pure trade between actors on the stock market. This weakened the Skandia board's statements or recommendations, including its view of the character of the bid (friendly or hostile). This partial decentering of the board's decision process was further enhanced by the way in which the arguments were elaborated (e.g. regarding index reshuffling), with the aim of influencing the financial flow (with no or few links to the operational dimension).

When it comes to various kinds of investors and their activities on the stock market – particularly their functioning on the market for corporate control – we have found in this empirical case study that, when it comes to finances, they tend to quite narrowly follow the theoretically expected rationales. Thus the investment decisions of most (perhaps all) of the mutual funds (Fidelity, Nordea Funds, SEB Funds and so on) were made in relation to an index. Thus performance became strongly linked to relative returns. This meant that they were acting just as short-term investors are usually supposed to do. They focused upon short-term capital gains and, consequently, supported the fraction of the Skandia board that sympathized with the classic short-term shareholder-value view, trying to raise the share price (without intervening in ways other than as buyers/sellers, or as [temporary] nomination committee members).

Among the mutual funds, however, not everybody acted as theoretically expected. Some of them left the passive entry/exit position and formed coalitions with the ambition to use voice and voting rights to enhance short-term or long-term returns. Such acting required some kind of leadership, since there was no standing and organized circles or coalitions ready to act. Such leadership could then be carried out by an actor at one of the mutual funds or be triggered by some outsider (in this case, an activist fund – Cevian – worked as the catalyst). It is also to be highlighted that many Swedish mutual funds have two independent branches; one led by a corporate governance general advocating a long-term shareholder-value perspective, the other led by a portfolio manager, instead acting according to a traditional index-tracking rationale founded on a short-term shareholder-value view (a de-coupling that could open up for organized 'hypocrisy'). This double rationale was present among some of the mutual funds that held stock in Skandia; several non-Swedish actors saw the presence of this double rationale as quite peculiar.[3]

Many of the state-owned national Swedish pension funds also acted in accordance with the aforementioned double rationale. The AP funds had an assignment to act solely in the best interest of their ultimate principals: the current and future Swedish pensioners (which should indicate the presence of a long-term investment horizon). However, their performances were concurrently evaluated against different indexes, thus enhancing the same short-term shareholder-value rationale that governed the mutual funds. This rationale implied quite a passive buy/sell actor stance in relation to the companies included in their investment portfolio. Moreover, despite their active stance on the 'no' side, neither AP4 nor AP2 increased their shareholding (as would have been expected). AP4 remained more or less neutral to the index, and AP2 merely made a symbolic investment.[4] However, there was another difficulty for the AP funds with this short-term shareholder-value action: there were some attempts in 2005 from Sweden's deputy minister of finance to persuade the state-controlled AP funds to act more in the interests of the Swedish nation. This meant adopting a longer-term perspective and stakeholder-like approach to the Old Mutual–Skandia process. However, other more important matters appeared on the political scene that stopped possible further proposals of the kind.

The hedge fund is a rather new kind of shareholding that, in a sense, can be seen as characteristic of the era of financial capitalism. Such funds also appeared in the Old Mutual–Skandia case. However, many funds fall into this category, both passive as well as active ones. There are also other kinds of investors on the global financial scene that express a similar rationale as many hedge funds, although they may be regulated differently (e.g. investment firms like Kauphting and Burdarás). Some of these funds and investors acted as catalysts and trading arbitrageurs in the studied takeover process; thus they became very important for its outcome. As with several other fund managers and (potential) investors in Skandia, some hedge fund managers participated in meetings and were on the phone talking to corporate insiders literally throughout the entire process (from May 2005 onwards). Although all investors are keen to seek information, the activities of these hedge funds seemed to be of a different, more intensive and systematic kind.

The more involved parts of the hedge fund and investor community supported Cevian's bid for a seat on the Skandia's board. This was based on its announced intention to work towards breaking up Skandia – as it presented its intentions in numerous meetings in 2004 and early 2005. Paulson, head of an arbitrage hedge fund carrying his name, had been involved in longer talks with Cevian's Christer Gardell, as had representatives from its analogue fund, Noonday. The latter also had straightforward negotiations with Old Mutual during the autumn of 2005, and participated in a joint hedge fund campaign to persuade Old Mutual to lower the bid condition of 90 per cent acceptances, in return for a promise to buy whatever shares other institutional investors sold off. All these activities were based on a rather straightforward short-term shareholder-value view that, through these efforts, made a strong impact upon the Old Mutual–Skandia takeover process.

The activist fund, as described in Chapter 1, is another category of investors that had dramatically increased and acquired a strong position on the global market for corporate control. Representatives of such a unit often campaign – even publicly – for substantial changes in 'attacked' companies, thus trying to obtain support from other investors. The power of the activist fund – in this case, that of Cevian – also depends a great deal on the composition of the shareholding of a targeted company. Therefore the chance of success is highest in a corporation such as Skandia that has an open shareholder structure, and in a country such as Sweden, which has a shareholder value oriented governance model that is open in character (by providing the opportunity to even moderately strong shareholders to influence the composition of the boards of [targeted] companies[5]).

In the Old Mutual–Skandia takeover process, the activist firm Cevian took a leading role by way of its two main actors: Christer Gardell and Lars Förberg. As can be seen from this case, Gardell's acting in particular was built upon his personal track record as a successful activist on the Swedish stock market. This was something that made many other market actors inclined to listen to what he suggested, and sometimes to walk in his footsteps, contributing to marked changes in share prices. Cevian was not restricted in its investment policy; however, it mostly looked for what it regarded as undervalued, rather large listed corporations on the SSE. Skandia soon became one such company; consequently Cevian acquired shares in Skandia. After Chair Magnusson had made his intentions of a Skandia being 'open to everything' publicly known, Cevian added to Skandia's heightened attention by making its rather small shareholding (of a mere few per cent) known to the public. A small rally in the stock was the immediate result, as was Gardell's co-option to the Skandia nomination committee in December 2004. This appointment was in accordance with the newer Swedish corporate governance principles where the largest shareholders – regardless of actual size – were supposed to have those positions.

Gardell also made several tours among potential supporters to raise their interest in participating in the Skandia race (such as US activist Icahn and several Icelandic investors). Successful talks would increase Cevian's opportunities to earn a healthy profit on its Skandia holding. We interpret Gardell's and Cevian's activities, taken together, as perhaps the most clear-cut example in our empirical material of a systematic (and successful) line of action based upon a short-term shareholder-value view. However, a most conspicuous component in Cevian's action base was the fact that some of the investors that expressed a differing basic view on the Old Mutual takeover effort (particularly AP1 and AP2) provided the major financing for its fund. The stance of those institutions was rather close to a long-term shareholder-value view and even touched a classic stakeholder perspective. One of the investors in Cevian (AP2) also made a late attempt to push the company to change its course, so that it better corresponded to a long-term shareholder view.

When the Old Mutual bid was finally on the table in September 2005, the basic argument to accept it from almost all of those actors that acted in a short-term shareholder perspective (be it directors like Skandia's Chair Magnusson, Deputy Chair Björnsson and Director Gardell, or outsiders like some mutual funds, hedge funds and activists) was that Old Mutual's offering at 42 SEK exceeded the current market value of Skandia. Another important reason for an acceptance of the bid was the perceived risk that otherwise the Skandia share – in the short-term perspective – could fall substantially, maybe as low as 35 SEK. Therefore, in their view, the bid should be accepted.

There were also several main actors in the struggle that expressed a long-term shareholder-value position, that is, one where the holding was also linked to a consideration of the other stakeholders' contributions, which was done to a significantly greater extent than by those more closely connected to the short-term shareholder-value view. Thus, for the Skandia directors who leaned more towards a long-term shareholder-value perspective, there were issues other than the (current and short-term) share prices that also had to be taken into account. They concentrated on building sustainable business structures; that is, they engaged in creating greater value for all shareholders alike (regardless of when an individual shareholding started or ended). These actors generally tended to support the Skandia stand-alone path (the naysayers on the Skandia board, and some of the Swedish institutional shareholders). The general idea was to 'immediately' launch efforts to improve the company's existing operations; by doing so, Skandia would concurrently build a platform of lasting values that would (over time) benefit all its shareholders. This would create better opportunities for its future strategic actions. Thus the main argument was that the market had yet to realize the true potential of the company, but would do so in due time; in the near future (a few years) the stand-alone path, including the Turbo plan, was expected to create more value to the shareholders than the actual bid on the table.

When Jeansson took over as Skandia chair and began to run the board's activities, it might have looked as though he carried forward certain aspects of the short-term shareholder-value perspective. For example, there were still quite a few lengthy discussions about stakeholder-oriented matters. This could be explained to a substantial extent by what had happened before he became chair, and by the fact that there was a current public bid for Skandia. The board's statements were also – and perhaps mostly – a consequence of the existing regulations that addressed takeover processes and demanded that the directors elaborate on particular predefined topics and followed certain prescriptions (see Section 22.6). As a consequence, many of these texts often focused on matters that were closer to the interests of the short-term shareholders. The case material, however, also indicates that for Jeansson and several other directors, the operational rationale was something important to consider in choosing the strategic path for Skandia. For example, the chair, several other directors and the CEO were all engaged in quite intense discussions during the autumn of 2005 with several of Skandia's shareholders, where the development of the business was claimed to be crucial for the company's future success. This attitude was in accordance with our interpretation of how Jeansson looked on his duty as Skandia chair (and as a board member in general): to act in the long-term interest of all company shareholders.

Jeansson and others considered Skandia to be in a cumbersome 'turnaround' process, although with a great deal of promising work having already been done, with more to come: some divestments, a structural integration of Skandia UK into the Skandia group, more product development, a few crucial management succession decisions, and a rebuilding of the company's reputation (particularly in Sweden). Skandia shareholders were addressed with a call to be patient. They were told that the business results would show the fruits of this labour within two to three years, and would be reflected in the future share price. The bid premium was argued to be low in light of this promising alternative.

Jeansson, as with other naysayers, saw the negative value gap between the Skandia share price and the Old Mutual bid price mostly as a reflection of the investors' uncertainty at the time regarding what would happen, and also as an outcome of their ignorance of what was actually being done in the company. This view could be contrasted with that of his predecessor, Bernt Magnusson, who came to the 'opposite' conclusion. Magnusson did not put much worth on the Skandia Turbo plan (the stand-alone alternative). His position was that it could – and should – be disregarded since the stock market had given the plan close to zero value, indicating that it added no substantial benefit for Skandia's (current) shareholders.

Significant attention was also given to part of the currency in the proposed transaction (i.e. to the Old Mutual shares). From the naysayers' perspective, the value of these shares could be questioned since Old Mutual's long-term management strategy and expected operational development was venturesome. Thus a takeover would increase the risk for those Skandia investors that had planned to remain long-term shareholders and were, thus, committed to take – and keep – Old Mutual shares as part of the payment. This argument, however, did not tie in with the short-term investor rationale on a market where hedge funds were ready to take arbitrage positions in order to facilitate mutual funds in selling shares at a price that would be fairly close to the expected final bid. Instead, the discussion mostly became a question of how much risk short-term activists and arbitrage funds would be willing to take.

The issue of whether Skandia should keep or sell Skandiabanken was treated in consensus between the two camps at the board: the bank represented a clear-cut long-term shareholder-value for the Skandia group (perhaps with some stakeholder-values involved as well). The Skandia board was united in trying to prevent Old Mutual shareholders from making a strategic mistake (selling off Skandiabanken if and when it secured control of Skandia). A concern for Skandia's employees and customers, who might lose from such a development, probably added to that conviction. However, it should be noted that, according to a radical short-term shareholder-value view, Skandia's shareholders should be expected to be indifferent to what an acquiring company does after an acquisition.[6]

The general impression from the activities that took place in the autumn of 2005 is that the Skandia board did not have much of a say in the takeover process, regardless of the perspective practised (shareholder or stakeholder). Several of the directors acted as if the board actually had some power; however, that journey was littered with disappointments. One cannot avoid the impression that several of the directors (and their allies) did not seem to have been prepared for the 'machinery' of contemporary financial capitalism. The ways the market for corporate control and hostile takeover processes worked seem to have come as a bit of a surprise. This also includes the new kind of shareholder rationales that became particularly visible in the Old Mutual–Skandia case. One could add the ambiguities that existed regarding the scope of the various institutional settings that had sprung up from different states or regions. This resulted in clashes that created action opportunities, particularly for those that had a more opportunistic relationship to rules and codes (see Section 22.6). This meant that the long-term view that the naysayers advocated during the autumn and winter of 2005 never became a powerful force in the struggle for control. The situation could have been different if the Swedish corporate governance legislation had provided the boards (in a target company) with a strong formal standing – particularly in takeover processes (see Section 22.5).

Some of the outsiders expounded the more tangible stakeholder-value views, most visibly through media debates (there was literally a campaign). For example, prominent business people publicly argued the importance of retaining high-salary and high-competence jobs in Sweden, declaring that much of the current corporate restructuring was driven mostly by financial speculation with little or no regard for long-term business success. The Swedish Shareholders' Association also acted to keep Skandia Swedish, as did prominent representatives from the Swedish unions. However, also a few of the Skandia directors (some of the 'naysayers' in the autumn of 2005) hinted at similar kinds of values by claiming that the company was 'particularly important to Sweden as a nation', and was of utmost concern for the viability of Stockholm as a Nordic financial centre. Some of the expressed views could also be interpreted as pleas for securing some measure of national control over other companies listed in Sweden (not least through Skandia Liv). All this arguing underpinned a view that favoured the stakeholders involved (who tended to be local or regional in their thoughts); it simply did not address the interests of the (current) shareholders.[7] From the point of view of certain stakeholders, the main argument regarding the bid in autumn 2005 was that there were important externalities linked to securing ongoing 'Swedish control' of Skandia. The (unknown) price to be paid at the time was neglecting an opportunity to make a short-term realization profit.

One might first conclude that the impact of the stakeholder-value view on the takeover process was limited (if there was any at all). This line of thought appeared to be rather controversial and not obviously legitimate – at least for many of the actors involved in the Old Mutual–Skandia takeover process. On the one hand, those associated with the core of the business community tended to keep such arguments private (some actually expressed such views publicly, but then often anonymously). On the other hand, those that were more loosely connected to the business community expressed their stakeholder views more frankly. However, no such issues really took off, not even the issue of nationalism, although distinguished actors put it both in the 'visible' (public) and in the 'invisible' (private) arenas.[8] This stakeholder failure came as a surprise to some of those who supported such values, since it is not at all unusual for stakeholder views to gain momentum and make an impact upon corporate governance and control processes.[9]

As mentioned in Chapter 1, the difference between a universal and a particular shareholding is important in determining which rationale an actor is supposed to execute when making an investment. In the Old Mutual–Skandia case, the 'universal' position can be found among investors such as AP funds, Fidelity, Nordea Funds and SEB Funds. The more 'particular' positions in the takeover struggle were instead found among investors like Cevian, activist supporters Burdarás and Kaupthing, hedge funds Noonday and Paulson, members of the Swedish Shareholders' Association, and individuals such as the Skandia directors. What happens in a larger context than that of a single company becomes very important for the investors that make use of a universal rationale, as their performances and achievements are usually linked to some index that represents a wider field (e.g. a nation or an industry). In such situations, it might be rational to also work for the interest of the larger sphere. Thus, investors applying a universal rationale are in a sense realizing some of the ideas and ideals that are associated with the stakeholder-value view. Despite that, however, we have seen that they still usually stick to the long-term shareholder rhetoric in legitimizing their actions, while, at the same time, applying a short-term shareholder-value view in their capital management decisions.[10]

In summarizing this section, it is fair to say that this study underlines the well-documented and highly problematic 'free-rider' problem on the market for corporate control in financial capitalism (see Chapter 1). Many institutional long-only investors characterize this situation with their accompanying strong demand for portfolio diversification (i.e. minimization of asset-specific risk). The difficulties with forming the coalitions for supporting (or rejecting) hostile bids are easily identified in the description of Old Mutual's bid for Skandia. Some Swedish institutions (AP2 and AP4) tried to take the lead in these efforts; however, traditional index behaviour and risk aversion made the other institutional investors reluctant to participate. Generally, this conservative allocation rationale makes long-term institutional shareholding problematic when it comes to corporate control and governance processes. A substantial amount of long-term shareholders are, therefore, prevented from effectively influencing takeover activities, such as the one studied in this book.

Skandia Liv's chair explained that the mutual firm, due to the great specific risk involved in an investment as large as a Skandia bid, could not act as the company's much-longed-for white knight. This is a striking example of the problem that stems from the 'obligation' to hold a diversified portfolio. Therefore an important conclusion from the case material is that for upcoming processes such as the one described in this book, there may be a need to have a negotiated order in place among institutional investors regarding how to distribute governance work. Otherwise, none of it will be done (see Section 22.5).

This case shows that some Swedish institutional shareholders moved from being 'long-only' and passive investors to being activist shareholders (while, at the same time, being restricted by laws and other regulations). Lars Idermark of AP2 and Björn Lind of SEB Funds were particularly vocal about the reasonableness of a structural solution to Skandia's situation. At the same time, they were prevented from letting their organizations make large financial bets on such an outcome. Thus it is important to note that some of the actors in the process expressed paths that they, themselves, could not follow in practice. Obviously, to some extent this weakened the impact of the values and ideas that such actors advocated. However, nothing prevented them from letting their values be expressed through the actions of others, to whom they gave their support. If this change from a passive to an active position among some of the shareholders was of somewhat lesser importance for the outcome of the takeover struggle, then one could say that the opposite was true for another development on the shareholding arena: the dramatic change in the Skandia holdings that occurred during a few months in 2005 in the more intense stages of the takeover process. This change meant that the shareholding moved from basically leaning towards long-term shareholder values to become more oriented towards short-term shareholder values. This shifting value base and action rationale of the shareholding constellations being in the driving seat in the process was such an important transformation of the takeover conditions that we regard it as close to a necessary circumstance for Old Mutual's acquisition of Skandia in late 2005/early 2006.

22.4 THE FINANCIAL RATIONALE DOMINATES THE SCENE

We discussed in the previous section the differences among the main actors regarding which kind of shareholder-value view they mostly endorsed in their actions: that which focuses upon a short-term perspective stressing the financial flow or that which centres upon a long-term perspective that adds considerations of the operational flow. We have found strong advocates of both throughout the Old Mutual–Skandia struggle, although those actors that applied the more short-term kind of rationale got the upper hand from early autumn 2005 and onwards. There were also some activities that were more the result of a stakeholder-value view; however, these initiatives never had a strong impact on the course of the takeover process.

Our main ambition in this section is to analyse how the two corporate flows – the capital-based and the operational-based one – worked in the Old Mutual–Skandia case (see Section 1.6). At the same time, we shall attempt to clarify their relative importance for the final outcome of the lengthy control struggle. The capital-based (i.e. financial) flow provided the main arena for the short-term shareholders. They tended to treat the corporation very much as a bundle of assets, possible to capitalize one by one or in its entirety. Note, for example, the actions of many of those that advocated a structural solution for Skandia. Moreover, some of the short-term shareholders participated in Skandia's financial flow primarily for speculative reasons, merely trying to capture some swift returns (cf. the acting of several hedge funds). The actors that instead maintained a long-term shareholder-value view stressed rather the importance of the business, and made the operational flow the nexus of their efforts.

Our flow analysis focuses on the actions of the most important (categories of) actors, and we try to identify in which of the two processes they tend to be more active. We also describe some of their differing rationales, as well as their varying degrees of eagerness to pursue their interests and ambitions. Our point of departure is an analysis of the actions of the potential as well as the current shareholders. We then continue our flow discussions by addressing the executive agencies involved: those of Old Mutual and Skandia. This section continues with a discussion on the impact made on the two flows by other categories of actors. In the financial flow, we find investments bankers, financial analysts, business journalists, credit-rating institutes, banks and other providers of credit, legislators, regulators and so on. If we turn instead to the operational flow, we find the executive bodies in Old Mutual and Skandia, strategic consultants, union representatives, customers, politicians and so on.[11] After that analysis, we continue by linking the two flows, the financial and operational, to the kinds of risks that some of the more leading actors either seek or try to avoid. In the end, we summarize the section by formulating three more general conclusions.

In this study, where Skandia became the target company, many kinds of potential and actual shareholders are involved: the acquiring company Old Mutual, pension funds, mutual funds, hedge funds, activist funds, members of the Swedish Shareholders' Association and so on. In early 2004, when our study of this particular process started, there was no stable dominating shareholder coalition in Skandia. The company was wide open for almost all kinds of shareholders trying to benefit from the situation and from those that, somewhat later, also tried to make gains during the upcoming bidding process or speculated on a particular outcome. Thus all the cooperating or competing shareholders that were involved in the Old Mutual–Skandia takeover addressed its financial flow, and their actions in that governance process were probably decisive for how this struggle ended.

In 2004, traditional Swedish long-only passive institutional investors 'controlled' Skandia; it was essentially pension funds and retail funds that formed the nomination committee, who were to suggest new board members at the April 2004 AGM. The implementation of that kind of shareholding usually occurred through the financial flows of the companies where they had made investments; they rather seldom expressed opinions regarding the ways operations were carried out. Basically, they also acted in that way in Skandia. Already during autumn 2004, some of them became interested in the possibility of finding a structural solution to Skandia's problematic situation. As time passed, they became more and more concerned about the rather unsatisfactory development of the Skandia share price.

Late in 2004 another (kind of) shareholder that more explicitly promoted a financially based restructuring of Skandia appeared on the Skandia scene: the activist fund Cevian. Soon after Chair Magnusson's announcement in the Swedish media in December that Skandia was 'open to everything', the fund announced its new shareholding in the company and its ambition to take an active part in the company's governance. Subsequently, Christer Gardell was co-opted to Skandia's nomination committee; just a few months later, he was appointed director of the company (April 2005). Some shareholders, including the Swedish Shareholders' Association, questioned this decision. However, several Swedish institutional investors actively supported Gardell's candidature, as did the new major Icelandic and US shareholders who had appeared on the scene following Cevian's entry as shareholder, thus taking part in its Skandia plan. Fidelity also gave its tacit consent, representing 5 per cent of the votes. Together, those who supported Gardell controlled about 25 per cent of the Skandia stock, which was enough for a practical majority at this AGM.

Fidelity had already been a relatively large shareholder in Skandia even before Cevian took a position in the company. However, it had usually refrained from being active in governance processes on the Swedish market; this policy of passivity also applied to its previous actions in Skandia. All of that changed in the winter of 2005, when Fidelity gave both formal and informal support to those actors that advocated an 'immediate' structural solution for Skandia. This strengthened the capital-based, more short-term kind of rationale in the struggle for control. However, Fidelity's way of arguing was to a large extent based also on presumed shortcomings in Skandia's operational flow (Skandia lacked the critical mass to be successful in the future insurance industry).

By May 2005, it was clear to the Skandia board and Morgan Stanley that there was only one seriously interested party left in the bid for the whole of Skandia: Old Mutual. From that time, the shareholding in Skandia gradually began to change, and the transformation then accelerated during the autumn and early winter of 2005. During the first two business days following the public bid on 2 September, Skandia's shares changed hands in heavy trading. Less than a week later, Swedish institutional investors had reduced their total shareholding in Skandia by ten percentage points. At the same time, international hedge funds substantially bought into the stock, as the spread between the value of the Old Mutual bid and the Skandia share turned the latter company into a lucrative place for short-term gamblers: activist funds, arbitrage funds, special event funds and so on. There were few deeper discussions about operational matters among these actors; consequently, no serious attempts to contribute to the development of that particular Skandia flow. Thus they all expressed a straightforward financial rationale in their activities.

In this autumn, several (kinds of) Swedish shareholders (as well as other categories of actors) began their attempts to stop Old Mutual's takeover of Skandia. For example, representatives for the Swedish Shareholders' Association, Folksam and AP4 – who all opposed Old Mutual's offer – stressed arguments that were linked to the operational flow. Some of the shareholders then focused on the importance of keeping both Skandia and its mutual subsidiary Skandia Liv in Sweden. This would ensure that crucial competencies stayed in the country. These arguments predominantly referred to operational matters; however, there were also demands that the SSE (the leading Nordic marketplace for financial flows) must be 'saved'. This was to be accomplished, *inter alia*, through having as many of the Swedish 'blue chips' as possible listed in the country. Some of the shareholders also stressed that it was a bad idea to entrust a large part of a nation's pension savings in the hands of a foreign company. These actions, which were built mostly on various kinds of operational rationales, had a limited impact upon the Old Mutual–Skandia takeover process in the end. What really mattered was the voting power of the two sides, which was fast turning in favour of those who were basically applying a financial rationale and working to gain control of Skandia's capital-based flow.

The changes in Skandia's shareholder base continued – and accelerated – throughout September. Several Swedish investors sold off their Skandia shares, which made foreign shareholding rise to close to 60 per cent by the end of the month. In September alone, 13 per cent of the Skandia shares 'had left the country'. Around 20 September Old Mutual claimed that it controlled more than 50 per cent of the Skandia shares, and that of those, around 60 per cent were in the hands of long-term investors, while the rest were held by short-term speculators. This meant that the takeover struggle had shifted from one that involved both Skandia's governance flows to one that merely influenced the financial one.

Several Swedish shareholders tried to establish a blocking minority. AP2 and AP4 led the formation of a group of core Swedish institutional investors, who together controlled more than 10 per cent of the capital in Skandia. This new coalition tried to create a block right at the heart of Skandia's financial flow (although the arguments were still mainly of an operational kind). The effect of this blocking effort was later eliminated on 1 December when Old Mutual, supported by activist funds and hedge funds, decided to lower the acceptance level to 50+ per cent. Thus, at this time, the control struggle almost solely addressed Skandia's financial flow.

Hedge fund heads such as Paulson & Co. had come to the same conclusion as many other actors in October 2005: a combined Old Mutual–Skandia would probably allow the two firms to compete more effectively on the global scale. These actors regarded Skandia as too small; a merged and enlarged Old Mutual would benefit from scale economies and a lesser country risk. Basically, that was a conclusion founded on operational and business considerations (or at least could be interpreted that way). However, besides that, Paulson & Co. was encouraged by the thought that a deal could result in both a takeover premium and a re-rating of the Old Mutual stock. Thus the hedge fund decided to bet that the deal would go through (positioning itself in Skandia's financial flow). Moreover, as Paulson & Co. at that time controlled about 5 per cent of the Skandia stock, the hedge fund was entitled to a seat in Skandia's nomination committee. Another hedge fund, Noonday, had also bought quite a few Skandia shares, trying to build up a position of a few per cent.

Old Mutual advisers continued to argue that it was pivotal to get hedge funds such as Paulson & Co. to support the bid. By November a bid withdrawal no longer seemed a realistic alternative for the Old Mutual board and management. This was the downside of drawing in many large hedge funds in the bid process, which also meant that they were involved as heavy traders in Old Mutual's stock. The investment bankers at Deutsche

Bank and Merrill Lynch expressed concern that if the bid were withdrawn Old Mutual's share would fall and hedge funds betting on the bid would experience substantial losses, thus spiralling further sellouts. This would make Old Mutual itself a target for a takeover.

The Swedish institutional investors did not increase their holdings in a similar way as, for example, the hedge funds did. The large bank-controlled mutual funds, that is, those linked to Handelsbanken, Swedbank and Nordea (that were negative to the bid), were all more or less index-trackers working solely in the financial flows of companies, and the same reasoning applied to the pension funds. SEB Funds (a supporter of the bid) was also a seller, as was Nordea. Therefore, when traders called round to potential investors, there was no one in Sweden ready to pick up the (blocks of) shares. Regulators had put the financial rationale at the forefront for most of them. Some of the Swedish institutional shareholders with holdings in Skandia (along with parts of the business elite) looked instead for a 'white knight'. For this reason, Skandia Liv was approached as a potential buyer of Skandia. From a portfolio perspective, however, such an acquisition could not be defended (almost regardless of possible business benefits).

Somewhat later in the process, Skandia Chair Jeansson and CEO Andersson launched a road show in an attempt to arouse interest in the stock market for a stand-alone future for Skandia. This would show the merits of the company's operational flow. They met both long-only shareholders and quite a large number of hedge funds on the tour. The former were impressed by the presentation of the company's operations, but could still not promise to stick to their Skandia shares (tied to a short-term financial rationale, they had triggering prices). The latter expressed no interest at all in Skandia as a long-term investment. Instead, their concerns lay with the probability that Old Mutual would pursue its bid. They were simply not willing to bet that there was a feasible stand-alone path, and they did not care about the operational flow. Instead, they were prepared to make massive bets on single events, acting in the financial flows surrounding Skandia. This concerned working with the difference between the price of acquiring Skandia shares and the value of the Old Mutual bid. They made arbitrage deals betting on the spread between the Old Mutual and Skandia share, buying Skandia and short selling Old Mutual.

In November 2005, the balance in favour for the naysaying Swedish long-only funds had clearly become a balance in favour of the short-sighted foreign hedge funds. The Swedish institutional investors who opposed the proposed deal began to admit to themselves that they were losing the financial battle. This trend prevailed; Swedish investment banks did the selling on behalf of their clients; foreign houses did the buying. Nine out of the ten largest net sellers were Swedish at that time, and hedge funds were still very active in early December. Short-term investors worked intensively to alter the conditions influencing the actions in Skandia's financial flow; first and foremost they tried to obtain assurance from Old Mutual that the company would drop the 90 per cent hurdle.

Turning to the executive agencies (i.e. the boards and CEOs) of the two focal firms, one could note that the agency in the driving seat differed between the companies. For Old Mutual, its top management was carrying out all the bidding and takeover activities, while in Skandia the initiative and actions in those areas were predominantly taken care of by the board, and particularly then by its chair (during most of the struggle this was Magnusson; later, to some extent, Jeansson), and also – but to a varying extent – by some of its directors. At the beginning of the whole process (i.e. from April 2004), Skandia's CEO was active both in the financial flow (e.g. handled suitors) and in the operations flow, but gradually his role in the former process became more modest.

Old Mutual's chair was by no means as active as his Skandia counterpart. The role of the Old Mutual board was essentially to approve (or possibly disprove of) what the company's management were proposing (this included the three executive directors). The case description indicates that Old Mutual's CEO Jim Sutcliffe, assisted by his advisers from Deutsche Bank and Merrill Lynch, was influential on the company's board. Despite a large number of sceptical media and analysts' comments, a growing Skandia resistance, and the obvious increase in the risk involved for Old Mutual, the non-executive board members (and, subsequently, the vast majority of shareholders) approved of the offer that the CEO endorsed.

When looking at the performances of the executive agencies, we shall find quite a few activities that mostly address the operational flows in the two firms: particularly, and not surprisingly, it occurs on the CEO level. Old Mutual's operational perspective was important to its CEO, since Sutcliffe was under heavy pressure from his shareholders to deliver on the strategic business plans for a European expansion that he previously had presented in public. This plan included business considerations; the company had decided that it needed to expand its operations outside South Africa. This implied a need to geographically rebalance its activities, and obtain more of the benefits of economies of scale. However, one could also see the growth ambition as an outcome of the pressure from actual as well as potential financial actors to get out of a highly risky position. South Africa represented both a currency risk and a political risk. Skandia looked like a perfect match. Skandia's UK Life business was particularly interesting with its growing and historically successful unit-linked operations. At the same time, Old Mutual would also obtain a Nordic business and certain other (minor) European businesses. Thus both operational and financial considerations created a great deal of pressure for Old Mutual's management to reach some sort of structural solution. That ambition was carried out through activities aiming to influence those actors deeply involved in Skandia's financial flow.

Turning to Skandia's executive agencies, Chair Magnusson held a prominent role up until September 2005, when the board revealed its split position and, in practice, became a 'caretaker unit'. Magnusson interacted mostly with people who were active in Skandia's financial flow, leaving the company's operations very much to the CEO. Thus the chair frequently talked with potential and actual bidders, larger shareholders, colleagues on the board, and with the CEO. Magnusson's growing concern regarding the merits of the stand-alone path (except as a fall-back alternative) appeared to be based on doubts regarding the vivacity of the company's operational flow. In his view, Skandia could not make it on its own: he believed that it did not have the strength (due to its scandals, the declining Swedish operations and the legal threats), the size (too small), and the business ('unit-linked' was becoming a 'mature' concept). Moreover, he noticed a high operational risk due to internal management conflicts (Skandia HQ versus Skandia Life UK). The material that Morgan Stanley provided supported his tentative conclusion, as did the analyses and judgements of several (actual and potential) investors. This included the well-respected Fidelity group. The fact that he did not exclude an acquirer whose expected synergies with Skandia were low indicated that a financial perspective dominated his actions. Therefore the operations as such were obviously not at the top of his agenda when he decided on which path to promote for Skandia. He seemed to look for (almost) any controlling shareholder that seemed to have the capacity to deal with the Skandia situation of 2004.

Since he was appointed chair of the Skandia board on 7 October 2005, Lennart Jeansson supported the idea of Skandia as a stand-alone company with a promising future, particularly when it included its bank business (Skandiabanken). The majority of the board and the CEO were also in agreement. As board member (and later as chair), Jeansson was not wholly absorbed by the contacts with the actors on the financial markets; rather, he also interacted with Skandia's other directors and top management. His view of financial engineering building up the auction process also became increasingly critical; he claimed that the board meetings focused too little on developing the Skandia stand-alone case and the company's operations flow. Hence the proposed deal with Old Mutual did not impress Jeansson. He could find no enthusiasm for a takeover that had so little business and operative synergies.

Turning to Skandia's other executive agency, the CEO level, we note that Hans-Erik Andersson comes to a different conclusion than that of Magnusson in his analysis of Skandia's situation and potential. However, the CEO, too, had strong backing from several other actors. First of all, his management team favoured the idea (excluding those in the UK), and so did most of the company directors and several of its long-term investors. Skandia was already a major player in the international unit-linked insurance industry in Andersson's and his supporters' more operationally influenced view. Thus its size was a good enough platform for the company's further development. Andersson also concluded that Skandia had an excellent opportunity to keep – or develop – a strong position in several national or regional unit-linked markets. He also saw the company as being in the middle of a turnaround that was not yet fully appreciated by the investment community. Andersson and his supporters' final conclusion was that Skandia did not need Old Mutual to successfully expand in the coming years.

Both of these conceptions of the best future for Skandia (the one that the chair advocated and that which the CEO promoted) circulated on the loosely organized market for corporate control. In the end, the notion of a Skandia being too small to make it on its own in a restructuring 'bankassurance' industry came out on top, not because it was necessarily 'true', but because those who turned out to be most powerful actors in the takeover struggle supported it.[12]

A situation where the leading representatives of the executive agencies in a company (the board and the top management team) simultaneously advocate opposing strategies is both uncommon in large business organizations and essentially unstable over time. Such a conflict becomes even more problematic if each of the positions taken is rooted in different corporate flows, making the necessary connection between the financial and the operational rationale problematic: on what organizational level should the meeting between the two flows occur? Skandia faced this integration problem, since Chair Magnusson, on the one hand, advocated a short-term structural solution, and acted mostly to influence the actors involved in the financial flow; the CEO, on the other hand, believed in the merits of a mid-term to long-term stand-alone path, making him committed to improve the crucial ingredients in the operational flow. Thus Skandia was a company where the two flows failed to integrate successfully, each basically developing independently of the other.

The case description further indicates that Skandia's executive agencies gave a great deal of attention to its federative-like structure, and also on sorting out some internal tensions in the operations of the company group, particularly those between the Skandia HQ and Skandia Life UK. As a consequence, there were many tough discussions on formal and informal arenas regarding the possibility for Skandia Life UK to obtain the opportunity to make it on its own. The senior managers in the UK operations were actually working out concrete plans to have the UK businesses separated from Skandia (i.e. create an autonomous financial unit). In other words, they advocated a solution that had to be implemented through a change in the company's financial flow; however, it was very much triggered by operational considerations (a lack of economies of scale and business synergies between Skandia Life UK and the rest of Skandia).

There was actually a shared understanding of the lack of fit between the operational flows of the two companies among those that advocated the stand-alone path and those that preferred selling Skandia. Both the 'yes' camp and the 'no' camp agreed that there seemed to be quite limited scale effects and synergies to expect from an Old Mutual–Skandia merger; that is, the operations rationale could not be the decisive factor for the outcome of the takeover process. However, there was a connection between the financial flow and the operational flow that actually seemed to be of importance for those that advocated the sellout of Skandia. The 'yes' camp proposed that a merger with Old Mutual might bring about a stronger capital base for further international growth of Skandia's cash-consuming unit-linked businesses. The 'no' camp also addressed this potential relationship between the two flows, but came to the opposite conclusion. They claimed that Skandia did not need such a cash flow from Old Mutual in order to expand. If the 'no' camp were right on this issue, an acquisition would not put additional pressure upon Old Mutual's financial situation. Judging from what actually occurred in the takeover struggle, it seems as though their view might have been shared by the credit-rating institute, Moody's and, perhaps, also by several South African actors.

Turning to other important actor categories that were active in either – or both – of the corporate governance flows, we find Old Mutual's and Skandia's advisers. Throughout the study, it has been easy to get the impression that they played important roles both for how the takeover process developed, and how it was brought to a close. In this case, one investment bank (Morgan Stanley) had an especially important function for Skandia – so vital that its contributions soon became a cause of conflict between two factions on the board. One of the main reasons for this tension was that some directors interpreted the adviser as more closely related to one of the emerging camps on the board, namely the one that favoured a structural solution for Skandia (with the stand-alone path reduced to a fall-back alternative). In most of its activities, the adviser also provided material that was well adapted to the functioning of Skandia's capital-based governance flow, offering many key calculations of both share prices and company values (e.g. FTV estimates based on various market assumptions). However, Morgan Stanley also contributed to the operational governance flow in Skandia by supplying, for example, an overview of the European insurance industry that had a particular focus on its more important markets. This material also included a benchmarking of Skandia against its main actual as well as potential competitors; this comparative analysis then contained analyses of both financial and operational flows. The adviser also provided industry forecasts; that is, its representatives presented how they believed the insurance industry would develop in the coming years.

As a result of Morgan Stanley's suggestion, the Skandia board also established a complicated auction process to enable interested parties other than Old Mutual to become active bidders. This was done in an attempt to raise the level of competition, thereby getting a better price for the whole or parts of Skandia. However, that process turned into a rather messy operation with a lot of complicated and ambiguous offerings. One could note, however, that operational considerations for these suitors seemed to be of paramount importance, particularly when they substantiated their price indications. Consequently, many of their offerings addressed solely those parts of Skandia that matched the individual bidder's own business.

Deutsche Bank and Merrill Lynch primarily assisted Old Mutual's executive team, predominantly through their activity in a process addressing the target company's financial flow.[13] Together with Old Mutual, the advisers constructed the (friendly) bid, and they did it in a way that over time created many options for both actual and potential shareholders. For example, their choice of financial construct made it possible for Old Mutual both to legally withdraw the offer at any level of acceptances below 90 per cent, as well as to stand by the offering at any level. Thus the bid construct created a playing field that was rich in possibilities: investors, analysts and media commentators could all speculate about a wide range of further actions and outcomes – and take positions accordingly. Consequently, this rather open kind of approach attracted many kinds of actors to the process; those with a short-term perspective acting out a financial rationale (e.g. hedge funds) as well as those with a longer perspective (also) considering the merits of Skandia's operations (e.g. AXA). However, quite soon, Old Mutual was the only party responding to Skandia's global invitation to structural deals with an indicative bid on the entire company, and with a price level implying a substantial premium to the current share price.

The credit-rating institute was another kind of outside actor that appeared to truly matter for the outcome of the takeover struggle. In this case, it was Moody's. Institutes of that kind basically serve lenders, which implies that they mostly review the financial flows of corporations. Moody's (and similar institutes') judgements and ratings influenced Old Mutual's cost for loans, and opportunities to carry out its operations. Moody's judgement regarding Old Mutual's financial standing even affected the possibility of the company making a bid at all. Finally, Moody's rating considerations and judgement were also rumoured to have played an important role when Old Mutual – rather unexpectedly and suddenly – changed its mind, and, having almost thrown in the towel, returned to the acquisition process. A credit-rating institute's activities usually focus on the capital-based flows of companies, and, judging from the Old Mutual–Skandia takeover, this was also the case for Moody's, whose judgement, based on a classical financial rationale, also, in practice, put a limit upon how far Old Mutual's long-term credit line could be stretched. The Skandia takeover then implied an explicit 'maximum' stretch of Old Mutual's borrowing capacity, thus creating the highest possible leverage and, at the same time, a dramatically increased long-run risk of corporate failure.

Business journalists lined up as both supporters and sceptics to the proposed deal. South African and UK journalists seem, on average, to have reported in somewhat more positive terms about the Old Mutual–Skandia deal than did those from Sweden. However, they all generally adopted a financial perspective rather than an operational one. The Swedish journalists who argued against the proposed affair usually did so on the grounds of a long-term shareholder-value view, then questioning the merger mostly on the basis of lacking synergies and mismatching business rationales. However, there were also some Swedish voices that actually backed a merger between the two companies (e.g. journalists at *Svenska Dagbladet*).

A great deal of the voluminous media coverage was not overt opinion pieces of business journalists or analysts; there was a substantial amount of 'plain news' reporting, too, besides anonymous as well as overt actor contributions from both factions or camps. Thus, leading actors in the takeover struggle used the media as a channel to promote their own interests and ambitions, trying to influence the expectations of certain actors regarding what the future would look like (e.g. attempting to manipulate the current pricing of the Skandia shares in particular). Some of these actors then used the media more extensively than others; some even gave interviews. One such example of great importance for the Old Mutual–Skandia takeover process was when Skandia Chair Magnusson made his view 'Skandia is open to everything' widely known through an interview published in early December 2004. Another obvious example was when Christer Gardell, head of the activist fund Cevian, systematically and successfully used the media for his and Cevian's purposes. He even made the fund's shareholding known through a stock exchange announcement that (in the end) was made public by the media, although the level as such did not call for any declarations. Thus, instead of secretly building a position, the activist fund head and Skandia director Gardell worked the other way round, trying to arouse an interest in the Skandia share among potential investors, claiming that it deserved a higher price.

The activity of the head of AP2 is yet another example of how the media was used to influence the takeover struggle. AP2 was a pension fund that was a large investor in Cevian, and its head tried to communicate to Gardell (and other Skandia shareholders) that such funds (i.e. their executive agencies) should act more according to the expressed preferences of their principals. In this case, AP2 publicly through the media advocated a stand-alone path for Skandia. A most striking media action in the Old Mutual–Skandia takeover struggle consisted of the remarkable leaking to business journalists that started in late August 2005, and focused on the proceedings in the Skandia board. News reporting actually turned many of the board discussions into a public drama. Business journalist Bengt Carlsson (*Dagens Nyheter*) almost continuously reported what had happened on the Skandia board, sometimes even within hours of the meetings.

Turning to the financial analysts, another important actor category in the Old Mutual–Skandia takeover process, it is probably no exaggeration to state that to them Skandia had been an interesting company for a long time, probably due to its runaway share price in 1996–2000 (cf. its AFS business and the 'IT hype'). Probably, this interest could also to some extent be explained by the gradual abandonment of voting restrictions in the 1990s. When the latter occurred (in stages), Skandia obtained an open shareholder structure and became a potential takeover target. Many global investment banks' analysts identified this opportunity, and contrasted it with treating the company as a potential stand-alone turnaround case. The latter position seemed to have dominated the process at the 'beginning', however, many within the financial community seemed to initiate a shift in their stance during the summer of 2004.[14] Early that same year, there were two story angles that dominated the headlines: one of an overcapitalized and uncertain Skandia regarding what the company intended to do with its capital, and one of Skandia as an interesting turnaround company in unit-linked savings. Skandia's message was that it would address the possibility of a cash dividend or buyback programme at the time of the 2004 Q2 report. Skandia made it publicly known on 13 August that there was no share redemption to expect from the company (and, consequently, the Skandia share price fell).

The outlook for Skandia participating in a deal was highlighted as the autumn and early winter passed. The analysts' dominating view of the company gradually became that of the more 'radical' restructuring alternative, which largely coincided with (or was stimulated by?) several occurrences. For example, one investment bank made a strategic review of Skandia and concluded that a structural deal could be an accretive value to Skandia shareholders. Other investment banks also signed contracts to represent potential Skandia suitors. Meanwhile, the Skandia chair tried to convince the board that such a structural deal could be an interesting option. In terms of a possible takeover, most analysts provided arguments that were conducive to a realized deal.

One has to keep in mind, however, that analysts generally have to act (calculate) on the financial information that is available, and in their advice they mostly turn to owners of capital supposed to be interested in investing in the collection of the companies assessed. Moreover, and as has been mentioned earlier, it is, relatively speaking, easier for distant actors to try to influence (or at least participate in) a company's financial flow with its predominantly number-based quantitative analyses. However, not even the official and publicly available or even 'informally acquired'[15] figures are always reliable, and high-quality information about the companies' operational flows is usually difficult to acquire. Therefore contemporary financial capitalism generally brings about a massive dissemination of stories in more or less closely tied networks (circles, coalitions as well as 'gatherings') upon which they have a bearing; for example, the movements of share prices. Insiders and outsiders alike tell and listen to such small talk. In most cases, such information is related to unique knowledge (financial as well as operational) of the actual businesses of the corporations to which the shares are connected. In some cases, however, this linkage is abandoned for a story that solely addresses the capital-based dimension: for example, saying that a share is headed for a revaluation because of its inclusion/exclusion in an important index.

Many actors that actively try to influence the company's financial flows advocate transparency, particularly those that – similar to analysts – act from an outsider position. The opposite is usually valid for those actors that are involved in the operational flows. This is so because several ingredients in a company's core business have to be kept secret in order to defend and develop comparative advantages and competitive power. The importance of such confidentiality was perhaps particularly visible in the Old Mutual–Skandia takeover process during the summer of 2005, when the Skandia board discussed intensely whether they should allow Old Mutual and other suitors to conduct due diligence (see Section 22.6).

Old Mutual focused a great deal on its risk situation. If one makes use of the distinction between risks that link to the operational flow and risks that links to the financial flow, as outlined in Chapter 1, it is possible to describe the differences between the main actors. Old Mutual could be interpreted as functioning as an 'entrepreneurial capitalist', since the acquisition of Skandia represented a simultaneous increase of both operational risk (moving to previously unfamiliar markets) and financial risk (increasing leverage and goodwill). However, Old Mutual could also be described as a reducer of these risks by its pushing of a geographic differentiation (away from South Africa and its currency).

Some actors acted more in the spirit of what we have denoted as 'industrial capitalism' instead: with a cautious approach to financial risk in combination with substantial operational risk-taking. Chair Lennart Jeansson and the other Skandia board members that rejected Old Mutual's offer expressed such a rationale, as did Skandia's management team. However, the vast majority of Skandia's shareholders showed only a modest inclination to accept the operational risks associated with the stand-alone case. Instead, they made short-term capital gains from selling their Skandia shares to the shareholders of Old Mutual. This is not particularly surprising, since the vast majority of those Skandia shareholders were actors working according to specific regulatory and cultural frameworks, based on the premise that they should avoid exposing themselves to asset-specific (i.e. operational) risks.

The sale of Skandia to Old Mutual was acheived by several kinds of intermediaries (supposedly in the interests of the ultimate shareholders): investment banks, hedge funds and activist funds; that is, by actors whose own operations are located almost exclusively in the financial markets. Activist Christer Gardell was such a mediator, exposing the Cevian fund to a significant asset-specific or operational risk (which is the essence of what an activist fund does). At the same time, however, he claimed, rightfully or not, that the fund controlled or compensated for its (poorly diversified-portfolio-related) financial risks by adding competence to the focal companies, thereby contributing to improved performances. Activists, then, at least in some cases, aspire to be able and interested to develop both the financial and operative flows in a targeted company. However, this did not eventually occur in the Old Mutual–Skandia case, since Cevian's holding was soon sold.

The rationale of activists might in some cases look somewhat similar to what has been traditionally associated with certain block-holding and controlling shareholders; for example, it matches those situations where a significant number of individuals and families sometimes retain large fortunes locked up in a specific business company. Our interpretation is, however, that the core competence of the activist (fund) is instead related

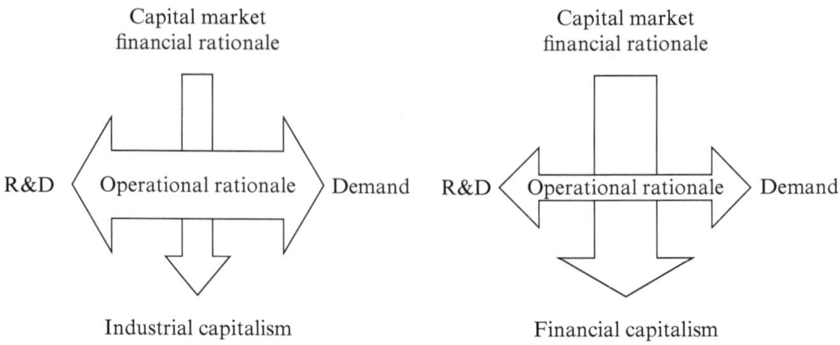

Figure 22.1 A changed relationship between the two corporate governance flows

to a capacity to shape events on the financial markets by intense and skilful storytelling in a wide-ranging network that is composed of both strong and weak ties. The activist fund shares this superior competence – the method of often working from inside the boards (which is one important way to influence the operational flow) – with investment banks in particular. Hedge funds, however, are usually not represented in corporate board meetings; they quite seldom claim any particular operational knowledge. What they offer their investors instead are opportunities to take asset-specific positions on financial markets. These risks are then 'managed' by intense communication with corporate managers, investments banks, activists and long-only institutional investors.

To sum up this section: those actors who had based their activities on the application of a financial rationale became stronger, predominantly because they had the interest, the financial capacity and the insight to deal with the new global market for corporate control. These actors' achievement is a strong indication that the financial flows have come to dominate the operational flows in corporations in the early twenty-first century. This is visible from the very outset of the Old Mutual–Skandia takeover (i.e. from spring 2004). In the later parts of the process – that is, during the autumn of 2005 – it became particularly visible. Figure 22.1 depicts this major change in the relative impact on corporate development of the financial and the operative flows.

A second general conclusion from the Old Mutual–Skandia case is that the shareholders, as a collective, have strengthened their position, at the same time as the two executive agencies (the board and the CEO) have become weaker. This could also be expressed as a state where the necessary balancing of the two governance flows has moved higher up the hierarchical ladder, from top management and boards to well-positioned shareholders.

A third general conclusion from the Old Mutual–Skandia case is that several (new) outside (categories of) actors play important roles in the struggle for corporate control. Some of these actors acted on bases, and in ways, that we interpret as decisive for the outcome of the whole acquisition process (e.g. investment banks, credit-rating institutes, hedge funds and activist funds). Therefore the governance process in Skandia was not just a matter for the current shareholders and the two executive agencies of the company. The governance efforts were manifested in flows that were also substantially influenced by other (categories of) outside actors.

Merging the second and third conclusions, one may propose that the judgements from many (kinds of) powerful outside actors formally and informally restrict the freedom of action for the agencies of a company – not the least because they tend to take each other's views and verdicts as fact and, therefore, act on them. Both the tendencies mentioned above – the move of power from the executive agencies to shareholders, and the empowering of outsiders in general – have been clearly visible in this case, which took place on one of the most benevolent and indulgent arenas for corporate control struggles: the contemporary financial scene in Sweden.

22.5 THE FUNCTIONING OF THE SKANDIA BOARD AND RELATED AGENCIES

As described in Chapter 1, the Swedish governance system has for long been based on a clear-cut distribution of functions – duties as well as responsibilities – between three different agencies: the shareholders (i.e. the AGM), the board of directors and the CEO. Many of the listed companies in Sweden have a controlling constellation of shareholders; however, this was not the situation for Skandia in the early twenty-first century. On the contrary, the company had quite recently abandoned its defence against 'undesired' shareholders by removing its old voting restrictions. This change made Skandia a possible takeover candidate, and it also meant that the company faced a more complicated organizing procedure than before when it formed its core agencies, and designed the financial and operational flows. This intricacy is visible in the relationships between Skandia's agencies, as well as in the ways in which its AGMs and changing nomination committees worked during 2004 and 2005.

According to Swedish regulations, it is the shareholders who appoint the directors at an AGM (all of them on one-year mandates). In addition to that, a few other board members are chosen by the local unions.

This means that even in a large listed company, the composition of an entire board may change almost instantly.[16] In this case, Skandia's board changed radically in the spring of 2004, making newcomers to the company dominate its agency.[17] Moreover, directors in Swedish firms are usually selected from other sources than its management;[18] they are supposed to be 'independent' of the corporation and its businesses (this rule also includes the chair).[19] Thus, in the Skandia case, the new directors lacked previous experience as Skandia managers (with the exception of Hammarkvist), although some of them had worked in the insurance industry. Instead, Swedish directors are 'dependent' upon (and chosen by) the large shareholders; they (or their representatives) are expected to be on the board, and often also to control the chair. However, the Anglo-Saxon regulations and traditions in this area are somewhat different from the Swedish ones, particularly with respect to important details.[20]

In the UK governance system, the board is composed of a mix of company managers (usually including the CEO and the CFO) and outsiders. The latter category is referred to as the 'independent directors'; its autonomy is then defined also in relation to the controlling shareholders.[21] It is these independent directors that suggest the new board members for whom the shareholders can vote.[22] This right of initiation is combined with a regulation stating that directors are elected for a one-to-three-year term (thus creating 'overlapping' boards).[23] All of this restricts shareholders' immediate influence in the Anglo-Saxon system. Compared to the Swedish system, it therefore takes a little longer to put intentions into practice.[24]

If one looks at the takeover regulations in Sweden, one finds that they are 'pretty inviting', even to hostile takeover bids. For example, a bidder can discuss matters and directly make a proposal to the shareholders of a target company. Thus Swedish company boards are given a rather passive role in the process – more like agencies supposed to carry out an advisory duty. This means that a board is only asked to make a recommendation, and that such a statement is made merely in order to assist the shareholders in their decision to accept or reject a bid. Moreover, such a board recommendation is not required before a formal bid is made, although it should be provided no later than two weeks before the close of a particular offering.

It is difficult to avoid getting the impression that the Skandia board was put in its rather weak position in the takeover process on more informal grounds as well, not least because of the tensions that were, over time, built up between several of its directors. One basis for the board split seems to have been the differing views regarding on which value basis companies in general, and Skandia in particular, should be controlled and governed (see Section 22.3). Another reason for the split, and the undermining of the agency, has to do with the information situation, which some of the board members conceived as increasingly problematic. Several of them expressed a sense of devaluation of their roles as directors, since many outsiders seemed to have had access to the same – or sometimes more or better – information than many of the board members regarding some of the crucial issues and processes. Thus the continuous more or less public discussion of strategic matters (based on a steady flow of new information) created problems for the Skandia board as an agency. However, this kind of more open or transparent information situation should be expected when the financial rationale takes precedence, and its advocates argue that they have a right to know what is going on in a company (this includes the board's work, too).

On top of that, and contributing to the board tensions, some of the directors had the impression that various advisers were 'pushing them around', and that it also to some of them seemed to be appropriate for single directors to travel around and in an uncoordinated way discuss with potential investors different strategic paths for the company (including structural changes).

We regard this kind of more or less intended 'sidestepping' of the board as the primary steward of the corporation as an important reason for the emerging crisis on the Skandia board. More generally, this bypassing also points to a growing problem within the core of the Swedish corporate governance doctrine. Chair Magnusson tried to solve part of that problem in Skandia, for example, with the introduction of frequent and extended 'pseudo-board' meetings (guests were invited) carried out particularly during the summer of 2005. This seems to have been one of his ways of trying to preserve one of the board's most basic functions: to make judgements on the strategic and operative running of the company on behalf of the collective of shareholders and stakeholders, based on privileged (and sometimes classified) information.

Magnusson's successor, Lennart Jeansson, acted strictly within Swedish governance regulations when he, for example, persistently argued that an interested party should come forth with a bid, which would then be evaluated by the board, and recommended (or not) to the shareholders. This action perhaps did not fully 'resonate' with the fact that a 'bid' (albeit an indicative one) had already leaked to the market in May 2005, and that a seemingly well-informed report about it also appeared in the media. Nor did his action take into account that the board might very well end up making a recommendation to a different set of shareholders from the ones that received the offer. This would make the board's views somewhat superfluous. Such a shifting stock market may also leave a board of directors in a very late – not to mention weak – position, which was basically also what happened to the Skandia board. The impression is that Jeansson and the other naysayers did not foresee the risk of a massive change in the shareholder base; thus they did not act to prevent this.

One must add that the dramatic changes in the Skandia shareholding during the bid process, particularly in its later stages, made the work of the board a complicated task; the directors did not really know, at any given moment, which shareholders they actually represented. These changes in the shareholding also made the relative strengths of the two sides rather uncertain; there was an assumed presumption of bid acceptance, but also a strong opposition sharing the conclusion of the board majority that Old Mutual's bid should be rejected. Thus the Skandia board was caught in a process characterized by tension between two opposite positions: on the one hand, that of a bidder and some of the shareholders wanting a deal; and, on the other, that of some of the other shareholders and the company's top management supporting the stand-alone path. Since a Swedish board is not allowed to act on its own account, it was obliged to respond to this difficult and variable shareholder pressure in one way or the other. However, a Swedish director cannot be penalized by criminal sanctions simply for making bad business decisions (in this case, for example, choosing to side with the 'wrong' camp, or pursue the 'wrong' strategic path).[25]

Three particular observations regarding cross-border takeovers can be made about the Old Mutual–Skandia case. The first deals with Old Mutual's way of approaching Skandia in May 2005. The differences between the UK's and Sweden's regulations and traditions meant that the leading Old Mutual managers perceived the role of a Swedish board differently than the Skandia directors did. The Brits might not have been aware that the Swedish directors saw their involvement in the bid process as being first and foremost to compile and communicate the shareholders' wishes; therefore they were not inclined to make any early statements of their own. The second observation is related to the first one and addresses the fact that Old Mutual decided to make a Skandia board recommendation a bid condition; this seemed to be partly a consequence of bowing to pressure from some of its own shareholders (particularly then certain South African ones), and partly a question of cost. In addition to that, one could note that it also was in line with UK traditions. Therefore the Old Mutual indicative offer on Skandia was presented to CEO Hans-Erik Andersson and director Christer Gardell as a 'friendly' takeover proposal. Thus Old Mutual sought a deal only if the Skandia board supported it. However, this line of action complicated the acquisition process for a long time, particularly because the Skandia board was (and remained) divided. The third observation is that Skandia's board of directors, which had already chosen the stand-alone alternative as the preferred path, could in that situation have said 'no': either forcing the bidder to present a public (hostile) bid or simply walk away. Instead, the board initiated an auction process and accorded due diligence.

In Sweden, the board appoints the CEO, who then is the person solely in charge of the operations of the company. He or she might be a member of the board, but this is not always the case. Sometimes such a proviso indicates the CEO's relative power versus the board; sometimes it is more a matter of principle.[26] The 2004 Skandia board inherited a newly appointed CEO, and that situation created a difficulty, as the newcomer was hurled into the infected media discussions about management bonuses and compensation systems, which contributed to the directors' doubts regarding the appropriateness of keeping him as CEO. However, in the end they decided that holding on to him was best for Skandia. Regarding the relationship between a board (particularly its chair) and a CEO, one could note that it is supposed to be characterized by a high degree of mutual confidence, and this is perhaps particularly true in Sweden, where only one manager is allowed as a formal board member. Throughout the takeover process, this ideal was practised when it came to the board majority; however, the relationship between the CEO and the chair, in time, lost some of that propitious quality.

The capacity of the AGM to exert influence is strong in Sweden. The agency has quite a direct influence on how a company is run; for instance, it is free to decide on any unannounced matter (yet its decisions remain constrained by law and the corporate constitution and requires (with some exceptions) consensus). The power of the Skandia AGM is particularly visible in the April 2005 session, where several important topics were debated and finally settled by shareholder voting.

A new 'independent' corporate governance body (listed companies only), which was positioned somewhere between the AGM and the board, was formalized in Sweden during the first few years of the twenty-first century: the nomination committee, an agency whose members represented the shareholders, and with the sole task of suggesting candidates for the board. Sweden's Code of Corporate Governance (and the SSE rules) also stated that at least two 'independent' directors should be elected to a company's board (this time 'independent' in the UK sense, that is, not associated with any of the dominant shareholders). This meant that the composition of the Swedish nomination committee differed significantly from its Anglo-Saxon counterpart, which is made up of 'independent directors' from the (current) company board.

Problems soon emerged in the interactions between the actors representing the four different basic agencies in Skandia (i.e. shareholders, directors, members of the nomination committee and the CEO). These inter-agency disputes then lasted – and in some cases even grew – all through the Old Mutual–Skandia takeover struggle. Basically, the entangled process started in April 2004, when the nomination committee voiced ideas about what kind of competencies were needed on the board to pull the company out of its crisis. The 2004 nomination committee members (SEB, AP2, Robur and Alecta) were not satisfied with Skandia's situation and current share price; they saw the company as undervalued, at least in the long term. Therefore the make-up of the 2004 Skandia board very much reflected the worries connected to this crisis situation, particularly when it came to the scandals and the impending legal processes. The suggested composition of the board can be described as the result of an ambition to create a 'board of trust'; the proposed directors were individuals that were seen as unblemished. With this specific ambition, in turn, Marcus Storch, Lennart Jeansson and Bernt Magnusson were approached. After some hesitation, Magnusson finally decided to accept to chair the troubled company. He was regarded as a competent business person, who came with quite a lot of experience from having handled complicated turnarounds. Furthermore, he was also known for acting in the interests of the shareholders.

We further interpret the Skandia board's composition as an attempt to signal to the public a genuine ambition and effort to 'clean up' the company's tarnished house. Thus Director Björn Björnsson was kept on the Skandia board, probably because of his strong track record as 'troubleshooter', and perhaps also for securing some continuity in the board activities (he was the only former board member left). The two women singled out for this difficult assignment also accepted to serve on the board: one was Birgitta Hedberg-Johansson, an experienced CEO with an impressive track record from several industries, including that of the financial sector; the other was Kajsa Lindståhl, a well-established fund manager.[27] All in all, when the institutional investors in charge of the nomination committee suggested their candidates for the board, they seem to have focused upon how to improve Skandia's share price in the short run, particularly focusing on how to deal successfully with the broader societal implications of the company's scandals and impending lawsuits.

The new 2004 Skandia board did not function particularly well. This became more and more obvious as the takeover process progressed. The case material leads us to believe that this problem could be explained to a substantial extent by the way in which it had been composed, that is, through the criteria and procedures put into practice by the nomination committee. It seems to have underestimated the need for creating a team quality in the group. There are no indications that they actually looked for candidates who had previously displayed the capacity – or had the reputation – of working well together. There was one visible exception: Chair

Magnusson and Deputy Chair Björnsson had worked together in a radical restructuring of a large Swedish forest company. However, this 'constellation' may have actually been more of a coincidence, since Magnusson was not the nomination committee's first choice for the Skandia chair.[28] Thus the board members resembled more of a 'gathering of individuals' than a deliberately formed team.

Thus with hindsight it was not surprising that the board quite soon began to express different positions regarding the future path for Skandia. There were also some early differences of opinion regarding how a board should operate. Somewhat later, it became apparent that there was not full agreement on the content of the positions of chair, deputy chair and director. These role ambiguities also materialized in an early clash between two directors (Hedberg-Johansson and Lindståhl) and the chair (Magnusson) regarding the board's information policy, that is, about what actors should be allowed to say publicly about the company. The Skandia board certainly could have got a better start.

We believe that the differences in opinions between the Skandia directors (at least as they were expressed from the beginning of 2005) were of such a magnitude that several board members – including the chair – would have been perfectly justified in making reservations to board decisions along the way. Some could even have chosen to resign, furnishing shareholders and the general public with very good reasons for such a decision. However, instead of leaving, all directors stayed and struggled according to their individual rationales. There were, however, some informal discussions among a few of them early in 2005 regarding whether they should resign or not. Such action was also recognized as reasonable by those who were involved in these informal conversations. However, they all decided that resigning would exacerbate the situation for the already troubled company.

For a long time, there was an ongoing process by which the directors became more divided in their opinions, but were still united in their (formal) decisions. In hindsight, perhaps several points of conflict that were brought up for discussion should have been more carefully followed up and clarified by all involved; their relationships with the advisers of the board, tensions within the board, the implications of the 2004 AGM's mandate to the chair, relations to the press, and the different grounds for valuing Skandia.

As mentioned earlier, there were both formal and informal ambiguities regarding the division of tasks and roles for the Skandia board that had been decided at the 2004 AGM. This uncertainty also included the board's relationship to the CEO. The board decided at the AGM that the chair and deputy chair should get extra compensation due to Skandia's very difficult situation and the heavy workload. However, the interpretations regarding the reasons for this differed. Magnusson appears to have interpreted the situation as giving the chair a more extended position, which would include some of the tasks usually performed by a Swedish CEO (at least during the era of industrial capitalism). This interpretation obviously brought the CEO's role more into line with that of a COO. One also gets the impression that Magnusson took his extended mandate seriously: he ran quite a few board meetings, many informal sessions (e.g. the ones during summer 2005), and organized many other special gatherings with various potential bidders, shareholders and advisers. Thus he was a most active and demanding chair, and expected the same level of dedication from most of the other actors as well, including the other Skandia directors.

Skandia's CEO, however, appeared to have interpreted his role in the company similarly to that of his predecessors, which corresponded to the standing of most CEOs in listed companies in Sweden. He did not act according to some kind of COO position. For example, he had responded to many proposals from suitors throughout 2004 and well into 2005, and turned them all down based on the board decision that Skandia should 'stand alone'. Therefore, following the April 2004 AGM, there were two continuously active, gradually less coordinated strategic actors in Skandia: a chair who was whole-heartedly committed to the strategic processes; and a formally appointed CEO who was also very active on the same scene. This dual control of the strategic process changed in 2005 in favour of the chair.

The tension between the chair and the CEO grew steadily during 2005, reaching the point where the CEO could have stepped down with very clear justification: he was at odds with the chair regarding the best way forward for the company. A chair and a CEO that do not cooperate closely (i.e. lack a shared view on how to divide the executive task, particularly its strategic component), express doubts regarding the merits of the conclusions drawn by the other party, and fail to walk in step may become a deleterious executive combination that can jeopardize the healthy development for any firm. However, such a simultaneous presence of opposing strategic views at the very top of a company's hierarchy should be expected to show up now and then, as strategic matters represent – to a substantial extent – outcomes of human judgement (as the presence of genuine uncertainty is a dominant factor in strategic considerations). This can be seen mostly in contexts where a chair and a CEO are relatively new to each other, where another (i.e. former) chair recruits a CEO, or when the two actors identify with – and work in – different governance flows. All three conditions were present in Skandia during the takeover struggle, and this may have contributed to the materialization of the two opposing strategies for the company: one that the chair (and his allies) endorsed, and one that the CEO (and his associates) promoted.

Our conclusion regarding strategic controversies such as the one described above is that there is no way of – with even close to certainty – knowing which path would have been the best: first, because all such conclusions basically are value based in character; and second, because it is simply not possible to make reliable *ex ante* calculations regarding a company's future; in such efforts there is always a need to make many arbitrary (at best reasonably enlightened) assumptions, making it impossible to come even near to safe conclusions. Finally, it is impossible to know how an alternative path to the one actually embarked would have developed had it been put into practice. For example, in this case, we will never know how a Skandia stand-alone path would have turned out, nor are we able to make any meaningful *ex post* comparisons with the actual performance of the enlarged Old Mutual.

Although it is collective with respect to its decision functions and responsibilities, any corporate board is made up of individual actors (with unique personalities). The mandate that each of them subjectively believes to have is usually formed in the context of their perceptions of the intentions of actual and potential shareholders, as well as in their relationships to top management. Other circumstances that regularly form these inferred mandates are type of directorship (chair, independent or other), the individual experiences and competencies, and the current organization of board's work.[29] Moreover, factors such as the directors' views and beliefs regarding the rationales and capabilities of the other directors, and the different circles or networks to which they belong, also shape the directors' construed mandates. In this case, it is possible to conclude that such individual interpretations and connections became an important basis for the emerging board problems in Skandia.

In the 1990s, the Swedish Shareholders' Association (through its CEO, Lars-Eric Forsgårdh) advocated an introduction of nomination committees in the Swedish corporate governance system. The general idea was that institutions should also have a say when the main shareholder(s) discussed candidates for the boards of listed companies. The association argued for what it regarded as an agency that strengthened the smaller shareholders vis-à-vis the larger shareholders, the boards and the CEOs. This new agency would then commit its members to a longer-term approach in their engagement in the corporation, since they would effectively be tied to it for one year into the future. The members of the committee were suggested to be chosen at the companies' AGMs (to be accountable), represent all (kinds of) shareholders, and then not necessarily be selected among those with the greatest shareholding. However, this view was cast aside when the Swedish Code of Governance was established. Instead, it was recommended that whoever the larger shareholders might be at a given time (usually six months ahead of an upcoming AGM), they would make up the nomination committee. One could note that this construct and soft regulation was not controversial at the time; for example, it was entirely in accordance with the current opinion of the institutional investors.

The intricate situation in Skandia (with ambiguities and tensions surrounding the executive agencies, the board and the CEO) had its roots in the works of its nomination committees. From the year 2000 and onward they were very short of long-term devotion to the company. This was taken to unusual levels with the formation of the nomination committees in the autumn of 2002, the autumn of 2003, the winter of 2004, and the autumn of 2004. As the shareholder base shifted significantly, new shareholder representatives literally walked in and out of the nomination committees. This impeded the quality of the work of monitoring the board in charge, as well as the search for new board members. This lack of long-term devotion to the company was mainly a consequence of Skandia's dispersed shareholding, making the largest holdings rather small – amounting to just a few per cent each. Therefore only relatively minor changes in holdings could 'produce' new committee members, opening the company board for activists and short-term investors that only controlled a few per cent of the stock. Moreover, many of those who held these small percentages of the Skandia stock were institutional investors, which were not at all interested in becoming involved in the running of the company. They basically relied on influencing companies by buying/selling their shares, usually in a continuous index-tracking race.

The nomination committee that was formed among Skandia shareholders in the autumn of 2004 turned out to be the perfect opportunity for a minor shareholder such as Cevian to gain a large impact in the company. In spite of its relatively low 3.4 per cent of the shares in Skandia, the fund received a voice on the nomination committee: Gardell became a co-opted member. This also made it possible to work more effectively for a board seat for Cevian (i.e. Gardell). The way in which this nomination committee functioned was the opposite of what the Swedish Shareholders' Association had envisaged when it began to promote this particular governance agency. This importation from an Anglo-Saxon tradition, modified and put into a Swedish governance system, turned into a vehicle for short-termism instead. In retrospect, it is not that difficult to grasp what might happen when ideas on how to strengthen shareholders, that originate within a governance regime tailored to tangible managerial direction, are injected into a governance regime that already affords great powers to shareholders. As we see it, the end result is a system that favours hyper-powerful and hyperactive shareholders.[30]

In a company with dispersed shareholders, and with an active nomination committee of minor shareholders in charge, it is sometimes difficult to procure leading actors who think in terms of sustainable business structures. It may also be hard to recruit a board of directors with a genuine interest in the company's long-term development, and who are able to act in a timely manner on crucial strategic challenges from outside actors. However, in spite of these difficulties, it was possible to recruit a board of competent directors in April 2004, composed of individuals with experience both in monitoring operations and in running complex strategic processes. The problem was rather that the board's possibility of influencing Old Mutual's takeover process had gradually faded away, as many of the important shareholders expressed their views long before the board was ready to give its recommendation.

All of this implies that a Swedish board of directors might become relatively marginalized in the era of financial capitalism and in takeover situations – almost to the point of being regarded as a 'turning buoy'. Informally, however, individual directors may act intensely in relation to shareholders and the financial market in general, thereby possibly exerting some influence. This formal and informal marginalization of the board provides plenty of room for the more passive directors to abstain from making a public and fully accountable judgement of a takeover proposition, as well as plenty of space for hyperactive directors to informally convey information to and from some, rather than all, investors.

Other important agencies were also involved in the control struggle. These were based on other bodies and regulations than those that formal organizing or legislation provides. For example, a distinct dominating coalition emerged that was composed of those who supported Old Mutual's bid: two Skandia board members (the chair and the deputy chair), a third Skandia director (who was also the head of an activist fund), three global investments banks, and at least one company (Old Mutual, represented by its top management). During the takeover process, communications were intense among these parties, thus giving rise to stronger relational ties between several who had previously not necessarily been acquainted. Notwithstanding their varying positions and stakes, these actors shared the view that a combination of Old Mutual and Skandia was a good idea.

The coalition opposing a deal was composed of many Skandia shareholders, including some of those with larger (relatively speaking) holdings, eight of its board members, and its group management. This bid-opposing coalition was actually formed later than the dominant one that supported the bid; its agency, therefore, tended to be more reactive. However, both coalitions were of a temporary kind and based on only one issue ('yes' or 'no' to Old Mutual's bid). Neither was an expression of an existing circle, clan, or some other kind of well-established network, although some duos in both camps represented such close relationships. Thus there were no existing structures on which the actors could base their joint actions. Instead, leadership had to be captured and earned, and the need for such a process made these coalitions rather fragile and unstable bodies for action.

By January 2005 two parallel strategic agendas for Skandia seemed to have emerged, each maintained by one of the two rather weakly tied coalitions described above. The majority of the board, the coalition of naysayers, who opposed any idea of a 'structural solution' (at least in the short run), seemed however to have been rather slow in realizing that another loosely coupled coalition of actors had been established. The naysayers had also been late recognizing that the 'yes' camp had been making substantial investments that supported an outcome in which Skandia would be sold to Old Mutual. At least the naysayers were rather slow at figuring out how to respond to the initiatives taken by that other coalition. We believe that this meagre preparedness for the 'acquisition path' was a consequence of four conditions within the work of the board (besides the aforementioned ones).

First of all, for quite some time there was an overwhelming focus on the Skandia board regarding the dealings with the previous scandals and the expected upcoming legal issues (although the deputy chair was allotted them as a special assignment). Second, there was also a 'systematic' difference among the Skandia directors regarding how much time they could spend on the Skandia assignment. Those who were in favour of a structural solution, and later supported Old Mutual's bid, worked (nearly) full-time. This was of course due to a substantial extent to their formal positions (chair and deputy chair), and the special assignments that had been given to them at the AGM in April 2004. The 'no' camp, however, worked less than full-time on Skandia; this was also for understandable reasons. They were 'simply' ordinary directors, who also were heavily engaged in other executive positions that claimed priority. The obvious exception in the 'yes' camp was Skandia's CEO and top management team, who devoted all of their time and efforts to Skandia.

Third, the formal position of the CEO, and his own interpretation of it, further contributed to the 'work-discrepancy' between the 'yes' camp and the 'no' camp on the board. The CEO was not a formal member of the board and acted accordingly: he kept a low profile, and only spoke when addressed or on issues that obviously related to the operational flow. Finally, the proactivity of Chair Magnusson put the naysayers in a defensive position. He had meetings with Old Mutual at an early stage of the process, and held many meetings with leading Skandia shareholders. Moreover, one of the Skandia directors, activist fund head Gardell, who shared the chair's strategic analysis, made tours to raise support for a 'yes' to a Skandia sales (to Old Mutual). These and several other activities almost forced the naysayers into a reactive agency. The 14 January 2005 board meeting was merely the first example of a string of meetings that ran up to August, in which the 'yes' camp simply ran ahead of the 'no' camp.

These coalitions having their roots (or tentacles; see below) in the Skandia board also included other actors. All advisers (investment banks, management consulting firms, legal firms, PR firms and 'independent advisers') belonged to the growing influential population of professional 'symbolic analysts' that prevail in – and partly create – increasingly globalized societies.[31] It is tempting to conceive of these as occupying the most elevated position in an informal hierarchy in the network of corporate governance actors in financial capitalism, mediating most actions of institutional investors with respect to the governance of corporations. While recognizing these coalitions and networks, the question arises whether the relationship could also be interpreted the other way round: as a process in which the institutional investors, for example the actual and potential shareholders in Skandia, or the executive agencies could be regarded as representatives and executors of the ideas and interests of their advisers instead. This is of course a radical and speculative thought; however, if one takes a closer look at the case material, it is difficult to categorically deny such a hypothesis.

If one picks out the more general insights from the analyses provided above, some conclusions (hypotheses) stand out in the material. First of all, it seems that the power of executive agencies tends to weaken in the context of financial capitalism, mostly because of the increasing influence from the (many new categories of) shareholders that follows from a global market system for corporate control. This effect is particularly visible in environments that already have a regulation in which openness is combined with a prescribed prominent shareholder position (in the first decade of the twenty-first century, Sweden represented such a context). As mentioned earlier, this situation makes room for hyper-powered and hyperactive shareholders, and there emerges a risk that the corporate boards gradually become marginalized. Sometimes, then, the board turns downwards in the hierarchy and limits the discretion of the CEO, turning her or his role into something similar to that of a COO. This places the balancing point of financial and operative governance flows at the level of the chair (or board) rather than at that of the CEO.

Looking at the Old Mutual–Skandia case, one also gets the impression that certain kinds of shareholding have grown in importance in corporate control and governance processes. It seems that short-term perspectives and acting play a much greater role in the early twenty-first century than they did during most of the twentieth century. Actors such as many sorts of mutual funds and hedge funds stimulate and intervene in company control struggles; their actions sometimes even become decisive for the outcomes and the investment banks play a role to enable this. Activists and private equity firms are also involved, both of which often claim the use of a slightly longer perspective (mid-term) when managing their holdings. However, as with most other kinds of shareholders, they still stand for a very different (time) perspective than their equivalents in corporations governed by families or dynasties. In the latter case, the time perspective is, at least in principle, eternal, making the company a kind of 'heirloom' for generation after generation of shareholders.

22.6 INSTITUTIONAL COMPETITION

In Chapter 1 we introduced the outline of a theory that suggested a crucial role for institutions in corporate control struggles and governance processes. A multitude of such institutions could be activated by individuals as grounds for their actions. Taken together, these institutions form what we have denoted a 'bricolage', meaning that institutionalized norms applicable to a certain situation may not only be numerous but also often conflicting or even contradictory to one another. In the following we shall address some of those institutions that enable or restrain the more important (categories of) actors involved in the struggle for control over Skandia, particularly the bidders that showed interest in buying (parts of) Skandia, and the other actors that also participated in the takeover process.

The Old Mutual–Skandia case illustrates a certain lack of knowledge among many actors regarding the 'new', changing, and differing Swedish and UK laws and regulations. However, such an ambiguous situation opens the way for something we have denoted 'rule arbitrage': the creative use of a situation where different norms essentially regulate the same phenomenon (originating, for example, from different countries). Such variations were frequent in the Old Mutual–Skandia case and they sometimes resulted in clashes. In this concluding chapter we have concentrated our analyses on just a few of them – those we believe to be the most important. Institutional ambiguities also produce plenty of opportunities for actor discretion (i.e. for strategic interpretations and manoeuvring); thus the decades surrounding the millennium have provided particularly favourable conditions for skilful agency, an aptitude for making use of other (countries) agents' historical legacy, and acting to obtain the benefits from it.

Since the takeover struggle addresses a Swedish company, we have decided to focus upon some of the legislation and codes of conduct in Sweden, and how all the various actors, with their differing backgrounds and interests, have related to these particular regulations. This means that some of the more important clashes between the two differing systems – the Swedish/Nordic and the UK/Anglo-Saxon one – will be analysed and discussed. Many of these regulations particularly address the way in which the capital-based financial flows are supposed to work, although they – to some extent – also apply to the operational dimension of corporate governance (e.g. by specifying the core agencies of a limited company).[32] As the Swedish market for corporate control and governance principles has been influenced by the UK interpretation of a governance system (a version of the Anglo-Saxon model), it is also important to know something about both the 'older' and the 'newer' Swedish governance model, to be able to understand why and how Old Mutual (in the end) acquired Skandia. The changing Swedish regulations, and the fact that some actors were better informed about some of these novelties than others, created competitive advantages in this takeover struggle.

The older Swedish model, which is associated with classical Nordic and continental European industrial capitalism, was built on a basically regional Swedish/Nordic market for corporate control. It was characterized by a long corporatist tradition that secured cooperation, mutual understanding and acting in concert between governments (mostly Social Democratic ones), unions and business elites (i.e. certain dynasties and bank spheres). However, the 'newer' Swedish model for corporate governance and control (outlined in Chapter 1) has begun to distance itself from certain ingredients of that kind of cooperation, adding in some – but far from all – components from the UK type of the Anglo-Saxon system.

As was mentioned in Chapter 1, individuals act very much through the use of the various 'toolkits' that their environments provide: laws and regulations, formulas for calculation, established arenas or networks, socially enforced custom and traditions. Regarding 'hard' regulation (i.e. legislation), we draw attention to the fact that such constructs basically deal with long-term processes, and therefore do not change that often. When a particular legislation is revised, the change almost always takes place after careful investigations and considerations. These can sometimes make legislation rather slow, at least if compared to some of the practices that might have emerged in the meantime.

There are also national 'soft' regulations. In Sweden there are *inter alia* the workings of the Swedish Securities Council, the workings of the Swedish Industry and Commerce Stock Exchange Committee, the code of corporate governance, and the Takeover Rules. Taken together, these (hard) laws and (soft) regulations form the basic toolkit for agency in the Swedish market for corporate control. Several of the hard and soft regulations of immediate relevance for actors involved in corporate control processes have been transformed in recent years. This also means that the Old Mutual–Skandia takeover process includes several novelties (i.e. new items for the Swedish market) such as nomination committees, due diligence procedures and soft irrevocables.

In the following, we describe several cases of what we claim to be illustrative examples of the decisive force of the institutions (hard and soft regulations) discussed above. There are many more to address, yet we shall focus on some of those that we believe played particularly important roles in the Old Mutual–Skandia takeover process. In our descriptions and analyses below we address in turn: the Swedish Companies Act, the Swedish Insurance Companies Act, the construct of a takeover bid as being either 'friendly' or 'hostile', the due diligence procedure, the rules enforced by the Swedish Securities Council, bid acceptance period regulations, rules addressing the use of advisers, and, finally, index behaviour. Two legal institutions play a particularly important role in the Old Mutual–Skandia struggle: the Swedish Companies Act (Aktiebolagslagen) and the Swedish Insurance Companies Act (Försäkringsrörelselagen), but there are also a number of other laws and regulations present, addressing, for example, insider trading in stocks and derivatives.

There were certain problems linked to a recent revision of the Swedish Companies Act in the studied takeover process. Among other things, its revised version provided a 66.7 per cent hurdle for forced mergers, instead of the 90 per cent that was previously enforced.[33] This change caused some turbulence among the naysayers to the bid, since there were several who did not recognize the circumvention of the minority protection rights. Old Mutual, however, used them to significantly strengthen its bargaining position in the takeover process.

Old Mutual decided on 1 December 2005 to lower the threshold from 90 per cent to 50 per cent acceptance[34] of its Skandia bid. Jeansson seems to have still believed that Old Mutual would abandon its offering if a 10 per cent minority among Skandia shareholders stood firm. Some Swedish institutional investors shared this belief and acted accordingly. However, this lowering of the acceptance rate undermined some of Jeansson's basic arguments, when he argued against a selling of Skandia shares (to enjoy the longer-term benefits of the Turbo plan). Instead, that argument backfired and worked in favour of holding on to Old Mutual shares. Additionally, since there was no longer much of a bargaining position related to such a (collected) holding, Old Mutual's decision instantly made the value of the last 10 per cent of the shares in Skandia drop. This applied, for example, to AP2's 3.0 per cent holding (that was kept until the 'bitter end'). This bargaining position was further undermined by the Swedish Insurance Companies Act, which provided a weaker set of rights for 10 per cent minorities than the Swedish Companies Act. However, this understanding was brought to the fore at a stage when Old Mutual had already secured a significant number of Skandia shares.

The question regarding whether the Old Mutual bid for Skandia should be regarded as either friendly or hostile is a third issue in the takeover process. It was important to Old Mutual that the bid was of the friendly kind (approved by Skandia's board and, consequently, recommended to the shareholders). Old Mutual officially refrained from using the word hostile all along.[35] There were several reasons why the UK company wanted the bid to be a friendly one: it was the usual practice in the institutional setting with which they were most familiar, and there was an obvious risk that the share price might otherwise fall (if a blocking minority of shareholders remained in Skandia, and management's resistance hampered a planned integration process). One can only speculate about the outcome of the takeover struggle if Old Mutual had already stated in May that it was ready to pursue a hostile offer. It would probably be fair to say that such a statement would have engendered resistance from the naysayers among the board of directors (limiting the possibility for Old Mutual to carry out a due diligence process), and also enabled the formation of a more potent blocking coalition. At the same time, Old Mutual's relationship to its own shareholders, as well as to the credit-rating institute Moody's, would have been more complicated.

A fourth institution that created some turbulence in the Old Mutual–Skandia takeover process was the one labelled 'due diligence' (see Chapter 13), through which the former company tried to get more, and altogether reliable figures, but also, and perhaps especially, a better understanding of the target company's operational flow.[36] Old Mutual's indicative offer for Skandia was therefore subject to this particular condition: the Skandia board invite Old Mutual to perform limited due diligence. The 45–48 SEK per share indication that Old Mutual and its financial advisers had established had been based entirely on public information; therefore the suggested price range was somewhat uncertain. In addition, both insurance-business accounting and embedded-value calculations are difficult matters, and there were also ongoing litigations that further contributed to the valuation problems. Hence there were comprehensible reasons for Old Mutual to demand limited due diligence. However, this request turned out to be a controversial issue for the Skandia board for many reasons: some of the demands did not correspond to the regulations in the Swedish takeover rules, and were expected to have negative effects on the

Skandia business during its execution. An extended limited due diligence procedure might also have an impact on its stock price.[37]

Swedish takeover rules stipulated at the time that a board should accept a limited due diligence if a bid seemed interesting enough for shareholders to take part in.[38] However, the board of a Swedish company did not have an obligation to enable such a procedure. Regulation has treated due diligence as a rather exceptional activity for listed companies.[39] The possibility of refusing such a procedure was however not fully recognized, so pending an expressed opinion from the Swedish Securities Council, a decision not to allow due diligence could be interpreted as implying a deterioration of the conditions for an offer. Therefore such a decision could, in the end, be regarded as a deleterious measure. Given that the Skandia share on 13 May had risen substantially, following the leak of Old Mutual's indicative 'bid', and considering Director Christer Gardell's concern that there otherwise existed some risk for legal actions, the board of directors, with good reason, felt themselves obliged to allow the due diligence. Apart from the fact that the board (probably) did not have to accord due diligence, almost any other counter-measure that the board of the target company took could be deemed injurious. 'Poison pills',[40] for example, are not legal in Sweden. Another issue addresses how much information should be provided to a bidder. In listed companies, due diligence is often carried out in a limited form. A bidder obviously wants to get as much information as possible, but what is given to one bidder must be given to the other bidders as well. The board must not take any measure that serves to give unfair advantages to any shareholder that are to the disadvantage of another.[41]

How to make public the information provided in the process is a third troublesome issue related to due diligence. In Sweden, relevant market-sensitive information must be made public during the due diligence process, or (at least) no later than when the bidder presents its full prospectus on the stock market. By this time, however, many other events may have influenced the stock price, including the fact that a bid may already have been publicly announced, and shareholders may already have sold their shares to other parties. This was the case for Skandia. Even if the information given is not market-sensitive, and not necessarily going to be made public, it does put the bidder in a stronger position than the seller. The fourth and final issue concerns the effect that a due diligence process has on the company in which it is being conducted. Opening up a company for such a procedure means that, during a period of time, senior management becomes involved in a time-consuming procedure on top of its day-to-day matters. As the maximum period was not regulated at the time, this activity could drag on for months in a Swedish company (and hurt operations), and, to some extent, that is what happened in Skandia.[42]

Another institution that created turbulence was the Swedish takeover rules as such, and the parallel works of the Swedish Securities Council (a self-regulatory body). The method of 'reinterpreting' (or disregarding) many of the self-regulating kinds of rules prevailing on the Swedish arena for corporate control seems to have been used almost systematically; for example, Old Mutual's disregard of the Swedish Securities Council decision to deem inappropriate the initial condition of a positive board recommendation for an upcoming bid. Further examples can be found in the disregard of the board's reservation of the bid in Old Mutual's abbreviated Swedish prospectus to Skandia's shareholders, and in the leaking to the media of the percentages of Skandia shareholders that supported the Old Mutual bid. The accompanying sanctions were simply (too) weak, making such violations close to costless (with the possible exception of reputational costs).

Yet another example of the workings of institutions is the various indices that strongly influence many of the actors in the Old Mutual–Skandia case (cf. index behaviour on the capital market; see Chapter 1). One such example is the effects following the composition of the Morgan Stanley index for European insurance companies. An inclusion of Old Mutual–Skandia in the Morgan Stanley insurance index – rather than in the Morgan Stanley emerging-markets index – created a need for institutional investors who tracked the former index to increase their exposure to the new Old Mutual share. They did, which resulted in a technically driven higher demand for the share, and a (short-term) rising price. At the same time, the construction of the main Swedish index, which included Skandia (and Swedish banks), worked in the opposite way. Old Mutual's move to back away from the condition of 90 per cent acceptances almost forced the (Swedish) institutional investors to sell substantial parts of their stakes in Skandia, since the share was to lose half of its weight in the index, and capital managers of mutual funds and pension funds could see their position turning from neutral/underweight in Skandia to one of overweight. Thus an index-based reshuffling of Old Mutual and Skandia shares took place.

Old Mutual's bid was prolonged several times; there was a 23-week period from the prospectus becoming public on 7 October to the last closing day on 14 March 2006. This was added to the period from 13 May, when an indicative 'bid' was leaked, to the formal and public bid on 2 September. This option to prolong and make revisions to an offering worked in favour of the bidder; at the time, such action was allowed in the Swedish institutional setting (no time limits were stated).[43]

Finally, the role of the investment bank when it is supposed to deliver fairness opinions in connection to a bid is a ninth example of institutional influence on takeover processes. In the Skandia case, Morgan Stanley prepared such a fairness opinion, while it had concurrently been enrolled by the board and entitled to receive a transaction fee that reflected the value of a bid. This brought to the fore a demand for more stringent rules regarding independence in such situations.

In a universe populated by multi-rational actors, there is certainly room for cognitive error, human laziness, incomplete or distorted information, as well as 'irrational' honesty and integrity. There is also room for the idea that all human actors are not alike: people often differ in terms of motivation and capacities. When we pursue this view of the multi-rational human being and, at the same time, conceive of a number of particular Swedish institutional conditions and add an open shareholder structure, the entire situation seems to tilt in favour of the 'yes' camp: the nomination committees, the board in their discussions of the stand-alone path/takeover bid, the due diligence, and the position taken by a few activists.

The presence of multi-rational actors opens the way for moral arbitrage, that is, individuals, who are prepared to do what others are not. These actors who break the institutionalized moral rules sometimes win, at least in the short term. One such example, which characterizes the Old Mutual–Skandia case, is the extensive leaking of confidential information. This disclosure initiated activities that became vital to the development of the whole takeover process, and also for the outcome. For example, the fund employee who leaked the information to the press on 12 May not only increased the tempo of the bid process;[44] he also benefited from it. Those who opposed the Old Mutual acquisition of Skandia also did quite a bit of leaking. Some of the leaks implied that the majority sidestepped the minority of the predominant opinion of the Skandia board regarding the company's immediate strategic plans (e.g., concerning the Turbo plan in late June 2005). This sidestepping is also an example of moral arbritrage. In our interpretation, certain tardiness and a slightly 'superior' morality contributed to the fact that the majority 'lost' the struggle. Another interpretation could be that they 'lost' because of weaker imagination.

Our conclusion here is that self-regulation functions merely in accordance with intent when, and only when, actors are bound by a common ethic, a perceived obligation to follow the rules, and regard the existing sanctions as trying or deterrent. As soon as actors not supporting such a shared ethical system appear on the scene, the phenomenon of moral arbitrage emerges.

As mentioned earlier, we regard corporate governance processes as taking place in the context of an institutional bricolage. We have also suggested that many actors find it necessary or valuable to follow the associated rules and norms, although others actually seem to prefer to breach some of them instead. One might qualify this conclusion by adding basic social science theory: established incumbents in power structures tend to uphold rules and regulations (which, at the same time, tend to serve their interests), while being challenged by 'newcomers' that exhibit non-traditional – call it unorthodox – styles of agency.[45] The result of these kinds of processes in the context of governance in Sweden is a transformed and transforming institutional bricolage. In this case, this means that those actors who, for a time, have (also) acted on the global arena with its free-flowing capital, have then been confronted with a variety of corporate governance regimes and regulations. Thus, by being familiar with alternative practices, some actors become more prepared to make use of the differing, changing or ambiguous institutions. This has probably added to their capacity to benefit from the situation. The Old Mutual–Skandia case also shows several such (categories of) actors who seem to have been much better prepared to use many of the opportunities (and 'tools') that financial capitalism provides. Some actors in Sweden, for example, make swift and clever use of this new toolkit of corporate governance, which includes nomination committees, takeover rules and due diligence on listed companies. The toolkit even includes 'new' interpretations of the roles and relationships for the basic agencies of a corporation (see Section 22.5).

We do not claim that all the institutional mismatches and clashes described above determined on their own the outcome of the takeover process; however, we believe that they did play an important role in what happened. It is difficult to imagine that Old Mutual would have been able to acquire Skandia if many of these institutional settings had looked differently, and if the multi-rational actors had not differed in their attitudes towards the rules and norms associated with these institutions. All in all, these new governance bodies and phenomena constitute legal and practical 'irritants' to the current governance regime. Undoubtedly, these irritants constitute a significant threat to some of the characteristics of this particular (Swedish) 'coordinated market economy', pushing it in the direction of tighter legal regulation, rather than increasing the share of non-governmental regulations upheld by shareholders, firms and their associations (cf. self-regulation).

Finally, one could add, as a concluding hypothesis, that transformations of institutional bits and pieces across national or regional borders generally face the risk of being rather harmful, since such partial or eclectic operations are interwoven in highly elaborated and differing cultural settings and traditions. This makes it very difficult to make changes even of minor components, without creating a plethora of unforeseen and unintended consequences.

22.7 WHERE DO WE GO FROM HERE?

We have discussed a number of themes: the drift towards short-termism; the predominance of the financial rationale; the permutations of corporate governance bodies; and institutional drift. All of these point to a shift in corporate governance away from industrial capitalism to financial capitalism: a corollary process to the move from socially embedded to disembedded capitalism. This transformation also challenges the European 'coordinated market economies' of the twentieth century. Instead, the new emerging global (financial) markets bear the stamp of the Anglo-Saxon liberal models, to a large extent carried by US-dominated professional services industries (e.g. hedge funds, investment banks, management consultants and audit companies). A substantial part of this 'professionalism' that has been exerted on capital (and other) markets is also – simultaneously – an outflow of speculation; this is how these markets work in order to be more 'effective'. Particularly in corporations with an open shareholder structure and a governance model that invite shareholder influence (such as the one prevailing in Sweden), however, the implication is that such corporations might be at risk of being stripped of most of their intended purpose: that of operational risk-taking in the name of invention and innovation, which is supposedly generative of material welfare.

A number of questions emerge from this study. A more comprehensive one could be formulated as follows: is it at all possible to construct an institutional setting for the market for corporate control and a corporate governance model that can organize large capital that active short-term speculators accumulate in such a way that the global population of corporations benefits in the long term? This problem could also be stated as: could there be an institutional setting that can deal with the predominantly short-term incentives (index-tracking, performance bonuses and so on) that dominate decision-making in hedge funds and activist funds, and spreads to the traditional long-only pension funds and mutual funds? The inclination among managers of long-term capital to support this short-term speculative action by, for example, joining them in their voting, or leaving the corporations, has become a serious problem for specific companies. However, the 'short-termists' also indirectly influence the governance of the population of listed companies at large. Thus there seems to be an acute shortage of shareholders upholding a long-term perspective (and exercising voting rights accordingly).

Another more general question emerges: should we reconsider the basic models for corporate governance; that is, should the core agencies and their interrelationships be reconsidered? This case has illustrated several differing models on the global scene, predominantly addressing institutions such as the ones that define shareholders' rights, the function of the AGM, the nomination committee's role and composition, the governing board's jurisdiction and tasks, and the CEO's standing and assignments. The Old Mutual–Skandia takeover process provides an excellent opportunity for studying such evolving toolkits of governance, the formation of corporate control rationales, and the emerging and reconfigured institutional bricolages. One theoretical hypothesis is that a corporate governance regime which originates in a context with dominating block-holding shareholders tend to put the control of corporations back into such hands, via processes that include some measure of both rule and moral arbitrage.

Yet another question relates to the ongoing academic debate, where it has been argued on innumerable occasions that the predominance of institutional investors as shareholders, together with the accompanying regulatory contexts, constitutes a problematic situation, since some regulations may stand in the way of large investors engaging in the beneficial oversight of corporations.[46] Thus is it time to rethink the ways in which people's pensions, (other) savings, and insurance capital are channelled to productive investments over which the true principals retain some sort of control?

A fourth question that calls for further studies addresses the roles of the intermediaries in corporate governance processes. Investment banks, now and then acting as creditors, underwriters, advisers, investors and even regulators, along with a wide range of specialized investment funds (hedge funds and the like), may be seen to have populated the financial markets, reproducing some of its basically speculative character. Concurrently, this establishes the conditions and 'rules' for all participants on their respective markets. The intermediaries tend to function like 'rational' destabilizers, working with and on the conceptions of the less professional investors.[47] Their actions may also produce certain negative externalities for people in their role as citizens; for example, a loss of a more direct control over capital formation, and over the production and distribution of material welfare. In our view, and in that of others,[48] corporate governance research has long hesitated to formulate the crucial (and most hard to solve) question: what are the overall societal implications of different governance regimes?

The Old Mutual–Skandia case also gives us reason to raise a more specific query, this time regarding hostile takeover processes, thus adding to the vigorous debates in the academic circles as to whether these are mechanisms in the service of 'efficient' markets or not.[49] This extends even further: what consequences in general pertain to hostile takeovers? The case studied provides a hypothesis: at least in certain cases, this kind of takeover may not add long-term value either to the shareholder or to the stakeholder. In 2004, Skandia was a company with a new management team that for several reasons (and in a far from effective market for corporate control) was turned over to another management team that took on substantial financial and operational risks. One could note that the acquisition took place in a market where several other investors – such as mutual funds and pension funds – were prohibited by law from borrowing money at all. They could, therefore, not finance any competing moves in the two shares involved without incurring the extraordinary risks associated with selling substantial amounts of other assets.

The Old Mutual–Skandia case also raises the problem of the procurement and diffusion of non-public information on the market for corporate control: is it possible to solve the insider problem on the market for corporate control (since everyone can talk informally to anyone at any given time)? This question could also be modified and phrased as follows: is it possible to protect the small shareholders or minorities from block holders of various kinds promoting their specific values in the governance processes? The economic incentives to commit insider crimes are considerable, and the risk of being caught is often negligible. The opportunities for any single actor to act on the financial markets from behind the walls of a boardroom, for example, are immense, regardless of whether or not it is illegal.[50] Thus there is every opportunity for everyone to talk to anyone, anywhere in the world, and then place financial bets on the value of a certain company's share.[51] Any such action is almost impossible to prove/disprove.

Apart from this, the opportunities to drive a legitimate agenda based on privileged information may also be disproportionate to the capital invested. Is it wise to make it easy for actors with small holdings to take seats on a board without having to state their intentions? Otherwise, there may be outsiders inside the boardroom whose rationales are hidden, with access to privileged and valuable information. These outsiders may also be capable of influencing actions on the financial markets to simultaneously create and capture value on the basis of this particular information. Others (perhaps also in the boardroom) could instead be described as insiders left outside: outside the opportunity to capture value. If (and how) all of this is done in and around corporations could hardly be studied keeping within the prevailing ethical codes of academic investigation.

The studied takeover struggle has illustrated a final basic question: why (and how) do socioeconomic institutions change? We claim that this book as a whole has addressed this crucial theme, as it presented itself from the outset as being about the transformation of an entire institutional setting from one state of affairs to another: from industrial capitalism to financial capitalism. This shift has been seen as having its constructive, destructive and reproducing mechanisms intentionally and unintentionally rooted in actors' agencies. We have focused on the institutional bricolage of the evolving corporate governance regime in the Swedish setting, but have not been able to provide an unconditional answer to the question of whether this particular bricolage was a result of intentional planning, or the not-so-intended consequence of separate acts and agencies over the course of time. Such an answer will depend on which specific weights are assigned to the power of actors, institutions and culture respectively, that is, through which basic perspective or historical narrative the world is understood.

Regardless of preferred theoretical approach, we argue that this study does, indeed, provide the kind of qualitative study of actual corporate governance practice – particularly at the level of the corporate board – called for by many academics.[52] In our view, this study has also moved beyond most qualitative approaches that have hitherto been published; we claim to have studied practice rather than merely actors' talk.[53]

As for the future of the Swedish and other corporate governance regimes, these might well be transformed again – perhaps even in a more planned and coherent manner than before. With regard to Sweden, European politics will probably establish itself as a decisive force for some time to come. Our belief and expectation is that the UK or the EU (and perhaps even the USA) will act in this field. We also think it might be wise if certain key institutional dimensions or aspects were put at the forefront – for example, the rules for cross border voting (cf. shareholder's rights), the regulation of previously basically unregulated financial actors (e.g. hedge funds), the incentive systems for long-term shareholding (e.g. pension funds and mutual funds), and the (relative) weights of prioritized stakeholder values. All in all, however, we claim that the crucial issue is to establish a better balance between short-term and long-term forces in a revised construct of the market for corporate governance and control.

NOTES

1. This is in defiance of the amassing evidence that takeovers do not generally seem to be a particularly efficient mechanism for creating economic value. The overarching impression from quantitative research is that, as in the case studied here, takeovers create short-term shareholder value for target company shareholders (see Maher and Andersson, 2002; Burkart and Panunzi, 2008).
2. Regarding Janusian rationality, see Sjöstrand (1997).
3. This double rationale had emerged in Sweden with the intention of enabling institutional minority shareholders to deal with governance issues that are otherwise controlled by a dominating shareholder. Some specific features of the model are highlighted when it is applied to a company with an open shareholder base involved in a cross-border struggle.
4. AP4's seemingly contradictory stance was a consequence of CEO Thomas Halvorsen's interpretation of his governance mandate to be more of the long-term shareholder

value kind, which enabled him and the fund to actively support the stand-alone path. This kind of action in the spirit of industrial capitalism was in line with what might be described as a particular tradition for this pension fund, established back in the early 1990s when AP4 took the lead in supporting Volvo's management in its attempts to stop a planned merger with Renault.

5. By getting a seat at a nomination committee.
6. It should also be kept in mind that at this relatively early stage of the takeover process, it was still all about a friendly deal, and Skandia's shareholders were then expected to receive approximately 27 per cent of an expanded Old Mutual.
7. It can also be noted, however, that the Swedish Companies Act has been written so as to make such interests dubious with regards to the law. According to the wording of the Act, any interest besides 'producing profit to owners' must be included in the Corporate Constitution. Everyday practice violates the spirit of this particular clause, essentially because it is extremely cumbersome to prove in a court of law that a business decision was motivated by something other than to make profit to its shareholders.
8. See Sjöstrand et al. (2001).
9. For example, such public attention could address pollution and the interests of those living in a affected area, or be about the hiring of cheap labour from abroad and violate the interests of the domestic employees, or deal with issues linked to protectionism or patriotism and the interests of a specific population or nation.
10. Hawley and Williams (2000) elaborate on the importance of externalities of corporate activity in terms of consequences for other corporations. Activities such as R&D, training, marketing efforts and infrastructure investments that are carried out by one corporation could have consequences for other corporations, most of them beneficial from an economic perspective. The universal shareholder with an encompassing portfolio of corporate shares will have an interest, for instance, in having individual portfolio firms abstain from too heavy R&D cost-cutting. This may spark spiralling effects for other firms in which it holds shares and, hence, drive down the value of the portfolio. A particular shareholder may have the completely opposite interest.
11. For a description of Skandia's operational flow, see Nachemsson-Ekwall and Carlsson (2004).
12. See also Blomberg (2004).
13. Old Mutual's board had its own advisers.
14. However, we have not completed a thorough analysis of all the analysts' reporting; it is very difficult for anyone to show with accuracy how such analyses come about.
15. There were also less 'visible' and informal arenas involved in the Skandia takeover process, where actors working in the financial governance flow assembled and discussed various critical matters.
16. A group of shareholders controlling 10 per cent of the votes can call for an EGM to change the board composition.
17. Only Björn Björnsson was kept on as board member, and he had been at the Skandia board merely one year.
18. The CEO may be a formal member of the board (see Chapter 1).
19. However, there are several cases in Sweden where a (former) CEO has been appointed chair in the same company (e.g. Sandvik, SCA, Electrolux, Nordea etc.).
20. The regulations also vary – sometimes significantly – between the UK and the USA, as well as among the USA's constituent states (e.g. Delaware).
21. In the UK, half of the members of the board must be independent of the company, that is, not related to the shareholders or their families, etc. Board membership for more than eight years also makes a director dependent. Usually both the CEO and the CFO are members of the board.
22. However, nothing prevents UK institutions from suggesting candidates to the nominating committee or straight to the shareholders' meeting, but that is rather unusual.
23. The first time a director is appointed for one year.
24. However, there are notable differences between the UK Anglo-Saxon governance

model and its US counterpart: for example, the latter has traditionally put more power in the hands of the CEO (who, historically, has also acted as chair).

25. However, a bad recommendation made by a board of directors in the USA, which lacks in explicit comparisons and discussions of the alternatives available when a bid is presented, can expose the directors to lawsuits from discontented shareholders.
26. Some actors claim that it would be inappropriate to have a CEO as a formal board member, as a key task for the board is to recruit and dismiss the CEO.
27. The appointment of two women also signalled an awareness of the importance of gender equality on these prestigious arenas. (See Sjöstrand and Petrelius, 2003).
28. This occurred before the millennium in the Swedish global paper and packaging company AssiDomän, when Magnusson was chair of the company and Björnsson was one of its directors. This turnaround case has been concluded, and a volume describing this process will be published (Sjöstrand, forthcoming).
29. See e.g., Kärreman (1999).
30. This could have expressed skilfulness on the part of Cevian actors in that they realized this effect before anybody else, and, thereby, acted on it. Herein, perhaps, lies one of Cevian's 'core competencies'.
31. Sassen (2001) is a very comprehensive empirical account and theoretical interpretation of the concentration of 'professional services work' in a limited number of 'global cities'. Anglo-Saxon dominance in global professional services has been seen as overwhelming for quite some time. The theme is intimately related to the concerns of Meyer and Jepperson (2000) to their attempt in formulate an encompassing Weberian understanding to be compared with, or complemented by, Sassen's more materialist Marxian interpretation of recent world history. In organization theory, Clegg et al. (2005, esp. ch. 13) give a few indications of some implications of this development.
32. Many regulations puts focus on the capital-based flow because they use a kind of principal–agent reasoning that puts the shareholders in the driver's seat.
33. In 2007, the forced merger legislation in the Swedish Companies Act was revised to ensure that it was only to be applicable if a takeover of a listed company were carried through by an exchange of shares (and voting rights) in the new entity. A bid on a listed company paid in cash is not allowed to use the 'forced merger approach' since that date.
34. However, the threshold of 50 per cent was also linked to two other target figures: a holding of 66.7 per cent or 75 per cent.
35. However, one could note that the management presentations that were made after the bid was finalized actually showed slides with the headline 'Old Mutual's Hostile Takeover of Skandia'.
36. When a corporation is seriously interested in acquiring a listed firm, it is usually not sufficient to rely on official or public material alone. That information may be biased in some way, or even not entirely reliable. Therefore, to take the final step and present a bid, the potential buyer usually also wants (needs) to carry out a due diligence procedure.
37. This discussion is based on Rydén (2006).
38. It can be argued that within the predominant rationale of Swedish corporate governance, such a demand for due diligence should more logically be made together with a public bid rather than in a confidential proposal to the board.
39. A statement by the Swedish Securities Council (AMN 2005: 47) eventually concluded that a target company is not obliged to take active measures to help the offering company make an offer. It also stated that a refusal to take part in the making of an offer is not, consequently, to be regarded as an unacceptable counter-measure. This particular decision, however, was made after the fate of Skandia was decided.
40. In publicly listed companies, various methods to avoid takeover bids are called 'poison pills' because they not only harm the bidder, but the target (or its shareholders) as well.

41. According to the Swedish Companies Act (Ch. 8, Sec. 41).
42. These kinds of costs were nowhere in regulatory texts said to be a legitimate reason for refusing, or cutting short, a due diligence process.
43. When the Swedish takeover rules were revised in 2009, it was decided that the acceptance period for a takeover bid should more closely resemble that of the UK system, and not be less than three weeks, and not more than ten weeks. At the same time it was stated that the total acceptance period could not exceed three months, and, if subject to approval by a public authority, the acceptance period could not exceed more than nine months.
44. In 2009, a Swedish prosecutor addressed the supposed leak.
45. E.g. Bourdieu (1980/90); Sjöstrand (1985); Fligstein (2001); Campbell (2004).
46. E.g. Fraser (1998); Mitchell (2001); Roe (2003).
47. Parenteau (2005).
48. E.g. O'Sullivan (2003).
49. Burkard and Panunzi (2008) argue that takeovers are not necessarily value-creating, and that obtaining a better understanding of the relative performance of different governance regimes is of some urgency. However, which measures of performance are to be included in these debates, and what, consequently, is meant by 'value', remains to be defined.
50. Or in other locations (see Sjöstrand et al., 2001).
51. Sjödin (2006).
52. Cf., e.g., Ezzamel (2005); Roberts et al. (2005); Huse (2007); Geale (2007).
53. Silverman (1985) refers to interviewing in its predominant form as a forum for 'moral storytelling' on the part of respondents. The very limited efforts that have been made at qualitative study of corporate governance processes have clearly been marked by this, although not all abstract or 'lofty' statements that knowledgeable practitioners make should be totally discounted.

Appendix A methodological note

The legitimacy of this and any other extensive case study rests on the assumption that one such single investigation can be used to provide evidence of social phenomena of a more general importance.[1] It also rests on the unique quality of the case-study format to convey an understanding of such general phenomena through their instantiations in a particular case, and the opportunity it might present to develop or revise connections between established as well as emerging – or even novel – explanatory concepts, often then formulated as empirically based theories. We claim that Chapters 3–21 in this book contain such an empirical foundation.[2]

Therefore some notes are warranted regarding the ways in which our materials have been co-produced by us and by others, and then further interpreted by us with the aid of yet others. This methodological note is brief for two reasons: this project has no ambition to make a significant methodological contribution; and our choice of methods and techniques is basically rather traditional, given the case-study format. As in most extensive case studies, the credibility of the empirical material presented (the story) rests on both how the material was produced (see below), and how it has been presented (clarity, internal consistency, accuracy etc.).

The basic idea with this study was described in Chapter 1: 'The theoretical purpose is to try to improve socioeconomic theories addressing corporate control and corporate governance, and the empirical ambition is to provide an extensive case study of a hostile cross-border takeover process that helps in understanding corporate control struggle practices in early financial capitalism'. To learn more about that we decided to study Old Mutual's hostile takeover of Skandia (formally in 2006), and the more concrete question we then addressed was, 'simply', 'Why did it occur?' This question prompted the perhaps more accessible empirical question: 'How did it occur?' Any answer to the 'why question' would rest on firmer ground in the presence of an empirically well-founded answer to the 'how question'.[3]

In accordance with the long research tradition in socioeconomics, we did not begin our study from some kind of *tabula rasa*. When this research effort started there was already a running research programme at the Stockholm School of Economics Centre for Management Studies addressing governance and control issues associated with the emerging global financial capitalism. One of the authors has since 1977, headed a research centre that has conducted a long series of longitudinal, multi-method studies of senior management and governance practice in many Nordic corporations. That same author has also served on boards of large listed companies and acted as senior adviser to many of the 'captains of Nordic industry'. This meant that there was an extensive, well-known and trustworthy network in place, making comprehensive empirical access possible (not least regarding more delicate and contentious research themes). That platform became even stronger as another of the authors was recruited to the research team on the merits of a journalistic career, involving both writings on financial capitalism in general, and on the target company in this study, Skandia, in particular.[4]

Because of our knowledge about the target company (Skandia), particularly about what had occurred in that firm since the 1980s and up to 2003, we could make both an early and quite accurate identification of who the main actors (probably) were in that company. As mentioned, we also had a privileged insight into the specific process studied, as one of the authors (as business journalist) had been covering the takeover intensively, often also functioning as an 'arena' for actor leakages, interests and argumentations. All this information and our already existing networks enabled us to contact all the important actors in Old Mutual's takeover of Skandia and invite them to participate. Then the sample of individuals predominantly included direct shareholders, shareholders' representatives, hedge or activist fund actors, board directors, members of managements, advisory firms' representatives, financial analysts and business journalists. Almost all of these individuals (Brits and Swedes, as well as actors from other countries[5]) received a letter outlining the purpose of the project, and also our promise to do all we could to secure the anonymity of anyone choosing to participate (or abstaining from participation).[6]

The intense and extensive empirical work directly involving the actors was carried out from December 2006 to May 2008, with follow-ups into May 2009. As a platform for these talks, based on the experience and information described above, we had a rough, preliminary structure describing events, involved actors, activity timings, crucial decisions or actions (such as a bid), and formal matters (such as a board meeting). This information was used as a kind of 'skeleton' in the interviews that always started as open-ended,[7] but gradually became more structured. That course was valid both for how individual interviews unfolded, and also when the same person was approached more than once. It also influenced the questioning, as the number of interviews accumulated.

We decided to start each interview with more general questions regarding the takeover process, and then gradually make use of the skeleton basis and information from previous interviews. As the interviews proceeded, we also made use of information from various kinds of writings (documents, articles, statistics etc). This 'funnel-like' technique to collect information from interviewees was chosen to enhance data quality, to enable new information to arise (i.e. information not expected by the interviewer), and to open the way for a cross-checking of information from a particular interviewee or between different interviewees. Thus all these bits and pieces of information were used to enrich and reconfigure the continuously developing hypothetical overarching case description of the takeover from which we started. A wide range of details was then followed up methodically (in spite of that, some figures and spellings of names may be incorrect, but we hope not the more important ones for understanding the basic issues in the study).

The interviews varied in length; some of them lasted up to six hours (then interrupted, for instance, by a lunch-break). A number of respondents have been interviewed more than once (in a few cases up to four or more times). During the interviews notes were taken by hand. None of the interviews was recorded, reinforcing the promised confidentiality and 'off-record' setting. The basic foundation for our case story is thus around 200 such interviews with around 75 different actors that have had a direct and profound involvement with the process covered.

The quality of the notes was improved by the fact that, on many occasions, two of us were doing the questioning and online documentation (in writing). The interview materials were transcribed in as much detail as possible within a few days. Most of those interviewed, and all those whom we found out to have played major parts in the process studied, have been given the opportunity to read our interpretations of their statements, and some have even read the semi-completed empirical material (see below).

The focus in the interviews was to get descriptions from those who were involved in some way in the process of: (i) what happened during the period leading up to the takeover discussions (see Part III); (ii) what occurred during the period after it had been publicly known that there was an interested bidder for Skandia (see Part IV); (iii) what happened after a bid had been put to the market (see Part V); and (iv) how Old Mutual finally bought Skandia (see Part VI). However, some interviews have covered much longer time spans than the ones directly addressed in Part III–VI, focusing on the longer history of Skandia.

There are also other sources of information building up the Old Mutual–Skandia case than the ones described above. There are written texts from the whole period, including documents produced (and published) by the involved companies, as well as most of what was reported in the leading business journals and daily papers in Sweden. There is also a selection of the more important written material in some of the media in the UK and South Africa addressing various stages of the takeover process. Moreover, quite a few of the analysts' reports evaluating Old Mutual and Skandia have also been used. However, the considerable presence of quotations from various newspapers and business journals must not be seen as a manifestation of an assumed importance of the media in the process (see Chapter 22). Instead, most of the accounts and quotations from such sources are used as 'substitutes' for an explicit presentation of statements through named and/or identifiable actors (the necessity to keep our informants anonymous made that use of the media a viable strategy). Furthermore, we have also read some diaries and many more private notes and correspondence, and our case material is even based on information that some of our informants perhaps might not have been permitted to provide. When all this is taken together and reflected on, it is our hope that readers will acknowledge the quality of the material, without being able to check the ultimate informants for specific pieces of text.

Thus the research process, predominantly driven by the theoretical interest (as described in Chapter 1) and the emerging empirical material, resembled a detective's procedure in that we were continuously looking for information in order to reconstruct a picture of a past (2004–06) takeover process using a particular lens (i.e. selecting information that was thought to be of importance for corporate governance and control issues). Crucial to this process was to continuously keep an open attitude towards the material, always ready to reconsider an assumption, a descriptive element, or a position if we acquired new and (more) reliable information. The interview process thus came to be founded on a quite traditional mix of the rationales of grounded theory, hermeneutics and critical theory, always going back and forth between the empirical material and the simultaneously evolving theoretical knowledge base, to gradually try to develop and improve existing theories in the relevant field. This is often called an 'abductive' approach, in terms more attuned to the terminology of analytical philosophy.[8]

As mentioned above, most interviewees, that is to say, all those we have regarded as the more important individuals in the processes studied, have been given the opportunity to read our first description of their parts and roles in the takeover process. During this second round several individuals have made elaborate comments, substantial additions, important corrections and provided well-founded criticism. This feedback from the informants has, at the same time, provided us with an opportunity for further interviewing. In this second round we were able to pose (even) more specific questions to fill gaps, check disagreements between informants, and eliminate discrepancies between certain texts and individuals' verbal statements.

We began gathering information by (temporarily) assuming that the written texts (of the more formal or published kind) were basically correct representations of what had occurred. We also (temporarily) assumed that what the informants were telling us, particularly when it came to 'facts' such as dates, persons, themes for discussions, were, on the whole, reliable data. However, we were from the beginning (and remained so) more 'open-minded' as to their explanations of motives and rationales (of self and others). To a large extent, that principle has proven fruitful in establishing a detailed (and basically uncontroversial) time-line of events (the 'time–place–actor–action skeleton'). To an overwhelming extent, we have been able to get confirmation from at least two reasonably independent informants on every single item included in the case text (so a wide range of claims made by [single] informants have not found their way into our description).

The entire material is finally presented as a (basically) chronological case description, providing quite detailed information on four of the five necessary dimensions of any completed narrative: actors, their actions, their tools for action, and the context for their action.[9] The fifth dimension, the overall 'purpose' or meaning of the story, is added by us in our composition of the case description (Chapters 2–21) as well as in our interpretations and theorizing in Chapters 1 and 22 (and perhaps also constructed by the individual reader[10]).

NOTES

1. Ragin and Becker (1992).
2. See Helenius (1990), and Flyvberg (2006).
3. We have tried to describe a complex process, relying heavily on chronology to make sense of it. The (lengthy) description is, by necessity, already an interpretation by us in terms of dramaturgy. This means that our narrative can be read or listened to according to at least four dramatic genres: realism, idealism, materialism and pragmatics. That is, we have focused on concrete acts (realism), accorded explanatory status to agents' competent, reflexive agency (idealism), as well as to their situation and incentive matrix (materialism) and to the tools to their disposition (pragmatics). See Burke (1945). The order in which we present events, and the choice of events presented, make up an interpretation of a higher order. As implied at the beginning of the book, we have attempted to enable readings according to many traditions of narrating.
4. Nachemson-Ekwall and Carlsson (2004).
5. However, we have not talked to actors from South Africa, and there are more Swedish sources than UK ones (cf. the nexus of the case). In Sweden there is also a tradition of considerable openness seldom found in the business communities elsewhere.
6. Some have also simply been asked to participate in face-to-face situations, and a few others have been asked over the phone (or by e-mail).
7. See Noaks and Wincup (2004, p. 80).
8. Alvesson and Sköldberg (2000).
9. Burke (1945).

10. We do not take the position of the ideal-typical realist novelist with the narrative voice that knows all. We do, however, claim to know quite a lot, leaving some readers with the harsher choice of letting go of their understanding of some aspects of the world or simply regarding much of what is stated in this book as erroneous.

References

Note: The letter 'å' and 'ä' have been treated as 'a'; and 'ö' and 'ø' have been treated as 'o' in this section.

Aglietta, Michel and Antoine Rebérioux (2005), *Corporate Governance Adrift. A Critique of Shareholder Value*, Cheltenham, UK and Northampton, MA, USA: Edward Elgar.

Alvesson, Mats and Kaj Sköldberg (2000), *Reflexive Methodology: New Vistas for Qualitative Research*, London and Thousand Oaks: Sage.

Aoki, Masahiro (2001), *Toward a Comparative Institutional Analysis*, Cambridge, MA: MIT Press.

Bartlett, Christopher, A. and Takia Mahmood (1996), *Skandia AFS: Developing Intellectual Capital Globally*, Boston, MA: Harvard Business School.

Baudrillard, Jean (1994), *Simulacra and Simulation*, Ann Arbor, MI: University of Michigan Press.

Bebchuk, Lucien A. (1988), 'The pressure to tender: an analysis and a proposed remedy', in John C. Coffee, Louise Lowenstein and Susan Rose-Ackerman (eds), *Knights, Raiders, and Targets*, Oxford: Oxford University Press, pp. 371–97.

Bebchuk, Lucien A. and Jesse Fried (2004), *Pay Without Performance: The Unfulfilled Promise of Executive Compensation*, Cambridge, MA: Harvard University Press.

Bengtsson, Elias (2005), *Shareholder Activism of Swedish Institutional Investors*, Stockholm: School of Business Stockholm University.

Berle, Adolf A. and Gardiner C. Means (1932/68), *The Modern Corporation and Private Property*, New York: Macmillan.

Blom, Martin (2007), *Aktiemarknadsorienteringens ideologi*, Lund: Lund Business Press.

Blomberg, Jesper (2004), *Finansmarknadens aktörer – ett 'organizational finance' perspektiv*, Malmö: Liber.

Blyth, Mark (2002), *Great Transformations. Economic Ideas and Institutional Change in the Twentieth Century*, Cambridge: Cambridge University Press.

Borglund, Tommy (2006), *Aktieägarvärden i focus. Internationell påverkan*

på intressentrelationer genom förvärv och fusion, Stockholm: Stockholm School of Economics Research Institute (EFI).
Bourdieu, Pierre (1980/90), *The Logic of Practice*, Stanford, CA: Stanford University Press (translated by Richard Nice).
Brealey, Richard A. and Stewart C. Myers (1991), *Principles of Corporate Finance*, 4th edn, New York: McGraw-Hill.
Brenner, Robert (2002), *The Boom and the Bubble: The US in the World Economy*. London and New York: Verso.
Brodin, Bengt, Leif Lundkvist, Sven-Erik Sjöstrand and Lars Östman (1995), *Styrelsearbete i koncerner*, Stockholm: Stockholm: EFI and IFL.
Brodin, Bengt, Leif Lundkvist, Sven-Erik Sjöstrand and Lars Östman (2000), *Koncernchefen och ägarna*, Stockholm: EFI and IFL.
Burchell, Graham, Colin Gordon and Peter Miller (eds) (1991), *The Foucault Effect: Studies in Governmentality*, London: Harvester Wheatsheaf.
Burkart, M. and S. Lee (2008), 'One share, one vote: the theory', *Review of Finance*, **12** (1), 1–49.
Burkard, Mike and Fausto Panunzi (2008), 'Takeovers', in Xavier Freixas, Philippe Hartmann and Colin Meyer (eds), *Handbook of European Financial Markets and Institutions*, Oxford: Oxford University Press, pp. 265–97.
Burke, Kenneth (1945), *A Grammar of Motives*, New York: Prentice-Hall.
Callon, M. and F. Muniesa (2005), 'Peripheral vision: economic markets as calculative collective devices', *Organization Studies*, **26**, 1229–50.
Campbell, John L. (2004), *Institutional Change and Globalization*, Princeton, NJ: Princeton University Press.
Carlsson, R.H. (2007), 'Swedish corporate governance and value creation: owners still in the driver's seat', *Corporate Governance – An International Review*, **15**, 1038–55.
Chandler, Alfred D. (1977), *The Visible Hand: The Managerial Revolution in American Business*, Cambridge, MA: Belknap.
Clarke, Thomas (ed.) (2004), *Theories of Corporate Governance. The Philosophical Foundations of Corporate Governance*, London and New York: Routledge.
Charkham, Jonathan and Anna Simpson (1999), *Fair Shares. The Future of Shareholder Power and Responsibility*, Oxford: Oxford University Press.
Clegg, Stewart, Martin Kornberger and Tyrone Pitsis (2005), *Managing and Organizations – An Introduction to Theory and Practice*, London: Sage.
Collin, Sven-Olof (1990), *Aktiebolagets kontroll*, Lund: Lund University Press.

D'Arista, J. (2008), 'U.S. debt and global imbalances', *International Journal of Political Economy*, **36** (4), 12–35.

Dodd, Randall (2005), 'Derivatives markets: sources of vulnerability in US financial markets', in Gerald A. Epstein (ed.), *Financialization and the World Economy*, Cheltenham, UK and Northampton, MA, USA: Edward Elgar, pp. 149–80.

Elmbrant, Björn (2005), *Dansen kring guldkalven. Så förändrades Sverige av börsbubblan*, Stockholm: Atlas.

Emling, Emil (2000), *Svenskt familjeföretagande*, Stockholm: Stockholm School of Economics Research Institute (EFI).

Englund, Karl (1982), *Försäkring och fusioner – Skandia-Skåne-Svea-Thule-Öresund 1855–1980*, Stockholm: Skandia Archives.

Epstein, Gerald A. (ed.) (2005a), *Financialization and the World Economy*, Cheltenham, UK and Northampton, MA, USA: Edward Elgar.

Epstein, Gerald A. (2005b), 'Introduction: financialization and the world economy', in Gerald A. Epstein (ed.), *Financialization and the World Economy*, Cheltenham, UK and Northampton, MA, USA: Edward Elgar, pp. 1–16.

Ericson, Mona (1990), *Iggesundsaffären: rationaliteter i en strategisk förvärvsprocess*, Stockholm: Stockholm School of Economics Research Institute (EFI).

Ezzamel, Mahmoud (2005), 'Introduction. Boards of directors: composition, dynamics and effects', in Mahmoud Ezzamel (ed.), *Governance, Directors and Boards, vol. 4*, Cheltenham, UK and Northampton, MA, USA: Edward Elgar, pp. xi–xxv.

Ezzamel, M., H. Willmott and F. Worthington (2008), 'Manufacturing shareholder value: the role of accounting in organizational transformation', *Accounting, Organizations and Society*, **33**, 107–40.

Fligstein, Neil (2001), *The Architecture of Markets: An Economic Sociology of Twenty-First Century Capitalist Societies*, Princeton, NJ: Princeton University Press.

Flyvberg, B. (2006), 'Five misunderstandings about case-study research', *Qualitative Inquiry*, **12**, 19–45.

Foucault, Michel (1975/77), *Discipline and Punish. The Birth of the Prison*, New York: Vintage.

Fraser, Andrew (1998), *Reinventing Aristocracy: The Constitutional Reformation of Corporate Governance*, Aldershot, UK and Brookfield, USA: Dartmouth/Ashgate.

Fristedt, Daniel and Sven-Ivan Sundqvist (2008), *Ägarna och makten i Sveriges Börsföretag*, Halmstad: SIS Ägarservice AB.

Froud, Julie, Sukhdev Johal, Adam Leaver and Karel Williams (2006),

Financialization and Strategy. Narrative and Numbers, London and New York: Routledge.
Gao, Bai (1998), 'Efficiency, culture and politics: the transformation of Japanese management in 1946–66', in Michel Callon (ed.), *The Laws of the Markets*, Oxford: Blackwell, pp. 86–115.
Geale, Patricia (2007), *Around the Board. Corporate Governance from the Board Director's Perspective*, Brisbane: The University of Queensland.
Geertz, Clifford (1973), *The Interpretation of Cultures*, New York: Basic Books.
Glete, Jan (1994), *Nätverk i näringslivet*, Stockholm: SNS Förlag.
González Guve, Bertil José (2003), *Att bestämma sig utan grund: om omdöme och övertygelse i riskkapitalinvesteringar*, Stockholm: Royal Institute of Technology and Arvinius.
Hall, Peter A. and David Soskice (2001). *Varieties of Capitalism: The Institutional Foundations of Comparative Advantage*, Oxford and New York: Oxford University Press.
Hawley, James P. and Andrew T. Williams (2000), *The Rise of Fiduciary Capitalism*. Philadelphia, PA: University of Pennsylvania Press.
Helenius, Ralf (1990), *Förstå och bättre veta: om hermeneutiken i samhällsvetenskaperna*, Stockholm: Carlsson.
Henrekson, Magnus and Ulf Jacobsson (2002), 'Ägarpolitik och ägarstruktur i efterkrigstidens Sveriige', in Lars Jonung (ed.), *Vem skall äga Sverige?* Stockholm: SNS förlag.
Hultkvist, Erik (2007), *Landskampen*, Stockholm: Näringslivets medieinstitut.
Huse, Morten (2007), *Boards, Governance and Value Creation*, Cambridge: Cambridge University Press.
Jackall, Robert (1988), *Moral Mazes. The World of Corporate Managers*, New York: Oxford University Press.
Jensen, M.C. (2001), 'Value maximization, stakeholder theory, and the corporate objective function', *Journal of Applied Corporate Finance*, **14** (3), 6–21.
Jensen, M.C. and R.S. Ruback (1983), 'The market for corporate control: the scientific evidence', *Journal of Financial Economics*, **11**, 5–50.
Johansson, Svante and Håkan Nial (2007), *Svensk associationsrätt i huvuddrag*, Stockholm: Norstedts juridik.
Jonung, Lars (2002), *Vem skall äga Sverige?*, Stockholm: SNS.
Karlsson Stider, Annelie (2000), *Familjen och firman*, Stockholm: Stockholm School of Economics Research Institute (EFI).
Kärreman, Matts (1999), *Styrelseledamöters mandat – ansats till en teori om styrelsearbete i börsnoterade företag*, Lund: Lund Business Press.

Kim, Kenneth A. and John R. Nofsinger (2007), *Corporate Governance*, 2nd edn, Upper Saddle River, NJ: Pearson Prentice Hall.

Knorr Cetina, Karin and Alex Preda (eds) (2004), *The Sociology of Financial Markets*, Oxford: Oxford University Press.

Krugman, Paul (2009), *The Return of Depression Economics and the Crisis of 2008*, London: Penguin.

Kurtz, Howard (2000), *The Fortune Tellers. Inside Wall Street's Game of Money, Media, and Manipulation*, New York: The Free Press.

La Porta, R., F. Lopez-de-Silanes and A. Shleifer (2000), 'Government ownership of banks', Cambridge, MA: Working Paper Series/National Bureau of Economic Research, 99-0429337-6; 7620.

Larsson, Soren and Jaak Saving (1990), *Nordstjernan innefrån 1890–1990*, Stockholm: Norstedts.

Lazonick, W. and M. O'Sullivan (2000), 'Maximizing shareholder value: a new ideology for corporate governance', *Economy and Society*, **29** (1), 13–35.

Lindberg, Nina (2005), 'Beordrad självreglering eller frivilliga direktiv? Hur man tog fram en svensk standard för ägarstyrning', in Karin Svedberg Nilsson, Roger Henning and Karin Fernler (eds), *En illusion av frihet? Företag och organisationer i regelsamhället*, Lund and Stockholm: Studentlitteratur and the Stockholm School of Economics Research Institute (EFI), pp. 27–48.

Lindqvist, Mats (1996), *Herrar i näringslivet. Om kapitalistisk kultur och mentalitet*, Stockholm: Natur och Kultur.

Lindqvist, Mats (2001), *Is i magen. Om ekonomins kolonisering av vardagen*, Stockholm: Natur och Kultur.

Lindstedt, Gunnar (2000), *Svindlande affärer. Historien om Trustor*. Stockholm: *Dagens Nyheter*.

MacKenzie, Donald (2006), *An Engine, not a Camera: How Financial Models Shape Markets*, Cambridge, MA: MIT Press.

Maher, Maria and Thomas Andersson (2002), 'Corporate governance: effects on firm performance and economic growth', in Joseph A. McCahery, Piet Moerland, Theo Raaijmakers and Luc Renneboog (eds), *Corporate Governance Regimes. Convergence and Diversity*, Oxford: Oxford University Press, pp. 386–418.

Mallin, Christine (ed.) (2006a), *Handbook of International Corporate Governance: Country Analyses*, Cheltenham, UK and Northampton, MA, USA: Edward Elgar.

Mallin, Christine (ed.) (2006b), *International Corporate Governance: A Case Study Approach*, Cheltenham, UK and Northampton, MA, USA: Edward Elgar.

Manne, Henry G. (2000), 'Mergers and the market for corporate control', in Robert I. Tricker (ed), *Corporate Governance*, Aldershot, UK and Darlington, USA: Ashgate/Dartmouth, pp. 27–37. Originally published as H.G. Manne, 'Mergers and the market for corporate control', *Journal of Political Economy* (1965), 110–20.

Mantzavinos, Chrysostomos (2001), *Individuals, Institutions, and Markets*, Cambridge: Cambridge University Press.

McCahery, Joseph, Piet Moerland, Luc Renneboog and Theo Raaijmakers (eds) (2002), *Corporate Governance Regimes: Convergence and Diversity*, Oxford: Oxford University Press.

McNiel, D. (1981), 'Economic analysis of contractual relations', *Northwestern University Law Review*, **75**, 854–906.

Meyer, J.W. and R.L. Jepperson (2000), 'The "actors" of modern society: the cultural construction of social agency', *Sociological Theory*, **18**, 100–20.

Micklethwait, J. and A. Wooldridge (2003/05), *The Company: A Short History of a Revolutionary Idea*, New York: Modern Library.

Mitchell, Lawrence E. (2001), *Corporate Irresponsibility: America's Newest Export*, New Haven, CT and London: Yale University Press.

Monks, Robert A.G. and Nell Minow (2004), *Corporate Governance*, 3rd edn, Malden, MA: Blackwell.

Nachemson-Ekwall, Sophie and Bengt Carlsson (2004), *Guldregn – sagan om Skandia*, Stockholm: Månpocket.

Noaks, Lesley and Emma Wincup (2004), *Criminological Research: Understanding Qualitative Methods*, London: Sage.

Olson, Mancur (1965), *The Logic of Collective Action: Public Goods and the Theory of Groups*, Cambridge, MA: Harvard University Press.

O'Sullivan, M. (2003), 'The political economy of comparative corporate governance', *Review of International Political Economy*, **10** (1), 23–72.

Östman, Lars (2009), *Towards a General Theory of Financial Control for Organizations*, Stockholm: Stockholm School of Economics Research Institute (EFI).

Palley, T.I. (2008), 'The fallacy of the revised Bretton Woods hypothesis', *International Journal of Political Economy*, **36** (4), 36–52.

Parenteau, Robert W. (2005), 'The late 1990s' US bubble: financialization in the extreme', in Gerald A. Epstein (ed.), *Financialization and the World Economy*, Cheltenham, UK and Northampton, MA, USA: Edward Elgar, pp. 111–48.

Pérez Caldentey, E. and M. Vernengo (2008), 'Global imbalances and economic development', *International Journal of Political Economy*, **36** (4), 5–11.

Pinkard, Terry (2000), *Hegel. A Biography*, Cambridge: Cambridge University Press.

Ragin, Charles C. and Howard S. Becker (eds) (1992), *What's in a Case? Exploring the Foundations of Social Inquiry*, Cambridge and New York: Cambridge University Press.

Ricœur, Paul (1983/84), *Time and Narrative* (K. McLaughlin and D. Pellauer, trans.), Chicago and London: The University of Chicago Press.

Roberts, J., T. McNulty and P. Stiles (2005), 'Beyond agency conceptions of the work of the non-executive director: creating accountability in the boardroom', *British Journal of Management*, **16**, S5–S26.

Roe, Mark J. (2003), *Political Determinants of Corporate Governance: Political Context, Corporate Impact*, Oxford: Oxford University Press.

Rydén, Karin (2006), *Due diligence-undersökningar i samband med offentliga uppköpserbjudanden*, Gothenburg: Gothenburg University, Institution of Law (assisted by Rolf Skog, Professor of Corporate Law, and Ragnar Boman, Swedish Securities Council).

Samuelsson, Per (2005), *Konkurrerande modeller för bolagsstyrning*, in Liber Amicorum Reinhold Fahlbeck, Lund, pp. 459-85.

Sassen, Saskia (2001), *The Global City. New York, London, Tokyo*, Princeton, NJ and Oxford: Princeton University Press.

Schütz, Alfred (1932/67), *The Phenomenology of the Social World*, Evanston, IL: Northwestern University Press.

Silverman, David (1985), *Qualitative Methodology and Sociology: Describing the Social World*, Aldershot, UK and Brookfield, USA: Gower.

Sjödin, Ulrika (2006), *Insiders' Outside/Outsiders' Inside: Rethinking the Insider Regulation*, Stockholm: Stockholm University.

Sjöstrand, Sven-Erik (1985), *Samhällsorganisation*, Lund: Doxa.

Sjöstrand, Sven-Erik (ed.) (1993), *Institutional Change: Theory and Empirical Findings*, Armonk, UK and London, UK: M.E. Sharpe.

Sjöstrand, Sven-Erik (1995), 'Towards a theory of institutional change', in John Groenewegen, Christos Pitelis and Sven-Erik Sjöstrand (eds), *On Economic Institutions*, Aldershot, UK and Brookfield, MA, USA: Edward Elgar, pp. 19–44.

Sjöstrand, Sven-Erik (1997), *The Two Faces of Management. The Janus Factor*. London: Thomson.

Sjöstrand, Sven-Erik et al. (2001), *Invisible Management*, London: Thomson.

Sjöstrand, Sven-Erik and Pernilla Petrelius (2003), *Rekrytering till koncernstyrelser*, Stockholm: Stockholm School of Economics Research Institute (EFI) and SNS förlag.

Sternberg, Elaine (2004), *Corporate Governance: Accountability in the Marketplace*, 2nd edn, London: Institute of Economic Affairs.

Sundquist, Sven-Ivan (1994), *Exit PG*, Stockholm: Fischer & Co.
Söderström, Hans Tson (ed.) (2003), *Ägarmakt och omvandling. Den svenska ägarmodellen utmanad*, Stockholm: SNS förlag.
Swedish Ministry of Finance (2006), *Ett reformerat system för försäkringsbolag*, September.
Tengblad, S. (2004), 'Expectations of alignment: examining the link between financial markets and managerial work', *Organization Studies*, **25** (4), 583–606.
Teubner, Gunther (2001), 'Legal irritants: unifying law ends up in new divergences', in Peter A. Hall and David Soskice (eds), *Varieties of Capitalism. The Institutional Foundations of Comparative Advantage*, Oxford: Oxford University Press, pp. 417–41.
Tricker, Robert I. (2000), 'The evolution of the company – how the idea has changed', in R.I. Tricker (ed.), *Corporate Governance*, Aldershot, UK and Darlington, USA: Ashgate/Dartmouth, pp. 1–21. Originally published as R.I. Tricker, *Corporate Governance: Practices, Procedures and Powers in British Companies and their Boards of Directors*, Aldershot: Gower, 1984, pp. 25–41, 282–5.
Turnbull, S. (1997), 'Stakeholder governance: a cybernetic and property rights analysis', *Corporate Governance – An International Review*, **5**, 11–23.
Weber, Max (1911–19/78), *Economy and Society: An Outline of Interpretive Sociology*, Berkeley, CA: University of California Press.
Windolf, Paul (2008), 'What is financial-market capitalism?', prepared for Glasshouse Forum.

NEWSPAPER ARTICLES, ANALYSTS' REPORTS AND INTERNET REFERENCES

Adler, J. (2005), 'Budet möter motstånd', *Dagens Industri*, 19 May.
Åkerhjelm, M. (2005), 'Skandia CEO would accept SEK 50 bid from Old Mutual–CNBC', *Dow Jones International News*, 17 November.
Alfvén, R. and F. Gutenbrant (2005), 'Skandia; damned if you do, damned if you don't', *Cheuvreux*, 3 November.
Aktiemarknadsnämnden [Swedish Securities Council] (AMN) (2005), 'Concerning certain conditions of withdrawal of a public offer (Old Mutual/Skandia)', 1 September, p. 33.
Almgren, J. (2005), 'Kritik i Old Mutual mot Skandia-bud', *Svenska Dagbladet*, 17 May.
Almgren, J. (2005), 'Kritik i Old Mutual mot Skandia-bud', *Svenska Dagbladet*, 19 May.

Aktiemarknadsnämnden [Swedish Securities Council] (AMN) (2005), 'Target company measures in public offer (Skandia, bid from Old Mutual)', 6 November, p. 47.

Almgren, J. (2005), 'Kommentar: Försäljningen av Skandia – Tuppfäktningen kring bolaget trappas upp', *Svenska Dagbladet*, 1 September.

Almgren, J. (2005), 'Fidelity trycker på för affär', *Svenska Dagbladet*, 22 September.

Almgren, J. (2005), 'Budet bör dras tillbaka', *Svenska Dagbladet*, 6 October.

Almgren, J. (2005), 'Ny storägare ger sig in i Skandiastriden', *Svenska Dagbladet*, 6 October.

Almgren, J. (2005), 'Paulson ny storägare i Skandia', *Svenska Dagbladet*, 7 October.

Almgren, J. (2005), 'Old Mutual gör eftergift', *Svenska Dagbladet*, 28 October.

Almgren, J. (2005), 'Doldis säger ja till bud på Skandia', *Svenska Dagbladet*, 12 November.

Almgren, J. (2005), 'Old Mutual möter kompakt motstånd', *Svenska Dagbladet*, 16 December.

Almgren, J. (2006), 'Sälj Skandia innan aktien är helt död', *Svenska Dagbladet*, 9 February.

Almgren, J., E. Bergin, A.-K. Storwall and E. Wahlin (2005), 'Styrelsen gick emot storägarna', *Svenska Dagbladet*, 30 August.

Andersson, J. (2005), 'Storägare positiva till Skandiaaffär', TT Nyhetsbanken, 30 August.

Andra AP-fonden (2006), 'Ägarrapport', www.ap2.se/upload/Agarrapport_060907.pdf.

Aronsson, C. (2005), 'Cheferna flyr Skandia', *Dagens Industri*, 1 July.

Aronsson, C. (2005), 'Trolles mål: Kicka Gardell', *Dagens Industri*, 15 November.

Aronsson, C. (2005), 'Trolles mål: Kicka Gardell', di.se, 15 November.

Aronsson, C. and S. Nachemson-Ekwall (2005), 'Utländskt nej till Old Mutual', *Dagens Industri*, 14 October.

Banknytt Online (2005), 'Robur tackar nej till Old Mutuals bud', 4 October.

Berglund, C. (2005), 'Christer Gardell – en playboy', *Veckans Affärer*, 11 April.

Bergström, R. and A. Felsted (2005), 'Old Mutual in talks over Skandia', *Financial Times*, 31 August.

Bergström, R. and H. Tricks (2005), 'Old Mutual launches SKr44.9bn bid for Skandia', *Financial Times*, 2 September.

Bergström, R. and H. Tricks (2005), 'Old Mutual in bid for Skandia', *Financial Times*, 3 September.

Billing, A. (2005), 'Tysk storbank i Skandiaräd', *Veckans Affärer*, 5 December.

Bjäringer, R. (2004), 'Bolagsslaktare in i Skandia', *Dagens Industri*, 14 December.

Blom, N. (2005), 'How low will Old Mutual go in its bid for Skandia?', *Business Day*, 4 October.

Borglund, T. (2005), 'Äntligen, Skandia', *Veckans Affärer*, 12 September.

Business Day (2005), 'Old Mutual's big bid', 7 September.

Carlsson, B. (2004), 'Skandiaaffär i huvudet på Nordeachefen' *Dagens Nyheter*, 29 June.

Carlsson, B. (2004), 'Skandia behöver inga soloåkare', *Dagens Nyheter*, 15 December.

Carlsson, B. (2005), 'Alecta har sålt alla sina Skandiaaktier', *Dagens Nyheter*, 19 March.

Carlsson, B. (2005), '50 kronor per aktie räcker inte', *Dagens Nyheter*, 14 May.

Carlsson, B. (2005), 'Skandia kunde erövrat världen utan stark ägare', *Dagens Nyheter*, 15 May.

Carlsson, B. (2005), 'Old Mutual vill växa med Skandia', *Dagens Nyheter*, 20 May.

Carlsson, B. (2005), 'Kontroversiella siffror i plan för styckat Skandia', *Dagens Nyheter*, 22 May.

Carlsson, B. (2005), 'Skandia klarar sig bra på egen hand, säger Skandiachefen', *Dagens Nyheter*, 11 June.

Carlsson, B. (2005), 'Oväntat svagt intresse för att lägga bud på Skandia', *Dagens Nyheter*, 14 August.

Carlsson, B. (2005), 'Skandia har två val för att rädda kursen', *Dagens Nyheter*, 17 August.

Carlsson, B. (2005), 'Oklart om det blir något bud på Skandia', *Dagens Nyheter*, 21 August.

Carlsson, B. (2005), 'Nu hoppas man att de dåliga nyheterna är bortsopade', *Dagens Nyheter*, 23 August.

Carlsson, B. (2005), 'Aktier som köpeskilling problem i Skandiaaffär', DN.se, 27 August.

Carlsson, B. (2005), 'Oenigt Skandia nobbar OM', DN.se, 28 August.

Carlsson, B. (2005), 'Skandiastyrelsen säger nej till OM', *Dagens Nyheter*, 29 August.

Carlsson, B. (2005), 'Flera storägare stödjer Old Mutual', *Dagens Nyheter*, 31 August.

Carlsson, B. (2005), 'Skandia blir prestigemärket', *Dagens Nyheter*, 2 September.

Carlsson, B. (2005), 'Budet bryter mot regler', *Dagens Nyheter*, 3 September.

Carlsson, B. (2005), 'Old Mutual riskerar skjuta sig själv i foten', *Dagens Nyheter*, 4 September.

Carlsson, B. (2005), 'Skandias styrelse fortfarande oenig till OM:s bud', *Dagens Nyheter*, 9 September.

Carlsson, B. (2005), 'Skandiastyrelsen ger inte klart besked om OM', *Dagens Nyheter*, 11 September.

Carlsson, B. (2005), 'Skandiabudet döms ut', *Dagens Nyheter*, 15 September.

Carlsson, B. (2005), 'Skandias styrelse enhälligt för "turboplanen"', *Dagens Nyheter*, 16 September.

Carlsson, B. (2005), 'Propagandakriget ännu en sida av Skandia', *Dagens Nyheter*, 18 September.

Carlsson, B. (2005), 'Detta är ett fientligt bud', *Dagens Nyheter*, 24 September.

Carlsson, B. (2005), 'Old Mutual fixar och trixar', *Dagens Industri*, 2 December.

Carlsson, B. and S. Nachemson-Ekwall (2005), 'Utlänningar sågar Old Mutuals bud', *Dagens Industri*, 16 November.

Carlsson, B. (2005), 'Skandia Liv vill kasta loss från moderbolaget', *Dagens Industri*, 10 December.

Carlsson, B. and S. Nachemson-Ekwall (2005), 'Michael Wolf kan bli ny Skandia-VD', *Dagens Industri*, 21 December.

Cathcart, M. and H. Spencer (2004), 'Skandia Forsakring. Q2 preview', Deutsche Bank, 10 August.

Cathcart, M. and H. Spencer (2004), 'Skandia Forsakring. Friday the 13th', Deutsche Bank, 13 August.

Coggan, P. (2003), 'The gin rummy school of management: Old story for Old Mutual', *Financial Times*, 28 October.

Connon, H. (2005), 'Old Mutual's risky Swedish connection', *The Observer*, 4 September.

Dagens Industri (2004), 'Miljardär går in i Skandia', 14 December.

Dagens Industri (2005), 'Skandia Livs ordförande är alltför godtrogen', comment signed by representatives of Grupptalan mot Skandia, 2 November.

Dagens Nyheter (2006), 'Andra AP-fonden lämnar Skandia', 9 February.

De Toytot A. (2003) 'Capital Adequacy at European Bancassurers: The Need to Look Beyond Regulatory Ratios', Standard & Poor's, 23 July.

Derby, R. (2005), 'In Brief – Company News', *Business Day*, 13 October.

Direkt (2004), 'Skandia: Merrill Lynch sänker rek till neutral', 10 September.
Direkt (2004), 'Skandia: Gardells Cevian storägare, vill in i styrelsen – *DI*', 13 December.
Dn.se (2005), 'Old Mutual: Majoritet för budet', 8 December.
Eklöv, B. (2005), 'Grupptalan målar en skräckbild', *Dagens Industri*, 29 October.
Eklöv, B. (2005), 'Brännpunkt', *Svenska Dagbladet*, 15 November.
Engzell-Larsson, L. '10 Frågor: 'Risk för negativa synergier', *Affärsvärlden*, 23 November.
Felsted, A. and R. Bergström (2005), 'Fidelity supports 3.3bn Old Mutual offer for Skandia', *Financial Times*, 6 September.
Felsted, A. and R. Bergström (2005), 'Old Mutual wins control of Skandia', *Financial Times*, 20 December.
Financial Times (2005), 'LEX COLUMN: Old Mutual/Skandia', 14 May.
Financial Times (2005), 'Lex: Skandia/Old Mutual', 30 August.
Finansdepartementet (2006), 'Ett reformerat solvenssystem för försäkringsbolag', Remissvar, available at www.sfs.se.
Forsberg, B. (2006), 'SKANDIA: räden blev en jackpot', *Veckans Affärer*, 31 January.
Forsgårdh, L.-E. (2005), 'Rädda Skandia från spekulanterna', *Svenska Dagbladet*, 2 September.
Frick, L. (2005), 'Splittrad styrelse – aktieägarna ska inte lita på turboplanen', *Svenska Dagbladet*, 24 September.
George, N. (2004), 'Icahn-backed fund builds up Skandia stake', *Financial Times*, 14 December.
Gohil, H. (2005), 'Old Mutual plc, Old Mutual Life (South Africa)', Fitch Ratings, 11 October.
Goksör, J. (2005), 'Ägarstriden i Skandia hettar till', TT Nyhetsbanken, 23 September.
Gripenberg, P. and D. Lucas (2004), 'Skandias ordförande öppen för försäljning', *Dagens Nyheter*, 2 December.
Gripenberg, P. and O. Sandström (2005), 'Old Mutual kritiseras av Skandiaägare', *Dagens Nyheter*, 28 June.
Gunnion, S. (2005), 'Old Mutual targets Swedish assurer Skandia', *Business Day*, 16 May.
Gunnion, S. (2005), 'Old Mutual woos shareholders to put Skandia purchase in motion', *Business Day*, 5 September.
Gunnion, S. (2005), 'Old Mutual chiefs take merger case to Skandia board', *Business Day*, 12 September.
Gunnion, S. (2005), 'Shareholders vote on Old Mutual green light for Skandia', *Business Day*, 14 November.

Gunnion, S. (2005), 'Results boost Skandia's spirits', *Business Day*, 16 November.
Hallåker, M. (2005), 'Skandia; Wait out Old Mutual's bid', Handelsbanken, 5 September.
Hammarström, M. (2005), 'Skandiachefen hoppas på snar strukturaffär', *Dagens Industri*, 1 June.
Hård, M. (2005), 'Skandia: Aktiespararna avvisar bud, avgå Gardell & Co', Nyhetsbyrån Ticker, 23 September.
Hård, M. (2005), 'Skandia: SHB Fonder tackar nej till budet från Old Mutual', Nyhetsbyrån Ticker, 5 October.
Hård, M. (2005), 'Skandia: Noonday ökar till 5,0% av kapitalet', Nyhetsbyrån Ticker, 28 December.
Hariharan, R. (2007), 'Old Mutual: Hoping for clean numbers', Fox-Pitt, Kelton, 23 February.
Haskel, A. (2005), 'Skandia säljs för billigt', *Veckans Affärer*, 12 September.
Haskel, A. (2005), 'Ge Skandia en chans', *Veckans Affärer*, 14 September.
Hedlund, M. (2005), 'Skandia kan vara sålt innan nyår', DN.se, 15 November.
Hellbom, O. (2005), 'Kamp om Skandia – på ministernivå', *Dagens Industri*, 16 September.
Hocking J. (2007), 'Insurance, wraps: The Insurers' Last Stand in the Savings Market?', Morgan Stanley, 17 January.
Huldschiner, H. and G. Larsson (2005), 'Näringslivet sågar försäljning', di.se, 30 August.
Huldschiner, H. (2005), 'De vill att Skandia förblir svenskt', *Dagens Industri*, 3 September.
Hunnissett, S. (2006), 'Analysis Old Mutual Plc', Moody's, October.
Isacsson, T. 2004, 'Trögstartad riskkapitalist har fått upp farten', *Dagens Industri*, 14 December.
Jonsson, J. and S. Nachemson-Ekwall (2005), 'Ställningskrig i Skandia', *Dagens Industri*, 15 November.
Ketola, R., O. Steel and V. Chapplan (2006), 'A simple puzzle; Life insurance', Deutsche Securities, January.
Lambridis, J. (2005), 'Old Mutual; Skandia Negotiations Drawing to a Close', Citigroup, 31 August.
Lambridis, J. (2006), 'Old Mutual; Skandia has Added Sales but Also Goodwill', Citigroup, 8 May.
Lambridis, J. (2006), 'Skandia; End of the Road', Citigroup, 9 February.
Larsson, G. (2005), 'Volvos trotjänare går efter 39 händelserika år', *Dagens Industri*, 17 June.

Lucas, D. and P. Gripenberg (2005), 'Old Mutual går vidare. Accepterar mindre än 90 procent av aktierna', *Dagens Nyheter*, 13 October.

Lundell, S. (2005), 'Gardell på ny pengajakt', *Dagens Industri*, 16 November.

Lundin, K. (2005), 'Vi tittar på Skandia', *Dagens Industri*, 31 May.

McCarney, J. (2005), 'Ideology and False Consciousness', www.Marxmyths.org/joseph-mccarney/article.htm.

McNulty, A. and R. Hill (2005), 'Old Mutual Plc; The Skandia Offer', UBS, 5 September.

McNulty, A. (2005), 'Old Mutual; A fair valuation for the combined group', UBS, 21 September.

Munter, P. (2005), 'Bid for Skandia meets emotive response', *Financial Times*, 19 September.

Nachemson-Ekwall, S. (2004), 'Skandias framtid – Vilken väg tar Skandia?', *Affärsvärlden*, 21 April.

Nachemson-Ekwall, S. (2005), 'Fokus: Carl Icahn – Ikonen Icahn', *Affärsvärlden*, 1 June.

Nachemson-Ekwall, S. (2005) 'Skandia-ledningen vill växa vidare själva', www.afv.se, 27 June.

Nachemson-Ekwall, S. (2005), 'Tveksamheter i budet från Old Mutual', *Dagens Industri*, 5 September.

Nachemson-Ekwall, S. (2005), 'Skandiaägare beredd att avstå kontanter', *Dagens Industri*, 5 September.

Nachemson-Ekwall, S. (2005), 'Budprocessen stinker', *Dagens Industri*, 9 September.

Nachemson-Ekwall, S. (2005), 'Nej-sägare i Skandia står fast', *Dagens Industri*, 12 September.

Nachemson-Ekwall, S. (2005), '. . . och ledningens trovärdighet analyseras', *Dagens Industri*, 13 September.

Nachemson-Ekwall, S. (2005), 'De kan rädda Skandia', *Dagens Industri*, 14 September.

Nachemson-Ekwall, S. (2005), 'Skandias VD träder fram', *Dagens Industri*, 16 September.

Nachemson-Ekwall, S. (2005), 'Skandias öde i hans händer', *Dagens Industri*, 20 September.

Nachemson-Ekwall, S. (2005), 'Svälta räv-spelet har just börjat', *Dagens Industri*, 24 September.

Nachemson-Ekwall, S. (2005), 'Han vill samla nej-sägarna', *Dagens Industri*, 8 October.

Nachemson-Ekwall, S. (2005), 'Han vill samla nej-sägarna', *Dagens Industri*, 10 October.

Nachemson-Ekwall, S. (2005), 'Gardell under hård press', *Dagens Industri*, 11 October.
Nachemson-Ekwall, S. (2005), 'AP-fond: 'Det är dags att dra sig ur', *Dagens Industri*, 12 October.
Nachemson-Ekwall, S. (2005), 'Old Mutuals vd lovar hårda tag', *Dagens Industri*, 2 December.
Nachemson-Ekwall, S. (2005), 'Marknaden tror på seger för Old Mutual', *Dagens Industri*, 9 December.
Nachemson-Ekwall, S. (2006), 'Han står bakom Gardell', *Dagens Industri*, 4 February.
Nachemson-Ekwall, S. and K. Svensson (2005), 'Skandiaägare byter sida inför slutstriden', *Dagens Industri*, 1 October.
Nachemson-Ekwall S. and J. Wäingelin (2005), 'Skandia nobbar Old Mutual', *Dagens Industri*, 23 September
Nachemson-Ekwall, S. and J. Wäingelin (2005), 'Skandia nobbar Old Mutual', di.se, 23 September.
Nachemson-Ekwall, S. and J. Wäingelin (2005), 'Striden är över', *Dagens Industri*, 8 December.
Nachemson-Ekwall, S. and J. Wäingelin (2005), 'Hemliga samtal kring Skandia', *Dagens Industri*, 20 December.
Näringslivets börskommitté (2005), 'Stockholmsbörsens Takeover regler'.
Öhlin, H. (2005), 'Skandia: Andra AP-fonden säger nej till Old Mutuals bud', Nyhetsbyrån Ticker, 23 September.
Öhrn, L. (2005), 'Hälften nog för Sutcliffe', *Dagens Industri*, 13 October.
Old Mutual, *Annual reports* 1999–2007, press releases.
Olsson, A. (2005), 'Starkt framåt för Skandia som håller tyst om friare', *Dagens Nyheter*, 1 June.
Paterson, G. and W. Hawkins (2005), 'Old Mutual's talks with Skandia: beginning the end game?', Keefe, Bruyette & Woods, 13 May.
Paulsson, L. (2005), 'Burdarás näst störst i Skandia', *Dagens Industri*, 18 May.
Reed, J. (2005), 'Skandia grills Old Mutual on Zimbabwe holdings', *Financial Times*, 5 September.
Rose, R. (2005), 'Old Mutual's offer for Skandia hits new hitch'. *Business Day*, 4 October.
Rose, R. (2005), 'Stery shareholder boosts Old Mutual bid', *Business Day*, 7 October.
Saigol, L. and R. Bergström (2005), 'Old Mutual confirms it is in talks to buy Skandia', *Financial Times*, 14 May.
Saigol, L. and A. Felsted (2005), 'Old Mutual in talks over Skandia', *Financial Times*, 12 May.

Saigol, L. and A. Felsted (2005), 'Suitors circle Skandia in hope of a break-up', *Financial Times*, 25 May.

Salmon, M. (2005), 'Old Mutual; A hope. A skip and a jump too far', Investec, 27 October.

Salmon, M. (2006), 'Looking to Skandia for growth', Investec, 13 April.

Shah, M. and J. Vo (2005), 'Old Mutual; Reinitiation of coverage: Dropping Anchor', Fox-Pitt, Kelton, 31 August.

Shah, M. and J. Vo (2005), 'Old Mutual: Full Steam ahead', Fox-Pitt, Kelton, 5 September.

Shah, M. and J. Vo (2005), 'Old Mutual; Skandia discloses stand-alone business plan', Fox-Pitt, Kelton, 15 September.

Shah, M. and J. Vo (2006), 'Unattractive prospect for Skandia minorities', Fox-Pitt, Kelton, 6 February.

Sigma (2003), 'Unit-Linked Life Insurance in Western Europe; regaining momentum', Swiss Re, no. 3.

SIS Ägarservice, 'Skandia ownership 2001–2006'.

Sjöshult, F. (2004), 'Bernt Magnusson tvekade länge innan han bestämde sig', *Dagens Industri*, 17 March.

Sjöström, C. (2004), 'Ny storägare tror på Skandia', *Tidningarnas Telegrambyrå*, 14 December.

Skandia, *Annual reports* 1999–2006, press releases.

Spikes, S. (2005), 'UPDATE: Old Mutual Cuts Skandia Acceptance Level', Dow Jones Newswires, 1 December.

Spikes, S. and L. Nordstrom (2006), 'Old Mutual–Skandia Deal Shows Hedge Fund Role', Dow Jones, 8 March.

Statistics Sweden (2008), 'Ownership of shares in companies quoted on Swedish exchanges', 28 August.

Strydom, M. (2005), 'Old Mutual Ltd; Vote No to Preserve Capital', Barnard Jacobs Mellet, 14 October.

Sundewall, C. (2000), 'Vi abdikerar inte från ägaransvaret', *Finanstidningen*, 12 December.

Sundström, A. (2005) 'Sälja ut Skandia skadar Sverige', *Dagens Industri*, 16 September.

Svensson, K. (2005), 'Spekulanter i huggsexa om Skandia', *Dagens Industri*, 4 May.

Svensson, K. (2005), 'Skandia är en fantastisk möjlighet', *Dagen Industri*, 17 May,

Svensson, K. (2005), 'Men Österberg oroar sig för AP-fonderna', *Dagens Industri*, 16 June.

Svensson, K. (2005), 'Ny spekulant redo ta upp kampen', *Dagens Industri*, 28 June.

Svensson, K. (2005), 'Robur säljer efter Skandias uppgång', *Dagens Industri*, 21 June.
Svensson, K. (2005), 'Han hoppas på snåla livbolag', *Dagens Industri*, 29 June.
Svensson, K. (2005), 'Total splittring i Skandia', *Dagens Industri*, 16 September.
Svensson, K. (2005), 'Skandias ägare oroade' *Dagens Industri*, 17 September.
Svensson, K. and J. Wäingelin (2005), 'Magnusson: Det finns många friare', *Dagens Industri*, 14 May (published on the web on 13 May).
Svensson, K. and J. Wäingelin (2005), 'Skärpning, Skandia', di.se, 30 August.
Syversen, E.B. and S. Håland (2005), 'Skandia; Old Mutuals flirt just the beginning?', ABG Sundal Collier, 16 May.
Tapper, G. (2004), 'Gardells hemliga plan för Skandia', *Dagens Industri*, 27 December.
Tapper, G. (2005), 'Han beställde ny analys', *Dagens Industri*, 15 September.
Tapper, G. (2006), 'Ingen tycker att Skandia är fint', *Dagens Industri*, 22 February.
TT Nyhetsbanken (2005), 'Ny storägare seglar upp i Skandia', 2 December.
Wahlin, E. (2005), 'Utlandsägandet ökar i Skandia', *Svenska Dagbladet*, 11 October.
Wäingelin, J. (2004), 'Det är fel att gå i pension vid 60 år', *Dagens Industri*, 9 July.
Wäingelin, J. (2005), 'Old Mutual mål: Bud före midsommar', *Dagens Industri*, 17 May.
Wäingelin, J. (2005), 'Inget tvingar oss till strukturåtgärder', *Dagens Industri*, 9 July.
Wäingelin. J. (2006), 'Stålmannens sista dag på jobbet', *Dagens Industri*, 22 April.
Wall Street Journal (2004), 13 December (European edition).
Wall Street Journal (2004), 14 December (European edition).
Wallén, M. (2005), 'De utmanar Skandia', *Dagens Industri*, 28 October.
Westin, H. (2003), 'Industrivärdens fiasko', *Dagens Industri*, 24 October.
Williams T. (2006), 'Principles of Ownership', Fidelity, September.

Name index

Ackerman, Josef 254
Agnew, James 148, 153, 177, 178, 181, 310, 319
Alfvén, Rodney 189
Almgren, Jan 240–41
Andersson, Anne 272, 282
Andersson, Hans-Erik 48–9, 67, 84, 91–4, 103, 107–8, 110, 114–16, 118–21, 123–4, 127–9, 130, 132–3, 135, 138, 140–43, 153–4, 160, 162–6, 168, 170–71, 179–82, 185–6, 192, 196–8, 208, 215, 217, 221–2, 230–32, 236, 244, 246, 254, 263–6, 275, 278–9, 286, 289, 290–91, 300–302, 304–6, 312–15, 322, 350, 353, 364, 368

Back, Jan-Erik 81, 92, 118, 127, 132, 179, 192, 208–9, 217, 266, 300, 322
Bane, Lars 145, 283, 302, 319
Bell, Katie 270
Bennet, Carl 249
Bexhed, Jan-Mikael 109, 127, 134, 173, 208, 252, 255, 322
Björgólfsson, Thor 171, 178, 321
Björnsson, Björn 49, 80–81, 83–5, 92–5, 97, 99–101, 105, 107, 109–10, 113–15, 117, 119, 121, 126–7, 130, 134, 137, 141–2, 161, 163–4, 166, 168, 170, 172–5, 177–9, 181, 186, 190, 197, 203–6, 208, 214, 217, 219–20, 222–3, 234, 236, 252, 255, 265–6, 272, 282, 289, 297–8, 319, 321, 340, 366–7, 386–7
Borglund, Tommy 256–7
Bradshaw, Paul 68–70, 151
Braun, Bengt 74, 80–85, 91–2, 119, 321
Brufer, Ramsey 94, 102, 110
Buffet, Warren 152
Burgess, Tony 121, 153, 177, 181, 217, 218
By, Carl-Olof 94

Capon, Frank 68
Carendi, Jan 58–9, 62, 67, 69–72, 115, 145, 153, 211
Carlsson, Bengt 144, 188, 191, 216, 235, 249, 254–5, 357
Cohen, Stewart 68
Collins, Christopher 295, 299, 307
Cranston, David 121

Dalborg, Hans 97, 108
D'Almeida, Eduardo 256
Deane, John 152–3, 161, 177, 181, 209
Dockered, Bo 98, 261–2
Douglas, Gustaf 239, 249
Duverne, Denis 130, 210

Ehrnrooth, Casimir 96, 104
Eiken, Odd 65
Eklöf, Bo 94–5, 104, 119, 134, 296–7
Engman, Gert 129, 132–5, 163, 208–9, 230, 254, 297, 322

Förberg, Lars 137, 139, 171, 175, 178, 237, 239, 289, 319, 339
Forsgårdh, Lars-Erik 76, 80, 92, 109, 174–5, 228–9, 239, 241, 253, 260, 275, 300, 308, 369

Gardell, Christer 48–9, 104, 106, 136–9, 143–6, 159–61, 171, 173–82, 185–6, 191, 193, 196, 203–4, 206–7, 216, 219–23, 233–4, 236, 241, 247, 252, 254–5, 262, 265, 272, 276, 278, 280–83, 285, 293, 298–9, 301, 304, 306–8, 321–2, 324, 339–40, 347, 356–7, 359, 364, 370, 373, 378

Garren, Mia 272, 282
Gibbs, Philip 189
Greenspan, Alan 303
Grefbäck, Staffan 106, 109
Grinbaum, Jacob 130, 201, 254
Gupta, Ashok 121, 192, 264
Gyllenhammar, Pehr G. 55, 58, 66, 98

Hagströmer, Sven 75, 136
Håland, Sigmund 195
Halvorsen, Thomas 222, 227–30, 239–40, 254, 271, 278, 295–6, 312, 315, 385
Hamilton, Greger 278, 306
Hammarkvist, Karl-Olof 49, 94, 97, 99, 101, 108, 110, 132, 142–3, 164, 170, 176, 178, 179, 193, 195, 197, 204, 220, 229, 232–3, 238, 245, 272, 362
Hardwick, Steve 132, 231
Haskel, Anders 204, 252, 255, 257
Heliövaara, Eero 77, 94, 104
Hillström, Per 122, 161, 164, 214, 289
Hogarth, Paul 119, 121, 180

Icahn, Carl 106, 137, 139–40, 144, 146, 340
Idermark, Lars 49, 95–6, 130–31, 139, 161, 172, 242–3, 260–61, 275, 285, 345
Isacsson, Torbjörn 144

Jeansson, Lennart 49, 94, 96–8, 104, 110, 164, 166, 176, 178, 181, 187, 190, 193, 195–7, 204, 206, 208, 216–18, 220–22, 232–7, 252, 254, 261, 271–3, 276, 282–3, 285, 290–91, 295–6, 299, 300, 302–3, 306, 312, 315–16, 318–19, 341–2, 350–52, 359, 363–4, 366, 376
Johansson, Fridrik 190, 240
Johansson-Hedberg, Birgitta 94, 98, 112–13, 164, 165, 170, 181, 196, 220, 229, 233, 238, 261
Johnson, Göran 228–9
Jonsson, Anders 261
Josefsson, Märtha 261–2
Jungkvist, Per 122, 165, 169, 177, 186, 204, 208, 212, 217, 231–2

Kudjoe, Sonto 277

Lambridis, Johny 189, 194, 251
Larsson, Gunnar 96, 261–2, 271, 276, 285, 295, 321
Lenkel, Göran 124
Lenner, Lars 45, 49, 165–6, 176, 180, 205, 221, 223, 239, 241–3, 310, 319, 321
Lilja, Maria 94, 104
Liljedahl, Arne 209, 254
Lind, Björn 49, 94, 96, 102, 110, 113, 130–31, 138, 161, 172, 202, 207, 215, 220, 231, 236–7, 239, 243, 303, 314, 345
Lindquist, Jakob 122, 161, 198, 201, 203, 219, 231, 264
Lindståhl, Kajsa 49, 96–7, 99, 110, 112–14, 164, 166, 170, 178, 193, 195, 197, 220, 229, 234, 238, 245, 252, 272, 314, 366–7
Lindvall, Karl Gunnar 131, 161
Löfqvist, Per 94, 161
Lundberg, Fredrik 296, 308
Lundin, Ingolf 272

Macleod, Jamie 121
Magnusson, Bernt 48–9, 96, 100–103, 105–6, 108–16, 122–7, 130–31, 137–43, 146, 153–4, 159, 161–8, 170, 172–82, 186–8, 190–93, 195–7, 202–3, 205–8, 215, 217–19, 220–23, 231–8, 241, 252, 255, 265, 272–3, 275, 277, 282–3, 293, 336, 340, 342, 347, 351–3, 356, 363, 366–8, 372, 387
Mann, Tim 129
Marthin, Tor 77–9, 83, 88
McDonald, Oonagh 77
McNulty, Andrew 190
Mesdag, Willem T. 77
Milberg, Lars 85, 257
Mpahwla, Mandisi 267
Munck, Johan 248
Munter, Päivi 258

Neiglick, Olof 131, 161
Nicolin, Thomas 104, 173, 178
Nilsson, Marianne 174, 204, 222, 236, 278, 316

Nordh, Gunnar 187, 231
Nordström, Lars G. 124, 191
Norman, Peter 315
Nuder, Per 229
Nyrén, Anders 80, 138

Öberg, Lars 94, 134
Odhnoff, Petter 205, 236, 239, 242–3, 260–61, 276, 291, 296, 299, 304, 306, 315–16, 319–21
Ohlsson, Robert 187, 196, 266
Oliw, Martin 138–9, 145
Olsson, Dan Sten 104, 296
Olsson, Jan 130, 153, 167, 176–7, 181, 205, 253–4
Österberg, Sven-Erik 229, 260, 262, 276–8
Östros, Thomas 267
Otterbeck, Lars 95, 104, 106, 296, 321, 324

Paterson, Greig 176, 190, 197
Paulson, John 281, 283, 303, 339
Pellegrini, Paulo 145, 281, 303, 316 17
Pereira, Paulo 170, 196, 231–2
Persson, Eva 261
Persson, Göran 267
Petersson, Lars-Eric 59, 60, 62–3, 65, 66, 71–2, 77, 80, 82–3, 85, 87–8, 91, 93, 111, 145, 160, 174
Phillips, Roger 121
Poole, James 185, 190–91, 270
Poyntz-Wright, Nick 118, 121–2, 125, 132, 179, 209, 264–6, 322
Purcell, Tom 128, 145

Qviberg, Mats 75, 136

Rafter, John 278, 306
Ramqvist, Lars 55, 65–7, 77–80, 104, 108, 111, 114, 160, 170, 172–4, 178
Ramstedt, Ola 65, 111
Reuterskiöld, Clas 78–81, 174
Rexrodt, Günter 77
Riegnell, Göran 185
Roberts, Jim 69, 121
Roberts, Julian 149, 152–3, 181, 185, 191, 205–6, 217, 244, 251, 269, 281, 283, 307, 311, 317, 320, 322–3, 325, 337
Rosén, Carl 49, 205, 271, 315–17, 321
Rudman, Peter 316, 320
Ruhle, Jennifer 129, 132, 322
Rydbeck, Otto 67, 84, 92, 111, 113, 160, 177
Rydén, Bengt 249, 387

Salmon, Mark 291–2
Sandberg, Alex 256, 271–2, 278
Sandeberg, William af 275, 315–16
Schörling, Melker 77, 292
Shear, Errol 256
Sheik al-Ahmoudi 182
Söderberg, Sven 55, 77, 85, 114
Spång, Ulf 60, 63–5, 71–2, 79, 111, 133
Spetz, Joachim 239, 315
Stadigh, Kari 82, 84, 138
Steward, Chris 251, 363
Stirling, Euan 189
Storch, Marcus 96, 366
Sullman, Mike 68
Sundén, Lennart 103
Sundström, Anders 257, 266
Sutcliffe, Jim 149, 150–51, 153–4, 161, 166–8, 176, 180, 181–2, 185–6, 189, 201, 205–6, 217–18, 221, 229, 237–9, 241–4, 249, 250–52, 254–5, 257, 269, 276, 278–9, 281, 283, 286, 288, 295, 297, 299, 302, 306–7, 310–11, 314–17, 320–23, 337, 351
Syversen, Espen Bruu 195

Taxell, Christopher 94, 104
Taylor, Simon 72, 119, 180
Thórisson, Ragnar 171
Tidström, Göran 84
du Toit, Hendrik 189

Ullberg, Anders 49, 96–7, 99, 105, 110, 126, 164, 166, 176, 178, 181, 193, 195–7, 206, 220, 232, 234, 238, 252, 272

Victorin, Leif 80–83, 91
Vos, Harry 171, 208, 300

Wahlroos, Björn 82–4, 88, 94, 96, 138, 182

Webster, Mark 189
Williams, Trelawny 49, 173, 206–7, 315
Wilson, Alan 68, 70–73, 81–2, 109, 118–19, 121–2, 125, 134
Wolf, Michael 81, 92–3, 129, 163, 230, 322
Wolrath, Björn 57, 59, 69, 70, 71, 74, 77–8, 99, 205

Subject index

Abbey Life 57, 68, 73
Abbey National 183
ABG Sundal 130, 195, 200
ABN Amro 81, 84, 191, 206, 264, 274, 300
Abu Dhabi Invest 314
acquisition (*see also* merger and takeover)
  of Bankhall *see* Bankhall
  path 372
  strategy 176
actor (*see also* the Name index)
  alliance 13, 229
  ambition 15, 21, 29, 50, 77, 92, 118, 127, 136, 138, 144, 148, 153, 164, 173, 185, 189, 192, 222, 241, 249, 331, 335–7, 346–7, 351–2, 366
  coalition 14, 40, 75, 330, 333–4, 337–8, 344, 347, 349, 358, 371–3, 374
  cognition 11–12
  dependency 13
  discretion 15, 21, 25, 30, 373–4
  emotions 11–12
  intention 11, 40, 46, 144, 161, 163, 202, 205, 210, 215, 232, 297, 312, 314, 319, 339–40, 362, 369, 380, 384–5
  intuition 11–12
  Janusian rationale 336
  judgement 11–14, 19, 352, 356, 361, 363, 368, 371
  limited liability of 14
  mixed rationale of 336
  multi-rational 12, 14, 31, 330, 380–81
  network 30, 45, 63, 71, 100, 249, 330, 333, 335, 358, 360, 369, 372–3, 375, 390
  rationale *see* rationale and rationality
  speculative 16, 43, 346, 373, 382–3
  toolkit 30, 46, 137, 375–6, 381, 383
  track record of 149, 180, 229, 304, 339, 366
activist
  rationality of 23, 136, 143–5, 159, 180, 302, 340–42, 344, 359, 370, 374, 380
adviser
  agreement 122, 161, 164–5, 289
  financial (*see also* relevant juridical persons) 204–5
  independent *see* Bankhall and IFA
  investment bank/bank (*see also* relevant juridical persons) 122, 132
  legal 8, 231
  public relation/PR (*see also* relevant juridical persons)
  role of 45, 144, 330, 337, 349, 354–5, 363, 367–8, 373, 376, 383
Aegon 43, 200
aesthetics 12
AFS business 357
AGA 79, 96
agency
  of AGM 365
  of board 77, 365, 373
  corporate 29–30, 46, 361, 365
  cost 6
  of executives 14, 45, 47, 334, 351–2, 362–3
  of nomination committee 365, 369–70
  theory 17
  toolkit for 376
Aktiefrämjandet 99
Albert E. Sharp 148
Alecta 80, 84, 94–5, 110, 172–4, 296, 321, 332, 366
Alfa-Laval 101

Alfred Berg 81, 165
Alliance & Leicester 148
Allianz 42–3, 145, 167, 203, 209
Amaranth 137, 143
ambiguity *see* uncertainty
American Fidelity 242
American Life 150
American Skandia 55, 58–9, 61–6, 68, 70–73, 78–9, 82, 109, 111, 138, 162, 174, 216
AMF/AMF Pension 75, 77, 82–3
Amnesty Business Group 99
analyst (*see also* relevant juridical persons and the Name index) 5, 19, 41, 44, 60–61, 99, 107–8, 116, 126–30, 134, 138, 145, 150–54, 162, 171–2, 176, 182, 184, 189–90, 195–8, 209, 214, 221, 244, 247, 251, 257, 260, 262, 265, 271, 276, 291, 311, 317, 323, 346, 351, 355–8, 390, 392
Anglo American 59, 147
Anglo-Saxon model/tradition 3, 4, 25–6, 28–30, 44, 46, 185, 331, 362, 365, 370, 375, 382
annual general meeting (AGM)
  British model of 28, 383
  general function of 28
  Swedish model of 28, 332, 361, 365, 369–70, 383
Aon UK Holdings 149
AP funds 228–9, 260–63, 276, 295–6, 319, 321, 338, 344
AP1 95, 137, 220–21, 223, 257, 262, 275–6, 285, 298, 315–16, 321, 340
AP2 45, 49, 95–6, 99, 130–31, 137, 139, 161, 172, 174–5, 181, 205, 207, 220–21, 223, 230, 236, 239, 242–3, 257, 260–62, 271, 275–7, 284–5, 287, 289, 291, 295, 298–9, 303–4, 306, 307, 313–17, 319, 321, 338, 340, 344–5, 349, 357, 366, 377
AP4 45, 49, 95, 97–9, 172, 220–23, 227–30, 236, 239–40, 254, 262, 271, 275–8, 295–6, 299, 312, 315–16, 338, 344, 348–9
AP6 98, 261
AP7 298, 307, 315
arbitrage
  deals 251, 311–12, 333, 350
  moral 30, 380, 383
  position/opportunity 23–4, 183, 342
  rule 30, 374
arena (for action)
  globalized 26, 381
  invisible (informal) 46, 330, 344, 353–4, 361
  visible (formal) 5–6, 16, 24, 30, 41, 45, 56, 136, 330, 344–6, 353–4, 361, 375, 379
Assa Abloy 239
asset(s)
  allocation of 19, 151
  bundle of (*see also* corporation) 17, 346
  contract 130
  manager 96–7, 99, 109, 256, 261
  management of 56, 61, 63–4, 79, 82, 111, 147–50, 152, 231, 262, 285, 317
  pools of 22
  price/pricing of 5, 30, 41
  return on 17
  underlying 4, 60
  value of 134
AssiDomän 100–103, 137, 139
Avesta 101
Avivia 42–3
AXA 42–3, 123, 130, 188, 200, 203, 209–10, 216, 219, 279, 355

Banco Funds 99
Banco Santander 183
Bankhall 63, 65, 71–2, 118–19, 125, 132, 162, 172, 180, 192, 200
Barclays Bank 151
Barloworld 147
bet/betting
  financial 61, 305, 311, 315, 345, 350, 384
bid
  acceptance of 201, 233, 300, 340, 364
  acceptance rate 244, 276–7, 273, 286–7, 300, 310–12, 322, 339, 355, 376, 379
  auction 51, 186, 197–8, 200–201, 203, 206–7, 215, 227, 229, 295, 352, 355, 365

hostile 3, 6–9, 29, 51, 74, 101, 136, 168, 235, 248–51, 269–80, 283, 286, 288, 304, 329, 331–2, 334, 337, 343–4, 362, 365, 376–7, 383
indicative 51, 177, 179–203, 363
level ('hurdle') 233, 244, 273, 276–7, 282–3, 286–7, 299–300, 306, 310–13, 317, 339, 349, 376
period 304, 306, 320, 322, 376
premium 74, 84, 185, 196, 219, 240, 272, 274, 290, 316, 342, 355
proposal 51, 130, 161, 164–5, 169, 177, 181, 185, 190–91, 198, 201–2, 215, 227, 240–41, 273–4, 290, 337, 362, 368
prospectus 276, 283–4, 286–90, 307, 378–9
recommendation of 51, 185, 190, 206, 219–21, 234–8, 242, 244–5, 270, 272–5, 278, 285, 287, 289–90, 300, 306, 316, 321, 337, 362–4, 371, 377, 379
withdrawal 311, 349
bidder (*see also* relevant juridical persons)
actual 29, 200–203, 208–10, 214–17, 265–6, 289, 330, 352, 355, 362, 378–9
potential 154, 166–7, 186, 188, 193, 196–8, 200–203, 265–6, 330, 352, 368
Billerud 100
Bloomberg 305
'blue chip' 229, 260, 348
board
as 'caretaker unit' 352
chair function *see* chair
composition 6, 23, 74–8, 96–103, 131, 175, 288, 315, 330, 333, 339, 362, 366, 383
fiduciary duty of 17, 136
functioning of 29, 166, 170, 175, 361–74
information policy 367
information situation 363
marginalization of 371
meeting
formal 71, 84, 94, 113–14, 118, 121–2, 124–7, 129–30, 143, 159–66, 168–70, 181, 187, 192, 196, 202–4, 206, 214–16, 219–21, 230–31, 235, 255, 264, 272, 282, 310, 312, 314, 352, 360, 373
informal 298, 368
'pseudo' 363
recommendation *see* bid recommendation
recruitment 27
reservation 274, 367, 379
sidestepping of 363, 380
Swedish *vs* UK regulations 6, 26–7, 29–30, 46, 331, 341, 361–4, 374–8, 380–81, 385
team quality of 100–101, 166, 366–7
Bonniers 74, 80
bonus programme 5, 55, 61–2, 68, 70, 77–88, 80, 84, 86, 92, 97, 109, 111, 133, 160, 365, 382
British Panel of Takeovers and Mergers 148
Brunswick 45, 270, 286
Burdarás 171, 173–4, 181, 190, 207, 221, 223, 230, 240, 243, 251, 277, 282, 289, 296, 313, 321–2, 338, 344
Bure Equity 100
business structure
sustainable 15, 335, 341, 371

Cadbury Report 76
CAI Cheuvreux Nordic 189
Capel Cure Myers 148
Capel Cure Sharp 148
capital market
deregulation of 27, 40
effective 17
global 16
transformation of 9
Capital Z 137
capitalism
entrepreneurial 19–20
financial 3–9, 16, 19–20, 22–4, 26–7, 30–31, 40, 86, 136, 329–32, 335, 338, 343–4, 358, 360, 371, 373, 381–2, 384
heirloom 20
industrial 7–9, 19–20, 23, 27, 336, 359–60, 368, 375, 382, 384
many kinds of 19–20
Carl Icahn Co. Investment 140

Carnegie 74
cash flow 41, 61–3, 66, 70, 82–3, 116–20, 122–3, 133, 169, 232, 239–41, 244, 255, 274–6, 299, 354
CEO/chief executive officer (*see also* the Name index)
  change of 333, 336, 365, 368
  position/role 7, 18, 27–9, 56, 333, 351–2, 360–62, 365, 367–70, 372–3, 383
Cevian 45, 48–9, 136–40, 143–5, 159, 161, 171–2, 174–5, 181, 192–3, 207, 221–3, 230, 236–7, 239–40, 243, 251, 253, 262, 276–7, 281–2, 285–6, 289, 303, 312–13, 319, 322, 338–40, 344, 347, 356–7, 359, 370
chair/chairman (*see also* the Name index)
  change of 65–6, 77–80, 85, 92, 96–8, 100, 109, 275, 277, 282–3, 341, 366, 368
  duty 160, 238, 273, 336, 341
  mandate/position 28, 102–3, 110, 113–14, 175, 295, 351–2, 362, 365, 367–9, 372
Chalmers University of Technology 98
Church of Sweden 172
Cigna 63
circle 13–14, 81, 86, 99, 101, 124, 235, 249, 296, 330, 332, 338, 358, 369, 372, 383
Citadel 300
Citigroup 189, 251
clan 13, 372
Class Action against Skandia Association 297
CNBC 305
company
  limited 14–15, 17, 21, 335, 375
compensation (*see also* incentive)
  board 175, 367
  committee 110
  executive 5–6, 41, 78, 234, 365
Confederation of Swedish Enterprise 98
contract(s)
  adviser (*see also* relevant juridical persons) 161, 164, 188, 204, 214, 255, 278, 289
  asset management 64, 79, 130
  derivative 23
  incomplete 15
  insurance 57, 63–4
  nexus of 15
  policy 61
  unit-linked 82
control *see* corporate control
COO/chief operating officer
  role of 368, 373
core business 18, 59, 358
core competence 5–7, 18, 26, 359
corporate constitution 28, 365
corporate flow *see* corporate governance
corporate governance
  Anglo-Saxon model 25
  capital-market based 6, 17, 26, 39, 337, 346–61, 373, 375
  flow 18–19, 346, 349, 353–4, 360–61
  German model for 25
  as a horizontal process 18–19
  ideals 7
  integration of 353, 373
  operational aspect of 18, 346, 348, 350–61, 372–3, 377
  regimes 25
  Swedish model for 26–7, 375
  as a vertical process 18–19
corporate path
  stand-alone type 47, 49–50, 83, 92, 116–35, 154, 165, 169–70, 179, 181, 195, 202, 220, 222–3, 227, 229, 233–4, 240, 247, 261–2, 264–5, 271, 273–5, 278–9, 290, 295–6, 301, 313, 341–2, 350, 352–4, 357, 359, 364, 369, 380
  structural deal/proposal/solution 50, 59, 74, 108, 116–35, 140–43, 153, 166, 170, 172–3, 176, 179, 181–2, 189–90, 195–8, 202–3, 206, 222, 233, 236, 295, 307, 311, 318, 323, 335, 339, 343, 345–8, 348, 352–5, 358, 361–3, 365, 368–9, 372, 378, 381–2
corporation/company (*see also* relevant juridical persons)
  as attractor of capital 16
  as a bundle of assets 17, 346
  comparative advantage of 358

competitive power of 112, 358
de-/listed 3, 5, 9, 16, 21–4, 27, 39, 42, 55, 60, 64–5, 76–9, 86, 97–8, 101, 110, 112, 117, 136–7, 139, 152, 182, 190, 195–6, 199, 209, 228–9, 239, 244, 248–9, 253, 262, 287–9
country 374
credit-rating institute (*see also* Fitch and Moody's) 346, 356
Crédit Suisse First Boston/CSFB 168, 305, 312–13, 319
culture
company 333
management 139
'societal' 10–11, 14, 25, 31, 45, 385
currency fluctuation (*see also* regulation) 154, 231, 275, 284, 292, 312, 323, 342, 351, 359
Custos 136–7, 139, 144–5

Danske Bank 42, 124, 305
debt
issue/ratio 20, 66, 107, 183–4, 200, 213–14, 244, 255, 291
and rating 213
Den Norske Bank 42, 64–5, 71, 79, 111, 130, 186, 199, 297
deputy chair (*see also* the Name index)
task 100, 110, 113, 367, 372
Deutsche Bank 45, 49, 128–30, 148, 153–4, 161, 166–8, 172, 176–7, 181–2, 184–5, 190, 205, 209, 213–15, 217–19, 221, 223, 237, 242, 253–4, 283, 286, 305, 310–11, 319, 350–51, 355
director (*see also* the Name index)
assignment 110–12, 129, 131, 170, 175, 330, 366, 372
independent 28, 44, 76–7, 121, 125, 133, 192, 261, 297, 320–21, 362, 365, 369
in-/outsider 76–7, 86, 221, 229, 235, 242, 248, 339, 358, 362
mandate of 29, 59, 86, 110–11, 113, 179, 248, 254, 364
position of 18, 28, 114, 136, 295, 342, 351, 363–4, 369, 371, 378
recruitment of 27–8, 76, 92, 96–103, 110, 145, 171, 175, 282, 287, 289, 312, 320, 343, 347, 351, 362, 371
time allocation of 41, 175–6, 208, 330, 371–2
trust between 51, 132, 164, 166, 170, 197, 219, 354, 362, 366, 369
DnB Nor/DnB *see* Den Norske Bank
due diligence
limited 30, 48, 152, 185–8, 193, 195–7, 201, 203, 205–7, 210, 217, 231, 265, 274, 334, 358, 365, 376–8, 380–81
time extension of 207–8, 210, 216, 230

economic system 8, 332
elite
business 148, 239, 296, 350, 375
political 261
embedded-value 40–41, 60–62, 65, 70, 80, 107, 116, 129, 134, 151, 159, 183, 189, 219–20, 231–2, 302, 377
Enron 92
Enskilda Securities 145
EQT 199
Ericsson 60, 77–80
Erneholm and Haskel 252, 255
ethics 46, 380
event 6, 8, 10–11, 31, 41, 44–5, 47–8, 50, 168, 273, 314–15, 348, 350, 360, 378

fairness opinion 201, 206, 264, 274, 300, 379–80
fair trading value (FTV) 169, 192, 198, 203, 219, 234, 263, 354
Fannie Mae 323
Farallon Group 145
'federative-like' organization 58, 66, 92, 108, 122, 204, 209, 334, 353
Fidelity 60, 95, 108, 131, 173–4, 181, 205–7, 215, 242, 252–3, 271, 277, 282, 288–9, 303, 314–15, 337, 344, 347–8
Fidelity & Guaranty Life 150
Fidelity Funds 145, 173, 313
Fidelity Group 131, 352
Fidelity International 45, 49, 131, 173–4, 206–7, 242, 253, 288, 303

financial engineering 138, 334, 337, 352
financial market *see* market
financial rationale *see* rationale
financial unit (*see also* relevant juridical persons) 16, 354
financial transparency 19, 129, 297, 358
'financialization' 4–5, 332
Fitch 184, 213
flow *see* corporate flow
Folksam 267, 348
force
  influencing corporate control 3–4, 6, 10, 17–18, 23, 45–6, 56, 76, 137, 257, 296, 306, 318, 331, 333, 343, 373, 375–7, 379, 385
FöreningsSparbanken 94, 98, 108
FöretagsJuridik Nord & Co 187, 231, 266
Fortune Global 500 151
foundation (*see also* relevant juridical persons)
  legal unit 24, 56, 74, 96, 149
Freddie Mac 323
free-rider problem 344
Friends Provident 42, 130, 186, 200, 210
FSA *see* UK Financial Services Authority
FTSE 100 149, 151
FTSE index 257, 270
fund (*see also* relevant juridical persons)
  activist 6, 8, 23–4, 41, 45, 47, 51, 137, 248, 301, 303, 332–4, 338–40, 347–9, 356–7, 359–61, 371, 373, 382, 390
  arbitrage 8, 248, 301, 314, 337–9, 342, 348
  hedge 5–6, 8, 23–4, 41, 45, 51, 60, 107, 136–7, 144–5, 183, 248, 279, 281–3, 286, 289–90, 301–6, 310–12, 314, 316, 319, 322, 332, 334, 337–40, 342, 344, 346–51, 355, 359–61, 374, 382–3, 385, 390
  mutual 22–3, 27, 57, 59, 72, 81, 111, 116, 133, 139, 147, 199, 207, 228, 284, 295, 310, 337–8, 340, 342, 347, 350, 374, 379, 382, 384–5
  pension 5, 22, 24, 27, 45, 108, 118, 228, 260, 332, 347, 350, 379, 382, 384–5
  retail 5, 22–3, 96, 332, 347
  sovereign wealth 24
  special event 348

Generali 43
Gerrard Group 149, 152
Gerrard Management Services 151
Glue plan 119, 192
Goldman Sachs 74, 77, 79, 94, 168, 200, 278–9, 290–91, 300–302, 306
goodwill 118, 162, 214, 359
Götaverken 99
governance *see* corporate governance
Government of Kuwait 314
Government of Singapore 95, 108, 300
Great-West Lifeco 200, 203, 209, 215–16, 219

Hafnia 74
Hagströmer and Qviberg 136
Halifax 148
Handelsbanken 42, 56, 78–9, 84, 92, 95, 97, 173, 220, 223, 239, 276, 278, 284–5, 290, 295–6, 305, 307, 315, 319–20, 350
Henderson Group 152
heuristics 12
Hexagon 281, 292
homo complexicus 12, 330
homo oeconomicus 11–12
HSBC Bank 108

ideal type construct 12, 19–20
If P&C 64, 82–4, 91, 93, 96, 107, 122
Ikanobanken 296
IKEA 296
Ilmarinen 78, 85
incentive programme (*see also* the specific programmes) 22, 45, 61–2, 70–71, 73, 110, 121, 125, 160, 175, 382, 385
index
  reshuffling 183–4, 319, 334, 337, 358, 379

tracking 22, 136, 228–9, 285, 295, 306, 338, 344, 350, 370, 376, 379, 382
individual *see* actor
Industrivärden 56, 78–82, 84–5, 94–6, 138
information
advantage 39
confidentiality of 195, 206, 208, 358, 380
delicate 14, 142–3
exclusive 22, 113–14, 175, 202, 207, 220, 223, 261, 384
financial 16, 19, 168, 198, 239, 272, 283, 358
hidden 23, 358, 378
informally acquired 339, 358, 371
lack of/late 76, 160, 166, 172, 189, 216, 287, 300, 307, 363, 380
leakage 41, 186, 190, 271, 380
official 133, 169, 195, 197, 265–6, 358
overload 208
private 14, 145
public 41, 109, 186–7, 198, 216, 235, 269, 274, 290, 377–8
ING 43
insider trading
crime 384
problem 193, 221, 229, 235, 242, 248, 339, 358, 384
regulation 30, 376
institution(s)/institutional (*see also* investor)
ambiguous 374, 381
bricolage of 6, 11, 86, 374, 380–81, 383, 385
changing 10, 25, 46, 381–2, 384
cross-national differences 24, 26, 30, 47, 331, 377, 379–80, 382
definition of 10, 46
export of 331
financial 4–5, 74–5, 147–8, 181
function/force 3, 8, 10–11, 14, 22, 31, 44, 331, 333, 374, 376–7, 379, 385
'irritant' 25
legal/regulatory 376, 379–80
productivity of 14
setting 7, 147, 330–31, 343, 377, 379–82, 384
insurance company (*see also* relevant juridical persons) 24, 39, 57
intermediary (*see also* relevant juridical persons)
kind of 5, 19, 21–2, 56, 321, 359
as rational destabilizers 383
International Shareholders' Services (ISS) 172
interpersonal/group (*see also* circle and coalition)
belief 13–14, 46, 82, 165, 222, 262, 369, 376
faith 13
trust 11, 13–14, 22, 41, 51, 72, 86, 102, 112, 127, 130, 166, 170, 173, 269, 275, 317, 366
Intrum Justitia 137, 171
Investec 189, 251, 291–2
investment bank/investment banker (*see also* relevant juridical persons)
role of 5, 8–9, 44, 81, 108, 130, 134, 142, 144, 165–6, 168, 184, 201, 208, 218, 221, 275, 332, 334, 337, 350, 357–61, 373, 379, 382–3
investment company (*see also* relevant juridical persons) 24, 56, 74, 76–8, 100, 136, 138, 143
investment policy 81, 228–9, 278, 339
Investor 56, 74, 76
investor (*see also* relevant juridical persons)
arenas 16, 22, 71, 176, 237, 254, 278, 281, 298, 300, 304, 307, 311
institutional 5–6, 9, 22–4, 44–5, 56, 76, 83, 95, 97–8, 102, 108, 122, 128–9, 131, 149, 174, 184, 192, 205, 220–21, 227–9, 233, 236–7, 242, 248, 281, 295, 298–9, 306–7, 312, 319–22, 332–3, 337, 347–8, 350, 370, 373, 376, 379, 383
long-term 24, 262, 271, 289, 342, 344, 349, 353
non-Swedish 27, 60, 78, 95, 107–8, 171, 173–5, 183–4, 189, 229, 242, 289–90, 301–5, 312, 319, 323

power 39, 56, 62, 75, 77–80, 95–6, 98, 102, 108, 110, 129, 131, 137, 144, 149, 171–2, 205, 207, 227, 248, 250–51, 262, 269–70, 275–6, 284, 288–90, 302–6, 313, 315, 318–19, 339–40, 345, 347–50, 366, 376, 383
rationale 22, 59–60, 62, 111, 136, 139, 145, 150–51, 342, 344
short-term 24, 84, 263, 271, 306, 313, 315, 322, 333, 337–8, 351, 370
ultimate 21–2, 47, 190, 229, 275, 321

Johannesburg Stock Exchange index 323
Johnson group 101
JP Morgan 168, 199
Jupiter Asset Management 189
juridical person 14, 202

K Capital Partners 300
Kaupthing 124, 171, 173–4, 181, 338, 344
Keefe, Bruyette & Woods 176, 190, 197, 292
Kreab 45, 185, 239, 244, 269–70, 278, 286, 288

Lancelot 99
Lantmännen 98, 170, 261
law/legislation
awareness/knowledge of 330
company/corporate 25–6, 28, 30, 39, 63, 65, 74, 117, 187, 288, 297–8, 331, 343, 345, 365, 375–6
emergence of 10, 375
environmental 25
function of 14, 27–8, 30, 46, 297, 371, 375, 384
labour (market) 25–7
local/regional 6, 109, 374
sidestepping of 380
taxation 27
Lazard 213, 310
Leica Geosystems 281, 292
Lenner & Partner 45, 49, 165, 176, 181, 205, 221
leverage 5–6, 23, 214, 356, 359
Lex column 188, 240
Liber 98
limited company *see* company
Linde 79
Lindex 98, 137, 139, 145, 171
Linklaters 45, 167, 215, 248, 289
Lundbergföretagen 296
London Stock Exchange 29, 42

M&A *see* merger and/or acquisition
management
accountability 15
team 372
market
emerging 40, 151, 184, 303–4, 320, 333, 379, 382
financial 3–5, 9, 16, 25–6, 41, 46, 62–3, 76, 79, 137, 149, 186, 260, 263, 306, 311, 331, 352, 359–60, 371, 382–4
regulation of 23, 26, 30, 65, 74, 96, 118, 331, 375–6, 381, 383, 385
McKinsey 81, 119–22, 136, 153, 159–60, 163, 192
Mercantile & General 91, 153
merger (*see also* acquisition)
cross-border 182
forced 293, 375–6
function of 6, 55, 74
'hurdles' 376
rationale behind 16
MeritaNordbanken 97
Merrill Lynch 45, 49, 128–9, 148, 167–8, 182–4, 200, 217, 219, 248, 278, 283, 286, 311, 350–51, 355
methodology 389–94
minority protection rights 244, 287, 298, 316, 318, 376
Monitor 120, 132, 163, 192
monitoring process (*see also* governance) 14, 113, 120, 370–71
Moody's 63, 184, 213–14, 218, 231, 310, 354–6, 377
Morgan Stanley 48, 84, 93, 122–7, 131–2, 153, 159–61, 163–6, 168–70, 172, 180–81, 184–8, 190–92, 195–8, 202–6, 208–10, 214–19, 221–2, 229, 231–3, 236–7, 247, 263–4, 275, 278, 289, 300, 311, 348, 352, 354–5, 379

Morgan Stanley Capital International Emerging Markets Index 184
Morgan Stanley insurance index 184, 247, 311, 379
Mutual & Federal 147, 152

narration/narrative 11, 41, 44–7, 332, 385, 393
nationalism 344, 348
NCC 101
Nedbank 147, 152, 292, 307
Nedcore 291
New York Stock Exchange 71
Nobel Foundation 96
nomination committee
 chair 131, 175, 202, 207, 220, 231, 236–7
 composition of 49, 77–9, 93–7, 110, 131, 160, 175, 277, 289, 302–3, 312, 317, 321, 340, 347, 349, 361, 365–6, 370
 construct of 28, 30, 96–7, 365, 370–71
 function of/task 83, 94–5, 99, 110, 113, 175, 315–18, 334, 365–6, 370, 383
 power of 110, 113, 139, 202, 236–7, 282, 285, 303, 315, 347, 349, 366, 370, 381
 regulation 277, 289, 369–70
Noonday 145, 283, 302, 306, 313, 315, 319–21, 339, 344, 349
Nordbanken 75, 97, 101
Nordea 42, 84, 95, 97, 101–2, 108, 124, 130, 167, 181, 186, 188, 191, 199, 200–204, 209, 216, 219–20, 227, 230, 254, 284–5, 290, 295, 298, 307, 313–14, 316, 318–20, 332, 350
Nordea Funds 80, 131, 161, 337, 344
Nordic Capital 136
Nordstjernan 101, 103
norm (*see also* institution) 10–11, 46–7, 61, 110, 299, 330–31, 374, 381
Norwich 148

occurrence *see* event
Old Mutual (no page numbers provided; referred to all over the text; *see* Contents)
OMX index 248
Oriflame 98

P&C *see* property and causality
Pacific Equity Partners 136
Paulson & Co 145, 281–3, 289, 292, 303, 306, 311–13, 316, 319, 339, 344, 349
Pohjola 64, 74–5, 77–9, 82, 85, 94–5
'poison pill' 29, 164, 378
portfolio
 diversification of 344, 359
 manager 338
power/influence
 of AGM 365
 in Anglo-Saxon system *see* Anglo-Saxon model
 board 275, 342, 365, 373
 centre 27, 97, 381
 CEO/managerial 25, 28, 39, 56, 86, 361, 365, 373
 hyper- 371, 373
 of outside actors 361
 political 27
 shareholder 15, 21, 23, 27, 39, 56, 312, 339, 343, 353, 361, 371, 373
 struggle 46, 62, 72
 in Swedish system *see* Swedish model
 voting 27, 29, 56, 303, 348
principal 17
principal-agent view 19
profit
 long-term 6
 short-term 6
property and causality/P&C (*see also* relevant juridical persons) 9, 43, 59–60, 64, 74–5, 82, 91
Prudential 5, 42–3, 61, 64, 66, 109, 111, 149, 162, 172, 174, 216
Public Investment Corporation 251
Putnam 60, 300

rating (*see also* credit-rating institute) 184, 213–14, 219, 232, 251, 276, 281, 292, 299, 315, 349, 356
rationale (*see also* rationality)
 calculative 11–13
 financial 5, 17–19, 296, 302, 310,

343, 345, 348–50, 355–6, 360, 363, 382
Janusian 336
long-term 16, 336–8, 344–6
operational ('business') 17–19, 71, 233, 236, 251, 274, 284, 341, 348, 353–6, 359–60
short-term 15, 336–8, 342, 345–6, 348
speculative 16, 43, 346, 382–3
value-based 13, 16, 22, 24, 46, 334
rationality (*see also* rationale)
bounded 12
human 12
regulation (*see also* law/legislation)
currency 27, 182, 232, 255, 257, 267
'hard' 30, 375
national 27, 46
self- 299, 380–81
'soft' 30, 46, 375–6
taxation 27, 29
Reinhold City 100
Rembrandt 147
Renault 9, 97, 228, 230
reputational cost 15, 379
rhetorics 5, 12, 27, 82, 114, 175, 252, 334, 344
Richemont 147
risk
allocation of 5, 14
asset-specific 344
attitude 4, 22, 151, 304
aversion 344,
country (incl. currency) 232, 274, 281, 284, 292, 349, 351, 359
financial 19–20, 78–9, 82, 184, 196, 213–14, 230–31, 235, 251, 275, 301–2, 333, 351, 359, 384
legal 177, 251, 262, 378, 384
level 25, 116, 145, 304, 360
high/low 25
in society 14, 61
managerial 220
operative 19–20, 57, 71, 159, 180, 191, 240, 251, 295, 352, 359, 384
political 275
specific 24, 345
-taking 5–6, 14
Robur 84, 94–5, 131, 161, 172–4, 181, 204, 220–23, 230, 236, 276, 278, 284–5, 296, 298, 307, 313, 316, 318–19, 332, 366
Royal Skandia 68, 72, 108, 116–18, 124–5, 139, 200
Rydbeck Report 92

Sampo 42, 64, 78, 82–5, 91, 93–6, 100, 107–8, 119, 122, 138, 182
Sanlam 148, 189, 256
SCA 100–101
Scudder 60
SEB 42, 56, 74–5, 92, 95, 98–9, 102, 117, 131, 133, 181, 220, 332, 366
SEB Funds 45, 49, 94, 96, 110, 113, 130, 138, 161, 172, 174–5, 202, 207, 215, 220–21, 223, 230, 236, 239, 243, 257, 284, 295, 314, 323, 332, 337, 344–5, 350
SEB Trygg Liv 117, 131, 174
Securitas 77, 239
Selestia 150–51, 184, 209, 244, 317
share
redemption 5, 16, 22, 127, 136, 138, 357
re-rating of 184, 219, 251, 281, 349
shareholder(s)
base 44, 77, 85–6, 93, 95, 149, 181–2, 184, 189, 233–4, 315, 317, 332, 349, 364, 370
current 15, 17, 196, 335–7, 342–3, 346, 361
discretion 15
hyperactive 371, 373
legitimacy of 21
potential 29, 355, 369, 373
profit ambition of 21
structure 23, 138, 339, 357, 380, 382
ultimate 21, 24, 359
undesired 361
shareholder behaviour (*see also* shareholder)
entry 25, 102, 182, 335, 337, 347
exit 25, 80, 102, 184, 337
voice 27, 78, 92, 107, 128, 337, 366, 370
shareholder value view/perspective 4, 9, 15–17, 21, 23–4, 26, 59, 143, 170, 176, 284, 329–30, 334–42, 344–6, 356

shareholding
composition of 23, 91, 95, 339
cross-holding of 27, 44
diluted 24
direct/indirect 21–2, 24, 29, 390
dominating (coalition/group) 28–9, 74, 76, 86, 103, 141, 332, 347, 371, 383
leadership of 338, 372
intermediary *see* intermediary
middleman 21, 24
minority (blocking) 271, 276, 278, 349, 377
'particular' 344
private 21, 24, 189, 275, 316
Sharetracker 59, 62, 85–6, 92, 109, 160
SIS Ägarservice 270
Skandia (no page numbers provided; referred to all over the text; *see* Contents)
Skandia Asset Management 64–5, 261
Skandia Deutschland 92
Skandia International 97
Skandia Life UK (no page numbers provided; referred to all over the text; *see* Contents)
Skandia Liv 9, 56, 59, 64–6, 68, 71, 79, 81, 93–4, 96, 100–101, 109, 111, 117, 119–20, 130, 133, 139, 171, 190, 202, 253, 296–8, 316, 343, 345, 348, 350
Skandia P&C 56
Skandia Shareholder Association 94
Skandiabanken 68, 120, 124, 134, 139, 162, 171, 199, 217–19, 232–3, 236, 241, 249, 254–5, 266, 292, 316, 322, 342, 352
Skandinaviska Banken 99
Skandinaviska Enskilda Banken 74
Södra Skogsägarna 98
'soft irrevocables' 30, 242–3, 245, 261, 334, 376
South African Mutual Life Assurance Society 148
South African Sanlam Asset Management 256
Sparbanken Sverige 75
sphere
bank 9, 27, 375
in general 86, 332, 344, 375
Handelsbanken 56, 80, 97, 295
shareholder 24, 27,
Wallenberg family 56, 97, 99
Spira 98
SSAB 96, 99, 126, 234
stakeholder value view/perspective
Standard Bank 147
Standard Life Investment 189
Stanlib Asset Management 256
State Street Global Advisors 189
Stena 98, 261, 296
Stockholm School of Economics 94, 97, 99, 136–7, 145, 389
Stockholm Stock Exchange/SSE 9, 39, 50, 55–6, 60, 66, 76, 86, 127, 130, 143–4, 193, 204–5, 216, 221, 227, 229, 248–9, 253, 284, 287, 289, 296, 306, 317, 319–20, 323, 339, 348, 365
Stockholm University 91, 99
Storebrand 42, 64, 82, 91, 93, 186, 199–200, 203, 215, 227
story (*see also* narrative)
building up 11, 44, 47, 51, 389, 391, 393
telling 55, 61, 65, 91–2, 107, 109, 173, 186–7, 204, 235, 238, 265, 271, 301, 314, 357–8, 360
strategic manoeuvring 30, 46, 374
strategic path *see* corporate path
strategic process
control of 45, 334, 368, 371
strategy
board's 127
chair's 114, 119, 122
company 5, 44, 81–2, 93, 119–20, 148–9, 162, 278
defence 279, 302
growth 129, 176, 204, 232
interpretation of 374
management's 122, 342
niche 99, 123, 126
opposing 368, 374
stand-alone *see* corporate path
Straumar-Burdarás 173
suitor (*see also* bidder) 153, 164–5, 167, 189, 198–202, 227, 239, 351, 355, 358, 368
Sun Life & Provincial Holdings 149
Suomi 78, 85

Sveaskog 98, 261
Swedbank 42, 59, 75, 84, 94, 186, 204, 236, 261, 295–6, 332, 350
Swedish Code of Corporate Governance 28, 365, 370
Swedish Companies Act 27–8, 232, 288, 298, 318, 376–7
Swedish Confederation of Industries 77
Swedish Farmers' Association 261
Swedish Financial Supervisory Authority 297–8
Swedish Industry and Commerce Stock Exchange Committee 30, 375
Swedish Insurance Companies Act 299, 376–7
Swedish Match 101, 103
Swedish Metalworkers' Union 343
Swedish model 26–30, 46, 56, 60–61, 76–7, 114, 121, 187, 219, 230, 232, 248–9, 256, 286–9, 295, 297–300, 310, 317–18, 331, 334, 338, 340, 343, 361–5, 368–71, 374–9, 381, 385
Swedish Securities Council 30, 248, 286–8, 299, 375–6, 378–9
Swedish Shareholders' Association 45, 76–7, 80, 85, 92, 108–9, 174, 228, 239, 241, 253, 257, 260, 275, 277–8, 287–8, 298, 300, 303, 305, 307, 313, 319, 321, 343–4, 347–8, 369–70
Swedish Social Democratic Party 27, 228, 249, 261, 267
Swedish Takeover Code 287
Swedish Television 84
synergy 189, 352

takeover
  break-up value of 192, 195
  context of 331–3, 345, 368
  cross-border 3, 7–8, 182, 329, 332, 364
  'friendly' 168, 364, 377
  hostile 3, 6–9, 29, 51, 74, 270, 278, 288, 329, 332, 334, 343, 362, 377, 383
  'lubricant'/'catalyst' 332, 338
  premium 274, 281, 284, 290, 349
  (control of) process 6, 46, 51, 182, 196, 260, 283, 304, 311, 321, 330–34, 336–85
  rationales behind/reasons for 74, 83, 210, 217, 239, 277, 292, 297, 317, 331, 337, 340, 358
  regulations 26, 29–30, 182, 248–9, 256, 286–7, 299, 310, 341, 343, 362, 375–9, 381
Takeover Rules 29, 30, 256, 286–7, 299, 310, 375, 377–8, 379, 381
target 40, 50, 55, 142–3, 311, 332, 334, 350, 357, 361
Telia 98
Teracom 100
Third Avenue 108, 145, 182, 290, 301, 305, 319
3i 199
TietoEnator 99
Tisbury 300
Trav & Galopp 261
trust *see* interpersonal
Trustor 100
Trygg Liv 98, 117, 131, 174
Tumba Bruk 99
Turbo Plan 162, 169, 191–3, 196–7, 204–5, 219–23, 229–30, 233, 240, 249–50, 261, 264–6, 290, 301, 314, 322, 341–2, 376, 380

UBS 190, 200, 257, 291
Uddeholm 101
UK Financial Services Authority/FSA 71, 117, 317
uncertainty
  actor 11, 21, 98, 202, 209, 231, 270, 301, 330, 333, 342, 367
  bid (*see also* bet and bid) 209
  country 274
  corporate 133, 198, 202, 209, 265
  genuine 45, 330, 333, 368
  interpersonal 11–14
  intrapersonal 11–14
Uni Storebrand (*see also* Storebrand) 59, 74–5
Unified Life 150
United Asset Management Corporation 149
unit-linked business 40–41, 43–4, 57–66, 68–72, 75–6, 81–2, 93, 97,

107–8, 116, 120, 123, 129, 133, 139, 150–51, 162–3, 184, 198, 333, 351–4, 357
University of Umeå 98
Uppsala University 100
US Federal Reserve 303
US Securities and Exchange Commission 23, 111

value-chain 18–19
Viking 60, 108, 128, 145, 300
Viking Global 108, 128, 145
Volvia 98
Volvo 9, 77, 94, 96–8, 196, 228, 230, 261
Volvo Car 98
voting
  power 27, 29, 56, 303, 348, 365, 382
  procedure 174, 207, 365
  right/rule 5, 27, 39–40, 56, 74–5, 77, 79, 254, 332, 337, 357, 361, 385
VPC 270

Wallenberg family 56, 97, 269
Warburg Dillon Read 148
Wealthbuilder 61–2, 70, 86, 109
Wolters Kluwer 98
Woolwich 148

Zurich Financial Services 137, 188